The Juvenile Justice System:
Law and Process, Second Edition

The Juvenile Justice System:
Law and Process, Second Edition

MARY J. CLEMENT, PH.D., JD/MSW

Bold Eagle, Director
www.bold-eagle.com

Boston • Oxford • Auckland • Johannesburg • Melbourne • New Delhi

Library of Congress Cataloging-in-Publication Data

Clement, Mary J., 1943–
    The juvenile justice system : law and process / Mary J. Clement.—2nd ed.
        p.   cm.
    Includes index.
    ISBN 0-7506-7353-2 (alk. paper)
    1. Juvenile justice, Administration of—Social aspects—United States.
    2. Juvenile delinquents—United States.   3. Parent and child—United
    States.   4. Child abuse—United States.   I. Title.
    KF9780.C58   2001
    364.36—dc21   2001025307

British Library Cataloguing-in-Publication Data
A catalogue record for this book is available from the British Library.

The publisher offers special discounts on bulk orders of this book.
For information, please contact:
Manager of Special Sales
Butterworth-Heinemann
225 Wildwood Avenue
Woburn, MA 01801-2041
Tel: 781-904-2500
Fax: 781-904-2620

For information on all Butterworth-Heinemann publications available, contact our World Wide Web home page at: http://www.bh.com

10 9 8 7 6 5 4 3 2 1

Printed in the United States of America

This book is dedicated to

Safeguarding Our Children

"And whosoever shall offend one of these little ones that believe in me, it is better for him that a millstone were hanged about his neck, and he were cast into the sea."
(Mark 9:42)

and to

SAMUEL, my son,

who, through his violent behavior as a young child, taught me to see the gaps in the criminological theory and to broaden my knowledge into newer, nontraditional treatment and prevention for juvenile delinquency. Thanks, Sam, for being the laboratory experience for the degree work. And later, thanks for supporting me in my efforts to obtain a dual degree in social work and law.

To my parents, Ken and Ethel Clement, who gave me life and supported that life, and most of all, to all those who took my classes in criminal justice departments at Virginia Commonwealth University and Wichita State University or in training academies in Kansas and Virginia—your questions and your concerns taught me and helped me to become a stronger advocate for children and their families.

Contents

Welcome

Welcome to an adventure—the juvenile justice system. Like a foreign country, the juvenile justice system in America has its own subculture and language. The language has been translated into simple English in the companion website called "Juvenile Law Dictionary," found at www.bh.com/companions. The website also includes names and addresses of affiliated agencies/groups that can be used to get good information quickly for class reports.

You can easily learn the material in this book, because it has been written by adapting the accelerated and whole brain learning methods developed in Europe by Dr. Georgi Lozanov. If you follow some of the suggestions, you will be using both the left and right hemispheres of your brain. The left brain is considered to be your analytical, logical, and conscious mind. This part learns the structure of language and lets you speak it. The right side of the brain is considered to be intuitive, holistic—your other-than-conscious mind. This part gets the "gist" of the story or the understanding of the court. Using both left and right brains—your whole brain—you will access more of your brain's limitless and natural power.

Your right brain loves symbols. The side margins of this book are for you to identify key ideas or trigger words. For example, whenever you see the Scales of Justice icon, you should be alerted that the information to follow describes extraordinary circumstances, sometimes positive and sometimes negative.

When you see a Question Mark icon in the side margins, be on the lookout for the major question the court is answering. Then, if you are asked to brief the case later, you will be able to locate the important issue easily.

You are also encouraged to add your own symbols and notes in the side margins. For example, when *Miranda* is discussed, write in the margin "the right to be silent" or some kind of symbol such as tight lips or a cross through an open mouth.

Use color. Color activates the right brain. Highlight key words. Underline and draw circles, squares, triangles, and fun shapes with colored pens or markers. Use one color to denote the facts of a law brief and use another color to identify the history of the case.

When reading the materials, close your eyes and vividly imagine the adventure in as much detail as possible. Some of the most interesting cases have been selected to capture your imagination. For example, when you read about the 8-year-old who goes into the neighbor's house and slaughters the goldfish on the kitchen countertop—**see** the sight, **smell** the aromas, **feel** the sensations, and **hear** the sounds. Then say aloud the concept or idea for which this example was used so you connect left and right brains.

Imagination is one of the most valuable tools in learning. Be curious. Ask questions before reading the materials. Wonder about how the court deals with children. Then let the chapter give you some answers. If your questions are not fully answered in one chapter, go to the next. The juvenile justice system is like an elephant—it is too big to be digested in one eating session.

Play with these materials. Divide your time into small units. Give yourself a 5 to 10 minute break every 20 minutes. Get a drink of water, exercise, walk, play with a softball . . .

Most of all—have fun and affirm your success. Having fun opens the right brain, where learning occurs, and where the greatest capacity for storage or memory is. As you think positively about learning law, your brain will turn on more learning power!

CHAPTER 1

History and Treatment

In 1876, the penitentiary's statistical report (State of Virginia) on deaths of prisoners listed one who died as a result of falling into a tub of boiling coffee. The prisoner's age was given as 10 years! (The Richmond Times-Dispatch, July 6, 1986).

The presence of so young a person in the state prison system in Virginia or elsewhere in the United States was not exceptional. As of 1876, the concept of juvenile delinquency was not yet defined in law. There was no separate juvenile court to process children who got into trouble or who were abused. The courts would sentence children to penitentiaries or prisons as they did adults. It was not until 1899 that a special court in Illinois was developed to route children out of the adult system into a separate system called "Juvenile Justice."

The purpose of this chapter is to give an understanding of how and why our society has defined children as needing special or separate treatment from adults. The redefining of children, combined with scientific research as to their growth and development, has continued to give us greater understanding of their needs. Yet that understanding of children's needs and patterns of maturing has not always been introduced into the laws and applied by persons dealing with youth.

It is a new idea in our society that children need treatment and special consideration according to their developmental stages. This chapter will discuss how children were treated in Hebrew, Greek, and Roman cultures, because these cultures are traditionally recognized as having a great impact upon Western society and its thoughts about social justice. The development of the criminal justice system, which dealt with wayward persons, was grounded in cultural values and definitions. Those definitions and the history of delinquency were interrelated with the definitions and history of dependent, neglected, and abused children. As Ashby argued, "harmful conditions that were once thought ameliorated or eliminated appear once again to plague children" (1997, xii), for it is children who pay the price for the lessons our society has forgotten.

INTRODUCTION

The beginning is the most important part of the work.
Plato

Figure 1.1
Used with permission of
Bob Gorrell, *The Richmond
Times-Dispatch.*

The second goal of this chapter is to see how, and under what legal concepts or authority, the present-day juvenile court was established. To better understand the present attitudes and law, we must understand the past and how "little people" (as children were called) used to be viewed.

SOCIAL HISTORY OF CHILDREN AND YOUTH

Our present system of juvenile justice dealing with delinquents and abused children is the result of four historical eras: (1) Biblical and Medieval Europe, (2) English History, (3) Early Colonial America, and (4) the Nineteenth-Century Reform Movement in the United States. Each era expressed different attitudes about the treatment of children. For example, English Common Law, imported by the American colonists to the New World, has descended from Hebrew, Greek, and Roman cultures. Thriving civilizations and systems of thought, as well as concepts of crime and justice, existed in all parts of the world during and before the period when the Bible was written, but the American juvenile justice system has more direct links to Western thought and traditions.

Biblical and Medieval Europe

Children = Property

The Superior man loves his soul, the inferior man loves his property.
Confucius

Power of the Father

Even though little is known about children in Biblical times, we do know that **adults sacrificed children**. The story of father Abraham and his son Isaac is a special example of how a father thought his God was different from the other pagan gods of the area, who required child sacrifice. When Abraham was told to sacrifice his son, he began the process, but in the end a ram was provided in place of the child. In the New Testament, Jesus' approach was an innovation because he showed compassion toward children. Children were considered **property—treated as nonpersons**. In Roman law, for example, the father had unlimited authority over his family. The father had unquestioned power to make life and death decisions about his children, the power to sell family members, and to marry his children to whomever he wished. Marriage in those times served family interests to strengthen alliances by having a daughter wed a neighboring king, for example. The father hoped that the grand-children would work together instead of warring with each other. In short, family life and society were **paternalistic**. The legal system of the Roman Empire established the absolute authority of the patriarch over his wife, who in law acquired the status of a daughter in relation to her husband when she married. The Roman law of persons provided for the *patriae potestas*, the power of the father. It included *just vitae necisque*, the power of life and death, and *a fortiori*, of uncontrolled corporal chastisement over wife, children, and other family members (Oppenlander 1981, 386).

As the Roman Empire expanded, forms of the *patriae potestas*, where it did not already exist, were incorporated into the legal systems of Britain, Europe, the Middle East, India, and eventually America. An example is the case of *Bradley v. State* (1824) in which the court held that a husband could chastise his wife with a rod not thicker than his thumb. This "rule of thumb" came from the English Common Law. William Blackstone, in his *Commentaries on the Laws of England* (1768, 444), stated that a man had the right to chastise his wife by enforced obedience to his lawful command. For children, it was the same—they had no legal protection from severe beatings until the 1970s (Child Protective Statutes). Interestingly, animals were protected under law from cruelty during the 1800s long before children were in the 1970s.

In medieval Europe, most mothers (especially among the well-born, not the lower classes) did not nurse their newborns nor did the children live near the family. Newborns were **nursed by wet nurses**. This meant that the child was breast-fed and cared for by someone other than his or her bio-logical mother during the early years of life. The child did not return home until age 3 or 4, and even then, went into the care of servants. At about age 7, the child went out to military service, apprenticeship, or school. Since antiquity, wet nurses have been acknowledged to have been thoroughly unreliable. Jacques Guilimeau (as documented by DeMause 1975) described how a nursing child might be "stiffled, overlaid, be let fall, and so come to an untimely death, or else may be devoured, spoiled, or disfigured by some wild beast." A clergyman told one British doctor about his parish that was "filled with suckling infants from London, and yet, in the space of one year, he buried them all except two." Of the 21,000 children born in Paris in 1780, 17,000 were sent into the country to be wet-nursed, 3,000 were placed in nursery homes, 700 were wet-nursed at home, and only 700 were nursed by their own mothers. Even those mothers who kept their infants at home often did not breast-feed them, giving them pap (water and grain) instead. One fifteenth-century mother, who had moved from an area in which nursing infants was common, was called "swinish and filthy" by her new Bavarian neighbors for nursing her child herself, and her husband threatened to stop eating if she did not give up this "disgusting habit" (DeMause 1975, 86). In addition, the wet nurses practiced **swaddling** the babies. This meant that the baby was wrapped entirely in bandages to prevent movement, but this also prevented their normal neurological and biological development. In the end, swaddling probably contributed to the high infant death rates because the child could not be kept clean. **Many children died in childbirth, in infancy, and in early childhood.**

Fear, not love, dominated the rearing of children.

Adults feared that children would turn into actual demons or be suscep- tible to the power of the devil. Historians of this period say that most parents and nurses used **terror and fear** in their moral lessons, employing imagi- nary figures, dummies, and corpses to frighten the children. As the child grew out of swaddling clothes, the parents, understandably, found it frightening to care for the child. Thus, caretakers took children to places where corpses were hanging and told them that this is what happens to bad children when they grow up. "Whole classes were taken out of school to witness hangings, and parents would often whip their children afterwards to make them remember what they had seen" (DeMause 1975, 86).

Adults regarded the young with indifference. Children became miniature adults who were subject to stringent rules. If a rule was broken, adults used that as a justification to severely beat any child. Any sign of disobedience or ill temper was also considered good cause. Adults expected children to enter the world of adults and function as adults at early ages without any training. Some adults **exploited** their children, some **ignored** them, and some **abandoned** them.

Many adults thought that children had the marks of the devil on them if they had a cleft palate or a club foot (both surgically correctable today). The poorer parents would abandon their children because the handicapped child might prove to be an embarrassment to the family and an economic drain. The children were put in dense forests with the hope that they would die. Some did. According to folklore, others were raised by animals. The children learned from the animals how to survive. In psychological litera- ture, these children are called **feral** children. We might also call them **throwaway children**: they do not run away, but they are pushed out of their homes.

Later, as the towns increased in size and the forests decreased in density, the half-animal-half-human lost its sanctuary. This creature was strange because it walked on all fours instead of upright. It stole food and frightened the townspeople. The people created cages outside of town where they held the grown feral child until its death. The "wild beast statutes," forerunners of the insanity defense, covered the problem of a human acting more like an animal. Thus, the criminal justice system excused these feral children for criminal acts of stealing. By caging them, they were not put into prisons for punishment but rather for safekeeping where they soon died.

Today, we view the abandonment of children in fairy tales and in legends, such as the origin of Rome by Romulus and Remus, as if it were all fantasy. Yet, in the Middle Ages—understandably referred to as the Dark Ages—abandonment, harsh punishment, and the use of fear and other life- inhibiting measures were all part of the era's social history, economics, and pattern of families.

Today, we understand the importance of the psychological bonding of children to their parents, but in those early days, the parents lacked under- standing and did not know how to rear their children. Today, the American Academy of Pediatrics (APA) has replaced its fifteen-year-old policy en- couraging six months of breast-feeding to one that urges all mothers to breast-feed for at least one year. La Leche League International, a breast- feeding advocacy group, hailed the policy shift as "overdue." The APA also recommends that insurance companies pay for services like lactation consultations to teach new mothers the basics of breast-feeding because this activity provides "significant social and economic benefits to the nation, including reduced health-care cost" (*The Richmond Times Dispatch*, Dec. 3, 1997, p. A9). In biblical and medieval times, however, the children were not seen as a distinct social group with unique needs and behaviors. If it were not for certain rights that evolved in England, the plight of children might still be the same today as it was in the early years of 1000 B.C.–1900 A.D.

English History

For the purposes of focusing on juvenile justice, two concepts that Americans inherited from England are key. The first deals with jurisdiction; the second deals with Poor Laws. First, let us consider jurisdiction. Jurisdiction is the power of the court to hear a case and to decide a result. Early English Common Law (the law of the people) followed the idea that children under the age of 7 were assumed incapable of criminal intent, which meant they could not be charged with crimes. Children aged 7 to 14 were presumed innocent of criminal intent unless it could be proved that they knew right from wrong. Judges tried them using the same procedures as they did for adults. There were no separate jails or courts for children.

Jurisdiction = Power to hear and decide a case

Today, in the United States, many states have upper age limits as well as lower age limits for jurisdiction. For example, some states use 18 as the cutoff age, after which time a person who commits a crime is tried as an adult. The juvenile court judge cannot hear that case nor does the juvenile court judge have the power to decide the case, that is, the **juvenile court lacks jurisdiction**.

In many U.S. states that follow English Common Law, children under age 8 are considered to be incapable of committing a crime and, therefore, are not amenable to or treatable by the juvenile court system. For example, a young child, age 5, goes over to play with a 4-year-old, hears a newborn cry, puts the baby into the washing machine, and turns on the machine while the father is asleep on the davenport. Because the 5-year-old lacks the required *mens rea* or **guilty mind**, the prosecutor might want to try the father for neglect but not the child for manslaughter or murder. Most people hold that losing a child in such a situation of neglect is punishment enough. More punishment would not necessarily correct the father's behavior in the future.

Today, age limits are very controversial. Some states have created a juvenile court to handle youths as young as 6 and 7. However, what does a state do with a 5-year-old who, while waiting for the school bus at the bus stop, hits other children with a two-by-four plank? Should the state prosecute the child under a petition of assault (as a delinquent) in the juvenile court? Should the state investigate the family under child protective statutes on the theory that a child is copying what is being done at home? In this latter example, **there is no limit on the age of the victim; the age limit for the juvenile court is used only when the child is the alleged offender**.

A noteworthy example of the problems of very young children committing criminal offenses is the case of Cameron Kocker from Pennsylvania. He would have been the nation's youngest murder defendant in the adult court in this century had not the Supreme Court of Pennsylvania in 1992 reversed a ruling that he be tried as an adult. At age 9, in 1989, he used his father's high-powered rifle to kill his playmate, age 8, as she rode a snowmobile past his house. The juvenile judge gave him probation through the juvenile court (*USA Today*, Sept. 3, 1992, 4A).

To summarize, **jurisdiction is the authority of the court to hear and decide a case**. Historical practice is the guide for setting juvenile age limits, not scientific studies or the developmental states of children. Under common law, a complete defense to crimes existed for children under 7 years of age. Children over age 14 were held responsible as adults. Children between the ages of 7 and 14 were "rebuttably presumed" to lack criminal capacity. Modern statutes have abolished the aforesaid common law presumptions and established specific minimum age criteria required for a criminal conviction. Juvenile courts now exercise either exclusive (original) or concurrent jurisdiction with criminal (adult) courts, depending on the offense committed and the age of the offender.

Guardianship = Legal authority to care and manage another person or his or her property

The second early English legal concept is guardianship under **Poor Laws**. As people left their kinship groups and moved from rural areas into the city, there were young people who were left destitute or neglected. As early as 1535, the English passed laws that allowed for the appointment of overseers or guardians to bind out destitute or neglected children as servants. The Elizabethan Poor Laws of 1601 created a system of church wardens and overseers who took into their control vagrant, delinquent, and neglected children. They undertook measures to put them to work in poorhouses or workhouses or to apprentice them to masters.

Equity Court

After the Magna Carta (1215), which guaranteed that no free man should be deprived of life, liberty, or property without due process of law, the English court system became so rigid with specific writs that many persons needing to settle disputes found that their particular problem did not fit the requirements for their case to be heard in a court of law. Thus the English created a court system called *equity* or *chancery*, which was separate from the law side of the court. Chancery was a court of equity. The chancellor, as the judge is called today as well as then, was not bound by the rules of the court of law. The chancellor used conscience to argue a case, not law. Equity court had no procedural formalities and could use an informal bill of complaint to hear a dispute. There was no jury. The judge also was free to fashion a remedy by coercing parties as long as it meant using the standard of conscience.

Parens Patriae

It was in this court of conscience or equity that *parens patriae* was used. *Parens patriae* literally meant "parent of the country." In practice it meant that the King was granted the guardianship over the children, especially those who owned property. The King made them wards of the state or of the Crown. Thus, as in any guardianship, the court was to exercise the power of the English Crown in guarding the young and their property. Guardianship never meant rigidity or punishment. It never meant the justification for intervention into children's lives and the lives of their families for the sake of the general welfare. It never meant total loss of liberty.

At that time (1601), however, the Poor Laws were passed to protect those who lived in the city and had the jobs (membership in the guilds) from this new "dangerous class" of peasants who were displaced from the land and went to the cities. Poor Laws prevented the new migrants from obtaining citizenship and closed the city gates to them. Vagrancy laws were created to control and punish those who seemed to be a threat to the social order (Krisberg and Austin, 1978, 8). Needless to say, the migration continued with the result that children were abandoned or released from traditional community restraints. Children then formed bands that engaged in thievery, begging, and other forms of misbehavior.

Because at this time in England family control of children was the dominant model for disciplining wayward youth, it was a logical extension for family government, with the father in the role of sovereign, to extend power over children without families. These children without families, through a system of *binding out*, were placed with other families. Poor children or those beyond parental control were apprenticed to householders for a specified period of time. Boys usually were assigned to farming tasks and girls to domestic service, because the master of the household was not obliged to teach his ward a trade (Krisberg and Austin 1978, 8).

Later, in 1899 in America, the new juvenile court used the *parens patriae* doctrine to place children in jails (secured facilities administered by the local authorities such as sheriffs) and detention facilities (a new name for the place where youth are housed to await their hearings) that are like jails. Again, English Common Law and the procedures of English courts came to America.

Early America

In the American colonies, the family was the basic social and economic unit. Parents expected children to work side by side with them, especially in rural areas where the wilderness was harsh. The Puritans believed it was necessary to reform and harness the child's inherent willfulness. The child was considered a "sinner" who could be saved if born again into obedience, discipline, and respect for the authority of religion, parents, and the state. Discipline was strict; there were no children's toys. Hard work was plentiful, education was useful, and the Sabbath day was holy.

New England Colonies

In the New England colonies in 1646, the Massachusetts General Court in the *Body of Liberties* stipulated that if a "stubborn" 16-year-old refused to obey his or her mother or father, the youth should be brought before the court where following the testimony of the parents "such a son shall be put to death." Also, the *Bodies of Liberties* acknowledged the possibility of child abuse by stipulating that if a "sixteen-year-old shall curse or smite their natural father or mother, he or she shall be put to death unless it can be sufficiently testified that the parents . . . so provoked them by extreme and cruel correction, that they have been forced thereunto, to preserve themselves from death or maiming" (Hawes 1991, 4–5).

For the most part, the misbehavior of children was the responsibility of parents, church leaders, and neighbors. Whipping in public was common for both children and adults. If a child was uncontrollable, the parents gave the child to church authorities. The church would place the child with another family. The family, church, and community acted as one. There was no need for elaborate legal machinery. For the most part, Puritans gave us law that defined child, parent, and state power relationships. That was the patriarchal rule of the father with children considered to be the property of the parents.

If children became wards of the state, they legally became state property, and the state had a sacred obligation to promote and enforce the work ethic. Thus, families who permitted their children the sin of idleness had their children removed from their homes. In 1737, selectmen in Watertown, Massachusetts, removed children older than age 7 from the homes of "negligent and indulgent" parents and placed them to work for other families (Hawes 1991, 7).

Erikson (1966) studied the court records of the early Puritan colonies. The following is one vivid example of how that society dealt with a youth as recorded in a diary:

*And after the time of the writing of these things
befell a very sad accident of the like foul nature in this
government, this very year, which I shall now relate.
There was a youth whose name was Thomas Granger
. . . He was this year detected of buggery [anal
intercourse], and indicted for the same, with a mare, a
cow, two goats, five sheep, two calves and a turkey . . .
Being upon it examined and committed, in the end he
not only confessed the fact with the beast at that time,
but sundry times before and at several times with all
the rest of the forenamed in his indictment . . . And
whereas some of the sheep could not so well be known
by his description of them, others with them were
brought before him and he declared which were they
and which were not. And accordingly he was cast by
the jury and condemned, and after executed about the
8th of September, 1642. A very sad spectacle it was.
For first the mare and then the cow and then the rest of
the lesser cattle were killed before his face, according to
law; and then he himself was executed. The cattle were
all cast into a great and large pit that was digged of
purpose for them, and no use made of any part of them.*
(Erikson 1973, 16)

The point of this example is that the way in which people define and handle what they consider deviant behavior is a reflection of the way in which they live the rest of their lives. Their reaction says something about their culture, attitudes, and values. The killing of the animals in public and before the youth's eyes made cultural sense only within that setting. Their belief was that sexual activity outside of a marital unit of husband and wife was very serious and punishable by death. The society valued adult authority, close supervision, and strict discipline of children. It also valued vocational education and monitored modesty.

Southern Colonies

Society was different for children to some degree in the settlement of Virginia because the society was more directly tied to economic considerations. Krisberg and Austin (1978, 9–11) report:

Studies of slavery often overlook the fact that most slaves were children. (Krisberg and Austin 1978, 10)

*There were persistent labor shortages, and the need for
labor prompted orders for young people to be sent over
from Europe. Some youths were sent over by Spirits,
who were agents of merchants or shipowners. The
Spirits attempted to persuade young people to emigrate*

to America. They often promised that the New World would bring tremendous wealth and happiness to the youthful immigrants. The children typically agreed to work a specific term (usually four years) in compensation for passage across the Atlantic and for services rendered during the trip. These agreements of service were then sold to inhabitants of the new colonies particularly in the South. One can imagine that this labor source must have been quite profitable for the plantations of the New World. Spirits were often accused of kidnapping, contractual fraud, and deception of generally illiterate, destitute, and young clientele.

Other children coming to the New World were even more clearly coerced. For example, it became an integral part of penal practice in the early part of the eighteenth century to transport prisoners to colonial areas. Children held in the overcrowded Bridewells and poorhouses of England were brought to the Americas as indentured servants. After working a specified number of years as servants or laborers, the children were able to win their freedom. In 1619 the colony of Virginia regularized an agreement for the shipment of orphans and destitute children from England.

. . . In 1609 officials of the Virginia Company were authorized to kidnap Native American children and raise them as Christians. The stolen youths were to be trained in the religion of the colonists, as well as in the language and customs. The early European colonists spread the word of the gospel to help rationalize their conquests of lands and people. But, an equally important motivation was their interest in recruiting a group of friendly natives to assist in trade negotiations and pacification programs among the native peoples. The early Indian schools resembled penal institutions, with heavy emphasis on useful work, Bible study, and religious worship.

The Puritans were not the only group who viewed children as miniature adults. In other colonies, children over age 7 were subject to the criminal law (same courtroom procedures and criminal penalties as adults). In some colonies, children who disobeyed their parents or stole a silver spoon from their masters received the death penalty. Such cases are rare, but there have been a few examples of death. As late as 1828, in New Jersey, a boy of 13 was hanged for an offense committed when he was 12 (Tenny 1969, 102).

In the eighteenth century, Christianity began to influence teachers and church leaders. Church leaders and teachers began to view children's **souls as immortal**. They thought children were **teachable**. They saw the child as **weak and innocent**. In their minds, the child needed the **protection, guidance, and instruction** of adults. In this manner then, **childhood** was extended **beyond the ages of 5 and 7**.

Because the law supported the families in the reasonable exercise of their disciplinary function, early institutional provisions were not necessary until

Children as Miniature Adults

the cities became larger and there were immigrants from other countries. In the eighteenth century, juvenile delinquency slowly ceased to mean a form of misbehavior common to all children and became instead a euphemism for the crimes and conditions of poor children. This was because those institutions that were developed by philanthropists did not discriminate among types of needy children, such as orphaned, destitute, and delinquent.

Greed

Children were now responsible to two masters—their fathers and their factory supervisors. (Krisberg and Austin 1978, 13)

By the end of the eighteenth century, the industrial revolution had come to America, and the home-based industry gave way to a labor or factory system where children comprised, for example, 47 to 55 percent of the labor force in the cotton mills. The use of child labor meant that the early industrialists were able to reap large profits and impoverish others—greed. Companies would provide temporary housing and supplies to workers at high prices and pay low wages such that families were always in debt. Needless to say, conditions of poverty continued to spread, child labor weakened family ties (the traditional form of social control), and the stage was set by those who feared this "dangerous class" to take more control over them (Krisberg and Austin 1978, 13).

In the seventeenth and eighteenth centuries, women typically had seven or eight children spread over twenty or more years of childbearing. However, by the end of the nineteenth century, the typical American family had three or four children. This decline in the size of rural and urban families was the result of the desire of parents to have more control over their own lives. It was not due to birth control devices by themselves, because the main methods of birth control were reduction in the frequency of sexual intercourse within marriage and withdrawal before ejaculation (Hamburg 1992, 28).

Immigrant families, on the other hand, still had large numbers of children and a value system that was different from the major society. In fact, some of the majority societal groups viewed the minorities as lacking control. This judgment by one societal group of another, along with public dissatisfaction with the legal system and the inability of many poor families to rear their own children, led to organized activity to develop houses of refuge (1825–1860) (Mennel 1973). The stage was set for the nineteenth-century reform movement.

Nineteenth-Century Reform Movement

New York House of Refuge

The first house of refuge was opened in New York City in 1825. It was the first time children and youth were separated from adults for punishment. The child still went through the same adult court system with its procedures as did adults, but instead of being sent to an adult prison, the child went to an institution specifically for children. "The system would avoid the cruelty of sending children to jail, but it would nonetheless insure that they were suitably corrected and reformed" (Mennel 1973, xxvii).

Other large cities like Boston and Philadelphia also developed houses of refuge for children: New Orleans, in 1847; Cincinnati, Ohio, in 1850; Colored House of Refuge, Philadelphia, in 1850; and the State Industrial

School for Girls, Lancaster, Massachusetts, in 1856 (Mennel 1973, 30). Unfortunately, there was no clear mission statement. Instead, there was confusion as to what was poverty and what was delinquency. This confusion was amplified by the houses of refuge being in competition for clients from other institutions like New York Orphan Asylum (1806) and Boston Asylum and Farm School for Indigent Boys (1814). Although there was confusion about the type of child needing their care, all unanimously agreed that the cause of both destitution and delinquency was parental neglect (Mennel 1973, 6).

Refuge house managers strengthened their position by legal means. They received children who had been convicted in state and local courts. Thus, state power was equal to parental power under the doctrine of *parens patriae*. The most significant legal case of that time, which contains words that are used today to justify the state doing whatever it wants with children, is *Ex Parte Crouse* (4 Whart 9 = citation). This case (1838) dealt with Mary Ann Crouse's father who, upon hearing about the violence in the Philadelphia House of Refuge decided that he wanted her out. She was not getting the promised training in skills. He tried to free her from the institution on a writ of habeas corpus. The Supreme Court denied his claim by saying:

> *The object of the charity is reformation, by training its*
> *inmates to industry; by imbuing their minds with*
> *principles of morality and religion; by furnishing them*
> *with means to earn a living; and, above all, by*
> *separating them from the corrupting influence of*
> *improper associates. To this end, may not the natural*
> *parents, when unequal to the task of education, or*
> *unworthy of it, be superseded by the parens patriae, or*
> *common guardian of the community? The infant has*
> *been snatched from a course which must have ended in*
> *confirmed depravity; and, not only is the restraint of*
> *her person lawful, but it would be an act of extreme*
> *cruelty to release her from it.* (Mennel 1973, 14)

Obviously, the judges believed what they had heard. If they visited these institutions, they would have found violence such as knife fights among youthful inmates and toward the officers. They would have seen burned-out buildings such as the cane-seating factory in Philadelphia. In like manner, state prison inspectors of the Boston House of Reformation filed a report in 1863 calling it "too much of a prison, too little an institution of instruction, too much the residence of law and punishment, too little the home of grace and culture" (Mennel 1973, 29).

There was little reformation of youth. Mennel (1973) found in a sample of 100 case histories taken from a two-year period (1839–1841) that 40 percent of the children in the New York House of Refuge absconded or repeatedly returned to the refuge. Although the idea of teaching children values of thrift, honesty, and individual responsibility was meritorious, reform institutions were huge, structurally modeled after adult institutions that permitted no individual treatment or educational facilities.

In addition, female delinquents and African-American delinquents of both sexes suffered acute forms of prejudice. Refuge managers viewed all female delinquents as sexually promiscuous with little hope for eventual

From the outset, the first special institutions for juveniles housed together delinquent, dependent, and neglected children—a practice still observed in most juvenile detention facilities today. (Krisberg and Austin 1978, 15)

Famous Law Case

reform. New York and Boston institutions were rigidly segregated. The education used in the institutions meant learning proper behavior such as neatness, diligence, and thrift. The institutions used the contract system to maintain order, provide revenue to the institution, and teach skills. That meant that boys were indentured to farmers and sea captains (and sailing at that time was not a safe occupation). Young women worked for prominent ladies in the community. Apprenticeships, supposedly to teach skills, accounted for 98 percent of the children released (Mennel 1973, 16–21).

These houses of refuge were for the reforming of the children, yet they could not begin to contain all of the troubled youth in their society. In some cities like New York, the children were victims of rapid urbanization and industrialization that tore some families apart. The city did have free public school systems but no compulsory attendance legislation. In addition, the poorer families needed the support of the children. The poor could not afford to send their children to school. Therefore, there were children on the streets selling newspapers, match covers, and fruits, and sleeping in the doorways at night. In 1852, the chief of police estimated that there were 10,000 homeless children out of a total population of 500,000. His statistics showed that four-fifths of the felony complaints were against minors (Wheeler 1983, 14).

"Tenement classes" were primarily immigrants crowded into urban centers where sporadic employment kept families in desperate poverty. Through a *padrone system* Italian families sent children to the United States as indentured laborers to stay with families who would return some of the children's earnings to their poor families in Sicily (Gordon 1988, 41). Children were used as beggars with a gimmick: organ grinders and dancing, begging monkeys. Alcoholism, prostitution, and thievery flourished among the youth in the streets such that respectable middle and upper classes did not venture into the streets of the so-called "dangerous classes."

What immigrant families needed most—decent jobs, housing, and health care—was not to be found. The social reformers with moral attitudes assumed that these immigrant families needed to emulate the standards of their new culture, regardless of the cultural and economic disruptions they were experiencing. Child reformers had at least two motives: (1) compassion for children, and (2) fear and ignorance of immigrant people. Thus, the legal and social power to remove children was in the hands of the reformers.

The reformers had better public relations, so they proclaimed the success of the houses of refuge. Many states then built similar institutions for delinquent and destitute youth and encouraged the general public to perceive delinquency as rising and being more serious.

The New York Children's Aid Society (a privately controlled organization subject to public support and backed by philanthropic-minded individuals), under the direction of Charles Loring Brace, a 26-year-old minister-turned-social worker, encouraged policemen or other agents to seize reluctant newsboys or match girls and bring them to his agency. Other "orphans" were brought by single mothers desperate to save their children from urban danger or the family's poverty. Then the agency would "place out" these children. Placing out meant that this state-chartered agency would take these children (some as young as 3 and others as old as teenagers), clean them up, and send them by "Orphan Trains" to Indiana, Illinois, Wisconsin, and then westward.

These "Orphan Trains" were met by other religious or community leaders of the western frontiers who would then hold a town meeting. Farmers from the area would come to decide which of the children could work best on their farms. The New York Children's Aid Society had existed since 1854. At first, the procedures were very informal. Later, due to the professionalism of social workers and the criticism of the program, the staff of the program inspected foster homes before placing children, and visiting agents carefully supervised them afterward. Because this was the first charitable organization "to make extensive and systematic use of placing out, the Children's Aid Society was to exert a major influence on child welfare policy for the next fifty years" (Wheeler 1983, 16).

Placing out was used for abused, neglected, vagrant, runaway, and delinquent children of immigrant working classes. The Children's Aid Society of New York placed out 100,000 children and the Boston Children's Mission and the Juvenile Asylum placed out thousands of others (Wexler 1995, 34).

Other cities tried a different approach. Boston, for example, had the efforts of John Augustus (1785–1859) to help the city with its children. In 1841, Mr. Augustus, a simple shoemaker, developed a rudimentary system of juvenile probation. He would attend the courts and provide bail for children and also for men convicted of drunkenness. In 1846, for example, he paid $3,000 bail for eleven boys, ages 9 to 13, who were arrested for larceny. Mr. Augustus provided clothing and temporary shelter, and sometimes he helped the youth get jobs (Mennel 1973, 43).

Carrying on the tradition of John Augustus, Massachusetts passed a law in 1869 providing for the presence of a visiting agent or officer of the state board of charity at the criminal trial of any child under 16. The officer was to investigate the case, attend the trial, protect the child's interest, and make such recommendations to the judge as might seem appropriate. The youths were often released on probation upon the condition of good behavior in the future. In 1870, Boston passed a law requiring separate hearings for the trials of juvenile offenders. Then, in 1877, a law was passed authorizing separate dockets and records. New York passed a similar law in 1877. Special handling of juvenile cases in criminal courts was thus being adopted in a number of states. However, the actual setting up of a new court specifically for juveniles to be viewed as wards of the state instead of criminals came in Chicago and Colorado in 1899 (Aumann 1995, 31–32).

Midway through the nineteenth century, state and municipal governments took over the administration of institutions for juvenile delinquents called reform schools. "In 1876, of the 51 refuges or reform schools in the U.S., nearly three-quarters were operated by state or local governments. By 1890, almost every state outside the South had a reform school, and many jurisdictions had separate facilities for male and female delinquents" (Krisberg and Austin 1978, 21).

Although institutions varied in their admissions criteria, their sources of referral, and the character of their inmates, most of the children were sentenced to remain in reform schools until they reached age 21—the **age of majority** (known as **continuing jurisdiction**)—or until they reformed. The length of confinement, as well as the decision to transfer unmanageable

Orphan trains contained children who had parents who sometimes did not know where they were!

youth to adult penitentiaries, then as well as now, was left to the discretion of reform school officials (Krisberg and Austin 1978, 21). Despite the building of these juvenile institutions in some states, in other states, as will be discussed, young people were still placed in adult prisons. Even today, young people can be sentenced to an adult prison. More of this will be discussed in Chapter 4 but remember that if a 12-year-old is waived into the adult court, then the youth will be sentenced to a prison with other adults. The only exception to this rule is if a particular state passes a new law of permitting the child to be tried as an adult and the judge has the option of sentencing (called blended sentencing) the youth to a juvenile correctional facility. (In the summer of 1998 my students visiting a female adult prison were amazed to see a 14-year-old who had been sentenced for 15 years for the death of her father. She and her father had been drinking and got into a fight in the kitchen except this time she defended herself with a knife. Unfortunately, the father, who had been abusive since her early childhood, was killed. She was prosecuted as an adult and convicted of manslaughter.)

Youth were in prison with adults, then and now.

As mentioned at the beginning of this chapter, some youths were placed in adult prisons because the states had no separate facilities for them. When the Civil War came to the South, some prisons were converted to factories to make war supplies. The Civil War nearly destroyed the prison system of the South. After the Civil War, black children were controlled under the disciplinary systems of slavery. "Southern whites used the notorious Black Codes and often trumped up criminal charges to arrest thousands of impoverished former slaves, placing them into a legally justified forced labor system" (Krisberg and Austin 1978, 23). The vagueness in state Black Codes resulted in blacks being leased out on contracts to railroad companies and manufacturers where they were treated miserably. Youths in prisons who had small hands, for example, had contracts with barrel companies because they could do the jobs easier, faster, and with more profits for the company (Keve 1986).

Contract labor in juvenile institutions continued to expand. An 1871 New York Commission on Prison labor found that refuge boys were paid $.30 per day for labor that would receive $4.00 a day on the outside. Some voices raised in protest charged that harnessing the labor of inmates had become the reason for the existence of the institutions rather than the reformation of the youth (Krisberg and Austin 1978, 22).

The western states, seeing the shortcomings of the eastern and southern institutions, located their prisons for youthful offenders, called "reformatories," in the rural areas. These institutions were organized around farm work, rudimentary programs of vocational education, military drill, and organization (Mennel 1973, 74).

Other eastern states also looked for different ways to redefine the institutional problems. The Massachusetts State Industrial School for Girls (1856) and the Ohio Farm School (1857) used a cottage system and family system to control the youths sent to them by the state (Mennel 1973, 52).

Some state governments set up reformatories for young men 16 to 30 years of age who were first-time offenders (Mennel 1973, 70). To do this, the state had to have a large population of youth and finances to support separate penal institutions. Hence, most state prisons for female juvenile offenders came toward the end of the nineteenth century.

The State Industrial School for Girls in New Jersey, for example, was legally established as a reform school in 1871. This school for females was modeled on the state law of 1865, establishing the State Reform School for Juvenile Offenders. This institution was for girls ages 7 to 16. A board consisting of the governor, the chancellor, and the chief justice of the state had the general control. The board then appointed six trustees for a term of three years who had direct control over the management of the institution for girls. In this capacity, the trustees had "power to indenture the inmates until they were 18 years of age, providing the proper stipulation was made as to the treatment and education of those thus bound out" (Barnes 1974, 270).

The State Home for Girls, as it was later called, used the cottage or family system model. By 1891, that model proved to be ineffective because of the increased population of the school. By the end of 1898, there were about 130 girls. So the state expanded the facility with new cottages and added a school. By the year 1916, there were 227 females. A few years later, the students took the Binet-Simon psychological test for intelligence. The results showed that of the 258 inmates tested, 36 were normal, 98 were borderline, and 125 were mentally retarded. As Barnes (1974, 275) so aptly stated, "about half of the inmates of the Home for Girls at Trenton do not belong at all in that institution, but rather at Vineland, or some other institution for custodial care of the mentally sub-normal."

To summarize, the new social problems of the cities and the states were war, industrialization, and immigration. Children went to local jails for petty offenses. They suffered in the jails, the county road gangs, and prison farms. The number of juvenile crimes and juvenile delinquents increased. By 1890, nearly every state outside of the South had some type of reform school for boys. The prosperous states had a separate institution for girls. These institutions housed both the delinquent child and the destitute child.

In the past, even though the number and variety of reform schools for juvenile delinquents multiplied, so did the problems. The period from 1880 to 1920, often referred to by historians as the Progressive Era, was a time of major social structure change for many reasons. "Pioneers in the natural and physical sciences provided new ideas about human behavior which gave interested citizens a different combination of perspectives for analyzing juvenile delinquency" (Mennel 1973, 77). Criminology, in its quest for scientific legitimacy, "borrowed both methodology and vocabulary from the medical profession, as metaphors such as pathology, infection diagnosis and treatment . . . because the ability to identify the causes of crime also implied the correlative ability to cure criminality" (Feld 1987, 475).

Krisberg and Austin (1978) show us how the Darwin Theory was misused. "While there was general agreement of the need for law enforcement to maintain social order, there was profound skepticism about attempts to alleviate miserable social conditions or reform deviant individuals. Some suggested that if society consisted of a natural selection process in which the fittest would survive, then efforts to extend the life chances of the poor or 'racially inferior' ran counter to the logic of nature" (Krisberg and Austin 1978, 24).

Misuse of Darwin's Theory

The mounting intensity of problems with the youth, coupled with the misguided actions of concerned citizens and child-saving philanthropies, created a heated social drama. The stage was set for reform in which the delinquents were to be removed from the processes of criminal law altogether. "The juvenile court movement attempted to remove children from the adult criminal justice and corrections system and to provide them with individualized treatment in a separate system of their own" (Feld 1987, 476). That reform is now known as the child-saving movement or the development of the juvenile court.

DEVELOPMENT OF JUVENILE COURT

In this section, we will discuss the development of the juvenile court and its procedures and philosophy. The first juvenile court was established in Chicago, Illinois.

Chicago Juvenile Court

It was not until 1899 in Cook County, Illinois, that the state legislators created the first juvenile court. Juvenile court in Illinois was a court specifically organized to process youth between the ages of 8 and 17. The court came into existence for at least five reasons: (1) the shift from an agrarian to an urban society, (2) violent and exploitative reform schools, (3) the child-saving movement, (4) court decisions, and (5) the Chicago Bar Association.

What were the benefits of a state-supported system of care and control? Are they the same today?

1. *The Shift from an Agrarian to an Urban Society.* The larger change in American life in late nineteenth century whereby an agrarian commercial country became an urban industrial nation resulted in a previously family-centered discipline shifting to a state-supported system of care and control. Late-nineteenth-century families, unlike the Puritan families discussed earlier, looked to the state for help.

2. *Violent and Exploitative Reform Schools.* Institutions such as reform schools and houses of refuge were violent and exploitative. The youth who were violent would fight with other children, set fire to the buildings, and stab the wardens. In fact, by the 1860s, the Chicago Reform School had worse conditions than the adult jail. It was a school for learning crime. Judges preferred to send first-time offenders to jail. By 1871, the reform school building burned to the ground (Fox 1970).

Portrait of a child saver: If a woman's place was in the home, she was certainly entitled to give her opinion on garbage disposal, cleanliness of the streets and the care and education of children. (Platt 1969, 79)

Platt's The Child Savers focuses on rule makers and rule making—How formal organizations define persons as "delinquent."

3. *The Child-Saving Movement.* Community leaders, professionals such as social workers, and civic-minded women (called child savers) raised concerns. Platt (1969) coined the term "child savers" for the group of disinterested reformers who were influenced by maternal values, especially middle-class women who extended their domestic role into public services and provided professional women with legitimate career openings. Between 1850 and 1900, they embraced John Dewey's democratic education philosophy and the belief in a child's natural innocence. One of their concerns dealt with better ways to handle the problems of juveniles. Another concern dealt with the state's power and jurisdiction over children who had not committed a crime other than being poor or neglected. This latter concern was voiced earlier in an 1870 Supreme Court of Illinois decision, *People v. Turner* (55 Ill. 280), in which the court ruled that a boy who committed no criminal offense could not be sent to the Chicago Reform School because it would brand him as a prisoner when he had done no wrong and give him a conviction without due process of law. Child savers advocated improved health care to reduce infant

mortality, supported mothers' pensions, and introduced compulsory education. Although this movement was viewed as a moral enterprise to strengthen and rebuild the moral fabric of the society, critics later saw it as hitting the urban poor with more control, restraint, and punishment—especially those who were experiencing premature independence. The child-saving movement was not benign nor were the child savers humanists because they "promoted correctional programs requiring longer terms of imprisonment, long hours of labor and militaristic discipline, and the inculcation of middle-class values and lower-class skills" (Platt 1969, 176).

4. *Court Decisions*. Other court decisions in other states voiced their distrust for *parens patriae* in the performance of reform schools. (See *State v. Ray*, 63 New Hampshire 405 [1886].) Thus there was a new appreciation for the natural parent. New York, Pennsylvania, and Massachusetts began to seek ways of reforming juvenile delinquents without incarcerating them (Mennel 1973). Some historians declared that the juvenile court was ready to be born. It was just a matter of time and the emergence of the circumstances in which it could begin.

5. *The Chicago Bar Association*. The Chicago Bar Association was an all-male association. In 1870, the Supreme Court of Illinois told Myra Bradwell (a lawyer from New Hampshire) that she could not become a lawyer in Illinois because she was more than a married woman; she was a woman (Morello 1986, 9).

Yet, in 1892, the Chicago Women's Club did a very daring thing. They asked the Chicago Bar Association to study the situation and draft a juvenile court bill. The Women's Club had several unique factors that helped them in this request to reconsider the method of handling juveniles. Besides the burning of the institution and the legal decision of *People v. Turner*, the Illinois system for handling delinquent children had virtually disappeared by 1890 (Mennel 1973). Judges put children back into jails and into prisons with adult offenders or into privately organized industrial schools.

The Chicago Women's Club recommended the creation of a juvenile court totally separate from the criminal court. It was a daring idea for that time and place. They had to gain the support of the 1898 convention of the Illinois State Conference of Charities and the Chicago Bar Association.

According to Mennel (1973), the Chicago Bar Association was influential but low-key. It was a Catholic philanthropic organization that provided some volunteer probation officers to the early juvenile court. Excluding female parishioners from this work altogether, that organization became the nucleus of the first association of probation officers that later developed into the National Council on Crime and Delinquency (NCCD, 1962).

The people of that time viewed the juvenile court as a "white-light-of-hope" to help save children from the sixty state and private reformatories that had developed since 1825 (Mennel 1973). Thus, many other states followed.

As expected, urban areas developed juvenile courts sooner than rural areas. Some states followed the New York state model in which the juvenile court encompassed all the issues related to youths and their families. It became known as the family court model. Other states limited their court jurisdiction to a narrower definition of youth and their problems.

The underlying legal principle was that under *parens patriae*, the state could become the guardian of the child and make the child a ward of the state to receive whatever services the state had to offer. Juvenile delinquency was broad in its definition so that a child would be adjudged delinquent if he or she violated any state law or any city or village ordinance. In addition, the court could hear cases of incorrigibility, truancy, and lack of proper parental supervision. The judge of the juvenile court, like a father to a child, was to determine the needs of the child. The judge was then to give sound advice to correct the child. The judge could use probation. The Illinois law at first provided for unpaid probation officers (later, in 1907, paid staff) who assisted the judges and supervised the youth (Krisberg and Austin 1978, 26, 28). Probation was a second chance to help the child. If that did not work, the judge could sentence the youth to one of the state penal institutions for juveniles that had been developed throughout the nineteenth century. In addition, the judge through the court had the authority to institutionalize children in orphanages or foster homes.

Power in the Juvenile Judge

It was the judge who dominated the juvenile court. An example of the interplay between the development of the court and the judge is found in Richmond, Virginia. In 1916, James Hoge Ricks (1886–1958) became a judge of the new court that handled juveniles and domestic relations but was not a full family court. A native of Caroline County, Virginia, and a lifelong Quaker, Judge Ricks studied at Guilford College in North Carolina (A.B., 1905) and T. C. Williams School of Law at the University of Richmond (LL.B., 1908). After being admitted to the bar in 1909, he became clerk and parole officer of the Juvenile Division of Police Court in 1912. When Judge Ricks took on the challenges of this new court, he was only 29 years old. Due to age and his activity in various "progressive" social movements, he served until his retirement in 1956. For 40 years he was the judge and his Quaker philosophy was part of the court system.

Each state, then, developed its own juvenile court so that there was diversity among the states and among the states' jurisdictions. There were few typical courts. Yet, in urban areas, the judge's role became more limited when the volume of cases greatly expanded. The dream of the reformers became a nightmare for the judges who, then as today, were unable to give close personal attention to each case. As caseloads soared with no expansion of existing personnel, the quality of probationary supervision deteriorated. Probation officers were forced to be more concerned with their paperwork than with their counseling of the youth.

Although most reformers of the period understood the relationship between poverty and delinquency, they responded with vastly different solutions. (Krisberg and Austin 1978, 27)

Some critics have viewed the juvenile court movement as an attempt to stifle the legal rights of children by creating a new adjudicatory process based upon the principles of equity law known as *parens patriae*. Others say that one needs to place the juvenile court movement in the context of changes taking place in American society at the time. There were some sincere social reformers and, of course, wealthy people, who felt the need for social control. This was an experimental time and the juvenile court was an experiment. "Some reformers supported large-scale experimentation with new social arrangements, such as the Cincinnati Social Unit Experiment, an early forerunner of the community organization strategy of the War on Poverty of the 1960s" (Krisberg and Austin 1978, 27–28).

Juvenile Court Procedure and Philosophy

The most distinguishing characteristics of the juvenile court in handling delinquents were (1) informal procedures, (2) a court of no record (no one was taking a transcript of the hearing), and (3) proceedings behind closed doors and not open to the public as were the adult criminal trials. The informal procedures would give the special judge the latitude necessary to accomplish rehabilitation. Therefore the process in hearing the case was not to be encumbered by indictments, prosecutors, defense attorneys, trials, criminal rules of procedure, or criminal rules of evidence. The probation officers considered themselves as servants of the judge who gathered what they regarded as the facts. These "facts" could be the opinions of others (hearsay, which is not permitted in a criminal trial) to help the judge make dispositions. In addition, the philosophy was different from criminal courts. Rehabilitation and personalized justice were paramount. But later, to use the words of the U.S. Supreme Court, there were grounds for concern.

Rehabilitation

The ultimate goal was **rehabilitation** instead of punishment. The juvenile court could not give a death sentence. Capital punishment was for the adult court. As such, juvenile courts developed a different vocabulary. Police did not "arrest" children; they "took them into custody." Judges did not have a "trial" for the youth; they held an "adjudicatory hearing." The judges did not "sentence" the youth; they gave a "disposition." (Disposition in juvenile court had many alternatives, such as foster care, group homes, probation, and time spent in a very structured program or institution operated by the department of corrections.) When an officer of the juvenile court checked on the child, it was called probation.

Personalized Justice

Another key idea was that the courts were to give personalized justice. Each child was to be individually diagnosed and treated. Professionals were called into the court proceedings to give advice and counsel.

   With the new court and new, relaxed procedures, the juvenile court had unexpected problems brought not only by the children themselves who were delinquent and/or neglected, but also from professionals both in the court and in the community. The courts were given jurisdiction over widely divergent problems, like a mother's pension and divorce. In addition, each year the courts had new responsibilities and an increased number of children with problems as illustrated by the following quotes:

*As of 1964, there were a total of 2,987 juvenile judges
in the United States, only 213 of whom were full time.
Half of them had no undergraduate degree, a fifth had
no college education at all, a fifth were not members
of the bar, and three-quarters of them devoted less
than one-quarter of their time to juvenile matters. A
quarter of the judges had no law school training.
Approximately one-third had no probation or social
work staff, and between eighty and ninety percent had*

no available psychologist or psychiatrist. In 1964, over 697,000 delinquency cases (excluding traffic offenses) were disposed of in juvenile court, involving 601,000 children or 2 percent of all children between 10 and 17. Undereducated, overworked, and understaffed, should one have expected juvenile judges to advocate sweeping reforms which would complicate and increase their burdens? (Piersma and Schiller 1974, 6)

Grounds for Concern

Landmark Case

The United States Supreme Court played the role of a hopeful, patient parent in that it permitted the juvenile court time to grow and mature from the time of its inception in 1898. In 1966, the U.S. Supreme Court was ready to hear a case called *Kent v. U.S.* (383 U.S. 541, 1967). Justice Abe Fortas voiced a warning by saying: "There may be grounds for concern that the child receives the worst of both worlds: that he gets neither the protection accorded to adults nor the solicitous care and regeneration treatment postulated for children" (*Kent v. U.S.*, 383 U.S. 541 at 556 (1966). *Kent* was first, then *Gault* (387 U.S. 1, 1967), then *Winship* (397 U.S. 358, 1970) and *McKeiver* (403 U.S. 528, 1971). These are known as landmark decisions.

The *Kent, Gault, Winship*, and *McKeiver* decisions drastically changed the juvenile court and gave it constitutional guidelines within which to operate. The *Kent* and *Gault* decisions in particular brought the demise of informal procedures, which had tremendous consequences.

Remember that this new juvenile court, like the reform schools and refuges of the nineteenth century, concentrated on salvageable children, "leaving the truly difficult child to the adult criminal system" (Mennel 1973, 133). Even today, if a child commits murder in the state of Wyoming, that child never sees the juvenile court. He or she is tried as an adult.

In other states, children are seen first in juvenile court (known as original jurisdiction), and then if all programs have been exhausted (the child is no longer amenable or treatable), the child, through a hearing process, is waived into the adult criminal court system (*Kent v. U.S.*, 383 U.S. 541, 1966). Levin and Sarri's (1974, 17) research showed that the juvenile courts in only twenty-eight states have exclusive or original jurisdiction. The other states have mandatory transfer to criminal court for homicides and/or other serious offenses by juveniles above a certain age, and concurrent jurisdiction with criminal court for certain offenders. (See footnote 4 after *Kent*.)

Please note that even though the following cases introduce procedural safeguards, the Supreme Court does not consider the entire procedural apparatus of juvenile justice, its jurisdictional reach, or its dispositional consequences. The Court narrowly confines its decision to the facts that each case brings before the Court.

NOTE ON READING LAW CASES

You are about to read your first law case, *Kent v. U.S.*, a case from the United States Supreme Court. There are three other levels of courts: the United States Courts of Appeals, state supreme courts, and intermediate appellate state courts. In this book, most of the example cases were heard by the U.S. Supreme Court because it has the final word in interpreting the United States Constitution and particularly the Bill of Rights.

Throughout the book there are excerpts and references or citations to cases from the United States Courts of Appeal. Those appellate courts deal with issues not yet decided by the Supreme Court. They apply the rules set by the Supreme Court to other cases.

You also will have cases or citations to state courts. State courts also interpret and apply their constitutional provisions. They are important because many criminal and civil cases originate, and frequently terminate, in state courts. Most of the work of the juvenile court is done in the state court system. The day-to-day decisions are done on the local level and then appealed to the next higher level within the state system before going on to the United States Supreme Court.

To make the task of reading these cases easier, please keep the following points in mind:

1. The title of the case has two names, one before the *v.* and one after. The first name refers to the party that brought the action. In the trial stage, it is the government that initiates all criminal cases. The *v.*, an abbreviation of the Latin *versus*, means "against." The second name refers to the party against which the action was brought. In *Kent v. U.S.*, the title tells us that *Kent* lost in the lower court and is now bringing suit against the federal court because he is in Washington, D.C. The District of Columbia does not have a state supreme court and must appeal to the United States Supreme Court.

2. The numbers and letters after the case are called a citation. They tell us what court heard the case, when the court decided the case, and where to find the case reported. It is like a footnote because it tells the source of the material. In legal citations, the numbers that appear before the title refer to a specific volume in a set of reports. Take, for example, *Kent v. U.S.*, 383 U.S. 541. This means that the law case *Kent v. U.S.* can be found in the *United States Reports*, abbreviated U.S., volume number 383, page 541. The *United States Reports* is the oldest publication of Supreme Court cases. Two other equally good publications are *Supreme Court Reporter*, abbreviated S.Ct., and *Lawyer's Edition*, abbreviated L.Ed. They will have different volume and page numbers because they are different publications.

3. Most of the cases in this textbook are appellate cases. This means that a lower court has already heard the case and taken some action. One of the parties did not like the result and is asking a higher court to review the lower court's action. To bring a claim means one has to argue that there were errors by the trial court. Convicted criminal defendants can appeal convictions, but the government cannot appeal acquittals.

4. The appellate courts refer to the **appellant**, which is a term derived from the word **appeal**. A **petitioner** is a defendant whose case has come to the higher courts by petition. The principal petitions are *certiorari*, Latin for "to be certified," and *habeas corpus*, Latin for "you should have the body." *Habeas corpus* is a separate proceeding from the criminal case itself. It requires jailers, prison administrators, and others who hold defendants in custody to justify the detention of defendants, who have petitioned the higher court to hear their cases. *In re Gault*, the second case you will read, deals with such a claim. Usually, in *habeas corpus* cases, you will find two persons' names instead of a government name, such as *Adams v. Williams* (Adams was the warden of the prison holding Williams;

Williams was the prisoner.) However, in juvenile cases, because juveniles cannot bring their own cases in their own names, their parents or someone in their place has to bring the case. Therefore, juvenile cases usually bear the words **In the matter of**, which is shortened to **In re**.

Certiorari is discretionary. The Supreme Court grants only a small number of such petitions because it cannot hear all the worthy cases. Yet these particular cases raise an important constitutional issue that will have an impact on many people—such as all the juveniles in the United States. Most appeals to the U.S. Supreme Court come through a *writ*, an old English term meaning a written order, that orders the lower courts to send up their proceedings for review. Four of the nine Supreme Court justices must vote to review a case. This requirement is known as the **rule of four**.

5. Most of the cases have two opinions—the majority and the minority. The **majority opinion** is at the beginning of the case; it is the law in the case. This means that five members agreed to that decision and the reasons. If a justice agrees with the decision but not the reason, then he or she writes a **concurring opinion**. An example of concurring opinions is found in *Stanford v. Kentucky*, which deals with capital punishment for juveniles in Chapter 4.

   A **plurality opinion** means that a majority of the justices agreed with the result but not the reasons, and several justices wrote their reasons. The dissenting opinions are written by those who voted against the decision to explain why they do not agree. Most textbooks omit the dissenting opinions, but they have been included here for several reasons. First, the dissents may, someday, become the majority opinion. (See *Stanford v. Kentucky* in Chapter 4.) Second, they give much information about the values of our society and how the criminal justice system is supposed to be working. Usually, the dissent gives additional information that should make you wonder about the entire adversarial process.

6. One of the best ways to read a law case is to answer the following questions as if you were briefing the case:

   a. What are the specific **facts** in this case? What happened to whom? The facts of the case make up the question or the issue about which the court is to make a decision.

   b. What is the **procedural history**? Identify the lowest level of the court system, that is, trial or juvenile court, and determine what was the result. Then identify which court came second and what was the finding. For example, watch for words that tell you whether the appeals court **affirmed** or **reversed** the trial court.

   c. What is the issue or question the court has to decide and how do the judges decide? Watch for words like: "the question before us is."

   d. What is the decision or holding in the case? Words like "affirm," "reverse," "reverse and remand" have been put in bold letters in these briefs so that you can see them. This decision usually comes just before the dissenting opinions. **Affirm** means that the court hearing the appeal upheld the lower court's decision or action. **Reversed** means that the court hearing the case set aside the lower court's judgment. **Remanded** means that the appellate court sent the case back to the lower court, usually with directions as to what has to be done to correct an error in the way the case was handled, or that some defect is to be corrected and the trial held again.

e. What arguments and reasons did the court give to support its decision?

7. Enjoy reading each law case as if it tells a story—for it does. As you get used to reading law cases, you will ask more questions and you will gain more understanding of legal definitions and theories.

KENT V. UNITED STATES

SUPREME COURT OF THE UNITED STATES

383 U.S. 541; 86 S. Ct. 1045; 16 L. Ed. 2d 84 (1966)

January 19, 1966, Argued March 21, 1966, Decided

Prior History: Certiorari to the United States Court of Appeals for the District of Columbia Circuit.

Disposition: 119 U.S. App. D. C. 378, 343 F.2d 247, reversed and remanded.

Syllabus: Petitioner was arrested at the age of 16 in connection with charges of housebreaking, robbery, and rape. As a juvenile, he was subject to the exclusive jurisdiction of the District of Columbia Juvenile Court unless that court, after "full investigation," should waive jurisdiction over him and remit him for trial to the United States District Court for the District of Columbia.

Petitioner's counsel filed a motion in the Juvenile Court for a hearing on the question of waiver, and for access to the Juvenile Court's Social Service file which had been accumulated on petitioner during his probation for a prior offense. The Juvenile Court did not rule on these motions. It entered an order waiving jurisdiction, with the recitation that this was done after the required "full investigation." Petitioner was indicated in the District Court. He moved to dismiss the indictment on the ground that the Juvenile Court's waiver was invalid. The District Court overruled the motion, and petitioner was tried. He was convicted on six counts of housebreaking and robbery, but acquitted on two rape counts by reason of insanity. On appeal petitioner raised among other things the validity of the Juvenile Court's waiver of jurisdiction; the United States Court of Appeals for the District of Columbia Circuit affirmed, finding the procedure leading to waiver and the waiver order itself valid. Held: The Juvenile Court order waiving jurisdiction and remitting petitioner for trial in the District Court was invalid. pp. 552–564.

Summary of Procedural History of Character of the Action

(a) The Juvenile Court's latitude in determining whether to waive jurisdiction is not complete. It "assumes procedural regularity sufficient in the particular circumstances to satisfy the basic requirements of due process and fairness, as well as compliance with the statutory requirement of a 'full investigation.'" pp. 552–554.

Reasons for Decision

(b) The parens patriae philosophy of the Juvenile Court "is not an invitation to procedural arbitrariness." pp. 554–556.

(c) As the Court of Appeals for the District of Columbia Circuit has held, "the waiver of jurisdiction is a 'critically important' action determining vitally important statutory rights of the juvenile." pp. 556–557.

(d) The Juvenile Court Act requires "full investigation" and makes the Juvenile Court records available to persons having a "legitimate interest in the protection . . . of the child. . . ." These provisions, "read in the context of constitutional principles relating to due process and the assistance of counsel," entitle a juvenile to a hearing, to access by his counsel to social records and probation or similar reports which presumably are considered by the Juvenile Court, and to a statement of the reasons for the Juvenile Court's decision sufficient to enable meaningful appellate review thereof. pp. 557–563.

(e) Since petitioner is now 21 and beyond the jurisdiction of the Juvenile Court, the order of the Court of Appeals and the judgment of the District Court are vacated and the case is remanded to the District Court for a hearing de novo, consistent with this opinion, on whether waiver was appropriate when ordered by the Juvenile Court. "If that court finds that waiver was inappropriate, petitioner's conviction must be vacated. If, however, it finds that the waiver order was proper when originally made, the District Court may proceed, after consideration of such motions as counsel may make and such further proceedings, if any, as may be warranted, to enter an appropriate judgment." pp. 564–565.

Majority Opinion

OPINION: MR. JUSTICE FORTAS delivered the opinion of the Court.

?

This case is here on certiorari to the United States Court of Appeals for the District of Columbia Circuit. The facts and the contentions of counsel raise a number of disturbing questions concerning the administration by the police and the Juvenile Court authorities of the District of Columbia laws relating to juveniles. Apart from raising questions as to the adequacy of custodial and treatment facilities and policies, some of which are not within judicial competence, the case presents important challenges to the procedure of the police and Juvenile Court officials upon apprehension of a juvenile suspected of serious offenses. Because we conclude that the Juvenile Court's order waiving jurisdiction of petitioner was entered without compliance with required procedures, we remand the case to the trial court.

More Facts

Morris A. Kent, Jr., first came under the authority of the Juvenile Court of the District of Columbia in 1959. He was then aged 14. He was apprehended as a result of several housebreakings and an attempted purse snatching. He was placed on probation, in the custody of his mother who had been separated from her husband since Kent was two years old. Juvenile Court officials interviewed Kent from time to time during the probation period and accumulated a "Social Service File."

On September 2, 1961, an intruder entered the apartment of a woman in the District of Columbia. He took her wallet. He raped her. The police found in the apartment latent fingerprints. They were developed and processed. They matched the fingerprints of Morris Kent, taken when he was 14 years old and under the jurisdiction of the Juvenile Court. At about 3 p.m. on September 5, 1961, Kent was taken into custody by the police. Kent was then 16 and therefore subject to the "exclusive jurisdiction" of the Juvenile Court. D.C. Code § 11–907 (1961), now § 11–1551 (Supp. IV, 1965). He was still on probation to that court as a result of the 1959 proceedings.

Upon being apprehended, Kent was taken to police headquarters where he was interrogated by police officers. It appears that he admitted his involvement in the offense which led to his apprehension and volunteered information as to similar offenses involving housebreaking, robbery, and rape. His interrogation proceeded from about 3 p.m. to 10 p.m. the same evening.

Some time after 10 p.m. petitioner was taken to the Receiving Home for Children. The next morning he was released to the police for further interrogation at police headquarters, which lasted until 5 p.m.

The record does not show when his mother became aware that the boy was in custody, but shortly after 2 p.m. on September 6, 1961, the day following petitioner's apprehension, she retained counsel.

Counsel, together with petitioner's mother, promptly conferred with the Social Service Director of the Juvenile Court. In a brief interview, they discussed the possibility that the Juvenile Court might waive jurisdiction under D.C. code § 11–914 (1961), now § 11–1553 (Supp. IV, 1965) and remit Kent to trial by the District Court. Counsel made known his intention to oppose waiver.

Petitioner was detained at the Receiving Home for almost a week. There was no arraignment during this time, no determination by a judicial officer of probable cause for petitioner's apprehension.

During this period of detention and interrogation, petitioner's counsel arranged for examination of petitioner by two psychiatrists and a psychologist. He thereafter filed with the Juvenile Court a motion for a hearing on the question of waiver of Juvenile Court jurisdiction, together with an affidavit of a psychiatrist certifying that petitioner "is a victim of severe psychopathology" and recommending hospitalization for psychiatric observation.

Petitioner's counsel, in support of his motion to the effect that the Juvenile Court should retain jurisdiction of petitioner, offered to prove that if petitioner were given adequate treatment in a hospital under the aegis of the Juvenile Court, he would be a suitable subject for rehabilitation.

At the same time, petitioner's counsel moved that the Juvenile Court should give him access to the Social Service file relating to petitioner which had been accumulated by the staff of the Juvenile Court during petitioner's probation period, and which would be available to the Juvenile Court judge in considering the question whether it should retain or waive jurisdiction. Petitioner's counsel represented that access to this file was essential to his providing petitioner with effective assistance of counsel.

The Juvenile Court judge did not rule on these motions. He held no hearing. He did not confer with petitioner or petitioner's parents or petitioner's counsel. He entered an order reciting that after "full investigation, I do hereby waive" jurisdiction of petitioner and directing that he be "held for trial for [the alleged] offenses under the regular procedure of the U.S. District Court for the District of Columbia." He made no findings. He did not recite any reason for the waiver. He made no reference to the motions filed by petitioner's counsel.

What did not happen is as important as what did happen.

We must assume that he denied, *sub silentio*, the motions for a hearing, the recommendation for hospitalization for psychiatric observation, the request for access to the Social Service file, and the offer to prove that petitioner was a fit subject for rehabilitation under the Juvenile Court's jurisdiction.

Where All the Errors Were That Now Need to Be Corrected

Presumably, prior to entry of his order, the Juvenile Court judge received and considered recommendations of the Juvenile Court staff, the Social Service file relating to petitioner, and a report dated September 8, 1961 (three days following petitioner's apprehension), submitted to him by the Juvenile

Probation Section. The Social Service file and the September 8 report were later sent to the District Court and it appears that both of them referred to petitioner's mental condition. The September 8 report spoke of "a rapid deterioration of [petitioner's] personality structure and the possibility of mental illness." As stated, neither this report nor the Social Service file was made available to petitioner's counsel.

The provision of the Juvenile Court Act governing waiver expressly provides only for "full investigation." It states the circumstances in which jurisdiction may be waived and the child held for trial under adult procedures, but it does not state standards to govern the Juvenile Court's decision as to waiver. The provision reads as follows:

"If a child sixteen years of age or older is charged with an offense which would amount to a felony in the case of an adult, or any child charged with an offense which if committed by an adult is punishable by death or life imprisonment, the judge may, after full investigation, waive jurisdiction and order such child held for trial under the regular procedure of the court which would have jurisdiction of such offense if committed by an adult; or such other court may exercise the powers conferred upon the juvenile court in this subchapter in conducting and disposing of such cases."

Procedural History

Petitioner appealed from the Juvenile Court's waiver order to the Municipal Court of Appeals, which affirmed, and also applied to the United States District Court for a writ of habeas corpus, which was denied. On appeal from these judgments, the United States Court of Appeals held on January 22, 1963, that neither appeal to the Municipal Court of Appeals nor habeas corpus was available. In the Court of Appeals' view, the exclusive method of reviewing the Juvenile Court's waiver order was a motion to dismiss the indictment in the District Court. *Kent v. Reid*, 114 U.S. App. D.C. 330, 316 F.2d 331 (1963).

Meanwhile, on September 25, 1961, shortly after the Juvenile Court order waiving its jurisdiction, petitioner was indicted by a grand jury of the United States District Court for the District of Columbia. The indictment contained eight counts alleging two instances of housebreaking, robbery, and rape, and one of housebreaking and robbery. On November 16, 1961, petitioner moved the District Court to dismiss the indictment on the grounds that the waiver was invalid. He also moved the District Court to constitute itself a Juvenile Court as authorized by D.C. Code § 11-914 (1961), now § 11-1553 (Supp. IV, 1965). After substantial delay occasioned by petitioner's appeal and habeas corpus proceedings, the District Court addressed itself to the motion to dismiss on February 8, 1963.

The District Court denied the motion to dismiss the indictment. The District Court ruled that it would not "go behind" the Juvenile Court judge's recital that his order was entered "after full investigation." It held that "The only matter before me is as to whether or not the statutory provisions were complied with and the Courts have held . . . with reference to full investigation, that does not mean a quasi judicial or judicial hearing. No hearing is required."

On March 7, 1963, the District Court held a hearing on petitioner's motion to determine his competency to stand trial. The court determined that petitioner was competent.

At trial, petitioner's defense was wholly directed toward proving that he was not criminally responsible because "his unlawful act was the product of mental disease or mental defect." *Durham v. United States*, 94 U.S. App. D.C. 228, 241, 214 F.2d 862, 875 (1954). Extensive evidence, including expert testimony, was presented to support this defense. The jury found as to the counts alleging rape that petitioner was "not guilty by reason of insanity."

Under District of Columbia law, this made it mandatory that petitioner be transferred to St. Elizabeth's Hospital, a mental institution, until his sanity is restored. On the six counts of housebreaking and robbery, the jury found that petitioner was guilty.

The painful result = harm

Kent was sentenced to serve 5 to 15 years on each count as to which he was found guilty, or a total of 30 to 90 years in prison. The District Court ordered that the time to be spent at St. Elizabeth's on the mandatory commitment after the insanity acquittal be counted as part of the 30- to 90-year sentence. Petitioner appealed to the United States Court of Appeals for the District of Columbia Circuit. That court affirmed. 119 U.S. App. D.C. 378, 343 F.2d 247 (1964).

The Harm

Before the Court of Appeals and in this Court, petitioner's counsel has urged a number of grounds for reversal. He argues that petitioner's detention and interrogation, described above, were unlawful. He contends that the police failed to follow the procedure prescribed by the Juvenile Court Act in that they failed to notify the parents of the child and the Juvenile Court itself; that petitioner was deprived of his liberty for about a week without a determination of probable cause which would have been required in the case of an adult; that he was interrogated by the police in the absence of counsel or a parent, cf. *Harling v. United States*, 111 U.S. App. D.C. 174, 176, 295 F.2d 161, 163, n. 12 (1961), without warning of his right to remain silent or advice as to his right to counsel, in asserted violation of the Juvenile Court Act and in violation of rights that he would have if he were an adult; and that petitioner was fingerprinted in violation of the asserted intent of the Juvenile Court Act and while unlawfully detained and that the fingerprints were unlawfully used in the District Court proceeding.

Arguments before the Appeals Court

These contentions raise problems of substantial concern as to the construction of and compliance with the Juvenile Court Act. They also suggest basic problems as to the justiciability of affording a juvenile less protection than is accorded to adults suspected of criminal offenses, particularly where, as here, there is an absence of any indication that the denial of rights available to adults was offset, mitigated, or explained by action of the Government, as parens patriae, evidencing the special solicitude for juveniles commanded by the Juvenile Court Act. However, because we remand the case on account of the procedural error with respect to waiver of jurisdiction, we do not pass upon these questions.

It is to petitioner's arguments as to the infirmity of the proceedings by which the Juvenile Court waived its otherwise exclusive jurisdiction that we address our attention. Petitioner attacks the waiver of jurisdiction on a number of statutory and constitutional grounds. He contends that the waiver is defective because no hearing was held; because no findings were made by the Juvenile Court; because the Juvenile Court stated no reasons for waiver; and because counsel was denied access to the Social Service file which presumably was considered by the Juvenile Court in determining to waive jurisdiction.

We agree that the order of the Juvenile Court waiving its jurisdiction and transferring petitioner for trial in the United States District Court for the District of Columbia was invalid. There is no question that the order is reviewable on motion to dismiss the indictment in the District Court, as specified by the Court of Appeals in this case. *Kent v. Reid*, supra. The issue is the standards to be applied upon such review.

We agree with the Court of Appeals that the statute contemplates that the Juvenile Court should have considerable latitude within which to determine whether it should retain jurisdiction over a child or—subject to the statutory delimitation—should waive jurisdiction. But this latitude is not complete. At the outset, it assumes procedural regularity sufficient in the particular circumstances to satisfy the basic requirements of due process and fairness, as well as compliance with the statutory requirement of a "full investigation." *Green v. United States*, 113 U.S. App. D.C. 348, 308 F.2d 303 (1962). The statute gives the Juvenile Court a substantial degree of discretion as to the factual considerations to be evaluated, the weight to be given them, and the conclusion to be reached. It does not confer upon the Juvenile Court a license for arbitrary procedure. The statute does not permit the Juvenile Court to determine in isolation and without the participation or any representation of the child the "critically important" question whether a child will be deprived of the special protections and provisions of the Juvenile Court Act. It does not authorize the Juvenile Court, in total disregard of a motion for hearing filed by counsel, and without any hearing or statement of reasons, to decide—as in this case—that the child will be taken from the Receiving Home for Children and transferred to jail along with adults, and that he will be exposed to the possibility of a death sentence instead of treatment for a maximum, in Kent's case, of five years, until he is 21.

We do not consider whether, on the merits, Kent should have been transferred; but there is no place in our system of law for reaching a result of such tremendous consequences without ceremony—without hearing, without effective assistance of counsel, without a statement of reasons. It is inconceivable that a court of justice dealing with adults, with respect to a similar issue, would proceed in this manner. It would be extraordinary if society's special concern for children, as reflected in the District of Columbia's Juvenile Court Act, permitted this procedure. We hold that it does not.

1. The theory of the District's Juvenile Court Act, like that of other jurisdictions, is rooted in social welfare philosophy rather than in the *corpus juris*. Its proceedings are designated as civil rather than criminal. The Juvenile Court is theoretically engaged in determining the needs of the child and of society rather than adjudicating criminal conduct. The objectives are to provide measures of guidance and rehabilitation for the child and protection for society, not to fix criminal responsibility, guilt, and punishment. The State is parens patriae rather than prosecuting attorney and judge. But the admonition to function in a "parental" relationship is not an invitation to procedural arbitrariness.

2. Because the State is supposed to proceed in respect of the child as *parens patriae* and not as adversary, courts have relied on the premise that the proceedings are "civil" in nature and not criminal, and have asserted that the child cannot complain of the deprivation of important rights available in criminal cases. It has been asserted that he can claim only the fundamental due process right to fair treatment. For example, it has been held that he is not entitled to bail; to indictment by grand jury; to a speedy and public trial; to trial by jury; to immunity against self-incrimination; to confrontation of his accusers; and in some jurisdictions (but not in the District of Columbia, see *Shioutakon v. District of Columbia*, 98 U.S. App. D.C. 371, 236 F.2d 666 (1956), and *Black v. United States*, supra) that he is not entitled to counsel.

While there can be no doubt of the original laudable purpose of juvenile courts, studies and critiques in recent years raise serious questions as to whether actual performance measures well enough against theoretical purpose to make tolerable the immunity of the process from the reach of constitutional guaranties applicable to adults.

There is much evidence that some juvenile courts, including that of the District of Columbia, lack the personnel, facilities, and techniques to perform adequately as representatives of the State in a parens patriae capacity, at least with respect to children charged with law violation. There is evidence, in fact, that there may be grounds for concern that the child receives the worst of both worlds: that he gets neither the protections accorded to adults nor the solicitous care and regenerative treatment postulated for children.

This concern, however, does not induce us in this case to accept the invitation to rule that constitutional guaranties which would be applicable to adults charged with the serious offenses for which Kent was tried must be applied in juvenile court proceedings concerned with allegations of law violation. The Juvenile Court Act and the decisions of the United States Court of Appeals for the District of Columbia Circuit provide an adequate basis for decision of this case, and we go no further.

3. It is clear beyond dispute that the waiver of jurisdiction is a "critically important" action determining vitally important statutory rights of the juvenile. The Court of Appeals for the District of Columbia Circuit has so held. See *Black v. United States,* supra; *Watkins v. United States,* 119 U.S. App. D.C. 490, 343 F.2d 278 (1964). The statutory scheme makes this plain. The Juvenile Court is vested with "original and exclusive jurisdiction" of the child. This jurisdiction confers special rights and immunities. He is, as specified by the statute, shielded from publicity. He may be confined, but with rare exceptions he may not be jailed along with adults. He may be detained, but only until he is 21 years of age. The court is admonished by the statute to give preference to retaining the child in the custody of his parents "unless his welfare and the safety and protection of the public can not be adequately safeguarded without . . . removal." The child is protected against consequences of adult conviction such as the loss of civil rights, the use of adjudication against him in subsequent proceedings, and disqualification for public employment. D.C. Code §§ 11-907, 11-915, 11-927, 11-929 (1961).

The net, therefore, is that petitioner—then a boy of 16—was by statute entitled to certain procedures and benefits as a consequence of his statutory right to the "exclusive" jurisdiction of the Juvenile Court. In these circumstances, considering particularly that decision as to waiver of jurisdiction and transfer of the matter to the District Court was potentially as important to petitioner as the difference between five years' confinement and a death sentence, we conclude that, as a condition to a valid waiver order, petitioner was entitled to a hearing, including access by his counsel to the social records and probation or similar reports which presumably are considered by the court, and to a statement of reasons for the Juvenile Court's decision. We believe that this result is required by the statute read in the context of constitutional principles relating to due process and the assistance of counsel.

The Court of Appeals in this case relied upon *Wilhite v. United States,* 108 U.S. App. D.C. 279, 281 f.2d 642 (1960). In that case, the Court of Appeals held, for purposes of a determination as to waiver of jurisdiction, that no formal hearing is required and that the "full investigation" required of the Juvenile Court need only be such "as is needed to satisfy that court . . . on the question of waiver." (Emphasis supplied.) The authority of *Wilhite,* however, is substantially undermined by other, more recent, decisions of the Court of Appeals.

In *Black v. United States,* decided by the Court of Appeals on December 8, 1965, the court held that assistance of counsel in the "critically important" determination of waiver is essential to the proper administration of juvenile proceedings. Because the juvenile was not advised of his right to retained or appointed

Famous Words in History Make Good Exam Questions

counsel, the judgment of the District Court, following waiver of jurisdiction by the Juvenile Court, was reversed. The court relied upon its decision in *Shioutakon v. District of Columbia*, 98 U.S. App. D.C. 371, 236 F.2d 666 (1956), in which it had held that effective assistance of counsel in juvenile court proceedings is essential. See also *McDaniel v. Shea*, 108 U.S. App. D.C. 15, 278 F.2d 460 (1960). In *Black*, the court referred to the Criminal Justice Act, enacted four years after *Shioutakon*, in which Congress provided for the assistance of counsel "in proceedings before the juvenile court of the District of Columbia." D.C. Code § 2-2202 (1961). The court held that "The need is even greater in the adjudication of waiver [than in a case like *Shioutakon*] since it contemplates the imposition of criminal sanctions." 122 U.S. App. D.C., at 395, 355 F.2d, at 106.

In *Watkins v. United States*, 119 U.S. App. D.C. 409, 343 F.2d 278 (1964), decided in November 1964, the Juvenile Court had waived jurisdiction of appellant who was charged with housebreaking and larceny. In the District Court, appellant sought disclosure of the social record in order to attack the validity of the waiver.

Importance of Social History Records

The Court of Appeals held that in a waiver proceeding a juvenile's attorney is entitled to access to such records. The court observed that "All of the social records concerning the child are usually relevant to waiver since the Juvenile Court must be deemed to consider the entire history of the child in determining waiver. The relevance of particular items must be construed generously. Since an attorney has no certain knowledge of what the social records contain, he cannot be expected to demonstrate the relevance of particular items in his request.

"The child's attorney must be advised of the information upon which the Juvenile Court relied in order to assist effectively in the determination of the waiver question, by insisting upon the statutory command that waiver can be ordered only after 'full investigation,' and by guarding against action of the Juvenile Court beyond its discretionary authority." 119 U.S. App. D.C., at 413, 343 F.2d, at 282. The court remanded the record to the District Court for a determination of the extent to which the records should be disclosed.

The Court of Appeals' decision in the present case was handed down on October 26, 1964, prior to its decisions in *Black* and *Watkins*. The Court of Appeals assumed that since petitioner had been a probationer of the Juvenile Court for two years, that court had before it sufficient evidence to make an informed judgment. It therefore concluded that the statutory requirement of a "full investigation" had been met. It noted the absence of "a specification by the Juvenile Court Judge of precisely why he concluded to waive jurisdiction." 119 U.S. App. D.C., at 384, 343 F.2d, at 253. While it indicated that "in some cases at least" a useful purpose might be served "by a discussion of the reasons motivating the determination," id., at 384, 343 F.2d, at 253, it did not conclude that the absence thereof invalidated the waiver.

What the Appeals Court Said It Did and Why

As to the denial of access to the social records, the Court of Appeals stated that "the statute is ambiguous." It said that petitioner's claim, in essence, is "that counsel should have the opportunity to challenge them, presumably in a manner akin to cross-examination." Id., at 389, 343 F.2d, at 258. It held, however, that this is "the kind of adversarial tactics which the system is designed to avoid." It characterized counsel's proper function as being merely that of bringing forward affirmative information which might help the court. His function, the Court of Appeals said, "is not to denigrate the staff's submissions and recommendations." Ibid. Accordingly, it held that the Juvenile Court had not abused its discretion in denying access to the social records.

We are of the opinion that the Court of Appeals misconceived the basic issue and the underlying values in this case. It did note, as another panel of the same court did a few months later in *Black* and *Watkins*, that the determination of whether to transfer a child from the statutory structure of the Juvenile Court to the criminal processes of the District Court is "critically important." We hold that it is, indeed, a "critically important" proceeding. The Juvenile Court Act confers upon the child a right to avail himself of that court's "exclusive" jurisdiction. As the Court of Appeals has said, "It is implicit in the [Juvenile Court] scheme that non-criminal treatment is to be the rule—and the adult criminal treatment, the exception which must be governed by the particular factors of individual cases." *Harling v. United States*, 111 U.S. App. D.C. 174, 177–178, 295 F.2d 161, 164–165 (1961).

Meaningful review requires that the reviewing court should review. It should not be remitted to assumptions. It must have before it a statement of the reasons motivating the waiver including, of course, a statement of the relevant facts. It may not "assume" that there are adequate reasons, nor may it merely assume that "full investigation" has been made. Accordingly, we hold that it is incumbent upon the Juvenile Court to accompany its waiver order with a statement of the reasons or considerations therefore. We do not read the statute as requiring that this statement must be formal or that it should necessarily include conventional findings of fact. But the statement should be sufficient to demonstrate that the statutory requirement of "full investigation" has been met; and that the question has received the careful consideration of the Juvenile Court; and it must set forth the basis for the order with sufficient specificity to permit meaningful review.

> Supreme Court judges telling other judges to do their jobs!

Correspondingly, we conclude that an opportunity for a hearing which may be informal, must be given the child prior to entry of a waiver order. Under *Black*, the child is entitled to counsel in connection with a waiver proceeding, and under *Watkins*, counsel is entitled to see the child's social records. These rights are meaningless—an illusion, a mockery—unless counsel is given an opportunity to function.

The right to representation by counsel is not a formality. It is not a grudging gesture to a ritualistic requirement. It is of the essence of justice. Appointment of counsel without affording an opportunity for hearing on a "critically important" decision is tantamount to denial of counsel. There is no justification for the failure of the Juvenile Court to rule on the motion for hearing filed by petitioner's counsel, and it was error to fail to grant a hearing.

> Role of Attorney

We do not mean by this to indicate that the hearing to be held must conform with all of the requirements of a criminal trial or even of the usual administrative hearing; but we do hold that the hearing must measure up to the essentials of due process and fair treatment. *Pee v. United States*, 107 U.S. App. D.C. 47, 50, 274 F.2d 556, 559 (1959). With respect to access by the child's counsel to the social records of the child, we deem it obvious that since these are to be considered by the Juvenile Court in making its decision to waive, they must be made available to the child's counsel. This is what the Court of Appeals itself held in *Watkins*. There is no doubt as to the statutory basis for this conclusion, as the Court of Appeals pointed out in *Watkins*. We cannot agree with the Court of Appeals in the present case that the statute is "ambiguous." The statute expressly provides that the record shall be withheld from "indiscriminate" public inspection, "except that such records or parts thereof shall be made available by rule of court or special order of court to such persons . . . as have a legitimate interest in the protection . . . of the child. . . ." D.C. Code § 11-929 (b) (1961), now § 11-1586 (b) (Supp. IV, 1965). (Emphasis supplied.) The Court of Appeals has held in *Black*, and we agree, that counsel must be afforded to the child in waiver proceedings. Counsel, therefore, have a "legitimate interest" in the protection of the child, and must be afforded access to these records.

We do not agree with the Court of Appeals' statement, attempting to justify denial of access to these records, that counsel's role is limited to presenting "to the court anything on behalf of the child which might help the court in arriving at a decision; it is not to denigrate the staff's submissions and recommendations." On the contrary, if the staff's submissions include materials which are susceptible to challenge or impeachment, it is precisely the role of counsel to "denigrate" such matter. There is no irrebuttable presumption of accuracy attached to staff reports. If a decision on waiver is "critically important" it is equally of "critical importance" that the material submitted to the judge—which is protected by the statute only against "indiscriminate" inspection—be subjected, within reasonable limits having regard to the theory of the Juvenile Court Act, to examination, criticism, and refutation. While the Juvenile Court judge may, of course, receive ex parte analyses and recommendations from his staff, he may not, for purposes of a decision on waiver, receive and rely upon secret information, whether emanating from his staff or otherwise. The Juvenile Court is governed in this respect by the established principles which control courts and quasi-judicial agencies of the Government.

Both federal courts erred—District and Court Appeals.

For the reasons stated, we conclude that the Court of Appeals and the District Court erred in sustaining the validity of the waiver by the Juvenile Court. The Government urges that any error committed by the Juvenile Court was cured by the proceedings before the District Court. It is true that the District Court considered and denied a motion to dismiss on the grounds of the invalidity of the waiver order of the Juvenile Court, and that it considered and denied a motion that it should itself, as authorized by statute, proceed in this case to "exercise the powers conferred upon the juvenile court." D.C. Code § 11-914 (1961), now § 11-1553 (Supp. IV, 1965). But we agree with the Court of Appeals in *Black*, that "the waiver question was primarily and initially one for the Juvenile Court to decide and its failure to do so in a valid manner cannot be said to be harmless error. It is the Juvenile Court, not the District Court, which has the facilities, personnel, and expertise for a proper determination of the waiver issue." 122 U.S. App. D.C., at 396, 355 F.2d, at 107.

What Might Have Happened

Ordinarily we would reverse the Court of Appeals and direct the District Court to remand the case to the Juvenile Court for a new determination of waiver. If on remand the decision were against waiver, the indictment in the District Court would be dismissed. See *Black v. United States*, supra. However, petitioner has now passed the age of 21 and the Juvenile Court can no longer exercise jurisdiction over him. In view of the unavailability of a redetermination of the waiver question by the Juvenile Court, it is urged by petitioner that the conviction should be vacated and the indictment dismissed. In the circumstances of this case, and in light of the remedy which the Court of Appeals fashioned in *Black*, supra, we do not consider it appropriate to grant this drastic relief. Accordingly, we vacate the order of the Court of Appeals and the judgment of the District Court and remand the case to the District Court for a hearing de novo on waiver, consistent with this opinion. If that court finds that waiver was inappropriate, petitioner's conviction must be vacated. If, however, it finds that the waiver order was proper when originally made, the District Court may proceed, after consideration of such motions as counsel may make and such further proceedings, if any, as may be warranted, to enter an appropriate judgment. Cf. *Black v. United States*, supra.

Decision

DECISION: REVERSED AND REMANDED.

Dissent by: Stewart

Dissent: Mr. Justice Stewart, with whom Mr. Justice Black, Mr. Justice Harlan, and Mr. Justice White join, dissenting.

This case involves the construction of a statute applicable only to the District of Columbia. Our general practice is to leave undisturbed decisions of the Court of Appeals for the District of Columbia Circuit concerning the import of legislation governing the affairs of the District. *General Motors Corp. v. District of Columbia*, 380 U.S. 553, 556. It appears, however, that two cases decided by the Court of Appeals subsequent to its decision in the present case may have considerably modified the court's construction of the statute. Therefore, I would vacate this judgment and remand the case to the Court of Appeals for reconsideration in the light of its subsequent decisions, *Watkins v. United States*, 119 U.S. App. D.C. 409, 343 F.2d 278, and *Black v. United States*, 122 U.S. App. D.C. 393, 355 F.2d 104.

NOTES AFTER KENT

1. The Progressives, who created the juvenile court, dreamed of a benevolent treatment agency staffed by expert judges and assisted by social services personnel. The informality, flexibility, and discretionary dispositions were to be in "the best interest of the child." As you read the facts in *Kent*, did you think that the "best interest of the child" was being met?

2. Lois G. Forer in *Money and Justice* (New York: W.W. Norton & Co., 1984) said that although the hasty, irregular procedures prevailed in juvenile court, there was a quiet revolution occurring in criminal law dealing with the right to counsel. In 1938 the U.S. Supreme Court held that an adult accused of a federal crime had the right to the assistance of counsel. In a series of other landmark cases, the right to counsel was extended to both federal and state crime violators for adults—not juveniles. "Appellate courts were, for the most part, unaware of the casual procedures in juvenile courts and the abominable conditions in many institutions to which children were committed by juvenile courts" (p. 139). Why do you think that happened?

3. There was, indeed, evidence that the children placed in correctional institutions were not getting the care and treatment that was supposed to be given to them. All across the country, citizens' groups, enraged parents, and journalists began to document the story. Documentary films like *This Child is Rated X* received awards for their work. Wooden (1976) described the horrors of the Indiana Boy's Home. One young man was tied to the bed with each foot and arm to a corresponding post of the bed. Then, he was given a shot of muscle relaxants and remained in that position for eight days. There were also class action suits such as *Nelson v. Heyne* (1972), which challenged the supervised beatings and indiscriminate use of tranquilizing drugs without competent medical supervision (Schwartz 1989, 5).

An example of one state's effort to improve conditions was in New York. Citizens' Committee for Children of New York, Inc. was a task force that reviewed the fourteen residential juvenile institutions. In its final report in December, 1969, the committee concluded that most of the monies were lavished on the buildings and, thus, too little for the care of the youth. The youths were doing time with few educational and treatment programs. Many children were given tranquilizers to make the work easier for the staff, and the television was used as a recreational program. Caretakers put the young people in stripped cells for days. Solitary confinement (under euphemisms, of course) was used in nearly all schools. The staff had neither the necessary background nor the in-service training to deal with troubled youths. This was all being done at an average cost of $8,000 per year per child with some programs as high as $11,000 per year per child (Citizens' Committee for Children of New York, Inc., 1969).

It is no wonder that the committee's recommendation was to do away with these large institutions far away from the homes of these youths. They recommended greater use of foster homes, day centers, small residences, community mental health services, and other means of rehabilitation. New York did not follow those suggestions as much as did the State of Massachusetts. In the early 1970s, following the leadership of Dr. Jerome Miller, Massachusetts closed its massive rural institutions built in the 1840s and replaced them with community-based corrections.

Krisberg, Schwartz, Litsky, and Austin (1986, 25) used data to show that although juvenile arrests have declined, the juvenile justice system has become more formal and restrictive and more oriented toward punishment. In their research, only Massachusetts and Vermont had virtually closed down their training schools (juvenile correctional facility = prison) substituting an array of community-based alternatives. Deinstitutionalization, as it has become known, was also employed by Kentucky, West Virginia, Alabama, and Utah. The highest training admission rates were found in Alaska, the District of Columbia, Maryland, New Hampshire, and Oregon.

4. The central issue of *Kent* is: How does a state, which has original jurisdiction over a child, end that jurisdiction and send the youth to the criminal court to be tried as if he or she were an adult? Only a very few states have exclusive jurisdiction over juveniles. As of 1997, 46 states and the District of Columbia have passed statutes allowing judicial waiver with 28 of those states excluding certain juvenile offenders from the juvenile court jurisdiction. There are three basic transfer mechanisms: judicial waiver, statutory exclusion, and concurrent jurisdiction. Judicial waiver is the kind of due process ceremony that Kent didn't get but the Supreme Court said he should have. Statutory waiver negates the *Kent* decision because the youth has no hearing. The statute permits the state to transfer the youth of a certain age, having committed a certain offense, and/or prior court history (no longer treatable in juvenile court) to go directly to the (adult) criminal court. Some 14 states at least hold a hearing in juvenile court to determine if the youth does fit the criteria of age and committed offense listed in the statute for mandatory waiver. Lastly, concurrent jurisdiction (also known as prosecutor discretion or direct filing) is when both the juvenile and criminal court have jurisdiction. The prosecutors can determine where to charge and prosecute. In 1997, there were 14 states and the District of Columbia that give prosecutors this "executive function" free from judicial review. According to state appellate courts, it is not required to meet the due process standards established by *Kent* (http://www.ojjdp.ncjrs.org/ojstatbb/qa088.html, 1 July 1999).

In addition, statutes in 13 states exclude large numbers of juvenile offenders due to their definition of juvenile. For example, North Carolina, Connecticut, and New York use age 15 as their cut-off age. A 16-year-old in those states is considered an adult for criminal court jurisdiction while many other states have the upper age of 17, making an 18-year-old an adult.

In Virginia, if the youth had committed a major offense such as murder, there is now a three-tier certification and transfer procedure. The first tier is a legislative waiver process that applies to juveniles 14 or older who are charged with murder and aggravated malicious wounding. In those types of cases, the preliminary hearing is held in the juvenile court but the case is tried in the adult court (Circuit Court). The judge in Circuit Court hears the case and fixes the sentence, except for capital murder, which has to be done by a jury.

The second tier of prosecutorial waiver applies to juveniles 14 or older charged with felony homicide, rape, forcible sodomy and object penetration, felony class mob violations, malicious wounding, malicious wounding of a law enforcement officer, poisoning, robbery, and carjacking. In these cases, the Commonwealth attorney (prosecutor) makes a written motion, and the juvenile court will certify the case to Circuit Court. Notice that this means there is no waiver hearing. There is no juvenile judge to decide. The decision-maker is the prosecuting attorney.

If the Commonwealth attorney elects not to make such a motion or withdraws the motion, the case will proceed as a judicial transfer process. This third tier is also known as reverse certification. In this hearing, a variety of factors that speak to the juvenile's being a "proper person" to be handled in the juvenile court are presented. Thus, if the child or child's attorney is successful, the child's case is then sent to juvenile court for the adjudicatory hearing and the sentencing using the dispositional options for youth.

5. What did Justice Fortas mean when he called the transfer of youth to adult criminal court a result of "such tremendous consequences"? Can a delinquent be sentenced to capital punishment in juvenile court?

(Answer: In the juvenile court, a youth cannot be given capital punishment because that option is not available. To receive that kind of punishment, the youth would have to be waived into the adult court and tried, found guilty of a capital crime, and then sentenced to capital punishment. If the youth were under 16 years of age, however, the recent Supreme Court decision *Kentucky v. Stanford* would prohibit the state from executing the youth.)

6. In the dissent written by Justice Stewart, to "vacate this judgment and remand the case to the Court of Appeals for reconsideration" means that if the judges in the Court of Appeals would change their decision of "affirm" to "reverse," this case would come back to the juvenile judge for his or her reconsideration. The result would be very different for anyone concerned except, possibly, for Kent. Because Kent is past the age of jurisdiction for the juvenile court, the juvenile judge may be able to not have any hearing. But, the whole messy case would go back down (in the hierarchy of the appellate courts), and juveniles, nationwide, would have no rights at the waiver stage. All those rights would be erased. Justice Stewart has reminded his other federal judges that they could change their minds by justifying their new decision by *Watkins* and *Black*, two earlier decisions.

IN RE GAULT ET AL.

SUPREME COURT OF THE UNITED STATES

387 U.S. 1; 87 S.Ct. 1428; 18 L.Ed.2d 527 (1967)

December 6, 1966, Argued May 15, 1967, Decided

Prior History: Appeal from the Supreme Court of Arizona.

Disposition: 99 Ariz. 181, 407 P. 2d 760, reversed and remanded.

Summary of Facts

Syllabus: Appellants' 15-year-old son, Gerald Gault, was taken into custody as the result of a complaint that he had made lewd telephone calls. After hearings before a juvenile court judge, Gerald was ordered committed to the State Industrial School as a juvenile delinquent until he should reach majority. Appellants brought a habeas corpus action in the state courts to challenge the constitutionality of the Arizona Juvenile Code and the procedure actually used in Gerald's case, on the ground of denial of various procedural due process rights. The State Supreme Court affirmed dismissal of the writ. Agreeing that the constitutional guarantee of due process applies to proceedings in which juveniles are charged as delinquents, the court held that the Arizona Juvenile Code impliedly includes the requirements of due process in delinquency proceedings, and that such due process requirements were not offended by the procedure leading to Gerald's commitment. Held:

1. *Kent v. United States*, 383 U.S. 541, 562 (1966), held "that the [waiver] hearing must measure up to the essentials of due process and fair treatment." This view is reiterated, here in connection with a juvenile court adjudication of "delinquency," as a requirement which is part of the Due Process Clause of the Fourteenth Amendment of our Constitution. The holding in this case relates only to the adjudicatory stage of the juvenile process, where commitment to a state institution may follow. When proceedings may result in incarceration in an institution of confinement, "it would be extraordinary if our Constitution did not require the procedural regularity and exercise of care implied in the phrase 'due process.'" pp. 12–31.

2. Due process requires, in such proceedings, that adequate written notice be afforded the child and his parents or guardian. Such notice must inform them "of the specific issues that they must meet" and must be given "at the earliest practicable time, and in any event sufficiently in advance of the hearing to permit preparation." Notice here was neither timely nor adequately specific, nor was there waiver of the right to constitutionally adequate notice. pp. 31–34.

3. In such proceedings the child and his parents must be advised of their right to be represented by counsel and, if they are unable to afford counsel, that counsel will be appointed to represent the child. Mrs. Gault's statement at the habeas corpus hearing that she had known she could employ counsel, is not "an 'intentional relinquishment or abandonment' of a fully known right." pp. 34–42.

4. The constitution privilege against self-incrimination is applicable in such proceedings: "an admission by the juvenile may [not] be used against him in the absence of clear and unequivocal evidence that the admission was made with knowledge that he was not obliged to speak and would not be penalized for remaining silent." "The availability of the privilege does not turn upon the type of proceeding in which its protection is invoked, but upon the nature of the statement or admission and the exposure which it invites. . . . Juvenile proceedings to determine 'delinquency,' which may lead to commitment to a state institution, must be regarded as 'criminal' for purposes of the privilege against self-incrimination." Furthermore, experience has shown that "admissions and confessions by juveniles require special caution" as to their reliability and voluntariness, and "it would indeed be surprising if the privilege against self-

incrimination were available to hardened criminals but not to children." "Special problems may arise with respect to waiver of the privilege by or on behalf of children, and . . . there may well be some differences in technique—but not in principle—depending upon the age of the child and the presence and competence of parents. . . . If counsel was not present for some permissible reason when an admission was obtained, the greatest care must be taken to assure that the admission was voluntary. . . ." Gerald's admissions did not measure up to these standards, and could not properly be used as a basis for the judgment against him. pp. 44–56.

5. Absent a valid confession, a juvenile in such proceedings must be afforded the rights of confrontation and sworn testimony of witnesses available for cross-examination. pp. 56–57.

6. Other questions raised by appellants, including the absence of provision for appellate review of a delinquency adjudication, and a transcript of the proceedings, are not ruled upon. pp. 57–58.

JUDGES: Warren, Black, Douglas, Clark, Harlan, Brennan, Stewart, White, Fortas

OPINION BY: FORTAS

OPINION: MR. JUSTICE FORTAS delivered the opinion of the Court. | Majority Opinion

This is an appeal under 28 U.S.C. § 1257 (2) from a judgment of the Supreme Court of Arizona affirming the dismissal of a petition for a writ of habeas corpus. 99 Ariz. 181, 407 P. 2d 760 (1965). The petition sought the release of Gerald Francis Gault, appellants' 15-year-old son, who had been committed as a juvenile delinquent to the State Industrial School by the Juvenile Court of Gila County, Arizona. The Supreme Court of Arizona affirmed dismissal of the writ against various arguments which included an attack upon the constitutionality of the Arizona Juvenile Code because of its alleged denial of procedural due process rights to juveniles charged with being "delinquents." The court agreed that the constitutional guarantee of due process of law is applicable in such proceedings. It held that Arizona's Juvenile Code is to be read as "impliedly" implementing the "due process concept." It then proceeded to identify and describe "the particular elements which constitute due process in a juvenile hearing." It concluded that the proceedings ending in commitment of Gerald Gault did not offend those requirements.

We do not agree, and **we reverse**. We begin with a statement of the facts. | Decision

I

On Monday, June 8, 1964, at about 10 a.m., Gerald Francis Gault and a friend, | Facts
Ronald Lewis, were taken into custody by the Sheriff of Gila County. Gerald was then still subject to a six months' probation order which had been entered on February 25, 1964, as a result of his having been in the company of another boy who had stolen a wallet from a lady's purse. The police action on June 8 was taken as the result of a verbal complaint by a neighbor of the boys, Mrs. Cook, about a telephone call made to her in which the caller or callers made lewd or indecent remarks. It will suffice for purposes of this opinion to say that the remarks or questions put to her were of the irritatingly offensive, adolescent, sex variety.

At the time Gerald was picked up, his mother and father were both at work. No notice that Gerald was being taken into custody was left at the home. No other steps were taken to advise them that their son had, in effect, been arrested. Gerald was taken to the Children's Detention Home. When his mother arrived home at about 6 o'clock, Gerald was not there. Gerald's older brother was sent to look for him at the trailer home of the Lewis family. He apparently learned then that Gerald was in custody. He so informed his mother. The two of them went to the Detention Home. The deputy probation officer, Flagg, who was also superintendent of the Detention Home, told Mrs. Gault "why Jerry was there" and said that a hearing would be held in Juvenile Court at 3 o'clock the following day, June 9.

Officer Flagg filed a petition with the court on the hearing day, June 9, 1964. It was not served on the Gaults. Indeed, none of them saw this petition until the habeas corpus hearing on August 17, 1964. The petition was entirely formal. It made no reference to any factual basis for the judicial action which it initiated. It recited only that "said minor is under the age of eighteen years, and is in need of the protection of this Honorable Court; [and that] said minor is a delinquent minor." It prayed for a hearing and an order regarding "the care and custody of said minor." Officer Flagg executed a formal affidavit in support of the petition.

Notice that the court does use footnotes. Most have been edited out except numbers 1–6.

On June 9, Gerald, his mother, his older brother, and Probation Officers Flagg and Henderson appeared before the Juvenile Judge in chambers. Gerald's father was not there. He was at work out of the city. Mrs. Cook, the complainant, was not there. No one was sworn at this hearing. No transcript or recording was made. No memorandum or record of the substance of the proceedings was prepared. Our information about the proceedings and the subsequent hearing on June 15 derives entirely from the testimony of the Juvenile Court Judge,[1] Mr. and Mrs. Gault and Officer Flagg at the habeas corpus proceeding conducted two months later. From this, it appears that at the June 9 hearing Gerald was questioned by the judge about the telephone call. There was conflict as to what he said. His mother recalled that Gerald said he only dialed Mrs. Cook's number and handed the telephone to his friend, Ronald. Officer Flagg recalled that Gerald had admitted making the lewd remarks. Judge McGhee testified that Gerald "admitted making one of these [lewd] statements." At the conclusion of the hearing, the judge said he would "think about it." Gerald was taken back to the Detention Home. He was not sent to his own home with his parents. On June 11 or 12, after having been detained since June 8, Gerald was released and driven home.[2] There is no explanation in the record as to why he was kept in the Detention Home or why he was released. At 5 p.m. on the day of Gerald's release, Mrs. Gault received a note signed by Officer Flagg. It was on plain paper, not letterhead. Its entire text was as follows:

"Mrs. Gault:

"Judge McGhee has set Monday June 15, 1964 at 11:00 A.M. as the date and time for further Hearings on Gerald's delinquency

"/s/Flagg"

---

[1] Under Arizona law, juvenile hearings are conducted by a judge of the Superior Court, designated by his colleagues on the Superior Court to serve as Juvenile Court Judge. Arizona Const., Art. 6, § 15; Arizona Revised Statutes (hereinafter ARS) §§ 8–201, 8–202.
[2] There is a conflict between the recollection of Mrs. Gault and that of Officer Flagg. Mrs. Gault testified that Gerald was released on Friday, June 12, and Officer Flagg that it had been on Thursday, June 11. This was from memory; Officer Flagg had no record, and the note hereafter referred to was undated.

At the appointed time on Monday, June 15, Gerald, his father and mother, Ronald Lewis and his father, and Officers Flagg and Henderson were present before Judge McGhee. Witnesses at the habeas corpus proceeding differed in their recollections of Gerald's testimony at the June 15 hearing. Mr. and Mrs. Gault recalled that Gerald again testified that he had only dialed the number and that the other boy had made the remarks. Officer Flagg agreed that at this hearing Gerald did not admit making the lewd remarks.[3] But Judge McGhee recalled that "there was some admission again of some of the lewd statements. He—he didn't admit any of the more serious lewd statements."[4] Again, the complainant, Mrs. Cook, was not present. Mrs. Gault asked that Mrs. Cook be present "so she could see which boy that done the talking, the dirty talking over the phone." The Juvenile Judge said "she didn't have to be present at that hearing." The judge did not speak to Mrs. Cook or communicate with her at any time. Probation Officer Flagg had talked to her once—over the telephone on June 9.

At this June 15 hearing a "referral report" made by the probation officers was field with the court, although not disclosed to Gerald or his parents. This listed the charge as "Lewd Phone Calls." At the conclusion of the hearing, the judge committed Gerald as a juvenile delinquent to the State Industrial School "for the period of his minority [that is, until 21], unless sooner discharged by due process of law." An order to that effect was entered. It recites that "after a full hearing and due deliberation the Court finds that said minor is a delinquent child, and that said minor is of the age of 15 years."

No appeal is permitted by Arizona law in juvenile cases. On August 3, 1964, a petition for a writ of habeas corpus was filed with the Supreme Court of Arizona and referred by it to the Superior Court for hearing.

At the habeas corpus hearing on August 17, Judge McGhee was vigorously cross-examined as to the basis for his actions. He testified that he had taken into account the fact that Gerald was on probation. He was asked "under what section of . . . the code you found the boy delinquent?"

His answer is set forth in the margin.[5] In substance, he concluded that Gerald came within ARS § 8-201-6 (a), which specifies that a "delinquent child" includes one "who has violated a law of the state or an ordinance or regulation of a political subdivision thereof." The law which Gerald was found to have violated is ARS § 13-377. This section of the Arizona Criminal Code provides that a person who "in the presence or hearing of any woman or child . . . uses vulgar, abusive or obscene language, is guilty of a misdemeanor. . . ." The penalty specified in the Criminal Code, which would apply to an adult, is $5 to $50, or imprisonment for not more than two months. The judge also testified that he

---

[3] Officer Flagg also testified that Gerald had not, when questioned at the Detention Home, admitted having made any of the lewd statements, but that each boy sought to put the blame on the other. There was conflicting testimony as to whether Ronald had accused Gerald of making the lewd statements during the June 15 hearing.

[4] Judge McGhee also testified that Gerald had not denied "certain statements" made to him at the hearing by Officer Henderson.

[5] "Q. All right. Now, Judge, would you tell me under what section of the law or tell me under what section of—of the code you found the boy delinquent?

"A. Well, there is a—I think it amounts to disturbing the peace. I can't give you the section, but I can tell you the law, that when one person uses lewd language in the presence of another person, that it can amount to—and I consider that when a person makes it over the phone, that it is considered in the presence, I might be wrong, that is one section. The other section upon which I consider the boy delinquent is Section 8-201, Subsection (d), habitually involved in immoral matters."

acted under ARS § 8-201-6 (d) which includes in the definition of a "delinquent child" one who, as the judge phrased it, is "habitually involved in immoral matters."[6]

Could this be an example of "Given to Sexual Irregularities" discussed in Chapter 2?

Asked about the basis for his conclusion that Gerald was "habitually involved in immoral matters," the judge testified, somewhat vaguely, that two years earlier, on July 2, 1962, a "referral" was made concerning Gerald, "where the boy had stolen a baseball glove from another boy and lied to the Police Department about it." The judge said there was "no hearing," and "no accusation" relating to this incident, "because of lack of material foundation." But it seems to have remained in his mind as a relevant factor. The judge also testified that Gerald had admitted making other nuisance phone calls in the past which, as the judge recalled the boy's testimony, were "silly calls, or funny calls, or something like that."

Procedural History

The Superior Court dismissed the writ, and appellants sought review in the Arizona Supreme Court. That court stated that it considered appellants' assignments of error as urging (1) that the Juvenile Code, ARS § 8-201 to § 8-239, is unconstitutional because it does not require that parents and children be apprised of the specific charges, does not require proper notice of a hearing, and does not provide for an appeal; and (2) that the proceedings and order relating to Gerald constituted a denial of due process of law because of the absence of adequate notice of the charge and the hearing; failure to notify appellants of certain constitutional rights including the rights to counsel and to confrontation, and the privilege against self-incrimination; the use of unsworn hearsay testimony; and the failure to make a record of the proceedings. Appellants further asserted that it was error for the Juvenile Court to remove Gerald from the custody of his parents without a showing and finding of their unsuitability, and alleged a miscellany of other errors under state law.

The Supreme Court handed down an elaborate and wide-ranging opinion affirming dismissal of the writ and stating the court's conclusions as to the issues raised by appellants and other aspects of the juvenile process. In their jurisdictional statement and brief in this Court, appellants do not urge upon us all of the points passed upon by the Supreme Court of Arizona. They urge that we hold the Juvenile Code of Arizona invalid on its face or as applied in this case because, contrary to the Due Process Clause of the Fourteenth Amendment, the juvenile is taken from the custody of his parents and committed to a state institution pursuant to proceedings in which the Juvenile Court has virtually unlimited discretion, and in which the following basic rights are denied:

1. Notice of the charges;
2. Right to counsel;
3. Right to confrontation and cross-examination;
4. Privilege against self-incrimination;

---

[6] ARS § 8-201-6, the section of the Arizona Juvenile Code which defines a delinquent child, reads:

" 'Delinquent child' includes:

"(a) A child who has violated a law of the state or an ordinance or regulation of a political subdivision thereof.

"(b) A child who, by reason of being incorrigible, wayward or habitually disobedient, is uncontrolled by his parent, guardian or custodian.

"(c) A child who is habitually truant from school or home.

"(d) A child who habitually so deports himself as to injure or endanger the morals or health of himself or others."

5. Right to a transcript of the proceedings; and
6. Right to appellate review.

We shall not consider other issues which were passed upon by the Supreme Court of Arizona. We emphasize that we indicate no opinion as to whether the decision of that court with respect to such other issues does or does not conflict with requirements of the Federal Constitution.

1. Previous juvenile court cases were declared moot when the juvenile was no longer under the jurisdiction of the juvenile court. One ACLU attorney recalled that there were several cases in the works. If **Gault** did not go, there would have been another case. Yet Jerry Gault was young enough. He was incarcerated for two years and was still under the jurisdiction of the juvenile court when his case came up to the Supreme Court. Thus the Supreme Court could not declare the case moot.

NOTES AFTER GAULT

2. When Gault was 15 years old, he was committed as a juvenile delinquent to the state industrial school for the period of his minority (until he reached age 21) for the act of making a lewd phone call to a neighboring woman. Applied to an adult, that act would have resulted in a $5 to $50 fine or imprisonment for not more than two months. Why was he sentenced to seven years in a state correctional facility for juveniles?

What do you think were the lewd words?

Although not in the transcript, Kittrie (1971, 122) said that Gault said he only dialed the phone number and his friend asked the following questions: "Do you give any?" "Are your cherries ripe today?" "Do you have big bombers?"

3. Someone had to play the role and advocate in the "best interest of the child." The American Parents' Association used its *amicus curiae* brief. *Amicus curiae* is Latin and means "friends of the court." It is a process in which an impartial bystander interposes and volunteers information upon some matter of law. It also means "advocate." It is a procedure in which weak and unpopular groups such as juvenile delinquents have a means of protecting and furthering their interests. Because the Supreme Court cannot overhaul the entire juvenile justice system, the Supreme Court judges must decide what cases come before them bringing the facts and legal questions based on the "fact pattern." The Supreme Court has the power to make changes in political and social areas and can create a national policy as a standard for all the 50 states; thus, the *amicus curiae* briefs have an impact on the decisions of the Supreme Court.

Several pressure groups responded to the question in *Gault*. They used the *amicus curiae* briefs to express their views. They desired to have the Supreme Court accept their arguments and thus follow their wishes. Each group crystallizes certain attitudes about children; thus, they are interesting to study.

The first group was the *Ohio Association of Juvenile Court Judges*. They represented the traditional view in which the juvenile court was to act as *parens patriae*. In their view, the judge was the wise parent who needed flexibility and freedom to act in the best interest of the child.

Table 1.1   SUMMARY OF AMICUS CURIAE BRIEFS FOR GAULT
GAULT QUESTIONS

Groups	Notice	Right to Counsel	Right to Cross-Exam & Confront	Priv. Against Self-Incrimination	Right to Transcript	Right to Appeal
Ohio Ass. of Juv. Court Judges	D	D	D	D	D	D
Nation. Legal Aid & Defender Assoc.	X	X	X	X		
Legal Aid Society	X	X		X		X
Amer. Parent's Comm.	X	X	X	X	X	X

CODE: X = Supports or agrees with that right.
D = Dissents or disagrees with that right.

Although this brief contains colorful metaphors such as "to burn the barn down to roast the pig," and "the child's welfare is the star to guide the court," the rhetoric and logic of their argument were, indeed, in keeping with the Pennsylvania decision in 1838 dealing with Mary Ann Crouse's father's attempt to free her from the Philadelphia House of Refuge. (Remember, that is the case in which the justices argued that not only did *parens patriae* give them the power to restrain her but also it would be an act of extreme cruelty to release her.)

In dealing with the six issues before the court (Table 1.1), this group disagrees (D = Disagrees) with giving any of these rights to juveniles. They do not want delinquent youth to have the rights to notice, to counsel, to confrontation and cross-examination, to privilege against self-incrimination, to access of a transcript, or to appeal. Remember, these are the judges who are undereducated, overworked, and understaffed. It would not have been in their interest to advocate change that would increase their own workload.

Defense Attorneys   The second group was the *National Legal Aid and Defender Association* with a letter of endorsement from the National Council of Juvenile Court Judges. That group supported its argument with original empirical research. It represented the interests of those who wanted some procedural safeguards in the juvenile court procedure but without setting up rigid guidelines for counsel. This group agreed with giving juveniles the right to notice, counsel, confrontation and cross-examination of the witness, and privilege against self-incrimination.

Social Workers   The third group was *The Legal Aid Society and Citizens' Committee for Children of New York, Inc.* The citizens' committee presented a logical argument with no empirical data. Using law cases dealing with mental illness such as *Baxstrom v. Harold*, the **amicus** brief served to introduce an attack on the vagueness of the Arizona statute dealing with conduct that endangers morals or health. Arguing from similarities for criminal prosecution in substance and impact and applying it to juveniles, the brief stated that the "point in determining safeguards required for the individual's protection against a misuse of State power, is whether he is subject to a restraint of liberty" (*Amicus Curiae* at 12).

The social work approach, blended with legal jargon, was reflected in this Legal Aid Society's brief. It saw this behavior as typical of children of this age because it was a petty violation of law by several children. Furthermore, it argued that the child before the court only admitted to a minor degree of involvement. (Gerald, known as Jerry to his friends, said that he only dialed the telephone number; it was his friend who said the words.)

This presence of social workers in the juvenile court has helped to make the court unique. From its beginning, social workers have been a part of the juvenile court. "Julia Lathrop, fresh from the battle which had resulted in the passage of the Illinois' juvenile court," became the first leader of the U.S. Children's Bureau (Stapleton and Teitelbaum 1972, 12). She and like-minded persons who succeeded her have worked for the development of the social work approach to the juvenile court. Establishing social work as a profession was also fostered to a substantial extent by the Children's Bureau. That professionalism in turn fostered the development of family courts.

As shown in Table 1.1, group 3 (Legal Aid Society and Citizens' Committee for Children of New York, Inc.) agreed with having notice, counsel, self-incrimination, and appeal. These rights are in keeping with civil court procedures that emphasize notice, hearing, and appeal as due process.

The last group, *The American Parents' Committee,* had Nicholas N. Kittrie | Parents as counsel. The parents' committee argued that the state will not be impaired with its aim of child rehabilitation by granting all six of the issues or rights to juveniles. Supported by legal authorities and secondary sources of empirical research, the parents' committee's brief suggested a balance between societal and individual interests. With persons like Jerry Gault in state institutions, experience had shown that more antisocial behavior was generated unless the child felt that he or she had been heard. "Darkness shrouds the court's operations in the absence of constitutional spotlights . . . The child needs to be heard for him to feel and develop a healthy attitude toward constitutional authority" (*Amicus Curiae* at 22).

To summarize Table 1.1, observe that the rights to notice, counsel, confrontation and cross-examination, and privilege against self-incrimination received the most endorsement. This is, of course, what the court decided to give the youth. This kind of research supports the theory that the Supreme Court is not a pacesetter; it is conservative.

Some noted authorities have argued that the juvenile court was illegitimate. Just as children who are born out of wedlock are called illegitimate and seen as the result of the error of the male and too much kindness of the female, some authorities saw an analogy. In their minds, the juvenile court was a product of a paternal error, which is the misinterpretation of the *parens patriae* concept, and of the maternal generosity of the child savers.

As has been discussed earlier, the changes in the juvenile justice system of the 1890s never fully developed. For society today, the result of what some authorities saw as illegitimacy or as a clandestine affair might be called a miscarriage—a miscarriage of justice. Justice Fortas called the juvenile court "the worst of two worlds."

More recently, Ira M. Schwartz, administrator of the Office of Juvenile Justice and Delinquency Prevention (OJJDP), called the juvenile court injustice and labeled his book (*In*) *Justice for Juveniles* (1989). He argued that the Juvenile Justice and Delinquency Prevention Act of 1974 succeeded in getting 40 percent of all youths who were status offenders and, to a lesser extent, dependent and neglected children, out of the adult jails, juvenile detention centers, youth prisons, and training schools. The hope was that states would follow Massachusetts' lead and close down large correctional institutions and use more community-based programs. Yet the opposite happened.

Get Tough Measures

"Public outrage over the juvenile crime problem precipitated an avalanche of 'get tough' measures in the states" and the rates of youth confined increased significantly (Schwartz 1989, 16). Most importantly, "many of these children are guilty of little more than running away from an intolerable and abusive home situation that often involves an alcoholic or sexually abusive family member" (Schwartz 1989, xii).

This "social experiment," as some people called this juvenile court, had no procedural safeguards for children. It had no real treatment. Social scientists began to argue for the decriminalization of the juvenile justice system.

4. The decision in *Gault* raised some issues regarding both costs and benefits for the court system, the social agencies, and the entire society. Impact studies do reveal that a more unified process came into being. However, the Supreme Court said little about the substantive issues such as the existence or the function of the juvenile court. Looking at Table 1.1, one could conclude that the court confined itself to the issues or rights on which there was the most support. They did not address society's need for a juvenile court.

Many people have thought that routing juveniles through the juvenile court might do more harm than good. This view became known as labeling theory, which holds that negative labels such as "delinquent" or "troublemaker" create a self-fulfilling prophecy. In time, the youth lives up to the label (conforms to the negative expectations) and looks for others who sympathize with his or her behavior and/or needs.

Using civil procedures as opposed to criminal procedures has resulted in what is known as a double-edged sword. Usually it means the following:

(1) Fewer procedural safeguards;

(2) Lower standards;

(3) More vulnerable people;

(4) Fewer civil rights; and

(5) Overcrowding in that particular organizational system (Kittrie 1971).

Changing the criminal law does not always change the public's values. Adding public indignation to the work of professional groups who want to define behavior in medical rather than criminal terms legitimizes the use of clinical explanations. The result is a double stigma. The mentally ill, for example, are "bad" and "mad." The delinquent youths are "bad" and "young." The stigmatizing effect of being declared delinquent can be noted by referrals for employment, public school records, and lack of admissions to Army officer's programs [*In re Winship*, 397 U.S. 358 (1970), **Amicus Curiae** at 4].

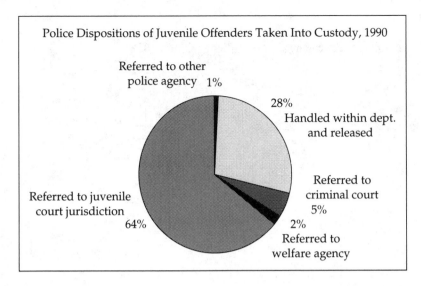

Police Dispositions of Juvenile Offenders Taken Into Custody, 1990

Referred to other
police agency 1%

28%
Handled within dept.
and released

Referred to
criminal court
5%

Referred to juvenile
court jurisdiction
64%

2%
Referred to
welfare agency

Figure 1.2
Source: U.S. Department
of Justice, *Arrests of Youth*
(1992:5).

5. In some juvenile courts, the system does everything it can to avoid labeling a child " bad" and "young." Figure 1.2 shows that not all juveniles
   come before a juvenile judge. Only 64 percent of the cases that were
   handled by the police in 1990 were referred to the juvenile court jurisdiction. The police used other diversion tactics within their departments
   or referred the cases to other agencies.

Sickmund (1992) used the findings from *Juvenile Court Statistics 1988* to
create a more complex flowchart in Figure 1.3. That chart shows what
happens to a young person once he or she comes into the juvenile
court. From the estimated 1,156,000 delinquency cases in 1988, notice
that most come from the police (84 percent). Yet, at the intake stage,
the intake worker disposed of the case informally 52 percent of the time.
Of the number that go to the judge, called a judicial decision, 40 percent
are dismissed or the sentence is suspended based on good behavior.
Mather (1974) concluded that due to discretion employed by police and
prosecuting attorneys, trial procedures do not determine guilt or nonguilt
as much as they determine how much punishment should be administered.
It is only the more mature youth, who has committed a serious crime, who
sees the juvenile judge. Then the youth is either punished or helped. Of the
youths found guilty of the charges at the adjudicatory hearing, 57 percent
were placed on probation. In 1992, the results were similar. See Figure
1.4 (Butts, Snyder, Finnegan, Aughenbaugh, Tierney, Sullivan, and Poole
1995, 9).

In addition, in 1996, "all measures of juvenile violence known to law
enforcement—the number of arrests, arrest rates, and the percentage of
violent crimes cleared by juvenile arrests—are down" (Synder 1997, 1).

In more recent years, the number of formally processed delinquency cases
has substantially increased between 1988 and 1997. However, the total
proportion of the delinquency cases that resulted in adjudication or waiver
has not changed. In 1997, even though there were more than 1.7 million
delinquency cases, youth were adjudicated delinquent or waived to criminal court in one-third of all delinquency cases referred to juvenile court.

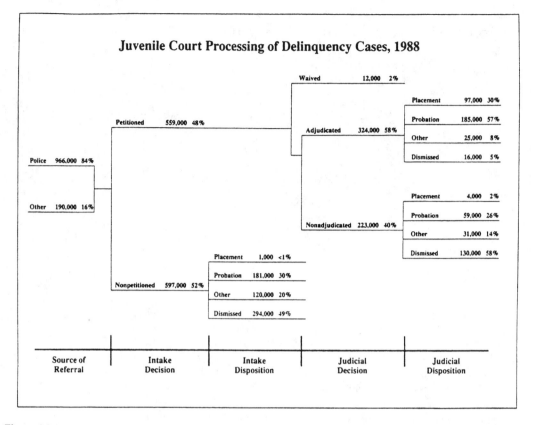

Figure 1.3
Source: Melissa Sickmund, "Offenders in Juvenile Court, 1998," in *OJJDP UPDATE ON STATISTICS*, U.S. Depart. of Justice, February 1992, p. 6.

Although the exact numbers in Figure 1.3 are different from the 1997 statistics (about 48% greater than 1988), what happens to the youth is about the same (http://www.ojjdp.ncjrs.org/ojstatbb/qa189.html, 30 September 1999).

6. What do we now know about the Supreme Court? We know, for example, that the Supreme Court is not known to be a pacesetter. In viewing Table 1.1, we came to the conclusion that the court chose to limit its granting of rights to juveniles to the first four rights because that is where there was the most support from the **amicus curiae** briefs.

In addition, the Supreme Court was extending rights to adult criminal offenders, so the extension of rights to juveniles may have been a logical next step. For example, *Gideon v. Wainwright* (372 U.S. 335, 1963) gave adults the right to counsel paid by the state if the person could not afford it, for felony trials that were not capital offenses. [The right to counsel for persons who are indigent, ignorant, illiterate, and persons arrested for a capital offense had been given in *Powell v. Alabama* (287 U.S. 45, 1932).] *Miranda v. Arizona* (384 U.S. 436, 1966) gave adult criminal offenders the right to remain silent; anything he or she says can and will be used against him or her in a court of law; right to the presence of an attorney during questioning; and if

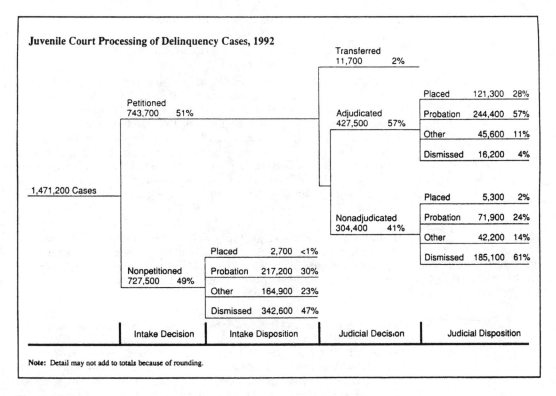

Figure 1.4
Source: *Juvenile Court Statistics* 1992, p. 9.

he or she cannot afford an attorney, one will be appointed for him or her prior to questioning if he or she so desires. *Gault* is considered by some to be *Miranda* for the youth because it gives them the right to an attorney and the right to remain silent (privileges against self-incrimination).

7. Notice the right to remain silent. When a law officer takes a child into custody and begins to interrogate the youth (when the youth is the prime suspect), the right to remain silent comes into action. In some ways *Gault* is the *Miranda* for youth. How?

8. The attorney who argued the case *Gideon v. Wainwright* before the Supreme Court in 1963 for Mr. Gideon because he was an imprisoned pauper (poor man) was Mr. Abe Fortas. The Justice of the Supreme Court who wrote the majority opinion for both *Kent* and *Gault* several years later was the same person—Abe Fortas.

9. Can anyone guess what Jerry Gault grew up to be? Right—an attorney!

IN RE WINSHIP

SUPREME COURT OF THE UNITED STATES

97 U.S. 358; 90 S. Ct. 1068; 25 L. Ed. 2d 368 (1970)

January 20, 1970, Argued March 31, 1970, Decided

Opinion: Mr. Justice Brennan delivered the opinion of the Court.

Constitutional questions decided by this Court concerning the juvenile process have centered on the adjudicatory stage at "which a determination is made as to whether a juvenile is a 'delinquent' as a result of alleged misconduct on his part, with the consequence that he may be committed to a state institution." *In re Gault*, 387 U.S. 1, 13 (1967). *Gault* decided that, although the Fourteenth Amendment does not require that the hearing at this stage conform with all the requirements of a criminal trial or even of the usual administrative proceeding, the Due Process Clause does require application during the adjudicatory hearing of "the essentials of due process and fair treatment." Id., at 30.

When briefing this case, this is the question or issue to be stated as a question with an answer of either yes or no.

This case presents the single, narrow question whether proof beyond a reasonable doubt is among the "essentials of due process and fair treatment" required during the adjudicatory stage when a juvenile is charged with an act which would constitute a crime if committed by an adult.

Procedural History

Section 712 of the New York Family Court Act defines a juvenile delinquent as "a person over seven and less than sixteen years of age who does any act which, if done by an adult, would constitute a crime." During a 1967 adjudicatory hearing, conducted pursuant to § 742 of the Act, a judge in New York Family Court found that appellant, then a 12-year-old boy, had entered a locker and stolen $112 from a woman's pocketbook. The petition which charged appellant with delinquency alleged that his act, "if done by an adult, would constitute the crime or crimes of Larceny." The judge acknowledged that the proof might not establish guilt beyond a reasonable doubt, but rejected appellant's contention that such proof was required by the Fourteenth Amendment. The judge relied instead on § 744 (b) of the New York Family Court Act which provides that "any determination at the conclusion of [an adjudicatory] hearing that a [juvenile] did an act or acts must be based on a preponderance of the evidence."[7] During a subsequent dispositional hearing, appellant was ordered placed in a training school for an initial period of 18 months, subject to annual extensions of his commitment until his 18th birthday—six years in appellant's case. The Appellate Division of the New York Supreme Court, First Judicial Department, affirmed without opinion, 30 App. Div. 2d 781, 291 N.Y.S. 2d 1005 (1968). The New York Court of Appeals then affirmed by a four-to-three vote, expressly sustaining the constitutionality of § 744 (b), 24 N.Y. 2d 196, 247 N. E. 2d 253 (1969). We noted probable jurisdiction, 396 U.S. 885 (1969).

Decision

We reverse.

I

What "Proof Beyond a Reasonable Doubt" Means

The requirement that guilt of a criminal charge be established by proof beyond a reasonable doubt dates at least from our early years as a Nation. The "demand for a higher degree of persuasion in criminal cases was recurrently expressed from ancient times, [though] its crystallization into the formula 'beyond a

---

[7] The ruling appears in the following portion of the hearing transcript:
Counsel: "Your Honor is making a finding by the preponderance of the evidence."
Court: "Well, it convinces me."
Counsel: "It's not beyond a reasonable doubt, Your Honor."
Court: "That is true . . . Our statute says a preponderance and a preponderance it is."

reasonable doubt' seems to have occurred as late as 1798. It is now accepted in common law jurisdictions as the measure of persuasion by which the prosecution must convince the trier of all the essential elements of guilt." C. McCormick, Evidence § 321, pp. 681–682 (1954); see also J. Wigmore, Evidence § 2497 (3d ed. 1940). Although virtually unanimous adherence to the reasonable-doubt standard in common-law jurisdictions may not conclusively establish it as a requirement of due process, such adherence does "reflect a profound judgment about the way in which law should be enforced and justice administered." *Duncan v. Louisiana*, 391 U.S. 145, 155 (1968).

Expressions in many opinions of this Court indicate that it has long been assumed that proof of a criminal charge beyond a reasonable doubt is constitutionally required. See, for example, *Miles v. United States*, 103 U.S. 304, 312 (1881); *Davis v. United States*, 160 U.S. 469, 488 (1895); *Holt v. United States*, 218 U.S. 245, 253 (1910); *Wilson v. United States*, 232 U.S. 563, 569–570 (1914); *Brinegar v. United States*, 338 U.S. 160, 174 (1949); *Leland v. Oregon*, 343 U.S. 790, 795 (1952); *Holland v. United States*, 348 U.S. 121, 138 (1954); *Speiser v. Randall*, 357 U.S. 513, 525–526 (1958). Cf. *Coffin v. United States*, 156 U.S. 432 (1895). Mr. Justice Frankfurter stated that "it is the duty of the Government to establish . . . guilt beyond a reasonable doubt. This notion—basic in our law and rightly one of the boasts of a free society—is a requirement and a safeguard of due process of law in the historic, procedural content of 'due process.'" *Leland v. Oregon*, supra, at 802–803 (dissenting opinion). In a similar vein, the Court said in *Brinegar v. United States*, supra, at 174, that "guilt in a criminal case must be proved beyond a reasonable doubt and by evidence confined to that which long experience in the common-law tradition, to some extent embodied in the Constitution, has crystallized into rules of evidence consistent with that standard. These rules are historically grounded rights of our system, developed to safeguard men from dubious and unjust convictions, with resulting forfeitures of life, liberty and property." *Davis v. United States*, supra, at 488, stated that the requirement is implicit in "constitutions . . . [which] recognize the fundamental principles that are deemed essential for the protection of life and liberty." In Davis a murder conviction was reversed because the trial judge instructed the jury that it was their duty to convict when the evidence was equally balanced regarding the sanity of the accused. This Court said: "On the contrary, he is entitled to an acquittal of the specific crime charged if upon all the evidence there is reasonable doubt whether he was capable in law of committing crime. . . . No man should be deprived of his life under the forms of law unless the jurors who try him are able, upon their consciences, to say that the evidence before them . . . is sufficient to show beyond a reasonable doubt the existence of every fact necessary to constitute the crime charged." Id., at 484, 493.

The reasonable-doubt standard plays a vital role in the American scheme of criminal procedure. It is a prime instrument for reducing the risk of convictions resting on factual error. The standard provides concrete substance for the presumption of innocence—that bedrock "axiomatic and elementary" principle whose "enforcement lies at the foundation of the administration of our criminal law." *Coffin v. United States*, supra, at 453. As the dissenters in the New York Court of Appeals observed, and we agree, "a person accused of a crime . . . would be at a severe disadvantage, a disadvantage amounting to a lack of fundamental fairness, if he could be adjudged guilty and imprisoned for years on the strength of the same evidence as would suffice in a civil case." 24 N.Y. 2d, at 205, 247 N. E. 2d, at 259.

Importance of This High Standard of Proof

The requirement of proof beyond a reasonable doubt has this vital role in our criminal procedure for cogent reasons. The accused during a criminal prosecution has at stake interests of immense importance, both because of the possibility that he may lose his liberty upon conviction and because of the certainty that he would be stigmatized by the conviction. Accordingly, a society that values the good name and freedom of every individual should not condemn a man for commission of a crime when there is reasonable doubt about his guilt. As we said in *Speiser v. Randall*, supra, at 525–526: "There is always in litigation a margin of error, representing error in fact finding, which both parties must take into account. Where one party has at stake an interest of transcending value—as a criminal defendant his liberty—this margin of error is reduced as to him by the process of placing on the other party the burden of . . . persuading the fact finder at the conclusion of the trial of his guilt beyond a reasonable doubt. Due process commands that no man shall lose his liberty unless the Government has borne the burden of . . . convincing the fact finder of his guilt." To this end, the reasonable-doubt standard is indispensable, for it "impresses on the trier of fact the necessity of reaching a subjective state of certitude of the facts in issue." Dorsen & Rezneck, *In re Gault* and the Future of Juvenile Law, 1 Family Law Quarterly, No. 4, pp. 1, 26 (1967).

Moreover, use of the reasonable-doubt standard is indispensable to command the respect and confidence of the community in applications of the criminal law. It is critical that the moral force of the criminal law not be diluted by a standard of proof that leaves people in doubt whether innocent men are being condemned. It is also important in our free society that every individual going about his ordinary affairs have confidence that his government cannot adjudge him guilty of a criminal offense without convincing a proper fact finder of his guilt with utmost certainty.

Lest there remain any doubt about the constitutional stature of the reasonable-doubt standard, we explicitly hold that the Due Process Clause protects the accused against conviction except upon proof beyond a reasonable doubt of every fact necessary to constitute the crime with which he is charged.

II

Questions Restated: Do Juveniles Get the Right?

We turn to the question whether juveniles, like adults, are constitutionally entitled to proof beyond a reasonable doubt when they are charged with violation of a criminal law. The same considerations that demand extreme caution in fact finding to protect the innocent adult apply as well to the innocent child. We do not find convincing the contrary arguments of the New York Court of Appeals. Gault rendered untenable much of the reasoning relied upon by that court to sustain the constitutionality of § 744 (b). The Court of Appeals indicated that a delinquency adjudication "is not a 'conviction' (§ 781); that it affects no right or privilege, including the right to hold public office or to obtain a license (§ 782); and a cloak of protective confidentiality is thrown around all the proceedings (§§ 783–784)." 24 N.Y. 2d, at 200, 247 N. E. 2d, at 255–256. The court said further: "The delinquency status is not made a crime; and the proceedings are not criminal. There is, hence, no deprivation of due process in the statutory provision [challenged by appellant]. . . ." 24 N.Y. 2d, at 203, 247 N. E. 2d, at 257. In effect the Court of Appeals distinguished the proceedings in question here from a criminal prosecution by use of what *Gault* called the "'civil' label-of-convenience which has been attached to juvenile proceedings." 387 U.S., at 50. But *Gault* expressly rejected that distinction as a reason for holding the Due Process Clause inapplicable to a juvenile proceeding. 387 U.S., at 50–51. The Court of Appeals also attempted to justify the preponderance standard on the related ground that juvenile proceedings are designed "not to punish, but to save the child." 24 N.Y. 2d, at 197, 247 N. E. 2d, at 254. Again, however, *Gault* expressly rejected this justification. 387 U.S., at 27. We made clear in that decision that civil labels and good intentions do not themselves obviate the need for criminal due process safeguards in juvenile courts, for "[a] proceeding where the issue is whether the child will be found to be 'delinquent' and subjected to the loss of his liberty for years is comparable in seriousness to a felony prosecution." Id., at 36.

Nor do we perceive any merit in the argument that to afford juveniles the protection of proof beyond a reasonable doubt would risk destruction of beneficial aspects of the juvenile process. Use of the reasonable-doubt standard during the adjudicatory hearing will not disturb New York's policies that a finding that a child has violated a criminal law does not constitute a criminal conviction, that such a finding does not deprive the child of his civil rights, and that juvenile proceedings are confidential. Nor will there be any effect on the informality, flexibility, or speed of the hearing at which the fact finding takes place. And the opportunity during the post-adjudicatory or dispositional hearing for a wide-ranging review of the child's social history and for his individualized treatment will remain unimpaired. Similarly, there will be no effect on the procedures distinctive to juvenile proceedings that are employed prior to the adjudicatory hearing.

The Court of Appeals observed that "a child's best interest is not necessarily, or even probably, promoted if he wins in the particular inquiry which may bring him to the juvenile court." 24 N.Y. 2d, at 199, 247 N. E. 2d, at 255. It is true, of course, that the juvenile may be engaging in a general course of conduct inimical to his welfare that calls for judicial intervention. But that intervention cannot take the form of subjecting the child to the stigma of a finding that he violated a criminal law and to the possibility of institutional confinement on proof insufficient to convict him were he an adult.

We conclude, as we concluded regarding the essential due process safeguards applied in *Gault*, that the observance of the standard of proof beyond a reasonable doubt "will not compel the States to abandon or displace any of the substantive benefits of the juvenile process." *Gault*, supra, at 21.

> Analysis of Outcome— No Large Impact

Finally, we reject the Court of Appeals' suggestion that there is, in any event, only a "tenuous difference" between the reasonable-doubt and preponderance standards. The suggestion is singularly unpersuasive. In this very case, the trial judge's ability to distinguish between the two standards enabled him to make a finding of guilt that he conceded he might not have made under the standard of proof beyond a reasonable doubt. Indeed, the trial judge's action evidences the accuracy of the observation of commentators that "the preponderance test is susceptible to the misinterpretation that it calls on the trier of fact merely to perform an abstract weighing of the evidence in order to determine which side has produced the greater quantum, without regard to its effect in convincing his mind of the truth of the proposition asserted." Dorsen & Rezneck, supra, at 26–27.

> Why They Do Not Go Along with the Lower Court

In sum, the constitutional safeguard of proof beyond a reasonable doubt is as much required during the adjudicatory stage of a delinquency proceeding as are those constitutional safeguards applied in *Gault*—notice of charges, right to counsel, the rights of confrontation and examination, and the privilege against self-incrimination. We therefore hold, in agreement with Chief Judge Fuld in dissent in the Court of Appeals, "that, where a 12-year-old child is charged with an act of stealing which renders him liable to confinement for as long as six years, then, as a matter of due process . . . the case against him must be proved beyond a reasonable doubt." 24 N.Y. 2d, at 207, 247 N. E. 2d, at 260.

Reversed.

> The Decision of the U.S. Supreme Court

DISSENT: MR. CHIEF JUSTICE BURGER, with whom MR. JUSTICE STEWART joins, dissenting.

The Court's opinion today rests entirely on the assumption that all juvenile proceedings are "criminal prosecutions," hence subject to constitutional limitations. This derives from earlier holdings, which, like today's holding, were steps eroding the differences between juvenile courts and traditional criminal courts. The original concept of the juvenile court system was to provide a benevolent and less formal means than criminal courts could provide for dealing with the special and often sensitive problems of youthful offenders. Since I see no constitutional requirement of due process sufficient to overcome the legislative judgment of States in this area, I dissent from further strait-jacketing of an already overly restricted system. What the juvenile court system needs is not more but less of the trappings of legal procedure and judicial formalism; the juvenile court system requires breathing room and flexibility in order to survive, if it can survive the repeated assaults from this Court.

What is the real issue: rights or lack of support for juveniles and judges?

Much of the judicial attitude manifested by the Court's opinion today and earlier holdings in this field is really a protest against inadequate juvenile court staffs and facilities; we "burn down the stable to get rid of the mice." The lack of support and the distressing growth of juvenile crime have combined to make for a literal breakdown in many if not most juvenile courts. Constitutional problems were not seen while those courts functioned in an atmosphere where juvenile judges were not crushed with an avalanche of cases.

My hope is that today's decision will not spell the end of a generously conceived program of compassionate treatment intended to mitigate the rigors and trauma of exposing youthful offenders to a traditional criminal court; each step we take turns the clock back to the pre-juvenile-court era. I cannot regard it as a manifestation of progress to transform juvenile courts into criminal courts, which is what we are well on the way to accomplishing. We can only hope the legislative response will not reflect our own by having these courts abolished.

MR. JUSTICE BLACK, dissenting.

The majority states that "many opinions of this Court indicate that it has long been assumed that proof of a criminal charge beyond a reasonable doubt is constitutionally required." Ante, at 362. I have joined in some of those opinions, as well as the dissenting opinion of Mr. Justice Frankfurter in *Leland v. Oregon*, 343 U.S. 790, 802 (1952). The Court has never clearly held, however, that proof beyond a reasonable doubt is either expressly or impliedly commanded by any provision of the Constitution. The Bill of Rights, which in my view is made fully applicable to the States by the Fourteenth Amendment, see *Adamson v. California*, 332 U.S. 46, 71–75 (1947) (dissenting opinion), does by express language provide for, among other things, a right to counsel in criminal trials, a right to indictment, and the right of a defendant to be informed of the nature of the charges against him. And in two places the Constitution provides for trial by jury, but nowhere in that document is there any statement that conviction of crime requires proof of guilt beyond a reasonable doubt. The Constitution thus goes into some detail to spell out what kind of trial a defendant charged with crime should have, and I believe the Court has no power to add to or subtract from the procedures set forth by the Founders. I realize that it is far easier to substitute individual judges' ideas of "fairness" for the fairness prescribed by the Constitution, but I shall not at any time surrender my belief that document itself should be our guide, not our own concept of what is fair, decent, and right. That this old "shock-the-conscience" test is what the Court is relying on, rather than the words of the Constitution, is clearly enough revealed by the reference of the majority to "fair treatment" and to the statement by the dissenting judges in the New York Court of Appeals that failure to require proof beyond a reasonable doubt amounts to a "lack of fundamental fairness." Ante, at 359, 363. As I have said time and time again, I prefer to put my faith in the words of the written Constitution itself rather than to rely on the shifting, day-to-day standards of fairness of individual judges.

Our Constitution provides that no person shall be "deprived of life, liberty, or property, without due process of law." The four words—due process of law— have been the center of substantial legal debate over the years. See *Chambers v. Florida*, 309 U.S. 227, 235–236, and n. 8 (1940). Some might think that the words themselves are vague. But any possible ambiguity disappears when the phrase is viewed in the light of history and the accepted meaning of those words prior to and at the time our Constitution was written.

"Due process of law" was originally used as a shorthand expression for governmental proceedings according to the "law of the land" as it existed at the time of those proceedings. Both phrases are derived from the laws of England and have traditionally been regarded as meaning the same thing. The Magna Carta provided that:

"No Freeman shall be taken, or imprisoned, or be disseised of his Freehold, or Liberties, or free Customs, or be outlawed, or exiled, or any otherwise destroyed; nor will we not pass upon him, nor condemn him, but by lawful Judgment of his Peers, or by the law of the Land."

Later English statutes reinforced and confirmed these basic freedoms. In 1350 a statute declared that "it is contained in the Great Charter of the Franchises of England, that none shall be imprisoned nor put out of his Freehold, nor of his Franchises nor free Custom, unless it be by the Law of the Land. . . ." Four years later another statute provided "that no Man of what Estate or Condition that he be, shall be put out of Land or Tenement, nor taken nor imprisoned, nor disinherited, nor put to Death, without being brought in Answer by due Process of the Law." And in 1363 it was provided "that no man be taken or imprisoned, nor put out of his freehold, without process of law."

Drawing on these and other sources, Lord Coke, in 1642, concluded that "due process of law" was synonymous with the phrase "by law of the land." One of the earliest cases in this Court to involve the interpretation of the Due Process Clause of the Fifth Amendment declared that "the words, 'due process of law,' were undoubtedly intended to convey the same meaning as the words 'by the law of the land' in Magna Carta." *Murray's Lessee v. Hoboken Land & Improv. Co.*, 18 How. 272, 276 (1856).

While it is thus unmistakably clear that "due process of law" means according to "the law of the land," this Court has not consistently defined what "the law of the land" means and in my view members of this Court frequently continue to misconceive the correct interpretation of that phrase. In *Murray's Lessee*, supra, Mr. Justice Curtis, speaking for the Court, stated:

"The constitution contains no description of those processes which it was intended to allow or forbid. It does not even declare what principles are to be applied to ascertain whether it be due process. It is manifest that it was not left to the legislative power to enact any process which might be devised. The article is a restraint on the legislative as well as on the executive and judicial powers of the government, and cannot be so construed as to leave congress free to make any process 'due process of law,' by its mere will. To what principles, then, are we to resort to ascertain whether this process, enacted by congress, is due process? To this the answer must be twofold. We must examine the constitution itself, to see whether this process be in conflict with any of its provisions. If not found to be so, we must look to those settled usages and modes of proceeding existing in the common and statute law of England, before the emigration of our

What Due Process Means

ancestors, and which are shown not to have been unsuited to their civil and political condition by having been acted on by them after the settlement of this country." Id., at 276–277.

Later in *Twining v. New Jersey*, 211 U.S. 78 (1908), Mr. Justice Moody, again speaking for the Court, reaffirmed that "due process of law" meant "by law of the land," but he went on to modify Mr. Justice Curtis' definition of the phrase. He stated: "First. What is due process of law may be ascertained by an examination of those settled usages and modes of proceedings existing in the common and statute law of England before the emigration of our ancestors, and shown not to have been unsuited to their civil and political condition by having been acted on by them after the settlement of this country.... [...means material edited out] "Second. It does not follow, however, that a procedure settled in English law at the time of the emigration, and brought to this country and practiced by our ancestors, is an essential element of due process of law. If that were so the procedure of the first half of the seventeenth century would be fastened upon the American jurisprudence like a straightjacket, only to be unloosed by constitutional amendment.... "Third. But, consistently with the requirements of due process, no change in ancient procedure can be made which disregards those fundamental principles, to be ascertained from time to time by judicial action, which have relation to process of law and protect the citizen in his private right, and guard him against the arbitrary action of government." Id., at 100–101.

In those words is found the kernel of the "natural law due process" notion by which this Court frees itself from the limits of a written Constitution and sets itself from the limits of a written Constitution and sets itself loose to declare any law unconstitutional that "shocks its conscience," deprives a person of "fundamental fairness," or violates the principles "implicit in the concept of ordered liberty." See *Rochin v. California*, 342 U.S. 165, 172 (1952); *Palko v. Connecticut*, 302 U.S. 319, 325 (1937). While this approach has been frequently used in deciding so-called "procedural" questions, it has evolved into a device as easily invoked to declare invalid "substantive" laws that sufficiently shock the consciences of at least five members of this Court. See, e.g., *Lochner v. New York*, 198 U.S. 45 (1905); *Coppage v. Kansas*, 236 U.S. 1 (1915); *Burns Baking Co. v. Bryan*, 264 U.S. 504 (1924); *Griswold v. Connecticut*, 381 U.S. 479 (1965). I have set forth at length in prior opinions my own views that this concept is completely at odds with the basic principle that our Government is one of limited powers and that such an arrogation of unlimited authority by the judiciary cannot be supported by the language or the history of any provision of the Constitution. See, e.g., *Adamson v. California*, 332 U.S. 46, 68 (1947) (dissenting opinion); *Griswold v. Connecticut*, supra, at 507 (1965) (dissenting opinion).

In my view both Mr. Justice Curtis and Mr. Justice Moody gave "due process of law" an unjustifiably broad interpretation. For me the only correct meaning of that phrase is that our Government must proceed according to the "law of the land"—that is, according to written constitutional and statutory provisions as interpreted by court decisions. The Due Process Clause, in both the Fifth and Fourteenth Amendments, in and of itself does not add to those provisions, but in effect states that our governments are governments of law and constitutionally bound to act only according to law. To some that view may seem a degrading and niggardly view of what is undoubtedly a fundamental part of our basic freedoms. But that criticism fails to note the historical importance of our Constitution and the virtual revolution in the history of the government of nations that was achieved by forming a government that from the beginning had its limits of power set forth in one written document that also made it abundantly clear that all governmental actions affecting life, liberty, and property were to be according to law.

First

Second

Third

For years our ancestors had struggled in an attempt to bring England under one written constitution, consolidating in one place all the threads of the fundamental law of that nation. They almost succeeded in that attempt, but it was not until after the American Revolution that men were able to achieve that long-sought goal. But the struggle had not been simply to put all the constitutional law in one document, it was also to make certain that men would be governed by law, not the arbitrary fiat of the man or men in power.

Our ancestors had known the tyranny of the kings and the rule of man and it was, in my view, in order to insure against such actions that the Founders wrote into our own Magna Carta the fundamental principle of the rule of law, as expressed in the historically meaningful phrase "due process of law." The many decisions of this Court that have found in that phrase a blanket authority to govern the country according to the views of at least five members of this institution have ignored the essential meaning of the very words they invoke. When this Court assumes for itself the power to declare any law—state or federal—unconstitutional because it offends the majority's own views of what is fundamental and decent in our society, our Nation ceases to be governed according to the "law of the land" and instead becomes one governed ultimately by the "law of the judges."

> Tyranny of Kings and Powerful Men

It can be, and has been, argued that when this Court strikes down a legislative act because it offends the idea of "fundamental fairness," it furthers the basic thrust of our Bill of Rights by protecting individual freedom. But that argument ignores the effect of such decisions on perhaps the most fundamental individual liberty of our people—the right of each man to participate in the self-government of his society. Our Federal Government was set up as one of limited powers, but it was also given broad power to do all that was "necessary and proper" to carry out its basic purpose of governing the Nation, so long as those powers were not exercised contrary to the limitations set forth in the Constitution. And the States, to the extent they are not restrained by the provisions in that document, were to be left free to govern themselves in accordance with their own views of fairness and decency. Any legislature presumably passes a law because it thinks the end result will help more than hinder and will thus further the liberty of the society as a whole. The people, through their elected representatives, may of course be wrong in making those determinations, but the right of self-government that our Constitution preserves is just as important as any of the specific individual freedoms preserved in the Bill of Rights. The liberty of government by the people, in my opinion, should never be denied by this Court except when the decision of the people as stated in laws passed by their chosen representatives, conflicts with the express or necessarily implied commands of our Constitution.

II

I admit a strong, persuasive argument can be made for a standard of proof beyond a reasonable doubt in criminal cases—and the majority has made that argument well—but it is not for me as a judge to say for that reason that Congress or the States are without constitutional power to establish another standard that the Constitution does not otherwise forbid. It is quite true that proof beyond a reasonable doubt has long been required in federal criminal trials. It is also true that this requirement is almost universally found in the governing laws of the States. And as long as a particular jurisdiction requires proof beyond a reasonable doubt, then the Due Process Clause commands that every trial in that jurisdiction must adhere to that standard. See *Turner v. United States*, 396 U.S. 398, 430 (1970) (BLACK, J., dissenting). But when, as here, a State through

> Limited Federal Government

its duly constituted legislative branch decides to apply a different standard, then that standard, unless it is otherwise unconstitutional, must be applied to insure that persons are treated according to the "law of the land." The State of New York has made such a decision, and in my view nothing in the Due Process Clause invalidates it.

NOTES AFTER WINSHIP

1. *Winship* is important because it changed the informal procedures of the juvenile court to the highest standard of proof used in the adult criminal court. The courts have three standards of proof, with "preponderance of evidence" as the lowest. In weighing the evidence this means that one side has 50.5 percent more than the other side. It is used in most civil proceedings and is thereby used as the standard on the television shows where people bring claims against others before a judge. The middle standard is "clear and convincing." This standard requires more proof than "preponderance" but certainly less than "proof beyond a reasonable doubt." The highest proof is "proof beyond a reasonable doubt" and is used in criminal trials.

2. Reading *Winship* and the amicus briefs, one can get the impression that the young boy did not take the money. He, or someone looking like him, was passing by the hallway when the woman went into the locker and found her money gone. She did not see him take the money. She only assumed it was he. The testimony from the parents of the child was that he earned money from a paper route and that he had no extra money like $112.00. What do you think?

3. If *Winship* means anything in history, it means that many children were indeed sent to institutions for being at the wrong place at the wrong time. The child or youth may not have done the deed at all.

McKEIVER ET AL. v. PENNSYLVANIA

SUPREME COURT OF THE UNITED STATES

403 U.S. 528; 91 S. Ct. 1976; 29 L. Ed. 2d 647 (1971)

December 10, 1970, Argued June 21, 1971, Decided*

*Together with No. 28, *In re Burrus* et al., on certiorari to the Supreme Court of North Carolina, argued December 9–10, 1970.

OPINION: MR. JUSTICE BLACKMUN announced the judgments of the Court and an opinion in which THE CHIEF JUSTICE, MR. JUSTICE STEWART, and MR. JUSTICE WHITE join.

?

These cases present the narrow but precise issue whether the Due Process Clause of the Fourteenth Amendment assures the right to trial by jury in the adjudicative phase of a state juvenile court delinquency proceeding.

I

The issue arises understandably, for the Court in a series of cases already has emphasized due process factors protective of the juvenile:

1. *Haley v. Ohio*, 332 U.S. 596 (1948), concerned the admissibility of a confession taken from a 15-year-old boy on trial for first-degree murder. It was held that, upon the facts there developed, the Due Process Clause barred the use of the confession. Mr. Justice Douglas, in an opinion in which three other Justices joined, said, "Neither man nor child can be allowed to stand condemned by methods which flout constitutional requirements of due process of law." 332 U.S., at 601.

2. *Gallegos v. Colorado*, 370 U.S. 49 (1962), where a 14-year-old was on trial, is to the same effect.

3. *Kent v. United States*, 383 U.S. 541 (1966), concerned a 16-year-old charged with housebreaking, robbery, and rape in the District of Columbia. The issue was the propriety of the juvenile court's waiver of jurisdiction "after full investigation," as permitted by the applicable statute. It was emphasized that the latitude the court possessed within which to determine whether it should retain or waive jurisdiction "assumes procedural regularity sufficient in the particular circumstances to satisfy the basic requirements of due process and fairness, as well as compliance with the statutory requirement of a 'full investigation.'" 383 U.S., at 553.

> Notice how later cases tell you about former cases.

4. *In re Gault*, 387 U.S. 1 (1967), concerned a 15-year-old, already on probation, committed in Arizona as a delinquent after being apprehended upon a complaint of lewd remarks by telephone. Mr. Justice Fortas, in writing for the Court, reviewed the cases just cited and observed, "Accordingly, while these cases relate only to restricted aspects of the subject, they unmistakably indicate that, whatever may be their precise impact, neither the Fourteenth Amendment nor the Bill of Rights is for adults alone." 387 U.S., at 13.

> Tells You about *Gault*

The Court focused on "the proceedings by which a determination is made as to whether a juvenile is a 'delinquent' as a result of alleged misconduct on his part, with the consequence that he may be committed to a state institution" and, as to this, said that "there appears to be little current dissent from the proposition that the Due Process Clause has a role to play." Ibid. *Kent* was adhered to: "We reiterate this view, here in connection with a juvenile court adjudication of 'delinquency,' as a requirement which is part of the Due Process Clause of the Fourteenth Amendment of our Constitution." Id., at 30–31. Due process, in that proceeding, was held to embrace adequate written notice; advice as to the right to counsel, retained or appointed; confrontation; and cross-examination. The privilege against self-incrimination was also held available to the juvenile. The Court refrained from deciding whether a State must provide appellate review in juvenile cases or a transcript or recording of the hearings.

5. *DeBacker v. Brainard*, 396 U.S. 28 (1969), presented, by state habeas corpus, a challenge to a Nebraska statute providing that juvenile court hearings "shall be conducted by the judge without a jury in an informal manner." However, because that appellant's hearing had antedated the decisions in *Duncan v. Louisiana*, 391 U.S. 145 (1968), and *Bloom v. Illinois*, 391 U.S. 194 (1968), and because *Duncan* and *Bloom* had been given only prospective application by *DeStefano v. Woods*, 392 U.S. 631 (1968), DeBacker's case was deemed an inappropriate one for resolution of the jury trial issue. His appeal was therefore dismissed. Mr. Justice Black and Mr. Justice Douglas, in separate dissents, took the position that a juvenile is entitled to a jury trial at the adjudicative stage. Mr. Justice Black described this as "a right which is surely one of the fundamental aspects of criminal justice in the English-speaking world," 396 U.S., at 34, and Mr. Justice Douglas described it as a right required by the Sixth and Fourteenth Amendments "where the delinquency charged is an offense that, if the person were an adult, would be a crime triable by jury." 396 U.S., at 35.

6. *In re Winship*, 397 U.S. 358 (1970), concerned a 12-year-old charged with delinquency for having taken money from a woman's purse. The Court held that "the Due Process Clause protects the accused against conviction except upon proof beyond a reasonable doubt of every fact necessary to constitute the crime with which he is charged," 397 U.S., at 364, and then went on to hold, at 368, that this standard was applicable, too, "during the adjudicatory stage of a delinquency proceeding."

From these six cases—*Haley, Gallegos, Kent, Gault, DeBacker,* and *Winship*—it is apparent that:

1. Some of the constitutional requirements attendant upon the state criminal trial have equal application to that part of the state juvenile proceeding that is adjudicative in nature. Among these are the rights to appropriate notice, to counsel, to confrontation and to cross-examination, and the privilege against self-incrimination. Included, also, is the standard of proof beyond a reasonable doubt.

2. The Court, however, has not yet said that all rights constitutionally assured to an adult accused of crime also are to be enforced or made available to the juvenile in his delinquency proceeding. Indeed, the Court specifically has refrained from going that far:

"We do not mean by this to indicate that the hearing to be held must conform with all of the requirements of a criminal trial or even of the usual administrative hearing; but we do hold that the hearing must measure up to the essentials of due process and fair treatment." *Kent*, 383 U.S., at 562; *Gault*, 387 U.S., at 30.

3. The Court, although recognizing the high hopes and aspirations of Judge Julian Mack, the leaders of the Jane Addams School, and the other supporters of the juvenile court concept, has also noted the disappointments of the system's performance and experience and the resulting widespread disaffection. *Kent*, 383 U.S., at 555–556; *Gault*, 387 U.S., at 17–19. There have been, at one and the same time, both an appreciation for the juvenile court judge who is devoted, sympathetic, and conscientious, and a disturbed concern about the judge who is untrained and less than fully imbued with an understanding approach to the complex problems of childhood and adolescence. There has been praise for the system and its purposes, and there has been alarm over its defects.

4. The Court has insisted that these successive decisions do not spell the doom of the juvenile court system or even deprive it of its "informality, flexibility, or speed." *Winship*, 397 U.S., at 366. On the other hand, a concern precisely to the opposite effect was expressed by two dissenters in *Winship*. Id., at 375–376.

II

Facts

With this substantial background already developed, we turn to the facts of the present cases:

No. 322. Joseph McKeiver, then age 16, in May 1968 was charged with robbery, larceny, and receiving stolen goods (felonies under Pennsylvania law, Pa. Stat. Ann., Tit. 18, §§ 4704, 4807, and 4817 (1963)) as acts of juvenile delinquency.

At the time of the adjudication hearing he was represented by counsel. His request for a jury trial was denied and his case was heard by Judge Theodore S.

Gutowicz of the Court of Common Pleas, Family Division, Juvenile Branch, of Philadelphia County, Pennsylvania. McKeiver was adjudged a delinquent upon findings that he had violated a law of the Commonwealth. Pa. Stat. Ann., Tit. 11, § 243 (4)(a) (1965). He was placed on probation. On appeal, the Superior Court affirmed without opinion. *In re McKeiver*, 215 Pa. Super. 760, 255 A. 2d 921 (1969).

Edward Terry, then age 15, in January 1969 was charged with assault and battery on a police officer and conspiracy (misdemeanors under Pennsylvania law, Pa. Stat. Ann., Tit. 18, §§ 4708 and 4302 (1963)) as acts of juvenile delinquency.

Facts of the Second Case Heard at the Same Time

Procedural History and Question

His counsel's request for a jury trial was denied and his case was heard by Judge Joseph C. Bruno of the same Juvenile Branch of the Court of Common Pleas of Philadelphia County. Terry was adjudged a delinquent on the charges. This followed an adjudication and commitment in the preceding week for an assault on a teacher. He was committed, as he had been on the earlier charge, to the Youth Development Center at Cornwells Heights. On appeal, the Superior Court affirmed without opinion. *In re Terry*, 215 Pa. Super. 762, 255 A. 2d 922 (1969).

The Supreme Court of Pennsylvania granted leave to appeal in both cases and consolidated them. The single question considered, as phrased by the court, was "whether there is a constitutional right to a jury trial in juvenile court." The answer, one justice dissenting, was in the negative. *In re Terry*, 438 Pa. 339, 265 A. 2d 350 (1970). We noted probable jurisdiction. 399 U.S. 925 (1970).

In each case the court found that the juvenile had committed "an act for which an adult may be punished by law." A custody order was entered declaring the juvenile a delinquent "in need of more suitable guardianship" and committing him to the custody of the County Department of Public Welfare for placement in a suitable institution "until such time as the Board of Juvenile Correction or the Superintendent of said institution may determine, not inconsistent with the laws of this State." The court, however, suspended these commitments and placed each juvenile on probation for either one or two years conditioned upon his violating none of the State's laws, upon his reporting monthly to the County Department of Welfare, upon his being home by 11 p.m. each evening, and upon his attending a school approved by the Welfare Director. None of the juveniles has been confined on these charges.

On appeal, the cases were consolidated into two groups. The North Carolina Court of Appeals affirmed. *In re Burrus*, 4 N. C. App. 523, 167 S. E. 2d 454 (1969); *In re Shelton*, 5 N. C. App. 487, 168 S. E. 2d 695 (1969). In its turn the Supreme Court of North Carolina deleted that portion of the order in each case relating to commitment, but otherwise affirmed. *In re Burrus*, 275 N. C. 517, 169 S. E. 2d 879 (1969). Two justices dissented without opinion. We granted certiorari. 397 U.S. 1036 (1970).

Two States with the Same Questions

III

It is instructive to review, as an illustration, the substance of Justice Roberts' opinion for the Pennsylvania court. He observes, 438 Pa., at 343, 265 A. 2d, at 352, that "for over sixty-five years the Supreme Court gave no consideration at all to the constitutional problems involved in the juvenile court area"; that *Gault* "is somewhat of a paradox, being both broad and narrow at the same time"; that it "is broad in that it evidences a fundamental and far-reaching disillusionment with the anticipated benefits of the juvenile courts system"; that it is narrow because the court enumerated four due process rights which it held applicable

What the State Court Argued

in juvenile proceedings, but declined to rule on two other claimed rights, id., at 344–345, 265 A. 2d, at 353; that as a consequence the Pennsylvania court was confronted with a sweeping rationale and a carefully tailored holding," id., at 345, 265 A. 3d, at 353; that the procedural safeguards "*Gault* specifically made applicable to juvenile courts have already caused a significant 'constitutional domestication' of juvenile court proceedings," id., at 346, 265 A. 2d, at 354; that those safeguards and other rights, including the reasonable-doubt standard established by *Winship*, "insure that the juvenile court will operate in an atmosphere which is orderly enough to impress the juvenile with the gravity of the situation and the impartiality of the tribunal and at the same time informal enough to permit the benefits of the juvenile system to operate" (footnote omitted), id., at 347, 265 A. 2d, at 354; that the "proper inquiry, then, is whether the right to a trial by jury is 'fundamental' within the meaning of *Duncan*, in the context of a juvenile court which operates with all of the above constitutional safeguards," id., at 348, 265 A. 2d, at 354; and that his court's inquiry turned "upon whether there are elements in the juvenile process which render the right to a trial by jury less essential to the protection of an accused's rights in the juvenile system than in the normal criminal process." Ibid.

They Bottom Line in More Ways Than One

Justice Roberts then concluded that such factors do inhere in the Pennsylvania juvenile system: (1) Although realizing that "faith in the quality of the juvenile bench is not an entirely satisfactory substitute for due process," id., at 348, 265 A. 2d, at 355, the judges in the juvenile courts "do take a different view of their role than that taken by their counterparts in the criminal courts." Id., at 348, 265 A. 2d, at 354–355. (2) While one regrets its inadequacies, "the juvenile system has available and utilizes much more fully various diagnostic and rehabilitative services" that are "far superior to those available in the regular criminal process." Id., at 348–349, 265 A. 2d, at 355. (3) Although conceding that the post-adjudication process "has in many respects fallen far short of its goals, and its reality is far harsher than its theory," the end result of a declaration of delinquency "is significantly different from and less onerous than a finding of criminal guilt" and "we are not yet convinced that the current practices do not contain the seeds from which a truly appropriate system can be brought forth." (4) Finally, "of all the possible due process rights which could be applied in the juvenile courts, the right to trial by jury is the one which would most likely be disruptive of the unique nature of the juvenile process." It is the jury trial that "would probably require substantial alteration of the traditional practices." The other procedural rights held applicable to the juvenile process "will give the juveniles sufficient protection" and the addition of the trial by jury "might well destroy the traditional character of juvenile proceedings." Id., at 349–350, 265 A. 2d, at 355. The court concluded, id., at 350, 265 A. 2d, at 356, that it was confident "that a properly structured and fairly administered juvenile court system can serve our present societal needs without infringing on individual freedoms."

IV

Watch this argument. Could we be there now?

The right to an impartial jury "in all criminal prosecutions" under federal law is guaranteed by the Sixth Amendment. Through the Fourteenth Amendment that requirement has now been imposed upon the States "in all criminal cases which—were they to be tried in a federal court—would come within the Sixth Amendment's guarantee." This is because the Court has said it believes "that trial by jury in criminal cases is fundamental to the American scheme of justice." *Duncan v. Louisiana*, 391 U.S. 145, 149 (1968); *Bloom v. Illinois*, 391 U.S. 194, 210–211 (1968). This, of course, does not automatically provide the answer to the present jury trial issue, if for no other reason than that the juvenile court proceeding has not yet been held to be a "criminal prosecution," within the meaning and reach of the Sixth Amendment, and also has not yet been regarded as devoid of criminal aspects merely because it usually has been given the civil label. *Kent*, 383 U.S., at 554; *Gault*, 387 U.S., at 17, 49–50; *Winship*, 397 U.S., at 365–366.

Little, indeed, is to be gained by any attempt simplistically to call the juvenile court proceeding either "civil" or "criminal." The Court carefully has avoided this wooden approach. Before *Gault* was decided in 1967, the Fifth Amendment's guarantee against self-incrimination had been imposed upon the state criminal trial. *Malloy v. Hogan*, 378 U.S. 1 (1964). So, too, had the Sixth Amendment's rights of confrontation and cross-examination. *Pointer v. Texas*, 380 U.S. 400 (1965), and *Douglas v. Alabama*, 380 U.S. 415 (1965). Yet the Court did not automatically and peremptorily apply those rights to the juvenile proceeding. A reading of *Gault* reveals the opposite. And the same separate approach to the standard-of-proof issue is evident from the carefully separated application of the standard, first to the criminal trial, and then to the juvenile proceeding, displayed in *Winship*. 397 U.S., at 361 and 365.

Thus, accepting "the proposition that the Due Process Clause has a role to play," *Gault*, 387 U.S., at 13, our task here with respect to trial by jury, as it was in *Gault* with respect to other claimed rights, "is to ascertain the precise impact of the due process requirement." Id., at 13–14.

All the litigants here agree that the applicable due process standard in juvenile proceedings, as developed by *Gault* and *Winship*, is fundamental fairness. As that standard was applied in those two cases, we have an emphasis on fact finding procedures. The requirements of notice, counsel, confrontation, cross-examination, and standard of proof naturally flowed from this emphasis. But one cannot say that in our legal system the jury is a necessary component of accurate fact finding. There is much to be said for it, to be sure, but we have been content to pursue other ways for determining facts. Juries are not required, and have not been, for example, in equity cases, in workmen's compensation, in probate, or in deportation cases. Neither have they been generally used in military trials. In *Duncan* the Court stated, "We would not assert, however, that every criminal trial—or any particular trial—held before a judge alone is unfair or that a defendant may never be as fairly treated by a judge as he would be by a jury." 391 U.S., at 158. In *DeStefano*, for this reason and others, the Court refrained from retrospective application of *Duncan*, an action it surely would have not taken had it felt that the integrity of the result was seriously at issue. And in *Williams v. Florida*, 399 U.S. 78 (1970), the Court saw no particular magic in a 12-man jury for a criminal case, thus revealing that even jury concepts themselves are not inflexible.

We must recognize, as the Court has recognized before, that the fond and idealistic hopes of the juvenile court proponents and early reformers of three generations ago have not been realized. The devastating commentary upon the system's failures as a whole, contained in the President's Commission on Law Enforcement and Administration of Justice, Task Force Report: Juvenile Delinquency and Youth Crime 7–9 (1967), reveals the depth of disappointment in what has been accomplished. Too often the juvenile court judge falls far short of that stalwart, protective, and communicating figure the system envisaged. The community's unwillingness to provide people and facilities and to be concerned, the insufficiency of time devoted, the scarcity of professional help, the inadequacy of dispositional alternatives, and our general lack of knowledge all contribute to dissatisfaction with the experiment.

[. . . more information deleted for this special edition, including 1–3]

4. The Court specifically has recognized by dictum that a jury is not a necessary part even of every criminal process that is fair and equitable. *Duncan v. Louisiana*, 391 U.S. at 149–150, n. 14, and 158.

5. The imposition of the jury trial on the juvenile court system would not strengthen greatly, if at all, the fact finding function, and would, contrarily, provide an attrition of the juvenile court's assumed ability to function in a unique manner. It would not remedy the defects of the system. Meager as has been the hoped-for advance in the juvenile field, the alternative would be regressive, would lose what has been gained, and would tend once again to lace the juvenile squarely in the routine of the criminal process.

6. The juvenile concept held high promise. We are reluctant to say that, despite disappointments of grave dimensions, it still does not hold promise, and we are particularly reluctant to say, as do the Pennsylvania appellants here, that the system cannot accomplish its rehabilitative goals. So much depends on the availability of resources, on the interest and commitment of the public, on willingness to learn, and on understanding as to cause and effect and cure. In this field, as in so many others, one perhaps learns best by doing. We are reluctant to disallow the States to experiment further and to seek in new and different ways the elusive answers to the problems of the young, and we feel that we would be impeding that experimentation by imposing the jury trial. The States, indeed, must go forward. If, in its wisdom, any State feels the jury trial is desirable in all cases, or in certain kinds, there appears to be no impediment to its installing a system embracing that feature. That, however, is the State's privilege and not its obligation.

7. Of course there have been abuses. The Task Force Report has noted them. We refrain from saying at this point that those abuses are of constitutional dimension. They relate to the lack of resources and of dedication rather than to inherent unfairness.

8. There is, of course, nothing to prevent a juvenile court judge, in a particular case where he feels the need, or when the need is demonstrated, from using an advisory jury.

9. "The fact that a practice is followed by a large number of states is not conclusive in a decision as to whether that practice accords with due process, but it is plainly worth considering in determining whether the practice 'offends some principle of justice so rooted in the traditions and conscience of our people as to be ranked as fundamental.' *Snyder v. Massachusetts*, 291 U.S. 97, 105 (1934)." *Leland v. Oregon*, 343 U.S. 790, 798 (1952). It therefore is of more than passing interest that at least 29 States and the District of Columbia by statute deny the juvenile a right to a jury trial in cases such as these. The same result is achieved in other States by judicial decision. In 10 States statutes provide for a jury trial under certain circumstances.

[Concurring opinion from Justice Harlan intentionally omitted.]

Dissent by: Brennan (In Part); Douglas

Dissent by Mr. Justice Brennan, concurring in the judgment in No. 322 and dissenting in No. 128.

. . . The Due Process Clause commands, not a particular procedure, but only a result: in my Brother BLACKMUN'S words, "fundamental fairness . . . [in] fact finding." In the context of these and similar juvenile delinquency proceedings, what this means is that the States are not bound to provide jury trials on demand so long as some other aspect of the process adequately protects the interests that Sixth Amendment jury trials are intended to serve.

In my view, therefore, the due process question cannot be decided upon the basis of general characteristics of juvenile proceedings, but only in terms of the adequacy of a particular state procedure to "protect the [juvenile] from oppression by the Government," *Singer v. United States*, 380 U.S. 24, 31 (1965), and to protect him against "the compliant, biased, or eccentric judge." *Duncan v. Louisiana*, 391 U.S. 145, 156 (1968).

Examined in this light, I find no defect in the Pennsylvania cases before us. The availability of trial by jury allows an accused to protect himself against possible oppression by what is in essence an appeal to the community conscience, as embodied in the jury that hears his case. To some extent, however, a similar protection may be obtained when an accused may in essence appeal to the community at large, by focusing public attention upon the facts of his trial, exposing improper judicial behavior to public view, and obtaining, if necessary, executive redress through the medium of public indignation. Of course, the Constitution, in the context of adult criminal trials, has rejected the notion that public trial is an adequate substitute for trial by jury in serious cases. But in the context of juvenile delinquency proceedings I cannot say that it is beyond the competence of a State to conclude that juveniles who fear that delinquency proceedings will mask judicial oppression may obtain adequate protection by focusing community attention upon the trial of their cases. For, however much the juvenile system may have failed in practice, its very existence as an ostensibly beneficent and noncriminal process for the care and guidance of young persons demonstrates the existence of the community's sympathy and concern for the young. Juveniles able to bring the community's attention to bear upon their trials may therefore draw upon a reservoir of public concern unavailable to the adult criminal defendant. In the Pennsylvania cases before us, there appears to be no statutory ban upon admission of the public to juvenile trials. Appellants themselves, without contradiction, assert that "the press is generally admitted" to juvenile delinquency proceedings in Philadelphia. Most important, the record in these cases is bare of any indication that any person whom appellants sought to have admitted to the courtroom was excluded. In these circumstances, I agree that the judgment in No. 322 must be affirmed.

The North Carolina cases, however, present a different situation. North Carolina law either permits or requires exclusion of the general public from juvenile trials. In the cases before us, the trial judge "ordered the general public excluded from the hearing room and stated that only officers of the court, the juveniles, their parents or guardians, their attorney and witnesses would be present for the hearing," *In re Burrus*, 4 N. C. App. 523, 525, 167 S. E. 2d 454, 456 (1969), notwithstanding petitioners' repeated demand for a public hearing. The cases themselves, which arise out of a series of demonstrations by black adults and juveniles who believed that the Hyde County, North Carolina, school system unlawfully discriminated against black schoolchildren, present a paradigm of the circumstances in which there may be a substantial "temptation to use the courts for political ends." Opinion of MR. JUSTICE WHITE, ante, at 552. And finally, neither the opinions supporting the judgment nor the respondent in No. 128 has pointed to any feature of North Carolina's juvenile proceedings that could substitute for public or jury trial in protecting the petitioners against misuse of the judicial process. Cf. *Duncan v. Louisiana*, 391 U.S. 145, 188, 193 (1968) (HARLAN, J., dissenting) (availability of resort to "the political process" is an alternative permitting States to dispense with jury trials). Accordingly, I would reverse the judgment in No. 128.

MR. JUSTICE DOUGLAS, with whom MR. JUSTICE BLACK and MR. JUSTICE MARSHALL concur, dissenting.

<aside>Oppressive Government or Biased Judge</aside>

These cases from Pennsylvania and North Carolina present the issue of the right to a jury trial for offenders charged in juvenile court and facing a possible incarceration until they reach their majority. I believe the guarantees of the Bill of Rights, made applicable to the States by the Fourteenth Amendment, require a jury trial.

Why do they want jury trials for juveniles?

In the Pennsylvania cases one of the appellants was charged with robbery (Pa. Stat. Ann., Tit. 18, § 4704 (1963)), larceny (Pa. Stat. Ann., Tit. 18, § 4807), and receiving stolen goods (Pa. Stat. Ann., Tit. 18, § 4817) as acts of juvenile delinquency. Pa. Stat. Ann., Tit. 11, § 246 (1965). He was found a delinquent and placed on probation. The other appellant was charged with assault and battery on a police officer (Pa. Stat. Ann., Tit. 18, § 4708) and conspiracy (Pa. Stat. Ann., Tit. 18, § 4302) as acts of juvenile delinquency. On a finding of delinquency he was committed to a youth center. Despite the fact that the two appellants, aged 15 and 16, would face potential incarceration until their majority, Pa. Stat. Ann., Tit. 11, § 250, they were denied a jury trial.

In the North Carolina cases petitioners are students, from 11 to 15 years of age, who were charged under one of three criminal statutes: (1) "disorderly conduct" in a public building, N.C. Gen. Stat. § 14-132 (1969); (2) "wilful" interruption or disturbance of a public or private school, N.C. Gen. Stat. §14-273; or (3) obstructing the flow of traffic on a highway or street, N.C. Gen. Stat. § 20-174.1 (1965 and Supp. 1969).

Imprisonment in a State Institution

Conviction of each of these crimes would subject a person, whether juvenile or adult, to imprisonment in a state institution. In the case of these students the possible term was six to ten years; it would be computed for the period until an individual reached the age of 21. Each asked for a jury trial which was denied. The trial judge stated that the hearings were juvenile hearings, not criminal trials. But the issue in each case was whether they had violated a state criminal law. The trial judge found in each case that the juvenile had committed "an act for which an adult may be punished by law" and held in each case that the acts of the juvenile violated one of the criminal statutes cited above. The trial judge thereupon ordered each juvenile to be committed to the state institution for the care of delinquents and then placed each on probation for terms from 12 to 24 months.

Youth in Jail with Adults

We held in *In re Gault*, 387 U.S. 1, 13, that "neither the Fourteenth Amendment nor the Bill of Rights is for adults alone." As we noted in that case, the Juvenile Court movement was designed to avoid procedures to ascertain whether the child was "guilty" or "innocent" but to bring to bear on these problems a "clinical" approach. Id., at 15, 16. It is, of course, not our task to determine as a matter of policy whether a "clinical" or "punitive" approach to these problems should be taken by the States. But where a State uses its juvenile court proceedings to prosecute a juvenile for a criminal act and to order "confinement" until the child reaches 21 years of age or where the child at the threshold of the proceedings faces that prospect, then he is entitled to the same procedural protection as an adult. As Mr. Justice Black said in *In re Gault*, supra, at 61 (concurring):

"Where a person, infant or adult, can be seized by the State, charged, and convicted for violating a state criminal law, and then ordered by the State to be confined for six years, I think the Constitution requires that he be tried in accordance with the guarantees of all the provisions of the Bill of Rights made applicable to the States by the Fourteenth Amendment. Undoubtedly this would be true of an adult defendant, and it would be a plain denial of equal protection of the laws—an invidious discrimination—to hold that others subject to heavier punishments could, because they are children, be denied these same constitutional safeguards."

Just as courts have sometimes confused delinquency with crime, so have law enforcement officials treated juveniles not as delinquents but as criminals. As noted in the President's Crime Commission Report:

"In 1965, over 100,000 juveniles were confined in adult institutions. Presumably most of them were there because no separate juvenile detention facilities existed. Nonetheless, it is clearly undesirable that juveniles be confined with adults." President's Commission on Law Enforcement and Administration of Justice, Challenge of Crime in a Free Society 179 (1967).

Even when juveniles are not incarcerated with adults the situation may be no better. One Pennsylvania correctional institution for juveniles is a brick building with barred windows, locked steel doors, a cyclone fence topped with barbed wire, and guard towers. A former juvenile judge described it as "a maximum security prison for adjudged delinquents." *In re Bethea*, 215 Pa. Super. 75, 76, 257 A. 2d 368, 369.

> Children in Prison

In the present cases imprisonment or confinement up to ten years was possible for one child and each faced at least a possible five-year incarceration. No adult could be denied a jury trial in those circumstances. *Duncan v. Louisiana*, 391 U.S. 145, 162. The Fourteenth Amendment, which makes trial by jury provided in the Sixth Amendment applicable to the States, speaks of denial of rights to "any person," not denial of rights to "any adult person"; and we have held indeed that where a juvenile is charged with an act that would constitute a crime if committed by an adult, he is entitled to be tried under a standard of proof beyond a reasonable doubt. *In re Winship*, 397 U.S. 358.

In *DeBacker v. Brainard*, 396 U.S. 28, 33, 35, Mr. Justice Black and I dissented from a refusal to grant a juvenile, who was charged with forgery, a jury trial merely because the case was tried before *Duncan v. Louisiana*, 391 U.S. 145, was decided. Mr. Justice Black, after noting that a juvenile being charged with a criminal act was entitled to certain constitutional safeguards, viz., notice of the issues, benefit of counsel, protection against compulsory self-incrimination, and confrontation of the witnesses against him, added:

"I can see no basis whatsoever in the language of the Constitution for allowing persons like appellant the benefit of those rights and yet denying them a jury trial, a right which is surely one of the fundamental aspects of criminal justice in the English-speaking world." 396 U.S., at 34.

I added that by reason of the Sixth and Fourteenth Amendments the juvenile is entitled to a jury trial "as a matter of right where the delinquency charged is an offense that, if the person were an adult, would be a crime triable by jury. Such is this case, for behind the facade of delinquency is the crime of forgery." Id., at 35.

Practical aspects of these problems are urged against allowing a jury trial in these cases. They have been answered by Judge De Ciantis of the Family Court of Providence, Rhode Island, in a case entitled *In the Matter of McCloud*, decided January 15, 1971. A juvenile was charged with the rape of a 17-year-old female and Judge De Ciantis granted a motion for a jury trial in an opinion, a part of which I have attached as an appendix to this dissent. He there concludes that "the real traumatic" experience of incarceration without due process is "the feeling of being deprived of basic rights." He adds:

> We teach them by the way we treat them.

"The child who feels that he has been dealt with fairly and not merely expediently or as speedily as possible will be a better prospect for rehabilitation. Many of the children who come before the court come from broken homes, from the ghettos; they often suffer from low self-esteem; and their behavior is frequently a symptom of their own feelings of inadequacy. Traumatic experiences of denial of basic rights only accentuate the past deprivation and contribute to the problem. Thus, a general societal attitude of acceptance of the juvenile as a person entitled to the same protection as an adult may be the true beginning of the rehabilitative process."

. . . [material deleted]

These cases should be remanded for trial by jury on the criminal charges filed against these youngsters.

APPENDIX TO OPINION OF DOUGLAS, J., DISSENTING

De Ciantis, J.: The defendant, who will hereinafter be referred to as a juvenile, on the sixth day of September, 1969, was charged with Rape upon a female child, seventeen years old, in violation of Title 11, Chapter 37, Section, 1, of the General Laws of 1956. . . .

TRAUMA

The fact is that the procedures which are now followed in juvenile cases are far more traumatic than the potential experience of a jury trial. Who can say that a boy who is arrested and handcuffed, placed in a lineup, transported in vehicles designed to convey dangerous criminals, placed in the same kind of a cell as an adult, deprived of his freedom by lodging him in an institution where he is subject to be transferred to the state's prison and in the "hole" has not undergone a traumatic experience?

The experience of a trial with or without a jury is meant to be impressive and meaningful. The fact that a juvenile realizes that this case will be decided by twelve objective citizens would allow the court to retain its meaningfulness without causing any more trauma than a trial before a judge who perhaps has heard other cases involving the same juvenile in the past and may be influenced by those prior contacts. To agree that a jury trial would expose a juvenile to a traumatic experience is to lose sight of the real traumatic experience of incarceration without due process. The real traumatic experience is the feeling of being deprived of basic rights. [In] *In the matter of Reis*, this Court indicated the inadequacies of the procedure under which our court operates. A judge who receives facts of a case from the police and approves the filing of a petition based upon those facts may be placed in the untenable position of hearing a charge which he has approved. His duty is to adjudicate on the evidence introduced at the hearing and not be involved in any pre-adjudicatory investigation.

It is contrary to the fundamental principles of due process for the court to be compelled, as it is in this state, to act as a one-man grand jury, then sit in judgment on its own determination arising out of the facts and proceedings which he conducted. This responsibility belongs with a jury.

BACKLOG

An argument has been made that to allow jury trials would cause a great backlog of cases and, ultimately, would impair the functioning of the juvenile court. The fact however is that there is no meaningful evidence that granting the right to jury trials will impair the function of the court. Some states permit jury trials in all juvenile court cases; few juries have been demanded, and there is no suggestion from these courts that jury trials have impeded the system of juvenile justice.

In Colorado, where jury trials have been permitted by statute, Judge Theodore Rubin of the Denver Juvenile Court has indicated that jury trials are an important safeguard and that they have not impaired the functioning of the Denver Juvenile Courts. For example, during the first seven months of 1970, the two divisions of the Denver Juvenile Court have had fewer than two dozen jury trials, in both delinquency and dependency-neglect cases. In Michigan, where juveniles are also entitled to a jury trial, Judge Lincoln of the Detroit Juvenile Court indicates that his court has had less than five jury trials in the year 1969 to 1970.

The recent Supreme Court decision of *Williams v. Florida* [399 U.S. 78] (June 22, 1970), which held that the constitutional right to trial by jury in criminal cases does not require a twelve-member jury . . .

. . . Among the benefits of a public trial are the following:

1. "Public trials come to the attention of key witnesses unknown to the parties. These witnesses may then voluntarily come forward and give important testimony."

2. "The spectators learn about their government and acquire confidence in their judicial remedies."

3. "The knowledge that every criminal trial is subject to contemporaneous review in the [forum] of public opinion is an effective restraint on possible abuse of judicial power." (p. 270.)

Justice Black has nothing to say on the question of whether a public trial acts as a deterrent to crime, but it is clear that he believes publicity to improve the quality of criminal justice, both theoretically and practically.

As for the juvenile trial issue, he writes:

"Whatever may be the classification of juvenile court proceedings, they are often conducted without admitting all the public. But it has never been the practice to wholly exclude parents, relatives, and friends, or to refuse juveniles the benefit of counsel." (p. 266.)

In fact, the juvenile proceedings as presently conducted are far from secret. Witnesses for the prosecution and for the defense, social workers, court reporters, students, police trainees, probation counselors, and sheriffs are present in the courtroom. Police, the Armed Forces, the Federal Bureau of Investigation obtain information and have access to the police files. There seems no more reason to believe that a jury trial would destroy confidentiality than would witnesses summoned to testify.

JUDGE'S EXPERTISE

The Court is also aware of the argument that the juvenile court was created to develop judges who were experts in sifting out the real problems behind a juvenile's breaking the law; therefore, to place the child's fate in the hands of a jury would defeat that purpose. This will, however, continue to leave the final decision of disposition solely with the judge. The role of the jury will be only to ascertain whether the facts, which give the court jurisdiction, have been established beyond a reasonable doubt. The jury will not be concerned with social and psychological factors. These factors, along with prior record, family and educational background, will be considered by the judge during the dispositional phase.

Taking into consideration the social background and other facts, the judge, during the dispositional phase, will determine what disposition is in the best interests of the child and society. It is at this stage that a judge's expertise is most important, and the granting of a jury trial will not prevent the judge from carrying out the basic philosophy of the juvenile court.

Trial by jury will provide the child with a safeguard against being prejudged. The jury clearly will have no business in learning of the social report or any of the other extraneous matter unless properly introduced under the rules of evidence. Due process demands that the trier of facts should not be acquainted with any of the facts of the case or have knowledge of any of the circumstances, whether through officials in his own department or records in his possession. If the accused believes that the judge has read an account of the facts submitted by the police or any other report prior to the adjudicatory hearing and that this may prove prejudicial, he can demand a jury and insure against such knowledge on the part of the trier of the facts.

WAIVER OF JURY TRIAL

Counsel also questions whether a child can waive his right to a jury trial or, in fact, whether a parent or counsel may waive.

When the waiver comes up for hearing, the Court could, at its discretion, either grant or refuse the juvenile's waiver of a jury trial, and/or appoint a guardian or legal counsel to advise the child.

My experience has shown that the greatest percentage of juveniles who appear before the court in felony cases have lived appalling lives due to parental neglect and brutality, lack of normal living conditions, and poverty. This has produced in them a maturity which is normally acquired much later in life. They are generally well aware of their rights in a court of law. However, in those cases where a child clearly needs guidance, the court-appointed guardian or attorney could explain to him the implications of a waiver. The juvenile's rights and interests would thus be protected every bit as stringently as they are today before he is allowed to plead guilty or not guilty to a complaint. A guilty plea is, after all, a waiver of the right to trial altogether.

Counsel is placed with the responsibility of explaining to the juvenile the significance of guilty and nolo contendere pleas, of instructing the juvenile on the prerogative to take the witness stand, and is expected to advise his client in the same manner as he would an adult about to stand trial. And now counsel suggests to the Court that counsel is not capable of explaining and waiving the right to a jury trial. The Court fails to see the distinction between this waiver and the absolute waiver, to wit, a guilty plea. Counsel should act in the best interest of his client, even if this may be in conflict with the parents. On a number of occasions this Court has appointed counsel for a juvenile whose parents could not afford to retain private counsel, and where the parents' interests were in conflict with those of the child. This procedure will be continued and the Court will continue to rely on the good judgment of the bar.

The Court could easily require that a waiver of a jury trial be made in person by the juvenile in writing, in open court, with the consent and approval of the Court and the attorney representing both the juvenile and the state. The judge could ascertain as to whether the juvenile can intelligently waive his right and, if necessary, appoint counsel to advise the youth as to the implications connected with the waiver. This could be accomplished without any difficulty through means presently available to the Court.

JURY OF PEERS

One of the most interesting questions raised is that concerning the right of a juvenile to a trial by his peers. Counsel has suggested that a jury of a juvenile's peers would be composed of other juveniles, that is, a "teenage jury." Webster's Dictionary, Second Edition, 1996, defines a peer as an equal, one of the same rank, quality, value. The word "peers" means nothing more than citizens, *In re Grilli*, 179 N.Y. S. 795, 797. The phrase "judgment of his peers" means at common law, a trial by a jury of twelve men, *State vs Simons*, 61 Kan. 752. "Judgment of his peers" is a term expressly borrowed from the Magna Carta, and it means a trial by jury, *Ex parte Wagner*, 58 Okl. Cr. 161. The Declaration of Independence also speaks of the equality of all men. Are we now to say that a juvenile is a second-class citizen, not equal to an adult? The Constitution has never been construed to say women must be tried by their peers, to wit, by all-female juries, or Negroes by all-Negro juries.

The only restriction on the makeup of the jury is that there can be no systematic exclusion of those who meet local and federal requirements, in particular, voting qualifications.

The Court notes that presently in some states 18-year-olds can vote. Presumably, if they can vote, they may also serve on juries. Our own legislature has given first passage to an amendment to the Constitution to permit 18-year-olds to vote. Thus, it is quite possible that we will have teenage jurors sitting in judgment of their so-called "peers."

CRIMINAL PROCEEDING

The argument that the adjudication of delinquency is not the equivalent of criminal process is spurious. This Court has discussed the futility of making distinctions on the basis of labels in prior decisions. Because the legislature dictates that a child who commits a felony shall be called a delinquent does not change the nature of the crime. Murder is murder; robbery is robbery—they are both criminal offenses, not civil, regardless and independent of the age of the doer. . . . It is noteworthy that in our statute there is not an express statutory provision indicating that the proceedings are civil. Trial by jury in Rhode Island is guaranteed to all persons, whether in criminal cases or in civil cases. That right existed prior to the adoption of the Constitution; and certainly whether one is involved in a civil or criminal proceeding of the Family Court in which his "liberty" is to be "taken" "imprisoned" "outlawed" and "banished" he is entitled to a trial by jury. (*Henry vs Cherry & Webb*, 30 R. I. 13, at 30).

This Court believes that although the juvenile court was initially created as a social experiment, it has not ceased to be part of the judicial system. In view of the potential loss of liberty at stake in the proceeding, this Court is compelled to accord due process to all the litigants who come before it; and, therefore, all of the provisions of the Bill of Rights, including trial by jury, must prevail.

The Court concludes that the framers of our Constitution never intended to place the power in any one man or official, and take away the "protection of the law from the rights of an individual." It meant "to secure the blessings of liberty to themselves and posterity." The Constitution was written with the philosophy based upon a composite of all of the most liberal ideas which came down through the centuries; The Magna Carta, the Petition of Rights, the Bill of Rights and the Rules of Common Law; and the keystone is the preservation of individual liberty. All these ideas were carefully inserted in our Constitution.

The juvenile is constitutionally entitled to a jury trial.

NOTES AFTER MCKEIVER

1. Up to this point in history, the Supreme Court was on a roll, in some people's mind, in giving juveniles many rights. When one reads the amicus curiae briefs, one gets a deeper understanding of why the court denied the right to a jury trial and has essentially backed away from issues dealing with the juvenile court. The commonwealth of Massachusetts, for example, in its amicus curiae brief, argued that the right to a jury trial would further "straightjacket" an already overly restricted system.

The most persuasive argument came from the state of California. It argued that the use of a jury trial should be a legislative decision set up as part of a comprehensive procedure. It reminded the Supreme Court that the juvenile could always waive his juvenile rights and go into a criminal (adult) court to obtain more procedural safeguards. It argued that juvenile courts were neither "criminal" nor "civil" in nature. It argued that juvenile courts were created by the statute with unique proceedings that required procedures appropriate to the special problems involved. Then, if that were not enough, the state of California argued that if the court did not stop trying to make the juvenile court more criminal in nature, the Supreme Court would have to handle the issue of vagueness. That was a real threat, for it meant giving precise definitions to such terms as neglect, abuse, dependent, and delinquent.

The Public Defender Service for the District of Columbia and Neighborhood Legal Services Program of Washington, D.C., argued that eleven jurisdictions already have jury trials. They said that having the right does not mean a person must use that right. It does not mean that a right should be so used that the increased numbers would clog the court.

In the end, the Supreme Court decided that states could give this right to juveniles. The court did not have to make it a national standard for all states. What do you think about juveniles having jury trials? (Use the majority and minority opinions to debate the issues.)

2. Even with procedural safeguards, the nature of children's crimes is changing. Krisberg et al. (1986, 16) argued that juvenile courts have a constant case load despite the sharply declining juvenile arrest rate. This is due in part to combined police and prosecution practices, more restrictive sanctions, and more serious offenses. It may be that juveniles who commit serious crimes are getting juries, but only because they are transferred into adult courts either through waiver hearings or mandatory waivers based upon the seriousness of the crime.

SUMMARY

In this chapter, the social history of children and youth and the development of the juvenile court were discussed. The beliefs that helped shape the juvenile court in America came from Biblical and medieval Europe, English common law, early Puritan colonists, and the nineteenth-century reform movement. The first juvenile court was developed in Chicago, Illinois, in 1899 with a special philosophy of rehabilitation and personalized justice. Platt (1969, 177) reminds us that this child-saving movement had its most direct impact on the children of the urban poor because these children were viewed as "troublesome" and were imprisoned "for their own good" under a paternalistic ideology that created a new vocabulary. To the child, however, it felt like control, restraint, and punishment. It took until 1966, however, as the landmark cases *Kent, Gault,* and *Winship* showed, before the U.S. Supreme Court would deal with the fact that there were grounds for concern that children were not getting the care nor the procedural safeguards to which they were entitled.

Kent gave youth the right to have a hearing for waiver with an attorney who has the right to view the social history records. The judge must also state on the record the reason for the waiver.

Gault gave youth the right to notice of the charges, the right to an attorney at the adjudicatory hearing, the right to remain silent, and the right to confront and cross-examine the witness. The case raised six issues, but the Court granted only four.

Winship raised the standard of proof in juvenile adjudicatory hearing (trial) to proof beyond a reasonable doubt, but *McKeiver* did not give juveniles the right to jury trials.

Paternalism continues today. There is no single principle or constitution for children's rights. What rights children do have do not flow from one coherent doctrine. For example, paternalism can explain why a 13-year-old girl may be required to obtain parental consent for marriage but no parental consent if she wishes to terminate a pregnancy by abortion. Consequently, what rights juveniles have had come through an appeal to the court system.

REFERENCES

Ashby, Leroy. *Endangered Children: Dependency, Neglect, and Abuse in American History.* New York: Twayne Publishers, c. 1997.

Aumann, F.R. "The Juvenile Court Movement in Ohio." *American Institute of Criminal Law* 22 (1931–32): 556–565. Reprinted in *The New Juvenile Justice,* edited by Martin L. Forst. Chicago: Nelson-Hall Publishers, 1995.

Barnes, Harry Elmer. *A History of the Penal, Reformatory and Correctional Institutions of the State of New Jersey.* New York: Arno Press, reprint edition, 1974.

Butts, Jeffrey A. "Offenders in Juvenile Court, 1992." *OJJDP Update on Statistics.* U.S. Department of Justice, October, 1994.

Butts, Jeffrey A., Howard N. Snyder, Terrence A. Finnegan, Anne L. Aughenbaugh, Nancy J. Tierney, Dennis P. Sullivan, and Rowen S. Poole. *Juvenile Court Statistics 1992, Statistics Report.* Washington, D.C.: Office of Juvenile Justice and Delinquency Prevention (OJJDP).

Citizen's Committee for Children of New York, Inc. *The New York State Training School System.* Unpublished task force report, 1969.

De Mauase, Lloyd. "Our Forebears Made Childhood a Nightmare," *Psychology Today,* April 1975: 85–88.

Erikson, Kai T. *Wayward Puritans.* New York: John Wiley, 1966.

———. "New Conceptions of Deviance." In *Symposium on Crime in America,* edited by Mary Jeanette Hageman. Oneonta, New York: Hartwick College, 1973, pp. 9–17.

Feld, Barry C. "The Juvenile Court Meets the Principle of the Offense: Legislative Changes in Juvenile Waivers Statutes." *The Journal of Criminal Law and Criminology* 78 (3)(1987): 471–533.

Fox, S. "Juvenile Justice Reform: An Historical Perspective." *Stanford Law Review* 22 (1970): 1187–1239.

Gordon, Linda. *Heroes in Their Own Lives.* New York: Viking, 1988.

Hamburg, David A. *Today's Children: Creating a Future for a Generation in Crisis.* New York: Random House, 1992.

Hawes, Joseph. *The Children's Rights Movement*. Boston: Twayne Publishers, 1991.

Keve, Paul. *The History of Corrections in Virginia*. Charlottesville, Virginia: University Press of Virginia, 1986.

Krisberg, Barry, and James Austin. *The Children of Ishmael*. Palo Alto, CA: Mayfield Publishing Company, 1978.

Krisberg, Barry, Ira M. Schwartz, Paul Litsky, and James Austin. "The Watershed of Juvenile Justice Reform," *Crime & Delinquency* 32 (1)1986: 5–37.

Kittrie, Nicholas N. *The Right to Be Different: Deviance and Enforced Therapy*. Baltimore, MD: The Johns Hopkins Press, 1971.

Levin, Mark, and Rosemary C. Sarri. *Juvenile Delinquency: A Study of Juvenile Codes in the U.S.* National Assessment of Juvenile Corrections. Ann Arbor, MI: University of Michigan, 1974.

Mather, Lynn M. "Some Determinants of the Method of Case Disposition: Decision-Making by Public Defenders in Los Angeles." *Law and Society Review* 8 (1974): 187–216.

Mennel, Robert M. *Thorns and Thistles*. Hanover, NH: University of New Hampshire, 1973.

Morello, Karen Berger. *The Invisible Bar: The Woman Lawyer in America 1638 to the Present*. New York: Random House, 1986.

N.C.C.C. *Procedure and Evidence in the Juvenile Court*. San Francisco, CA: 1962.

Oppenlander, Nan. "The Evolution of Law and Wife Abuse." *Law and Policy Quarterly* 3 (4)(1981): 382–405.

Piersma, Paul, and Wendy Schiller. *Juvenile Court and Children's Institutions: Current Legal Issues*. St. Louis, MO: National Juvenile Law Center, Saint Louis University School of Law, 1974.

Platt, Anthony. *The Child Savers: The Invention of Delinquency*. Chicago: University of Chicago Press, 1969.

Rubin, H. Ted. *Juvenile Justice: Policy, Practice, and Law*. 2d ed. New York: Random House, 1985.

Schwartz, Ira M. *(In)justice for Juveniles*. Lexington, MA: Lexington Books, 1989.

Sickmund, Melissa. "Offenders in Juvenile Court, 1988." *OJJDP Update on Statistics*. U.S. Department of Justice, February, 1992.

Snyder, Howard N. "Juvenile Arrests 1996." *OJJDP Juvenile Justice Bulletin*, November 1997.

Stapleton, William V., and L. Teitelbaum. *In Defense of Youth: A Study of the Role of Counsel in American Juvenile Courts*. New York: Russell Sage Foundation, 1972.

Tenney, Charles W., Jr. "The Utopian World of Juvenile Courts." *The Annals* 383 (1969): 102–118.

Wexler, Richard. *Wounded Innocents*. Buffalo: Prometheus Books, 1995.

Wheeler, Leslie. "The Orphan Trains." *American History Illustrated* 18 (Dec.)(1983): 10–23.

Whitcomb, Debra. *When the Victim Is a Child*. 2d ed. Washington, D.C.: National Institute of Justice, 1992.

Wooden, Kenneth. *Weeping in the Playtime of Others*. New York: McGraw Hill, 1976.

CHAPTER 2

The Definition of Juvenile Delinquency, Status Offenses, Abuse, and Developmental Stages

There are *now* three major classes of children who come before the juvenile court for services: (1) delinquents, (2) status offenders, and (3) the abused and neglected. There are others who also come for services before the juvenile court depending on the breadth of jurisdiction. Some courts, called family courts, handle everything that pertains to families, including the granting of divorce or the dissolving of marriages. Because each class has different procedures and laws, Chapter 4, "Process for Delinquent (Criminal) Youth," will discuss delinquency, and Chapter 5, "Child Abuse and Neglect," will be concerned with abuse and neglect.

This chapter will cover the definitions of delinquency, status offenders, abuse, and other noncriminal behavior. It also covers the informal and formal procedures used with status offenders. Then the chapter will close with a discussion of the developmental stages of children and how this knowledge impacts on investigation, witnesses, and treatment of children. We will begin with delinquents because the court was created to deal with these youths.

Legal Definition

The legal definition of a delinquent is one who has committed an act for which he or she could be arrested if he or she were an adult. All fifty states, the District of Columbia, and Puerto Rico have laws delimiting delinquency. Yet all states vary in how they define what acts are prohibited. For example, some states define rape very narrowly, such as a man having sexual intercourse with a woman against her will if she is not his wife. Other states have a broader law to cover both men and women as aggressors. Some states include the use of objects under "sexual penetration by objects" as a form of rape. Only a few states permit people who are married to each other to charge the partner with rape.

Early Definitions

In 1968, Sussman and Baum documented the following thirty-four acts or conditions that were used to define delinquency for which a child could be taken into custody and processed as a delinquent:

1. Violates any law or ordinance

2. Habitually truant

3. (Knowingly) associates with thieves, or vicious or immoral persons

4. Incorrigible

5. Beyond control of parent or guardian

6. Growing up in idleness or crime

7. So deports self as to injure or endanger self or others

8. Absents self from home (without just cause) without consent

9. Immoral or indecent conduct

10. (Habitually) uses vile, obscene, or vulgar language (in public place)

11. (Knowingly) enters or visits house of ill repute

12. Patronizes or visits policy (lottery) shop or gaming place

13. (Habitually) wanders about railroad yards or tracks

14. Jumps train or enters car of engine without authority

15. Patronizes saloon or dram house where intoxicating liquor is sold

16. Wanders streets at night, not on lawful business

17. Patronizes public poolroom or bucket shop (place where stocks and bonds are traded or sold)

18. Immoral conduct around school (or in public place)

19. Engages in illegal occupation

20. In occupation or situation dangerous or injurious to self or others

21. Smokes cigarettes (or uses tobacco in any form)

22. Frequents place whose existence violates law

23. Is found in place for permitting which adult may be punished (If an adult is in a place to which the law permits punishment, then a youth can also be punished.)

24. Addicted to drugs

25. Disorderly

26. Begging

27. Uses intoxicating liquor

28. Makes indecent proposal

29. Loiters, sleeps in alleys, vagrant

30. Runs away from state or charity institution

31. Found on premises occupied or used for illegal purposes

32. Operates motor vehicle dangerously while under influence of liquor

33. Attempts to marry without consent, in violation of law

34. Given to sexual irregularities (Sussman and Baum 1968, 12)

This accumulated list of thirty-four acts came about for many historical reasons. First, parents had access to courts to give legal sanctions against wayward behavior before the establishment of the modern juvenile court.

Puritan Definitions

Early Massachusetts statutes had harsh penalties for disobedient, idle, or stubborn children. The Protestant view was that man is essentially wicked and needs stern discipline in order to produce a godly or goodly society. Because the family was the center of the Puritan society, the society supported the parents in their task of discipline. The Colonial Law of 1654 in Massachusetts made criminal any disobedience by children and servants toward their parents, masters, and governors (*Commonwealth v. Brasher*, 359 Mass. 550, 270 N.E.2d 389 [1971]).

Erikson (1973, 15), who documented his study on *Wayward Puritans* with the court documents of early Puritan society, gives the following example of "stern discipline":

It is ordered, that Phillip Ratcliffe shall be whipped,
have his ears cut off, fined forty pounds, and banished
out of the limits of this jurisdiction, for uttering
malicious and scandalous speeches against the
government and the church of Salem, as appeareth
by a particular thereof, proved upon oath.

> People need stern punishment.

Reformers of Nineteenth Century

In their development of the juvenile court, unfortunately, the reformers of the nineteenth century made no distinction between criminal and noncriminal behavior. All antisocial behavior was labeled "delinquency." The juvenile court invention of 1899 was not concerned with guilt or nonguilt. Its philosophy was what can be done in the interest of the state (*parens patriae*) and the youth to save this child from a life of crime.

> Juvenile court handled all children the same—neglected, abused, and delinquent.

Early Twentieth Century

In the early part of the twentieth century the statutes that were used in many states to give legal authority to the juvenile courts contained phrases like "found begging," "destitute," and "home unfit." The following are some of the typical phrases used in the former § 700 of the California Welfare and Institutions Code, 1937 Cal. Stat. ch. 369, p. 1030, § 700, as amended.

The jurisdiction of the juvenile court extends to any person under the age of 21 years who comes within any of the following descriptions:

> *Whoever controls the media—the images—controls the culture.*
> *Allen Ginsberg*

1. Who has no parent or guardian; or who has no parent or guardian willing to exercise or capable of exercising proper parental control; or who has no parent or guardian actually exercising such proper parental control, and who is in need of such control.

2. Who persistently or habitually refuses to obey the reasonable and proper orders or directions of his parents, guardian, or custodian; or who is beyond the control of such person.

3. Who habitually visits, without parent or guardian, a public billiard room or public poolroom, or a saloon or a place where any spirituous, vinous, or malt liquors are sold, bartered, exchanged, or given away.

4. Who is afflicted with syphilis, gonorrhea, or chancroid and is in need of medical and custodial care, or both.

Reforming Statutes

In the 1960s, California and New York took the lead in reforming their statutes. They began to divide juvenile misbehavior into two areas: criminal (delinquency) and noncriminal (persons in need of supervision or beyond control). Thus began the movement for status offenders. In addition, all thirty-four previously listed acts of behavior became challenged for (1) statutory vagueness, (2) equal protection, and (3) sex-based discrimination.

Statutory Vagueness

Easily Misunderstood Because of No Certainty

The argument raised in the 1970s was that the terms "stubborn" or "incorrigible" child are vague and indefinite. It permitted judges and jurors to decide without any legally fixed standards what is prohibited and what is not in each particular case.

In *Commonwealth v. Brasher*, 359 Mass. 550 (1971), for example, Dianne Brasher was considered to be a stubborn child after refusing to submit to the lawful commands of Michael T. Walsh. The Superior Court ordered her to be committed to the custody of the youth service board, suspended execution of the order for three years, and placed her under probation on condition that she be placed in the home of another named individual. The Supreme Judicial Court of Massachusetts did not at that time see the statutes as vague and indefinite and beyond the police power of the state.

For some parents, the mere expressions of disagreement or differences of views or opinions between parent and child brought fear. They wanted the courts to make the child obey every word of the parent.

The courts recognized the need to maintain the proper functioning of a family unit but they wanted greater clarity of specific offenses for which a child could be prosecuted. They wanted the legislators to rewrite the codes to protect children as well. (Remember, this was the era when reasonable adults differed in their views on African Americans' rights, women's rights, students' rights, and the war in Vietnam. The dilemma was that some children were not bad but were thinking people who might come to a different conclusion on these social issues than their parents.)

Equal Protection Challenges

Another challenge to all the definitions of delinquency was under the legal concept of "equal protection." A person suing in a court of law who claims that a statutory classification denies him or her equal protection bears the burden of persuading the court that the legislative classification has no rational basis. If the statute is rationally related to a legitimate legislative purpose, the courts will permit the legislative judgment to stand and the challenge to fail. If the person complaining of unequal treatment can show that he or she is a "suspect classification," then the courts will use a strict judicial scrutiny. This means the burden is shifted to the state to demonstrate a compelling state interest to justify the inequality of treatment.

Equal = Same conditions and rights as others

In this area of equal protection, youth and their advocates were wondering why youth who leave home are considered "runaways" but adults are not. Why do students in colleges and universities not have truant officers knocking on their dormitory doors to see if they are attending classes? Why are adults allowed to smoke cigarettes and die of lung cancer but juveniles are not? If the behavior, per se, is not wrong and it is only a matter of time, namely, growing up, then why make the behavior criminal for children and not for adults?

For example, in *In re Walker*, 282 N.C. 28, 191 S.E.2d 701 (1972), the question was raised again: How can a child be incarcerated when he has committed no criminal offense, while adults are subjected to incarceration only for actual criminal offenses? When the Supreme Court of North Carolina said the statutes did not violate the Equal Protection Clause of the Constitution, a lot of other advocates saw that it did.

Thus the federal government and behavioral scientists had to begin to educate the judges and the courts. In addition, lawmakers began to see that some behaviors, such as running away and truancy, were better classified as status offenses instead of delinquent or criminal offenses.

Sex-Based Discrimination

Of all the challenges to state statutes, it was sex-based discrimination that is and was the one most in need of removing. Sex-based discrimination was evident in several ways.

In Oklahoma girls were permitted to continue under the jurisdiction of the juvenile court until they were age 18, but boys had to use the adult court after age 16. In *Lamb v. Brown* (456 F.2d 18, 1972), Danny R. Lamb was tried as an adult when he was 17 years of age for the act of burglary. He contended that he should have been tried in the juvenile court. The Tenth Circuit of the United States Court of Appeals agreed with the youth's argument and reversed and remanded the case. They said that the statute did not present any logical constitutional justification. The court did not support the state which, in its brief and oral argument, defined the unexplained statute as "demonstrated facts of life."

In the previously cited case, girls got the better end of the deal than boys, but in other cases girls were more severely punished because the state wanted to protect them. That meant that the state would let young men "sow their wild oats" but would send young women to the state reformatories, learning centers, or juvenile correctional facilities.

Another area where sex-based discrimination has been evident has been with the term "immoral conduct." In *E.S.G. v. State* (447 S.W.2d 225, 1969), the court noted that in thirty-three states a child could be found delinquent if he or she is guilty of immoral conduct. The case before them on appeal dealt with a 14-year-old female who was absent from her home for days at a time and lived with a young woman reputed by the appellant's mother to be a prostitute. In addition, she began hanging around a Greyhound Bus Station and other public places. She was brought to the Juvenile Court after her mother had located her in a downtown transient apartment with a young adult male.

The lower court adjudicated the girl as delinquent and committed her to the custody of the Texas Youth Council for an indefinite term not extending beyond her 21st birthday. The appeals court of Texas affirmed the lower court.

E.S.G. gives you an understanding of why so many status offenders are female. Could there be any other ways to control sexual behavior than incarceration in a juvenile correctional facility for seven years, as was given to E.S.G.?

✳ BRAIN EXERCISE

In the list of thirty-four original acts of delinquent behavior, notice number 34: "given to sexual irregularities." What does that mean? Is it vague? Is it equal protection? Is it sex-based discrimination? Is it all three?

Number 27 of the 34 acts says "uses intoxicating liquor." What about possession of alcohol? Is possession of alcohol by a minor considered a delinquent act? You bet, especially if the youth was already adjudicated as delinquent and possession of alcohol was a violation of imposed probation (*In the Interest of C.P.*, 458 S.E.2d 166, 1995).

Washington State Model

In 1977, Washington State became the first state to drastically revamp its juvenile justice philosophy from treatment alone to determinate sentencing for juvenile offenders. "The juvenile court is to view itself primarily as an instrument of justice rather than as a provider of services" (Forst and Bloomquist 1992, 2).

Other States

California and Minnesota also revamped their statutes. California's "statutory revisions enacted in the past ten years have made accountability, victims' rights, and public safety high priorities in the juvenile justice system" (Forst and Bloomquist 1992, 2).

Likewise, Minnesota's juvenile law uses phrases like "promote public safety" and develop "individual responsibility for lawful behavior." Regardless of the state, the result was a disenchantment with the old system and a lack of clarity in the emerging concepts. One concept that won political favor was "public safety."

Definition

"Status offender" is a legal description used to describe a juvenile who commits an act that is a law violation only for a juvenile. If the youth were an adult and committed the act, he or she would never be arrested or processed for that act. An example is running away from home.

Depending on the locality, status offenders are also known by such names as persons in need of supervision (PINS), minors in need of supervision (MINS), and children in need of supervision (CHINS). In the state of Virginia, for example, a **child in need of services** is different from a **child in need of supervision**. A child in need of services is one who is absent without good reason from school or is continuously disobedient to parents or their equal, who remains away from his or her family, and whose behavior could result in physical damage to the child by the family or by the child.

The child in need of supervision means, for example, that under compulsory school law, the child is continuously absent from school, the child has been offered to receive an education, and the school has tried without result to effect the child's attendance. Or the child, without parental consent, remains away from home, or equal and such action may result in physical damage to the child, and the family is in need of treatment, and the intervention of the court is the only remedy. The judge can hold a child who is in need of supervision but cannot hold a child in need of services.

These status offenders (generic term) are brought to the attention of criminal justice agents by the parents who ask, for example, that the police do something about their child who is "going around with the wrong crowd" or is dating someone the parents "worry about." The young people resent the unrealistic limits placed on their behavior as if to say "What's the matter? Don't you trust me?"

The youth's poor schoolwork, truancy, conflict with teachers, and fights with peers and parents are expressed behaviors. The behavior speaks for itself. It tells people the youth cannot handle life.

Although these youths do not consider themselves as delinquents, their behavior draws attention to the fact that all is not well. Their behavior may consist of drunkenness, unauthorized use of motor vehicles and credit cards, and running away. These youths who are angry with their parents may turn to alcohol, marijuana, and other drugs (prevalent in both middle-class and lower-class offenders). Therefore, courts and social agencies use informal procedures to assist these families.

Informal Procedures

The following case study, with different real names for reasons of confidentiality, shows some of the problems of these youths and how the Family Crisis Intervention Program of Clark County, Washington (Anderson et al. 1979, 23–24), worked:

Tim, a 13-year-old boy, resided with his natural mother, Jenny, and her boyfriend, Ray, along with two older sisters, Lucy (15), Tina (14), and two younger stepbrothers, Bill (6), and Jim (5). Jenny had been married twice, both marriages ending in divorce. She was employed as a bartender in a tavern. Ray was an unemployed carpenter.

Tim ran away from home for two days, hiding in the woods until he was found by the police. He was brought to juvenile detention because he refused to return home. He stated that Ray drank excessively and abused him physically. Tim stayed in Interim Care pending the impact session one day later. During the session the family established two goals: (1) to keep Tim from running away, and (2) to develop a higher level of trust among family members.

The family crisis team focused on some major areas of conflict within the family. Due to Jenny's evening job, she was away from home before the children returned from school. She left Lucy in charge of the family and household. It was apparent that Jenny avoided her family by using work and free time as an escape. Jenny felt that without her two "good girls," the family would fall apart. Tim had not seen his natural father, who had been in prison for a long time. Bill had been diagnosed as having dyslexia (a learning disability) and did poorly in school. The team discovered that the children resented Ray and wanted him to leave them alone. Ray and Jenny drank excessively and fought, causing a lot of unrest for the children.

Jenny and Ray admitted that their lives had excluded the children. They agreed to become more involved in family activities and to be home more often. Jenny decided to reduce her working time to three evenings a week. The team recommended that she and Ray seek alcohol counseling and that they work more closely on managing the family. Tim was returned home and encouraged to communicate his frustration with the family. All the children agreed to talk and reduce their yelling at one another.

Follow-up indicates that Jenny did reduce her working time and is more actively involved in the family. Ray is presently employed. Tim has not returned to the juvenile court and has not run away again.

Programs developed in communities to aid with these offenders have centered around two themes: (1) providing shelter with or without counseling for the youths, and (2) providing training in parenting and communication skills for the parents—a theme that has permitted the growth of a new field of psychotherapy called "family therapy." The shelters, sometimes called "crisis centers," focus on giving youths in trouble food, clothing, a safe place to sleep, referrals to other community services, and, when possible, counseling to help return youths to their families.

Some of these crisis centers, like the Berkeley Youth Alternatives of Berkeley, California (Wall et al. 1981, 20), receive referrals from police, probation, schools, and other agencies. In addition, this program has a 24-hour hotline telephone emergency service. This program also permits youths and families to "drop in" at the center.

Another program called *Homebuilders*, which began in Tacoma, Washington, in 1974, is now replicated in many states. The program uses therapists who actually intervene in the homes of families to provide short-term, intensive, education-based therapy designed to improve family interactions and preserve family structure. The counselor works with two client families at a time and is available on a 24-hour basis. In short, the counselors do "house calls" to show parents better ways to communicate and develop cooperation among family members. Children do not have to be put into foster care, group homes, psychiatric hospitals, or correctional facilities. Because placement into these group homes or correctional facilities is more costly, keeping children at home is more cost-effective and beneficial to the family in the short and long run.

Runaways create an unusual challenge for criminal justice agencies. It is hard to distinguish between youths who have physically relocated and those who are victims of foul play. Since 1973, mass murders of young boys have caused parents and interested citizens and professionals to put more pressure on the police. Some of the murdered youths in a suburb of Chicago (1980) and those in Atlanta, Georgia (1981), had not really "run away." They had been lured away with, perhaps, promises of making money.

The interaction between a group of angry mothers in Atlanta, Georgia, and the police department, news media, and so forth, showed a lack of credibility in the police department. Editorials in the newspaper pointed to the police department's "mismanaging the missing persons bureau" and to city officials for playing "their favorite game, cover-your-tail (a—), instead of leveling with the citizenry" (Levinson 1981, 48). Other police departments across the nation are realizing the need to update the techniques and operations of their missing persons bureau.

In addition to the youths in Atlanta, on May 25, 1979, Etan Patz vanished from the streets of New York City on his way to school. The massive search brought nothing except a momentum that moved elected officials, child advocates, families of missing children, and concerned citizens from coast-to-coast. Thus, in 1982, President Ronald Reagan signed into law the Missing Children Act, and in 1983, he proclaimed May 25 National Missing Children's Day. The National Center for Missing and Exploited Children (NCMEC) began in 1984. It is a national clearinghouse of information about the problem of missing and exploited children developed by John Walsh. John Walsh's son, Adam, disappeared in 1981 from a shopping mall while shopping with his mother. To Mr. Walsh's amazement, the FBI could not aid him unless there was a ransom note or evidence of his son being taken over state lines. He was told that if it had been a missing automobile the FBI could have helped.

Missing Children Act

Later, the police found only the skull of the young boy in a canal over 100 miles from the shopping center. With the loss of his son and his own mistreatment in the process, John Walsh pushed for the enactment of federal laws to aid in recovering missing children. It was his driving effort that educated both the public and the Congress about missing children. NCMEC has a toll-free hotline at 1-800-THE-LOST or 1-800-843-5678. Their new address is 699 Prince Street, Arlington, VA 22201; www.ncmec.org. NCMEC works with the U.S. Justice Department's Office of Juvenile Justice and Delinquency Prevention and is now the world headquarters of the newly formed International Center for Missing and Exploited Children. The center recommends action in the areas of child abduction, sexual victimization of children, child pornography and prostitution, services for child victims, and prevention. (For more details, see *A Report Card to the Nation: Missing and Exploited Children, 1984–1994*, published by the U.S. Justice Department Office of Juvenile Justice and Delinquency Prevention.)

NCMEC

Generally speaking, status offenses include truancy, running away, smoking, drinking alcohol, and violation of curfew. Again, there is no national code. States vary even though there has been a national concerted effort to remove status offenses from the juvenile court (Schwartz 1989).

Figure 2.1
Used by permission of the artist Bob Gorell, *The Richmond Times-Dispatch.*

Most state codes try to handle the behavior of youth that others think is "incorrigible," "immoral," and "beyond the control."

✳ BRAIN EXERCISE

What do parents do when they know their daughter is seeing older men and there is the risk of a pregnancy? Does the state charge the man with a criminal offense or the daughter?

In *Stump v. Sparkman* (435 U.S. 349, 1978), the mother requested the circuit court judge to have a tubal ligation done on her 15-year-old "somewhat retarded" daughter. (It is questionable how retarded the daughter was. She passed every year in school!) The mother wanted this operation because the daughter was associating with older youth and had stayed out overnight on several occasions. According to the court record, the mother wanted to prevent "unfortunate circumstances." The judge, without talking to the girl or ordering a home study, ordered the operation.

Several years later, the daughter married. She and her husband figured out that the earlier operation was not to remove the appendix, as the daughter had been told. They sued the mother, her attorney, the judge, the doctors who performed and assisted in the tubal ligation, and the hospital. One result of that decision was that now a judge cannot be sued. But what is more important is how society, through its courts, deals with these problems. Were there any other ways to deal with the issue of a daughter dating older men other than by performing tubal ligations?

Formal Procedures

Each state and each jurisdiction within states varies in its formal procedures. Let us take a case in the make-believe state of Euphoria. We will use some statutes and write a script for how a social worker in the court and a defense counselor might do their jobs in helping a juvenile judge deal with a problem child and his or her family. In short, let us "walk a case through."

In the state of Euphoria, the legislators have made it the intention of the law that in all proceedings the welfare of the child and the family is the paramount concern. The judge will, therefore, possess all necessary and incidental power and authority, whether legal or equitable, to benefit all concerned. Some of the purposes (Juvenile Code § 16.1–227) will be as follows:

a. To divert from the juvenile justice system, where possible, without harm to public safety, those children who can be cared for or treated through alternative programs.

b. To provide judicial procedures through which the provisions of this law are executed and enforced, and in which the parties are assured a fair hearing and their constitutional and other rights are recognized and enforced.

c. To separate a child from that child's parents, guardian, legal custodian, or other person standing in loco parentis only when the child's welfare is endangered or it is in the interest of public safety.

d. To protect the community against those acts of its citizens that are harmful to others and to reduce the incidence of delinquent behavior.

Let us pretend that Lucy Smith has gone before Judge Charlie Brown on January 20, 1994, and has admitted to being a "child in need of supervision" (similar to the Virginia definition). That means that her behavior was not delinquent and can only be covered by the statute 16.1–227 (c) as listed above. Her father Snoopy Smith had gone to the juvenile court. He filed a petition with the juvenile intake worker that Lucy (age 14) was carrying on a relationship with a divorced man (age 25). She is eager to wed this man, Beethoven Schroder. Schroder thought that Lucy was over 21. Snoopy, her father, is irate. He says that Lucy does not even look 18. In fact, he says that she has not even begun to sexually develop even though she does wear a training bra.

Judge Brown orders that Lucy be detained by the Division of Youth Services for an evaluation pending the dispositional hearing on February 26, 1994, at 2:00 p.m. Judge Brown orders the court staff to conduct an investigation.

Social History Investigation

The court staff conducted an investigation of the family and wrote up their findings in what is called a **Social History Investigation**. This legal document is very important because it gives the judge, supposedly, all the information the judge needs in order to make a decision that will be in the "best interest of the child." The court staff and probation officers are to explore all avenues—biological, psychological, sociological, and spiritual. Watch for all that information.

SOCIAL HISTORY INVESTIGATION

<u>Name</u>: Lucy Smith
<u>Address</u>: 20 Doghouse Road,
Anytown, Euphoria, USA
<u>Date of Birth</u>: 9/10/80
<u>School</u>: Pigpen Senior High
<u>Judge</u>: Charlie Brown
<u>Charge</u>: CHINS
<u>Finding</u>: CHINS
<u>Father</u>: Snoopy Smith
<u>Address</u>: Same as above.
<u>Siblings</u>:

<u>Race</u>: White
<u>Sex</u>: Female

<u>Religion</u>: Great Pumpkin
<u>Grade</u>: 9 <u>Employed</u>: No
<u>Hearing Date</u>: 1/20/94

<u>Dispositional Date</u>: 2/26/94
<u>Mother</u>: Peppermint Patty Smith
<u>Address</u>: Same as above.

Linus Smith, Male, 1/12/74
Curtis Smith, Male, 12/29/74
Denise Smith, Female, 8/27/76
Jacqueline Smith, Female, 7/14/77
Beverly Smith, Female, 9/25/78

Medical

Present Charge

Petition alleges that the respondent is a "child in need of supervision" because she is ungovernable and is a runaway. By definition, a child in need of supervision is one who, without reasonable cause and without consent of his or her parents, remains away from home. Such behavior presents a clear and substantial danger to the child's life or health, and the child's family is in need of treatment, rehabilitation, or services not presently being received.

Respondent's Account of the Case

The respondent admitted to carrying on a relationship with a divorced man that she has known for over four years. He is 25. Despite the difference in their ages, Lucy claims to be in love with, and eager to wed, Beethoven Schroder, a/k/a "Buba," of E. Mainstreet (first floor front). Mr. Schroder is currently on parole or probation, but the respondent feels that he is incapable of such behavior. Lucy readily admitted to running away from her parents to spend time with this man whom she says she is "going with." She sees nothing wrong with their relationship nor wrong with the difference in their ages. She explains away the fact that "Buba" has not worked nor has any training in a trade except for playing the piano. The respondent admits to kissing Mr. Schroder but, in my presence, she denies any sexual contact. This is contrary to the statements she made in open court. Lucy takes $10 or $20 per week from him. Together they purchase paint and solvents from which they inhale the intoxicating vapors.

Previous Court Appearances

A search of the records of the Court was initiated by this worker. That search revealed that there are no past petitions alleging delinquency against Lucy Smith in the city of Anytown in the state of Euphoria.

Respondent

Lucy Smith is a 14-year-old female Caucasian. She is a slender (5'1" 103 lbs.), curly-haired youngster with adolescent acne. She is physically less mature than other girls her age, and so she appears somewhat younger than her stated age. She was born on September 10, 1980, in Anytown, Euphoria. (Birth certificate #74-26158.) Her birth was an uncomplicated delivery after a full-term, uneventful pregnancy.

All of the respondent's developmental milestones were within normal limits. She was using words in sentences at 2 years of age and completed toilet training at about age 2. Her menstrual period began in 1989 (the exact date is easily recalled by the respondent) and is regular. The respondent had all of the required inoculations and all of the usual childhood illnesses.

Lucy stated that she had difficulty falling asleep despite being easily tired. She denied having nightmares but did describe headaches and dizziness. The respondent admits to the consumption of alcohol and the "huffing" of paint fumes. Due to the inhalation of these fumes, she was hospitalized at Anytown Memorial Hospital for a drug-induced psychotic reaction. Psychiatric intervention was suggested at an early age, but no appointment was made or kept.

The respondent was interviewed at the Reception and Diagnostic Center of Euphoria's Division of Youth Services. She was quite verbal and very cooperative. She presents herself as a depressed child but capable of moments of lighter moods. These shifts were not sudden or inappropriate. She was oriented in all spheres and denies having hallucinations or suicidal ideation, except when under the influence of paint fumes. However, she has been heard making suicidal threats in the past when she was not intoxicated. Dynamically, these self-destructive desires are manifested in her rebellious behavior, her obviously stressful interaction with her parents in terms of her living with Buba. She impressed me as a stubborn, selfish, and narcissistic individual who can see only her needs as being worthy of satisfaction. She is immature and refuses to recognize the responsibility of guarding her health.

Lucy is a quiet, shy child whose anxiety is seen in her nail-biting. She is a loner who has always played by herself and avoided others. She sulks when she cannot get her way, or she has tantrums. She rationalizes and blames others for her difficulties. With the availability of Mr. Schroder's house as a refuge, she can always run from conflict and confrontation.

Lucy angers easily and responds with death threats to her antagonists. She has done so frequently enough to instill in her sister a fear of sleeping alone with the respondent. Lucy, however, stated that she could not really kill anyone. Lucy further stated that she is not an aggressive person at all. Linus, the older brother, said that Lucy is always doing something mean like taking his blanket away.

She is angered when Mr. Schroder reprimands her or when any restrictions on her movements are made. Lucy takes her relationship with him seriously and would not voluntarily stay in an environment that would not allow her to see him.

This would mean that a secure setting might be indicated if residential treatment were recommended. The respondent said that the only time that she was sad was when her grandmother died. She also described being "down" about her parents filing the CHINS petition against her. She felt that she was right and that her parents should let her stay with Mr. Schroder.

The respondent's free time is spent with Mr. Schroder instead of agemates. If she has the money to get to his house, she will "talk about things" with him or get high.

Lucy's plans for her future are to get married to Mr. Schroder, find an apartment, and seek employment as a waitress or as a receptionist in a psychiatrist's office.

Needless to say, the respondent is anything but enamored of her parents. She described her father's behavior as being of a routine nature, that on return home from work, he is "put in the doghouse," so to speak, by her mother and he goes to bed. He gives money to his wife and then ignores her.

Lucy stated that the undisputed boss in her home is her mother. The respondent hates and fears her. When drunk, the mother becomes dangerously assaultive and strikes her children with her fist, according to Lucy. The relationships with her siblings are equally poor.

School Adjustment

Lucy is a ninth-grade student at Pigpen Senior High. We have requested a report from the school, and it will be included in the respondent's folder, for the court's information, *upon its receipt. Lucy says that her grades are in the 80th to 90th percentile but that she does fail an occasional examination or paper. Her trouble in school comes from, Lucy says, her misbehavior in class.*

Family Evaluation

The respondent lives with her parents and three of her five siblings. The dwelling is a two-story affair in the French Quarter of the Public Housing Project. The family has lived there for 18 years and pays $384.40 per month rent. The home is cluttered and in minor disrepair, but the kitchen has a microwave oven. Mr. Smith's salary is the only source of family income.

Mrs. Peppermint Patty Smith was educated through the eighth grade and has never been employed. Mr. Snoopy Smith has completed two years of college. He gave up flying airplanes and has been a long-distance truck driver for 22 years. Due to his long-term employment and recent heart surgery, he is near retirement. He is on the road a great deal of the time. He is rarely home more than three days in a row.

During my interview with Mr. and Mrs. Smith, he said he feels like he leads a dog's life. Mrs. Smith is a large woman with a deep, gruff voice, and a tattoo spelling her name appears on her right arm. She described her family and their various problems in a matter-of-fact way and gave me the impression that she was not at a point where she had no control over her daughter. Both agree that Lucy is more sexually involved with Buba than Lucy described to me. Mrs. Smith would like to have Mr. Schroder arrested for contributing to the delinquency of a minor. She cannot make Mr. Schroder see how inappropriate this relationship is. When he appears at her door, she throws him out.

Dispositions

Now, with the completion of the investigation into the home life of the young woman, the **Judge** will hold a **dispositional hearing** to give a **disposition**. With this **Social History Investigation** report and any other pertinent reports from the school, medical doctors, or court psychologist, Judge Charlie Brown is now ready to have a hearing. At this hearing, he will hear arguments from defense counsel and court workers as to what would be in the best interest of the child. Because the child is not charged with delinquency, the prosecuting attorney has no interest in the case. In addition, the statute of the state limits what the judge can do. For example, the judge may not send this youth to a facility in which other children who have been found delinquent reside. Yet, as you will see in this fictional case, there are many other alternatives.

This hearing will determine what will happen to Lucy. The court worker, the defense counsel, the family, and the Judge will all take part. The defense attorney will stand before the judge and probably give the following recommendations with the appropriate justification:

Go after the whole family. The child's behavior is sometimes the result of poor communication between husband and wife.

1. Family therapy, family counseling, and parenting classes as ordered by the court through the City of Anytown Mental Health. This is justified because this is a dysfunctional family in that both parents abuse alcohol and their power. The parents misuse their power in a physical way and, in so doing, abuse the children. The expressions of anger are out of control. Lucy is **not running to** something as much as she is **running from something**.

Mrs. Smith is also co-dependent. She feels responsible for everything and everyone, yet feels powerless and unworthy. There is too much reliance on the coping skills of passivity, suffering, blaming, and hope that God will take care of everything. Lacking both physical and emotional health and well-being, the co-dependent has no energy to deal effectively with the problems in the family. Feeling tired, weak, and fearful is both a cause and consequence.

Mrs. Smith is a passive-aggressive woman who had six children in a five-year period of time. This woman was sexually abused in a marital situation. Newborns are very tiring; they require a lot of attention. When one child is quickly followed by another child, there is little time and energy to help or assist the child with developmental tasks because of the demands of the youngest child. The mother could not possibly meet the emotional needs of each child without additional support from others, namely, husband, extended family members, older children.

The first one to two years of life for a child's development are crucial. The process of getting needs met establishes a basis of trust. Lucy was the youngest in her family. She was at the end of the family line in more ways than one. Her psychosocial development was hindered at an early age.

Lucy is the sixth child. According to the birth order theory of dysfunctional families, she has learned a certain role in the family. She is in the role of the scapegoat or rebel. Her relationship with a man much older than herself, her sexual and drug experiences, and her running away are all examples of her rebelliousness.

Although the preference of the parents for Lucy would be to remain in the home, the reality is that the home is not stable nor is it safe for her. The kinds of difficulties that the Smiths are experiencing, even with the most intensive counseling and highest motivation, will take more than one year to resolve. Therefore, a more structured placement is required.

2. Placement at Little Red-Head Girl's Finishing School. This school has a special cottage with a director, Diane MacGladiator. She is skilled in the treatment of substance abuse and troubled youth. The program involves the parents as part of the treatment. In this structured program, the youth are given consistency, such as set meal times, so that they can begin to trust others. Decision-making skills, impulse control, anger control, and assertiveness are also taught.

Deal with the unique needs of the client.

In addition, Lucy needs help with her sexual identity. She is using it to manipulate men to get some of her needs met. By having role models and involvement with female counselors, this need can be addressed.

This special program includes some wilderness experiences that help youth learn to work as a team to accomplish goals for the betterment of the group. In addition, learning to survive in the out-of-doors elevates self-esteem and gives youth a sense of betterment and higher self-worth. All of these things are extremely important to Lucy's growth and development.

School is taught on the campus but there are no high walls, and Lucy could attend a nearby high school if she desired. This might also help in maintaining positive ties to the community.

3. Ask her boyfriend, Mr. Schroder, to come to court. It is recommended that she be told she cannot see this man without parental consent until she is 18 years of age. Her continuation of the relationship with him without parental consent should result in a contempt of court citation

Deal with the boyfriend.

against her. This means that if she is found to be in contempt of court, she could be found guilty and placed in a secure facility in which others who have criminal violations are placed.

Mr. Schroder could, and should, be charged with contributing to the delinquency of a minor. For him to argue, Your Honor, that she looked like she was 21 and talked like she was 21 when she has a flat chest is unreal on his part. He should be sentenced to 12 months in jail, with the sentence suspended upon condition that he stay away from Lucy. Lucy needs to understand that if he does not, he will be put in jail. If she really likes him and does not want to see him go to jail, she will stay away from him.

The defense attorney will end her or his statements and then sit down. The court social worker will then give her or his statements. The judge will ask some questions, not to investigate, but rather to see if there is agreement and if the family is willing to go to counseling. Then the judge will so order the programs and ask for reports from the social agencies dealing with the family. Judge Brown's hope will be that all those involved will cooperate and the agencies and their staff will function appropriately. Then the agencies will send reports that all is progressing well. The case will be closed. And all will live happily ever after.

Real Life

Now, in real life, the defense counsel may not have extensive knowledge of social agencies in the community. Or, even worse, the community may have no alternatives for children who are having troubles within the family. In addition, in some states there are more services for boys than for girls. Moreover, the limited programs that do exist are overcrowded. By the time there is room in these facilities, the child sometimes has grown past the jurisdiction age of the court. In one case, *Larry L. v. State of West Virginia* (444 S.E. 2d 43, 1994), the Supreme Court of Appeals of West Virginia reversed the circuit court by stating that a court could not remove a juvenile from the custody of his guardian and place him in a juvenile facility for a status offense without any record of a psychological, physical, or diagnostic evaluation no matter how disruptive the child was for the parents or the school attendants.

Throwaway Children

In some families, the abuse is so great that the children run away and live on the streets. In the 1970s, young people went to large cities like San Francisco because their lifestyle was different from their parents. Today, young people run or are pushed out of their homes because of family problems that our society has not recognized or has been unable to handle by mobilizing resources to provide other alternatives such as independent living places.

Some abused children get married and create their own dysfunctional families. Some may not get married but they do have children. Some of these young people take drugs or drink alcohol while carrying a fetus; they have now produced a generation of children with a very preventable condition that cannot be fixed: fetal alcohol syndrome (FAS). FAS has now been shown to affect the brain and its development so that some children with FAS have no understanding of right and wrong and long-term consequences.

In this chapter, a fiction was created by using the state of Euphoria and a make-believe family problem of Lucy Smith before Judge Charlie Brown. Yet, in reality, each state varies in what it defines as status offenses and what procedural rights are granted. Societies differ in their enlightenment and the resources available to assist parents with the task of raising their children. The parents themselves may not have had very mature, responsible parents.

Deinstitutionalization

In 1974, Congress responded to child advocates who showed that runaways were often jailed—or put in detention homes or other secure facilities—by passing the Juvenile Justice and Delinquency Prevention (JJDP) Act. This act labeled runaway children, school truants, alcohol users, and incorrigible children as "status offenders," and required them to be "deinstitutionalized."

The federal government, through its Juvenile Justice and Delinquency Prevention (JJDP) Act, brought pressure on states to deinstitutionalize status offenders and separate them from the delinquents. Once the states wrote statutes to specifically handle status offenders, the statutes were challenged. The District of Columbia Court of Appeal in *District of Columbia* (appellant) *v. B.J.R.* (appellee), *332 A.2d 58 (1975), was called upon to judge the new language of a CHINS statute. The pertinent portion of § 16-2301 reads as follows:

(8) The term "child in need of supervision" means a child who—(A) . . . (iii) is habitually disobedient of the reasonable and lawful commands of his parent, guardian, or other custodian and is ungovernable; and (B) is in need of care or rehabilitation.

The appellee (B.J.R.) was specifically charged with "absconding" from home in April and October of 1969, in June and August of 1972, and on February 26, 1973.

The issue of question before the court was: Did the language pass constitutional muster? The court found that it did.

That court argued that the statute as drafted was the product of highly competent, contemporaneous legal expertise. The definition of "children in need of supervision" is substantially identical to that of the Uniform Juvenile Court Act (U.L.A.) 2(4) (1973) and the Legislative Guide for Drafting Family and Juvenile Court Acts 2(p) (Dept. of H.E.W., Children's Bureau Pub. No. 472-1969). The court even mentioned that the 1970 statute drop-ped some of the troublesome language such as "immoral activities" of the Code 1967.

What the courts across the United States were trying to do was differentiate between youth who had committed a serious criminal act and a child who was having disagreements or problems with parents.

First, they were trying to decide: if the juvenile court did intervene, what would they do to appease those who did not want both kinds of youth in the same detention or secure facilities?

A second objective was for juveniles to be separated from the sight and sound of adults in jails. Later, the objective was to remove all youth from

Some children are in jails and prisons who do not need to be there.

---

*When the court has a child before it, it will use initials so as not to fully identify the child by name to the public. In other cases, the court will give fictitious names to protect the identity of the appellee such as *Roe v. Wade*. Roe was not her real name nor was a later case when the court used the name of Jane Doe.

jails. Thus, children had a right to freedom from custody of their parents or legal guardians. While some children got help, others were free to leave at their leisure, regardless of the risks and dangers on the street.

By 1980, Congress permitted Courts to enforce their own valid court orders so that a child was given "one free runaway." Courts could not detain a first-time runaway. "If the child returned home voluntarily, was placed under court orders to remain at home, but later violated the order by running away, he or she then could be detained" (U.S. Dept. of Justice 1986, 3).

By 1984, the mood of the nation and Congress had drastically changed . . . The abduction and murder of Adam Walsh, the series of child murders in Atlanta, the serial murders of runaway children in Texas, the "Minnesota Connection" of runaways to the streets of New York City, have all vividly alerted our N(n)ation to a much larger problem—children who are out of legal, parental custody . . .

In October 1984, Congress began to change the direction of the JJDP Act by amending the Act to incorporate the Missing Children's Assistance Act . . . Parents, schools, child-serving agencies, and professionals of all disciplines are justifiably worried about the nature, scope, and resolution of problems surrounding America's missing children. (U.S. Dept. of Justice 1986, 3)

Application of Newer Laws

In the state of New York, a petition which alleged that Cassandra R. was in need of supervision was dismissed because it **lacked sufficient particularity**. The petition contained six allegations. These allegations stated that the juvenile had left home (absconded) on a certain date; that she had absconded three times in the past; that she was truant from school; that she smoked cigarettes; that she drank alcohol; and that she was disobedient and beyond the petitioner's (mother's) control. However, only one of the allegations set forth a specific date and time. The petition had to be dismissed because a single act could not form the basis for an adjudication that an individual is "a person in need of supervision" (*Matter of Cassandra R.*, 589 N.Y.S.2d 739 [Fam. Ct. N.Y.C.N.Y. July 1992]).

ABUSED AND NEGLECTED

I believe in life after birth. Maxine Dunham

Definition

All fifty states have defined abused and neglected children in their statutes. Each state varies as to degrees of abuse, but generally speaking, abuse is defined as nonaccidental injury to a child by a caretaker. It involves a child whose physical or mental health or welfare is harmed, or threatened with harm, by the acts or omissions of the parents or someone who has control over the child as a caretaker. The abuse can be physical, like a broken arm, or sexual, or emotional. Each kind of abuse has different criteria for proof. (Chapter 5, "Child Abuse and Neglect," and Chapter 6, "Crimes Against Children," will discuss these issues in greater detail.)

For example, *In re Interest of T.M.B.*, 491 N.W. 2d 58 (Neb. Sup. Oct. 1992) the father argued that his activity of corporal punishment was protected by the freedom of religion under the First Amendment. The court found that the forty to sixty strikes with a belt per week to the body of the child was excessive and constituted abuse under Nebraska law. The court also noted that child abuse was not a constitutionally protected activity.

Neglected children, on the other hand, have been physically or emotionally abandoned by parents or those who are supposed to care properly for them as required for normal human growth. A brain scan of a neglected orphan compared with that of a normal child shows much less activity in the connections responsible for feeling, learning, and remembering. Neglected children are at high risk for physical disabilities and developmental delay along with poor social or emotional skills to establish supportive relationships. An example might be a 3-year-old child who is not being fed by his parents. The neighbors may find themselves feeding a child and then calling Child Protective Services (CPS). CPS would investigate the complaint and provide needed services or file charges depending upon the situation and the willful intent of the parent(s). If, for example, the parents are out of work and do not know about applying for Food Stamps (a federal governmental agency food supplement program), then the parents would be assisted by referrals to other agencies. (How CPS investigates is explained in detail in Chapter 5.)

Despite difficulties in definitions, child abuse and neglect rates remain high according to the National Committee to Prevent Child Abuse (NCPCA), based on their 1996 Annual Fifty State Survey. "Consistent with data from prior years," a vast majority of children die due to maltreatment: 82 percent were under the age of five, and "42 [percent] were less than one year old at the time of their death" (*Together for Children*, published by Prevent Child Abuse, Virginia, Summer 1997, 3).

Prenatal Abuse

Some states have had to define neglect or include prenatal care in their definition of abuse. In Maryland, for example, the Appellant Court upheld a trial court decision that a mother neglected an unborn child. Their decision was based on evidence that the mother was addicted to drugs, had failed in previous drug treatment programs, took phencyclidine, cocaine, and engaged in unprotected sex while pregnant. Therefore, the mother was unable to provide sufficient and adequate care for her child [*In re Dustin I.*, 614 A.2d 999 (Md. Spec. App. Oct. 1992)].

Dependency

Dependency usually is distinguished from neglect in that dependency involves the inability, as opposed to the willful failure, of parents to provide for their children. These children might be the sole survivors of an automobile accident or a shooting or hostage situation.

Ritualistic Abuse

Ritualistic abuse of children, adolescents, and adults involves repeated physical, sexual, psychological, and/or spiritual abuse. The abuse utilizes rituals. Rituals can be religious, social, cultural, sexual, and so forth. Ritualistic abuse does not necessarily have to do with religion. The ritual is necessary for the abuser or criminal because it fulfills a need. For example, most mutilation in homicides is the result of sexual ritualism. The offender is doing it because it arouses him or her sexually.

In all neglect and abuse cases, it is well to remember that some states give greater authority for immediate removal of the child by police and others demand that a child protective service worker do the investigation. States vary.

CAUSATION

Abused children may become delinquent. Why?

See "Victim Becomes Offender" in Chapter 6.

The line between delinquents, status offenders, and abused and neglected children are not always solid lines. Some children may be abused first and then become delinquents. Some delinquents may so frustrate their parents that they may also be abused after doing criminal acts. Abused children do have more problematic and aggressive behavior than children who are not abused. Yet, some abused children continue to internalize the pain and continue to inflict the pain upon themselves, thereby becoming self-destructive. Some get professional help.

Where we do have case histories of children killing their parents, the child is usually severely abused sexually, physically, or verbally. Torture is probably a better word to describe the abuse. In addition, when a child is raised in a family with drug dependence or other dysfunction, the violence in the child's family escalates, and the youth becomes increasingly vulnerable to stressors in the home environment. In some cases there has been a confrontation in which one of the parents has said to the child that it was either the parent or the child who would be killed. In addition, most of the youth had ready access to a firearm (Mones 1991).

Researchers are trying to sort out these connections of abuse, neglect, and delinquency. Various studies have found that between 8 and 26 percent of delinquents have been abused. Self-report studies (studies in which the individuals report for themselves) have higher rates—from 51 to 69 percent. We do know that not all children who grow up in violent homes become violent adults. The road from abuse to delinquent, violent, or criminal behavior is not straight or certain. Factors such as the frequency and duration of abuse and the age of the child need to be studied. We do know that abuse increases the risk. Youth who join gangs may do so as a result of being abandoned or neglected by their parents. Other predictors are lack of parental supervision and parental rejection, either physical or emotional (Wright and Wright 1994).

Widon (1995) examined criminal records on more than 1,500 individuals and found that a childhood history of physical abuse predisposes the survivor to violence in later years. Physical abuse was the most likely to be associated with arrest for a violent crime later in life. But the group next most likely to be arrested were those who experienced neglect. Although neglect is often considered a more "passive" form of maltreatment, neglect is associated with an array of developmental problems.

To study childhood sexual abuse, Widon (1995) examined the official criminal histories of those whose sexual victimization during childhood had been validated and who were processed through the courts between 1967 and 1971. Then victims of sexual abuse were compared to cases of physical abuse and neglect and to a control group of individuals who were closely matched in age, race, sex, and approximate family socioeconomic status.

Victims of childhood sexual abuse in that study were at higher risk of arrest for committing crimes as adults, including sex crimes, than were people who did not suffer sexual or physical abuse or neglect during childhood. Compared to victims of childhood physical abuse and neglect, victims of childhood sexual abuse were at greater risk of being arrested for prostitution than any other type of sex crime.

Even if states do make a legal distinction between and among delinquents, status offenders, and abused and neglected children, what is the end result? If states did take these children out of juvenile correctional facilities used for delinquents, where would they put them? The reality is that all of these children are housed together in juvenile detention or adult jails with a special section for youth in some states or localities. Rubin (1985) and Schwartz (1989) argued that some states do not have adequate facilities. Due to the geographic location of the child's home, it is easier and administratively convenient to house these youth with delinquents.

OTHER NONCRIMINAL BEHAVIOR

The juvenile court judge has jurisdiction within the corporate limits of the cities and the boundaries of the counties for which they are appointed or elected to hear cases dealing with other noncriminal behavior. The general jurisdiction includes children who may be subject to the following: entrustment agreement (an agreement for someone to be responsible for a child); controversy regarding custody, visitation, or support; proceedings that seek termination of parental rights; traffic infraction charges; and proceedings that commit mentally ill persons or certify mentally retarded persons.

In addition, the judge may have to give consent for emergency surgery or medical treatment for children whose parents or guardians are incapable of consenting or are unwilling to give consent. This emergency order can deal with children who need blood transfusions but whose parents do not believe in it. The judge takes temporary custody of the child, orders the treatment, and then returns the custody back to the parents.

The juvenile court judge deals with anything that deals with children. That may mean work permits and petitions for emancipation. It may mean persons absent without permission or escapees from either court-ordered placement or a "commitment to the Department of Corrections." It may also mean that the child is the victim of a crime and the adult is the offender.

> Emancipation means surrender to the right to care, custody, and earnings of a child before the child is 18.

Family courts and courts of domestic relations also deal with all offenses or warrants regarding the actions of one family member against another family member. Family includes husband-wife, parent-child, brother-sister, grandparent-grandchild, regardless of whether the parties reside in the same home. With domestic violence comes spousal protection orders.

To summarize to this point, the juvenile court judge hears and has the power to decide (jurisdiction) cases dealing with children as offenders (delinquency), as status offenders, and as abused and neglected. In addition, the court has jurisdiction over a lot of family matters and even adult criminal cases when the child is the victim (see Chapter 6, "Crimes Against Children").

DEVELOPMENTAL STAGES OF CHILDREN

A child's life is like a piece of paper on which every passer-by leaves a mark. Chinese Proverb

Many professionals have documented the developmental stages of children. Medical doctors, for example, have a body of research they use to determine when a baby should lift her head and roll over. When children fail to do the tasks that many other healthy babies do, the doctors then begin to suspect and ask questions in order to prevent or to identify some kind of biological delay or illness. In addition to biological developmental theories, there are psychological and social theories, with the most acclaimed being that of Eric Erikson (1968).

Psychosocial Theory

An important idea in understanding and defining delinquency and abuse has been the research and knowledge that children grow and develop in different stages. Developmental theory, based upon assumptions of the needs and capacities of children, should become the basis for policy and policy decisions about children as they go through childhood.

In each stage there are important tasks to master.

Ages	Tasks
Birth to 12–18 months	TRUST, EMOTIONAL DEVELOPMENT
18 months to 3 years	AUTONOMY, SELF-CONTROL
3–6 years	INITIATIVE, EARLY MORAL DEVELOPMENT
6–12 years	INDUSTRY, COOPERATION, TEAM PLAY
Adolescence	IDENTITY, SEX-ROLE IDENTITY
Young adult	INTIMACY, WORK

Erikson's (1968, 94) psychosocial theory is predicated on the idea that each one of us goes through critical stages during development. Even though the above table shows six stages and one major task for each stage, Erikson's psychosocial theory has eight stages from birth to old age, addressing the development throughout the life span. Each stage has more tasks than those presented here. Yet, for our purposes, we can see how the lack of mastery of just the listed tasks produces challenges for the child and social service practitioners who deal with children.

Lack of Mastery

If there are difficulties at one age, that unresolved conflict will continue as the child physically matures. This is called a lack of mastery. Two key tasks are trust and autonomy.

Stage 1—Trust

The ability to trust has important consequences for children. For example, if a child has parents who provide consistent, warm, loving care and nourishment, the child learns to trust (Stage 1). The child can later apply this memory and skill to friends, an intimate partner, or the government. If this stage is hampered, then any of the following might occur:

☐ Fear of intimacy

☐ Needing—but being afraid of—physical affection

☐ Continual need for oral gratification (eating, smoking, drinking)

☐ Fear of acknowledging needs because of the fear that they will not be met

☐ Inability to trust even in trustworthy situations (Taylor 1991, 43).

Stage 2—Autonomy

During ages 18 months to 3 years, children strive to accomplish things independently. This accomplishment provides them with feelings of self-worth and self-confidence. If the child at this age is restricted or punished or told such things as "can't you do anything right?," shame and guilt take over. Self-doubt replaces self-confidence. If our parents were confused about their own boundaries, they would not have been able to help us learn. So parents may give mixed messages about acting independently and so affect the child's autonomy.

Marriage counselors see this lack of mastery in stage two as "isolaters" or "fusers" (Hendrix 1988). If the parent needs the child to remain dependent, then when the little girl wanders out of the room, the insecure mother might call out, "Don't go into the next room! You might get hurt!" The dutiful child comes back to the mother's lap but pays the price of being afraid. Her inner drive for autonomy was denied, and she now fears that she will be forever trapped in a symbiotic union—engulfment. Thus, in her later years, she becomes an "isolater"—a person who unconsciously pushes others away to gain freedom.

On the other hand, "fusers" are the product of caretakers who were not equipped to handle any needs but their own and the child grew up feeling emotionally abandoned. Thus, they want to "do things together" all the time. They crave physical affection and reassurance and often stay in constant verbal contact. As strange as it may seem, isolators and fusers tend to grow up and marry each other. That begins a marriage of push and pull that is not satisfying to either partner and does not provide the proper emotional environment for rearing children.

Another place we see this lack of mastery of stage two is in *co-dependency*. Co-dependency is the condition in which someone meets another's needs at the sacrifice of his or her own. This adult response in intimate relationships is usually a pattern developed in childhood in which the child learned that if he or she expressed his or her independence, the caretaker broke into tears or expressed a feeling of rejection. The child would probably develop the belief system that expressing independence causes suffering to others; therefore, the child would suppress individuality to do as others expected. The lesson learned was that the caretaker's needs were more important than the child's.

Co-dependency is a major problem in families with alcohol, drug, or other addictions. Members of the family literally help the addict to be an addict because there are no boundaries.

> Meeting Another's Needs at the Sacrifice of One's Own

Separating boundaries are extremely important to begin to separate right from wrong, good from bad. In some families, called *dysfunctional*, the boundaries are not clear. This is especially true in families where incest or sexual abuse is present. Usually in families, there are rules and privileges for those who are a generation older than the children, and thus, some kind of boundaries are set. Needless to say, not all children have separated boundaries in their family of origin.

Some children cannot honor another's boundaries because they never had any for themselves. There was no privacy. The child does not know where he or she ends and another begins. The child's emotions were merged with the caretaker's. We call this enmeshment. So the child feels overly responsible for other people's needs and feelings whether it be mother's happiness or father's sobriety.

In terms of treatment, the importance of this information on Stages 1 and 2 is that it is basic to the emotional foundation of the child. The unmet needs and the beliefs the child developed because of them have to be addressed in therapy in order for the child to make wiser and better choices.

Child Witnesses

Knowledge about developmental stages also helps us in investigating crimes in which children are witnesses or victims or survivors. In child sexual abuse, for example, Goodwin (1982, 59–73) specifically described age categories and what one could expect victims to say:

- □ Victims age 2–3: "I hurt," or "Daddy hurt my pee."

- □ Victims age 4–6: "This is the third time it happened. Only this time, daddy wiped it."

- □ Victims age 7–10: fear telling the secret for fear of losing families or hurting their parents.

- □ Victims age 11–13: dread of sexual encounter, feel trapped by father's threats.

- □ Victims 14 and over: blame themselves.

In addition to understanding the fact that children master different tasks at different ages, we also need to be aware that age has several dimensions: biological, mental, and emotional. The lower the biological age, such as 2 and 3, the greater are the chances for all three dimensions to be developmentally the same. However, it is possible to have a child be biologically 6 but emotionally and socially much younger due to the effects of the first sexual abuse experience, which traumatized the child and hindered the emotional and social development. (One 11-year-old girl I interviewed as a child protective worker took on all the emotions of a 6-year-old. Even though she was now physically bigger than her grandfather who was molesting her, she still saw herself as a 6-year-old who could not scream or run for help.)

Young children are the most difficult to interview unless one remembers that their sense of time is limited. One has to use birthdays, holidays, and schools attended as benchmarks to help identify first sexual contact when investigating sexual abuse. In addition, one has to develop a vocabulary for talking about sexuality. What does a child call his or her anus, for example? Children will differ in their understanding of events and their ability to express themselves. This is why very young children are a special challenge as witnesses in the criminal/juvenile justice system (Whitcomb 1992).

Placing Children Outside Home

Knowledge about developmental stages is also important for placing children outside of the home or determining child custody in marital disputes or divorces. Goldstein, Freud, and Solnit (1979), and more recently Goldstein, Solnit, Goldstein, and Freud (1996), were instrumental in helping to form legislative, judicial, and executive decisions on the placement of children when the parent-child relationship required state intervention. The following are some of their key ideas:

1. Children change constantly from one state of growth to another, unlike adults whose psychic functioning proceeds on more or less fixed lines. Demands for care and support, stimulation, guidance, and restraint vary as the child matures and begins to need independence.

2. Children, unlike adults who measure the passing of time by clock and calendar, have their own built-in sense of time based on the urgency of their instinctual and emotional needs.

3. Children experience events in an egocentric manner as if it were happening solely with reference to their own person, unlike adults who are generally able to see occurrences in a relatively realistic perspective.

4. Children are governed in much of their functioning by the irrational parts of their minds—such as primitive wishes and impulses—instead of by reason and intellect, as are many adults.

5. Unlike adults, who are generally capable of maintaining positive emotional ties with a number of different individuals, unrelated or even hostile to each other, children lack the capacity to do so.

6. Children, unlike adults, have no psychological conception of relationship by blood-tie until quite late in their development (Goldstein et al. 1979, 11–12).

One of the greatest contributions of Goldstein et al. (1979) was the concept of the psychological parent, who is the person who had developed an emotional bond with the child because of his or her willingness to meet the child's needs for being fed, washed, changed, and loved on a daily basis. This relationship could be damaged. For example, if the court takes the young child from the person meeting the child's needs and places the child with a person who is biologically related but has not been involved in child-rearing practices, attachment and trust can be affected. The arguments of Goldstein et al., supported by research and social work practice, is that where psychological parenting is inadequate, there are deficits in the child's emotional growth. When the psychological parenting is adequate, it is best to keep the child in that setting until he or she can mature and be more easily moved.

It is ideal when the psychological parent and the biological parent are the same person. In the real world that does not always happen. Some addicted

Psychological Parent

mothers may not be available physically or emotionally to meet the needs of an infant. They forget to feed the baby and the baby does not thrive. Then the state has to intervene to protect the welfare, safety, and health of the child.

For example, in *Painter v. Bannister*, 258 Iowa 1390 (1966), the mother died in an automobile accident. The surviving father gave the surviving son to the maternal grandparents to rear for many years. Meanwhile, the father went to California to be a photographer and to watch the waves roll in on the beaches. Later, when the father remarried and got a good job, he wanted the child to live with him. The court then had to decide—should they continue to use the law, which says that the biological parent has the highest claim over any other interested adult? Or, should they recognize the child's attachment to and trust in the grandparents and permit the grandparents to win custody of the child? What really are the "best interests of the child?" The Iowa Supreme Court reversed the trial court's decision to give the father custody of the son because the son had developed a father-son relationship with the grandfather. Even though the grandparents won the case, the father came to see the son with his new wife. As the father and son developed their relationship on that visit, the young boy asked his grandfather if he could go live with his father. The grandfather had enough love in his heart that he said yes.

Critical Guidelines

Continuity

To assist the court in making decisions concerning "child placement" (procedures include birth certification, neglect, abandonment, battered child, foster care, adoption, delinquency, as well as custody in annulment, separation, and divorce), Goldstein et al. (1979) gave two very critical guidelines: (1) continuity and (2) least detrimental alternative. The first was to give *continuity* when and wherever possible because the child's sense of time is different. Instead of divorced parents thinking of dividing the custody of the child exactly in half, the parents should give thought to a young child's need to have continuity. Instead of sending a young child on an airplane to visit the father, for example, the father gets on the airplane and visits the young child.

A good application of this theory is found in the Delta Airlines brochure regarding air travel by unaccompanied children (Figure 2.2). Their age categories restrict some kinds of unaccompanied travel arrangements. For example, children ages 1 to 4 cannot travel alone. Children ages 5 to 8 can fly alone only on nonstop flights that do not require a connection. Children ages 8 to 12 may fly on itineraries that require a change of planes.

The second guideline is to use the *least detrimental alternative*. For example, if the child has to be away from the biological parent because of abuse or neglect, instead of foster care, is there any other relative who has had some contact with the child who would be willing to take the child temporarily?

Goldstein et al. (1996, xv) realize that the "best interest" test is not clearly defined, so that existing policies and practices are not formulated to give the guidelines for professional participants to use their expertise. In some cases, the judges have been usurpers of parental autonomy and confused the child by acting like the parent. Thus, Goldstein et al. advocate that the

Unaccompanied Children Don't Travel Alone On Delta

▲ *DELTA*
The Official Airline For Kids.

Unaccompanied Minor Guidelines

What If Your Child Becomes Ill?

Each one of our flight attendants has received extensive first aid training. Should your child become ill en route, they are ready to provide assistance and reassurance.

In the event of a serious illness, we can quickly reach a location where emergency services are available. On Delta's domestic system, an airport can be reached in 20 minutes.

We're Glad You've Chosen Delta For Your Child's Solo Flight.

We hope we've answered most of your questions and removed any possible sources of concern. But if you have any additional questions – or a special request – just call Delta or your favorite Travel Agent.

Remember, you'll be giving your child more than just a wonderful trip. You'll be giving memories that last a lifetime.

Children are special passengers, and we've adopted special policies to insure their well-being. It's important that you share in observing these policies and make all of the necessary arrangements at each end of your child's flight.

When Can A Child Travel Alone?

Delta will accept an unaccompanied minor for any flight – domestic or international – as long as the child and the flight meet the conditions outlined in this chart:

Travel Restrictions For Minors	Ages 1–4	Ages 5–7	Ages 8 and over
Child may travel alone.	No	Yes	Yes
Child must be accompanied by a responsible person at least 12 years old.	Yes	No	No
Flight restricted to one-plane through service.	N/A	Yes	No
Child may use Delta flights connecting with another airline. (Reservations Required.)	N/A	No	Yes
At time reservation is made you must supply the name, address, and phone of the responsible adult who is bringing child to airport as well as the name, address, and phone for the adult who is responsible for meeting child at the destination airport.	N/A	Yes	Yes
Your child's age must be given, and proof of age may be required.	N/A	Yes	Yes
Unaccompanied child pays full adult fare.	N/A	Yes	Yes

Check with The Delta Connection® carriers for their specific restrictions.

Additional Restrictions For International Flights:
Your child must possess and carry the necessary travel documents...i.e., passport, visas, etc. If your child is under age 8, you may not choose a flight that stops in a country other than the country of origin or destination.
For travel to Mexico, your child is considered a minor through age 18. Your child must have your written, notarized permission for travel to Mexico. The written requirements are very specific, so call your Delta agent for the exact details.
A Delta reservations agent will be happy to provide full details and fare information regarding your child's international travel.

©1989 Delta Air Lines, Inc.
Printed in U.S.A.

0432-01994
Brochure 3/89

Figure 2.2
Reprinted by permission of DELTA AIRLINES, INC., 1994.

state must leave parents to minister to the child's needs until such time the family fails to provide nurture and protection based upon minimum societal standards. Once the family ceases to function for a child, the child should be considered separate and apart from the interests of the family and the state should intervene, putting the child's interest first and over even the most "deserving" of adults. These decisions need to be done quickly and with the least harmful alternative. "Having intervened, it is the obligation of the state to provide for the child, with all deliberate speed, a safe and secure place in a family in which she feels wanted and which holds the promise of providing her with continuity of affectionate care and safety. The placement should be unconditional," with no further intervention, unless the family fails to meet society's minimum standards of child care.

Child Development-Community Policing (CD-CP)

Child Development-Community Policing has been developed by the New Haven Police Department, Connecticut, and the Yale Child Study Center through funding from the Office of Juvenile Justice and Delinquency Prevention (OJJDP). Through community-oriented policing, the New Haven Police Department has moved away from a reactive, incident-based response to a community-based, proactive approach to problem solving and crime prevention. Of particular concern was the fact that large numbers of urban children witnessed violent crimes, yet small numbers received psychological support to cope with the effects of violence and crime. For children, the impact of crime can disturb eating patterns, create depression, and increase fear and helplessness (OJJDP National Satellite Teleconference, December 1995).

Since the impact of crime on children can be devastating and long lasting, the CD-CP program means that mental health professionals, psychiatrists, and police officers work together in the community to assist, protect, and intervene on behalf of children and families who are most affected by community violence. The partnership gives police officers more strategies to respond to community violence and more immediate responses from the mental health professionals to deliver psychological services. Officers, when doing investigation, are able to recognize a child's emotional needs, understand the family dynamics, and effectively intervene.

The CD-CP has four components: child development fellowship, training seminars, consultation service, and program conferences. For example, police "Fellows" spend several hours each week in the mental health setting. Mental health professionals introduce and familiarize officers with developmental concepts and patterns of psychological disturbances, methods of clinical intervention, and settings for treatment and care. Through clinical rotations, officers observe and discuss mental health services for children and families. Clinicians accompany police on ride-alongs to observe officer response to calls, engage in casual encounters with neighborhood residents, and collaborate with officers. Thus, both groups learn about the work of the other and develop ways to be supportive.

Training seminars are led by a core team of mental health and police "Fellows." The nine-week course covers the various developmental stages of children from infancy through adolescence. Special topics are the effects of separation and trauma on children, issues of race and class in child development, and community-policing and community mental health resources.

Through the consultation service, clinicians are available 24 hours a day, providing officers with immediate access to clinical services and consultation. This also promotes clinical referrals to other services—such as emergency rooms, inpatient facilities, and outpatient clinics—and interagency collaboration with schools, therapists, pediatricians, and child welfare professionals.

The last component, program conference, gives officers and clinicians an opportunity to discuss broad program issues, difficult and/or perplexing cases, reasons for law enforcement interaction, types of services needed or required, and problems. This component provides the structure to integrate diverse program elements into a consistent, coherent process.

In conclusion, it is in the early ages, when the child is developing, that the child is like a sponge. The children are absorbing all that is around them—all that they hear, see, and feel. Children learn how to control unacceptable behavior or to delay gratification or to respect the rights of others by the actions of those around them and the way they are treated themselves. Wright and Wright (1994, 32–33) said:

Apparently, a healthy home environment is the single most important factor, an environment characterized by parents' affection, cohesion, and involvement in their children's lives. Children need the love, support, and acceptance that parents can provide. When these elements are missing, that is, when parents are harsh, unloving, overly critical and authoritarian, healthy development is impeded and the child's risk of delinquency increases . . . Children who grow up in homes with considerable conflict, marital discord, and, perhaps, even violence are also at greater risks of becoming delinquent. . . . it is also important to recognize that observation of marital discord is a more powerful predictor of delinquency than divorce or single-parent family structure. Family relations, not just the separation, influence delinquency.

Children have biological needs, psychological needs, social needs, and spiritual needs. We term these needs "bio/psycho/social/spiritual." The way adults or parents permit the healthy unfoldment and the stimulation of each child's needs determines to a large degree the type of adult the child will become. "Children then are not adults in miniature. They are beings per se, different from their elders in their mental nature, their functioning, their understanding of events, and their reactions to them" (Goldstein et al. 1979, 13).

SUMMARY

This chapter discussed the definition of three types of youth who use the juvenile court: (1) delinquent, (2) status offender, and (3) abused. The newest definition of delinquents is youth who have committed an act for which, if they were adults, they could be arrested. Earlier definitions of delinquents were developed by the Puritans, and later by reformers of the nineteenth century and early twentieth century. Because many of those definitions made no distinction between criminal and noncriminal behavior, they were challenged as being vague, a violation of equal protection, and/or as sex-based discrimination. Washington, California, and Minnesota revised their statutes to include such phrases as "promote public safety" and "develop individual responsibility for lawful behavior."

Status offenders were defined as juveniles who committed acts that were a law violation only for juveniles. In some places, they are also known as PINS (persons in need of supervision), MINS (minors in need of supervision), and CHINS (children in need of supervision). Examples of violations are running away, truancy, drunkenness, and unauthorized use of motor vehicles and credit cards. Informal procedures included a discussion of crisis intervention programs and *Homebuilders*. To illustrate the formal procedures of status offenders, an actual case, written in fictional terms, was discussed showing a social history investigation and what kinds of alternatives and dispositions a judge may be asked to consider. Finally, the chapter discussed the need to deinstitutionalize (get youth out of jails and other secure facilities).

The term "abused children" was defined as "nonaccidental injury to a child by a caretaker." The abuse can be physical, sexual, and emotional. If the abuse occurs before the child is born, then states must have special prenatal statutes. Dependency, unlike neglect, was defined as the inability of parents to provide for their children. Ritualistic abuse includes repeated physical, sexual, psychological, and/or spiritual abuse by the use of rituals.

In terms of causation, the road from abuse to delinquent, violent, or criminal behavior was shown not to be a straight or certain path. Factors such as the frequency and duration of abuse and the age of the child need to be studied. Yet we do know that abuse increases the risk.

Although this chapter focuses mainly on three classes of youth, it also points out that many other children and their families come before the judge seeking a resolution or permit. This other noncriminal behavior may involve child custody or support, traffic infractions, work permits, and emancipation.

Information on the developmental stages of children is important to those who choose to work in this area in order to adequately advocate their needs, develop programs, and make judicial decisions. In this area, the psychosocial theory of development was discussed along with the problems that arise due to lack of mastery of trust and autonomy. Developmental stages were then applied to child witnesses, placing children outside of the home, and community policing. The two critical guidelines for a child's placement are continuity and "least detrimental alternative" so as not to negatively impact the child's developmental stage of trust.

To recap and pull together Chapters 1 and 2, you should now know the following:

1. Our society, for various reasons, has always mistreated children. Child protection laws, services, and education for parents are modern inventions.

2. The old juvenile court of "mix and stir" no longer worked. Supreme Court decisions and advocates who were educated in the

developmental stages of children demanded more clarity in classifying youthful behavior and formal procedures to protect and balance a child's rights, the rights of the parents, and the safety of society.

a. The rules of procedures regarding children who have committed criminal acts are now mandatory for professionals working with youth. Chapter 3, "Search, Seizure, Investigation, and Interrogation," and Chapter 4, "Process for Delinquent (Criminal) Youth," will give you some basic information.

b. The rules, guidelines, and procedures for children who were abused and neglected are different from delinquent youth. Chapter 5, "Child Abuse and Neglect," will give you more details.

REFERENCES

Anderson, Patricia S. et al. *Family Crisis Intervention Program, Clark County, Washington*. Washington, D.C.: U.S. Dept. of Justice, 1979.

Erikson, Eric. *Identity: Youth and Crisis*. New York: Norton, 1968.

Erikson, Kai T. "New Conceptions of Deviance." In *The Negley K. Teeters Symposium on Crime in America*, edited by Mary Jeanette Hageman. Oneonta, NY: Hartwick College, 1973, pp. 9–17.

Forst, Martin L., and Martha-Elin Bloomquist. "Punishment, Accountability, and the New Juvenile Justice." *Juvenile & Family Court Journal* 43 (1992): 1–9.

Goldstein, Joseph, Anna Freud, and Albert J. Solnit. *Beyond the Best Interests of the Child*. New York: The Free Press, 1979.

Goldstein, Joseph, Albert J. Solnit, Sonja Goldstein, and Anna Freud. *The Best Interest of the Child: The Least Detrimental Alternative*. New York: The Free Press, 1996.

Goodwin, Jean. *Sexual Abuse: Incest Victims and Their Families*. Littleton, MA: John Wright, PSG Inc., 1982.

Hendrix, Harville. *Getting the Love You Want: A Guide for Couples*. New York: Harper Perennial, 1988.

Levinson, Marc. "A Beleaguered Department Faces Its Toughest Test." *Police Magazine* 4 (1981):3.

Mones, Paul. *When a Child Kills*. New York: Pocket Star Books, 1991.

National Center for Missing and Exploited Children. *A Report Card to the Nation: Missing and Exploited Children, 1984–1994*. Arlington, VA: U.S. Dept. of Justice, 1994.

Rubin, H. Ted. *Juvenile Justice: Policy, Practice and Law*, 2d ed. New York: Random House, 1985.

Schwartz, Ira M. *(In)justice for Juveniles: Rethinking the Best Interests of the Child*. Lexington, MA: Lexington Books, 1989.

Sussmann, Frederick B., and Frederic S. Baum. *Law of Juvenile Delinquency*, 3d ed. Dobbs Ferry, NY: Oceana Publications, 1968.

Taylor, Cathryn L. *The Inner Child Workbook*. Los Angeles, CA: Jeremy P. Tarcher, 1991.

U.S. Dept. of Justice. *America's Missing and Exploited Children: Their Safety and Their Future*. Washington, D.C., 1986.

Wall, John S. et al. *Reports of the National Juvenile Justice Assessment Center. Juvenile Delinquency Prevention: A Compendium of 36 Program Models*. Washington, D.C.: U.S. Dept. of Justice, 1981.

Whitcomb, Debra. *When the Victim Is a Child*, 2d ed. Washington, D.C.: National Institute of Justice, 1992.

Widon, Cathy S. "Victims of Childhood Sexual Abuse—Later Criminal Consequences." *Research in Brief.* National Institute of Justice, March, 1995.

Wright, Kevin N., and Karen E. Wright. *Family Life, Delinquency, and Crime: A Policymaker's Guide. Research Summary.* Washington, D.C.: Office of Juvenile Justice and Delinquency Prevention, 1994.

CHAPTER 3

Search, Seizure, Investigation, and Interrogation

B.B., a learning disabled 12-year-old, was arrested at about midnight outside a store where the display window had been smashed and some jewelry taken. He told the arresting officer at the scene he knew "nothing about it." He said he was on his way home from a friend's house where they had been watching videos, but he can't remember where his friend lives. B.B. was taken to the police station where he was questioned for about an hour and made some statements implying he had done the crime (mildly inculpatory statements), after being read his Miranda rights. You are the attorney for the youth. What grounds, if any, would you raise to suppress the oral statement?

INTRODUCTION

This chapter is about when a juvenile can be searched. You will find answers to the question: Can school officials search the purse of a 14-year-old student? Can parents consent to police searching the room of their child?

Search is important because it leads into seizure, and then the evidence tends to speak against the alleged offender. Search thus leads to investigation and interrogation, and then to an arrest and possible conviction. So, what rights do juveniles have?

Juveniles have as much right to be secure in their persons from unreasonable searches and seizures as do adults. When police officers are operating as agents of the government, then they must follow certain rules and procedures that United States Supreme Court justices say is covered under the United States Constitution. In some situations, such as being transported from the scene of a crime, juveniles are to be treated differently, that is, they cannot be transported in the same vehicle with an alleged adult offender. However, in these particular areas of investigation—search, seizure, and interrogation—the police powers and the restrictions placed on those powers do not differ with juveniles. To better understand this very highly litigated area, some of the adult cases will be discussed and applied to juveniles.

SEARCH AND SEIZURE

The way police or agents of the state search people is governed by courts' interpretation of the Fourth Amendment in the Bill of Rights, which reads:

4th Amendment

The right of the people to be secure in their persons, houses, papers, and effects, against unreasonable searches and seizures, shall not be violated, and no warrants shall issue, but upon probable cause, supported by oath or affirmation, and particularly describing the place to be searched, and the persons or things to be seized. (Fourth Amendment, Constitution of the United States)

The question or action of a search is very important. If the evidence obtained in a search is found to be the result of an illegal search, then the evidence cannot be used against the alleged suspect. Without evidence or a confession, the case is usually dropped by the prosecutor. The defendant is then released without any record because one was never established.

Protects Citizens and Limits Police Power

In short, the Fourth Amendment helps protect citizens from overzealous agents of the government. To our forefathers, this was not just a fear. It was a reality that they themselves had experienced, and they wanted the right to limit the government's powers. In fact, of the twenty-three separate rights noted in the first eight Amendments, twelve deal with criminal procedure.

In addition to the protection of civil liberties, there "has been a recognition of the need for especially close judicial scrutiny where the burdens of governmental regulation fall upon 'discrete and insular minorities' who cannot count on the protection of the political process" (Israel and LaFave 1993, 27). Accused persons constitute a highly unpopular minority, usually having few desirable friends, and they therefore need the special watchdog of the courts for infringements of criminal procedures. Children, because they are children, are even more vulnerable. Therefore, the courts set the guidelines to make sure law officers do not overstep their powers. We thereby become a nation of law and justice. One of those guidelines is a search warrant.

Figure 3.1
Used with permission of Bob Gorrell, *The Richmond Times-Dispatch.*

Search Warrant

A search warrant is required if an agent of the state is going to take a person's property as evidence of a crime. To obtain a search warrant, the officer must have probable cause (PC). PC constitutes facts or apparent facts that are reliable and generate a reasonable belief that a crime has been committed. With this PC, an officer goes to a magistrate and gets a written order directing a law officer to search a specific location for a specific item or person. Usually the search warrant is for weapons or other objects used in the commission of a crime; unlawful articles; stolen property or fruits of any crime; mere evidence like documents, books, papers, records, or bodily fluids constituting evidence of the crime; or a person in another person's house.

PC

Any judge, magistrate, or other person having authority to issue criminal warrants may issue a search warrant. The warrant has to be based upon a complaint on oath supported by an affidavit. The supporting affidavit must reasonably describe the place, thing, or person to be searched and the things to be searched. The affidavit must also allege material facts to constitute probable cause and state how this item or person that is to be seized relates to a criminal offense, and that it is evidence necessary for criminal prosecution.

Copy of an affidavit for search warrant is included in the teacher's manual. ASK TO SEE IT.

The search warrant cannot be a general warrant for a search nor an invitation for the state to go into someone's home and search for anything in the hope of finding something that is illegal. Courts do not favor the police when they pretend to have a search warrant and search a house until they find something incriminating, such as pornography in an attic trunk, in order to charge, and hopefully convict, the occupant of possession of pornographic materials. (See *Mapp v. Ohio*, 367 U.S. 643 [1961].)

What if the affidavit is supported by a sleazy informant and one could argue "hearsay"? What if there are no direct witnesses to support an affidavit for a search warrant? If there is an informant (usually for drug buys) or a trained drug dog alerts the police, the magistrates use a **totality of circumstances test**. This means that the judge or person issuing the warrant looks to the totality of the surrounding facts, namely, the reliability and credibility of the informer or the dog—that person's or dog's basis of knowledge. What is required is a common-sense evaluation of all the considerations (all the surrounding events) that may be intertwined to determine whether or not probable cause exists.

Totality of Circumstances Test

Once the warrant is issued, it is given to another sheriff or police officer who has the appropriate jurisdiction. The officer is then authorized to search the designated place and seize the items described in the warrant, if they are found. If found, the seized property—or person in whose possession it is found—is brought before the court having jurisdiction over the offense. If the warrant is not executed within a reasonable time after its issuance, it becomes void. Reasonable time is set by statute in the various states. In federal cases, it is ten days.

If the officers of the government rely on a search warrant issued by a detached and neutral magistrate but ultimately find the search warrant was unsupported by probable cause, the search is still permitted. It is called the **good faith exception** (*U.S. v. Leon*, 104 S. Ct. 3405 [1984]).

Today, there is controversy over a "no-knock" warrant. Police are expected in their first attempt to gain admittance peaceably by announcing their presence. Obviously, if they believe that they will be in peril by announcing their presence or that people will escape or destroy evidence, then the police can resort to forced entry. It is not the magistrate who gives authority for a forced entry; rather, it is a judgment call on the part of the police.

The way the police act is governed in part by rules established by the U.S. Supreme Court. In *Boyd v. U.S.* (1886), the Supreme Court pointed out that the Fourth Amendment becomes linked to the Fifth Amendment in that what is searched for and found (Fourth Amendment) are fruits of crime and speak against a person (Fifth Amendment). Thus, it is important to understand some of those cases.

Supreme Court Decisions

During the 1960s, the Supreme Court held that certain rights within the Bill of Rights were fundamental and applicable to the states under the same standards applied to the federal government. For example, the freedom from unreasonable searches and seizures and the right to have excluded from criminal trials any evidence obtained in violation thereof, *Mapp v. Ohio* (1961); the privilege against self-incrimination, *Malloy v. Hogan* (1964); the right to the assistance of counsel, *Gideon v. Wainwright* (1963); the right to confront opposing witnesses, *Pointer v. Texas* (1965); and the prohibition against cruel and unusual punishment, *Robinson v. Calif.* (1962).

Prior to 1967, the cases that the Supreme Court heard defined the term "search" as a governmental trespass into a constitutionally protected area. The result was that law enforcement officers could use electronic surveillance and physical surveillance as long as they did not trespass into constitutionally protected areas such as homes and offices.

Katz v. U.S.

Katz to Protect Persons, Not Places

In 1967, in *Katz v. U.S.*, 389 U.S. 347, the Supreme Court had to deal with the question of whether a public telephone booth is a constitutionally protected area so that evidence obtained by attaching an electronic listening recording device to the top of the booth is in violation of the right to privacy of the user of the booth. The petitioner was under an eight-count indictment charging him with transmitting wagering information by telephone from Los Angeles to Miami and Boston.

Two Tests: Does a person have an expectation of privacy, and is society prepared to recognize that expectation as reasonable?

From *Katz*, the Supreme Court said that for a search to be unreasonable, there must be two requirements. First, the person has to have a (subjective) expectation of privacy. Second, the expectation is one that society is prepared to recognize as "reasonable." Thereafter, searchers were required to protect people, not places.

To better understand privacy and place, let us discuss what is not included in a reasonable expectancy of privacy. Then, we will discuss the place.

Reasonable Expectancy of Privacy

The Supreme Court has said that there is **no reasonable expectation of privacy in such places as an open field, fly-overs, discarded trash, and dog**

sniffs. The lead case for open fields was *Oliver v. U.S.*, 466 U.S. 170 (1984). Two officers, acting on a tip that marijuana was being grown on the defendant's farm, went to the farm to investigate without a search warrant. While there, they ignored a "No Trespassing" sign and locked gate, and they located a marijuana field approximately one mile from the defendant's house. The marijuana was seized and the defendant was arrested. He was charged with manufacturing a controlled substance. If he could argue that the search was unreasonable, the evidence would have been suppressed and there would have been nothing to convict him.

The Supreme Court said that open fields do not provide the setting for those intimate activities that the Fourth Amendment was intended to shelter from government interference or surveillance. Society does not have an expectation of privacy in open fields. Thus, there could be warrantless entries into open fields. Fly-overs were then an extension of open fields. In a fly-over case, the police used an airplane and a camera to take pictures of a backyard that had a ten-foot high fence built around it. The point is that there is no reasonable expectation of privacy.

In general, things that are out in the open are just that—open to others to see and, therefore, not protected. These include trash on the sidewalk, trash left in containers for the sanitation workers, and parked car(s) outside that can be seen. Therefore, there is no privacy and no protection. Samples of paint from a parked car can be taken to investigate a hit-and-run accident and used as evidence without a warrant.

Can a person in a public airport, caught carrying drugs when a narcotics dog alerts officers, be permitted to use the argument that because the police had no warrant, the evidence seized came from an illegal search and the evidence cannot be used in a court of law? NO!

Why? Because dogs have a greater sense of smell than humans. (Where you and I might smell spaghetti sauce cooking, a dog would smell the meat, the onions, the tomatoes, the oregano, and the garlic.) Dogs smell each item and, therefore, putting talcum powder on drugs does not confuse a dog. Dogs that are trained for detection of narcotics or bombs are permitted to sniff anything in the air. No warrant is needed. Air is free. There is no reasonable expectation of privacy in air. The dog only identifies drugs or bombs. The dog does not identify the person, his or her social security number, or his or her address. In short, there is no violation of one's privacy.

No Expectation of Privacy in the Air

Reasonable Place for Privacy

Society is not always willing to recognize certain places as places of privacy. So, even if you behaved at the bus station as you normally do in the privacy of your bedroom, the courts would not recognize that behavior in a public place as one that society is prepared to condone or honor.

Valid Search

When faced with a question of a legal or illegal search, one must first ask the question: "Has a search taken place?" The second question is whether the search was based upon a valid warrant; was there probable cause and was the search conducted in a reasonable manner? If not, then look to see if this search comes under one of the seven general exceptions to the rule of a search warrant.

General Exceptions

There are seven general exceptions that are recognized by law as not needing a warrant. They are as follows:

H   Hot pursuit and other emergencies

I   Incident to a lawful arrest

P   Plain view

C   Consent

A   Automobiles

R   (Highly) Regulated industry

S   Stop and frisk

(HIP CARS is not a legally recognized concept. This is a mnemonic—a technique to assist in the memory process.)

Hot Pursuit and Other Emergencies

Hot pursuit usually means the police have seen the alleged offender do something and they are chasing the person either on foot or in a car. The police are permitted to search the suspected criminal. If the person is out in public and then runs into a private dwelling, the police may still search first without having to get a search warrant (*U.S. v. Santana*, 427 U.S. 38 [1976]).

Other emergencies can be anything from burning fires and bomb threats to contaminated food or drugs. Once the fire is out, however, and the building is cooling, if someone wants to search for evidence of arson, then he or she is required to apply for a search warrant. If he or she does not, then the evidence seized cannot be used in a court of law to prosecute someone for the criminal charge of arson. The same reasoning applies after a murder. A warrant is required to search a murder scene (*Mincey v. Arizona*, 437 U.S. 385 [1978]).

Incident to a Lawful Arrest

Incident to a lawful arrest permits the officer to search a person lawfully arrested and the area within the arrestee's control in which he or she might gain possession of a weapon or destroy the evidence (*New York v. Belton*, 453 U.S. 454 [1981]; *Chimel v. Calif.*, 395 U.S. 752 [1969]). A search incident to an arrest, however, must happen in the time and place that the arrest is happening. The search must be contemporaneous in time and place. The police may also make a protective sweep of the area beyond the defendant's wingspan if they believe accomplices may be present (*Maryland v. Guie*, 110 S. Ct. 1093 [1990]).

Plain View

For police to claim the **plain view** exception, the officer must first legitimately be on the premises where the object is seized and discover the object in plain view. The plain view exception formerly applied only if the evidence was inadvertently discovered, but inadvertence is no longer a requirement. In other words, surprise is not needed. However, the object has to be seen, heard, or smelled without handling it. In *Texas v. Brown*, 460 U.S. 730 (1983), for example, the officer stopped an automobile. In the back seat were some opaque balloons that contained narcotics. The court permitted the plain view exception because the officer suspected narcotics based on his knowledge and experience, even though the connection with contraband would not be obvious to the average person looking at the opaque balloons.

Consent

Consent is saying "Yes" to the question: "May we search?" In one case, the defendant, whom police believed was a major Colombian trafficker of cocaine, consented to the search of a pickup truck. The surprised officers discovered inside the truck more than 400 pounds of cocaine (*People v. Carvajis*, 202 Cal. App. 3d 487 [1988]). In order for the search to be valid under the consent exception to the warrant rule, there must be several key factors: (1) voluntariness, (2) authority to permit the search, and (3) scope of the consent.

Voluntariness

Voluntariness is a question of fact to be determined from the **totality of the circumstances**. Totality of circumstances means the surrounding circumstances under which the consent was given. For adults, it may mean such things as whether the individual was advised of **Miranda** rights, whether the consenting person was in custody, and whether the consent was given in response to an express or implied assertion of authority. The police are not required to inform the consenting person of his or her right not to consent to a search of property or person. What the court is looking for is coercion, because when there is coercion, there cannot be consent.

A combination of all the factors show the court that consent was voluntary, not one factor per se. A police officer's drawn gun will not alone invalidate a consent to search. Neither will large numbers of officers present at the time of the request. Now, if the SWAT team has the house surrounded, the canine patrol is there, four patrol squad cars with four officers in each car, a helicopter overhead with the big light on your house, and you are asked if you would be willing to consent to a search, then the court may have some difficulty believing it was voluntary.

Totality of Circumstances Test

Authority to Permit the Search

As a general rule, voluntary consent by a joint owner or occupier is valid when the joint owner or occupier has "common authority" over the property. Examples come from cases in which the husband or wife gives lawful consent to search the family home.

The general rule is that both husband and wife have "common authority" over their home and its contents. The parent can consent to have police enter a child's bedroom and conduct a search even when the child is not a minor. If there is an area in which the child or the parent has "exclusive control," like a zipped-up bag or a locked toolbox, then consent is invalid.

The test is whether the police officers, reasonably and in good faith, believe that the consenting person has the authority to consent to the search. In one case, officers were approaching a house when the person came out the front door and greeted the officers. The officers asked if they could come in and search. The person agreed. A few minutes later, the person left the house to the police. The police found some evidence, but the person giving consent was no longer there. Later, it turned out the person giving the consent was a burglar. Obviously, at the time of getting the consent, the police believed the person in the house to be a rightful owner, not a burglar. So, to protect both the police and citizens, the court upheld that consent as valid under a theory of "good faith." (See *Frazier v. Cupp* [1969]; and *United States v. Matlock* [1973].)

Scope of the Consent

A person who gives consent may limit the search. For example, if consent is limited to a particular room or container, a search that exceeds this scope cannot be based on consent.

Automobile

The **automobile** exception to a warrant is permitted if the officer has probable cause to believe that a vehicle is carrying contraband or the fruits or instruments of a crime, and if the officer believes the vehicle might be moved. Obviously, the police do not reasonably expect citizens to stand by their auto filled with drugs while the police go off to get a search warrant and return to the car. Therefore, the police have this exception, which applies to any vehicle that has the same attributes of mobility as motor homes. If the police have probable cause to justify a warrantless search of an automobile, they may search the entire car and open any packages or luggage found there that could reasonably contain the items for which they have probable cause to search (*U.S. v. Ross*, 456 U.S. 7987 [1982]).

Highly Regulated Industries

A search warrant is not required for searches of businesses in highly **regulated industries** such as liquor and gun stores and automobile junkyards. Public interest overrides privacy. In addition, the theory is that a business has implied consent to warrantless searches by entering into a highly regulated industry. Most notably, courts have generally upheld searches of airline passengers prior to boarding. Passengers generally consent to searches as a condition to boarding the aircraft. These safety procedures were put into place after the many airplane hijackings in the 1960s and 1970s. If a person wanted to avoid the search, the person could avoid planes and travel by some other means.

Stop and Frisk

Stop and frisk was the result of the case *Terry v. Ohio*, 392 U.S. 1 (1968). An officer may stop a person without probable cause for arrest if she or he has an **articulable and reasonable suspicion** of criminal activity. The officer is

---

Role-play some of these searches and their exceptions to get the feel for what is a good search.

Contrast this with *U.S. v. Pierre*, 932 F.2d 377 (1991), which said that in order for officers to stick their heads into a vehicle, there is a search.

allowed to conduct a protective frisk (something less than a full search for evidence) only if he or she reasonably believes that the person may be armed and be presently dangerous. The scope of the intrusion is a **pat-down of outer clothing** for concealed instruments of assault. Limited intrusion does not require probable cause. But the stop must be brief and temporary, and the person has a right not to answer questions.

To summarize this section, there are seven general exceptions to the requirement that a search warrant be obtained before searching anyone and taking the item or the person into custody for use as evidence in a criminal court of law. They are: (1) hot pursuit and other emergencies, (2) incident to a lawful arrest, (3) plain view, (4) consent, (5) automobile, (6) highly regulated industries, and (7) stop and frisk. In order for consent to be valid, it must be done under conditions of voluntariness, authority to permit the search, and scope. Day by day, the U.S. Supreme Court continues to add to and change these rules. For example, "plain touch" has now been analogized to plain view for some purposes, but ordinarily the touching will itself constitute search activity for which a justification must be shown (*Minnesota v. Dickerson*, 113 S. Ct. 2130 [1993]).

In addition, there are some unique searches. Searches of residential and commercial premises for fire, health, and safety violations may not be undertaken without a search warrant unless the occupant consents to the inspection. These search warrants do not require a showing of probable cause, and occupants are free to challenge the inspector's decision to search without the risk of suffering criminal penalties for refusal. However, border searches and license-registration checks may occur without a warrant and, therefore, they need some special discussion.

Unique Searches

The Fourth Amendment has been held to apply to a variety of searches, but the standards have been somewhat different for regulatory searches as opposed to those in a criminal investigation. For example, in border searches, a person crossing the border of any country may be required to submit to a warrantless search of the person, baggage, and vehicle as a general course of action. If there is a reasonable suspicion, authorities can detain a suspect at the border and have the suspicion verified or dispelled.

For example, in 1985, in *U.S. v. Montoya de Hernandez* (105 S. Ct. 3304), Rosa Elvira Montoya de Hernandez arrived at Los Angeles International Airport shortly after midnight from a direct ten-hour flight from Bogota, Colombia. Her visa was in order, so she passed through Immigration and proceeded to the customs desk. At the customs desk, the inspector noticed that she had made at least eight recent trips to either Miami or Los Angeles. She was referred to a second inspector who asked questions about her and the purpose of her trip. Ms. Montoya de Hernandez spoke no English and had no family or friends in the United States. She had $5,000 in cash, mostly $50 bills, and no billfold. She said in Spanish that she had come to purchase goods for her husband's store in Bogota. Although she had made no appointments with merchandise vendors, she planned to ride around Los Angeles in taxicabs, visiting retail stores such as J.C. Penney and K Mart in order to buy goods. A female customs inspector was requested to conduct a pat-down and strip search. Although no contraband was noticed, the inspector saw that she was wearing two pairs of elastic underpants with a paper towel lining the crotch area. Suspecting she was a "balloon swallower" (one who attempts to smuggle narcotics into this country hidden in her alimentary canal), the inspectors gave her the choice to return to Colombia on the next available flight or be X-rayed at a hospital or remain in detention until she had a bowel movement. When she refused the flight home and the X-ray arguing that she was pregnant, she was detained until she did have a bowel movement. She produced over eighty-eight bags of cocaine!

In like manner, when police observe a traffic violation, they may stop the vehicle and demand to see the driver's license and vehicle's registration and vehicle identification number. The police can also have license-registration checkpoints but cannot randomly stop an auto and detain the driver in order to check the license and registration. Checkpoints may also be used to seek out intoxicated drivers, but these checkpoints must be carefully planned by police supervisory personnel, operate with a maximum of discretion by on-the-scene officers, and detain individuals only briefly.

✳ BRAIN EXERCISE

Take the following set of facts and decide for yourself if there was an illegal search:

A juvenile and his companions were stopped after the officer observed them make a "rolling stop" at an intersection. The officer stopped the juvenile's vehicle. After a search, the officer obtained from the vehicle a large amount of cocaine, a firearm, and a box of ammunition. The juvenile was adjudicated delinquent based on a conspiracy to violate a federal controlled substance law and possession of a controlled substance with intent to distribute. In order to avoid these charges, the juvenile, through his attorney, argued that the evidence against him was the fruit of an illegal search and should be suppressed. If the evidence was suppressed, the case would be dismissed and the youth would go free.

You are the judge. What would you decide and why?

Do not look for a federal case addressing whether the "exclusionary rule" applies to proceedings in juvenile court. The exclusionary rule states that evidence secured by federal agents through an illegal search and seizure is inadmissible in a federal prosecution (*Weeks v. U.S.*, 232 U.S. 383 [1914]). There is none. Instead, ask these five questions: (1) Was there a search? (2) Is this a recognized exception to the search warrant rule? (3) If there is no exception, was there a need for a search warrant? (4) Was there probable cause? (5) Was the search conducted in a reasonable manner?

Write your answer. Then compare it to *United States v. Doe*, 801 F. Supp. 1562 (U.S.D. Tex. July 1992) wherein the court agreed with the juvenile and stated that the sole deterrent to violation of the Fourth Amendment rights of juveniles is to make sure that evidence from an illegal seizure is not

Ask: (1) search? (2) exception? (3) no exception—was there a need for a search warrant? (4) PC? (5) search reasonable?

Practice writing your own answer.

permitted in a court of law. (This is called the exclusionary rule.) The failure to adhere to the exclusionary rule in delinquency cases would reduce significantly the effectiveness of the rule's general deterrent value. If the exclusionary rule were not enforced in a delinquency proceeding and the police were rewarded for illegal searches, then the police might feel less likely to follow the Constitution.

Furthermore, the court said that the juvenile has a **reasonable expectation of privacy** in the vehicle. There was **no valid consent to search the entire vehicle**, and there was no **probable cause to search the vehicle**, so the search was illegal. The court was simply not convinced that the officer should have made a custodial arrest for a "rolling stop" violation by a juvenile.

> These words in bold should have been in your answer for full credit.

In other words, the "rolling stop" was not enough of a violation to permit the officer to make an arrest. Therefore, anything found could not be seized and used in court. If there had been a violation such as not stopping at the stop sign or failure to use turn signals, then the court would have supported the police in its stopping the youth for a violation and then the search that resulted in illegal items to be seized.

School Searches

Under what conditions would there be an expectation of privacy in a place like a public school? If you are in the third grade and your desk has no lock on it, should you think that you can hide your drug money in your desk or money you have stolen from the teacher without the teacher looking for it in your desk or the teacher needing a search warrant? What about junior high school and a locker in which the student owns the lock? What are the rules? To understand this area, let us first consider the case *In re Ronald B.,* 61 A.D.2d 204 (1978).

In re Ronald B.

In re Ronald B. dealt with a 14-year-old boy who was enrolled in his public school in Queens, New York, and who argued in juvenile court that the seizure of his gun should be suppressed because it was discovered as a result of an unconstitutional search. Sometime during that eventful day, a school official was conversing with Ronald in the hallway of the school. Another school official came up to Ronald and told him that he had been informed that Ronald had a gun. Ronald denied it and refused a search even though he had his right hand in his pocket. When Ronald was asked to withdraw his hand, he refused. Then, Ronald made a sudden movement with his hand and the two school officials grabbed his arm and withdrew it slowly from the pocket. Ronald had a .32-caliber pistol. The gun was taken and turned over to the police for evidence. If you were the defense attorney or the prosecuting attorney what would your arguments sound like? What facts would you use? What law cases would you cite? What do you think the judge would say?

In writing your opinion, first, think about the legal concept of "reasonable expectation of privacy." Second, think about school officials. Do school officials have the same status as police officers who are mandated by the Constitution to have a search warrant? Or are school officials more like people acting in place of parents (*in loco parentis*)? (Ask any parent of a 4-

year-old leaving a grocery store if the parent has a right to pat the child down for non-purchased candy.) Or are school officials more like private citizens? Or are school officials like government officials who only need a "reasonable suspicion" to search (*State v. Young*, 34 Ga. 488 [1975])? Can one argue that school officials have "common authority" to consent to a search? Needless to say, with all these different ways to label school officials and teachers, school systems decided that there had to be better ways to provide a safe public school environment. They chose to use policy.

Policy Instead of Law

Some school systems are more willing to use policy as a form of getting control over the schools instead of trying to use law to determine who is an agent of the state and needs a search warrant. Policies have been developed to deal with fights, assaults, homicides, drive-by shootings, weapons, and general disruption to the educational environment.

The policy approach begins by telling the parents and children the need for such a policy. Letters are sent home to the parents to describe what is and is not permitted and why it is necessary to limit these items in the school. There are contracts for both the parents and the children to sign. These contracts or agreements serve to give notice as to what specifically cannot be brought to school, such as particular kinds of guns, other weapons, and illegal drugs.

With the consent and agreement of both parents and children, the lockers become the property of the school, and random searches can be done to maintain safety. Accordingly, if a reeking smell is coming from a particular locker (something is successfully decaying like a forgotten sandwich or worn gym clothes), then the school officials have reasonable suspicion to open the locker and dispose of the contents.

The policy can also spell out what role the evidence taken will have in disciplinary functions in the school and in juvenile court. In this manner, protections for both teachers and students are maintained. In addition, liability on the part of the school can be reduced. Some school officials sense they have a duty to provide a safe environment. But school safety is another issue.

The big debate is whether school districts have the right to randomly drug test students who participate in sports. In some schools, the Student Athlete Drug Policy authorizes random urinalysis drug testing of students who participate in athletic programs. It is equated with a physical exam required to play sports. The other side argues that the drug testing should be reserved for those students who are suspected of using drugs at school. To open children up to a bodily search, in some people's minds, violates the requirement of individualized suspicion. Taking that a step further, a new policy at Appalachian State University allows campus police to search a dormitory room for drugs without a student's permission or a warrant. Reasonable suspicion means noticing an odor or seeing towels crammed under a doorway. Yet students who complain say that police are "overzealous," invading the privacy of students by entering dorm rooms for any reason and not always finding what they hope. The school counters by saying that the drug cases are handled with the university's judicial system and not the courts, and thus the punishment is not great enough to come under

Figure 3.2
Used with permission of
Bob Gorrell, *The Richmond
Times-Dispatch*.

"IF CONGRESS GOES AHEAD WITH SCHOOL PRAYER, WILL THAT INCLUDE LAST RITES?"

the Fourth and Fourteenth Amendments (*The Chronicle of Higher Education*, March 22, 1996, A36).

School Safety

The presence of drugs, gangs, and violence on school grounds has made security a major concern for educators, students, and parents. School systems across the nation have had to deal with "crack" cocaine and youth gangs. There is no easy answer.

According to a 1988 study conducted in Florida school districts, "Almost 87% of the students who had brought weapons to school got them right out of their own home. Another 6% got the gun from a friend or relative's home, and another 6% acquired the gun from other sources, including school" (Baron and Wheeler 1994, 28). Schools are places to recruit gang members (ibid., 29).

Some schools have had to develop crisis drills as part of the regular part of school operations. Having drills saved lives according to Patricia Busher, principal of Cleveland Elementary School in Stockton, California, where five children were killed and twenty-nine others were wounded by an adult sniper on January 17, 1989. She stressed in an article on school safety that the previous drills had improved the children's response to the directives of adults and, thus, saved lives (Blauvelt 1990). Today, the snipers may be the students themselves.

Some schools employ local police. Some schools use access control techniques like metal detectors or X-ray machines and telephones in the classroom. Some schools have "No Locker" and "No Bookbag" policies (Chase 1993). Some contract a guard service and some hire security professionals. Some invite the local police with a dog to help clean up the school of drugs. Unfortunately, dog searches have special rules. Early law cases tell us of some of the problems.

Dog Searches

After *Doe v. Renfrow*, 475 F. Supp. 1012 (1979), caution is advised in using dogs. In a Highland, Indiana, school system, the school was alarmed by

Teacher Abuse—Teacher Threatened and Harassed by Student Wins $33,700 Jury Award in Ludlow (KY). *USA Today*, August 29, 1995, p. 3A

What if a high school student's gun is seen in his car on the school grounds, the school wants to expel him, but the parents argue that he has attention deficit disorder (which is why he forgot the gun was in the car) and that removing him would be a violation of federal laws banning discrimination against the handicapped?

general reports of drug users but nothing was found. School officials requested the help of police with a trained dog sniffer. They made the error of permitting the dog to go into the classroom and sniff each person in front of all the other students. After an alert by the dog, a student was asked to empty his or her pockets or purse. If the dog continued to alert when the pockets were empty, then a body search was done.

In this case, a female student was asked to go to the nurse's office for the body search. Again, nothing was found. No marijuana or other drugs were found in her possession. The only other reasonable explanation for the dog's behavior was that the plaintiff had been playing with one of her dogs that morning of the search and that her dog was in heat.

The court agreed that nude searches were more than just a mild inconvenience like a pocket search. The court said that school systems should look at such factors as the student's age, the student's history and record in school, the seriousness and prevalence of the problem to which the search is directed, and the exigency requiring an immediate warrantless search. Using these factors, one can better determine the reasonableness of a student search.

New Jersey v. T.L.O.

New Jersey v. T.L.O., 469 U.S. 325 (1985), dealt with a teacher at Piscataway High School in Middlesex County, New Jersey, who discovered two girls smoking in a lavatory. One of the two respondents was T.L.O., a 14-year-old freshman. Because smoking in the lavatory was a violation of a school rule, the teacher took the two girls to the principal's office. The vice principal asked if they had been smoking. The companion admitted that she had, but T.L.O. claimed she did not smoke at all. He asked her into his private office and demanded to see her purse.

Opening her purse, he first found a pack of cigarettes. Then he noticed a package of cigarette rolling papers. Then he found a small amount of marijuana, a pipe, a number of empty plastic bags, a substantial quantity of money in one-dollar bills, an index card that appeared to be a list of students who owed money, and two letters implicating her in dealing marijuana. The school turned the evidence over to the police.

The state brought delinquency charges against her. Her lawyer argued to suppress the evidence found in her purse as well as her confession given to the police because they were tainted by the allegedly unlawful search.

When the juvenile court denied the motion to suppress, she appealed to the Supreme Court of New Jersey, which reversed the judgment of the Appellate Division and ordered the suppression of the evidence found in her purse. New Jersey, on a petition of *certiorari*, went to the United States Supreme Court. The question before that court was: Does the exclusionary rule operate to bar consideration in juvenile delinquency proceedings of evidence unlawfully seized by a school official without the involvement of law enforcement officers?

To that question and the broader issue of the Fourth Amendment, the court reversed the New Jersey Supreme Court and said that the search did not violate the Fourth Amendment. First, public school officials are not covered by the Amendment's prohibition on unreasonable searches and seizures. Second, reasonableness of the search should be the standard, because there is a substantial need of freedom for teachers and administrators to maintain order in the schools while accommodating the privacy of school children.

To determine reasonableness, the court developed a two-pronged test. First, one must consider if the action was justified at its inception. Second, one must consider if it was reasonable in scope to the circumstances that justified the interference in the first place.

Yet the dissent in this case is very interesting. In the dissent by Justice Stevens, with whom Justice Marshall joined, and with whom Justice Brennan joined as to Part I, concurring in part and dissenting in part, Justice Stevens said that the question presented by the state's petition for *certiorari* would have required affirmation of a state court's decision to suppress evidence. But the U.S. Supreme Court disregarded the doctrine of judicial restraint. The Supreme Court avoided the result in this case by ordering reargument and directing the parties to address a constitutional question that the parties, with good reason, had not asked the Court to decide. In addition, Justice Stevens argued that a search of the young woman's purse by a school administrator was a serious invasion of her legitimate expectations of privacy.

Then, Justice Stevens pointed to the *amicus curiae* briefs, which relied heavily on empirical evidence of a contemporary crisis in American schools of violence and unlawful behavior that is seriously undermining the process of education; he argued that a standard that was better attuned to this concern would be to permit searches when teachers and school administrators believe that the search will uncover evidence that the student is violating the law or engaging in conduct that is seriously disruptive of school order or the educational process.

With that standard in mind, Justice Stevens said the vice principal overreacted to what appeared to be nothing more than a minor infraction. Smoking in the bathroom was not unlawful nor significantly disruptive of school order or the educational process. Therefore, there was an invasion of privacy associated with the forcible opening of T.L.O.'s purse, which was entirely unjustified because it was not justified at its inception.

Present Rule

Because of *T.L.O.*, the Court now permits a **"reasonable suspicion" standard** for school searches as opposed to the more stringent "probable cause" standard. This is **only for school officials. Once the law officer is the initiator or it is done in conjunction with the police, the standards are again higher—probable cause has to precede a search warrant, and a search warrant has to be obtained in order for the items searched and seized to be entered as evidence against a person.**

Reasonable Suspicion Less Than PC Test

Another critical variable to consider is whether the evidence seized will be used only for discipline within the school or whether it will be turned over to the police for charges in a court of law. For example, a small amount of drugs is found on a young person. If the drugs are used to identify a student who has a drug problem and the results are such things as parents being notified and referrals to drug counseling, the student's cries of unlawful search will probably go unheard.

✻ BRAIN EXERCISE

A college student was ill during the regular time to take a three-hour final exam. She asked and was given permission to take a make-up test. When she went to the professor's office to take the exam, she was told to leave all her notes behind with the department secretary. Then the secretary took her to a private room to take the exam. Sometime during the exam, the student went to the bathroom. When the secretary went into the bathroom to check on the student's whereabouts, she heard the rustling of papers. After the student left the restroom, the secretary found some notes stuffed in the trash container in the individual stall. The secretary told the professor, and when the student returned to the exam, they both confronted the student about cheating. The college student was requested to go with the secretary for a strip search. Do you think that cheating on an exam is enough of a crime under *T.L.O.* for school officials to conduct a strip search without a warrant? See *Carboni v. Meldrum, Sonenberg, Waldrom and Armstrong*, 949 F. Supp. 427; 1996 U.S. Dist. Lexis 8196.

INVESTIGATION

Investigation is when an officer comes to your door and asks questions about a recent criminal activity, such as: "Do you know anything about the recent break-in?" At this point, the officer is investigating. The officer is just asking questions. When the investigation turns to interrogation, when the youth is **not free to leave** and he or she is the **suspect** for the crime, then custodial interrogation has begun.

INTERROGATION

*No person . . . shall be compelled in any criminal case
to be a witness against himself.* (Fifth Amendment,
U.S. Constitution)

*In all criminal prosecutions the accused shall enjoy the
right . . . to have the assistance of counsel for his
defense.* (Sixth Amendment, U.S. Constitution)

The purpose of interrogation is to get someone to confess. A confession, whether written, oral, or recorded, is a statement by a person admitting to the violation of the law. Yet this confession is supposed to be voluntary. Court cases tell us that this has not always happened. To better understand voluntary confessions, we will discuss court cases. After a discussion of court cases, we will direct our attention to the rules for a confession: whether the parent has to be present, the age of the child, and the role of the probation officer. Notice when the behavior of the police is "notification" and not "questioning." (See "Notification versus Questioning" later in this chapter.)

Court Decisions

In *Brown v. Mississippi*, 297 U.S. 278 (1936), the Supreme Court said that states could no longer use coerced confessions to convict persons of crimes. They heard a case in which three African-Americans were arrested for the murder of a white man without any other evidence than their coerced confessions. They were sentenced to death.

The defendants had been tied to a tree, whipped, twice hung by a rope from a tree, and told that the process would continue until they confessed. The record of the testimony showed that the signs of the rope on the neck of one of the defendants was plainly visible during the so-called trial. The other two defendants endured whippings that continued until the confessions had been obtained word-for-word as desired by the mob. The defendants were told that if they changed their story at any time, in any respect from that last stated, they would again be given the same treatment.

The sheriff of the county of the crime admitted that he had heard of the whippings. He, of course, had no personal knowledge. Yet he admitted that one of the defendants, when brought before him to confess, was limping and did not sit down. The defendant later stated that he had been strapped so severely that he could not sit down. The other defendant had rope burns on his neck. At the trial, the confessions were viewed as free and voluntary.

The Court in *Brown* said that the state is free to regulate the procedure of its courts unless it offends some fundamental principle of justice. A state may dispense with a trial by jury but cannot substitute trial by ordeal. The rack and torture chamber are not to be substituted for the witness stand in our system of justice.

> Confessions are not a trial by ordeal.

Later, in the 1960s, there were a series of Supreme Court decisions that united the Fifth and Sixth Amendments and strengthened defendants' rights. Some of the most important cases using these amendments were *Escobedo v. Illinois*, 378 U.S. 478 (1964), which gave an accused the right to have an attorney present during police interrogation, and *Miranda v. Arizona*, 384 U.S. 436 (1966). *Miranda* said that prior to any **questioning** during which the person is in **custody**, the person must be warned that he or she has a right to remain silent; any statement he or she does make may be used as evidence against him or her, and he or she has a right to the presence of an attorney, either retained or appointed. The defendant can waive these rights, but the waiver must be done **voluntarily, knowingly, and intelligently**.

When the defendant is an adult, the court protects those rights. When the defendant is a youth—an easy victim of the law—then special care needs to be exercised. Justice Douglas in *Gallegos v. Colorado*, 370 U.S. 49 (1962), described the test to be employed. The test is **totality of circumstances**, which means that the youth's age, long detention, the failure to send for his parents, the failure to immediately bring him before the judge of the juvenile court, the failure to see to it that he had the advice of a lawyer or a friend, have to be considered as a whole with regards to all the surrounding events. In this particular case, all of these above factors in combination were too much for the 14-year-old convicted of crimes in a criminal court.

> ? + prime suspect + custody = *Miranda* rights

In *Quick v. State*, 599 P.2d 712 (1979), the Alaskan court stated that just because the defendant is a minor does not make him or her incapable of making a knowing and voluntary waiver. Surrounding circumstances have to be considered in each case with each particular juvenile. Among the factors they suggested were age, intelligence, length of the questioning, education, prior experience with law enforcement officers, mental state at the time of the waiver, and whether there had been any prior opportunity to consult with a parent, guardian, or attorney.

In *Com. v. Philip S.*, 611 N.E.2d 226 (Mass. Sup. Jud. April 1993), the order that suppressed the statements made by the 12-year-old juvenile in reference to a charge of manslaughter had to be reversed. In other words, the juvenile's confession should not have been suppressed by the trial court. The appeals courts said that investigating officials may interview a juvenile suspected of a crime. If a statement is the product of that interview and is knowing and voluntary, it may be admitted at trial against the juvenile. However, courts have to proceed with special caution when reviewing a purported waiver of constitutional rights by juveniles. In the case of a juvenile under the age of 14, the Commonwealth had to show that a parent or an interested adult was present, understood the warnings, and had the opportunity to explain to the juvenile his rights so that the juvenile understood the significance of the waiver of these rights.

Interested Adult Test

The court said that the interrogating officials should not be expected to know of the psychological atmosphere of the juvenile's home or any undisclosed problems in his relationship with the parent or interested adult. All that is required is that the prosecutor demonstrate an opportunity to discuss the juvenile's rights with an interested adult. In this case the child and his mother were given the *Miranda* warning. They were left alone for from five to fifteen minutes. They were specifically instructed to discuss the juvenile's rights.

In addition, in this case, there was nothing to show that the juvenile was mentally or physically impaired. There was no evidence of the investigating officials using threats, promises, or subterfuge to induce the juvenile to speak. Although a juvenile's age and inexperience with police procedures are factors to be considered in determining the admissibility of a juvenile's confession, age and lack of encounters with the police, standing alone, would not warrant suppression.

In contrast, in *Matter of Robert H.*, 599 N.Y.S.2d 621 (N.Y. Sup. App. Div. June 1993), the statement made by the juvenile, after he showed the police where the body of the shooting victim was hidden, was inadmissible. The court said that under the circumstance, a reasonable 15-year-old youth would not have believed that he was free to leave the scene. There were approximately eight police officers present and the juvenile was not advised of his rights, but he admitted to the shooting and showed the police where the body was hidden. In addition, at the police precinct, the court could not say that there was a definite, pronounced break in the interrogation so that the juvenile could be said to have returned, in effect, to the status of one who was not under the influence of questioning. Therefore, the juvenile's statement at the precinct was also subject to suppression.

Rules for a Confession

Indiana, like many states, has set forth certain rules or guidelines for taking a confession or statement from a juvenile. IC 31-6-7-3 codifies those guidelines as follows:

(a) Any rights guaranteed to the child under the Constitution of the United States, the Constitution of Indiana, or any other law may be waived only:

(1) by counsel retained or appointed to represent the child, if the child knowingly and voluntarily joins with the waiver; or

(2) by the child's custodial parent, guardian, custodian or guardian ad litem if: (A) that person knowingly and voluntarily waives the right; (B) that person has no interest adverse to the child; (C) meaningful consultation has occurred between that person and the child; and (D) the child knowingly and voluntarily joins with the waiver.

Role of Parent(s)

States do not all agree on the use and function of parents in interrogation. Some states require parents to be present and others do not. Attorneys argue that if one is to waive the right to an attorney, the best person to consult is an attorney, not the parent, unless she or he is an attorney. *In re Patrick W.*, 104 Cal. App. 3d 615, 1980, a young man had intentionally shot and killed his father, a police officer. He obviously declined to face his mother, whom he had just widowed. Even though she was his mother, she would not have been the best person to advise him even if she were what the court called an "interested adult."

The mere absence of a parent or counsel does not render the *Miranda* waiver invalid. Although it is a significant one, it is only a factor to be considered when looking at the totality of the circumstances. (See *Roberts v. Commonwealth*, 18 Va. App. 455 [1994].)

Age

Age is clearly the most critical factor used by the courts to determine the voluntariness of the confession, the waiver of rights, and the need for a parent's presence. Yet age is more than biological age; it is mental and emotional age as well. For example, a 14-year-old boy with an IQ of 67, who attended school for mentally retarded children, functioned on a third-grade level, and exhibited the behavior of an 8-year-old child, was held to be incompetent to make a knowing, understanding waiver of *Miranda* (*State ex rel. Holifield*, 319 So. 2d 471 [1975]). On the other hand, a confession by a ninth-grader who had an IQ of 52 and a mental level "below the age" was held admissible because he did understand the meaning of "silent" and was streetwise enough to understand his right not to speak (*People v. Morris*, 49 Ill. App. 3d 284 [1977]).

Determining whether a child is mentally retarded or criminally insane needs the expertise of trained professionals. One counsel had to argue that his client, a 16-year-old female who had been found emotionally retarded in three earlier tests, needed the court to pay for an independent psychiatric and psychological testing. The judge denied the motion and she was transferred from the juvenile court to the adult court. Upon appeal, the higher court reversed and remanded the juvenile judge because the denial of an independent psychological evaluation of a juvenile to determine competency to stand trial was considered a denial of juvenile due process (*Anderson v. Commonwealth*, 15 Va. App. 226; 421 E.E. 2d 900 [1992]).

Role of Probation Officer

In *Fare v. Michael C.*, 442 U.S. 707 (1979), the youth, when asked questions about a murder, said he wanted to have his probation officer present. The police officer specifically asked: "Do you want to give up your right to have an attorney present here while we talk about it?" Michael asked: "Can I have my probation officer here?"

Probation officers are not lawyers.

The Supreme Court said that a probation officer, by virtue of his working for the court, was not the type of person (a lawyer independent of the court who could advocate for the youth) to whom a minor was entitled within the purpose of *Miranda*. The state had created a statutory duty on the part of the probation officer to protect the interest of the juvenile. But that did not mean that the probation officer was capable of rendering legal assistance to the juvenile or of protecting his legal rights. In fact, there was a legal duty on the part of the officer to report wrongful behavior by the juvenile and to serve the ends of the juvenile court system. In effect, the youth was asking for help from someone who would have to be on the side of the prosecution and thus against his side. The Supreme Court concluded that the question as to whether the statements obtained during subsequent interrogation of a juvenile who has asked to see his probation officer, but who has not asked to consult an attorney, is to be resolved on the **totality of circumstances** surrounding the interrogation. Thus, the case was reversed and remanded.

Waiver of an Attorney—
Totality of Circumstances
Test

Notification versus Questioning

Most states require the police to notify a juvenile's parents when the juvenile is taken into custody, which is the step before interrogation. When a juvenile is residing in his or her parents' home, the police have an obligation to establish and maintain procedures so that the juvenile is not deliberately or inadvertently held beyond the reach of the parents. (*Gault* gives parents a right to notice of the charges and some idea of where their child is.) However, in some states, there is no requirement that a parent be present during questioning. In other states, the requirement that the parent be present is based upon the age of the child (such as 16 years of age and older).

See, for example, *Surles v. State*, 610 So. 2d 1254 (Ala. Crim. App. Sept. 1992). The juvenile requested to be excused during the custodial interrogation and his request was denied. The juvenile court held that his statement to the police was voluntary. The youth claimed that his request to be excused was an attempt to exercise his right to call his guardian, but there was no evidence in the record and the juvenile never claimed that he told the officers that he wanted to call anyone. Moreover, he was told that he could remain silent and that he could contact his parent or guardian if he so desired. Because he did not indicate that he was trying to exercise either the right to remain silent or contact his parent or guardian, the court held that the juvenile's confession was admissible.

✳ BRAIN EXERCISE

Roach, age 17 years, was charged with the murder of his 70-year-old neighbor by a gunshot wound to her chest during a robbery. Roach had been familiar with her habits and had helped her with household chores. On the night she was killed, her purse, containing a Discover credit card and approximately $60 in cash, was taken from her home as well as her 1981 Buick Regal. The next day in another state, Roach attempted to use her Discover bank card at an automated teller machine. A videotape from the machine showed him attempting to withdraw cash from the account. The next day and in another state, the 1981 Buick Regal was being driven 69 miles per hour in a 55 mile per hour zone. When the state trooper activated the lights on the patrol car, the driver drove the automobile over to the left shoulder of the road, got out of the car, ran into the woods at the side of the road, and escaped. The impounded vehicle was traced to the murder victim. An aunt encouraged Roach to return home and give himself up.

A total of three days after the murder, Roach and his father went to the Sheriff's office. There, the Sheriff advised Roach of his *Miranda* rights in the presence of Roach's father. Roach waived his rights, and both he and his father signed the waiver form. The Sheriff then questioned Roach out of his father's presence. An acquaintance of the Roach family and an employee of the Department of Alcoholic Beverage Control was present during the interview. At first Roach blamed the crime on his friend. The sheriff told Roach that he was having a difficult time believing him due to all the discrepancies in the story. The family friend told the youth that he was lying and that "this is a heavy burden to carry on your shoulders for the rest of your life. If you committed this act, you need to tell the Sheriff, and you need to unburden yourself." The youth then said he had gone over to the woman's house, saw her counting the money from her social security check, used the shotgun laying at the door, shot her, took the money and the car and left. The question for you as a judge is: "Was Roach's confession made knowingly, voluntarily, and intelligently? See *Roach v. Commonwealth*, 251 Va. 324, 468 S.E. 2d 98 (1996).

Conclusion

Once the investigation turns to interrogation and the focus is on a particular suspect and the suspect is in custody, then *Miranda* or *Gault* rights come into play. The intent of interrogation is to obtain a confession and/or gather evidence. When a juvenile is not represented by a parent, guardian, or custodian during an interrogation, he or she has a right to have an attorney present. If the parents are present, the parent(s) and the youth can waive the right to an attorney if the waiver is done knowingly, intelligently, and voluntarily. In some states, like Indiana, the provisions to safeguard the rights of juveniles are **strict compliance**.

What happens when there is no strict compliance? What happens if there is error by the police in the search, investigation, or interrogation?

If there is error, that error can impact what happens to the juvenile once he or she enters the juvenile court. Take for example the case of *Palmer v. State*, 626 A.2d 1358 (Del. Sup. June 1993). The juvenile was taken into custody and was transported to the police station where he was **Mirandized** at approximately 6:45 p.m. The youth, who was a suspect in a homicide, gave his name, address, and age. A contested fact was whether he also gave the police his grandmother's phone number. The juvenile was not cooperative in answering further questions. He was then taken to an interview

? + prime suspect + custody = *Miranda* rights

room where he spent the night handcuffed to a bench. After the arrest of the juvenile's cohorts, several of them gave statements. At approximately 5:02 a.m., ten and one-half hours after his arrest, the juvenile gave a statement in which he implicated himself in a plan to sell drugs. The juvenile was not presented to the family court commissioner until approximately 8:00 a.m.

The juvenile moved to suppress his statement on the grounds that the police failed to immediately present him to the family court commissioner as required by the law of the state of Delaware and to suppress his statement to the police on the grounds that it was involuntary. The trial court denied the motions and convicted on all counts based on accomplice liability.

The Delaware Supreme Court, however, reversed. The higher court rejected the arguments of the state that they were too busy. The court said that as soon as a child was in "custody" of the police, then the police should immediately notify the child's custodian. The court also found the same excuses offered by the state unpersuasive in establishing the reasonableness of the delay in presenting the youth before the commissioner of the family court. Delaware requires presentation without unnecessary delay.

The result was that the case had to be remanded for a new trial. The lesson to be learned is that a failure to observe the special statutory requirements of a particular state can result in a reversal of an otherwise valid finding of delinquency. In cases of confessions, once the case is returned to the lower court and the confession is thrown out, there may be no other evidence to convict on that charge or a lesser charge. The result is that the defendant now goes free because the case is dismissed.

Please do not think that courts restrict all good confessions; there are some exceptions. Known as "spontaneous statements" by a suspect, the courts permit children and adults to give confessions such as at the scene of the crime if the investigating officer has asked: "What happened?" If someone replied that he or she did it, then the confession is good. A second exception to *Miranda* warnings is the "inevitable discovery." The courts do not want police to deliberately elicit incriminating evidence from an accused while in custody in the absence of the lawyer. If the youth tells where the body is while in custody without the lawyer, then the confession is not allowed in the court. However, if the police were searching in the direction where the body lay and it was an "inevitable discovery" then the evidence of the body itself can be entered into a court of law. Lastly, considerations for public safety can override *Miranda* warnings. If a suspect escapes into a store and the apprehending police notice the suspect is wearing an empty shoulder holster, they are allowed to ask: "Where's the gun?" The public's safety need negates the advisement of rights prior to limited questioning which focuses on the need to prevent further harm.

Another example is that if a juvenile is in juvenile hall or juvenile detention on one matter and says to the police officials that he or she committed another criminal act, the new confession stands. What the court will look for is whether the admission was voluntary. (See *Ex Parte Smith*, 611 S.so. 2d 1023 [Ala. Sup. Dec.1992].)

In a more recent case from North Carolina, the appeals court held that even a judge has to be held to the high standard of making sure the juvenile's admission was proper. In *Matter of Kenyon N.*, 429 S.E. 2d 447 (N.C.

App. May 1993), the court reversed and said that the adjudication of delinquency based on the juvenile's admission or confession to a misdemeanor assault with a deadly weapon had to be vacated. The trial judge had to address the juvenile personally on the following: (1) informing him that he has a right to remain silent and that any statement he makes may be used against him; (2) determining that he understands the nature of the charge; (3) informing him that he has a right to deny the allegations; (4) informing him that by his admissions he waives his right to be confronted by the witnesses against him; (5) determining that the juvenile is satisfied with his legal representation; and (6) informing him of the most restrictive disposition (sentence) on the charge. Because the record did not reflect that these inquires and statements had been made, the adjudication of delinquency based on the juvenile's admission had to be reversed.

The next chapter will discuss more fully the critical stages in the juvenile court for youth with criminal charges against them. Yet it is clear that what happens with search, seizure, investigation, and interrogation affects what can happen in the juvenile court.

SUMMARY

The Fourth Amendment requires police officers or others acting as governmental officials to have search warrants based upon probable cause if items or persons are to be seized and used as evidence in a criminal court. Prior to 1967, the term "search" meant a governmental trespass into a constitutionally protected area. After *Katz*, a search was considered unreasonable if there was a reasonable expectancy of privacy and society recognized the place as private.

The chapter then discussed these seven general exceptions to the warrant rule:

1. hot pursuit and other emergencies,

2. incident to a lawful arrest,

3. plain view,

4. consent,

5. automobiles,

6. highly regulated industry, and

7. stop and frisk.

In addition, three factors were discussed to determine if consent was valid: (1) voluntariness, (2) authority to permit the search, and (3) scope of the consent.

School searches become special conditions of the general rules. Some school officials have moved to using policies with contracts or agreements to get parents and students to help maintain the school environment as a learning environment. School searches were discussed in terms of policy, school safety, and dog searches. From *T.L.O.*, school officials are permitted to search even a female's handbag, if there is reasonable suspicion.

After search came investigation and interrogation. Court cases were discussed along with the rules for a confession from juveniles, the role of the parent, age of the child, the role of probation, and the difference between notification and questioning. When the child is the prime suspect and he or she is in custody (not free to leave), then before questioning can begin, the child must be told his or her rights, such as the right to remain silent, that anything she or he says can and will be used against her or him, and her or his right to have an attorney present. If the suspect or child cannot afford one, an attorney will be provided for the purpose of determining if the child should speak. In addition, in some states, parents or an interested adult are required to be present.

The four bases on which to exclude statements and confessions are: (1) voluntary approach from due process clause of Fifth and Fourteenth Amendments, (2) *Miranda*, (3) right to counsel of the Sixth Amendment, and (4) fruit of illegal conduct. All in all, juveniles have the same rights as adults when it comes to search, seizure, investigation, and interrogation. Errors on the part of professionals during these stages can affect the outcome of the youth's case before the court.

REFERENCES

Baron, Anthony D., and Eugene D. Wheeler. *Violence in Our Schools, Hospitals and Places.* San Bernardino, CA: Borgo Press, 1994.

Blauvelt, Peter D. "School security: 'Who you gonna call?'" *School Safety* Fall (1990): 4–8.

Chase, Anne. "School Violence: Two Ways to Fight Back." *Governing* 6 (March 1993): 20–21.

Israel, Jerold H., and Wayne R. LaFave. *Criminal Procedure: Constitutional Limitations.* St. Paul, MN: West Publishing, 1993.

APPENDIX 3A

In answering the question at the beginning of this chapter, consider using the following guidelines:

1. Identify the main question, issue, or right.

2. Give the general rule as to what is supposed to happen under that particular right.

3. Give the legal theory or the result of a specific Supreme Court case.

4. Show how the facts of the new situation fit the facts of the cited law case.

5. Argue the result you want by law or logic.

Using the above guidelines, the written answer might look like the following:

The main issue in this problem with B.B. is a violation of *Miranda* rights. Under the *Miranda* decision, the U.S. Supreme Court extended the rights of an alleged suspect to say that certain rights (the right to be silent; the right to know that anything you say can be used against you; and the right to an attorney even if you cannot afford one) have to be given to the accused when these two situations come together: (1) when the

accused is in custody and is not free to leave, and
(2) when the questioning has become an
interrogation and the person is being accused of
the crime. An interrogation is when the accused is
the prime suspect or defendant and the police are
questioning with the hope to gain a partial or full
confession or inculpatory statements. In addition,
In re Gault gave juveniles the right to remain
silent.

In this case, B.B. was (1) in custody because he
was arrested, and (2) he was the prime suspect. In
fact, he was questioned **for one full hour** before
the rights were given to him. If the right to remain
silent is to mean anything, it has to be given
immediately upon event no. 1 (being taken into
custody and not free to leave) and no. 2 (the start
of the questioning).

The test to determine voluntariness of
confessions is **totality of circumstances**. Even
though I do not have all the surrounding events
in this situation, I do know that he is young (age
12), has a learning disability, is at a police station
late at night, and is a first-time offender. Without
his parents present, these events taken as a whole
are probably too much for this youth. He
probably would have confessed to anything
including being the Boston Strangler if it would
give him a chance to go home. Under *Miranda*
and *Gault*, I would argue for the suppression of
the oral statements.

CHAPTER 4

Process for Delinquent

(Criminal) Youth

*Kevin Stanford committed the murder on January 7, 1981, when he was approxi-
mately 17 years and 4 months of age. He and his accomplice repeatedly raped and
sodomized a 20-year-old gas station attendant. They drove her to a secluded area
near the station where Stanford shot her point-blank in the face and then in the back
of the head. The proceeds from the robbery were roughly 300 cartons of cigarettes,
two gallons of fuel, and a small amount of change. (Stanford, v. Kentucky, 494 U.S.
361 [1989])*

INTRODUCTION

What do you do with youth who commit criminal acts? Children who
are arrested for such acts are processed in the juvenile courts under a petition of delinquency. The process of the juvenile court is divided into five
stages called **intake, detention, waiver, adjudicatory**, and **disposition**. See
Table 4.1.

The purpose of this chapter is to explain each of the five stages. Each stage
will be discussed in terms of: purpose, decision-maker, rights, standard of
proof, qualifications, and the role of the attorney. The actual step-by-step
flow chart is in Table 4.1. (For an overview and a summary of the process
for delinquent youth, see Figure 4.2.)

Formal and Informal
Ways to Handle Youth

As you read, please keep several things in mind. First, every case that
comes before the juvenile court is unique and therefore handled differently
to some degree. The **court has formal and informal procedures** and both
can be used. **Discretion** is often used where appropriate. In addition, these
formal and informal procedures will vary from community to community,
depending upon the interpretation of the local police department, probation officers, and judges, plus the resources of the community at the disposal of the court.

Decisions by U.S.
Supreme Court Can be
Law

State Lawmakers—State
Code

Second, the laws that affect juveniles can change. The **United States
Supreme Court** and state courts of appeals can hear a case and make a decision that becomes a landmark case, such as *Kent* or *Gault*. They may also

	INTAKE	DETENTION	WAIVER	ADJUDICATION	DISPOSITION
PURPOSE	1. File petition 2. Divert a. Informal adjustment b. Referral to a non-court social service agency "Discretion"	1. Predict the probability of an individual committing a crime if released 2. Probable cause	To end juvenile court jurisdiction; to be tried as an adult in criminal court	To sustain the charges	To treat and reduce criminal behavior
DECISION-MAKER	Intake officer	Judge	Judge	Judge	Judge
RIGHTS?	1. Notice (*In re Gault*) 2. *Breed v. Jones*. If case goes to adj. hearing the case may not also be waived to adult court. This would be double jeopardy.	1. Hearing within 72 hours 2. No right to counsel 3. Bail permitted in some states	*Kent v. U.S.* 1. Right to attorney 2. Attorney has right to social history 3. Right to waiver hearing 4. Reasons for waiver have to be stated on the record	*In re Gault* 1. Notice of charges 2. Right to counsel 3. Right to confrontation and cross-examination 4. Privilege against self-incrimination	*In re Jose P.* (California case) "It is an abuse of discretion not to consider lesser restrictive placements before commitment to" . . . youth authorities, i.e., Dept. of Corrections
STANDARD OF PROOF		1. Clear and convincing evidence	1. Preponderance of evidence or clear and convincing 2. Not proof beyond a reasonable doubt	Proof beyond a reasonable doubt (*In re Winship*) contrasted with termination of parental rights that is clear and convincing (*Santrosky v. Kramer*)	
QUALIFICATION			1. Age 2. Mental and physical 3. Amenability (treatability) 4. Nature of the offense 5. Safety of the public		
ROLE OF ATTORNEY	1. Arrange restitution 2. Interpret the proceedings 3. Collect and present relevant school, medical, and social records 4. Assess and make recommendations or treatment		1. Right to an active role and may have access to social history files (*Kent*) 2. Rules of evidence *not* followed because waiver hearing is dispositional—not a hearing to determine guilt	Waiver of Attorney 1. Totality of circumstance test 2. Interested adult	Counsel can present to the court reasonable alternative dispositions

Figure 4.1
Used with permission of
Bob Gorrell, *The Richmond
Times-Dispatch.*

"JUVENILE CRIME IS REALLY GETTING OUT OF HAND! ... SOME KIDS JUST TOOK
A BITE OUT OF MCGRUFF!"

remand the case to the lower court, directing the case to be reheard, and for the rehearing to be consistent with their opinion. Thereby, they **make laws**. Usually, however, it is the state lawmakers who reinterpret and add to the Juvenile Code. States may, through their codes, give juveniles more rights than are mandated by the U.S. Supreme Court decisions. Yet they must give juveniles the rights required by the Supreme Court, as in waiver hearings (*Kent*) and adjudicatory hearings (*Gault*).

**Court and Records
Closed to General Public**

Third, in most states, **the general public is not allowed to attend juvenile court hearings**. In some states, the general public can attend only a certain kind. The public is not allowed to see or read the records of the juvenile court. These records are kept confidential so that the juvenile will not be labelled for the rest of his or her life.

Last, this chapter is not a substitute for a lawyer. If there is an actual situation involving a juvenile, it would be best to talk to an attorney who specializes in juvenile law.

JUVENILE COURT

Custody

Once an officer of the law takes a youth into custody (arrest), the youth may be placed in a temporary "lockup" for a period not to exceed six hours. Juveniles taken into custody for status offenses are to be held in nonsecure custody, such as in an unlocked multipurpose area, lobby, office, or report writing room. The status offenders and nonoffenders are limited to nonsecure custody only long enough for identification, investigation, processing, release to parents, or arranging transfer to appropriate juvenile facility or court. They are to be under continuous visual supervision until released, and never physically secured to a cuffing rail or other stationary objects.

Unlike status offenders and nonoffenders, federal regulations of delinquent offenders (juveniles accused of committing criminal-type offenses) permit a six-hour period of **secure** detainment in an adult jail or lockup. This six-hour period is used for identification, processing, release to parents or guardian, or transfer to juvenile court officials or to a juvenile facility when a juvenile court and its detention center are not near. While in a secure detainment, the juvenile must be separated from adult offenders at all times. This means both sight and sound separation so that juveniles

The Juvenile Justice System*

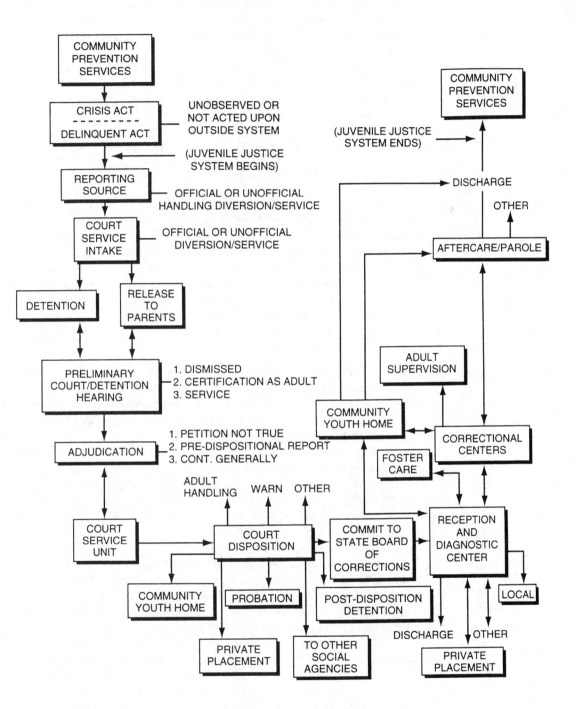

*Modeled after the Commonwealth of Virginia's Juvenile System

Figure 4.2
Juvenile Case Processing.

and adults cannot speak to each other. Written police departmental policies and procedures for handling delinquent offenders are usually developed and followed. For example, records must be maintained, documenting the length of time a juvenile is in secure custody in the event of a lawsuit.

In larger cities, the police take the youth directly to a juvenile court complex in which the court, intake offices, and detention facilities are located. Once the youth comes before the intake officer of the court service unit (a part of the juvenile court), another part of the system begins. We will discuss this stage of the process or procedures in terms of the following: **intake**, **detention**, **waiver**, **adjudicatory**, and **disposition**.

Intake

Intake is the first stage in the processing of the juvenile in the juvenile justice system. By bringing the youth to the intake officer of the juvenile court, the police officer is asking the juvenile court to invoke its jurisdiction. The jurisdiction of the juvenile court also can be invoked by parents and other citizens who come before the intake officer and fill out a petition against a juvenile. We will discuss intake in terms of its purpose, the decision-maker, the rights of the juvenile, the standard of proof, who qualifies for intake qualifications, and the role of the attorney.

Purpose

The main purpose of intake is to decide whether a child's act is severe enough that a petition has to be filed or whether the child can be "diverted." Notice in Figure 4.3 how, of the 1,338,200 cases processed by juvenile courts in 1991 on delinquency charges, 50 percent were nonpetitioned and the other 50 percent were petitioned by the intake worker.

Nonpetitioned or unofficial handling refers to cases where formal charges are not filed against the child. If the child's act can be adjusted in an informal way, such as paying for or repairing damages done to a neighbor's yard, then that will be considered. The purpose is to provide planning, counseling, and treatment to juveniles who have come to the attention of the court.

The intake officer will conduct an interview with the child and his or her parent(s) or guardian(s). Some of the questions will center around the child's understanding of the behavior being unlawful, the purpose of the behavior, and the ability of the parent(s) to correct the behavior. The officer of the court is trying to determine if this is a one-time occurrence or if the child's behavior is a sign of more serious trouble requiring special help.

Some juvenile courts provide programs of their own to help with troubled youth and their families. Some programs include educational services for specific age groups and their parent(s) on drug and alcohol abuse and communication skills to help them problem solve. Programs range from in-depth family counseling to mediation to recreational opportunities such as wilderness programs where the youth can develop self-esteem in challenge and discovery activities. These programs are usually called in-house diversion programs.

Petition

Petitioned or official handling occurs when a petition is sworn against the youth and the youth is required to appear before the judge. A **petition**

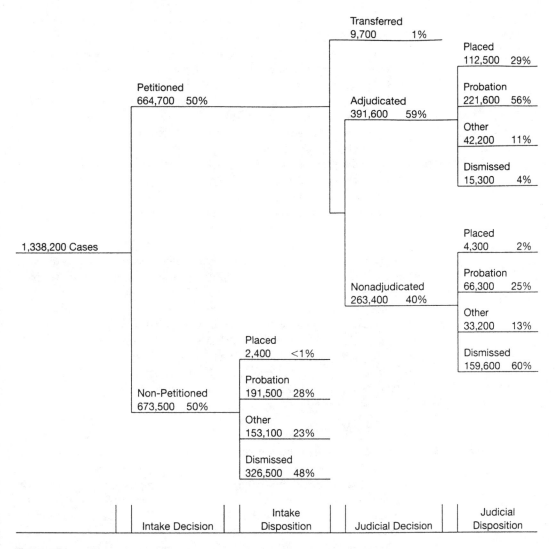

Figure 4.3
Juvenile Court Processing of Delinquency Cases, 1991. Note: Detail may not add to totals because of rounding.
Source: *Juvenile Court Statistics* 1991, 9.

is usually written by a juvenile court intake officer. It states for the record the specific charges and is signed by the person making the complaint, the intake officer, or by the commonwealth's attorney or prosecuting attorney. Juvenile courts have more flexibility in this task than adult criminal courts. For example, changing the petition from second-degree to first-degree criminal mischief simply to reflect the dollar amount of the damage done, or from burglary III to second-degree burglary is not viewed as prejudice to the juvenile. See *A.E. v. Com.*, 860 S.W.2d 790 (Ky. App. July 1993).

In order for a petition to be legally sufficient, however, it must set forth a *prima facie* case (on its "face of the paper") of the alleged offense. Besides the names and residences of the child and parent(s) or guardian(s), the petition must contain a statement of the facts that allegedly bring the child within the purview of the law. It has to be verified and may be based upon secondhand information. Each state has specific rules and forms that have to be filled out as to what constitutes a petition.

One young man in New York, through appeal, had his case dismissed because there was no support for the element that the weapon in question was operable (*Matter of Shannon G.*, 600 N.Y.S.2d 478 [N.Y. Sup. App. Div. July 1993]). The arresting officer's statements did not reveal that the officer actually saw the appellant fire the weapon. Without a ballistics report, the petition was declared by the higher court as legally insufficient to establish that the weapon was operable.

Warrant

A **warrant**, on the other hand, is issued by a police magistrate who has power similar to an intake officer's. Usually, warrants are issued against adults. If, however, the court service unit is closed and neither the judge nor intake officer is available, then a warrant can be written for a juvenile.

Citation

A **citation** is usually written by a police officer at the scene, such as a traffic stop, and it is called a summons. While a citation requires the juvenile to appear in court on a certain date, he or she is not arrested or detained.

Summons

In most cases, the juvenile is released. A summons can also be a legal document issued by a court clerk or other court officer, notifying the juvenile and his or her parent(s), guardian(s), or custodian(s) that a legal action has been filed against or involves the juvenile. The summons also provides notice of any dates set for hearing and deadlines for responding to the complaint or petition. The purpose of a summons is simply to notify the persons concerned; it does not require court attendance.

Decision-Maker

Intake Worker

The intake worker is the person who has the discretion to divert informally or formally to other noncourt social service agencies. Sometimes the intake officer does informal counseling, which helps to resolve the situation so that a petition does not have to be filed. The intake officer (depending on the seriousness of the offense) decides if the youth may be released until the adjudicatory hearing.

This position of intake worker has tremendous discretion. The intake worker who is part of the court services unit or probation staff has to decide if this case really merits going to the judges for an adjudicatory hearing (trial). In some cases, an intake worker may file a petition of delinquency. If the worker decides to refuse to write a petition, the complainant must be notified in writing that he has a right to apply to the magistrate for a warrant. The complainant can then go before a magistrate. If the magistrate finds probable cause for an offense that, if committed by an adult, would constitute a felony or Class 1 misdemeanor, the magistrate will issue a warrant returnable and delivered to the juvenile court. Upon receipt, the intake officer must accept the warrant and file a petition based upon the warrant.

Although most of the cases before the juvenile court come through law enforcement agencies, the complainant can be anyone. In *Gault*, the complainant against Jerry Gault was the female neighbor who said she had received an obscene phone call.

Once a petition is filed, if it is a felony (a serious crime that if convicted requires punishment over one year in a state correctional facility), the intake officer has the duty of notifying the prosecuting attorney for the state. This puts the attorneys for the state on notice.

In some cases the intake worker tries to resolve the situation instead of charging the child with delinquency, such as declaring the child neglected. One such unusual case comes from Washington state. An 8-year-old and some other boys were trespassing on the victim's property. They were told to leave but they did not immediately leave. In fact, they said, "In a minute." The victim replied, "Not in a minute; now! Get out of here now!" The boys ran off, but three days later the 8-year-old entered the victim's home without her permission during the daylight hours, pulled a live goldfish from her fishbowl, chopped it into several pieces with a steak knife, and smeared it on her kitchen counter. Then he went into the bathroom and clamped a plugged-in hair curling iron onto a towel. He was charged with burglary and adjudicated "delinquent." However, that was reversed by the Washington Court of Appeals, which said there was no clear and convincing evidence that the juvenile understood that the act of burglary was wrong (*State v. K. R. L.*, 840 P.2d 210 [Wash. App. Nov. 1992] as cited in **Juvenile Law Reports**, Vol. 15, p.26). The youth did not have the necessary *mens rea* (guilty mind) intent necessary to satisfy one of the elements of burglary to be found guilty of the crime. Even though the youth is not considered delinquent, he does have a serious anger-control problem and the court should do referrals to individual and family counseling. If not, then he may move from goldfish to torture cats and dogs before he starts on humans.

> Common Law Burglary:
> 1. Breaking and 2. Entering 3. Dwelling Place 4. of Another 5. at Nighttime 6. with Intent 7. to Commit a Felony

The intake officer usually uses the following factors in deciding if official handling is warranted:

- ☐ Age
- ☐ Current Offense (Felony)
- ☐ Prior Offenses
- ☐ History of Problems
- ☐ On Probation
- ☐ Parental Control
- ☐ Insistence of Complainant
- ☐ Repeated Complaints

If the case is handled on an official basis, this means that the youth must go to the adjudicatory hearing (trial) where the judge decides whether the child is guilty of the charge. If the child is placed in detention (the next stage), the adjudicatory hearing must be held within a specific number of days. For example, in Virginia, it is 21 days (Va. Code §16.1–277). If the youth is not detained, the hearing must take place within 120 days or the youth goes completely free.

Rights

In re Gault (1967) does give the right to notice of the charges at intake but not for an attorney. Juveniles have no right to counsel at intake because it is not considered a part of the adjudication process. Individual states, however, through their own statutes, may request attorneys.

All information discussed with the intake officer during the intake interview is confidential. It cannot be used as evidence during the adjudicatory hearing. However, information given to others, such as a psychiatrist or psychologist, can be used as evidence in the adjudicatory hearing.

Standard of Proof

There is no standard of proof at this stage of intake. Intake is viewed as an informal forum for the free exchange of ideas among the intake officer, the child, the child's parent(s) or guardian(s), and perhaps the complaining witness who may be a neighbor or a police officer. The parent(s) may hire an attorney if desired, but an attorney's presence is not required by a United States Supreme Court decision.

Qualifications

Children younger than 16 or 17 years old, who have committed their first offense, and whose offense is less serious so that it might be considered a misdemeanor if committed by an adult, are more likely to be informally diverted. The attitude and willingness of the parent(s) and the child to restitute and/or pay damages also play a part in becoming informally diverted.

Role of the Attorney

Four Important Roles

The role of the attorney can be an important role. The lawyer can arrange restitution, interpret the proceedings to the child and the parent(s) or guardian(s), as well as collect and present relevant school, medical, and social records and make recommendations for treatment.

The attorney's presence could introduce objectivity into an otherwise unilateral decision by the intake worker. Because there are no reports, records, or transcripts made at this stage, the attorney has the opportunity to make concrete suggestions for treatment of the child. Intake workers with advanced degrees tend to be therapeutically oriented and favor informal treatment based on individual need. Yet many intake workers are overwhelmed with the number and the complexity of the problems. To have someone else do some of the work in seeking alternative social services would be welcomed by the intake officer. It is a role the attorney could play, helping all concerned.

The intake officer usually will talk to the child and the parent(s) or guardian(s) about the need to have legal representation. It is important to have a professional who knows and understands the system to work for the interest of the child. If the family cannot afford to hire a lawyer, the court can appoint one.

If the family asks for court appointment, they have to sign statements saying that they cannot afford to hire an attorney. That usually includes a financial statement. If the court later determines that the family qualifies for court appointment, the court can request that the family pay the costs of the lawyer. In the end, it is the youth and the parent(s) or guardian(s) who have the right to make the final decision as to whether they want to have an attorney or waive that right.

Detention

Detention is the place that usually looks like a jail, but only young people are housed in the cells. A "secure facility" means that the youth loses **ALL** his or her liberty until there is a hearing. A child may be placed in detention **awaiting** a procedural hearing called a detention hearing.

Awaiting Adjudicatory Hearing

In 1984 in *Schell v. Martin*, 104 U.S. 2403, the U.S. Supreme Court held constitutional the New York state statute that detained a juvenile prior to the adjudicatory hearing (trial). The majority opinion saw detention as prevention—is the youth a serious risk who will commit an act that if, committed by an adult, would be considered a crime, or who will not return for the set court date? The dissenting opinion (Justices Marshall, Brennan, and Stevens) thought preventive detention of juveniles constituted poor public policy. They thought the balance of harms outweighed any possible benefits either to society or the juveniles themselves.

When a child is taken into custody, a detention hearing has to be given within a specific number of hours, such as 72 hours. Oral or written notice must be given to the parents or guardians of the child if they can be located. "Notice" specifies time, place, and purpose of the hearing.

Detention is a very serious matter. So serious that the 1988 Amendments to the Juvenile Justice and Delinquency Prevention (JJDP) Act requires the administrator of the Office of Juvenile Justice and Delinquency Prevention (OJJDP) to submit summaries and analyses of the juveniles in custody. This annual report must be made to Congress. Furthermore, separate reports must be presented for delinquent offenders, status offenders, and nonoffenders. The reports must describe the specific type of facility (secure detention, correctional facility, jail, lockup), plus offense, race, sex, and age.

In Chicago, a young man in a group shower bent over to get a bar of soap from the floor of the shower. Instead of getting the soap sent to him by one of the other older juveniles, he got something more and later died of internal bleeding to the anus.

What is important to realize is that these detention or juvenile halls can be very similar to adult jails. Youth commit suicide (seven in 1988) or kill other children (two in 1988) (*Juveniles Taken Into Custody: 1990*). This is why there is national attention focused on trying to keep youth in the community and still protect the community from the youth who is out of control.

Purpose

The purpose of the detention hearing is to determine if the youth should appear for an adjudicatory hearing. It is not a trial. Thus, if a youth commits another crime while released, then his or her chance of release is low. During this hearing the judge advises the parties (1) of the right to counsel, (2) of the child's right to remain silent with regard to any allegation of delinquency, and (3) of the content of the petition against the child.

There are three forms of detention. The first form is *outreach detention* where the juvenile lives at home under the custody of the parent(s) or guardian(s). There is intensive supervision by court staff. In some places, electronic monitoring is used to assist the staff. In this form of detention, the youth must follow very specific rules. If there is a violation of the rules, then the youth may be returned to the court and placed in more secure detention.

Three Forms of Detention

The second form is *less secure detention* in houses that have no barred windows or locked cells. Residents are closely supervised. Some communities that have very rural populations, like Genessee County, Michigan, have provided other methods that are less expensive, yet still reduce risks to the public (Krisberg, Schwartz, Litsky, and Austin 1986, 29).

The third form is *secure detention*. These youths are under lock-and-key for twenty-four hours, seven days a week. They are required to follow strict rules and attend the school provided within its structure. Every part of the juvenile's life is structured into times for eating, times for being locked into a shower room for a shower, and being locked up for sleep. Secure detention is total confinement by a total institution (in the Goffman sense of the word) with the subsequent loss of being able to make choices. Secure detention centers are usually the most expensive to build and operate. The estimated cost for a facility in northern Virginia in 1990 was $70,000 per person, per bed, for one year.

Since not all youth need a secure facility, other arrangements can be made. In some situations the reason the youth cannot go home is because the charge against the child has been brought by the parent.

Usually, "detention" is a special building for youth, but a judge can place youths in jail if their behavior warrants it. One industrious young man, while in lockup in the juvenile court awaiting to be placed in juvenile detention, escaped through the fan system in the ceiling. He followed the system through the ceiling until he hit a weak spot and fell through the ceiling. He landed in the juvenile court judge's chambers. The judge thought the youth needed a more secure facility like the county jail.

Not all detention facilities follow the state mandates and provide youth with the services they need, as evidenced by the following class-action lawsuit. The state of Delaware and an attorney for the ACLU National Prison Project have reached an agreement to settle a class-action lawsuit. *John A. and Mary B. v. Michael N. Castle* alleged that juvenile institutions in Delaware were overcrowded, and the youths were subjected to beatings, use of Mace, and excessive use of physical restraints. In addition, the education and health-care programs were inadequate. The agreement lays out detailed requirements for reforms in discipline procedures, education and other programs, staffing levels, suicide prevention, medical care, mental health, safety, and hygiene. The resulting New Castle County Detention Center is called "state of the art." In addition, the state is directed to use screening methods upon admission to the new detention facility to promote the use of less restrictive alternatives to incarceration (*Criminal Justice Newsletter*, 25:5, May 16, 1994).

Decision-Maker

The judge has to make the decision to detain. He or she has to decide within a reasonable time if a child before him or her has committed a specific crime. The judge has to determine probable cause. In some states the juvenile can be released on bail or recognizance. Or, the judge may issue a detention order or a warrant to a secure facility.

PC + Felony or threats to run away

Usually the judge has **probable cause to believe the child committed the alleged act** and (1) the crime is a **felony** and release of the child constitutes **unreasonable danger to the person or property of others, or the child's own life or health**; or (2) the **child has threatened to leave the jurisdiction**. Other factors may be that (3) the child has already run away from the court;

(4) the child is a fugitive from a jurisdiction outside of the state; or (5) the child failed to appear in court after having been served with a summons alleging that the child committed a delinquent act.

Standard of Proof

The judge usually uses a standard of "clear and convincing." This is not a trial, so *Winship* does not apply. The judge does not have to use proof beyond a reasonable doubt. If the judge does find adequate probable cause but does not believe full-time detention of the child is warranted, the court can place the child in the custody of a parent or guardian under the court's supervision. There can be restrictions regarding travel, companions, and bedtimes. This is called a *conditional release*. Thus, evidence that is relevant and material to the question of detention can be admitted even though that same evidence may not be admissible on the petition at the adjudicatory hearing.

Role of the Attorney

Even if the child is placed in detention, the attorney may request the judge to reconsider the evidence. If the attorney can find someone responsible to look after the child, the child may be released to that caretaker's custody. In one particular case, the attorney made such a compassionate plea to the judge, and arguing why the detention home was not appropriate for the special needs of his client, the judge released the child to the arguing attorney for control and safekeeping (personal experience).

Waiver

When the juvenile court was first established, it provided for some children to be processed by the juvenile court. Other children, unfortunately, due to the seriousness of their offenses, never saw the juvenile court. In short, they remained in the adult court.

States that developed "exclusive jurisdiction" waived youth out of the juvenile court into the adult court based solely upon the nature of the crime. Waiver is usually applicable to those states that have what is known as *exclusive* or *original jurisdiction*. Waiver or transfer is the process by which the juvenile court sends the youth's case to the adult court "to be tried as an adult." Generally speaking, a juvenile's criminal case under a petition of delinquency can be waived or certified to criminal court for trial as an adult in one of three ways: (1) judicial waiver, (2) prosecutorial discretion, and (3) statutory exclusions. Today, in a given state, one, two, or all three transfer mechanisms may be in place. "From 1992–1997, 44 states and the District of Columbia passed laws making it easier for juveniles to be tried as adults" (http://www.ojjdp.ncjrs.org/ojstatbb/qa091.html, 1 July 1999). States also vary in specifying a minimum age for transfer. Sixteen states set the minimum age at 14 but others use age 10, 12, 13, 15, and no minimum age. Many of these changes were due to politicians wanting to give the impression that they are tough on crime. Refer back to Chapter 1 on *Kent* or read ahead to Chapter 8 where this will be discussed in greater detail. For now, waiver will be discussed in terms of purpose, decision-maker, rights, standard of proof, qualification, and role of the attorney.

Purpose

The purpose of the waiver hearing is to **end juvenile court jurisdiction**. In the states where the juvenile court is the only court with power to hear this child's case (called original jurisdiction), that jurisdiction must end for the child to be transferred, waived, or certified into the adult court to be tried as if he or she were an adult. Juvenile judges hold a hearing usually in response to a request by the prosecutor. Upon completion of this hearing, if the youth's case is to be transferred to the adult criminal court, the youth is said to be "certified as an adult."

Most states mandate age and/or offenses that impact the decision. For example, in the state of Virginia, a youth must be 14 years or over and charged with an offense which, if committed by an adult, could be punishable by confinement in the penitentiary.

Transfer is contingent on the court making two decisions. The first is **probable cause** (that the child committed the delinquent act). The second is that the child is not **amenable** (treatable). If the court finds that both are true, interests of the community require that this child be placed under legal restraint.

In some ways the transfer or waiver hearing is similar to a preliminary hearing in the criminal division in that it determines probable cause. However, the juvenile court has a greater function—to determine whether a particular juvenile will benefit most from treatment as a child in juvenile court or as an adult in criminal court. The question is—has the child exhausted all the resources of the juvenile court? Concern is given to the child's responses to past treatment efforts. If the child has had several different placements, and if he or she has caused trouble in each, the prosecutor may argue that the court has no more programs willing or able to take his or her youth.

In the early juvenile courts, the decision to transfer was made by a juvenile court judge based upon the individual circumstances in each case. In the 1970s and continuing to the present, state legislatures have created statutes that move youth into criminal court based on age and the seriousness of the offense, such as murder, rape, robbery, and so forth. This means that in some cases, the juvenile charged with murder, for example, never sees a juvenile judge because the state—through state law—permits the youth to go directly to the adult criminal court. In one-quarter of the states, the prosecutors have the discretion to charge certain offenses either in juvenile or criminal court. So states now determine by statutes the specific ages and offenses requiring youth to be transferred.

Today, one of the "buzzwords" in criminal and juvenile justice is restorative justice. It is a justice model that promotes maximum involvement of the victim, the offender, and the community in the justice process (Bazemore and Umbreit 1994). The balanced and restorative justice model means more accountability to community protection—public safety. Even though a minor has committed only one offense and has not used the services or treatment in the juvenile court, if the offense is serious, the youth can be waived. In some states, by statute or state law, it is automatic and there is no hearing.

Decision-Maker

The judge presides over the waiver hearing. Also present will be the defense attorney, the prosecuting attorney, probation staff, and witness(es).

Before making the decision, the judge will order a "transfer hearing report." This report is prepared by the probation officer. The transfer hearing report contains information about the youth's home life, background, past offenses, previous commitment to the corrections system, plus recommendations made by the probation officer. It was this set of documents that the attorney in *Kent* wanted to see, for help in representing his client, and was denied. If the judge has access to this information—should not the attorney who is to defend the youth have the same opportunity?

Rights

According to *Kent v. U.S.* (see Chapter 1, "History and Treatment"), the juvenile has a right to (1) a hearing in which there is (2) an attorney. In the waiver hearing the attorney has a right to (3) social history reports. The judge must (4) state on the record the reason for the transfer.

Standard of Proof

The standard of proof is "preponderance of evidence" or "clear and convincing." Remember, preponderance of the evidence is equal to 50.5 percent—a standard used in civil courts to determine that one person has more blame than another. It is not "proof beyond a reasonable doubt," because this is not a hearing to determine if the youth did the crime (that is assigned to the adjudicatory hearing). The waiver or transfer hearing determines if the youth has exhausted all the treatment programs of the juvenile court and should now be treated as an adult. Because this waiver hearing is a dispositional hearing, which is a final decision that can pass the control of the juvenile court to another court, **illegally seized evidence can be admitted into the hearing**.

Qualifications

Most states put some limits on the age of the child who can be transferred to adult court (Feld 1987). Maryland's code lists the following factors that influence the decision:

1. Age of child

2. Mental and physical condition of child

3. Child's amenability to treatment available to delinquents

4. Nature of the offense

5. Safety of the public

Not all five of the above factors are necessary for waiver. In some states, the nature of the offense makes a "mandatory waiver." This approach was pioneered in Florida in the early 1980s as part of the state's "get tough" response to juvenile crime. When a mandatory waiver is required, there is no discretion for the juvenile justice system.

Louisiana expressly places within the criminal court jurisdiction, regardless of the age of the offender, such offenses as murder, manslaughter, rape, robbery, burglary, and kidnapping. North Carolina permits the adult court control only if the child is 14 or older and she or he could receive the death penalty.

Besides the nature of the offense, other variables to be considered are mental and physical age, the youth's prior record and past efforts to treat and rehabilitate, and the availability of programs and facilities within the juvenile justice system. The most important is the issue of treatability.

Under Massachusetts law, if a child is charged with murder in the first or second degree and there is a finding of probable cause, there is **"rebuttable presumption" that the child presents a significant danger to the public. As such, the child is not amenable to rehabilitation or treatable within the juvenile justice system.** This means that the juvenile has to produce evidence showing that she or he is not a danger to society and is able to be treated in the juvenile justice system to overcome the presumption.

In recent years, society has demanded more often the incarceration of violent juvenile offenders—especially those who commit heinous or serious violent crimes, provoking strong community emotions and fear for safety. Legislatures in many states have enacted statutes to guide the juvenile courts in the transfer decision.

Since the end of the year 1992, in all states except Nebraska and New York, juvenile court judges may waive jurisdiction over a juvenile case and transfer it to adult criminal court through statutory exclusion or prosecutorial discretion (Sickmund 1994, 1). Prosecutorial discretion is given by statute so that prosecutors can file certain juvenile cases in either juvenile or criminal court under concurrent jurisdiction. Original jurisdiction, in effect, is shared by both criminal and juvenile courts for youths of certain ages and with certain offenses.

Another important part of waiver is the determination of mental retardation. What do you do with a juvenile who functions with an I.Q. in the high 60s or low 70s and is considered "educably mentally retarded"? (See *Russell v. Commonwealth*, 432 S.E.2d 12 [Va. App. June 1993].)

The dissenting opinion in *Bobby J. Wills v. Texas*, 114 S. Ct. 1867 (1994), argued that the court's imposition of the death penalty on Wills was inappropriate because the jury was not allowed to consider the defendant's mental retardation. The Eighth Amendment is clearly violated if the jury cannot consider the mitigating effect to the defendant's mental state.

Thus, transfer or waiver of hearings to determine if a youth should be sent to adult criminal court can have extremely serious results. If the youth does go into the adult criminal court and is found guilty, the youth can be sentenced to adult prison, have a permanent criminal record, and upon reaching adulthood, lose some of his or her civil rights such as the right to vote, run for public office, and serve on a jury. In *Harris v. Wright*, 93 F.3d 581, 1996 U.S. App. Lexis 20643, 96 Cal. Daily Op. Service 6150 (1996), a mandatory sentence of life imprisonment without the possibility of parole does not violate the Eighth and Fourteenth Amendments on cruel and unusual punishment when applied to punish an offense committed when the youth was less than 16 years of age. The theory is that by sending the youth into the adult system, the youth will get more punishment. Is that always true?

Present-day research into the kinds of punishment youth get in adult courts has brought some interesting findings. Keiter (1973) looked at the sentencing patterns of juvenile waivers into adult court. The profile of juveniles transferred was: usually black, male, 16 years of age, charged with murder, several prior police contacts, at least two previous court contacts, and adjudicated delinquent at least once previously. Using data from social histories, his study revealed that nearly one-third had spent time in a state juvenile institution and that a significant number were involved with neighborhood street gangs.

Later, Bortner (1986), using 214 juveniles in a western metropolitan county during 1980–81, showed that those who received jail terms in the adult system were given times of nine months and less. Those who were sentenced to prison received five years or less. His conclusion was that "remand does not provide extensive protection, nor does remanding juveniles result in a high percentage of incarceration or long periods of incarceration" (Bortner 1986, 56).

Most recently, Houghtalin and Mays (1991) examined 49 cases that were transferred during the period of 1981 through 1990 in New Mexico. Their profile was: male, 16 to 17 years of age, in the juvenile justice system several prior times, charged with a serious offense such as murder or armed robbery, and at least once adjudicated and placed on probation. Of the 49 cases waived, 39 (79.6 percent) were convicted. Twenty-five (64.1 percent) received prison sentences, and 11 (28.2 percent) were placed on probation with the adult court. Three were still pending final sentencing.

Clement (1993, 1997) used a five-year study of juveniles in Richmond, Virginia, waived from juvenile court into the adult court, by following each case through each court and then into the correctional database. Thus, her research is the most complete, overcoming many of the other research studies that only use a court database (Poulos and Orchowsky 1994) or a correctional database (Fritsch, Caeti, and Hemmes 1996). For example, from November 1986 to December 1991, 65 out of 250 cases received no sentences. They were found not guilty, nolle processed (prosecutor declares that he or she will proceed no longer to prosecute), and dismissed. Clement also found the sentencing to be creative—using ISS-KPGB. ISS-KPGB means the imposed sentence is suspended if the youth keeps the peace and shows good behavior.

One youth, for example, was accused of the following:

1. Robbery
2. Use of a firearm in commission of a felony
3. Abduction
4. Use of a firearm in commission of a felony
5. Robbery
6. Use of a firearm in commission of a felony
7. Abduction
8. Use of a firearm in commission of a felony

After being waived into adult court, he received the following sentences for the specific charges listed above:

Profile of Waived Youth

1. ISS (Imposed Sentence is Suspended)

2. Nolle prosequi

3. Five years prison

4. Two years prison

5. ISS

6. Four years prison

7. Five years prison

8. Nolle prosequi

This means that charges no. 1 and no. 5 were given a sentence but not imposed. The sentences were suspended with the hope that the youth would correct his behavior. If the youth does not and returns to the adult court for not having kept the peace or maintained good behavior, the ISS is revoked and the youth has some more time to serve.

Clement's data showed that the prior record of a youth was critical. Prior record was defined as the number of petitions or appearances made by these youths before the juvenile court. They ranged from 1 to 34. In fact, four youths had 34 previous petitions. Yet the average number of previous appearances in juvenile court was 10. This statistic supports the idea that the juvenile court did in fact try to work with the youth and attempt treatment before sending them to adult court. Clement found that those who did commit crimes of rape and murder got much more time in the adult system than they could have gotten in the juvenile system. However, most of the youth transferred were for property crimes, not crimes of violence.

Some national groups also realize that the criminal courts have their own problems and are not the cure-all that the public wants. For example, the National Association of Juvenile Court Judges, citing research done by the RAND Corporation, the American Institute of Research, and the Federal Office of Juvenile Justice and Delinquency Prevention, said that sanctions received do not vary greatly whether the youngster is prosecuted in juvenile or adult court. In fact, in New York, some criminal courts dismiss 50 percent or more of the juvenile cases sent to them (*Criminal Justice Newsletter*, 25 [Mar. 1, 1994]: 2).

Role of the Attorney

The role of the attorney is very important at the waiver hearing. According to *Kent*, the attorney has a right (1) to review the social history of the youth, and (2) to have a hearing on the question of transfer. This is a very active role for the attorney. Besides assuring the child every chance to remain in the juvenile court, the attorney must make sure things are done properly.

Double Jeopardy   One type of error is called "double jeopardy." A waiver hearing is held first. If the child is amenable (treatable in the juvenile court), then the child should remain in that court and go to the adjudicatory hearing. If the adjudicatory hearing is held first, and if it determines that the child is no longer treatable and tries to waive the child into adult court, the juvenile's rights have been violated (*Breed v. Jones*, 421 U.S. 519 [1975]). The child will have had to defend him- or herself on the same offense twice—double jeopardy. When this occurs, once in juvenile court and once in adult court for the same exact charge, it is considered by the Supreme Court as double jeopardy.

The Supreme Court decision in *Kent* established a juvenile's due process rights to (1) a hearing to determine waiver, (2) an attorney, (3) access to the court documents, and (4) reasons for the transfer to be written on the documents so that the youth can form an appeal if necessary. The Court's decision did not make juvenile courts adhere to all the procedural requirements of an adult criminal trial. But court watchers will tell you this waiver hearing looks like and feels like a full-blown trial with all witnesses and attorneys representing the youth and the state. States are free, within due process limits, to design their own model of waiver because the U.S. Supreme Court has not established age and/or offense requirements for juvenile court waivers.

Being an attorney for juveniles and protecting their rights is a challenge. Take, for example, *Mosby v. Commonwealth of Virginia*, 23 Va. App. 38 (1996). The youth was accused of malicious wounding, and a transfer hearing was held in the juvenile court and the youth was certified to (adult) circuit court. At the trial, several witnesses for the prosecutor failed to appear, and the prosecutor requested a nolle prossed for the indictment. The youth was again indicted on the same malicious wounding charges, but no additional petition was filed in the juvenile court and no transfer hearing was held. At the sentencing, the attorney had to argue by moving to set aside the verdict on the grounds that the nolle prossed applied to the first indictment and the charge of malicious wounding was terminated at that time. Because the defendant was a juvenile, any further proceedings had to start with a filing of a second petition in the juvenile court, and then a second transfer hearing needed to be conducted. Because the court didn't agree, the attorney had to appeal the case. The court of appeals then reversed and remanded the case because the second petition and transfer hearing didn't precede the sentencing.

The most severe sentencing in adult courts is a death penalty or capital punishment. The U.S. Supreme Court, in a series of cases, has had to deal with the situation when youths act like adults in committing crimes, but they are not legally considered adults (age 18 or older). In *Thompson v. Oklahoma*, 108 S.Ct. 2687 (1988), the Supreme Court prohibited execution of persons below age 16. Earlier, in 1982, the Supreme Court overturned the death penalty for a 16-year-old who killed a highway patrol officer on the grounds that the trial court had failed to consider such mitigating factors as age and the youth's emotional state and troubled childhood (*Eddings v. Oklahoma*, 455 U.S. 104). In *Eddings*, the Court said that adolescents are less mature and self-disciplined than adults and are less able to anticipate the future results of their behavior. The sentencer (the judge) may not refuse to consider any relevant mitigating evidence offered by the defendant. The judge may determine how much weight to be given to the mitigating circumstance, such as the psychologist's report, the divorce of the parents, and the youth living with an alcoholic mother who set no limits on his or her own behavior.

In *Stanford v. Kentucky*, 492 U.S. 361 (1989), the Court said that the death penalty could only be given to youths 16 or older because there was no national prohibition against it. Whether a particular punishment violates the Eighth Amendment depends on whether it constitutes one of those acts of punishment considered cruel and unusual at the time that the Bill of Rights was adopted. Stanford (age 17) and Wilkins (age 16) (two cases heard together) did not argue that their sentences would have been considered cruel and unusual punishment in the eighteenth century. In fact, common law tradition did not view it as cruel and unusual punishment because at least 281 offenders under age 18 and 126 under age 17 have been executed in this country. *Stanford* means that it is not a violation of the Eighth Amendment for 16- and 17-year-olds who have committed a felony to receive a death sentence—capital punishment. Thus, the minimum age for receiving the death penalty is 16. Because society as a whole has not formed one opinion on the death penalty for juveniles, states are free to impose the death penalty for juveniles age 16 or over who commit capital offenses.

Because juvenile courts do not give capital punishment, the only way a youth could get the death penalty would be to be waived into the adult court and found guilty of a capital offense with no mitigating circumstances in a state that favored the death penalty. Truly, waiving a youth to adult criminal court as stated in *Kent* has "tremendous consequences."

✳ BRAIN EXERCISE

Take the following set of facts and decide for yourself whether there is an error to which the juvenile can appeal:

Bud Wiser was arrested and charged with driving an automobile while under the influence of alcohol and grand larceny—of an auto. Because Bud Wiser was 17 years of age at the time of the commission of the offense, he was tried before the Juvenile and Domestic Relations Court of the appropriate city. His petitions were sustained, and he was committed to the Department of Youth Corrections to spend time in the juvenile correctional center.

The prosecuting attorney for the city presented the case to the grand jury, which returned an indictment on grand larceny. While Bud Wiser was in detention awaiting his transfer to the state correctional center for juveniles, he was taken to the adult criminal court where he was tried before the Circuit Court and found guilty of grand larceny.

His attorney argued that the trial before the Circuit Court constituted double jeopardy. His motion was denied, and Bud was tried and sentenced to two years in the state penitentiary. Bud Wiser now appeals to the Supreme Court of his state.

How should the Supreme Court rule on his appeal? Why?

STANFORD V. KENTUCKY

SUPREME COURT OF THE UNITED STATES

492 U.S. 361; 109 S.Ct. 2969; 106 L.Ed.2d 306; (1989)

March 27, 1989, Argued June 26, 1989, Decided*

Together with No. 87-6026, *Wilkins v. Missouri*, on certiorari to the Supreme Court of Missouri.

PRIOR HISTORY: CERTIORARI TO THE SUPREME COURT OF KENTUCKY.

SYLLABUS: Petitioner in No. 87-5765 was approximately 17 years and 4 months old at the time he committed murder in Kentucky. A juvenile court, after conducting hearings, transferred him for trial as an adult under a state statute permitting such action as to offenders who are either charged with a Class A felony or capital crime or who are over the age of 16 and charged with a felony. Petitioner was convicted and sentenced to death. The State Supreme Court affirmed the death sentence, rejecting petitioner's contention that he had a constitutional right to treatment in the juvenile justice system, and declaring that his age and the possibility that he might be rehabilitated were mitigating factors properly left to the jury. Petitioner in No. 87-6026, who was approximately 16 years and 6 months old when he committed murder in Missouri, was certified for trial as an adult under a state statute permitting such action against individuals between 14 and 17 years old who have committed felonies. He pleaded guilty and was sentenced to death. The State Supreme Court affirmed, rejecting his contention that the sentence violated the Eighth Amendment.

Held: The judgments are affirmed. | Decision

JUSTICE SCALIA delivered the opinion of the Court with respect to Parts I, II, III, and IV-A, concluding that the imposition of capital punishment on an individual for a crime committed at 16 or 17 years of age does not constitute cruel and unusual punishment under the Eighth Amendment. | Rules to Determine This Case

(a) **Whether a particular punishment violates the Eighth Amendment depends on whether it constitutes one of "those modes or acts of punishment . . . considered cruel and unusual at the time that the Bill of Rights was adopted,"** *Ford v. Wainwright*, 477 U.S. 399, 405, or is contrary to the "evolving standards of decency that mark the progress of a maturing society," *Trop v. Dulles*, 356 U.S. 86, 101. Petitioners have not alleged that their sentences would have been considered cruel and unusual in the 18th century, and could not support such a contention, since, at that time, the common law set the rebuttable presumption of incapacity to commit felonies (which were punishable by death) at the age of 14. In accordance with this common-law tradition, at least 281 offenders under 18, and 126 under 17, have been executed in this country.

(b) **In determining whether a punishment violates evolving standards of decency, this Court looks not to its own subjective conceptions, but, rather, to the conceptions of modern American society as reflected by objective evidence.** E.g., *Coker v. Georgia*, 433 U.S. 584, 592. The primary and most reliable evidence of national consensus—the pattern of federal and state laws—fails to meet petitioner's heavy burden of proving a settled consensus against the execution of 16- and 17-year-old offenders. Of the 37 States that permit capital punishment, 15 decline to impose it on 16-year-olds and 12 on 17-year-olds. This does not establish the degree of national agreement this Court has previously thought sufficient to label a punishment cruel and unusual. See *Tison v. Arizona*, 481 U.S. 137, 154. | Major Reasons for the Decision

(c) **Nor is there support for petitioners' argument that** a demonstrable reluctance of juries to impose, and prosecutors to seek, capital sentences for 16- and 17-year-olds **establishes a societal consensus that such sentences are inappropriate**. Statistics showing that a far smaller number of offenders under 18 than over 18 have been sentenced to death reflect in part the fact that a far smaller percentage of capital crimes is committed by persons in the younger age group. Beyond that, it is likely that the very considerations that induce petitioners to believe death should never be imposed on such young offenders cause prosecutors and juries to believe it should rarely be imposed, so that the statistics are no proof of a categorical aversion.

JUSTICE SCALIA, joined by THE CHIEF JUSTICE, JUSTICE WHITE, and JUSTICE KENNEDY, concluded in Parts IV-B and V that:

Mitigating Factor Test

1 There is no relevance to the state laws cited by petitioners which set 18 or more as the legal age for engaging in various activities, ranging from driving to drinking alcoholic beverages to voting. Those laws operate in gross, and do not conduct individualized maturity tests for each driver, drinker, or voter; an age appropriate in the vast majority of cases must therefore be selected. In the realm of capital punishment, however, individualized consideration is a constitutional requirement. Twenty-nine States, including Kentucky and Missouri, have codified this requirement in laws specifically designating age as a mitigating factor that capital sentences must be permitted to consider. Moreover, the determinations required by transfer statutes such as Kentucky's and Missouri's to certify a juvenile for trial as an adult ensure individualized consideration of the maturity and moral responsibility of 16- and 17-year-olds before they are even held to stand trial as adults. It is those particularized laws, rather than the generalized driving, drinking, and voting laws, that display society's views on the age at which no youthful offender should be held responsible.

2 The indicia of national consensus offered by petitioner other than state and federal statutes and the behavior of prosecutors and juries cannot establish constitutional standards. Public opinion polls, the views of interest groups, and the positions of professional associations are too uncertain a foundation for constitutional law. Also insufficient is socioscientific or ethicoscientific evidence tending to show that capital punishment fails to deter 16- and 17-year-olds because they have a less highly developed fear of death, and fails to exact just retribution because juveniles, being less mature and responsible, are less morally blameworthy. The audience for such arguments is not this Court but the citizenry. Although several of the Court's cases have engaged in so-called "proportionality" analysis—which examines whether there is a disproportion between the punishment imposed and the defendant's blameworthiness, and whether a punishment makes any measurable contribution to acceptable goals of punishment—those decisions have never invalidated a punishment on that basis alone, but have done so only when there was also objective evidence of state laws or jury determinations establishing a societal consensus against the penalty.

JUSTICE O'CONNOR, although agreeing that no national consensus presently forbids the imposition of capital punishment on 16- or 17-year-old murderers, concluded that this Court has a constitutional obligation to conduct proportionality analysis, see, e.g., *Penry v. Lynaugh*, ante, at 335–340, and should consider age-based statutory classifications that are relevant to that analysis.

?

These two consolidated cases require us to decide whether the imposition of capital punishment on an individual for a crime committed at 16 or 17 years of age constitutes cruel and unusual punishment under the Eighth Amendment.

I

The first case, No. 87-5765, involves the shooting death of 20-year-old Barbel Poore in Jefferson County, Kentucky. Petitioner Kevin Stanford committed the murder on January 7, 1981, when he was approximately 17 years and 4 months of age. Stanford and his accomplice repeatedly raped and sodomized Poore during and after their commission of a robbery at a gas station where she worked as an attendant. They then drove her to a secluded area near the station, where Stanford shot her point-blank in the face and then in the back of her head. The proceeds from the robbery were roughly 300 cartons of cigarettes, two gallons of fuel, and a small amount of cash. A corrections officer testified that petitioner explained the murder as follows: "'He said, I had to shoot her, [she] lived next door to me and she would recognize me. . . . I guess we could have tied her up or something or beat [her up] . . . and tell her if she tells, we would kill her. . . . Then after he said that he started laughing.'" 734 S. W. 2d 781, 788 (Ky. 1987).

Facts

After Stanford's arrest, a Kentucky juvenile court conducted hearings to determine whether he should be transferred for trial as an adult under Ky. Rev. Stat. Ann. §208.170 (Michie 1982). That statute provided that juvenile court jurisdiction could be waived and an offender tried as an adult if he was either charged with a Class A felony or capital crime, or was over 16 years of age and charged with a felony. Stressing the seriousness of petitioner's offenses and the unsuccessful attempts of the juvenile system to treat him for numerous instances of past delinquency, the juvenile court found certification for trial as an adult to be in the best interest of petitioner and the community.

Procedural History

Stanford was convicted of murder, first-degree sodomy, first-degree robbery, and receiving stolen property, and was sentenced to death and 45 years in prison. The Kentucky Supreme Court affirmed the death sentence, rejecting Stanford's "demand that he has a constitutional right to treatment." 734 S. W. 2d, at 792. Finding that the record clearly demonstrated that "there was no program or treatment appropriate for the appellant in the juvenile justice system," the court held that the juvenile court did not err in certifying petitioner for trial as an adult. The court also stated that petitioner's "age and the possibility that he might be rehabilitated were mitigating factors appropriately left to the consideration of the jury that tried him."

The second case before us today, No. 87-6026, involves the stabbing death of Nancy Allen, a 26-year-old mother of two who was working behind the sales counter of the convenience store she and David Allen owned and operated in Avondale, Missouri. Petitioner Heath Wilkins committed the murder on July 27, 1985, when he was approximately 16 years and 6 months of age. The record reflects that Wilkins' plan was to rob the store and murder "whoever was behind the counter" because "a dead person can't talk." While Wilkins' accomplice, Patrick Stevens, held Allen, Wilkins stabbed her, causing her to fall to the floor. When Stevens had trouble operating the cash register, Allen spoke up to assist him, leading Wilkins to stab her three more times in her chest. Two of these wounds penetrated the victim's heart. When Allen began to beg for her life, Wilkins stabbed her four more times in the neck, opening her carotid artery. After helping themselves to liquor, cigarettes, rolling papers, and approximately $450 in cash and checks, Wilkins and Stevens left Allen to die on the floor.

Facts

Because he was roughly six months short of the age of majority for purposes of criminal prosecution, Mo. Rev. Stat. §211.021(1) (1986), Wilkins could not automatically be tried as an adult under Missouri law. Before that could happen, the juvenile court was required to terminate juvenile court jurisdiction and certify Wilkins for trial as an adult under §211.071, which permits individuals between

Procedural History

14 and 17 years of age who have committed felonies to be tried as adults. Relying on the "viciousness, force and violence" of the alleged crime, petitioner's maturity, and the failure of the juvenile justice system to rehabilitate him after previous delinquent acts, the juvenile court made the necessary certification.

Wilkins was charged with first-degree murder, armed criminal action, and carrying a concealed weapon. After the court found him competent, petitioner entered guilty pleas to all charges. A punishment hearing was held, at which both the State and petitioner himself urged imposition of the death sentence. Evidence at the hearing revealed that petitioner had been in and out of juvenile facilities since the age of eight for various acts of burglary, theft, and arson, had attempted to kill his mother by putting insecticide into Tylenol capsules, and had killed several animals in his neighborhood. Although psychiatric testimony indicated that Wilkins had "personality disorders," the witnesses agreed that Wilkins was aware of his actions and could distinguish right from wrong.

Determining that the death penalty was appropriate, the trial court entered the following order:

"The court finds beyond reasonable doubt that the following aggravating circumstances exist:

"1. The murder in the first degree was committed while the defendant was engaged in the perpetration of the felony of robbery, and

"2. The murder in the first degree involved depravity of mind and that as a result thereof, it was outrageously or wantonly vile, horrible or inhuman." App. in No. 87-6026, p. 77.

On mandatory review of Wilkins' death sentence, the Supreme Court of Missouri affirmed, rejecting the argument that the punishment violated the Eighth Amendment. 736 S. W. 2d 409 (1987).

Question

We granted certiorari in these cases, 488 U.S. 887 (1988) and 487 U.S. 1233 (1988), to decide whether the Eighth Amendment precludes the death penalty for individuals who commit crimes at 16 or 17 years of age.

II

What the Offenders Argue

The thrust of both Wilkins' and Stanford's arguments is that imposition of the death penalty on those who were juveniles when they committed their crimes falls within the Eighth Amendment's prohibition against "cruel and unusual punishments." Wilkins would have us define juveniles as individuals 16 years of age and under; Stanford would draw the line at 17.

Neither petitioner asserts that his sentence constitutes one of "those modes or acts of punishment that had been considered cruel and unusual at the time that the Bill of Rights was adopted." Ford v. Wainwright, 477 U.S. 399, 405 (1986). Nor could they support such a contention. At that time, the common law set the rebuttable presumption of incapacity to commit any felony at the age of 14, and theoretically permitted capital punishment to be imposed on anyone over the age of 7. See 4 W. Blackstone, Commentaries *23–24; 1 M. Hale, Pleas of the Crown 24–29 (1800). See also In re Gault, 387 U.S. 1, 16 (1967); Streib, Death Penalty for Children: The American Experience with Capital Punishment for Crimes Committed While Under Age Eighteen, 36 Okla. L. Rev. 613, 614–615 (1983); Kean, The History of the Criminal Liability of Children, 53 L. Q. Rev. 364, 369–370 (1937). In accordance with the standards of this common-law tradition, at least 281 offenders under the age of 18 have been executed in this country, and at least 126 under the age of 17. See V. Streib, Death Penalty for Juveniles 57 (1987).

Thus **petitioners are left to argue that their punishment is contrary to the "evolving standards of decency that mark the progress of a maturing society,"** *Trop v. Dulles,* 356 U.S. 86, 101 (1958) (plurality opinion). They are correct in asserting that this Court has "not confined the prohibition embodied in the Eighth Amendment to 'barbarous' methods that were generally outlawed in the 18th century," but instead has interpreted the Amendment "in a flexible and dynamic manner." *Gregg v. Georgia,* 428 U.S. 153, 171 (1976) (opinion of Stewart, Powell, and STEVENS, JJ.). In determining what standards have "evolved," however, we have looked not to our own conceptions of decency, but to those of modern American society as a whole.

As we have said, "Eighth Amendment judgments should not be, or appear to be, merely the subjective views of individual Justices; judgment should be informed by objective factors to the maximum possible extent." *Coker v. Georgia,* 433 U.S. 584, 592 (1977) (plurality opinion). See also *Penry v. Lynaugh,* ante, at 331; *Ford v. Wainwright,* supra, at 406; *Enmund v. Florida,* 458 U.S. 782, 788–789 (1982); *Furman v. Georgia,* 408 U.S. 238, 277–279 (1972) (BRENNAN, J., concurring). This approach is dictated both by the language of the Amendment—which proscribes only those punishments that are both "cruel and unusual"—and by the "deference we owe to the decisions of the state legislatures under our federal system," *Gregg v. Georgia,* supra, at 176.

III

"First" among the "'objective indicia that reflect the public attitude toward a given sanction'" are statutes passed by society's elected representatives. *McClesky v. Kemp,* 481 U.S. 279, 300 (1987), quoting *Gregg v. Georgia,* supra, at 173. Of the 37 States whose laws permit capital punishment, 15 decline to impose it upon 16-year-old offenders and 12 decline to impose it on 17-year-old offenders. This does not establish the degree of national consensus this Court has previously thought sufficient to label a particular punishment cruel and unusual. In invalidating the death penalty for rape of an adult woman, we stressed that Georgia was the sole jurisdiction that authorized such a punishment. See *Coker v. Georgia,* supra, at 595–596. In striking down capital punishment for participation in a robbery in which an accomplice takes a life, we emphasized that only eight jurisdictions authorized similar punishment. *Enmund v. Florida,* supra, at 792. In finding that the Eighth Amendment precludes execution of the insane and thus requires an adequate hearing on the issue of sanity, we relied upon (in addition to the common-law rule) the fact that "no State in the Union" permitted such punishment. *Ford v. Wainwright,* 477 U.S., at 408. And in striking down a life sentence without parole under a recidivist statute, we stressed that "it appears that [petitioner] was treated more severely than he would have been in any other State." *Solem v. Helm,* 463 U.S. 277, 300 (1983).

Since a majority of the States that permit capital punishment authorize it for crimes committed at age 16 or above, petitioners' cases are more analogous to *Tison v. Arizona,* 481 U.S. 137 (1987), than *Coker, Enmund, Ford,* and *Solem.* In *Tison,* which upheld Arizona's imposition of the death penalty for major participation in a felony with reckless indifference to human life, we noted that only 11 of those jurisdictions imposing capital punishment rejected its use in such circumstances. Id., at 154. As we noted earlier, here the number is 15 for offenders under 17, and 12 for offenders under 18. We think the same conclusion as in *Tison* is required in this case.

Use Federal Laws

Petitioners make much of the recently enacted federal statute providing capital punishment for certain drug-related offenses, but limiting that punishment to offenders 18 and over. The Anti-Drug Abuse Act of 1988, Pub. L. 100–690, 102 Stat. 4390, § 7001(1), 21 U.S.C. § 848(1) (1988 ed.). That reliance is entirely misplaced. To begin with, the statute in question does not embody a judgment by the Federal Legislature that no murder is heinous enough to warrant the execution of such a youthful offender, but merely that the narrow class of offense it defines is not. The congressional judgment on the broader question, if apparent at all, is to be found in the law that permits 16- and 17-year-olds (after appropriate findings) to be tried and punished as adults for all federal offenses, including those bearing a capital penalty that is not limited to 18-year-olds. See 18 U.S.C. § 5032 (1982 ed., Supp. V). Moreover, even if it were true that no federal statute permitted the execution of persons under 18, that would not remotely establish—in the face of a substantial number of state statutes to the contrary—a national consensus that such punishment is inhumane, any more than the absence of a federal lottery establishes a national consensus that lotteries are socially harmful. To be sure, the absence of a federal death penalty for 16- or 17-year-olds (if it existed) might be evidence that there is no national consensus in favor of such punishment. It is not the burden of Kentucky and Missouri, however, to establish a national consensus approving what their citizens have voted to do; rather, it is the "heavy burden" of petitioners, *Gregg v. Georgia*, 428 U.S., at 175, to establish a national consensus against it. As far as the primary and most reliable indication of consensus is concerned—the pattern of enacted laws—petitioners have failed to carry that burden.

IV

A

Application of law =
Contemporary society

Wilkins and Stanford argue, however, that even if the laws themselves do not establish a settled consensus, the application of the laws does. That **contemporary society views capital punishment of 16- and 17-year-old offenders as inappropriate is demonstrated, they say, by the reluctance of juries to impose, and prosecutors to seek, such sentences.** Petitioners are quite correct that a far smaller number of offenders under 18 than over 18 have been sentenced to death in this country. From 1982 through 1988, for example, out of 2,106 total death sentences, only 15 were imposed on individuals who were 16 or under when they committed their crimes, and only 30 on individuals who were 17 at the time of the crime. See Streib, Imposition of Death Sentences for Juvenile Offenses, January 1, 1982, through April 1, 1989, p. 2 (paper for Cleveland-Marshall College of Law, April 5, 1989). And it appears that actual executions for crimes committed under age 18 accounted for only about two percent of the total number of executions that occurred between 1642 and 1986. See Streib, Death Penalty for Juveniles, at 55, 57. As Wilkins points out, the last execution of a person who committed a crime under 17 years of age occurred in 1959. These statistics, however, carry little significance. Given the undisputed fact that a far smaller percentage of capital crimes are committed by persons under 18 than over 18, the discrepancy in treatment is much less than might seem. Granted, however, that a substantial discrepancy exists, that does not establish the requisite proposition that the death sentence for offenders under 18 is categorically unacceptable to prosecutors and juries. To the contrary, it is not only possible, but overwhelmingly probable, that the very considerations which induce petitioners and their supporters to believe that death should never be imposed on offenders under 18 cause prosecutors and juries to believe that it should rarely be imposed.

B

This last point suggests why there is also no relevance to the laws cited by petitioners and their amici which **set 18 or more as the legal age for engaging in various activities**, ranging from driving to drinking alcoholic beverages to voting. It is, to begin with, absurd to think that one must be mature enough to drive carefully, to drink responsibly, or to vote intelligently, in order to be mature enough to understand that murdering another human being is profoundly wrong, and to conform one's conduct to that most minimal of all civilized standards. But even if the requisite degrees of maturity were comparable, the age statutes in question would still not be relevant. They do not represent a social judgment that all persons under the designated ages are not responsible enough to drive, to drink, or to vote, but at most a judgment that the vast majority are not. These laws set the appropriate ages for the operation of a system that makes its determinations in gross, and that does not conduct individualized maturity tests for each driver, drinker, or voter. The criminal justice system, however, does provide individualized testing. In the realm of capital punishment in particular, "individualized consideration [is] a constitutional requirement," *Lockett v. Ohio*, 438 U.S. 586, 605 (1978) (opinion of Burger, C. J.) (footnote omitted); see also *Zant v. Stephens*, 462 U.S. 862, 879 (1983) (collecting cases), and one of the individualized mitigating factors that sentences must be permitted to consider is the defendant's age, see *Eddings v. Oklahoma*, 455 U.S. 104, 115–116 (1982). Twenty-nine States, including both Kentucky and Missouri, have codified this constitutional requirement in laws specifically designating the defendant's age as a mitigating factor in capital cases. Moreover, the determinations required by juvenile transfer statutes to certify a juvenile for trial as an adult ensure individualized consideration of the maturity and moral responsibility of 16- and 17-year-old offenders before they are even held to stand trial as adults. The application of this particularized system to the petitioners can be declared constitutionally inadequate only if there is a consensus, not that 17 or 18 is the age at which most persons, or even almost all persons, achieve sufficient maturity to be held fully responsible for murder; but that 17 or 18 is the age before which no one can reasonably be held fully responsible. What displays society's views on this latter point are not the ages set forth in the generalized system of driving, drinking, and voting laws cited by petitioners and their amici, but the ages at which the States permit their particularized capital punishment systems to be applied.

V

Having failed to establish a consensus against capital punishment for 16- and 17-year-old offenders through state and federal statutes and the behavior of prosecutors and juries, petitioners seek to demonstrate it through other indicia, including public opinion polls, the views of interest groups, and the positions adopted by various professional associations. We decline the invitation to rest constitutional law upon such uncertain foundations. A revised national consensus so broad, so clear, and so enduring as to justify a permanent prohibition upon all units of democratic government must appear in the operative acts (laws and the application of laws) that the people have approved.

We also reject petitioners' argument that we should invalidate capital punishment of 16- and 17-year-old offenders on the ground that it fails to serve the legitimate goals of penology. According to petitioners, it fails to deter because juveniles, possessing less developed cognitive skills than adults, are less likely to fear death; and it fails to exact just retribution because juveniles, being less mature and responsible, are also less morally blameworthy. In support of these claims, petitioners and their supporting amici marshal an array of socioscientific

No Individualized
Maturity Tests

evidence concerning the psychological and emotional development of 16- and 17-year-olds.

If such evidence could conclusively establish the entire lack of deterrent effect and moral responsibility, resort to the Cruel and Unusual Punishments Clause would be unnecessary; the Equal Protection Clause of the Fourteenth Amendment would invalidate these laws for lack of rational basis. See *Dallas v. Stanglin*, 490 U.S. 19 (1989). But as the adjective "socioscientific" suggests (and insofar as evaluation of moral responsibility is concerned perhaps the adjective "ethicoscientific" would be more apt), it is not demonstrable that no 16-year-old is "adequately responsible" or significantly deterred. It is rational, even if mistaken, to think the contrary. The battle must be fought, then, on the field of the Eighth Amendment; and in that struggle socioscientific, ethicoscientific, or even purely scientific evidence is not an available weapon. The punishment is either "cruel and unusual" (i.e., society has set its face against it) or it is not. The audience for these arguments, in other words, is not this Court but the citizenry of the United States. It is they, not we, who must be persuaded. For as we stated earlier, our job is to identify the "evolving standards of decency"; to determine, not what they should be, but what they are. We have no power under the Eighth Amendment to substitute our belief in the scientific evidence for the society's apparent skepticism. In short, we emphatically reject petitioner's suggestion that the issues in this case permit us to apply our "own informed judgment," Brief for Petitioner in No. 87-6026, p. 23, regarding the desirability of permitting the death penalty for crimes by 16- and 17-year-olds.

We reject the dissent's contention that our approach, by "largely return[ing] the task of defining the contours of Eighth Amendment protection to political majorities," leaves "'constitutional doctrine [to] be formulated by the acts of those institutions which the Constitution is supposed to limit,'" post, at 391, 392 [citation omitted]. When this Court cast loose from the historical moorings consisting of the original application of the Eighth Amendment, it did not embark rudderless upon a wide-open sea. Rather, it limited the Amendment's extension to those practices contrary to the "evolving standards of decency that mark the progress of a maturing society." *Trop v. Dulles*, 356 U.S., at 101 (plurality opinion) (emphasis added). It has never been thought that this was a shorthand reference to the preferences of a majority of this Court. By reaching a decision supported neither by constitutional text nor by the demonstrable current standards of our citizens, the dissent displays a failure to appreciate that "those institutions which the Constitution is supposed to limit" include the Court itself. To say, as the dissent says, that "'it is for us ultimately to judge whether the Eighth Amendment permits imposition of the death penalty,'" post, at 391 (emphasis added), quoting *Enmund v. Florida*, 458 U.S., at 797—and to mean that as the dissent means it, i.e., that it is for us to judge, not on the basis of what we perceive the Eighth Amendment originally prohibited, or on the basis of what we perceive the society through its democratic processes now overwhelmingly disapproves, but on the basis of what we think "proportionate" and "measurably contributory to acceptable goals of punishment"—to say and mean that, is to replace judges of the law with a committee of philosopher-kings.

While the dissent is correct that several of our cases have engaged in so-called "proportionality" analysis, examining whether "there is a disproportion 'between the punishment imposed and the defendant's blameworthiness,'" and whether a punishment makes any "measurable contribution to acceptable goals of punishment," see post, at 393, we have never invalidated a punishment on this basis alone. All of our cases condemning a punishment under this mode of analysis also found that the objective indicators of state laws or jury determinations evidenced a societal consensus against that penalty. See *Solem v. Helm*, 463 U.S., at 299–300; *Enmund v. Florida*, supra, at 789–796; *Coker v. Georgia*, 433

U.S., at 593–597 (plurality opinion). In fact, the two methodologies blend into one another, since "proportionality" analysis itself can only be conducted on the basis of the standards set by our own society; the only alternative, once again, would be our personal preferences.

* * *

We discern neither a historical nor a modern societal consensus forbidding the **imposition of capital punishment on any person who murders at 16 or 17 years of age**. Accordingly, we conclude that such punishment **does not offend the Eighth Amendment's prohibition against cruel and unusual punishment**.

The judgments of the Supreme Court of Kentucky and the Supreme Court of Missouri are therefore **Affirmed**.

Decision

CONCUR: JUSTICE O'CONNOR, concurring in part and concurring in the judgment.

Last Term, in *Thompson v. Oklahoma*, 487 U.S. 815, 857–858 (1988) (opinion concurring in judgment), I expressed the view that a criminal defendant who would have been tried as a juvenile under state law, but for the granting of a petition waiving juvenile court jurisdiction, may only be executed for a capital offense if the State's capital punishment statute specifies a minimum age at which the commission of a capital crime can lead to an offender's execution and the defendant had reached that minimum age at the time the crime was committed. As a threshold matter, I indicated that such specificity is not necessary to avoid constitutional problems if it is clear that no national consensus forbids the imposition of capital punishment for crimes committed at such an age. Id., at 857. Applying this two-part standard in *Thompson*, I concluded that Oklahoma's imposition of a death sentence on an individual who was 15 years old at the time he committed a capital offense should be set aside. Applying the same standard today, I conclude that the death sentences for capital murder imposed by Missouri and Kentucky on petitioners Wilkins and Stanford respectively should not be set aside because it is sufficiently clear that no national consensus forbids the imposition of capital punishment on 16- or 17-year-old capital murderers.

In *Thompson* I noted that "the most salient statistic that bears on this case is that every single American legislature that has expressly set a minimum age for capital punishment has set that age at 16 or above." Id., at 849. It is this difference between *Thompson* and these cases, more than any other, that convinces me there is no national consensus for bidding the imposition of capital punishment for crimes committed at the age of 16 and older. See ante, at 370–372. As the Court indicates, "a majority of the States that permit capital punishment authorize it for crimes committed at age 16 or above. . . ." Ante, at 371. Three States, including Kentucky, have specifically set the minimum age for capital punishment at 16, see Ind. Code § 35-50-2-3(b) (1988); Ky. Rev. Stat. Ann. § 640.040(1) (Baldwin 1987); Nev. Rev. Stat. § 176.025 (1987), and a fourth, Florida, clearly contemplates the imposition of capital punishment on 16-year-olds in its juvenile transfer statute, see Fla. Stat. § 39.02(5)(c) (1987). Under these circumstances, unlike the "peculiar circumstances" at work in *Thompson*, I do not think it necessary to require a state legislature to specify that the commission of a capital crime can lead to the execution of a 16- or 17-year-old offender. Because it is sufficiently clear that today no national consensus forbids the imposition of capital punishment in these circumstances, "the implicit nature of the [Missouri] Legislature's decision [is] not . . . constitutionally problematic." 487 U.S., at 857. This is true, a fortiori, in the case of Kentucky, which has specified 16 as the minimum age for the imposition of the death penalty. The day may come when there is such general legislative rejection of the execution of 16- or 17-year-old capital murderers that a clear national consensus can be said to have developed. Because I do not believe that day has yet arrived, I concur in Parts I, II, III, and IV-A of the Court's opinion, and I concur in its judgment.

I am unable, however, to join the remainder of the plurality's opinion for reasons I stated in *Thompson*. Part V of the plurality's opinion "emphatically reject[s]," ante, at 378, the suggestion that, beyond an assessment of the specific enactments of American legislatures, there remains a constitutional obligation imposed upon this Court to judge whether the " 'nexus between the punishment imposed and the defendant's blameworthiness' " is proportional. *Thompson*, supra, at 853, quoting *Enmund v. Florida*, 458 U.S. 782, 825 (1982) (O'CONNOR, J., dissenting). Part IV-B of the plurality's opinion specifically rejects as irrelevant to Eighth Amendment considerations state statutes that distinguish juveniles from adults for a variety of other purposes. In my view, this Court does have a constitutional obligation to conduct proportionality analysis. See *Penry v. Lynaugh*, ante, at 335–340; *Tison v. Arizona*, 481 U.S. 137, 155–158 (1987); *Enmund*, 458 U.S., at 797–801; id., at 825–826 (O'CONNOR, J., dissenting). In *Thompson* I specifically identified age-based statutory classifications as "relevant to Eighth Amendment proportionality analysis." 487 U.S., at 854 (opinion concurring in judgment). Thus, although I do not believe that these particular cases can be resolved through proportionality analysis, see *Thompson*, supra, at 853–854, I reject the suggestion that the use of such analysis is improper as a matter of Eighth Amendment jurisprudence. Accordingly, I join all but Parts IV-B and V of the Court's opinion.

DISSENT BY: BRENNAN

DISSENT: JUSTICE BRENNAN, with whom JUSTICE MARSHALL, JUSTICE BLACKMUN, and JUSTICE STEVENS join, dissenting.

Dissenting Opinions

I believe that to take the life of a person as punishment for a crime committed when below the age of 18 is cruel and unusual and hence is prohibited by the Eighth Amendment.

The method by which this Court assesses a claim that a punishment is unconstitutional because it is cruel and unusual is established by our precedents, and it bears little resemblance to the method four Members of the Court apply in this case. To be sure, we begin the task of deciding whether a punishment is unconstitutional by reviewing legislative enactments and the work of sentencing juries relating to the punishment in question to determine whether our Nation has set its face against a punishment to an extent that it can be concluded that the punishment offends our "evolving standards of decency." *Trop v. Dulles*, 356 U.S. 86, 101 (1958) (plurality opinion). The Court undertakes such an analysis in this case. Ante, at 370–373. But JUSTICE SCALIA, in his plurality opinion on this point, ante, at 374–380, would treat the Eighth Amendment inquiry as complete with this investigation. I agree with JUSTICE O'CONNOR, ante, at 382, that a more searching inquiry is mandated by our precedents interpreting the Cruel and Unusual Punishment Clause. In my view, that inquiry must in this case go beyond age-based statutory classifications relating to matters other than capital punishment, cf. ante, at 382 (O'CONNOR, J., concurring in part and concurring in judgment), and must also encompass what JUSTICE SCALIA calls, with evident but misplaced disdain, "ethicoscientific" evidence. Only then can we be in a position to judge, as our cases require, whether a punishment is unconstitutionally excessive, either because it is disproportionate given the culpability of the offender, or because it serves no legitimate penal goal.

I

Our judgment about the constitutionality of a punishment under the Eighth Amendment is informed, though not determined, see infra, at 391, by an examination of contemporary attitudes toward the punishment, as evidenced in the actions of legislatures and of juries. *McCleskey v. Kemp*, 481 U.S. 279, 300 (1987); *Coker v. Georgia*, 433 U.S. 584, 592 (1977) (plurality opinion). The views of organizations with expertise in relevant fields and the choices of governments elsewhere in the world also merit our attention as indicators whether a punishment is acceptable in a civilized society.

Expert Organizations, World Governments

A

The Court's discussion of state laws concerning capital sentencing, ante, at 370–372, gives a distorted view of the evidence of contemporary standards that these legislative determinations provide. Currently, 12 of the States whose statutes permit capital punishment specifically mandate that offenders under age 18 not be sentenced to death. Ante, at 370–371. When one adds to these 12 States the 15 (including the District of Columbia) in which capital punishment is not authorized at all, it appears that the governments in fully 27 of the States have concluded that no one under 18 should face the death penalty. A further three States explicitly refuse to authorize sentences of death for those who committed their offense when under 17, ante, at 370, making a total of 30 States that would not tolerate the execution of petitioner Wilkins. Congress' most recent enactment of a death penalty statute also excludes those under 18. Pub. L. 100–690, § 7001(1), 102 Stat. 4390, 21 U.S.C. § 848(1) (1988 ed.).

Twelve states forbid capital punishment under age 18.

Total of 30 states would not execute Wilkins.

In 19 States that have a death penalty, no minimum age for capital sentences is set in the death penalty statute. See *Thompson v. Oklahoma*, 487 U.S. 815, 826–827, and n. 26 (1988), and n. 1, supra. The notion that these States have consciously authorized the execution of juveniles derives from the congruence in those jurisdictions of laws permitting state courts to hand down death sentences, on the one hand, and, on the other, statutes permitting the transfer of offenders under 18 from the juvenile to state court systems for trial in certain circumstances. See *Thompson*, supra, at 867–868, and n. 3 (SCALIA, J., dissenting). I would not assume, however, in considering how the States stand on the moral issue that underlies the constitutional question with which we are presented, that a legislature that has never specifically considered the issue has made a conscious moral choice to permit the execution of juveniles. See 487 U.S., at 826–827, n. 24 (plurality opinion). On a matter of such moment that most States have expressed an explicit and contrary judgment, the decisions of legislatures that are only implicit, and that lack the "earmarks of careful consideration that we have required for other kinds of decisions leading to the death penalty," id., at 857 (O'CONNOR, J., concurring in judgment), must count for little. I do not suggest, of course, that laws of these States cut against the constitutionality of the juvenile death penalty—only that accuracy demands that the baseline for our deliberations should be that 27 States refuse to authorize a sentence of death in the circumstances of petitioner Stanford's case, and 30 would not permit Wilkins' execution; that 19 States have not squarely faced the question; and that only the few remaining jurisdictions have explicitly set an age below 18 at which a person may be sentenced to death.

B

... Adolescent offenders make up only a small proportion of the current death-row population: 30 out of a total of 2,186 inmates, or 1.37 percent. NAACP Legal

Only 1.37 percent of death row inmates are youths.

Defense and Educational Fund, Inc. (LDF), Death Row, U.S.A. (Mar. 1, 1989). Eleven minors were sentenced to die in 1982; 9 in 1983; 6 in 1984; 5 in 1985; 7 in 1986; and 2 in 1987. App. N to Brief for the Office of the Capital Collateral Representative for the State of Florida as Amicus Curiae (hereafter OCCR Brief). Forty-one, or 2.3 percent, of the 1,813 death sentences imposed between January 1, 1982, and June 30, 1988, were for juvenile crimes. Id., at 15, and App. R. And juvenile offenders are significantly less likely to receive the death penalty than adults. During the same period, there were 97,086 arrests of adults for homicide, and 1,772 adult death sentences, or 1.8 percent; and 8,911 arrests of minors for homicide, compared to 41 juvenile death sentences, or 0.5 percent. Ibid., and Apps. Q and R. . . .

C

American Bar
Association

National Council of
Juvenile and Family
Court Judges

Further indicators of contemporary standards of decency that should inform our consideration of the Eighth Amendment question are the opinions of respected organizations. *Thompson*, 487 U.S., at 830 (plurality opinion). Where organizations with expertise in a relevant area have given careful consideration to the question of a punishment's appropriateness, there is no reason why that judgment should not be entitled to attention as an indicator of contemporary standards. There is no dearth of opinion from such groups that the state-sanctioned killing of minors is unjustified. A number, indeed, have filed briefs amicus curiae in these cases, in support of petitioners. The American Bar Association has adopted a resolution opposing the imposition of capital punishment upon any person for an offense committed while under age 18, as has the National Council of Juvenile and Family Court Judges. The American Law Institute's Model Penal Code similarly includes a lower age limit of 18 for the death sentence. And the National Commission on Reform of the Federal Criminal Laws also recommended that 18 be the minimum age.

Our cases recognize that objective indicators of contemporary standards of decency in the form of legislation in other countries is also of relevance to Eighth Amendment analysis. *Thompson*, supra, at 830–831; *Enmund*, 458 U.S., at 796, n. 22; *Coker*, 433 U.S., at 596, *Trop v. Dulles*, 356 U.S., at 102, and n. 35. Many countries, of course—over 50, including nearly all in Western Europe—have formally abolished the death penalty, or have limited its use to exceptional crimes such as treason. App. to Brief for Amnesty International as Amicus Curiae. Twenty-seven others do not in practice impose the penalty. Ibid. Of the nations that retain capital punishment, a majority—65—prohibit the execution of juveniles. Ibid. Sixty-one countries retain capital punishment and have no statutory provision exempting juveniles, though some of these nations are ratifiers of international treaties that do prohibit the execution of juveniles. Ibid. Since 1979, Amnesty International has recorded only eight executions of offenders under 18 throughout the world, three of these in the United States. The other five executions were carried out in Pakistan, Bangladesh, Rwanda, and Barbados. In addition to national laws, three leading human rights treaties ratified or signed by the United States explicitly prohibit juvenile death penalties. Within the world community, the imposition of the death penalty for juvenile crimes appears to be overwhelmingly disapproved. . . .

III

There can be no doubt at this point in our constitutional history that the Eighth Amendment forbids punishment that is wholly disproportionate to the blameworthiness of the offender. "The constitutional principle of proportionality has been recognized explicitly in this Court for almost a century." *Solem v. Helm*, 463 U.S. 277, 286 (1983). Usually formulated as a requirement that sentences not be "disproportionate to the crime committed," id., at 284; see, e.g., *Weems v. United*

States, 217 U.S. 349 (1910); *O'Neil v. Vermont*, 144 U.S. 323, 339–340 (1892) (Field, J., dissenting), the proportionality principle takes account not only of the "injury to the person and to the public" caused by a crime, but also of the "moral depravity" of the offender. *Coker*, supra, at 598. The offender's culpability for his criminal acts—"the degree of the defendant's blameworthiness," *Enmund*, supra, at 815 (O'CONNOR, J., dissenting); see also id., at 798 (opinion of the Court)—is thus of central importance to the constitutionality of the sentence imposed. Indeed, this focus on a defendant's blameworthiness runs throughout our constitutional jurisprudence relating to capital sentencing. See, e.g., *Booth v. Maryland*, 482 U.S. 496, 502 (1987) (striking down state statute requiring consideration by sentencer of evidence other than defendant's record and characteristics and the circumstances of the crime, which had no "bearing on the defendant's 'personal responsibility and moral guilt'"); *California v. Brown*, 479 U.S. 538, 545 (1987) (an "emphasis on culpability in sentencing decisions has long been reflected in Anglo-American jurisprudence. . . . Lockett and Eddings reflect the belief that punishment should be directly related to the personal culpability of the criminal defendant") (O'CONNOR, J., concurring).

Proportionality analysis requires that we compare "the gravity of the offense," understood to include not only the injury caused, but also the defendant's culpability, with "the harshness of the penalty." *Solem*, supra, at 292. In my view, juveniles so generally lack the degree of responsibility for their crimes that is a predicate for the constitutional imposition of the death penalty that the Eighth Amendment forbids that they receive that punishment.

Proportionality Analysis
Defined

A

Legislative determinations distinguishing juveniles from adults abound. These age-based classifications reveal much about how our society regards juveniles as a class, and about societal beliefs regarding adolescent levels of responsibility. See *Thompson*, 487 U.S., at 823–825 (plurality opinion).

The participation of juveniles in a substantial number of activities open to adults is either barred completely or significantly restricted by legislation. All States but two have a uniform age of majority, and have set that age at 18 or above. OCCR Brief, App. A. No State has lowered its voting age below 18. Id., App. C; see *Thompson*, supra, at 839, App. A. Nor does any State permit a person under 18 to serve on a jury. OCCR Brief, App. B; see *Thompson*, supra, at 840, App. B. Only four States ever permit persons below 18 to marry without parental consent. OCCR Brief, App. D; see *Thompson*, supra, at 843, App. D. Thirty-seven States have specific enactments requiring that a patient have attained 18 before she may validly consent to medical treatment. OCCR Brief, App. E. Thirty-four States require parental consent before a person below 18 may drive a motor car. Id., App. F; see *Thompson*, supra, at 842, App. C. Legislation in 42 States prohibits those under 18 from purchasing pornographic materials. OCCR Brief, App. G; see *Thompson*, supra, at 845, App. E. Where gambling is legal, adolescents under 18 are generally not permitted to participate in it, in some or all of its forms. OCCR Brief, App. H; see *Thompson*, supra, at 847, App. F. In these and a host of other ways, minors are treated differently from adults in our laws, which reflects the simple truth derived from communal experience that juveniles as a class have not the level of maturation and responsibility that we presume in adults and consider desirable for full participation in the rights and duties of modern life.

. . . Moreover, the very paternalism that our society shows toward youths and the dependency it forces upon them mean that society bears a responsibility for the actions of juveniles that it does not for the actions of adults who are at least theoretically free to make their own choices: "youth crime . . . is not exclusively the offender's fault; offenses by the young represent a failure of family, school, and the social system, which share responsibility for the development of America's youth." Task Force 7.

Developmental Stages of Children

To be sure, the development of cognitive and reasoning abilities and of empathy, the acquisition of experience upon which these abilities operate and upon which the capacity to make sound value judgments depends, and in general the process of maturation into a self-directed individual fully responsible for his or her actions, occur by degrees. See, e.g., G. Manaster, Adolescent Development and the Life Tasks (1977). But the factors discussed above indicate that 18 is the dividing line that society has generally drawn, the point at which it is thought reasonable to assume that persons have an ability to make, and a duty to bear responsibility for, their, judgments. Insofar as age 18 is a necessarily arbitrary social choice as a point at which to acknowledge a person's maturity and responsibility, given the different developmental rates of individuals, it is in fact "a conservative estimate of the dividing line between adolescence and adulthood. Many of the psychological and emotional changes that an adolescent experiences in maturing do not actually occur until the early 20s." Brief for American Society for Adolescent Psychiatry et al. as Amici Curiae 4 (citing social scientific studies).

B

There may be exceptional individuals who mature more quickly than their peers, and who might be considered fully responsible for their actions prior to the age of 18, despite their lack of the experience upon which judgment depends. In my view, however, it is not sufficient to accommodate the facts about juveniles that an individual youth's culpability may be taken into account in the decision to transfer him or her from the juvenile to the adult court system for trial, or that a capital sentencing jury is instructed to consider youth and other mitigating factors. I believe that the Eighth Amendment requires that a person who lacks that full degree of responsibility for his or her actions associated with adulthood not be sentenced to death. Hence it is constitutionally inadequate that a juvenile offender's level of responsibility be taken into account only along with a host of other factors that the court or jury may decide outweigh that want of responsibility.

Immaturity that constitutionally should operate as a bar to a disproportionate death sentence does not guarantee that a minor will not be transferred for trial to the adult court system. Rather, the most important considerations in the decision to transfer a juvenile offender are the seriousness of the offense, the extent of prior delinquency, and the response to prior treatment within the juvenile justice system. National Institute for Juvenile Justice and Delinquency, United States Dept. of Justice, Major Issues in Juvenile Justice Information and Training, Youth in Adult Courts: Between Two Worlds 211 (1982). Psychological, intellectual, and other personal characteristics of juvenile offenders receive little attention at the transfer stage, and cannot account for differences between those transferred and those who remain in the juvenile court system. See Solway, Hays, Schreiner, & Cansler, Clinical Study of Youths Petitioned for Certification as Adults, 46 Psychological Rep. 1067 (1980). Nor is an adolescent's lack of full culpability isolated at the sentencing stage as a factor that determinatively bars a death sentence. A jury is free to weigh a juvenile offender's youth and lack of full responsibility against the heinousness of the crime and other aggravating factors—and, finding the aggravating factors weightier, to sentence even the most immature of 16- or 17-year-olds to be killed. By no stretch of the imagination, then, are the transfer and sentencing decisions designed to isolate those juvenile offenders who are exceptionally mature and responsible, and who thus stand out from their peers as a class.

It is thus unsurprising that individualized consideration at transfer and sentencing has not in fact ensured that juvenile offenders lacking an adult's culpability are not sentenced to die. Quite the contrary. Adolescents on death row appear typically to have a battery of psychological, emotional, and other problems going to their likely capacity for judgment and level of blameworthiness. A recent diagnostic evaluation of all 14 juveniles on death rows in four States is instructive. Lewis et al., Neuropsychiatric, Psychoeducational, and Family Characteristics of 14 Juveniles Condemned to Death in the United States, 145 Am. J. Psychiatry 584 (1988). Seven of the adolescents sentenced to die were psychotic when evaluated, or had been so diagnosed in earlier childhood; four others had histories consistent with diagnoses of severe mood disorders; and the remaining three experienced periodic paranoid episodes, during which they would assault perceived enemies. Id., at 585, and Table 3. Eight had suffered severe head injuries during childhood, id., at 585, and Table 1, and nine suffered from neurological abnormalities, id., at 585, and Table 2. Psychoeducational testing showed that only 2 of these death-row inmates had IQ scores above 90 (that is, in the normal range)—and both individuals suffered from psychiatric disorders—while 10 offenders showed impaired abstract reasoning on at least some tests. Id., at 585–586, and Table 3 and 4. All but two of the adolescents had been physically abused, and five sexually abused. Id., at 586–587, and Table 5. Within the families of these children, violence, alcoholism, drug abuse, and psychiatric disorders were commonplace. Id., at 587, and Table 5.

Failure of Our Society to Identify and Early Treat These Individuals on Death Row

The cases under consideration today certainly do not suggest that individualized consideration at transfer and sentencing ensure that only exceptionally mature juveniles, as blameworthy for their crimes as an adult, are sentenced to death. Transferring jurisdiction over Kevin Stanford to Circuit Court, the Juvenile Division of the Jefferson, Kentucky, District Court nevertheless found that Stanford, who was 17 at the time of his crime, "has a low internalization of the values and morals of society and lacks social skills. That he does possess an institutionalized personality and has, in effect, because of his chaotic family life and lack of treatment, become socialized in delinquent behavior. That he is emotionally immature and could be amenable to treatment if properly done on a long term basis of psychotherapeutic intervention and reality based therapy for socialization and drug therapy in a residential facility." App. in No. 87-5765, p. 9.

At the penalty phase of Stanford's trial, witnesses testified that Stanford, who lived with various relatives, had used drugs from the age of about 13, and that his drug use had caused changes in his personality and behavior. 10 Record in No. 87-5765, pp. 1383–1392, 1432. Stanford had been placed at times in juvenile treatment facilities, and a witness who had assessed him upon his admission to an employment skills project found that he lacked age-appropriate social interaction skills; had a history of drug abuse; and wanted for family support or supervision. Id., at 1408; see also id., at 1440–1442.

Heath Wilkins was 16 when he committed the crime for which Missouri intends to kill him. The juvenile court, in ordering him transferred for trial to adult court, focused upon the viciousness of Wilkins' crime, the juvenile system's inability to rehabilitate him in the 17 months of juvenile confinement available, and the need to protect the public, though it also mentioned that Wilkins was, in its view, "an experienced person, and mature in his appearance and habits." App. in No. 87-6026, p. 5. The Circuit Court found Wilkins competent to stand trial. Record in No. 87-6026, p. 42. Wilkins then waived counsel, with the avowed intention of pleading guilty and seeking the death penalty, id., at 42, 55, and the Circuit Court accepted the waiver, id., at 84, and later Wilkins' guilty plea, id., at 144–145. Wilkins was not represented by counsel at sentencing. See id., at 188–190. Presenting no mitigating evidence, he told the court he would prefer

If the youth was incompetent to waive his rights, then is Wilkins really mature enough for death?

the death penalty to life in prison, id., at 186–187—"one I fear, the other one I don't," id., at 295—and after hearing evidence from the State, the Court sentenced Wilkins to die. Wilkins took no steps to appeal and objected to an amicus' efforts on his behalf. The Missouri Supreme Court, however, ordered an evaluation to determine whether Wilkins was competent to waive his right to appellate counsel. Concluding that Wilkins was incompetent to waive his rights, the state-appointed forensic psychiatrist found that Wilkins "suffers from a mental disorder" that affects his "reasoning and impairs his behavior." App. in No. 87-6026, p. 74. It would be incredible to suppose, given this psychiatrist's conclusion and his summary of Wilkins' past, that Missouri's transfer and sentencing schemes had operated to identify in Wilkins a 16-year-old mature and culpable beyond his years.

Juveniles very generally lack that degree of blameworthiness that is, in my view, a constitutional prerequisite for the imposition of capital punishment under our precedents concerning the Eighth Amendment proportionality principle. The individualized consideration of an offender's youth and culpability at the transfer stage and at sentencing has not operated to ensure that the only offenders under 18 singled out for the ultimate penalty are exceptional individuals whose level of responsibility is more developed than that of their peers. In that circumstance, I believe that the same categorical assumption that juveniles as a class are insufficiently mature to be regarded as fully responsible that we make in so many other areas is appropriately made in determining whether minors may be subjected to the death penalty. As we noted in *Thompson*, 487 U.S., at 825–826, it would be ironic if the assumptions we so readily make about minors as a class were suddenly unavailable in conducting proportionality analysis. I would hold that the Eighth Amendment prohibits the execution of any person for a crime committed below the age of 18.

IV

Under a second strand of Eighth Amendment inquiry into whether a particular sentence is excessive and hence unconstitutional, we ask whether the sentence makes a measurable contribution to acceptable goals of punishment. *Thompson*, supra, at 833; *Enmund v. Florida*, 458 U.S., at 798; *Coker v. Georgia*, 433 U.S., at 592; *Gregg v. Georgia*, 428 U.S., at 173. The two "principal social purposes" of capital punishment are said to be "retribution and the deterrence of capital crimes by prospective offenders." *Gregg*, supra, at 183; see *Enmund*, supra, at 798. Unless the death penalty applied to persons for offenses committed under 18 measurably contributes to one of these goals, the Eighth Amendment prohibits it. See ibid.

"Retribution as a justification for executing [offenders] very much depends on the degree of [their] culpability." Id., at 800. I have explained in Part III, supra, why I believe juveniles lack the culpability that makes a crime so extreme that it may warrant, according to this Court's cases, the death penalty; and why we should treat juveniles as a class as exempt from the ultimate penalty. These same considerations persuade me that executing juveniles "does not measurably contribute to the retributive end of ensuring that the criminal gets his just deserts." Id., at 801. See *Thompson*, supra, at 836–837. A punishment that fails the Eighth Amendment test of proportionality because disproportionate to the offender's blameworthiness by definition is not justly deserved.

Nor does the execution of juvenile offenders measurably contribute to the goal of deterrence. Excluding juveniles from the class of persons eligible to receive the death penalty will have little effect on any deterrent value capital punishment may have for potential offenders who are over 18: these adult offenders may of course remain eligible for a death sentence. The potential deterrent effect of juvenile executions on adolescent offenders is also insignificant. The deterrent value of capital punishment rests "on the assumption that we are rational beings who always think before we act, and then base our actions on a careful calculation of the gains and losses involved." Gardiner, The Purposes of Criminal Punishment, 21 Mod. L. Rev. 117, 122 (1958).

As the plurality noted in *Thompson*, supra, at 837, "the likelihood that the teenage offender has made the kind of cost-benefit analysis that attaches any weight to the possibility of execution is so remote as to be virtually nonexistent." First, juveniles "have less capacity . . . to think in long-range terms than adults," Task Force 7, and their careful weighing of a distant, uncertain, and indeed highly unlikely consequence prior to action is most improbable. In addition, juveniles have little fear of death, because they have "a profound conviction of their own omnipotence and immortality." Miller, Adolescent Suicide: Etiology and Treatment, in 9 Adolescent Psychiatry 327, 329 (S. Feinstein, J. Looney, A. Schwartzberg, & A. Sorosky eds. 1981). See also, e.g., Gordon, The Tattered Cloak of Immortality, in Adolescence and Death 16, 27 (C. Corr & J. McNeil eds. 1986) (noting prevalence of adolescent risk taking); Brief for American Society for Adolescent Psychiatry et al. as Amici Curiae 5–6 (citing research). Because imposition of the death penalty on persons for offenses committed under the age of 18 makes no measurable contribution to the goals of either retribution or deterrence, it is "nothing more than the purposeless and needless imposition of pain and suffering," *Coker*, supra, at 592, and is thus excessive and unconstitutional.

V

There are strong indications that the execution of juvenile offenders violates contemporary standards of decency: a majority of States decline to permit juveniles to be sentenced to death; imposition of the sentence upon minors is very unusual even in those States that permit it; and respected organizations with expertise in relevant areas regard the execution of juveniles as unacceptable, as does international opinion. These indicators serve to confirm in my view my conclusion that the Eighth Amendment prohibits the execution of persons for offenses they committed while below the age of 18, because the death penalty is disproportionate when applied to such young offenders and fails measurably to serve the goals of capital punishment. I dissent.

> Summary of All the Reasons

1. Footnote no. 14 said the following about Wilkins' past:
   "Mr. Wilkins . . . was raised in a rather poor socioeconomic environment [and] reportedly had extremely chaotic upbringing during his childhood. He was physically abused by his mother, sometimes the beatings would last for two hours. . . . As a child, he started robbing houses for knives and money and loved to set fires. Mr. Wilkins' mother worked at night and slept during the day, thus the children were left alone at night by themselves. He claims that he was started on drugs by his uncle [at age six]. Apparently he used to shoot BB guns at passing cars. Mr. Wilkins indicated that his mother's boyfriend had a quick temper and that he hated him. He also started disliking his mother, not only because she punished [him], but also because she stood up for her boyfriend who was unkind towards [him]. He then decided to poison his mother and boyfriend by placing rat poison in Tylenol capsules. They were informed by his brother about the situation. They secretly emptied the capsules and made him eat them. He was afraid of death and attempted vomiting by placing [his] fingers in his throat. Then he ended up getting a beating from his mother and boyfriend. At the age of ten, Mr. Wilkins

> **NOTES AFTER STANFORD**

was evaluated at Tri-County Mental Health Center and Western Missouri Mental Health Center. He stayed there for a period of six months. He was then sent to Butterfield Youth's Home and then to East Range, a residential facility for boys. He started using drugs quite heavily. . . . He also started drinking hard liquor. . . .

"At Butterfield, he was very angry at the teachers because they considered him to be 'dumb.' He showed rather strange behavior there. When he became depressed he would dance with a net over his head. On another occasion he cut his wrist and claimed to have had frequent thoughts of suicide. Prior to going to Butterfield, he had jumped off a bridge but the car swerved before he was hit. At Butterfield, he attempted to overdose with alcohol and drugs and another time with antipsychotic medication, Mellaril. Mr. Wilkins was placed on Mellaril because he was 'too active.' . . . for three and one half years between the ages of 10 through 13½. After that, he was transferred to Crittenton Center since it was closer to his mother's residence. He stayed there only for four or five months and was then kicked out. The court gave him permission to go home on probation. At this time his mother had started seeing another boyfriend and Mr. Wilkins apparently liked him. He continued the usage of alcohol and drugs while at school, continued to break into houses stealing money, jewelry, and knives, and generally stole money to spend at the arcade. On one occasion he ran away to Southern California. He was introduced to amphetamines there and spent all his money. . . . After his return [home, he] was charged with a stolen knife and was sent to [a] Detention Center. . . . At age 15, he was sent to the Northwest Regional Youth Services in Kansas City. There, an attempt at prescribing Thorazine (major tranquilizer) was made. After this, Mr. Wilkins was placed in a foster home. He ran away from the foster home. . . . Beginning in May of 1985 he lived on the streets. . . .

"Records from Butterfield . . . indicated that Mr. Wilkins' natural father was committed to a mental institution in Arkansas, and there was considerable amount of physical abuse that existed in the family. . . . In the educational testing, he gave rather unusual responses. For example, when asked the reasons why we need policemen, he replied, 'To get rid of people like me.' He also revealed plans to blow up a large building in Kansas City [and] made bizarre derogatory sexual comments towards women prior to visits with his mother. He had episodes of hyperventilation and passed out by fainting or chest squeezing. . . . On one occasion in September of 1981, he put gasoline into a toilet and set fire to it, causing an explosion. Mr. Wilkins' brother was diagnosed to be suffering from schizophrenia when he was admitted along with Mr. Wilkins in 1982 at Crittenton Center. Mr. Wilkins was often noticed to be fantasizing about outer space and supernatural powers. In the fall of 1982, [the Crittenton psychiatrist] recommended placement on Mellaril because of a 'disoriented thinking pattern and high anxiety.' In 1983, his condition started deteriorating. . . . His final diagnoses in November of 1983 when he was discharged from Crittenton were Borderline Personality and Passive-Aggressive Personality. Psychological testing at Crittenton indicated isolated episodes of paranoid functioning."

2. Prosecutors argue that this murder of Wilkins was premeditated, that is, "a dead person can't talk." They are not mistakes of youth but planned acts of heinous violence. Wilkins was in fact six months short of majority in Missouri. In *Wilkins v. Bowersox*, 933 F. Supp. 1496; 1996 U.S. Dist. Lexis 15970 (1996), the court permitted a writ of habeas corpus for Wilkins from the state correctional facility because there was substantial

and injurious error on the outcome. The court found it "incredulous to imagine a former defense attorney, privy at one time to the thoughts of a juvenile defendant so disturbed that he is committed to a mental institution, to then turn prosecutor and accuser seeking the death penalty for his former client without disclosing the relationship to the court and to counsel. This is particularly disturbing in this case because petitioner waived counsel, entered a guilty plea to a capital charge, waived mitigation and was sentenced to death" (p. 1523). The serious student might want to find out what really happened to Heath A. Wilkins.

3. Age, maturity, and chances for rehabilitation are considered as mitigating factors. How amenable to treatment is someone whose heart is so cold that he or she murders?

4. Since 1642 to "the 1990s, approximately 285 juveniles (that is, under the age of eighteen) have been lawfully executed in the United States. The youngest person to be executed in the United States was ten years old; however, the vast majority have been over the age of fourteen" (Forst 1995, 281). Despite thousands of convictions of juveniles for capital offenses, today there are only 32 juveniles on death row out of a total population of some 1,800 (Scott 1990, 852). Under what conditions and ages would you be willing to permit capital punishment?

5. Between 1973 and 1991, there were only 91 cases in which a juvenile under the age of 18 years has been sentenced to death. The word "trouble" provides a convenient umbrella for a variety of problems ranging from physical abuse to an unstable childhood. See Robinson, "Patterns of Mitigating Factors in Juvenile Death Penalty Cases," *Criminal Law Bulletin*, 28 (1992):246–259. Bard, Feldman, Lewis, Pincus, Prichep, Richardson, and Yeager (1988) did comprehensive assessment on approximately 40 percent of 37 juveniles waiting execution and found eight subjects had head injuries that were severe enough to result in hospitalization, and/or indentation of the cranium, 9 subjects were documented with serious neurological abnormalities, 4 had histories consistent with diagnoses of severe mood disorders, and 3 experienced paranoid ideation.

6. In terms of the fact that the United States is one of the few nations that permits the execution of offenders, some citizens in Cincinnati and Columbus, Ohio, through telephone surveys, were found to have an inverse relationship between belief in the effectiveness of rehabilitation programs and support for the death penalty. Respondents who expressed greater belief in the effectiveness of rehabilitation programs were less likely to support the juvenile death penalty (Skovron, Scott, and Cullen 1989).

7. This case shows the controversy over children's rights. One camp believes that children lack the capacity to care for themselves or make effective independent decisions. For these children, people argue for more positive or protective rights and immunities. Others believe that the protectionists' assumptions are masks for paternalism. This second group believes that children can decide just as well as adults what is in their best interest. The second group believes children should be granted more liberties and power rights. A legal brief drafted by the American Civil Liberties Union (ACLU) for the U.S. Supreme Court appeal of a 15-year-old killer (*Thompson v. Oklahoma*, 487 U.S. 815 [1988]) argued that persons under 18 should not be given the death penalty because they lack the capacity to make rational decisions about committing capital

offenses. (As in this case of *Stanford*, the argument is that he really could not have made a rational decision; it was more impulsive.) At the same time the ACLU was working on the draft for *Thompson*, another group of lawyers within the ACLU were arguing abortion rights cases before the Court and saying that teenage girls do have the capacity to make rational decisions to have abortions. After failing to reconcile the two positions, the ACLU declined to file a brief in *Thompson* (Stafford 1995, 123–124).

The controversy for the ACLU is also a controversy for our society. Is there any middle ground? Are there situations where a person in the past was acting "impulsively" but now is more rational?

Adjudication

Equal to Trial Stage in
Adult Criminal Court

The adjudication hearing in juvenile court is equal to the trial stage in the adult criminal court. It is a trial on the merits. We will discuss it in terms of purpose, decision-maker, rights, standard of proof, and role of attorney.

Purpose

The purpose of adjudication is to have a hearing and determine if the youth did commit the act for which she or he is charged. This is similar to the trial stage for adults. The attorney for the state is called the *commonwealth attorney* in Virginia and Kentucky, but the *prosecuting attorney, state's attorney*, or *district attorney* in other states. The prosecuting attorney represents the state. His or her job is to prove the case to the judge. The defense attorney defends the youth. The defense attorney may be obtained by the youth, may be appointed by the state, or may be part of a public defender's office.

The police officer and any other complainants and/or witnesses for either the state or the defense also will be present at the hearing to give their testimony. All will be sworn to tell the truth, for it is a fact-finding hearing.

If the child does not appear in court on the scheduled date, she or he can be found in "contempt of court." "Contempt of court" is a crime and can be added to the charges the youth already faces. If there is a valid reason for not appearing, such as illness or a death in the family, the youth is supposed to notify the attorney and the court for permission to postpone the case. Only the court can postpone the date.

There are also time limitations for this hearing. In New York, for example, the hearing had not commenced within the sixty-day time limit set by the Family Court Act; thus the petition had to be dismissed (*Matter of Shannon FF*, 596 N.Y.S.2d 219 [N.Y. Sup. App. Div. April 1993]).

As mentioned earlier when discussing intake, the actual time limit varies from state to state. All states usually start the clock running from the juvenile's initial appearance on the first petition filed.

Decision-Maker

Judge

The judge makes the decision based upon hearing all the facts of the case. It is the judge's responsibility to determine whether the youth is guilty or not.

In *Matter of Herbert TT*, 597 N.Y.S.2d 194 (N.Y. Sup. App. Div. April 1993), the record clearly showed that the Family Court judge failed to advise the juvenile of his right to a fact-finding hearing. In addition, the judge failed to ascertain from the juvenile, his mother, or his law guardian whether the juvenile had actually committed the acts to which he was admitting. Therefore, the order of disposition was reversed and remanded.

If found not guilty or the charges cannot be proven beyond a reasonable doubt, the youth will be free to go. The youth will be released unless, of course, she or he has other pending charges. If found not innocent (guilty), the judge will request an investigation by the probation officer. The probation officer will write a social history report (see example in Chapter 2) containing information about the child's family, friends, health, neighborhood, religion, and school progress. The officer of the court may include other information that would help the judge and staff working with the family and the youth to make an informed and appropriate decision. The information in the social history is confidential. This information will be used to assist the judge in the disposition stage.

Thus, after a guilty or not innocent verdict, the judge will set the date for the dispositional hearing. The judge may detain the youth in detention depending upon the facts of the case and the likelihood of the youth running away or committing another offense.

Social History Report

Rights

After the petition has been filed, the court shall direct the issuance of summonses. One goes to the child if he or she is age 12 or over and others to the parent(s) or guardian(s) and any other such persons as appear to be proper and necessary to the court. The summons requires the person(s) named to appear personally before the court at the fixed time and to answer or testify with regard to the allegation in the petition.

The summonses advise the parties of their right to counsel, and a copy of the petition for the initial proceedings accompanies each summons. Notice of subsequent proceedings will be provided to all parties. Service of notice to an attorney representing a party is sufficient to constitute notice to the party unless the attorney has notified the court that s/he no longer represents that party. These summonses are at the heart of notice. They are mandatory and must be followed or waived in a proper manner.

The juvenile has all the rights resulting from *In re Gault*: the right to have an attorney present at the hearing, to confront and cross-examine the witness, and to refrain from being a witness against him- or herself. There are no jury rights under *McKeiver v. Pa.* (See Chapter 1 for greater detail and briefs of these cases.)

Waiver of an attorney can only be done if the youth had the opportunity to consult with an interested adult or waived rights knowingly and willingly ("totality of the circumstances" test). *In re J.B.*, 618 A.2d 1329 (Vt. Sup. Nov. 1992), the Supreme Court reversed the adjudication of delinquency because the juvenile was denied effective assistance of counsel. Under the Vermont Constitution, the juvenile must be given the opportunity to consult with an adult, and the adult must be one who is generally interested in the welfare of the juvenile and completely independent from and disassociated with the prosecution. The independent interested adult must be informed and be aware of the rights guaranteed to the juvenile. In this case the juvenile's attorney indicated that he did not provide the juvenile or his parents

Waiver of Attorney; Totality of Circumstances; Interested Adult Test

with any meaningful consultation before waiving the juvenile's right to remain silent.

The U.S. Supreme Court developed the concept of "effectiveness of legal counsel" when it stated that the necessity of counsel was so vital and imperative that the failure to make effective appointment of counsel was a denial of due process. The scope of the right to counsel was redefined to include the class of defendants who are financially unable to retain legal counsel. As a result, nearly half of all persons accused of a crime in the United States each year are represented by indigent counsel. This enormous caseload fosters the question of whether clients of indigent counsel (adults) are receiving effective assistance of counsel (Hanson et al. 1992; Krantz 1979).

Only more recently has attention been given to the juvenile. Federal and state courts, various levels of government charged with providing defense services, and professional groups such as the American Bar Association (ABA) (1986) are struggling with the development of principles and training for attornies for effective counsel. Some critics believe that the role of attorney is more important at intake because there is a better chance to get a better result. Regardless of the stage, many parents and youth waive their rights to an attorney, especially ethnic and minority youth. Future research will give us greater insight as to why this is done.

Standard of Proof

Beyond a Reasonable Doubt

According to *In re Winship*, the youth is to be judged according to the highest standard of proof. The highest standard is proof beyond a reasonable doubt. It is the same standard used in the adult criminal court trial stage.

Role of Attorney

The role of the attorney is crucial in the adjudicatory hearing. The only way a **waiver of an attorney** can be given is if it is **done with the advice of an interested adult or the "totality of the circumstances" test. Totality of the circumstances test** means that the waiver was done knowingly and willingly, given all the surrounding circumstances. One young, frustrated woman, when asked if she wanted to waive her son's right to an attorney, said, "Your honor, no one but Jesus could help that kid!" With that statement, the judge waived the right and she signed the papers. Yet, her son needed an attorney because he had no "interested" adult—only one worn-out mother!

The role of the attorney is especially confusing when representing a child who is in conflict with her or his parent or parents. It is not easy if the parents are overwhelmed and feel frustrated. These adults are normally the ones who make decisions regarding the child and may even pay for the services of the attorney.

Canon 5 of the **Code of Professional Responsibility** states that a lawyer should exercise independent professional judgment on behalf of a client. This is more difficult when the child is the client and the parent(s) are paying the fee.

The effective representation of a child in any court proceeding may require different skills and more intensive efforts than with adults. For example, the attorney may have to spend more quality time with a child client to gain the client's trust and confidence. In addition, the attorney will have to be far more explicit in describing the attorney's role and ethical obligations to a child. It may be to the attorney's advantage to have some understanding of children's developmental stages and the way children deal with life and their stresses. It also would be important for the attorney to know what other social agencies exist so that the attorney can justly represent the needs of the child, adequately defending the child against unjust punishment demanded by the victim(s) as payment for the pain or suffering caused by the child.

Disposition

Disposition follows the adjudicatory hearing. It will be discussed in terms of purpose, decision-maker, rights, and role of attorney.

Purpose

The purpose of the disposition hearing is to determine what can be done with the youth in order to treat and reduce his or her criminal behavior. It is similar to the sentencing stage for the adult.

Once the game is over, the king and the pawn go back into the same box. Italian Proverb

Decision-Maker

It is the judge's responsibility to establish the treatment. He or she is aided by the probation staff (investigative unit) who provide a social history.

The social history is a written report containing information about the youth's family, friends, health, neighborhood, religion, and school progress. It is used to help the judge and other staff working with the youth to make informed and appropriate decisions for treatment. The judge has broad powers in fashioning a remedy by balancing the rehabilitative interests of the juvenile with the best interests of the public. The exact dispositional remedies for delinquents are set out in statutes. In making the decision, besides using the social history report, the judge will consider the seriousness of the crime, prior offenses, the home environment, the youth's physical and mental health, and any other relevant factors. The judge may order other alternatives such as substance abuse treatment, family counseling, restitution, and community service.

The judge may defer disposition for up to twelve months. After that time, the charge may be dismissed if the child exhibits good behavior during the period of deferred disposition. Sometimes, the judge will require the youth to return to the court and bring his or her report card. If the progress in school is satisfactory and the behavior better, the judge will dismiss the charge. Some judges suspend the motor vehicle and operator's license. This gets the attention of the youth and motivates his or her desire for cooperation.

The judge also can order the youth to more structured placement with a person like a probation officer. Juvenile probation is similar to adult probation in that it comes with certain conditions. If the youth does something that is in violation of the terms of probation, the probation officer can request the judge to reconsider the placement on probation. In other words, the probation can be revoked.

In California, a juvenile was on probation in relation to a previous charge. Yet he agreed to submit to searches and seizures by law officers as part of the probation. The juvenile was stopped and subjected to a pat-down for weapons during which he dropped a quantity of rock cocaine. He wanted to suppress this evidence, and the trial court granted the motion, but the California Court of Appeals upheld the search (*In re Thomas M.*, 18 Cal.Rptr.2d 710 [Cal. App. April 1993]).

The judge also may use structured placements such as a foster home or group home. Some states have "camps." What makes them camps is that they are located in very rural areas. A "camp" is not a camp in the usual sense—it is not to be misconstrued as a fun place to visit.

Commitment to the state facility (the state Department of Corrections or the Department of Youth) is the ultimate in structure and control over youth beyond a certain age, such as 10. It is a prison for youth.

In some states, a juvenile is sent to the Department of Corrections for a period of time not to exceed his or her 21st birthday. This is called **continuing jurisdiction**.

For example, in Louisiana, a youth age 16, pursuant to a plea agreement, pleaded guilty to simple burglary and was sent to a correctional facility until age 21. Even though he appealed, he had such a history with the juvenile court that he did not win. The record showed that he had a history of delinquent behavior beginning at age 13; that he had been placed in group homes or detention facilities because of complaints by his mother, who could not control his behavior; and that he showed a pattern of a recalcitrant youth. Also, he frequently manifested episodes of disruptive behavior in schools and other settings where he was placed (*State In Interest of KH*, 612 So.2d 1036 [La. App. Jan. 1993]).

In Washington state, the appeals court permitted the juvenile court to impose a disposition outside the standard range if the court determined that a disposition within the standard range would effectuate a manifest injustice. In this case, the female offender was arrested for prostitution. She had a long history of drug and alcohol abuse and was found with two syringes hidden in her vagina. Community-based treatment professionals testified that the probation system had exhausted the community resources available to treat the juvenile and commitment to the state prison facility for youth was the best place to get needed treatment (*State v. N.E.*, 854 P.2d 672 [Wash. App. July 1993]).

In other states, the juvenile court may extend beyond the upper age of original jurisdiction and impose adult correctional sanctions. Legislatures have permitted the courts to have a set of sanctions (dispositional options) known as **blended sentencing** under the rhetoric of the "best interests of the juvenile and the public."

Juveniles can be placed in jails (operated by the city or county authorities) and in prisons (operated by state authorities usually for felons doing more time than 1 year). See Table 4.2 and Figure 4.4. Table 4.2 shows the number of youth who have been placed in public and private facilities from 1978 to 1988. At that time, there was a decline in the use of state juvenile correctional facilities sometimes called training schools. Between 1988 and 1997, "there has been a substantial increase in the number of cases in which the youth was placed on probation or ordered to a residential facility" (http://www.ojjdp.ncjrs.org/ojstatbb/qa190.html, 30 September 1999). In

Table 4.2 NUMBER OF JUVENILE ADMISSIONS TO PUBLIC AND PRIVATE JUVENILE FACILITIES BY FACILITY TYPE, 1978–1988

Public Facilities

	1978 Number	%	1982 Number	%	1984 Number	%	1986 Number	%	1988 Number	%	% Change 1978–1988
Admissions	568,802	100	530,200	100	527,759	100	590,654	100	619,181	100	8.9
Detention centers	451,859	79	411,201	78	404,178	77	467,668	79	499,621	81	10.6
Shelters	12,472	2	14,008	2	17,212	3	22,126	4	14,949	3	19.9
Reception/diagnostic centers	13,037	2	15,751	3	16,493	3	13,313	2	13,924	2	6.8
Training schools	65,513	12	59,732	11	61,706	12	61,399	11	62,824	10	-4.1
Ranches/camps or farms	16,753	3	18,962	4	17,062	3	13,248	2	14,146	2	
Halfway houses/group homes	9,168	2	10,546	2	11,108	2	12,900	2	13,717	2	49.6

Private Facilities

	1978 Number	%	1982 Number	%	1984 Number	%	1986 Number	%	1988 Number	%	% Change 1978–1988
Admissions	69,507	100	88,806	100	101,007	100	125,954	100	141,463	100	103
Detention centers	1,923	3	3,189	4	5,813	6	7,873	6	9,106	7	373
Shelters	20,209	29	40,160	45	47,817	47	66,387	53	75,459	53	273
Reception/diagnostic centers	1,218	2	2,045	2	2,192	2	2,881	2	3,126	2	156
Training schools	5,210	8	5,712	6	7,225	7	7,952	6	9,161	7	75
Ranches/camps or farms	12,706	17	8,636	10	8,924	9	6,858	6	6,030	4	-50
Halfway houses/group homes	28,871	41	20,064	33	29,036	29	34,003	27	38,581	27	33

Source: The 1979–1989 Census of Public and Private Juvenile Detention, Correctional and Shelter Facilities: Admissions for Calendar Years 1978, 1982, 1984, 1986, and 1988.

Source: Juveniles Taken into Custody 1990, 50.

Figure 4.4
U.S. Juvenile Admissions
by Type of Facility
(*Juveniles Taken into
Custody*, 1990, 84).

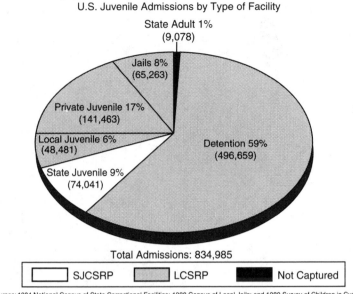

U.S. Juvenile Admissions by Type of Facility

Total Admissions: 834,985

Sources: 1984 National Census of State Correctional Facilities; 1988 Census of Local Jails; and 1989 Survey of Children in Custody.

1997, formal probation was ordered in about 55% of all adjudicated delinquency cases whereas residential placement was used in 28% of the cases. In addition, other types of sanctions like community service and restitution have also increased and may be a part of the other sanctions imposed by the court.

Rights

There are no Supreme Court decisions that give youth any rights at this stage. There is state case law that lays a foundation for what is known as "lesser restrictive placements." The California court *In re Jose P.*, 101 Cal.App.3d 52 (1980), made a list of dispositions that went from the least to the most severe in restriction. They were as follows:

1. any reasonable order

2. supervision of the probation officer

3. commitment to the custody of a reputable person consenting thereto

4. award of custody to a public or private entity designed to care for minors

5. foster home

6. commitment to juvenile home (detention), ranch camp, or forestry camp

7. confinement to juvenile hall or detention

8. all of the above, plus restitution and participation in uncompensated work programs

9. commitment to a sheltered care facility

10. commitment to the Youth Services that maintain the correctional center, reformatory or training schools, or other secure facilities

Once a youth is committed to the custody of the state corrections department, the youth is appointed an **aftercare worker** in some states and a parole officer in others. The aftercare worker may be the person who served as the probation officer prior to the youth's commitment or may be a person newly assigned to the case.

In essence, aftercare is parole in that there are rules to follow and supervision, which may last as long as two years. If the youth violates the aftercare or parole rules or has a new delinquent charge, the youth may be taken back to court. The aftercare status or parole can be revoked and the youth recommitted to the state juvenile correctional facility.

Role of Attorney

The attorney has an advocacy role at this stage. The attorney can give suggestions and help his or her client through the maze to get the treatment the child client needs.

The attorney can also help with an appeal if one is necessary. The juvenile may appeal the juvenile court's findings and disposition to the next higher court. Yet the sanction imposed by that new court may also be greater as well as lesser than that decided upon by the lower court.

The attorney may also be used to file charges against the Department of Corrections for the conditions of the buildings, lack of programs, or inhuman treatment. In 1989, there were 33 deaths in public juvenile facilities, mostly in juvenile detention centers and training schools. There were 23 deaths in private facilities like halfway houses and group homes (*Juveniles Taken into Custody* 1990). These "out-of-mind" places need the watchful eyes of someone who can use the legal system if necessary to improve the care and services.

DELINQUENCY IN THE COMPUTER AGE

Today, as well as in the future, we can identify at least eight major kinds of delinquent (criminal) juvenile offenders: (1) situational offenders, (2) chronic offenders, (3) sex offenders, (4) gangs, (5) emotionally disturbed children, (6) substance abusers, (7) naive or mentally retarded children, and (8) learning-disabled. At the moment, most juvenile courts prosecute youth on the crime of the youth, and not the underlying causation or motivations. Yet, to prosecute a gang member for only the crime and then return the youth to the same social situation only sets him or her up to fail again. As you read about these youth offenders, think about what could or should be done to curb juvenile crime. Then you, too, will get a sense about what the future of the juvenile court should be.

Situational Offender

The situational offender is, in many respects, different from the chronic offender. To be sure, both are involved in serious antisocial behavior, such as armed robbery, burglary, or battery. The situational offender, however, lacks a commitment to crime as a way of life. He or she is more prone to do acts that are charged as petty larceny, possession of alcohol, trespassing, or grand larceny. This offender depends on or needs the peer group. In groups of two or three, the individual offender is "bored" and seeks new thrills.

Figure 4.5
Used with permission of
Bob Gorell, *The Richmond
Times-Dispatch.*

Drifts into crime—peer
pressure

Matza (1964) developed the image of a situational delinquent as one who "drifted" into the world of crime. It also means that this type of youth could easily move back into conventional society. The delinquent, according to Matza, is an actor who was *"neither compelled nor committed to deeds nor freely choosing them; neither different in any simple or fundamental sense from the law abiding, nor the same; conforming to certain traditions in American life while partially unreceptive to other more conventional traditions ..."* (Matza 1964, 28).

As some of these youths grow up, they outgrow their desire to commit malicious mischief. In their adult years, they assume mature responsibilities of work, marriage, and family life. Youths who are situational delinquents and processed by the juvenile court are deterred from future antisocial behavior by the experience of dealing with the juvenile court and perhaps a probation officer. On the other hand, others who have been processed by the court begin to accept the label of being a delinquent and may consequently continue their antisocial behavior. At that point, the offender is no longer considered as a situational. Instead, he or she is classified a chronic or habitual offender.

Chronic Offender

5 or more offenses

Serious and violent offenders are a group of offenders who contain others who are called violent offenders and chronic offenders and a subgroup that is both violent and chronic. Although their numbers are few, they are responsible for a disproportionate amount of crime. Regardless of the name, these youth start at early ages (age 7) and progress to moderately serious behavior problems at age 9.5. They tend to have multiple problems such as substance abuse and mental health difficulties in addition to truancy, suspension, expulsion, and dropping out of school. One of the accepted working definitions used by researchers is that this juvenile has five or more offenses or charges on his or her official record usually with serious crimes against persons and property.

Chronic offenders can be divided into two groups. One group includes those who, through the process of labeling and lack of rehabilitation in the system, became willing to accept the self-definition of a "loser." At each stage of the processing, these individuals seemed to have made the decision to continue their involvement in crime. The second kind, on the other hand, grow up in an environment of crime and may, therefore, be absorbed in a way of criminal life before they have contact with the justice system. Often these youths feel rejected and thereby have no trust, as explained in discussion of child development stages in Chapter 2. Their attitude of hostility and suspiciousness makes it hard for them to develop warm, meaningful relationships with other human beings. The research on child abuse and sexual assault suggests that many chronic and violent offenders have experienced those conditions in their lives.

Self-fulfilling prophecy: the proposition that people behave in a manner that brings about the results that they or others have expected of themselves or others

Birth Cohort Study

The classic study on chronic juvenile offenders was done by Wolfgang, Figlio, and Sellin (1972), who studied all the boys born in Philadelphia in 1945 (called a birth cohort study). They traced the boys through the school and police records. These researchers subdivided the delinquents into single, multiple, and chronic offenders. They defined a chronic offender as a person who committed more than five violations. As mentioned before, the incredible fact was that these chronic offenders represented only 6.3 percent of the total population but were responsible for 51 percent of all offenses and about two-thirds of all violent offenses. In addition, nonwhites and lower-class boys were more likely to be chronic offenders than whites and middle-class boys. Chronic offenders also made more residential moves and had lower IQ scores and less education than either single or multiple offenders.

Small Numbers Responsible for Large Amounts of Crime

Current studies on chronic offenders continue to indicate that a small proportion of juvenile delinquent offenders commit most of the serious and violent juvenile crimes. For example, the U.S. Department of Justice has requested and sponsored research on career criminals. The Justice Department's most recent report is called *Guide for Implementing the Comprehensive Strategy for Serious, Violent, and Chronic Juvenile Offenders* (Howell 1995). The report explains how these youth begin to break the law at an early age (age of onset) and how they have multiple risk factors. The suggested strategy is comprehensive, beginning with prevention while the child is still a fetus (prenatal) and moving through the child's development with other prevention programs in the community. For the juvenile courts, the recommendation is for graduated sanctions from immediate intervention to secure corrections, depending upon the results used by risk assessments. Risk assessments, if well designed, are able to identify a group of high-risk offenders who are four or five times more likely to commit a new offense than the identified low-risk offenders. See Figure 4.6 for a juvenile probation and aftercare parole (after the youth has been in a juvenile correctional facility) assessment of risk (Howell 1995).

Early Age

Graduated Sanctions

While research continues in the area of criminal-chronic juvenile offenders, some states and communities have already set up programs that range from community alternatives to nonresidential to institutional. To locate these programs, Arthur D. Little, Inc. of Washington, D.C., with a grant from

Select the highest point total applicable for each category.

1. Age at First Adjudication _____
    16 or older 0
    14 or 15 3
    13 or younger 5

2. Prior Criminal Behavior _____
    No prior arrests. 0
    Prior arrest record, no formal sanctions. 2
    Prior delinquency petition sustained; no offenses classified as assaultive 3
    Prior petition sustained for an assaultive offense. 5

3. Institutional Commitments or Placements of 30 Days or More _____
    None. 0
    One. 2
    Two or more 4

4. Drug/Chemical Use _____
    No known use or no interference with functioning. 0
    Some disruption of functioning 2
    Chronic abuse or dependency. 5

5. Alcohol Abuse _____
    No known use or no interference with functioning. 0
    Occasional abuse, some disruption of functioning 1
    Chronic abuse, serious disruption of functioning. 3

6. Parental Control _____
    Generally effective 0
    Inconsistent and/or ineffective 2
    Little or none. 4

7. School Disciplinary Problems _____
    Attending, graduated, GED equivalence 0
    Problems handled at school level. 1
    Severe truancy or behavioral problems 3
    Not attending/expelled. 5

8. Peer Relationships _____
    Good support and influence. 0
    Negative influence, companions involved in delinquent behavior 2
    Gang member. 4

Figure 4.6
Juvenile Probation and Aftercare Assessment of Risk (Howell 1995, 192).

the U.S. Department of Justice's Office of Juvenile Justice and Delinquency Prevention, made extensive phone calls to practitioners working with criminal youths. The published information was to be a resource for communities so that new programs would meet specific communities' needs. No evaluations were done on the programs. Examples from those materials include programs like the one in St. Paul, Minnesota, called Serious Juvenile Offender Programs (SJO). SJO was set up in correctional facilities to provide public safety in addition to treatment. Then, existing social and correctional services were coordinated to better meet the needs of individual offenders. A third component of the program, which of course is used by many other programs, is called accountability on the part of the offender through the use of contracts. The entire program works this way:

A youth spends a total of eighteen months in the Serious Juvenile Offender program, six in the institution, six in the community, and, theoretically, six months can be given in good time, thus decreasing his/her stay to a year. Most youth, however, spend the full eighteen months in the program. A youth designated a serious offender can opt to spend his/her eighteen months in an institution rather than join the program, although this has not occurred. A youth who chooses to enter the program is assigned a case manager who works closely with the youth while in the institution and upon release.

The case manager negotiates a contract with the youth that is predicated on attainable, concrete goals such as completion of the GED, acquisition of a driver's license, or participation in vocational training. Youth are tested to insure that the goals are appropriate and obtainable. The youth must have 90 incident-free days prior to parole as well as having met the conditions of the contract before being discharged. Behavioral contracts are used with all clients and are the mechanism by which youth move through the program, i.e., from security to discharge. Both monetary and symbolic restitution is used in the contracts for the community. While in the institution, youth provide their case manager with the names of three people with whom they would want to spend time upon release. These names are screened carefully, and one individual is chosen as a community liaison worker. The community liaison worker must spend 18 hours a week with the paroled youth in face-to-face contact, and is compensated at a rate of $5.50 an hour and 19 cents a mile for any transportation. The community liaison worker must have been free of crime for at least a year. Although many are involved in youth or human service work, some have had no previous formal training or work in these areas. The case manager supervises the community liaison worker. The community liaison worker must know the whereabouts of the youth while on parole and play the dual role of providing community supervision and support. Since the community liaison worker is one of the unique aspects of the program, in this capacity he or she must provide intensive supervision for at least the first six months of the youth's return to the community. (Program for the Serious and Violent Juvenile Offender 1981, 6–7)

Other programs working with criminal juvenile offenders operate with youths and staff sharing the responsibilities of living together (therapeutic community) in a community-based operation. Such a house, for example, is Nexus of Minnetonka, Minnesota.

Another successful type is the Associated Marine Institutes, Inc. of Tampa, Florida, where staff go as far as treating youths in their own homes and communities. The services provided by this nonprofit, public program involve:

educational and vocational activities. Since most of the youth have a history of poor performance in school, the program emphasizes the basic academic skills so that a majority of youth coming out of the program have attained their GED. They are also simultaneously involved in marine-related work. The staff teaches them about seamanship, SCUBA diving, and other ocean sciences. Each youth receives individual, group, and crisis counseling. Therapy is available to respond to a youth's need as it arises. The program utilizes a behavior modification system that emphasizes performance preceding rewards, which develops a pattern of success. This facet of the program emphasizes privileges, overnight trips, and other motivational tools to reinforce positive behavior. Recidivism rates over the past twelve years have averaged 18 percent or below, and the adjustment of each client is followed up for a minimum of three years.

The staff at the Institute are unique in that they are primarily recruited from marine-related backgrounds. They are ship captains, scientists, marine technicians, SCUBA diving instructors, general contractors, and the like. Some have had business experience. As in the program's beginning, the Institute is still a scientific marine firm engaged in work other than its work with youth. There are 90 permanent staff members including administrative staff. At a given time, the program also makes use of about 10 to 15 volunteers, who are often interns from the universities or volunteers from the communities. Each location also has a Board of Trustees in addition to the Board of Trustees who oversees the program as a whole. There are approximately 120 Board members, and they are very active and integral to the success of the program. They facilitate relations with the communities, which are excellent in all locations, secure funding and equipment, and make policy decision. (Programs for the Serious and Violent Juvenile Offender 1981, 15–16)

By 1985, this program was expanded to five additional sites and has "continued to maintain the lowest reoffenses rate for successful releases from all programs—23 percent over an 18-month period. Program cost approximated $2,500 to $3,000 per youth for the 5- to 6-month experience" (Rubin 1985, 19–20).

To be sure, none of the twenty programs described in the material on *Programs for the Serious and Violent Juvenile Offender* recommend excusing serious and violent criminal juvenile offenders from their behavior. They do advocate youths taking responsibility for their behavior. In addition, to accomplish that goal, many programs include community services and involvement of community people to help with the challenge.

Besides nonprofit organizations, the federal government in 1984 developed through the Office of Juvenile Justice and Delinquency Prevention (OJJDP) a new initiative known as the Habitual Serious and Violent Juvenile Offender Program (HSVJOP) at thirteen locations nationwide. The program, modeled in part after "Career Criminal" programs directed at adult offenders, concerns itself with vertical prosecution (the same prosecutor or team was to remain with a case from start to finish), limited charge and sentence bargaining, and, if convicted, more correctional services such as enhanced diagnostic assessment, individual treatment plans, and continuous case management. The program was a success in the sense that it opened up lines of communication to other agencies about problems of mutual concern and encouraged a problem-solving program. Obviously, the problem is more complex and could not redress the lack of suitable correctional alternatives for serious offenders.

Today, the Serious Habitual Offender Comprehensive Action Program is known as SHOCAP. The recommendation is to develop interagency programs where police, schools, human services, corrections, courts, and prosecution are the core agencies working together to more effectively deal with chronic youth offenders (Crowe 1991).

> SHOCAP

Sex Offender

Historically, juvenile sex offenders were viewed as young people experimenting. Yet studies, at first done by Groth (1977) and now by others (Abel, Mihelman, and Becker 1985; Freeman-Longo 1983), show that adult sex offenders began as youth; as many as 60 to 80 percent report offending as adolescents. In addition, there is research to show that there is a progression of offenses such that obscene phone calls, voyeurism, or stealing undergarments are not necessarily harmless juvenile pranks.

> Was Jerry Gault really a sex offender?

Groth (1977) found that some of the adults themselves had been victimized as children. Because of that connection between sexual abuse and delinquent behavior, more of the research and programs on juvenile sex offenders are discussed in Chapter 6, "Crimes Against Children," under "Victim Becomes Offender Cycle."

Gangs

The importance of gang membership and the tendency of youths to engage in group criminal activities have been the research interest of sociologists for decades. Beginning with the Chicago School of Sociology in the early 1930s until now, the studies help us understand that these youth commit crimes for different reasons. Their ages vary depending on the city and the scale of gang activity. Usually a gang is loosely knit, without structure, and with the strongest or boldest member being the leader. The gang has a name and a dress style, and it claims a territory of the neighborhood. Its members can have different levels of involvement. Some are on the periphery with connections into the gang but not very strong ties. Others are associated, and others are dedicated or hardcore.

> Shaw and his associates in Chicago attributed variations in delinquency rates to demographic or socioeconomic conditions in different areas of cities due to the breakdown of spontaneous or natural forces of social control (Shaw 1930, Shaw 1936, and Shaw and McKay 1942).

Since there is no accepted standard definition of a gang, state and local jurisdictions tend to develop their own to distinguish gangs from other law-violating youth groups and other collective youth groups. This is necessary because most juvenile delinquency is committed in groups of at least two or three persons.

Regardless of a standard definition, in 1991 there were 4,881 gangs with 249,324 members with an estimated 46,359 criminal gang incidents. Twenty-seven cities reported female gangs with an estimate of 7,205 female gang members (Howell 1994).

Gang members range in age from 12 to 25 years old with the peak age at 17. In cities beginning to report gang activity, the members are usually juvenile, but in cities with a long history of gang activity, the members are usually adults (Howell 1994). (For a real understanding of gangs, see Brown 1965.)

Gangs have always been a part of American history, both in cities (Asbury 1928) and in the uncharted land of the West. Although there are some similarities, the gangs of today are also different.

From the late 1940s through the 1950s, teenage gangs in nearly every urban area caused trouble for the police and fear for private citizens. Today, gang activity also seems to be at a high level. Miller (1975, 41), who conducted the first national study of youth gangs and young gang violence, concluded that the "prevalence, use, quality and sophistication of weaponry in the gangs of the 1970s far [surpass] anything known in the past and [weaponry] is probably the single most significant characteristic distinguishing today's gangs from [their] predecessors." Short (1973, 47), another noted researcher of gang activity in Chicago, said:

A decade ago, when we were studying our Chicago gangs, The Egyptian Cobras had an interesting relationship with certain prostitutes in the Maxwell Street area. The boys knew the girls well and they regularly avoided rolling potential tricks until after the girls had first crack at them. One of these boys graduated from that gang into running policy numbers and several were involved in a variety of minor hustles. Then drugs become a big thing among a fairly large number of gang youngsters, both as users and as pushers. Some are inclined to attribute the decline in fighting activity in Chicago to drug use. A former "gang banger" in Chicago was recently quoted in the New York Times *to this effect: "Gang banging in itself is dying off. Now too many brothers are busy nodding on the junk."*

Besides guns and violence, the gangs of today are representative of minority groups such as Hispanic, Asian, and African-American. All have their own street talk, graffiti, hand signals, and rap music (Carondelet Management Institute 1992a).

Street talk is a mixture of English and street slang. It is likened to "jive talk" among black gangs. Example: "I took one time out with da tray eight." Translation: "I took the police out with my .38 handgun." Hispanic gang members, or zoot-suiters, combined Spanish and English languages gener-ations ago to form a street talk called "calo."

Example: "The juras got Joker torcido."
  Translation: "The police have Joker arrested."
(Carondetet Management Institute 1992a, 6)

Graffiti is a gang's "newspaper" of the street. It marks gang territories and rivalries. Moreover, hand signs are rising in popularity. They are used to challenge rival gang members or to insult the police (Carondelet 1992a, 6).

Gangster rap music was born out of the emotional pain and death surrounding the African-American experience in the inner-city ghettos. Its expressions and rhythmic lyrical cadence are reflective of a subculture of gangs and the activities of pimping, prostitution, drug usage and dealing, alcohol abuse, burglary, robbery, assaults, and so forth. The primary themes, which change very little from rapper to rapper, are as follows:

1. Glorification of the gang lifestyle and mentality.

2. Violence to society as a whole and the police in general.

3. Racism against the government and its agents, especially against the black police officer. The rap talks of the true villains being the police who are waging a war of genocide by systematically exterminating the race by depriving them of basic needs such as educational opportunities. (Don't see or hear "Funk the Police" by NWA and "Straight Outta Compton" and "I Wanna Kill Sam" by Ice Cube.)

4. Psychotic personality.

5. Black male sexual stereotype of a superlover.

6. Sexism and misogynist attitude toward women. (Don't see or hear "Findem, Fuckem, and Flee," "Niggaz 4 Life," and "One Less Bitch" by NWA.) Women in these rap songs are sexual objects to be used, abused, and killed, if necessary, to make way for the next conquest (Carondelet 1992b, 3–5,11).

Present-day gangs tend to extort local merchants, engage in robberies, shake down students for money, intimidate local residents, sell stolen goods, kill each other, and victimize adults and children. They seem to be moti-vated by (1) desire for material gain and (2) control over public facilities or territory.

Some gang activity is focused around the business of selling drugs. For example, youth from New York, where the jurisdictional age for juvenile court ends at age 16, can set up their own businesses in the state of Virginia where the adult court begins at age 18. If caught, the New York youth has to be first seen by the juvenile court. If found guilty, the disposition (sen-tence) is usually lighter (called "peanut butter time"). Another group is Asian youth, especially Vietnamese, who have two ages. One is the age reported to the officials, which is younger than their real age. The dual age system was adopted in refugee camps in Southeast Asia where parents dis-covered that placement in school systems depended upon age. The age of children was reduced to give the youth a chance in the school system. Yet this practice also served the criminal element well (Carondelet 1992a, 16).

Gang members are primarily male, from low-income communities, range in age from 10 to 21, and are largely black and/or of Hispanic origin. Gang memberships of a variety of Asian origins are also present as well as white groups that have an "Aryan"-type mentality. There has been a shift to exclusive ethnic minority membership. Moreover, that shift is matched with a shift toward the money-making aspects of crime, such as selling drugs and stealing cars. In this new gang activity, protection of turf is not as important as competition. Gang members seemingly engage in more organized, criminal activity (Carondelet 1992a).

The most acclaimed program dealing with black gangs during the 1970s, 1980s, and 1990s came from Philadelphia, Pennsylvania—House of UMOJA.

House of UMOJA in Philadelphia, Pennsylvania, was founded 12 years ago by journalist Sister Falaka Fattah as a communication by-product of the third Black Power Conference, which was held in Philadelphia in 1968. House of UMOJA's first client population were gang members who were invited to live in the house by the founder and her husband, David, when they discovered one of their six sons was involved in a gang in 1969. The Fattahs felt that it was necessary to provide services to youthful gang members who were otherwise ignored by the system. Thus, the residential component of the House of UMOJA began to take shape.

. . . House of UMOJA operates on the premise that the family structure is an important, natural process. The program is operated like a family, and the support mechanisms and structure are reflective of this premise. As youth enter the home and accept responsibility, they earn their African name. It is not until youth have completely made a commitment in the program that they earn their last African name, Fattah. Heritage and background are keys to the success of the program, and youth are taught to respect and acknowledge their own heritage. The program tries to grow boys into men, making them responsible, contributing members of the community.

. . . Residents in the home are provided with the support mechanisms of a surrogate family. While in residence, the youth attend local schools and are provided with counseling, shelter, job readiness and survival skills, as well as actual on-the-job experience if they are ex-offenders. The majority of the residents live on their own once leaving the program, and therefore preparation for independent living is an important aspect of the program. On Friday or Saturday "truth sessions" are held with the staff and residents sharing opinions, each of which holds an equal weight. If rules of the home are broken, the resident chooses his own consequences and punishment.

The program serves males between the ages of 15 to 18, who reside in or around Philadelphia. Eighty percent of the population served have been gang members, while the remaining 20 percent were dependent or emotionally disturbed. The program has served over 500 residents between 1969 and 1981, serving between 15 to 30 residents at any given time. Youth in the program have been either self-referred, or are referred from court or another social agency and remain in the program for an average of one year; the House of UMOJA has a 75 percent to 80 percent success rate.

The basic premise behind the program is that youth are in the program to provide a service, not merely receive services. Many youth feel that society owes them something and the program goal is to turn that thought around and have the youth provide some type of concrete service to the community. The rules which govern the operation of the program were created by the youth themselves and include personal discipline, self-respect, and responsibility to the larger community.

. . . Residents of House of UMOJA who participate in on-the-job training receive 120-hour training in crime prevention, e.g., security techniques which would allow them to be security officers in actual jobs. Actual on-the-job training is also an essential part of this crime prevention program. This training program has been supported by CETA and is expected to end due to federal budget cuts. House of UMOJA has continually been planning for self-sufficiency and is already prepared to deal with CETA cutbacks through the development of a Boys Town Project.

. . . House of UMOJA owns 23 houses within a city block which are being developed for Boys Town. Half of the houses are being utilized for economic development, while the other half will be used for social development. It is within this structure that youth will receive on-the-job training in seven businesses to be developed and operated by the residents. Included in Boys Town will also be a residential quarters, and services provided to the residents will include art, photography, and music instruction and appreciation. (Programs for the Serious and Violent Juvenile Offender, pp. 40–42)

This program uses community resources to provide for the special needs of the youth. In this manner, then, this program can be developed in other cities. Anytime various community groups get together to plan ways to decrease the social disorganization and involvement in drugs and antisocial behavior, the greater are the chances for success.

Today, there has been a shift in strategies in dealing with gangs. In the 1950s and 1960s, there were social intervention approaches. In the 1970s to 1990s, there were suppression strategies. Today, the National Youth Gang Suppression and Intervention Program, sponsored through the Office of

Shift in Strategies

Juvenile Justice and Delinquency Prevention, helps communities to understand that gang problems are (1) chronic and (2) emerging. Thus, different strategies are needed, both through the courts and in the community at the grassroots level. Using the lack of social opportunities theory (youth in gangs lack the social opportunities that middle-class youth have), Dr. Irving Spergel and his colleagues at the University of Chicago have conducted the first comprehensive national survey of organized agency and community group responses to gang problems in the United States. Their research also developed a comprehensive intervention model.

Chronic Gangs; Emerging Gangs

For cities with chronic-gang problems, opportunities provision was the most effective strategy, followed by community organization approaches. For cities with emerging-gang problems, community organization was perceived as the most effective strategy. Suppression strategies work best in conjunction with other approaches (Howell 1994; Hatchell 1990).

Remember that gang membership is also related to higher levels of serious, violent, chronic offending. Reducing gang involvement also reduces gang violence. OJJDP (Office of Juvenile Justice and Delinquency Prevention) that has been implementing prevention programs by targeting key risk and protective factors with programming has highlighted some promising programs. One is the Little Village Gang Violence Reduction Program operated by the Chicago Police. Law and probation officers increase surveillance and provide a wide range of social service and opportunities for targeted gang members to transition out of gangs. A second program developed by the Bureau of Alcohol, Tobacco and Firearms is a prevention program being tested and evaluated in 42 schools across the country. The Gang Resistance Education and Training (GREAT) Program uses a structured curriculum taught by trained officers to discourage youth from joining gangs (*Juvenile Justice Bulletin*, May 1998, p. 5).

New Code Provisions for Prosecution

In terms of prosecution, prosecutors in thirty-six states use existing criminal codes to proceed against street gangs. In fourteen states, they work under newly enacted code provisions on street gangs. These new code provisions are necessary because state juvenile codes were not designed for the serious violence that characterizes street gang crime, such as drive-by shootings and brandishing weapons. In addition, victim and witness cooperation and protection are major challenges because today's victim may become tomorrow's perpetrator seeking revenge (Johnson, Webster, and Connors 1995). Yet, in some places the "anti-gang violence" policies in the schools are coming under attack because those writing the policies have not clearly defined what behavior, what colors, or what symbols are considered gang activities, yet they still expel the youth from school. See *Sephenson v. Davenport Community School System*, 110 F.3d 1303 (8th Circuit 1997).

Emotionally Disturbed Children

Definitions of children with this behavior vary somewhat. Generally speaking, emotionally disturbed children are the youths whose coping styles severely interfere with their everyday functioning. They seem to be characterized by two important behavior patterns: (1) psychological state, labeled as emotionally disturbed, psychotic, or schizophrenic, and (2) an acting-out behavior.

The most common mental health disorders in juvenile justice populations are depression, bipolar disorder, attention deficit, conduct disorders, oppositional defiant disorder, and general frontal lobe activity problems. The latter may include low impulse control, aggression, disinhibition, agitation, immature behavior for age, and poor socialization processing (Pratt 1995).

These youths either have continual behavior problems or are involved in shocking crimes. Usually, these youths are referred to mental health facilities and may spend time as patients in psychiatric hospitals.

Sometimes these youth are noted for doing "strange" activities. For example, an Indiana teenager tried to break into an apartment clubhouse in Richmond, Virginia. He got stuck in the chimney and fire-fighters had to remove him. The juvenile judge released the boy to the custody of the parent in Indiana with the order to continue psychiatric treatment (*Richmond Times-Dispatch* Oct. 27, 1992, B3).

Others are more violent. For example, Richette (1969) wrote a very descriptive account of one of her clients in the Juvenile Court in Philadelphia. Because it is still true today, it is important to know about the behavior of emotionally disturbed individuals. She described Vincent (not his real name) as a youth whose anger toward his parents mounted over the years. He had never been a troublemaker. He had even been an altar boy. Although his parents expected perfection from him, they would run naked through the house, keep pornographic books around the house, have sexual intercourse in front of him, and provide no doors to any of the bedrooms. The child tried to channel his rage into the Catholic religion, which in the long run only made him feel guiltier. Then, one day, he took matters into his own hands and killed both parents.

A more recent example comes from the legal folders on juvenile offenders who have been transferred (waived into the adult court) to the Circuit Court in Richmond, Virginia. This 15-year-old white male went into a large bank with a .38-caliber revolver. He told everyone to lie down on the floor, cross their legs, and place their arms above their heads. From the teller of this large bank, he got $4,833.00 in U.S. money. The reason why this robbery was not a smart crime was the teenager's oversight of the fact that the incident was recorded by the bank's video equipment, which is used as standard practice in most banks today. Moreover, he then rode off on his bicycle and later threw the money away. Again, not a very smart thing to do.

When we look behind the actual crime, we find more information in the folder. The teenager reported that it was like someone else was inside of his body during the event; it was as if he was observing himself carrying out the robbery. At school his grades had been dropping over the years. He would sleep at his classroom desk. In the legal file, someone was able to point to the family as being dysfunctional. For example, the family was known to Protective Services because the father was an alcoholic. The mother, who had acute hysterical episodes and depression, was a frequent client in local mental health hospitals. Neither parent had control of the children. Violent arguments occurred between the parents, between the parents and the children, and between the siblings. The family life also was wrecked by alcohol abuse and attempted suicides, especially by the older brother.

These three examples indicate that some juveniles are not breaking the law to please their peers. In fact, they are operating alone, whereas many other youth commit their crimes in twos or threes. Certainly, some of these youths are capable of committing horrible crimes, as in the preceding example of Vincent. Their delinquency results from personal problems, not because of a desire for fame or toughness as is the case for some youth. They are not committed to crime as a way of life as are youthful drug dealers who are equipped with beepers and in possession of large sums of money and drugs. In summary, these native youths get in trouble with the law because they lack internal controls.

Substance Abusers

Substance abuse has become a widespread problem among youths. The fact that both girls and boys perceive the use of alcohol, for example, as normal has contributed to the increased use of drugs such as cocaine, crack, and marijuana. Beer and marijuana are used most often because they are easier to obtain and less costly. In recent years, inhalants, such as paint thinners, gasoline, airplane glue, and aerosol cans have gained popularity.

Some studies indicate that adolescent drug abusers have different characteristics than adults who abuse the same drugs. For example, adolescents have less involvement with opiates and engage in shorter periods of abuse. That means they tend to use more alcohol, marijuana, and multiple drugs than adults (OJJDP 1992, 1). Sickmund (1991) conducted a National Juvenile Court Data Archive study of nearly 300,000 court records describing drug and alcohol cases processed from 1985 through 1988 in 841 courts in 17 states. As one might expect, there is a decrease in cases, especially with drunk driving. Yet our society still has a mental attitude that tolerates youth experimentation such that more than three-quarters of all drinking cases were handled informally by an intake department. On the other hand, three-quarters of all driving-under-the-influence cases were formally charged and seen by a judge.

Law enforcement agents who work on the highways know the devastating effect of young drunken drivers on other people's lives and property. Youth who are driving under the influence are more likely to be petitioned and placed in a residential facility or on probation. The attempts by more recent citizens' pressure groups to streamline drunken driving laws exemplify the seriousness of this problem and the need for cooperation between citizens and police, and for the education of law enforcement agencies in the struggle against drunken driving. Grassroots programs like Mothers Against Drunk Driving (MADD) are part of a nationwide educational effort aimed at intervening in crimes and alcohol usage.

In addition to the changing attitudes produced by MADD and Students Against Driving Drunk (SADD) through their national media and state legislative educational programs, many states have enacted stricter laws. With greater awareness about alcohol impairment, states are passing laws that lower the blood alcohol concentration (BAC). Today, no state is higher than 0.10 percent, and thirteen states have ratified 0.08 percent BAC. Maine, for example, saw a 19 percent decline in nighttime alcohol-related fatalities three years after it passed its 0.08 BAC law. Because teenage drivers are disproportionately involved in auto crashes compared to drivers in other age groups, thirty-two states and the District of Columbia now have low-BAC or zero-BAC limits for teenage drivers. In addition, in eleven states and the District of Columbia, there is a keg registration that puts purchasers on notice that they face penalties if minors drink from their keg (Bohen 1996).

The criminal alcoholic, unlike the alcoholic, has usually committed a murder, assault, and/or rape. Studies seem to show that the adult criminal alcoholic typically has had a history of violent behavior and involvement with alcohol starting during adolescence or even earlier. For adolescents, drug use is preceded by family, social, and psychological problems. "Significantly, teenage substance abusers also tend to have a higher incidence of family deviance and a history of psychological treatment" (OJJDP 1992, 1).

Unlike alcohol-related crimes, drug cases are considered more serious and are dealt with more severely. Generally, young drug dealers and/or users, if caught, are not dealt with at the informal level at intake, leading to either placement outside the home in a residential facility or dismissal of the charges. Instead, the decision-maker is a judge in the juvenile courtroom.

Not at the Informal Level

What do typical drug dealers look like? They come in all shapes and sizes. The common characteristics involve drugs packaged in small units, large sums of money in different denominations, and a gun. One young drug dealer in the court records, when caught, had over $3,500 on his person with more than $1,500 in his shoes (Personal Observation). When they come to court, they argue that the drugs were for personal use only. Therefore, they should be charged with possession versus trafficking. For the youth, the court tries probation or placement in a nonsecure treatment facility.

Depending upon the state and the available resources, some youth may, indeed, see the judge in the adult court even though they have little history of treatment in the juvenile court.

Programs that have been developed for this area of crime involvement have had to address pharmacological issues, socioeconomic factors, personality factors, and situational components. The newer approaches advocate "holistic" or "multimodality" approaches. The future trend is to develop community-based operations that consolidate alcohol and narcotic addiction programs because of the similarities in the problems and treatment modalities.

The Office of Juvenile Justice and Delinquency Prevention (OJJDP) teamed up with the American Probation and Parole Association to develop *Drug Testing Guidelines for Practice for Juvenile Probation and Parole Agencies* (1992). Using the drug-testing policies and procedures from more than 125 probation and parole agencies across the nation, they developed drug-testing policies and procedures to assist juvenile agencies in identifying abuses and withstanding the legal challenges to drug testing. Detection among juveniles is different because they are not prone to inject hard drugs—they use more soft drugs. Yet, intervention at this early stage could have positive effects both in terms of prevention of a lifestyle affected by hard drugs and adult criminal behavior.

Drug screening can be used for both the time period of the probation and the treatment process to identify relapses and assist juveniles in abstaining from drug use for longer periods of time. The scientifically reliable drug test permits the agencies and juvenile court to initiate appropriate sanctions.

Two law cases are important concerning this issue. *In re C.J.W.*, 727 P.2d 870 (Colo. Ct. App. 1986), the Colorado Court of Appeals upheld the testimony of a probation officer to rule that the juvenile had violated conditions of probation in that the juvenile failed to submit to a urine test as required by conditions of probation. California even took it a step further by upholding the inclusion of drug testing as a condition of probation for a juvenile who was found to have disturbed the peace and committed a battery on school property and who had a history of admitted substance abuse, coupled with no parental supervision in the evening hours (*In re Jimi A.*, 257 Cal. Rptr. 147 [Cal. Ct. App. 1989]).

It is important to understand that rehabilitation of drug-abusing juveniles is facilitated by sobriety—by getting the youth to be chemically free so as to engage in many of the psychological treatment modalities. Successful treatment is contingent on stabilizing the biochemical dimensions so that other treatment modalities can be applied.

As explained in Chapter 1, "History and Treatment," juveniles now have more rights in the juvenile court systems. Some of the legal issues raised by defense attorneys who concentrate their efforts on youth have been violations of the right against unreasonable search and seizure, the right to due process, the right to confrontation and cross-examination, and the right against self-incrimination.

Claims for due process of law are unsuccessful when an agency develops proper procedures and notifies a youth prior to drug testing. The officer must explain to the juvenile why he or she was selected—for instance, because the youth has a history of drug use, a previous positive test result, a rearrest for a drug-related offense, and behavior cues such as intoxication or an acute hangover, mood swings, needle marks, rapid weight loss, and chronic running nose (OJJDP 1992, 37). Reliable information that the juvenile is using drugs can always be used as well.

The juvenile should be informed in writing how the drug-test results will be used and what the consequences of a positive result are. Although there is no case law on this exact point, courts are stipulating that a failure or refusal to cooperate in providing a urine specimen within a reasonable time period is a violation, and that this violation will be reported to the court or aftercare (parole) and may result in revocation (taking away one's liberty in the community and sending that person back to the institution) or other administrative sanctions (OJJDP 1992).

Reasonable Suspicion Test

Another legal defense that has not gained the desired result for defendants concerns the right against unreasonable search and seizure. If a defendant can claim that law enforcement officers obtained evidence through violation of search procedures, then the fruits of what the officer found can be suppressed as evidence. If there is lack of sufficient evidence or no evidence, the case is usually dismissed. But, in probation cases, the trend is to permit a **less stringent standard of reasonable suspicion** for the probation officer to search. That means the probation officer needs only to be able to point to specific and articulate facts leading to a rational inference that a condition of probation has been violated (*State v. Smith*, 540 A.2d 679 [Conn. 1988]). A probation officer could say the client was unable to speak clearly, his eyes were bloodshot, and he could not stand up. Given the history of that probation officer's work with that particular client, the courts would usually support the officer's decision (OJJDP 1992).

To be sure, parents are not considered agents of the state, and they do not need probable cause to search. In one observed court case, the mother was angry that her son was not obeying the juvenile court's house arrest. The son was not coming home at the required hour; he took the neighbor's car and drove it around the community when he did not have a driver's license. The final blow came when he tried to dry his marijuana in her microwave oven! The mother and father collected the evidence and brought the son and the "grass" (the drug) into the court for help in gaining control in their lives and their family.

There are many cases supporting drug testing with adults that will, no doubt, be used to support drug testing for juveniles. The crimes associated with drug use and drug trafficking have increased so significantly, and the crimes have permeated every level of our society, that many people have been calling for protection from both adults and juveniles. Drug testing seems to be a way to monitor those who come through the court systems in order to preserve public order and to mandate treatment and punishment where individuals are unwilling and/or unable to receive those services for themselves.

Drug screening, however, does not get to the cause and core of the problem. There are many treatment programs, but those that seem to get the best results have included some kind of biological and nutritional treatment, even vitamins and minerals and a sugar-free diet, along with other multiprograms. There seems to be no easy answer.

Drug addiction is complex, because psychological variables such as peer influence may cause a youth to begin, but once taking the drug, the individual's own biological, chemical make-up may cause an immediate attraction and, thus, a strong addiction. Medical doctors and scientists prefer longitudinal, double-blind studies to determine cause and treatment. Parents and loved ones, however, who watch their children become less than human while on the drugs cry for immediate action.

One of the precursors of addiction seems to be an excess of sugar in the diet or a hypersensitivity to sugar. Yet the literature about hypersensitivity to sugar in children is inconclusive and controversial. But ask any parent who has a child who has a so-called allergy to sugar, and that parent will tell you about the violent behavior that occurs before the child experiences the down side. Some doctors are now viewing and treating alcoholism as a food allergy to B-complex vitamins and sugar. Several techniques dealing with food allergies are elimination diets, rotation diets, and serums. Dr. Devi S. Nambudripad's technique, as explained in the best-selling book *Say Goodbye to Illness*, is the newest and most acclaimed of these approaches (Nambudripad 1993).

Nontraditional treatments have been used with successes in some individual cases. For example, acupuncture has been used with cocaine addicts. The National Institutes of Health, through its Office of Alternative Medicine (OAM), is answering this need by developing a database of researchers and practitioners to assist with grant applications for research into this area (letter dated February 27, 1995).

Perhaps one of the most important breakthroughs has been the research using positron emission tomography (PET), better known as a brain scan, which shows that "addiction is a brain disease" (Leshner 1998). From that scientific research, virtually all drugs, legal and illegal, have common effects on the mesolimbic reward system within the brain. Changes occur in all levels of the body—molecular, cellular, structural, and functional—that create long-lasting brain changes. On the basis of this research, the argument is that addiction (any addiction) is a prototypical psychobiological illness that demands treatment strategies of biological, behavioral, and social context elements. Like other brain diseases, including stroke, schizophrenia, and Alzheimer's disease, addictions should be addressed as a chronic, relapsing disease of the brain. Imprisoning youth and adults for a brain disease without treatment is futile. Policy strategies focusing solely on the social or criminal justice aspects of drug use and addiction will continue to be unsuccessful because they are missing the core of the problem—the changed brain.

Besides treatment for addicts, the society needs to develop policies that integrate strategies. Such a lesson comes from the research linking alcohol consumption with homicide rates. Parker (1998, 14) held that factors associated with violence were constant among individuals, neighborhoods, cities, and states: "Holding poverty, income, and the proportion of males ages 15–24 constant, homicide rates for both whites and nonwhites were found to be related to alcohol consumption over this 62-year period" since the repeal of Prohibition. In each case, alcohol consumption led the homicide rate and "declining alcohol consumption has played a role in the decline in homicide and other types of violence in the United States" (14). Locations with large concentrations of alcohol outlets are "hot spots" because they attract all kinds of people for both legal and illegal activities. People who live in and around such areas drink more alcohol on the average. Since there is a research link between alcohol consumption and homicide, planing and zoning rules that regulate the density of alcohol outlets and their placement in neighborhoods can have an impact on the quality of life. In addition, enforcement against underage drinking may also result in a significant drop in youth violence.

In conclusion, historic policy strategies and treatment focusing only on the voluntary behavior of the individual are grossly inadequate. A more holistic approach to treatment and prevention by many experts living and working in a community is vital for the quality of life of that community and its members.

Naive or Mentally Retarded Children

The distinction between certain forms of mental illness and mental retardation among youth is not always clear. Probation Officer William Beer (1976), of San Bernardino, California, mentioned that latent and incipient schizophrenics are often misdiagnosed. For example, schizophrenics score poorly on IQ tests because of their lack of interest in reality, not because they are mentally retarded.

When a youth's mental condition has reached the state of a catatonic stupor (frozen and immobile like a statue) or is characterized by florid hallucinations and delusions, the diagnosis of schizophrenia is easy. Yet the probability of a cure is extremely low.

Beer (1976) recommends using casework such as interviews with the child and others to gather information on hallucinations or delusions. Then, have the child diagnosed by a mental health professional. Sometimes, hospitalization can be avoided with good outpatient services. This kind of treatment is important because the youth's behavior may be a "cry for help rather than delinquency per se" (Beer 1976, 27).

Like dependent and neglected children, mentally retarded children become victimized by the fact that the state or local communities have no other placements available or lack an understanding of how to deal with these special youth. When they do crimes of murder, the courts often support the state's right to execute a brain-damaged child (*Dalton Prejean v. Larry D. Smith*, 889 F.2d 1391, 1989) or a mentally retarded person (*Bobby J. Wills v. Texas*, 114 S. Ct. 1867, 1994). See especially the dissent in *Wills*.

Learning Disabled

The learning disabled are protected under the Americans with Disabilities Act (ADA) and other civil rights acts. Their problem is not legal protection; it is the early identification, prevention, and remedial care that are missing in their lives. The juvenile justice system is often confronted with young people who have a learning disability that has not been previously detected. If not detected, the youth is not properly tested and the school will do nothing to remedy the situation.

See the beginning problem of B.B. that introduced Chapter 3.

For most children and adults, the fundamental skills of reading, spelling, writing, and arithmetic, once learned and practiced, come easily. For the learning disabled that is not true. However, having a learning disability does not mean that a person is mentally retarded.

Learning Disabilities Are not Mental Retardation

For children with a learning disability, materials and schoolwork suitable for others without learning impairments can be frustrating and difficult. But some compensate for their disabilities so well that they do not become noticeable until the individuals reach adolescence. Another problem is that there are various types or forms of learning disabilities and each has a slightly different effect on a person's physical or mental performance. If a child has a learning disability, it must be made clear what the specific condition is and how much the person's performance and ability to do something independently are affected. Professional testing aids in clarification.

For example, Attentional-Deficity Hyperactivity Disorder (ADHD) may be separate from a learning disability or it may be part of it. There is great controversy over the use of drugs such as Ritalin for controlling the youth. Parents have turned to other alternatives including nutritional supplements such as Mannatech where the medical research has shown symptoms of ADHD to be reduced by the addition to the diet of saccharides used by the body in glycoconjugate synthesis (Dykman and Dykman 1998).

Children with a learning disability face more than learning problems. The condition may be compounded by sensory disorder, emotional disturbance, or deficits in basic psychological processes that interfere with a person's memory, attention, language, perception, and coordination. Because learning disabilities are not outgrown, a large segment of the adult population may also be regarded as learning disabled. In *Clement v. Virginia Board of Bar Examiners* (case No. 3:96CV363 [1996]) dealing with an adult learning disabled person requesting double-time to take a bar exam instead of the traditional time and one-half), the United States District Court Judge for the Fourth Circuit permitted the bar examiners to prevail on a statute of limi-

The videotape *Retarding America—The Imprisonment of Potential* from the U.S. Department of Justice talks about different learning styles and the need for phonics for reading.

tations claim and through summary judgment. In his mind, the accommodations were reasonable, even though the experts were trying to instruct him through their affidavits that this particular student needed double time. His own confusion between a learning disability and mental impairment is evident from the following statements he made at the hearing for summary judgment:

It seems to me a sort of a sad commentary that there's
a person who probably could never pass the Bar, I
mean could never effectively practice law even if she
passed the Bar, and it looks like just passing the Bar
was sort of a trophy sort of pursuit of her which is
commendable. But, it seems to me that, she had a
Ph.D., a J.D., was a college professor, and has all sorts
of degrees bestowed upon her, there is a limit to what
can be done to accommodate people. (p. 13a)

In terms of the process in the juvenile court, a learning disabled suspect may be more susceptible, or have less resistance, to the influence of a person in authority, and may be less capable of understanding in that atmosphere of confrontation any explanation of his or her rights. The youth may nod his or her head in agreement but without fully knowing to what he or she has given consent.

The most crucial problem is that there are many hidden learning disabled persons. Officers on the street or in the court face the great challenge of not violating the principles of justice when dealing with learning disabled youth by seeing that the accused are guaranteed their constitutional rights. A judge, for example, must satisfy him- or herself when accepting a plea and rendering adjudication. A judge will have to consider all of the circumstances, including the age of the young person and the apparent degree of intelligence. A judge will have to be "cautious about simply accepting assurances of a young person who may state that he or she understands for any number of reasons: out of sheer naiveté; a desire not to appear 'stupid'; an attempt to appear cooperative; a wish to expedite and settle the matter; or to respond to peer or parental pressure" (Kirvan 1986, 52).

Caused by Many Factors

Learning disabilities can be caused by many factors. Before birth, the fetus's brain development can be altered by the foods or drugs ingested by the expectant mother. After birth, the baby can be affected by a host of things. The most severe would be a blow to the head, intentional or accidental. Other less severe, but just as damaging, influences include a lack of stimuli, such as light, sound, or people talking with or holding the child.

Highly Correlated with Low Birth Weight

Learning disabilities are highly correlated with babies who are born premature or with low birth weight. Some of those conditions stem from inadequate and insufficient prenatal care or the denial of such care to poor expectant mothers, the growing rate of drug and alcohol abuse among pregnant women, and the age of the mother giving birth.

Learning disabilities will or should be a concern for the future juvenile court. Like some of the other types of juvenile offenders, the problems of youth with learning impairments are diverse and multifaceted and thus demand the involvement of professionals like psychologists, neurologists, pediatricians, psychiatrists, teachers, speech and language pathologists, occupational therapists, and social workers. Optometrists do not conceptualize all reading and learning disabilities in terms of a single factor theory. Johnson, Nottingham, Stratton, and Zaba (1996) found a statistical significance between students who were academically and behaviorally at risk with lower scores on tracking of their eyes, stereopsis, hyperopia, and color vision subtests. Visual perception is not the same thing as "needing glasses." Eyes do more than receive impulses. They are gateways to the brain where the process of extracting and organizing information from the environment takes place. So the inability to perform at the visual perceptual level affects visual memory, symbolization, and conceptualization and thereby impacts the child's ability to respond to classroom instruction.

Bleything (1997, 211), in an extensive review of the literature on the health profile of the juvenile delinquent, notes that many juvenile offenders show an unusually high prevalence of dental problems, neurological problems, and vision/hearing anomalies because of prenatal/perinatal complications and head trauma. He concluded that many **visual dysfunctions could be viewed as neural dysfunctions** that become risk factors for juvenile delinquency. He strongly suspects that they are "causal factors" given the right set of circumstances.

The 1999 National PTA (Parent and Teacher Association) at their national convention was asked to support a resolution wherein they provide information to educate members, educators, administrators, and public health officials about learning-related visual problems and the need for more comprehensive visual skill tests in school vision screening programs. Tests for learning-related visual skills are necessary for children to be successful and learn effortlessly in classrooms.

The School for Contemporary Education (SCE), founded in 1967, is a good example of a professional multidisciplinary team approach to academic learning, emotional growth, and vocational training for children and adolescents with multiple learning and behavioral disabilities. Currently, ages at the school range from 5 to 21. A unique plan is made for each child with input from parents. The plan is enhanced by supervised real-life experiences in the community. For older children, independent living is developed by teaching functional skills in the on-site apartment and in the community. Serving the families in the Washington, D.C., metropolitan area, SCE, as a private, nonprofit organization, receives funding from United Way, local businesses, community groups, and members of the Chamber of Commerce.

In summary, each of these eight different types of offenders may engage in criminal activity, but the motivations or drives behind the crime vary from case to case. It is logical then to conclude that if the motivation is different, should not the treatment be administered on a case-by-case basis? Thus, the future of the juvenile court lies in its ability to identify and provide the proper treatment. Yet that is not easy. One reason is that the more chronic offender takes a great deal more of the resources of the state and its courts. Another reason is that courts are overburdened with cases and must try to dispose of them quickly to avoid an increasing backlog of juvenile cases. Plus, the public, including legislators, in their rush to see delinquents brought to justice, are looking for easy answers for very troubled youth.

Lastly, juvenile delinquency has roots in biological, psychological, and social factors, and thus, many disciplines need to be involved for prevention and treatment. For example, the research has consistently shown that birth complications are strongly related to violent criminal offending (Seward 1993), causing groups to advocate primary and secondary prevention, such as affordable prenatal care and medical attention for brain injuries and developmental problems. Child advocates have pointed to the need for programs that address the violent, abusive households that rear the violent youth as well as parenting skills. For example, a youth's perception and feeling about the mother's employment is more important than the actual employment. According to Cernkovich, Giordano, and Desmond (1997), if the youth are strongly bonded to the family and school, maternal employment did not appear to result in an increase of delinquency in 942 youth. Yet, weakly bonded children of working mothers were more likely to be delinquent than weakly bonded children of unemployed mothers.

FUTURE JUVENILE COURT

In the future, besides the need to identify specific youth needs and match youth with the programs discussed above, the courts will have to address four major concerns with delinquent youth: (1) increasing juvenile violence and crime rates; (2) disposition programs; (3) racial and sexual disparity in court practice; and (4) the expanded role of others in the court process and the judges in the community.

Increase in Violence and Expected Crime Rates

One of the greatest concerns for the future is the interplay between the increase of violence among juveniles and the expected population growth. In 1992, less than one-half of 1 percent of juveniles in the United States were arrested for a violent offense. But, as more of the population of young children grow into the teen years, there will be an increase in teenagers at a time when our society has become more violent. Let's look more closely at how that might play out.

Data gathered from a variety of sources show that a major turning point occurred in the mid-1980s when there was an increase in drug trafficking and when the use of guns became a function of crime. The figures also show a connection between youth and crime, noting that the younger years of life—age 18 and younger—have become the years of high rates for murder, the type of offense that traditionally was committed by young people aged 18 to 24. Age-specific crime rates have usually showed that they peak for juveniles in the late teen years and decline with advancing age. In regard to robbery, for example, the peak age of offending has been about 17. But, since 1985, rates of homicide, the number of gun-related homicides, and the rates in arrests of nonwhites for drug offenses have doubled. Blumstein (1995, 6) attributes the reason to the rapid growth of crack cocaine markets in the mid-1980s, because "To service the growth, juveniles were recruited, they were armed with the guns that are standard tools of the drug trade, and these guns then were diffused into the larger community of juveniles."

Snyder and Sickmund (1995b, iv), who wrote an extensive statistical analysis called *Juvenile Offenders and Victims: A National Report*, "estimate that by the year 2010 the number of juvenile arrests for a violent crime will more than double and the number of juvenile arrests for murder will increase nearly 150%" if both population growth and arrest rates continue to increase. Remember that some states with high juvenile arrest rates for some violent crimes do not necessarily have high juvenile arrest rates for all violent crimes. In 1992, for example, the states of New York, Florida, New Jersey, Maryland, and California had the highest juvenile violent crime arrest rates (Synder and Sickmund 1995a, 4).

Another dimension of this challenge is the fact that a person's race, sex, age, and socioeconomic status have a great deal to do with whether that individual will become a victim of a serious crime. Overall, any juvenile aged 12 to 17 is more likely to be the victim of a violent crime than any person past his or her mid-20s, because most offenders who victimize juveniles are family members, friends, or acquaintances. Also, whites are much more likely to be victims of property crimes, especially personal theft, than Hispanics or blacks, while black youth are more likely than whites to be victims of violent crimes, according to 1991 reports on victimization patterns. In fact, young black males have the highest homicide victimization rate of any race or sex group (Snyder and Sickmund 1995b)!

From the National Crime Victimization Survey in 1991, victimization of juveniles took place frequently—56 percent—within school or on school property, and the home ranked as the number two place of victimization. Equally important, few juvenile victimizations are reported to law enforcement, so there are, indeed, some hidden statistics. One reason is that most juvenile victims know their attacker, and young children are typically too afraid to report their experiences as victims. In effect, one in four violent attacks are committed against those under 12 (Snyder and Sickmund 1995b, 22–28).

Another reason for the lack of reporting victimization may well be that among the older youth, both the victim and the attacker were carrying a weapon. This finding is supported by a study done in 1990 by the Centers for Disease Control who asked a nationally representative sample of students in grades 9 through 12 how many times they had carried a weapon. According to those reporting, knives or razors were carried more often (55 percent) than clubs (24 percent) or firearms (21 percent). Usually males carried a firearm—a handgun. Fifty-four percent of black males who carried weapons, however, carried a firearm (Snyder and Sickmund 1995b, 52).

A recent longitudinal study of high-risk urban youth in Rochester, New York, shows a strong connection between illegal gun ownership, involvement in street crime, drug use, and gang activity. Compared with youth who had legal guns (3 percent), boys who owned illegal guns (7 percent) were more likely to be involved in street crime (74 percent vs. 14 percent), drug use (41 percent vs. 13 percent), and gang membership (54 percent vs. 7 percent) (Snyder and Sickmund 1995b, 25). Related research suggests that most weapon-related violence in schools occurs because the social worlds of some students encourage the use of weapons. Schools do not generate weapon-related violence. The students do not leave their disputes at the schoolhouse door but bring them in. Thus, even though the schools may prevent the violence through metal detectors and increased security, the source of trouble lies outside and out of the school (Sheley, McGee, and Wright 1995).

Snyder and Sickmund (1995c) recommend a 3 p.m. as opposed to a 10 p.m. curfew. Based on their research, adult violent crime increased through the nighttime hours, peaking between 10 p.m. and midnight. On the other

Curfews or Supervision after School

hand, violent crime by juveniles peaked between 3 p.m. and 4 p.m.—right after school!

Besides this increase in violence by juveniles, the juvenile population is growing—especially among racial and ethnic minorities who will produce different demands on the juvenile justice system. Of those racial and ethnic minorities, many live in poverty in the central cities. In 1992, for example, the poverty rates for African-American juveniles (47 percent) and those of Hispanic origin (40 percent) were far greater than the rates for white juveniles (17 percent). Children in single-parent families are more likely to be in poverty than those in two-parent families (Snyder and Sickmund 1995b, 6–8).

In addition, what some people call "babies" (very young women) are having babies themselves. "In 1960, 1 birth in 20 was to an unmarried woman; by 1990 it was 1 birth in 4" (Snyder and Sickmund 1995b, 10). These babies are more likely to have a low birth weight. Low birth weight is related to a smaller brain and defects in the neurological development of the child. Low birth weight is then highly correlated with developmental problems and school performance for the child. Thus the cycle of poverty continues when newborns do not have the potential to learn at the same rate as others and later will face barriers or constraints limiting their future choices in employment and the kind of money they will make.

All of this will produce different demands on the juvenile justice system. Paternity (see Chapter 7, "Other Hearings in Juvenile Court: Child Custody, Support, and Termination of Parental Rights") is only one of the spin-offs when juvenile judges use support issues as a prevention technique for delinquency.

Others will argue a "get-tough" approach. Some of the measures may be that states will lower the age for waiver. Some states may do away with the age requirement for waiver. Other states that have original jurisdiction are thinking of permitting the prosecutor to elect to indict the juvenile and proceed in adult court so that the burden is on the youth to remand the case back to juvenile court by showing that it would serve the public interest. In addition, some people are thinking of doing away with the juvenile court despite the growing research supported by federal and state monies that juveniles who are transferred to the adult court are more likely to reoffend.

Get-tough legislators are making the child seem more like a demon by calling the child a "punk." In one state, the new bills to be passed run the gamut of "5 unexcused absences in a school year means suspension of a minor's driving license" to leaving juvenile delinquents to the mercy of the prosecutor and transferring the "serious offender" from a juvenile correctional center to an adult facility after the youth reaches age 18 to complete his or her sentence (age of majority).

Thus, another issue involves the kinds of programs the juvenile court has for chronic, serious, and violent career youth. To better understand that problem, let us look at the different types of programs usually offered by the juvenile court as treatment.

Dispositional Programs

"Put Resources in the Playpen Instead of the State Pen." Robert E. Shepherd, Jr.

Dispositional programs are those programs that juvenile courts create to treat or reduce the criminal behavior of the youth found guilty of a criminal offense. As mentioned earlier, some courts put the resources at the front of the system so that the treatment really becomes early intervention and prevention. Other courts, lacking those resources, have treatment only for those adjudicated. Due to future restrictive budgets, the future juvenile court will have to be more creative in developing treatment programs for youth. Given the cost of keeping youth in correctional facilities, child advocates are suggesting that it would be more cost-effective to put money and other resources in the playpen instead of the state pen.

Dispositional programs as seen in Figure 4.2 show community youth homes, private placement, probation, other social agencies, and post-disposition detention as alternatives to commitments to state boards of corrections. Missing from Figure 4.2 are the more structured "boot camps" that are not camps. Boot camps were created in many states as the answer to juvenile crime only to find that juvenile robbers could now do a better job of outrunning the police and that shock incarceration with a mean drill leader did nothing to deal with drug addictions. Professionals, not politicians, argued for the movement away from large institutions and into community-based services. Community youth homes are nonsecure facilities. As expressed earlier in *In re Jose*, less restrictive placements need to be used before using the maximum secure facilities—prisons for youths. Some of the newer approaches in probation, diversion, secure confinement, and boot camps will be discussed.

Probation

When the juvenile court was first established, the chief so-called "treatment" for the child was probation. At first, probation was very informal. It was more like a second chance with a warning from the judge to correct one's behavior. Later, after World War II, all states had formalized adult probation staff and thus some of those newer ways of interviewing and establishing "case management" for the client trickled down into the juvenile court.

Today, probation staff usually do the intake functions and the social history investigation but have little time left to actually do any counseling. "On probation," as it is called, means the youth is released into the community, back with all of his or her friends, with the same parental controls, and so forth. The probation officer is supposed to be watching or supervising the juvenile, calling the school to make sure the youth has attended, and talking with the parents. In theory, it sounds good. In reality, there are too many youths with too many needs.

Thus, a new approach to probation has been intensive supervision or probation. It was developed to permit one juvenile probation officer to carry a reduced load of cases and thereby actually be able to meet with the child on a weekly basis to do counseling with the goal of keeping the youth from returning to the juvenile court with additional charges.

Some juvenile courts realize that waiting for the probation officer is too late. As a result, some courts have sought other remedies, such as diversion.

Diversion

Diversion is the process of taking certain children out of the process of the juvenile court and channeling them into formal or informal programs in the

PAL—Police Athletic Leagues

community. Some diversion programs may be sponsored by the police, such as police athletic leagues. These programs are offered pre-custody—before the juvenile court.

When we look at intake and disposition, we often find courts offering similar programs, except that more monies and resources are used at the intake stage than at the dispositional stage. An example of an intake diversion program is an educational program for families of 13- to 17-year-olds charged with minor drug, alcohol, or less serious offenses. It might be a seven-week, two-hour-per-week program for drug and alcohol awareness and improvement of interpersonal relationships. Another program would offer these services to younger children and their families. Other programs may provide wilderness activities or mediation. Mediation has worked well in such family matters as divorce and custody disputes, as well as in setting less violent criminal charges (Galaway and Hudson 1990).

Wilderness Mediation

The Michigan State Diversion Project for arrested juveniles uses college students as the principal caseworkers. The reasons for its success have been the fact that the youth respond better if treated outside the juvenile justice system, that the youth are in a natural context for intervention, and that service delivery by nonprofessionals is more effective and less costly (Howell 1995, 146).

In 1976, the Office of Juvenile Justice and Delinquency Prevention (OJJDP) began the movement to early diversion programs for youth who were at risk by creating eleven model diversion programs. The evaluation showed that the programs were clearly distinct from the justice system. Based on the reports of clients and service providers, the programs were less coercive, less controlling, and more oriented to meeting clients' needs than comparable justice agencies. Yet there was evidence that only three such programs had reduced the penetration of youth through the court system. In addition, although the programs succeeded at meeting many of the criteria of true diversion, they were no more successful in avoiding stigma or reducing delinquent behavior (Dunford, Osgood, and Weichselbaum 1982).

Perhaps part of the problem lies in our inability to get to the root causes of the pain for the child. A second challenge is: If we do find the cause, how do we match the child with a specific program or create a program to deal with the needs? For example, females studied in Clark County (Nevada) Juvenile Court Services in 1985 (N = 129) and 1988 (N = 219) who had been charged with a violent crime were given program referrals in only 29.5 percent of the cases. Yet more females (89.1 percent) were charged with assault and battery (fighting) than males (67 percent) (Tracy and Shelden 1992).

More progressive communities have developed community-based diversion in such settings as schools, or have directed their attention at family-guidance programs such as parenting classes. Some schools offer conflict resolution and violence prevention curricula, peer mediation, peer counseling, and special one-on-one tutoring by older students, adult volunteers, and trained paraprofessionals. Schools are also developing behavior management strategies to monitor and reinforce attendance, academic progress, and school behavior. In addition, special educational placements have had to be created for disruptive, disturbed, and learning disabled students. Other diversion programs provide a variety of family services, including parenting skills training, intensive family preservation, and marital and family counseling (Howell 1995).

Community and national agencies also have begun to organize diversion programs. For example, in 1992, Congress authorized the National Guard to develop and implement pilot programs to aid high school dropouts in acquiring life-value enhancing and employable skills. An example is ChalleNGe, which was founded in 1992 and which had branches in sixteen states in 1994. The program targets 16- to 18-year-old youth who are drug-free, are not on probation or parole, and have never been convicted of a felony offense. These youth are provided with an opportunity to attend a twenty-two-week military school offering life and job skills, physical education, and coursework in areas of teamwork. In addition, the youth take GED (Graduation Equivalency Degree) preparatory courses so they can obtain a GED certificate and receive a scholarship of $2,200 for further education.

ChalleNGe

Secure Confinement

Secure confinement means total security—being locked up. In some cases, confinement means that the youth is sent back into detention for a period of six months. Usually, confinement means going to a state facility called a correctional center—a prison for youth. Some states are now using boot camps, modeled after the Army and shock incarceration programs, to teach youth life skills in communication and use of time. The biggest drawbacks to the program are its shortness and lack of aftercare.

Altschuler and Armstrong (1994) developed a theoretical model that integrates strain, social learning, and social control theories to assist youth in their reintegrative process. Figure 4.7 shows how the service areas mesh with the program elements to increase responsibility and freedom for the youth while the community develops new resources, supports, and opportunities. They recommend the use of risk assessment tools (like the one in Figure 4.6). The model helps to identity both the potential safety issues for the community and the special needs that should be addressed to assist the youth and his or her family.

Intensive aftercare or parole involves individual case planning, and the use and involvement of many individuals, agencies, and resources from the community. If the conditions of the parole or aftercare relate to the offender's needs, the conditions will be taken more seriously than will a laundry list of unenforceable conditions. However, electronic monitoring and drug and alcohol testing, as mentioned earlier, preclude the aftercare or parole officer from active involvement with the parolee and the family.

Boot Camps

Boot camp prisons began in Georgia in 1983 and Oklahoma in 1984. By 1988, fifteen programs were operating (Parent, Chaiken, and Logan 1989). By October 1991, there were over 34 programs in 23 states involving over 4,000 convicted felons (MacKenzie and Souryal 1991).

Boot camp is a shock incarceration correctional practice, usually for three to six months, with a demanding and rigorous schedule, strict discipline, military-style drill and ceremony, and physical exercise and labor. Usually it is for young offenders convicted of less serious, nonviolent crimes who

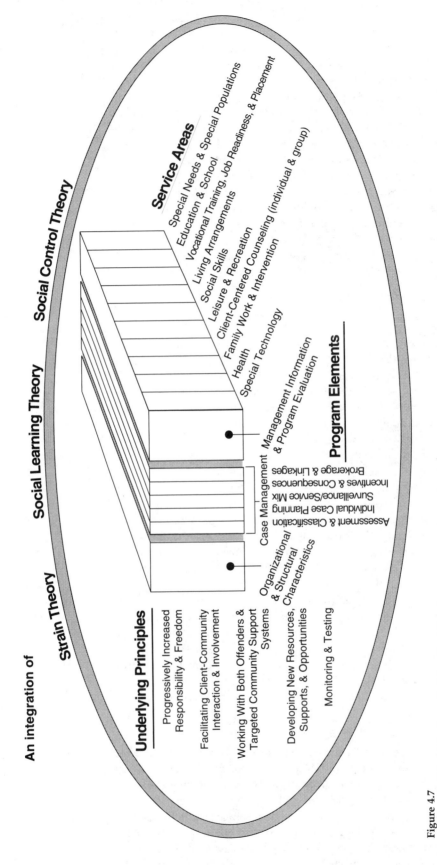

Figure 4.7
Intervention Model for Juvenile Intensive Aftercare.
Source: Altschuler and Armstrong 1994, 3.

have not been imprisoned. Since it is less confining than a traditional prison, hence the term camp, it is known as one of several "intermediate sanctions" that are currently popular. However, according to MacKenzie and Souryal (1991), there are no statistical data to support its effectiveness. Instead, the driving forces for the concept, especially for its use with juveniles, is society's need to punish offenders ("just deserts") and discipline them at a reduced cost to the state.

In short, although some states are moving toward bigger juvenile institutions or military-style institutions, the research supports short-term incarceration with long-term reintegration. To have a major expansion of juvenile justice institutions without a like expansion in community-based services or programs to support children and their families is a disservice to the youth and to the public. To build only prisons is to play upon the public's fear of crime and to give them a sense of safety that is false.

The bottom line is that it takes a whole village to raise a child. If we do not do it to begin with, we do it by default. Perhaps we should see the juvenile court as another segment of our society instead of looking to it to solve all the juveniles' problems. This, of course, will require cooperation among courts, criminal justice, and social agencies, as well as civic and church groups. Such cooperation can help in providing more effective intervention strategies in areas of problem-solving, case management, and referral. The Weaversville Intensive Treatment Unit is such an example for it is operated under a contract with the Commonwealth of Pennsylvania and by Career System Development Corporation, Division of Redirection Programs from New York for twenty-three chronic violent male juvenile offenders (Eisenbauch and Freeman 1992). Yet, take, for example, those parents who never had their emotional or physical needs met. Is it then realistic to expect that these parents can raise their children in a nurturing environment without some kind of teaching, training, or assistance? Clearly not. Therefore, the future of the juvenile court depends upon its ability to interrelate and integrate all possible services and resources and to advocate the needs of children.

It takes a whole village to raise a child. African Proverb

Hope for the Future—Restorative Justice

Restorative justice is one of those new philosophies that operate through the criminal justice system to provide protection for the public by strengthening the community and also holding the offenders accountable. It is a shift from using the power of the state with its warehousing of youthful offenders to repair the harm resulting from the crime. In this type of thinking, the restorative-justice model requires the youthful offender to earn his or her way back into the community by making amends to the victim and the community with the assistance of the community. This model may mean programs of mediation between the victim and the offender before the case actually goes to court, similar to a diversion program. Minnesota, Montana, Pennsylvania, and Vermont call it a family group conference with the victim, the offender, the family and friends of both, and in some cases a mediator. In Canada, circle sentencing has been used with a judge, prosecutor, defense attorney, victim, offender, supporters for both, and interested community member who all consider the issues of the crime and the impact on the community so as to develop a plan for the offender to be held accountable and make amends. It is the community that helps turn the theory into practice, so it will look different from community to community. Yet the guiding principles permit restorative measures that are free from racism or other biases that promote separation instead of inclusion and community problem-solving. (See *The Plan for Restoring Justice* prepared by the South Carolina Justice Fellowship Task Force, P.O. Box 24648, Columbia, South Carolina 29224.)

Racial and Sexual Disparity

Inconsistency in court practice and judiciary decisions account for racial disparity. Some of it has not been reported. Of that which is reported, Pope and Feyerherm (1993), in researching racial disparity in the empirical literature of the social sciences, conclude that bias does exist. It can appear at any stage of juvenile processing. In some cases, what are seemingly small racial differences can accumulate and become more pronounced as minority youth proceed farther into the juvenile justice system.

For example, Bishop and Frazier (1990) used statewide data over a three-year period to examine case processing through Florida's juvenile justice system and found that race (for nonwhites) did make a difference. According to Bishop and Frazier (1990, 3):

Nonwhite juveniles processed for delinquency offenses in 1987 received more severe (i.e., more formal and/or more restrictive) dispositions than their white counterparts at several stages of juvenile processing. Specifically, we found that when juvenile offenders were alike in terms of age, gender, seriousness of the offense which prompted the current referral, and seriousness of their prior records, the probability of receiving the harshest disposition available at each of several processing stages was higher for nonwhite than for white youth.

Likewise, Kemph, Decker, and Bing (1990), who studied eight juvenile circuit courts in the Missouri juvenile justice system, found that in urban courts African-American youth were more likely than their white counterparts to be held in detention and more likely to be referred for felony offenses. One of the reasons was parental influence. Parental influences included such outcomes as whether the parents were willing to provide family support for the youth and whether the youth resided in an intact home. That, in turn, had a bearing on the court's decision-making when dealing with youth offenders. For example, in rural courts, African-Americans received more severe punishments at the disposition stage. They were more likely than white youth to be placed out of the home. The researchers stated that legal decision processes have been systematically disadvantaging youths who are either black, female, or both.

Secret and Johnson (1997, 445), in examining Nebraska Crime Commission data from 1988–1993, found that "black youths are usually more likely to receive harsher treatment than whites in regard to prehearing detention and final penalty. With regard to judging an accused youth to be delinquent or a status offender, the analysis reveals a reversal of this relationship between race and harshness of outcomes: whites are more likely to be found delinquent."

Racial disparity also extends to Southeast Asians and Hispanics—a growing minority but the research is minimal except for gangs. For example, Ying, Akutsu, Zhang, and Huang (1997) interviewed 2,234 Vietnamese, Cambodian, Laotian, Hmong, and Chinese-Vietnamese refugees to try to understand how and why they are able to mediate the effects of external stressors. It maybe that we as a nation can learn from some of their strengths in terms of their families and their practices and beliefs in Buddhism. (See also Zhou and Bankston III [1998], *Growing Up American: How Vietnamese Children Adapt to Life in the United States*.)

Bishop and Frazier (1992) showed that female status offenders were more likely to be petitioned into the juvenile court than were males. They argued that a "double standard" was operating instead of the Juvenile Justice Delinquency and Prevention Act of 1972, which was to equalize males and females.

Juvenile crime among girls under age 18 has been greatly increasing over the years. The arrest rates, according to the *Uniform Crime Report*, have more than tripled between 1960 and 1975. In contrast, prior to that period, females were arrested for activities exclusively related to sexual activity. Today, females are arrested not only for incorrigibility, running away, and promiscuity, but also for more aggressive and criminal behavior, namely, murder, robbery, aggravated assault, and larceny-theft (Chesney-Lind and Shelden 1992, 7–14).

Some females operate alone. Some work with other people, especially males. In fact, it is usually a female who carries the drugs for a male because they both think that she, if caught, will get a more lenient sentence.

In some states, women are even arrested for forcible rape because they have helped men to violently force other women. In addition, some females form gangs and cause trouble for police and citizens. In some large cities, like Philadelphia, female cliques, ranging from a few to several dozen members, engage in typical male gang activity, such as the Black Persuaders and the Sedgewick Sisters. There have always been girl gangs, but the majority have seemed to be female branches of the male gangs. These affiliates serve as the social leg of male gangs. For example, the *Vice Ladies* is a gang of girls organized with the *Vice Lords* in New York City. The Ladies' responsibility is to be wherever needed when needed. For example, they carry weapons such as razors and guns in their bras.

Once a female juvenile offender is arrested, she enters the juvenile justice system much like a male. Yet the processing and decision-making concerning females in many localities and states reflect a "double standard." The earliest and most comprehensive research on sex discrimination in police arrest practice was conducted by Chesney-Lind (1973) and in some places remains true today. Her research suggests that police treat girls more leniently when they are accused of criminal offenses, but less leniently when they are accused of status offenses. For example, girls tend to be arrested for offenses that are less serious than those committed by boys. In fact, about one-half of all girls are either arrested for larceny-theft (shoplifting) or running away from home. Of the girls who go to runaway shelters or juvenile detention facilities, two-thirds to three-fourths are victims of child sexual abuse. Police and officers of the juvenile court seem to be parental in their attitudes and overly concerned about female misbehavior, which would appear to endanger a young woman's reputation. Perhaps the perception in the minds of law enforcement officers is that there is a dualism among women—good women and bad women—and that their greatest efforts should be directed at helping good girls become better women. The end result is that in 1987 only 3 percent of the boys in detention facilities were being held on status offenses as opposed to nearly 20 percent of the females (Chesney-Lind and Shelden 1992).

Programs for troubled, youthful female offenders have existed for centuries. Examples of early programs included the Magdalen Society (Teeters 1956, 157–158) of Philadelphia, Pennsylvania, in 1800, and the Female Humane Association of Richmond, Virginia. The Female Humane Association was a nonsectarian home for virtuous and indigent females begun by Chief Justice John Marshall's wife, Mary Marshall, and Clara Hoxall.

The Good Shepherd Center in Baltimore, Maryland, is a continuation of a program established in 1864 by the Sisters of the Good Shepherd. They handle girls who have a high risk of becoming delinquents, in addition to being emotionally disturbed and in need of special education. Court adjudicated CHINS (or PINS) and delinquents are also helped. Throughout the years, different kinds of services and programs have been developed to help young women receive education and psychological treatment so that they can make responsible and knowledgeable decisions. The residential treatment program is the usual group living experience in a therapeutic environment. *MacTavish Apartment* is a newer program begun in 1980 for girls who have been through the residential treatment program and need to strengthen their independent living skills. The obvious goals are to help these young women live alone, take a job, or develop their educational skills so they can go on to college. In addition to the residential and apartment living programs, there are day programs and outreach programs that offer both counseling and assistance with home management to young girls and their families.

Some of the programs for female youthful offenders are centered in institutions and others are community-based. Some deal with those adjudicated. The following, located in Tucson, Arizona, is an example of a nonresidential program:

The Direct Services Program of New Directions for Young Women is a short-term, nonresidential program that serves young women between the ages of 12 and 25. The average time spent with each client is about 14 hours per week. The program began in 1976, with funds from the Office of Juvenile Justice and Delinquency Prevention, with the intent to provide alternatives to secure confinement for young women in trouble and to advocate for positive change within institutions and organizations that have the greatest effect on the lives of these young women.

The program deals primarily with young women who are at-risk of delinquency. Approximately 90% of the population served are girls who are pregnant, have experienced sexual abuse or incest, or are having severe family problems and have run away or are considering it as an option. The average age of the client served is 16, although, as stated previously, the age range has been as wide as 12 to 25. Out of the 1,700 clients served by the program in 1980, approximately 600 were aided with individual counseling specifically. The remaining 1,100 girls received group counseling in the center as well as outside the center in their school or home. New Directions provides services from the feminist view-point, and they are designed for young women who need support, information, and guidance, rather than therapy. Through the Educational Program, Groups, Individual/Family Counseling, and Retreat Program, New Directions staff help girls deal with the issues directly affecting them, such as birth control, sexuality, rape, the job market, and local cultural and educational opportunities. The Direct Services program components are available in local schools, agencies, and organizations. The staff makes every effort to establish close relationships with teachers, counselors, and others in the community who affect the lives of the young women in question. In fact, the majority of young women served receive services in their schools. (Programs for Young Women in Trouble, 5–6)

Many of the early delinquency theories reflect traditional notions of class and masculinity. Therefore, some authors do not believe that we can continue to understand female delinquency just by taking old theories and "add-women-and-stir" (Chesney-Lind and Shelden 1992). Other dimensions that need to be included are the fact that many of the young women have been victimized and have poor self-images, relatively low expectations from life, and low confidence in themselves. Many victims have low self-esteem because of the influence of adults imposing sexual activities upon children disrupts psychosexual development of children. That means that if a child is "taught" at age 5 to have sexual intercourse with someone, that child's development is arrested emotionally at age 5, even though the body grows to adulthood. This may lead into prostitution.

Teenage prostitution can be both commercial and survival sex. Survival sex is the term given to acts of sex in which the female or male receives housing, food, clothing, and even drugs. Survival sex is what one does in return for what one needs. The director of **Children of the Night**, an agency in Hollywood that tries to help teenage prostitutes, says that the girls are getting younger (40 percent were under age 15) and come from dysfunctional families characterized by alcoholism or drug abuse, physical abuse, and neglect (Chesney-Lind and Shelden 1992, 38).

Simons and Whitbeck (1991) used a sample of 40 adolescent girls and a sample of 95 homeless women to study the direct and indirect effect of sexual abuse on prostitution. Their research suggests that early sexual abuse only indirectly affects the chances of victimization. For example, repeated child sexual abuse provides training for a young girl to use the technique of "emotional distancing," which is useful in the trade of prostitution.

Yet we know that not all sexually abused women become prostitutes on the streets. Some get married. Some stay single, and some may change their sexual orientation. Some may even inflict their pain as physical or sexual abuse on their own children as well as others.

Therefore, there must be some other sociological variables that assist boys and girls in learning the trade of prostitution. One has to learn the street culture, the language, and the differences between cops and johns in order to survive.

It has only been more recently that professionals who work with young women are documenting an addiction to sex and to rage. They are creating programs that are sensitive to their special needs. In addition, research on young, pregnant African-American women showed that young women with a history of sexual victimization were more symptomatic, had lower self-esteem, and had a more external locus of control than the non-victimized woman (Rhodes, Ebert, and Meyers 1993). In short, the link between sexual victimization and psychological distress in pregnant and parenting adolescents needs to be addressed to stop the cycle. It is hoped that more will be done in the future.

Expanded Role

In the future, there will be an expanded role in the juvenile court for several key players. The first is the public, who will make more demands upon the juvenile justice system. Others will be the attorney and the court itself. First to be discussed is how the public will ask for more involvement through the press.

The Public

The juvenile court is not totally public like the adult criminal court, and press personnel do not have the access they desire. Appendix 4A has a copy of a legal brief written to support the motion that a newspaper reporter be permitted to see the juvenile court record of a particular "hit man" for drug dealers. The juvenile had been waived into adult court, but the case was dismissed because the material witness did not appear to testify. Later, the youth was killed with four "hits" to the back of his head—street justice. The police suspected that the youth himself was a hit man for drug dealers. Since this youth was so deep into criminal activity, the reporter was hoping to get access to the juvenile's record to write a story. The motion was denied.

The U.S. Supreme Court, in a series of decisions (*Davis v. Alaska*, 415 U.S. 308 [1974], *Oklahoma Pub. Co. v. District Court*, 430 U.S. 308 [1977], *Smith v. Daily Mail Pub.*, 443 U.S. 97 [1979], *Penna. v. Ritchie*, 480 U.S. 39 [1987]), has ruled that there is no categorical right to complete confidentiality or to publicity. The public does have a right to access to criminal trials, but that right must be balanced against juvenile and state rights. Information lawfully obtained out of court cannot be restrained. On the other hand, constitutional rights can outweigh state and juvenile rights. Thus, juvenile judges must employ an *in camera* (in chambers) review of the situation, balancing the needs of both parties before ruling on access (in states that permit judicial discretion).

Some states are seeking to pass laws that require all proceedings and records maintained by the juvenile or family courts regarding juvenile crime and traffic offenses to be open to the public. The court may, with the consent of the accused, close the proceedings only if it finds that to do so is necessary to protect the interests of the victim or witness. By passing a law, the states see themselves as being able to bypass some of the above mentioned Supreme Court decisions.

The key buzzword will be accountability. The public may become more involved in judge selection and retention. Some of their involvement, especially in the case of citizen groups assisting the court, may be welcome.

Attorneys

Although *Gault* gave juveniles the constitutional entitlement to the assistance of counsel, Feld (1993, 72) found that half of the jurisdictions for which data were available are not in compliance. In Nebraska, Minnesota, and North Dakota, nearly half or more of delinquent and status offenders appear without lawyers. Many youth who were adjudicated delinquent and received out-of-home and secure confinement had no attorney. In Minnesota, "in only six of Minnesota's 87 counties are even a majority of juveniles involved in delinquency proceedings represented, and in 68 counties, a total of only 19.3 of such juveniles have counsel" (Feld 1993, 241).

The issue is: What factors get youth sent to correctional facilities? Feld's (1993) statistical analysis of data shows no powerful, explanatory relationship between the legal variables and dispositions. Present offense and prior record, typically the most powerful explanatory legal variables, account for only about 25 percent of the variance in sentencing.

One might interpret that to mean there is true "individualized justice" in that the judge considered both legal and social variables. Others disagree with that interpretation. Court watchers suggest that there is no rationale to dispositional decision-making. Guesswork and hunches become euphemisms for subjectivity, arbitrariness, and discrimination.

Minor offenders can receive much more severe dispositions than serious offenders. Youth who have the same present offense or prior record can receive markedly dissimilar dispositions depending upon the county in which they are tried, the judge before whom they appear, the manner in which their guilt is determined, or their race or gender.

The way we treat youth in the name of the state cuts to the heart of the juvenile court as an institution. If we do not treat youth fairly and meaningfully, where will they ever learn those qualities?

An expanded role for attorneys would be more competence to have more competent attorneys who understand child development stages. California, Pennsylvania, and New York provide legal counsel for the vast majority of young offenders. What is more impressive is the fact that very low numbers of uncounseled juveniles receive out-of-home placement or secure confinement dispositions. So what can the other states do?

Would mandatory and nonwaivable counsel help? Would a prohibition on waivers of counsel without prior consultation with and the concurrence of counsel on the record help to make waiver "knowing, intelligent, and voluntary"?

Feld's (1993, 256) research shows that:

many unrepresented juveniles are routinely adjudicated delinquent and removed from their homes or incarcerated. In addition, within each offense category, first offenders have the lowest rate of representation, thereby increasing the probability that any subsequent sentences they receive will be based upon those prior, uncounseled convictions. Status offenders have the lowest initial rate of representation. If they return to juvenile court for violating a condition of probation or a court order, then they may be adjudicated delinquent and sentenced to an institution like any other delinquent despite the absence of counsel at their original hearing for the status offense (L.E.A. v. Hammergren, 294 N.W.2d 705 [Minn. 1980]). *Moreover, earlier dispositions are consistently the most important variable explaining later ones. Finally, it is undoubtedly the case that many of these unrepresented juveniles will later be tried as adults and have their prior, uncounseled convictions included in their adult criminal history scores.*

In addition to the role of attorneys being expanded, the services that an attorney can give need to be expanded to a meaningful representation for youth. Youth are not like other clients. Attorneys will need much more training, education, and sensitivity than what present law schools are giving in order to effectively represent youth—especially troubled youth who have difficulty trusting others. Youth will have to be shown they are worth the investment.

Involvement of Judges

The juvenile court, since the *Gault* decision, is first and foremost a legal entity engaged in formal social control. That means that certain "fairness" and rules need to be followed, including the right to attorney. To have only 25.1 percent of the 77 rural counties in Minnesota with legal counsel for juveniles (Feld 1993, 247) is sad for Minnesota youth. But Minnesota is probably not that unusual in comparison to other states.

 In addition to seeing to the legal needs of children, judges will need to be more involved in the communities. Crime is a complex phenomenon demanding that many agencies and private and public groups get together as a united front to put limits on people's behavior and provide equality services while holding people accountable for the services they receive.

In the past, some progressive juvenile judges have used the power of their position and their innate ability to persuade to create exciting, innovative programs such as Homebuilders and Court Appointed Special Advocates (CASA). Today, more can be done to include more of the community in partnerships with public, private, and nonprofit corporations.

SUMMARY

This chapter looked at how the juvenile court handled youth who are charged with crimes. The juvenile court was discussed in terms of **intake**, **detention**, **waiver**, **adjudication**, and **disposition**. Each of the five stages was discussed in terms of purpose, decision-maker, rights, standard of proof, qualification, and the role of the attorney. (See Table 4.1 at the beginning of the chapter for a summary.) The chapter concluded with delinquency in the computer age and the future of the juvenile court. (See Figure 4.2 for a summary of the entire juvenile justice system—from the reporting source, through the courts, to probation or secure facilities, and then to aftercare.)

To recap, Chapters 3 and 4 have shown you that delinquent youth have specific rights that translate into specific job demands for those who arrest and work with youth. These rights are very different from those of abused and neglected children, as you will see in Chapter 5.

REFERENCES

Abel, G.G., M.S. Mihelman, and J.B. Becker. "Sex Offenders: Results of Assessment and Recommendations for Treatment." In *Clinical Criminology: Current Concepts*, edited by H. Ben-Aaron, S. Hacker, and C. Webster. Toronto: M & M Graphics, 1985.

Altschuler, David M., and Troy L. Armstrong. *Intensive Aftercare for High-Risk Juveniles: Policies and Procedures. Program Summary*. Washington, D.C.: Office of Juvenile Justice and Delinquency Prevention, 1994.

American Bar Association. *An Introduction to Indigent Defense Systems*. Chicago: ABA, 1986.

Asbury, Herbert. *The Gangs of New York*. New York: Knopf, 1928.

Bard, Barbara, Marilyn Feldman, Dorothy Lewis, Jonathan Pincus, Leslie Prichep, Ellis Richardson, and Catherine Yeager. "Neuropsychiatric, Psychoeducational, and Family Characteristics of 14 Juveniles Condemned to Death in the United States." *American Journal of Psychiatry* 145 (1988): 584–589.

Bazemore, Gordon, and Mark S. Umbreit. *Balanced and Restorative Justice, Program Summary*. Washington, D.C.: U.S. Department of Justice, Office of Juvenile Justice and Delinquency Prevention, 1994.

Beer, William. "Probation Supervision of the Schizophrenic Adolescent." *Federal Probation* 40 (1976): 21–28.

Bishop, Donna M., and C. E. Frasier (1990). "A Study of Race and Juvenile Processing in Florida." A report submitted to the Florida Supreme Court Racial and Ethnic Bias Study Commission and quoted in Carl E. Pope and William Feyerherm, *Minorities and the Juvenile Justice System, Research Summary*. Washington, D.C.: Office of Juvenile Justice and Delinquency Prevention, 1993.

Bishop, Donna M., and Charles M. Frazier. "Gender Bias in Juvenile Justice Processing: Implications of the JJDP." *Journal of Criminal Justice*, 82 (4): 1163–1185, 1992.

Bleything, Willard B. "The Health Profile of the Juvenile Delinquent," *Journal of Optometric Vision Development*, 28 (1997): 204–212.

Blumstein, Alfred. "Why the Deadly Nexus?" *National Institute of Justice Journal*, Issue 229. Washington, D.C.: U.S. Department of Justice, Office of Justice Programs, National Institute of Justice, 1995.

Bohen, Jim. "Drunk Driving," *Geico Direct*, 10 (1996): 8–10.

Bortner, M.A. "Traditional Rhetoric Organizational Realities: Remand of Juveniles to Adult Court." *Crime and Delinquency* 32 (1986): 53–69.

Brown, Claude. *Manchild in the Promised Land*. New York: New American Library, 1965.

Carondelet Management Institute. *Gangs*. Tucson, Arizona: Author, 1992a.

———. "An Introduction to 'Gangster' Rap Music and Its Correlation to the Gang Environment." Unpublished manuscript. Tucson, Arizona, Author, 1992b.

Chesney-Lind, Meda. "Judicial Enforcement of the Female Sex Role." *Issues in Criminology* 8 (1973): 51–70.

Chesney-Lind, Meda, and Randall G. Shelden. *Girls, Delinquency, and Juvenile Justice*. Pacific Grove, CA: Brooks/Cole Publishing Company, 1992.

Clement, M. "Juvenile Waiver." Unpublished paper presented at American Society of Criminology national meeting, November 1993. Revised "A Five-Year Study of Juvenile Waiver and Adult Sentencing: Implications for Policy." *Criminal Justice Policy Review* 8 (2/3): 201–219, 1997.

Cernkovick, Stephen, Peggy C. Giordano, and Scott Desmond. "Maternal Employment and Delinquency." Unpublished paper presented at Academy of Criminal Justice Sciences 1997.

Crowe, Timothy D. *Habitual Juvenile Offenders: Guidelines for Citizen Action and Public Responses*. Washington, D.C.: Office of Juvenile Justice and Delinquency Prevention, 1991.

Dunford, F.W., D.W. Osgood, and H.E. Weichselbaum. *National Evaluation of Diversion Projects. Executive Summary*. Washington, D.C.: U.S. Dept. of Justice, 1982.

Dykman, Kathryn, and Roscoe A. Dykman. "Effect of Nutritional Supplements on Attentional-Deficity Hyperactivity Disorder," *Integrative Physiological and Behavioral Science* 33 (1998): 49–60.

Eisenbuch, Arthur J., and Michael H. Freeman. "The Weaversville Intensive Treatment Unit Effective Programming for Chronic, Violent Juvenile Offenders." Unpublished paper presented to the Academy of Criminal Justice Sciences, 1992.

Feld, Barry C. "The Juvenile Court Meets the Principle of the Offense: Legislative Changes in Juvenile Waiver Statutes." *Journal of Criminal Law and Criminology* 78 (3) (1987): 471–533.

——. *Justice for Children. The Right to Counsel and the Juvenile Courts*. Boston: Northeastern University Press, 1993.

Forst, Martin L. *The New Juvenile Justice*. Chicago, IL: Nelson-Hall Publishers, 1995.

Freeman-Longo, R.E. "Juvenile Sex Offenders in History of Adult Rapists and Child Molesters." *International Journal of Offender Therapy and Comparative Criminology* 27 (2) (1983): 150–155.

Fritsch, Eric J., Tony J. Caeti, and Craig Hemmens. "Spare the Needle But Not the Punishment: The Incarceration of Waived Youth in Texas Prisons." *Crime and Delinquency* 42 (1996): 593–609.

Galaway, Burt, and Joe Hudson. *Criminal Justice, Restitution, and Reconciliation*. Monsey, NY: Criminal Justice Press, 1990.

Groth, N. *Men Who Rape: The Psychology of the Offender*. New York: Plenum Press, 1977.

Hanson, Roger A., William E. Hewitt, Brian J. Ostrom, and Christopher Lomvardias. *Indigent Defenders: Get the Job Done and Done Well*. Williamsburg, VA: National Center for State Courts, 1992.

Hatchell, Billie S. *Rising Above Gangs and Drugs*. Lomita, CA: Community Reclamation Project, 1990.

Houghtalin, M., and G.L. Mays. "Criminal Dispositions of New Mexico Juveniles Transferred to Adult Court." *Crime and Delinquency* 37 (1991): 393–407.

Howell, James C. "Gangs." In *Fact Sheet #12*. Washington, D.C.: Office of Juvenile Justice and Delinquency Prevention, 1994.

Howell, James C., ed. *Guide for Implementing the Comprehensive Strategy for Serious, Violent, and Chronic Juvenile Offenders*. Washington, D.C.: Office of Juvenile and Delinquency Prevention, 1995.

Johnson, Claire, Barbara Webster, and Edward Connors. "Prosecuting Gangs: A National Assessment." In *Research in Brief*. Washington, D.C.: National Institute of Justice, 1995.

Johnson, Roger A., Derick Nottingham, Randi Stratton, and Joel N. Zaba. "The Vision Screening of Academically and Behaviorally At-Risk Pupils." *Journal of Behavioral Optometry* 7 (2) (1996): 39–42.

Juvenile Law Reports. Warrensburg, MO: Knehans-Miller Pub., 1993.

Juveniles Taken into Custody: Fiscal Year 1990 Report. Washington, D.C.: Dept. of Justice and Juvenile Justice and Delinquency Prevention, 1991.

Keiter, Robert. "Criminal or Delinquent? A Study of Juvenile Cases Transferred to the Criminal Court." *Crime and Delinquency* 18 (1973): 528–538.

Kemph, K.L., S.H. Decker, and R.L. Bing. *An Analysis of Apparent Disparities in the Handling of Black Youth within Missouri's Juvenile Justice System*. University of Missouri-St. Louis: Department of Administration of Justice, 1990, and quoted in Carl E. Pope and William Feyerherm, *Minorities and the Juvenile Justice System, Research Summary*. Washington, D.C.: Office of Juvenile Justice and Delinquency Prevention, 1993.

Kirvan, Mary-Anne. "Commentary on the Implications of the *Young Offenders Act* for Treatment and Rehabilitation." In *Learning Disabilities and the Young Offender: Arrest to Disposition*, edited by Howard Stutt. Ottawa, Ontario: The Canadian Association for Children and Adults with Learning Disabilities, 1986.

Krantz, Sheldon. *Right to Counsel in Criminal Cases: The Mandate of Argersinger v. Hamlin*. Cambridge, MA: Ballinger Publishing Company, 1979.

Krisberg, Barry, Ira M. Schwartz, Paul Litsky, and James Austin. "The Watershed of Juvenile Justice Reform." *Crime and Delinquency* 32 (1) (1986): 5–37.

Leshner, Alan I. "Addiction Is a Brain Disease—and It Matters." *National Institute of Justice Journal* October 1998, 2–6.

MacKenzie, D.L., and C.C. Souryal. "Boot Camp Survey: Rehabilitation, Recidivism Reduction Outrank Punishment as Main Goals." *Corrections Today* 53 (1991): 90–96.

Matza, David. *Delinquency and Drift*. New York: John Wiley & Sons, 1964.

Miller, Walter. *Violence by Youth Gangs and Youth Groups as a Crime Problem in Major American Cities*. Washington, D.C.: U.S. Government Printing Office, 1975.

Nambudripad, Devi S. *Say Goodbye to Illness*. Buena Park, CA: Delta Publishing Company, 1993.

OJJDP, and American Probation and Parole Association. *Drug Testing Guidelines and Practices for Juvenile Probation and Parole Agencies*. Washington, D.C.: U.S. Department of Justice, 1992.

Orchovsky, Stan, and Tammy M. Poulos. "Serious Juvenile Offenders: Predicting the Probability of Transfer to Criminal Court." *Crime and Delinquency* 40 (1) (1994): 3–17.

Parent, D.G., M. Chaiken, and W. Logan. *Shock Incarceration: An Overview of Existing Programs*. National Institute of Justice, 1989.

Poe-Yamagata, Eileen, and Jeffrey A. Butts. *Female Offenders in the Juvenile Justice System*. Washington, D.C.: U.S. Dept. of Justice, Office of Juvenile Justice and Delinquency Prevention, June 1996.

Pope, Carl E., and William H. Feyerherm. *Minorities and the Juvenile Justice System. Research Summary*. Washington, D.C.: OJJDP and U.S. Dept. of Justice, 1993.

Poulos, Tammy M., and Stan Orchowsky. "Serious Juvenile Offenders: Predicting the Probability of Transfer to Criminal Court," *Crime and Delinquency* 40 (1) (1994): 3–17.

Pratt, George W. "Mental Health Services for Court Serviced Chronic Juvenile Offenders." Paper presented at 1995 JJDP Conference in Virginia, 1995.

Programs for the Serious and Violent Juvenile Offender. Washington, D.C.: U.S. Department of Justice, 1981.

Programs for Young Women in Trouble. Washington, D.C.: U.S. Department of Justice, 1981.

Richette, Lisa Aversa. *The Throwaway Children.* New York: Dell Publishing Company, 1969.

Rhodes, Jean E., Lori Ebert, and Adena B. Meyers. "Sexual Victimization in Young, Pregnant and Parenting, African-American Women: Psychological and Social Outcomes." *Violence and Victims* 8 (2) (1993): 153–163.

Robinson, Dinah A. "Patterns of Mitigating Factors in Juvenile Death Penalty Cases." *Criminal Law Bulletin* 28 (1992): 246–275.

Rubin, H. Ted. *Juvenile Justice: Policy, Practice, and Law*, 2d ed. New York: Random House, 1985.

Scott, Steven M. "Evolving Standards of Decency and the Death Penalty for Juvenile Offenders: The Contradiction Presented by *Stanford v. Kentucky.*" *Capital University Law Review* 19 (1990): 851–867.

Secret, Philip E., and James B. Johnson. "The Effect of Race on Juvenile Justice Decision Making in Nebraska: Detention, Adjudication, and Disposition, 1988–1993," *Justice Quarterly* 14 (1997): 445–478.

Seward, James D. "Brain Injury and Violence: Implications for Criminal Justice." *Journal of Police and Criminal Psychology* 9 (1993): 48–55.

Shaw, Clifford R. *Brothers in Crime.* Chicago: University of Chicago Press, 1936.

——. *The Jackroller: A Delinquent Boy's Own Story.* Chicago: University of Chicago Press, 1930.

Shaw, Clifford R., and Henry D. McKay. *Juvenile Delinquency and Urban Areas* (rev. ed.) Chicago: University of Chicago Press, 1942.

Sheley, Joseph F., Zina T. McGee, and James E. Wright. *Weapon-Related Victimization in Selected Inner-City High School Samples.* Washington, D.C.: National Institute of Justice, 1995.

Short, James F., Jr. "Gangs and Politics: Images and Realities." In *Symposium on Crime in America*, edited by Mary J. Hageman. Oneonta, NY: Hartwick College, 1973.

Sickmund, Melissa. "Juvenile Court Drug and Alcohol Cases: 1985–1988." *Update on Statistics*, OJJDP, 1991.

——. "How Juveniles Get to Criminal Court." *OJJDP Update on Statistics, Juvenile Justice Bulletin*, October (1994).

Simons, Ronald L., and Les B. Whitbeck. "Sexual Abuse as a Precursor to Prostitution and Victimization Among Adolescent and Adult Homeless Women." *Journal of Family Issues* 12 (1991): 361–379.

Skovron, Sandra Evans, Joseph E. Scott, and Francis T. Cullen. "The Death Penalty for Juveniles: An Assessment of Public Support." *Crime and Delinquency* 35 (4) (1989): 546–561.

Snyder, Howard N., and Melissa Sickmund. *Juvenile Offenders and Victims: A Focus on Violence.* Washington, D.C.: Office of Juvenile Justice and Delinquency Prevention, 1995a.

——. *Juvenile Offenders and Victims: A National Report.* Washington, D.C.: Office of Juvenile Justice and Delinquency Prevention, 1995b.

——. "Time-Related Characteristics of Violent Crime." Unpublished manuscript presented at the annual conference of the American Society of Criminology in Boston in November, 1995c.

Stafford, Mark C. "Children's Legal Rights in the U.S." *Marriage & Family Review* 21 (3/4) (1995): 121–140.

Teeters, Negley K. "The Early Days of the Magdalen Society in Philadelphia." *Social Service Review* 30 (1956): 157–158.

Tracy, Sharon, and Randell Shelden. "The Violent Female Juvenile Offender: An Ignored Minority within the Juvenile Justice System." *Juvenile and Family Court Journal* 43 (3) (1992): 33–39.

Wolfgang, Marvin E., R. Figlio, and T. Sellin. *Delinquency in a Birth Cohort.* Chicago: The University of Chicago Press, 1972.

Ying, Yu-Wen, Phillip D. Akutsu, Xiulan Zhang, and Larke N. Huang. "Psychological Dysfunction in Southeast Asian Refugees as Mediated by Sense of Coherence," *American Journal of Community Psychology* 25 (1997): 839–860.

Zhou, Min, and Carl L. Bankston III. *Growing Up American: How Vietnamese Children Adapt to Life in the United States.* New York: Russell Sage Foundation, c. 1998.

APPENDIX 4A

VIRGINIA:

IN THE CIRCUIT COURT FOR THE CITY OF RICHMOND
Manchester Division

In re Richmond Newspapers, Inc.

Memorandum In Support of Motion
For Access To Court Records

Richmond Newspapers, Inc. ("Richmond Newspapers") has moved the Court for access to sealed court records relating to Raykie Cloyd. This memorandum supports the motion.

Facts

As reported in the July 30, 1988 (copy attached), issue of the Richmond Times-Dispatch, on July 27 seventeen year old Raykie Cloyd was found dead in an alley, shot four times from behind. Before his death, Mr. Cloyd had been a defendant in this Court on a murder charge, which was eventually dismissed when a critical witness failed to appear. Mr. Cloyd was also a suspect in numerous other murders in Richmond; police believed him to be a "hit man" for certain drug dealers.

Mr. Cloyd's case in this Court (No. 88-179-F) had been transferred from the Juvenile and Domestic Relations District Court pursuant to Section 16.1–269 of the Virginia Code. While much of his court file is open for public inspection, it also contains a sealed envelope with documents forwarded by the Juvenile Court. Attached to this envelope is an unsigned form stating that pursuant to Section 16.1–296 of the Virginia Code, the documents may be examined only by the Court, the Commonwealth's Attorney, or the defendant's counsel. Because of the great public interest in Mr. Cloyd's case, reporters for Richmond Newspapers, Inc. now wish to inspect the sealed records.

Argument

I. Absent The Most Compelling Need For Secrecy, The Press and *Public Have a Constitutional Right to Inspect Court Records*

"One of the demands of a democratic society is that the public should know what goes on in the courts by being told by the press what happens there. . . . *Richmond Newspapers, Inc. v. Virginia*, 448 U.S. 555, 573 n. 9 (1980) (Burger, C.J.). In an unbroken line of cases starting in 1980, the United States and Virginia Supreme Courts have given meaning to this principle, recognizing that, in all but the most unusual circumstances, what goes on in the courts must be open to public view. See *Richmond Newspapers, Inc. v. Virginia*, 448 U.S. 555 (1980) (Richmond Newspapers I); *Globe Newspaper Co. v. Superior Court*, 457 U.S. 596 (1982); *Press Enterprise Co. v. Superior Court*, 464 U.S. 501 (1984); *Press Enterprise Co. v. Superior Court*, 478 U.S., 92 L.Ed. 2d 1 (1986); *Richmond Newspapers, Inc. v. Commonwealth*, 222 Va. 574 (1981) (Richmond Newspapers II).

These cases have all held that absent a compelling need for secrecy, the First Amendment to the United States Constitution and Article 1, Section 12 of the Virginia Constitution require that trials and pre-trial proceedings be open to the public and the press. Among the reasons cited by these courts for this rule is that observation of judicial proceedings has "therapeutic value, as an outlet for community concern when a shocking crime occurs . . ." Richmond Newspapers II, 222 Va. at 585.

The role played by the press in attending judicial proceedings enhances the structural functions of the First Amendment and Article 1, Section 12 in our democratic form of government.

[I]n a society in which each individual has but limited time and resources with which to observe at first hand the operations of his government, he relies necessarily upon the press to bring to him in convenient form the facts of those operations. . . . With respect to judicial proceedings in particular, the function of the press serves to guarantee the fairness of trials and to bring to bear the beneficial effects of public scrutiny upon the administration of justice. (Citation omitted).

. . . The commission of crime, prosecutions resulting from it, and judicial proceedings arising from the prosecution . . . are without question events of legitimate concern to the public and consequently fall within the responsibility of the press to report the operations of government.

Cox Broadcasting Corp. v. Cohn, 42Q U.S. 469, 491–92 (1975); *see Richmond Newspapers I*, 448 U.S. at 475 n.9.

There is no principled reason to distinguish between physical access to judicial proceedings, such as trials and pretrial hearings, and access to the records filed in connection with such proceedings. See *Associated Press v. United States District Court*, 705 F.2d 1143, 1145 (9th Cir. 1983) ("There is no reason to distinguish between pretrial proceedings and the documents filed in regard to them."); *Vermont v. Mitchell*, 1G; vied. L. Rep. 2442, 2446 (Vt. Dist. Ct. 1984) ("Assuming that there is a first Amendment right of access to judicial proceedings in general, it follows logically that documents relating to those proceedings should likewise be accessible."). The United States Supreme Court has explained that "official records and documents . . . are the basic data of governmental operations." *Cox Broadcasting Corp.*, 420 U.S. at 491–92. In the context of judicial proceedings, "court records often provide important, sometimes the only, basis or explanations for a court's decision." *Brown and Williamson Tobacco Corp. v. Federal Trade Commission*, 710 F. 2d 1165, 1787 (6th Cir. 1983), *cert. denied*, U.S., 80 L.Ed 2d 127, 104 S.Ct. 1595 (1984); see *In re Knicht Publishing Co.*, 743 F.2d 231, 235 (4th Cir. 1984).

Recognizing the important functions served by wide public access to judicial records, the vast majority of courts that have examined the issue have concluded that such access is protected by the First Amendment, or the comparable state constitutional provision.[1] See, e.g., *In re Coordinated Pretrial Proceedings*, 10 Med. L. Rep. 2430 (9th Cir. 1984); *Brown and Williamson Tobacco Corp. v. Federal Trade Commission*, 710 F. 2d 1165 (6th Cir. 1983); *In re Knoxville News-Sentinel Co., Inc.*, 723 F.2d 470, 474–76 (6th Cir. 1983); *U.S. v. Werrlein*, 10 Med. L. Rep. 1319 (C.D. Calif. 1984); *In re Agent Orange Litigation*, 9 Med. L. Rep. 1840 (Flat Cir. Ct. 1984); *Placuemines Parish Commission Council v. Delta Development Company, Inc.*, 11 Med. L. Rep. 2353 (La. 1985); *Journal Newspapers, Inc. v. Maryland*, 54 Md. App. 98, 456 A.2d 963 (Md. Ct. Spec. App. 1983), *aff'd. sub. mon.*, *Buzbee v. Journal Newspapers, Inc.*, 297 Md. 68, 246i A.2d 426 (1983).

(1. Recently, the Virginia Supreme Court held that absent unusual circumstances, most civil court records must be open to the public under Section 17–43 of the Virginia Code. *Shenandoah Publishing House, Inc. v. Fanning*, 235 Va. ____, 4 V.L.R. 2424 (1988). Although the Court did not reach the constitutional issue, the opinion may be fairly read as suggesting that the Court would ultimately adopt the view that the First Amendment requires broad access to court records.)

II. The State's Interest Is Insufficient To Justify Confidentiality of All Juvenile Court Records, Nor Does The Virginia Code Impose Such a Requirement.

The State's concern for the well-being of children unquestionably is a compelling governmental interest. It is this compelling interest to save the child from a downward career that led to the creation of the juvenile court system. See *In re Gault*, 387 U.S. 1, 14–15 (1967). The primary objective of juvenile courts is rehabilitation, Rooke, *The Kent Case and Juvenile Courts in Virginia*, 2 U. of Rich. L. Notes 366, 375 (1967), and if the benevolent and rehabilitative purposes of the juvenile court system are actually to be served, confidentiality of proceedings is desirable, see Hopper and Slayton, *The Revision of Virginia's Juvenile Court Law*, 13 U. of Rich. L. Rev. 847, 880–81 (1979). To enhance the rehabilitative function of the juvenile courts, the General Assembly of Virginia has enacted various provisions providing for confidentiality of records under certain circumstances.

The records in the instant case were apparently sealed by an interpretation of Section 16.1–296 of the Virginia Code which requires that all records be sealed, regardless of the circumstances. There are numerous difficulties with this view, however.

First, a blanket rule sealing all juvenile court records, regardless of the circumstances, goes too far in impinging on the public's constitutional access right. *Globe Newspapers Co. v. Superior Court*, 457 U.S. 596 (1982), presents an analogous case. In *Globe Newspapers* a Massachusetts trial court, pursuant to a statute, excluded the public and the press from the courtroom while minor victims of a sex crime were testifying. The Massachusetts Supreme Judicial Court construed the statute as an absolute, requiring trial judges in all "trials for specified sexual offenses involving a victim under the age of 18, to exclude the press and general public from the courtroom during the testimony of that victim." Id. at 598. Recognizing that valid state interests for the welfare of children lay behind the statute, the United States Supreme Court nonetheless held that the statute, so construed, was unconstitutional as violative of the First Amendment right of the public and press to attend criminal proceedings. Regarding the State's interest, the Court wrote:

. . . [S]afe-guarding the physical and psychological well-being of a minor . . . is a compelling one. But as compelling as that interest is, it does not justify a *mandatory* closure rule, for it is clear that the circumstances of a particular case may affect the significance of the interest.

Id. at 607–08 (emphasis in original).

By the same token this Court has recognized on at least two occasions that the Commonwealth's interest in the confidentiality of juvenile court records as furthering rehabilitative purposes does not justify an automatic rule of secrecy in all cases. *In re Richmond Newspapers, Inc.*, No. N-5055-2 (July 28, 1987) (copy of transcript attached); *Commonwealth v. Talley* (Cir. Ct. of Richmond 1986) (copy of Order attached); see also *Commonwealth v. Mayton* (Cir. Ct. for Amherst County 1987).

Second, constitutional principles aside, Section 16.1–296 of the Virginia Code provides no authority for sealing records transmitted to this Court from the Juvenile Court. That section simply governs the jurisdiction and procedure in appeals from the Juvenile Court; it contains no provision for secrecy of records once they are transmitted to a circuit court. Moreover, the instant case was not appealed under Section 16.1–296; it was transferred pursuant to Section 16.1–269 of the Virginia Code.

The only provision of the Virginia Code that provides any authority for a circuit court to seal records received from a juvenile court is Section 16.1–307 of the Virginia Code, but that section applies only in cases "in which the circuit court deals with the child in the same manner as a case in the juvenile court." By the order transferring Mr. Cloyd's case to this Court, the determination was made to treat Mr. Cloyd as an adult, not a child, and thus section 16.1–307 could not possibly have any application.

Finally, even if Section 16.1–307 were applicable, it would not require record secrecy in all cases. Rather, Section 16.1–307 adopts the confidentiality provisions of Section 16.1–305 of the Virginia Code which provide access to juvenile court records to "[a]ny other person, by order of the court, having a legitimate interest in the case or in the work of the court. . . ." This Court has already interpreted that section as requiring courts to unseal juvenile records in appropriate cases. See *In re Richmond Newspapers, Inc.* (transcript attached). Thus, even in cases where secrecy may have been called for at an earlier time, where subsequent events have created a legitimate public interest in the records, disclosure is required.

III. Denial of Access In The Instant Case Would Be *Both Unconstitutional And An Abuse Of Discretion*

The circumstances surrounding Mr. Cloyd's case are not isolated or unusual; they are, unfortunately, common and repetitive. Richmond has one of the highest murder rates in the United States. See e.g., Richmond Times-Dispatch, May 10, 1987, at B-1. The City's leaders are justifiably outraged, and the public is deeply concerned about how to eradicate this blight from the community's landscape. See, e.g., **The Richmond News Leader**, May 2, 1987, at 4.

This Court has recognized that "the public has a right to the information about . . . whether the juvenile system is working . . . and the only real way we can find out about that is through the newspapers. . . ." *In re Richmond Newspapers, Inc.* (attached transcript at 31). The Supreme Court of Virginia has explained that dissemination of information about the criminal justice system serves "both a therapeutic value, as an outlet for community concern when a shocking crime occurs . . . and as a means for the public to see that all citizens are treated equally." Richmond Newspapers II, 222 Va. at 585 (citing Richmond *Newspapers* I). In a community like Richmond, plagued by its murder rate, the need for a therapeutic outlet is particularly acute.

The public sees that most of the murders in this community are committed by young men with criminal records. See, e.g., Richmond Times-Dispatch, March 25, 1987, at B-1. It also sees that Mr. Cloyd's career apparently fits this pattern. Some suggest that courts have been too lenient in their treatment of this new breed of young, recidivist criminal. See, e.g., id.

Without access to the records sought by Richmond Newspapers, the public will be left to speculate about Mr. Cloyd and his experiences in the juvenile justice system. Unable to see how the system worked, public confidence in its institutions may be undermined, and respect may be lost. Mr. Cloyd's record strongly suggests inadequacies in the criminal justice system to deter foreseeable criminal conduct. The public has a legitimate interest in knowing whether the juvenile system is protecting the citizenry as well as pursuing its rehabilitative goal, and this interest can be served only by inspecting juvenile records in appropriate cases like this one. The United States Supreme Court has recognized that "[a] result considered untoward may undermine public confidence, and where the trial has been concealed from public view an unexpected outcome can cause a reaction that the system at best has failed and at worst has been corrupted." *Richmond Newspapers* I at 571. It is precisely such a result that the constitutional right of access seeks to prevent.

Continued confidentiality of the sealed records regarding Mr. Cloyd will serve no useful purpose. The public knows Mr. Cloyd's identity and the crimes for which he was charged. Mr. Cloyd is now deceased, and even before his death, the Juvenile Court's Order of March 31, 1988, transferring his case to this Court recognized that he "is not amenable to treatment or rehabilitation as a juvenile." Thus, any hope had long since vanished that the benevolent, rehabilitative objectives of the juvenile justice system could be served by continued confidentiality.

An infringement of First Amendment liberties can never be tolerated if it realistically cannot accomplish its intended purposes. See *Nebraska Press Association v. Stuart*, 427 U.S. 539, 565–67 (1976); *Smith v. Daily Mail Publishing Co.*, 443 U.S. 97, 104–05 (1979); id. at 110 and n.3 (Rehnquist, Jr., concurring). Thus when the evidence that a criminal defendant seeks to suppress has been widely disclosed, the Constitution will not allow a court in its discretion to forbid the press from publishing that evidence. See *Nebraska Press*, supra. Nor when the identity of an alleged juvenile delinquent has been disseminated through the broadcast media will a law punishing a newspaper for disclosing the juvenile's identity survive constitutional challenge. See *Smith*, supra. It follows that this Court should no longer deny access to the records sought.

RICHMOND NEWSPAPERS INC.

BY Counsel
Alexander Wellford
David C. Kohler
Christian, Barton, Epps,
Brent & Chappell
1200 Mutual Building
909 East Main Street
Richmond, Virginia 23219
(804) 644-7851

CERTIFICATE

I certify that on this _____ day of August, 1988, I hand delivered a copy of the foregoing Memorandum In Support of Motion For Access To Court Records to Aubrey Davis, Esquire, Commonwealth Attorney, Richmond Commonwealth Attorney's Office, John Marshall, Courts Building, 800 East Marshall Street, Richmond, Virginia, 23219

David C. Kohler

Figure 4.8
Determination of Whether to Release or to Detain a Juvenile.

DETERMINATION OF WHETHER TO RELEASE OR TO DETAIN A JUVENILE

In order to make a determination about whether or not a juvenile should be released or should remain under the jurisdiction of the court, the authorities take a number of things into account including:

- Whether or not the juvenile is a threat to himself or herself.

- Whether or not the juvenile is a threat to others.

- Whether or not the juvenile is likely to run away prior to any scheduled court hearing.

- The juvenile's age.

- The offense for which the juvenile is being held.

- The juvenile's past history.

- The juvenile's school record.

- Where and with whom the juvenile is currently living.

Criteria for Detention according to VA Code:

- Is either a felony or a Class 1 misdemeanor, and there is clear evidence that:

- the release of the child constitutes a threat to himself to the person or property of others.

- the release of the child would present a clear and substantial threat of serious harm to the child's life or health; or

- the child has threatened to abscond from the court's jurisdiction during the pendency of the proceedings or has a record of willful failure to appear at a court hearing within the immediately preceding 12 months.

- the child has absconded from a detention home or facility where directed to participate per the order of the court.

- the child is a fugitive from a jurisdiction outside the commonwealth and arrangements are made to return the child to the other state.

- the child has failed to appear in court.

YOU BE THE JUDGE

Figure 4.9
You Be the Judge.

You are the juvenile court judge who has to decide a disposition for the following cases. Choose the decision you think is best. You must give reasons to support the decision you make. Remember, every judge has a responsibility to protect the community. This responsibility must be weighed against the desire to help the juvenile.

Michael, age 15, was found guilty of burglarizing a home while the owners were at work. He was working with two other men, ages 19 and 21. Detectives who searched a garage rented by the 21-year-year-old found eight color television sets, seven stereos, four video recorders, and large quantities of jewelry such as twenty, 20 inch, 14 kt. gold herringbone chains. Michael has no past record, has been truant occasionally, but otherwise attends school on a regular basis. Reportedly, there are no academic performance is fair. His mother reports his required curfew is 12:00 midnight. Most of the time she says, he returns around 11:30 p.m., but sometimes at 1:00 or 2:00 a.m.

Walter, age 16, and three friends were bored and decided to rob a convenience store. One of the members of the group stated he was not going unless he could a gun, but promised to use it only as a threat. During the holdup, one of the employees panicked and was shot by the friend. Walter and his friends were all arrested for the charge of malicious wounding. What punishment would you choose for Walter? Walter has dropped out of high school, works temporary construction assignments, and lives with his mother.

Leisha, age 15, was found guilty of possession of three grams of cocaine. The drugs were spotted by a security guard while she was at her locker. Leisha has no prior record, but has a poor academic record, and school attendance. What disposition would you recommend for Leisha?

Jerry, age 17, was found guilty of selling drugs at an elementary school playground. Jerry lives with both parents, attends school on a regular basis, makes good grades, and is a peer counselor in his high school. What disposition/services would you recommend as a result of this offense.

Figure 4.9 *Continued*   Waiver (Transfer) of juvenile cases

1. The seriousness of the offense (For example, was the act committed in a violent or willful manner, and did it result in damage to property or injury to persons?)

2. The amount of evidence supporting the allegation (that is, is there strong evidence to indicate that the juvenile did commit the offense?).

3. Adult involvement (for example, is there an adult who is an accomplice in the offense? Should the juvenile be treated the same as the adult who is involved?).

4. The maturity of the juvenile (for example, what is the juvenile's age, does the juveile appear and act as an adult in most situations? Does the juvenile understand the difference between right and wrong?).

5. Previous juvenile record (for example, has the juvenile been in trouble with the law on previous occasions? How often has the juvenile been in juvenile court? What has the court decided in the past offenses and has the juvenile obeyed the court's decisions?).

6. The likelihood of rehabilitation if treated as a juvenile offender (for example, if kept in juvenile jurisdiction, will the juvenile correct his or her behavior? Does the juvenile have family support? Does the juvenile have a good school record?).

Summary of the requirements for a Waiver

1. Age at time of offense (In Virginia, 14 years of age, as of July 1, 1994)
2. Seriousness of offense and previous offenses
3. Mental and Physical amenability
4. Determination of whether the youth can be treated in the juvenile justice system/or has exhausted the services of the juvenile system.
5. What services are available in the juvenile system versus the adult system
6. Juvenile history (criminal history and were there any previous cases certified)
7. In some states, and specifically in Virginia, as of July 1, 1994, a juvenile case will be waived to the adult system if a case was previously waived to the adult system.

CHAPTER 5

Child Abuse and Neglect

What happens to children who are systematically tortured? What is child abuse and how and when does the state intervene? In 1996, the National Center on Child Abuse and Neglect (NCCAN) reported that nearly 3 million cases of maltreatment towards children were reported. NCCAN, established as a national data collection program on child maltreatment, annually collects information on cases handled by each state's Child Protective Services (CPS) agency. Of the nearly 3 million cases reported, only 2 million are actual children because the counts are duplicated when an individual child is the subject of more than one report during a year. In that 1996 national summary data, 80% of the perpetrators were parents of the victims and an estimated 1,077 children died as the result of the maltreatment. Nineteen percent of the victims were age 2 or younger, 52% were age 7 or younger, and 7% were age 16 or older (Snyder and Sickmund 1999, 45).

All the world is full of suffering, it is also full of overcoming it. Helen Keller

Yet that statistic of 2 million is a low figure; there are more cases. Some of the reasons for low reporting will become apparent as you read this chapter. Before we discuss physical and sexual child abuse, let us discuss some important aspects of the investigation of a complaint and its process.

The process and procedure for child abuse and neglect cases are different from those that originate under a delinquency petition, as discussed in Chapter 4, "Process for Delinquent (Criminal) Youth." As shown in the **Flow Chart** of Figure 5.1, the process begins by a complaint received. The actual process is set by the law of each state. Therefore, it may vary from state to state.

INTRODUCTION

Process

Under law, the Child Protective Services (CPS) investigates, usually within 24 hours of receiving any report of abuse or neglect. A few States rely exclusively on law enforcement for after-hours emergency response, but most jurisdictions use law enforcement only with serious cases involving serious injury, sexual assault, and death. Many statutes authorize home visits for the purpose of interviewing the child without obtaining a warrant or first

Figure 5.1
The process begins by a complaint received. Note: This flowchart represents only the small proportion of CPS cases where legal intervention is required and may vary from jurisdiction to jurisdiction.

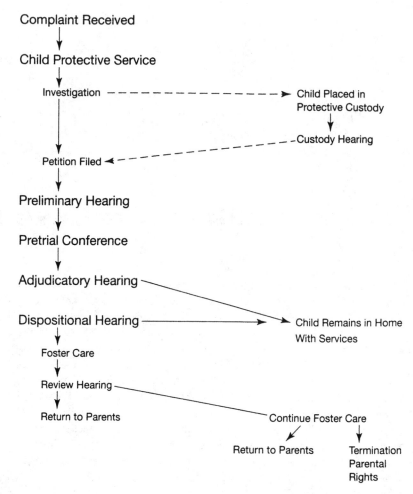

establishing reasonable cause. If consent to enter is denied, the CPS worker can use legal authority to enter and may summon the police or obtain a court order. If there is reason to believe that a child is in danger, the police may use reasonable force to gain entry, and the police may take the child into protective custody.

Protective Custody

If the child is in serious danger, the child can be taken into "protective custody," which means the child is taken somewhere else. The worker has 72 hours in which to address the court and explain the need for the removal of the child. This is called an **emergency removal**.

Danger. No Preventive Services. No Alternative. Best Interest Test.

The key findings needed to support an emergency removal of a child from his or her home are (1) imminent danger; (2) reasonable efforts were made to prevent removal, or there was no reasonable opportunity to provide preventive services; (3) no less drastic alternative; and (4) the best interests of the child are served by removal. Within 72 hours, the worker comes before the court where a hearing is held. It is known as a protective custody hearing.

Legal Custody vs. Physical Custody

At the protective custody hearing, the court decides who should have physical custody of the child. The parents may maintain legal custody, but the child might be placed in a medical facility that the parents can visit. In this manner, parents cannot take the child home and into their complete control. The child is protected.

If the case does not necessitate emergency removal to protect the life of the child, then the worker has 45 days in which to make an investigation before a petition is filed in juvenile court. An investigation means making announced and unannounced home visits, interviewing family members, and contacting other professionals who have had some involvement with the family. The role of the worker is to use the power of the position to help families get the services they need and thus avoid going through the court system. Services might include family counseling, parenting courses offered by the agency, and/or referrals to other community agencies like mandatory attendance of meetings held by Parents Anonymous (a group of adults discussing parenting problems with the help of a trained counselor).

Usually within 45 days, the worker will submit a report to the state's Child Abuse and Neglect Central Registry. Usually, the CPS worker will come to one of the three following conclusions:

1. **Founded**: After a complete investigation, the worker has preponderance of evidence that the child has been abused or neglected. The information remains in the Central Registry for 10 years after the child's 18th birthday.

2. **Unfounded**: After a complete investigation, the worker has not found any evidence of abuse or neglect. All information regarding the complaint is destroyed.

3. **Unfounded, but with reason to suspect**: A complete investigation reveals no clear and convincing evidence that abuse or neglect occurred; however, the worker has reason to suspect the child may be at risk of being abused or neglected. This information is stored for one year. If within a year no additional complaints are "founded" or "unfounded but with reason to suspect," all the information is destroyed.

> Preponderance is the lowest standard of proof. All states except one use this lowest standard. CPS argues that this standard permits them to serve families at an earlier stage in the abuse cycle.

Most "founded" cases of child abuse and neglect never result in a petition to the court. Instead, the cases are managed through services and supervision with the family. When the worker decides that court intervention is necessary, additional decisions must be made on whether the situation is so serious that immediate court action is warranted, or immediate court action requires removal of the child from the home or protective services to the home.

This actual case will give you an idea of how an agency works with a family. In February of 1986, a department of social services received a complaint that the Turners were leaving their four children alone for 30 to 40 minutes while Mrs. Turner drove Mr. Turner to work. On April 28, 1988, the Turners were again referred to the department for possible child abuse. Mr. Turner allegedly hit his daughter on her face with his fist. On November 23, 1988, Mr. Turner pulled a nickel-sized plug of hair from the head of his daughter, then 3 years old. (Pulling hair from the head of a small child is very serious because it causes internal bleeding on the skull.) Based on that complaint, on May 15, 1989, the Commissioner of the Department of Social Services determined that a complaint of child abuse against Mr. Turner was "founded." Mr. Turner appealed the Commissioner's decision to the circuit court, which sustained the "founded" disposition of child abuse. Upon that court's affirming the Commissioner, Mr. Turner appealed to the Appeals Court claiming that the hearing officer applied the incorrect burden of proof and improperly admitted evidence of prior abuse by Mr. Turner, that the circuit court applied the incorrect standard of review, that the Commissioner lacked statutory authority to adopt the child protective services guidelines, that the circuit court erred in finding that the statue and guidelines were unconstitutionally vague, and that his due process rights were violated. To all those questions, the Appeals Court said "No" and thus affirmed the lower courts (*Turner v. Jackson*, 417 S.E. 2d 881 [1992]).

If the parent denies the allegation and is unwilling to cooperate, the worker does not use an informal system as shown in the above case but uses the full force of the juvenile court by filing a petition. The petition forces the judge to hold a preliminary hearing to inform the family of the nature of the charge. A pretrial conference is held with the hope of settlement. If there is no settlement, then an adjudicatory hearing to hear the evidence is held, followed by a disposition hearing. During the adjudicatory and disposition hearings, the child may remain in the home with services provided by the social worker of the court or a special child advocate.

In some states, it is the abuser who must leave the home instead of the child. In other states, the child is put in a foster home. If a single parent is the abuser, a foster home may be the only reasonable thing to do because there is no one inside the home to help protect the child.

If the family needs long-range assistance through court orders, the child may be placed in foster care until the child can be reunited with the family. Foster care is often reviewed with specific guidelines so that children are not dumped and lost and forgotten. For example, in some states, if the child is under age 2, the social worker has only one year to develop a plan and has the full cooperation of the parents for reintegration. If the child is older, the worker has up to two years. See Appendix 7B: Mock Trial in Chapter 7, "Other Hearings in Juvenile Court: Child Custody, Support, and Termination of Parental Rights."

It is important to note that having court involvement doesn't always benefit the child, as noted by a four-year study on 206 children through the Boston Juvenile Court system:

Two thirds of all parents were found to be poor, 84% had one or more psychiatric disorders, and 81% had been known to the Department of Social Services prior to their court appearance. The average age of children at the start of the court process was 4.2 years, and the average length of temporary foster care was 2.3 years. Judges' decisions to return children to parental custody or to order permanent removal were most strongly predicted by parental compliance with court-order services. Of the 63 cases dismissed from court and thus returned to biological parents, 18 (29%) had substantiated reports of new mistreatment over an approximately 3-year follow-up period. We concluded that children are often poorly served by the current delays in the social service/legal system, and that further clinical research would provide needed

empirical data on how to best protect mistreated
children. (Jellinek, Murphy, Poitrast, Quinn,
Bishop, and Goshko 1992)

If reintegration is not possible, then a petition to terminate parental rights is heard by the court so that the child may have a chance for adoption while still young. (Chapter 7 will deal with custody and termination of residual parental rights.)

Power of Parents

You may be wondering why parents have so much power and so many rights. The power of the parent(s) came from the traditions explained in Chapter 1, "History and Treatment." They also became law in the U.S. Supreme Court decision *Meyer v. Nebraska* and in the way that case was later interpreted.

MEYER v. STATE OF NEBRASKA

SUPREME COURT OF THE UNITED STATES

262 U.S. 390, 67 L. Ed. 1042; 43 S. Ct. 625; 29 A.L.R. 1446

Argued February 23, 1923. June 4, 1923 Decided

OPINION: Mr. Justice McREYNOLDS delivered the opinion of the Court.

Plaintiff in error was tried and convicted in the District Court for Hamilton County, Nebraska, under an information which charged that on May 25, 1920, while an instructor in Zion Parochial School, he unlawfully taught the subject of reading in the German language to Raymond Parpart, a child of ten years, who had not attained and successfully passed the eighth grade. The information is based upon "An act relating to the teaching of foreign languages in the State of Nebraska," approved April 9, 1919, which follows [Laws 1919, c. 249.]:

Facts and Procedural History

"Section 1. No person, individually or as a teacher, shall, in any private, denominational, parochial or public school, teach any subject to any person in any language other than the English language.

"Sec. 2. Languages, other than the English language, may be taught as languages only after a pupil shall have attained and successfully passed the eighth grade as evidenced by a certificate of graduation issued by the county superintendent of the county in which the child resides.

"Sec. 3. Any person who violates any of the provisions of this act shall be deemed guilty of a misdemeanor and upon conviction, shall be subject to a fine of not less than twenty-five dollars ($25), nor more than one hundred dollars ($100) or be confined in the county jail for any period not exceeding thirty days for each offense.

"Sec. 4. Whereas, an emergency exists, this act shall be in force from and after its passage and approval." The Supreme Court of the State affirmed the judgment of conviction. 107 Neb. 657. It declared the offense charged and established was "the direct and intentional teaching of the German language as a distinct subject to a child who had not passed the eighth grade," in the parochial school maintained by Zion Evangelical Lutheran Congregation, a collection of biblical stories being used therefore.

How the Other Court Held

And it held that the statute forbidding this did not conflict with the Fourteenth Amendment, but was a valid exercise of the police power. The following excerpts from the opinion sufficiently indicate the reasons advanced to support the conclusion.

"The salutary purpose of the statute is clear. The legislature had seen the baneful effects of permitting foreigners, who had taken residence in this country, to rear and educate their children in the language of their native land. The result of that condition was found to be inimical to our own safety. To allow the children of foreigners, who had emigrated here, to be taught from early childhood the language of the country of their parents was to rear them with that language as their mother tongue. It was to educate them so that they must always think in that language, and, as a consequence, naturally inculcate in them the ideas and sentiments foreign to the best interests of this country. The statute, therefore, was intended not only to require that the education of all children be conducted in the English language, but that, until they had grown into that language and until it had become a part of them, they should not in the schools be taught any other language. The obvious purpose of this statute was that the English language should be and become the mother tongue of all children reared in this state. The enactment of such a statute comes reasonably within the police power of the state. *Pohl v. State*, 132 N.E. (Ohio) 20; *State v. Bartels*, 181 N.W. (Ia.) 508.

"It is suggested that the law is an unwarranted restriction, in that it applies to all citizens of the state and arbitrarily interferes with the rights of citizens who are not of foreign ancestry, and prevents them, without reason, from having their children taught foreign languages in school. That argument is not well taken, for it assumes that every citizen finds himself restrained by the statute. The hours which a child is able to devote to study in the confinement of school are limited. It must have ample time for exercise or play. Its daily capacity for learning is comparatively small. A selection of subjects for its education, therefore, from among the many that might be taught, is obviously necessary. The legislature no doubt had in mind the practical operation of the law. The law affects few citizens, except those of foreign lineage. Other citizens, in their selection of studies, except perhaps in rare instances, have never deemed it of importance to teach their children foreign languages before such children have reached the eighth grade. In the legislative mind, the salutary effect of the statute no doubt outweighed the restriction upon the citizens generally, which, it appears, was a restriction of no real consequence."

?

The problem for our determination is whether the statute as construed and applied unreasonably infringes the liberty guaranteed to the plaintiff in error by the Fourteenth Amendment. "No State shall . . . deprive any person of life, liberty, or property, without due process of law."

Majority Opinion

While this Court has not attempted to define with exactness the liberty thus guaranteed, the term has received much consideration and some of the included things have been definitely stated. Without doubt, it denotes not merely freedom from bodily restraint but also the right of the individual to contract, to engage in any of the common occupations of life, to acquire useful knowledge, to marry, establish a home and bring up children, to worship God according to the dictates of his own conscience, and generally to enjoy those privileges long recognized at common law as essential to the orderly pursuit of happiness by free men. Slaughter-House Cases, 16 Wall. 36; *Butchers' Union Co. v. Crescent City Co.*, 111 U.S. 746; *Yick W v. Hopkins*, 118 U.S. 356; *Minnesota v. Barber*, 136 U.S. 313;

Allgeyer v. Louisiana, 165 U.S. 578; *Lochner v. New York*, 198 U.S. 45; *Twining v. New Jersey*, 211 U.S. 78; *Chicago, Burlington & Quincy R.R. Co. v. McGuire*, 219 U.S. 549; *Truax v. Raich*, 239 U.S. 33; *Adams v. Tanner*, 244 U.S. 590; *New York Life Ins. Co. v. Dodge*, 246 U.S. 357; *Truax v. Corrigan*, 257 U.S. 312; *Adkins v. Children's Hospital*, 216 U.S. 525; *Wyeth v. Cambridge Board of Health*, 200 Mass. 474. The established doctrine is that this liberty may not be interfered with, under the guise of protecting the public interest, by legislative action which is arbitrary or without reasonable relation to some purpose within the competency of the State to effect. Determination by the legislature of what constitutes proper exercise of police power is not final or conclusive but is subject to supervision by the courts. *Lawton v. Steele*, 152 U.S. 133, 137.

The American people have always regarded education and acquisition of knowledge as matters of supreme importance which should be diligently promoted. The Ordinance of 1787 declares, "Religion, morality, and knowledge being necessary to good government and the happiness of mankind, schools and the means of education shall forever be encouraged." Corresponding to the right of control, it is the natural duty of the parent to give his children education suitable to their station in life; and nearly all the States, including Nebraska, enforce this obligation by compulsory laws.

Practically, education of the young is only possible in schools conducted by especially qualified persons who devote themselves thereto. The calling always has been regarded as useful and honorable, essential, indeed, to the public welfare. Mere knowledge of the German language cannot [reasonably] be regarded as harmful. Heretofore it has been commonly looked upon as helpful and desirable. Plaintiff in error taught this language in school as part of his occupation. His right thus to teach and the **right of parents** to engage him so to instruct their children, we think, are within the liberty of the Amendment.

The challenged statute forbids the teaching in school of any subject except in English; also the teaching of any other language until the pupil has attained and successfully passed the eighth grade, which is not usually accomplished before the age of twelve. The Supreme Court of the State has held that "the so-called ancient or dead languages" are not "within the spirit or the purpose of the act." *Nebraska District of Evangelical Lutheran Synod v. McKelvie*, 187 N.W.927. Latin, Greek, Hebrew are not proscribed; but German, French, Spanish, Italian, and every other alien speech are within the ban. Evidently the legislature has attempted materially to interfere with the calling of modern language teachers, with the opportunities of pupils to acquire knowledge, and with the power of parents to control the education of their own.

It is said the purpose of the legislation was to promote civic development by inhibiting training and education of the immature in foreign tongues and ideals before they could learn English and acquire American ideals; and "that the English language should be and become the mother tongue of all children reared in this State." It is also affirmed that the foreign born population is very large, that certain communities commonly use foreign words, follow foreign leaders, move in a foreign atmosphere, and that the children are thereby hindered from becoming citizens of the most useful type and the public safety is imperiled.

That the State may do much, go very far, indeed, in order to improve the quality of its citizens, physically, mentally and morally, is clear; but the individual has certain fundamental rights which must be respected. The protection of the Constitution extends to all, to those who speak other languages as well as to those born with English on the tongue. Perhaps it would be highly advantageous if all had ready understanding of our ordinary speech, but this cannot be coerced by methods which conflict with the Constitution—a desirable end cannot be promoted by prohibited means.

For the welfare of his Ideal Commonwealth, Plato suggested a law which should provide: "That the wives of our guardians are to be common, and their children are to be common, and no parent is to know his own child, nor any child his parent.... The proper officers will take the offspring of the good parents to the pen or fold, and there they will deposit them with certain nurses who dwell in a separate quarter; but the offspring of the inferior, or of the better when they chance to be deformed, will be put away in some mysterious, unknown place, as they should be." In order to submerge the individual and develop ideal citizens, Sparta assembled the males at seven into barracks and intrusted their subsequent education and training to official guardians. Although such measures have been deliberately approved by men of great genius, their ideas touching the relation between individual and State were wholly different from those upon which our institutions rest; and it hardly will be affirmed that any legislature could impose such restrictions upon the people of a State without doing violence to both letter and spirit of the Constitution.

The desire of the legislature to foster a homogeneous people with American ideals prepared readily to understand current discussions of civic matters is easy to appreciate. Unfortunate experiences during the late war and aversion toward every characteristic of truculent adversaries were certainly enough to quicken that aspiration. But the means adopted, we think, exceed the limitations upon the power of the State and conflict with rights assured to plaintiff in error. The interference is plain enough and no adequate reason therefore in time of peace and domestic tranquility has been shown.

Now the Questions!

The power of the State to compel attendance at some school and to make reasonable regulations for all schools, including a requirement that they shall give instructions in English, is not questioned. Nor has challenge been made of the State's power to prescribe a curriculum for institutions which it supports. Those matters are not within the present controversy. Our concern is with the prohibition approved by the Supreme Court. *Adams v. Tanner*, supra, p. 594, pointed out that mere abuse incident to an occupation ordinarily useful is not enough to justify its abolition, although regulation may be entirely proper. No emergency has arisen which renders knowledge by a child of some language other than English so clearly harmful as to justify its inhibition with the consequent infringement of rights long freely enjoyed. We are constrained to conclude that the statute as applied is arbitrary and without reasonable relation to any end within the competency of the State.

As the statute undertakes to interfere only with teaching which involves a modern language, leaving complete freedom as to other matters, there seems no adequate foundation for the suggestion that the purpose was to protect the child's health by limiting his mental activities. It is well known that proficiency in a foreign language seldom comes to one not instructed at an early age, and experience shows that this is not injurious to the health, morals or understanding of the ordinary child.

The judgment of the court below must be reversed and the cause remanded for further proceedings not inconsistent with this opinion.

Decision

Reversed.

NOTES ON MEYER

1. *Meyer* deals with teaching a foreign language to children. What is important about *Meyer* is not its decision about teaching a foreign language to children but how it gets used after 1923 and cited in later cases to support more rights for parents. For example, in 1925, *Meyer* was used to support

parents choosing to send their children to a private school instead of the public school to meet the compulsory school attendance rules (*Pierce v. Society of Sisters of the Holy Names of Jesus and Mary*, 268 U.S. 510). Later, in *Stanley v. Illinois*, 405 U.S. 645 (1972), *Meyer* was cited to refer to the importance of families and the "rights to conceive and to raise one's children" as essential.

Loving v. Virginia, 388 U.S. 1 (1967), which struck down the state's statutory scheme to prevent marriages between persons solely on the basis of racial classifications (miscegenation), cited *Meyer*. In *Loving*, *Meyer* was cited to represent the proposition that the Fourteenth Amendment defined the outer boundaries for state regulation of marriage and family life in general.

2. *Meyer* has become the key case on due process in family law. It is the granddaddy, so to speak, of family law. It gives families rights to do some things without the state intervening. So when you combine law with the custom explained in Chapter 1, "History and Treatment," of the father having rights to discipline a child, you can better understand the importance of the case law. Yet the power to discipline was abused by some. Research by medical doctors in the 1960s helped us understand that some children were not being disciplined—they were being tortured. This began the movement to protect children from death at the hands of their own parent(s).

History

In the 1960s, two physicians, Kempe and Helfer, systematically identified a medical syndrome that resulted from physical beatings administered to children. From full-body X-rays, the doctors identified broken bones at different stages of healing and established that the children had been repeatedly beaten.

The doctors coined the term "battered child" to describe victims of the syndrome and joined with social workers to pressure state legislators to protect children by adopting statutes that defined, prohibited, and punished child abuse. The resulting legislation covered **nonaccidental physical injury** resulting from acts of either commission or omission **by the parent(s), guardian(s), or person(s) having charge over a child.**

Prior to 1975, statutory definitions of child abuse primarily dealt with battery and only indirectly, if at all, with sexual abuse. Sexual abuse was included later in the statutes.

Other signs of physical abuse are unexplained burns, bites, bruises, and black eyes. If faded bruises or other marks are evident after an absence from school, then there may be physical abuse. If the child reports an injury by a parent or other adult caregiver and the adult offers conflicting, or unconvincing, information or no explanation for the child's injury, this may be a sign of abuse.

Causes of injury can be more than just the typical cigarette burn, the dipping in hot water, or the beating of the body. For example, Andrew Dominick Diehl, age 13, died of multiple, forceful blows to the head by restraining his nude body by a pipe cleaner on one hand and handcuffs on the other with a rope around his feet and using a wooden paddle to both buttocks and the head (*Diehl v. Commonwealth of Virginia*, 9 Va. App. 191, 1989).

Some newer possibilities are as follows:

PHYSICAL CHILD ABUSE AND NEGLECT

Battered Child Syndrome

1. Dehydration: This occurs when liquids are withheld or there is excessive ingestion of salt.

2. Toxic Ingestion: Included in this category are illicit, prescription, or non-prescription drugs given to the child, or through neglect of adequate supervision, the child eats them.

3. Pancreas Injuries: Serious injury of the pancreas alone rarely occurs from falls or other forms of minimal abdominal trauma. It is usually due to a deep, penetrating blunt trauma such as a broomstick or deeply placed fist.

4. Tin Ear Syndrome: This is unilateral ear bruising with CAT scan evidence of brain swelling and hemorrhages in the eye. Like the word "tin ear" in the boxing world, this kind of blow to the head of a young child frequently causes death (*Update* June 1992, 1).

The most recent serious but unusual form is called **Munchausen Syndrome by Proxy** (MSP). Munchausen Syndrome refers to a practice of repeatedly inducing or feigning physical illness and seeking medical attention for the self-produced affliction. Munchausen Syndrome by Proxy refers to the practice of inducing or fabricating an array of medical ailments in another person, usually in a child ranging from birth to 9 years. In a typical scenario, the mother presents her child to medical personnel in differing locales with an array of medical ailments with the purpose of getting attention and sympathy for herself.

The most common MSP physical symptoms are apnea (breathing abnormalities), fictitious bleeding from body orifices, claimed seizures, diarrhea, fever, rashes or vomiting. They are induced most frequently by near-suffocation, placement of blood on underwear, injection or poisoning. While the perpetrator deliberately creates the medical emergency, she is eager to deny any knowledge of the symptoms' etiology and to be of a possible assistance in caring for the patient. Nevertheless, it is common to find that when the victim is separated from the perpetrator, symptoms dissipate or disappear. Separation may come too late for the victim's recovery. Many children die before foul play is suspected. (Update December 1994, 1)

Continue to soil your bed and you will one night suffocate in your own waste. Chief Seattle 1844

In the past, when children were killed at the hands of their parents, the parents were prosecuted under a charge of manslaughter. "So far, 13 states have amended their first degree or capital murder statutes to eliminate the intent-to-kill requirement when a child's death results from abuse. Prosecutors in these states must instead prove that defendant physically abused the child and the abuse caused the child's death" (*Update* September 1992, 1).

Effects of Child Abuse on Children

In addition, research continues to show the negative effects of child abuse and neglect on the child's development. Infants who experience failure-to-thrive in conjunction with physical abuse showed significant delays on measures of mental and motor ability. Between groups of preschool and school-age children, language comprehension skills are significantly different for those who were physically abused or neglected. Emotionally, there is a relationship between childhood neglect and increased insecure patterns of infant-caretaker attachment, which then promotes different styles of social interaction with peers such as isolation, apathy, withdrawal, and dependency in social interactions.

Because there are short-range and long-range consequences, one of the major tasks for a CPS worker is to determine the risk to the child. To help you better understand how a worker goes about his or her job, an actual case study will show you how a worker takes a complaint and tries to collect evidence to either prove or disprove the allegations. At the same time, the worker knows that she or he needs to assist families so the child can safely remain with its own parents. As you read this case, ask yourself how you would have handled this. Would you have gone into a public housing project with no backup or gun to investigate a complaint of a woman shooting a .357-caliber Magnum in her house?

CPS CASE STUDY

In this particular case, the standard format for process reporting as established by Child Protective Services will not be followed. Rather, the case will be described for purposes of social work practice and to show the style of this particular caseworker. The case will cover events before the visit, the actual home visit, analysis of the worker, and other factors, as told by the caseworker.

Before the Visit

From the photocopy of the complaint, I had identified four specific issues: (1) bruise on jaw of the oldest child, (2) firing a gun in the house, (3) mother fighting with the boyfriend as a part of the overall emotional neglect, and (4) smoking marijuana and using cocaine. I discussed this case with the field instructor to make sure I fully understood the complaint. Then, in my mind I prioritized the issues with the idea that one issue would be easier to start with and be easier to verify. As it turned out, I did begin with the first issue—bruise on jaw of the oldest child.

In terms of my own thoughts and feelings, I wondered what she would look like—this woman who used a .357-caliber Magnum gun to handle anger and frustration. Having fired many different handguns and shotguns, I have a healthy respect for guns. I know how hard it is for me to hold a .357. I use two hands!

I was also aware of my own feeling of resistance going into the project area (welfare public housing) because it was unfamiliar to me. Then, I remembered the warm memories of a friend of mine who used to live on that very same street. So I used the warmth of her memories to focus me into a feeling of warmth and friendliness for this new experience.

Home Visit

When I got out of the car at the noted address, I saw that the shades on the windows were all drawn and that the house seemed very quiet. At first I feared that no one was home. Then I noticed that the screen door was locked from the inside. So I knocked harder and called her by name.

She came to the door in her night clothing and acted as if she had just been awakened. I felt embarrassment at seeing her in her night clothing. I also remembered how I feel when I am first awakened and how much I hate loud noises. I spoke softly and lightly but still audible.

"Are you Mrs. X?" I asked.

She replied that she was. She was much smaller in appearance than I had expected.

I maintained an attitude of "you have nothing to fear" by telling her my name and saying, "I am from Child Protective Services. Can I come in and talk with you, please?"

As she unlocked the screen door and permitted me entrance, I thanked her and apologized for waking her.

She didn't say anything as I proceeded into the darkened room. I remembered what my field instructor had said—that many of our clients were used to social workers coming in and out of their homes. Yet I felt concern because I wasn't sure she was fully awake nor was I sure she understood I was from Child Protective Services.

Once inside the living room, I took the time to let my eyes adjust to the dim lighting and to permit her some time and space. I saw a davenport sofa against the wall in front of me, a soft, matching chair against the left wall, and a love seat and soft chair with plastic covering against the wall to my right. All the furniture was modern and new. There were no pictures on the walls. The living room seemed sparsely furnished considering the space. There was also a TV with tape equipment on a stand. There was no clutter or mess and she had three children all under age 4!

I felt uneasy about how close I should sit to her. I remembered thinking that the davenport doesn't give us much distance but the soft chair to the left is so far away that if I needed to give her something, like our brochure, I would have to get up and down. So I asked her if she wanted me to sit in the chair on the left. She nodded her head.

I realized that I had interrupted her sleep. I also realized that this was nearly 11:00 a.m. on a nice day. So, I gently asked, "Are you not feeling very well?"

She mumbled something about a sore throat and I said something to the effect of did she have the flu. I was thinking I could engage her in a topic of polite conversation.

I expressed my concern to her by saying I was sorry to hear she wasn't feeling very well. Then, I also explained I was hoping she would have called me and set up an appointment.

She had such a blank expression on her face that I backtracked and asked if she had gotten something in the mail from me. I stated her name again to make sure I had the correct client. I showed her our brochure and asked if she had received anything like this in the mail. I didn't feel she was playing dumb, but I was curious as to what had happened to the mail. Her lack of familiarity with the brochure gave me reassurance and I decided to proceed with the interview and come back to this issue of the mail later, if need be.

When I handed her the brochure and told her I was from CPS, she had a look of shock on her face. I saw the whites of her eyes. I now felt she was awake.

I felt the need to lessen the impact of my visit. I explained how we had received a complaint last week and how I had sent her a letter with the brochure in the mail last Friday. Since today was Wednesday, I had expected her to call me by now. I reassured her that it was OK that she didn't call. I just wanted her to know what I had done so it would not be such a shock to her.

By saying the word "shock," I gave her permission to express her feelings which also verified my perception. She repeated the word "shock" as if to say "you bet." I supported her by taking her position and giving more words to her expression by saying that this wasn't a very nice way to be awakened.

At this point, I felt she was fully awake and ready to work with me in the problem-solving process of determining the verification of the complaint. I began by telling her what I needed to do today with her. I needed to introduce who I was, who the agency was, and why I had to talk with her. I talked about confidentiality and reassured her that what she said to me was not shared with others—meaning outsiders. She seemed to like that idea because she not only nodded her head but also said something to the effect of affirming that idea. I stated that it meant I would have to ask some questions. After I asked these questions, I would summarize whatever I had found or whatever we were going to do.

At that point, I took the same brochure I had originally given her but which she had given back when she said she never saw anything like that. I explained it in greater detail. I also explained that I was a graduate student in social work. I asked her permission to continue to record our conversation. I stated that its use was to help the people who were watching me and helping me learn to be a good social worker. I told her it was for no other purposes. Then I specifically asked if it was OK if we had it [the tape recorder] on. She moved her head and verbally said OK. I thanked her and shared my appreciation.

In terms of the brochure, I explained how the law required people to call and report suspected cases of child abuse. I put special emphasis on the word "suspected." I got up from my chair to show her the next part that dealt with the three outcomes of the investigation: (1) founded, (2) unfounded, and (3) reason to suspect and unfounded. I explained our procedure—especially the 45-day time frame to complete the investigation. I also discussed parental responsibility and cooperation for the purpose of helping the child.

To begin the middle phase of this interview, I again stated that someone had called in a complaint last week. I said, "I would really like to know from you what is going on because often, when people call in, we are not sure what's going on."

She replied that they were crank calls. Building on that trust, I said, "Well, you can help me with that. OK?" She agreed.

I began by asking how many children she had, their ages, etc. This also helped to verify data. The house was obviously quiet. My next spontaneous question was: "Where were the children?" She explained they were in the house, upstairs, sleeping. Since I never was able to keep my son in bed in the early mornings, I wondered what her secret was. When she first said that they were sleeping, I said, "You're kidding. How do you get them to sleep so long?"

She replied that they stay up half of the night. I accepted that reply and decided to come back to it later because I felt this was an issue where she might need some help.

For right now, I felt more concern to see just how much of this complaint was valid. Going back to the complaint, I explained that the caller was saying something about how the oldest child—the 4-year-old—had a jaw that was swollen and purple. "Did he get hit somehow?" I asked.

She shook her head. I rephrased my question. I used this week and last week as a reference point and still got negative replies. I used more global questions like did he fall down or get hurt in any way. All of these questions were done softly and slowly. I felt perplexed and used some other questions to probe to see if there was any way that someone could have seen her son hurt. Since there didn't seem to be any way and I knew I would be seeing the child, I moved on to the issue of the boyfriend and the gun.

I used the technique used in death notification wherein the helper gives the information slowly and in parts, with each new part having more information. It sounded like the following:

"The complaint also says that—you were really upset—with a boyfriend—you were so upset with the boyfriend that when he left you—you were using a gun. You were shooting the gun off in the house."

"Oh, no," she replied.

"Do you remember anything like that?"

"I don't even have a gun," she said with excitement.

I had already come to the conclusion that the most gun this woman could handle was a .38 because she was so physically small. The walls didn't show any marks at all let alone bullet holes. I explored with her possible other explanations such as had she even said something to make people think she had a gun.

She replied, "I don't have a gun. I'm scared to death of a gun!"

I began to explore the boyfriend breakup. Again she replied negatively and added information that he was at his mother's house.

I was silent. I felt awkward. There was nothing to verify the complaint.

Then, I felt for her. She must have thought I was a real crazy person. First, I wake her and then I tell her stories.

To check this impression, I began to express my nonverbal feelings by shaking my head and looking at her. At which point, we both did a little laugh and I explained, "I'm not doing this to cause you pain and frustration. I'm doing it because there is a child involved. I'm not making this stuff up!"

With that we both relaxed more and I stated in a matter-of-fact way that the complaint was saying that she was so upset with her boyfriend that she was firing a gun in the presence of her children. I commented on how scary that is for children.

She talked more about how she was afraid of guns; she said, "I would not shoot around my children." Then she ended with a very appropriate expression: "Lord, have mercy!"

"Do you use any kinds of drugs—or anything like marijuana or cocaine?"

"No," she said. "I don't even smoke cigarettes."

I noticed there were no ashtrays and nothing to suggest any smoking equipment. I was also at a loss as to what to do. I was silent.

After the silence, I said, "Well, as I told you, I'm just here to share with you what the complaint says and get from you what your impressions are. Now that I have said some of this, is there any way that you think—somehow, I have to explain why this other person called in and sometimes we do something with people but they get a wrong impression—they get a false impression." Still, nothing jogged her memory.

I thought about how I might verify this situation. I asked her about talking with her boyfriend. As I asked the question I realized that wasn't a very swift idea. In this discussion, I also noticed there was no sense of anger or frustration when we talked about the boyfriend. Those feelings would have been quite normal if they, indeed, had broken up.

I broke the silence this time by requesting to see the oldest child and reassuring her that I would not awaken him. We went upstairs to his bedroom.

I sensed the order of the room and the care of the room. The children slept on the floor on a mattress covered with a sheet. Everything was very neat. I became aware of the awed feeling I have when I see sleeping children.

We talked in whispers and she moved his face very gently so that I could see both sides of his mouth. There was nothing there. I nodded my head in approval of her gesture and got up off my knees and went into the hallway.

In the hallway, she touched my upper arm and motioned me to another room and said with pride, "I want you to see my baby."

As I followed her into this second bedroom I realized how much her touching me told me about her essence. She was a very gentle woman.

When we returned to the downstairs, I told her I saw no bruises on the oldest child nor anything that even suggested what the complaint had alleged. I gave her support for the efforts she has put forth to care for her children. I gave her specific examples of what I saw that gave me that impression so that she would know I was being sincere. I told her I knew it wasn't easy to raise three children under 4 years of age.

That led to her talking more about how she really enjoys these children and how her mother often wants her to leave a child with the mother so that the younger mother could have some time to herself. This information told me she had a support system.

At this point, I felt I had her confidence and cooperation so I used the momentum to discuss the issue of the children staying up so late. First, I made sure that I knew what the situation was. Since she gave me what a typical evening pattern was, I had no need to ask that particular question nor to ask for greater clarification or detail. When she talked about how much they like the stimulation of the TV and how it propels them into late hours, I nodded my head that her observations were accurate. I gave information and suggested other ways she could help keep the children happy, which I felt was one of her main concerns because of one of her statements, and still set realistic limits for bedtime. I realized that she was doing very well with her children and I wanted to be as supportive as possible. I asked if she thought our parenting classes would also help. She didn't hurt my feelings with her refusal.

We went back to the late-time bed-hour issue. I told her I wasn't being critical of her. I was looking ahead to next year when the oldest child would have to go to school. I acted and talked like I was just sharing the wisdom of my child-rearing experiences and my thinking. I explained the importance of deciding now to ease the children into this different sleeping pattern and gave suggestions in a manner that said that these might not be the exact answers. Yet she was smart enough to adapt them. I remembered her financial limitations, for she was a welfare mother living in one of the projects, and I geared my suggestions accordingly.

To end our interview, I summarized what I had seen or didn't see. I said I found no evidence to support (1) the bruised jaw, nor (2) the gun, nor (3) marijuana and/or cocaine use. "We did talk a little bit of what you (she) could do to help your children go to bed earlier at night. If that is the only difficulty you (she) are having . . . ," I was stopped by the sound of a crying baby. I asked, "Which one is that one—the baby?"

She went upstairs and came back with the baby and a change of pampers. Our conversation then centered around the child who was very tall for his age of 1 year. I spent a few minutes talking with the child with both my eyes and voice. The child had bright eyes and a sweet disposition. Once he checked in with his mother and felt there was no need to cry—even for this stranger—he got down from his mother's lap and began to walk around, exploring his world.

I have often used my interaction with the client's children as a way to establish rapport with the parent. This technique is useful in giving needed attention to the child. In this situation, connecting with the client had already been established and I was now seeking to end that.

I then brought the conversation back to my summarizing. I restated we had 45 days in which to continue and watch this complaint if that was what we needed to do. I also stated that I would, of course, check with my field instructor. If we (my field instructor and I) felt the case was unfounded, we would "unfound" the case and she would get a letter in the mail to that effect. If we felt the case needed to be watched for the remainder of the 45-day limit, it would mean that she would not get a letter immediately and I would come back and visit again.

Then I asked her if she had any questions. She said she didn't. I made sure she had my name card with its phone number. Since she was getting phone service installed, I made her responsible for calling me if she had any additional questions.

I also stated I was still curious as to what happened to that letter I sent her. I said, "I am still somewhat surprised as to why you didn't get that letter. I mailed it Friday, and you say you haven't seen anything like it at all?"

She went to the front door where the mail had been dropped through the mail slot earlier that day. In opening one of the envelopes, we found the letter I had sent. For me, it was important for her to receive that letter. I reflected on how this delay in the mail was probably better because if she had received it earlier, it would have worried her unnecessarily. I got up from the chair and checked the postmark. I had mailed it Friday, but it was postmarked Tuesday. I felt satisfied.

We then began to process what had happened, how I came and talked with her. She explained that she thought a neighbor had made a complaint because the neighbor woman didn't like her. She told how she had just moved to this address—about a month and a half earlier. She expressed her amazement when she had put her clothes on the outside line to dry—in the daytime—and someone had stolen them. Gone. Twice.

She then told how she has to make other arrangements to do the washing. She goes to her mother's and comes back and stays in the house.

I listened and said that must make you feel very isolated. Would she like to have friends? Then we talked about the elderly people around her in the public housing and how she can continue to build on that support.

To end this interview, I again thanked her for her cooperation. We then began to process this shocking situation for her. In my laughing with her, I asked what was her former impression of CPS workers and she replied, "They come get your children."

"No, no, no," I said. "We also come out and do just what I did—we talk to people. We don't take children unless they are at risk." Then I explained what situations might call for intervention. As a reasonable person, she also agreed on that judgement call.

As I moved toward the front door, I restated how she would hear from me. I also thanked her for her cooperation and told her I was sorry I shocked her.

Analysis of the Worker

I used the tape recorder to record the conversation. I then listened to the recorder and tried to remember what thoughts I had and/or feelings at different points in the conversation. This particular process report was written with the idea of showing the integra-

tion of course work, reading, and social work practice. This method permitted me to more accurately describe what did happen as opposed to my writing what I thought had happened.

The following key concepts of social work practice with examples were utilized:

(1) Ventilate—She said, "I can hardly wait until my mother comes home from work so that I can tell her what happened to me today."

(2) Verbalization of feelings—An example is where I effectively used the word "shocked" to help her express what I thought I saw her express through body language.

(3) Reassurance—I gave reassurance in the very beginning of the interview when I said it was OK not to call me, especially if she didn't get my letter. I gave reassurance and support in terms of the positive things I saw her doing with her children.

(4) Explanation—I used explanation mostly in dealing with the late-bedtime issue as well as in explaining my purpose for talking with her.

(5) Confrontation—I used confrontation in raising each of the issues of the complaint. The manner in this particular situation was slow and gentle.

I particularly liked how I created a relationship with the client. Once there was "connectedness," I used it to give advice and information to assist with her parenting; of setting a more realistic bedtime for the children. I also used this situation to activate a client to feel through and think through these potential problems of bedtime and neighbors.

In terms of preconceived notions, I was fearful at first. The thought passed through my mind that there was a gun involved. I also knew my time to leave this earth had not come. I also thought about the unfamiliarity of the area. I was glad I remembered past warm experiences and could use that energy to influence this situation.

I suppose I also envisioned a lot of resistance. Now, as I reflect, I realize that when a client believes the complaint is unfounded, they will do everything in their power to cooperate, get me verification and get me out of the house as fast as possible. This certainly was the case in another situation.

In terms of principles of casework, I used a nonjudgmental attitude and acceptance. I accepted her as an ADC [Aid to Dependent Children] mother and treated her with respect, as I have treated all my other clients.

Other Factors

The risk factor would have been quite high if the mother did have a gun and even higher if she had a lot of angry, frustrated feelings. The ages of the children would have also added to the equation because they could not have protected themselves by running to a neighbor's house.

In terms of bio/psycho/social factors, I did not see anything that suggested severe mental illness. The woman was working on such tasks as raising a family and gaining a life style. She had accomplished the tasks of later adolescence (18–22) with her sex-role identity, internalized morality and career choice. She seemed to thrive on being a mother. Others might say that there is a weak ego development in the sense that she has had the same boyfriend for five years and they have never married even though they have 3 children. She gets stuck with all the responsibilities of raising the children. I saw her as having a strong ego because she was more successful than unsuccessful in the mastery of everyday tasks.

This case was unfounded.

✳ BRAIN EXERCISE

A 28-year-old woman told officials that she has been a heroin and cocaine addict for twelve years. To alleviate the suffering of her 4-month-old baby, she was feeding a small amount of heroin to the child by mouth. She has been charged with permitting serious injury to a minor child and forcibly administering heroin to a minor child.

Some medical personnel believe that giving small doses of heroin might have saved the child's life. A baby born addicted to drugs—heroin, cocaine, pain pills—could go through withdrawal serious enough to cause death.

What would you do with the mother?

Most state statutes protect the born child but what about the unborn? Should there be laws for prenatal care? Should mothers who expose their unborn children to illegal drugs be held criminally accountable or should they be treated under medical models called "Center for Perinatal Addiction?" In some states, a woman who is pregnant and realizes she has a problem can go to any treatment center available and not be automatically referred to jail. But, when that rational ability is gone and the mother feels no obligation toward her child, should the legal power of the state be brought to bear in an effort to help the child? If so, how much?

To better understand how our society became aware of child sexual abuse, it is important to discuss its history and the various groups that discovered its ongoing existence. Then, based on that history, this section will discuss risk assessments. Characteristics of families that are healthy will be contrasted with families that are dysfunctional in order to understand how sexual abuse can exist—and continue—within a family.

SEXUAL CHILD ABUSE

Today . . . we know that all living beings who strive to maintain life and long to be spared pain—all living beings on earth are our neighbors. Albert Schweitzer

History

After 1975, child abuse began to include sexual abuse as well. Prior to 1975, societal attitudes—including those of professionals—toward incest and sexual abuse were expressed, for the most part, as silence or denial. To better understand this area, we will discuss the fantasy hypothesis, father-daughter rape, and a *prima facie* case of sexual abuse before discussing the rates of sexual abuse today and the reporting statutes.

Fantasy Hypothesis

Professionals were influenced by now-disproved Freudian concepts, which suggested that children indulged in sexual fantasies, so much so that the literature of the 1970s seemed devoted to debunking this myth. Some studies described cases of only a few victims of sexual abuse (Adelman 1974; Award 1976; Dixon, Arnold, and Calestro 1978; Gutheil and Avery 1977; Herman and Herschman, 1977), while others gave accounts of several hundreds (Armstrong 1978; Butler 1978; Forward and Buck 1978; Geiser 1979; Justice and Justice 1979). Whatever the numbers involved, the conclusions were very similar: sexual abuse exists.

In retrospect, it is obvious that the fantasy hypothesis should have been tested instead of simply being accepted, yet untested acceptance seems to have been the norm. Had research and testing been done earlier, the defining, identifying, preventing, or punishing of child sexual abuse might have resulted sooner.

Psychoanalysts, besides oversubscribing to the childhood sexual-fantasy theory, also adopted a concept of children's cognitive and developmental stages. This led to negative, unhelpful views of children's qualifications to serve as witnesses in court proceedings. Sexual abuse and the characteristics of its victimizers and victims had to be more widely studied and understood before any special consideration for the child victim-witness could be given.

Types of Rape

The establishment of rape crisis centers around the country in the 1970s raised public consciousness about child sexual abuse due to unexpected and unsolicited information from adults who were sexually molested and raped as children. Incest was described as "father-rape." The women's movement and child protection lobbies gained political power and won public credibility, enabling them to expand child protective statutes to include sexual abuse (Finkelhor 1980).

Some groups such as the René Guyon Society lobbied for the age of consent to be reduced so that adult-child sex can occur. Using the slogan, "Sex before eight, or it's too late," this group recommends incest. They argue that the lack of premarital sex leads to divorce, drug abuse, crime, and suicide. Justice and Justice (1979, 269) say that no valid evidence has been presented nor studies offered to prove their theory. Existing literature documents only negative consequences of incest.

Although father-daughter incest may be the most prevalent (Brownmiller 1975; Peters 1976; Weeks 1976; Browing and Boatman 1977; Herman and Herschman 1977; Stucker 1977; Armstrong 1978; Butler 1978), other forms of incest occur, such as mother-son, sibling, grandfather-granddaughter, mother-daughter, and father-son (Award 1976; Burgess et al. 1978; Dixon et al. 1978; Forward and Buck 1978; Justice and Justice 1979).

Unlike physical abuse, sexual abuse often has few, if any, physical indications that may alert a professional. A study based on pediatric emergency-room records and clinical experience in the 1970s recommended that all children seen for genital injury, irritation, and infection be considered sexually misused. Children under age 12 with venereal disease, primarily gonococcal infections of the genitourinary tract, the throat, and the anal canal were to be considered prime suspects of having been sexually abused.

Thus, many states passed statutes having these elements as a *prima facie* case of sexual child abuse:

☐ under age 12

☐ venereal disease

☐ of any opening

An example would be a 3-month-old baby with gonorrhea of the mouth (an actual case). The baby was taken to the hospital with a sore throat and an inability to gain weight. Then, the real infection was found!

Today, professionals in the field say that sexual abuse occurs to 1 out of 3 females and 1 out of 5 males before the 18th birthday. Healthy sexual relationships between two persons usually have these qualities and characteristics:

☐ giving and receiving

☐ sense of worth

☐ sense of self-esteem

☐ mutual

☐ consensual

☐ partnership

☐ peers

But child sex is not mutual. It is nonconsensual with someone who is a nonpeer. There may be part compliance but there is no commitment. So the need for being consistently accepted and respected as an individual is not met by the offender.

In *State v. Salata* (859 S.W.2d 728 [1993]) the Supreme Court of Missouri denied to hear a case from the Court of Appeals because the court found no errors in the conviction of Salata. Salata had taken J. R., a 4-year-old, to his van, took nude photographs after covering the young boy with excrement for the purpose of the sexual stimulation or gratification of an individual viewing the nude photographs.

The proof of the unequal power in a sexual abuse relationship is that children will suffer from physical problems and emotional trauma, such as post-traumatic stress disorder (PTSD). They will go through behavioral changes, which will negatively affect their family and other social interactions. They may have poor interactions with peers, a sudden interest in sex, mimic sexual behavior in play, and express hostility and fear.

From the research done on adult survivors (n = 135) of sexual abuse who reported themselves for outpatient psychotherapy at a university-affiliated mental health center serving the suburbs of a large metropolitan area in the southeast, we gain a bigger picture of the problem. Of the 127 who could remember how old they were at the onset of the abuse, 46% were 5 years or younger. The average duration of the sexual abuse was 5.05 years, ranging from less than a year to 28 years. The most common forms of abuse were fondling (92%), digital penetration (63%), vaginal intercourse (59%), masturbation of the perpetrator (54%), and performing oral sex on the perpetrator (51%). Sixty-one percent reported having more than one perpetrator, with 37% having three or more. Perpetrators were males with a few females, and 7% were being victimized by both males and females (Gold, Hughes, and Swingle 1996).

Reporting

It seems that most of the reporting is done by someone close to the family. Like physical abuse, there are no known special social or psychological indexes that readily identify these families (Holder 1980). No family, despite its level of income or education, is free from the potential of abuse.

All fifty states have child protective statutes that require certain occupations to report. In fact, courts have upheld lawsuits against professionals who failed to detect and report signs of child abuse. In 1976 in *Landeros v. Flood*, 17 Cal. 3d 399, the California Supreme Court held that a child may sue a physician for injuries received from a parent after the physician examined the child. The question to the Supreme Court was: "Does the standard

Reporting Statutes

Figure 5.2
Child Abuse and Neglect:
Criminal Prosecution of
Child Abuse Cases.

Child Abuse & Neglect
Criminal Prosecution of Child Sexual Abuse Cases

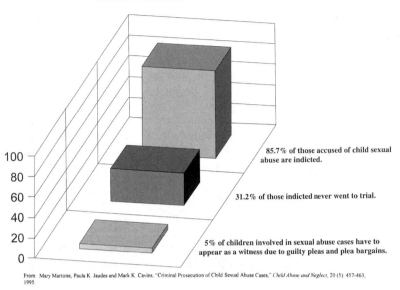

85.7% of those accused of child sexual abuse are indicted.

31.2% of those indicted never went to trial.

5% of children involved in sexual abuse cases have to appear as a witness due to guilty pleas and plea bargains.

From: Mary Martone, Paula K. Jaudes and Mark K. Cavins, "Criminal Prosecution of Child Sexual Abuse Cases," *Child Abuse and Neglect*, 20 (5) 457-463, 1995.

of care include a requirement that the physician(s) know how to diagnose and treat the battered child syndrome?" The obvious answer by the court was "Yes."

In addition, most states define child pornography as a form of abuse rather than a form of obscenity (Baker 1980), and most provide immunity for those who report it. Reporting does not mean one has to prove the abuse occurred. Reporting only means you suspected something. The reporting agency then considers the merits of your report. See Figure 5.2 to see what happens next.

Yet cases do go unreported. Not until the child is an adult and safely away from the family situation does she or he, through the support of others, disclose the pain. This delay, unfortunately, is used by others to suggest that the report is a "false memory" when in fact the delay is a psychological mechanism to deal with the trauma of the event.

Most charges of sex abuse are reported during custody hearings.

Reporting is not the same thing as disclosure. Reporting means to contact an official agency. Disclosure, on the other hand, refers to the victim. Sometimes the victim will be spontaneous in that the child deliberately and quickly tells adults of an incident. In other cases, the child may accidentally refer to an event during a conversation with an adult. For example, "when a three-year-old began to masturbate vigorously, her mother told her to stop (but) the child protested, 'But my daddy puts his finger in there'" (Ceci and Bruck 1995, 75). Many sex abuse cases come while the parents are divorcing and are part of custody decisions. Custody will be discussed in Chapter 7, "Other Hearing in Juvenile Court: Child Custody, Support, and Termination of Parental Rights."

Risk Assessment

Risk assessments are done to determine the amount of risk the child is in. The assessment is usually done by the CPS worker who has to take into

Sexual Activity

	Low	Medium Low	Medium	Medium High	High	Extreme High
Activities	Fondling with clothes on	Fondling with clothes off	Fellatio	Cunnilingus	Sexual intercourse	Ritual sexual intercourse

Bio/Psy/Social

	Low	Medium Low	Medium	Medium High	High	Extreme High
Bio Age	16–18	13–15	9–12	5–8	1–4	Birth
Mental Age	16–18	13–15	9–12	5–8	1–4	Birth
Social	16–18	13–15	9–12	5–8	1–4	Birth

Family Dynamics

Activities	Very Strong	Strong	Average	Weak	Dysfunctional
1. Dealing with tensions					
2. Clear boundaries					
3. Equal powers					
4. Open communications					
5. Understanding by others					
6. Negotiation skills					
7. Acceptance of change					

Figure 5.3
The Risk Check (RIC) List.

account: (1) the types of sexual activities, (2) the biopsychosocial factors of the child, and (3) the family dynamics. (See **Risk Check (RIC) List** in Figure 5.3 and Table 5.1.)

Types of Sexual Activity

Incest is any overtly sexual contact between persons who are biologically or socially related. Although a female victim is not biologically related to her stepfather, she is socially related. Due to this social relationship, some courts view the sexual misconduct as "incest" as opposed to statutory rape. Some states have modified their statutes to define it as sexual assault.

Sexual child abuse can run the gamut from fondling with clothes on to fellatio, cunnilingus, sodomy, and/or sexual intercourse. Force is not always necessary because the child is often too young to understand the significance of what is happening. The parent's or caretaker's authority is used to acquire compliance. If that does not work, stronger threats and/or force are used.

Table 5.1   ASSESSMENT OF RISK

Factors	Low Risk	Intermediate Risk	High Risk
Child			
Age	Adolescent	Lower elementary school age	Infant
Physical and mental abilities	Cares for and protects self without adult assistance	Requires adult assistance to care for and protect self	Completely unable to care for or protect self without assistance
Caretaker			
Level of cooperation	Aware of problem; works with social services agency to resolve problem and protect child	Overly compliant with investigator	Doesn't believe there is a problem, refuses to cooperate
Physical, mental, and emotional abilities or control	Realistic expectations of child; can plan to correct problem	Poor reasoning abilities; may be physically handicapped; needs planning to protect child	Poor conception of reality or severe mental or physical handicaps
Perpetrator			
Rationality of behavior	Accidental injury; adequate supervision	Minor injury resulting from excessive corporal discipline	Injury, the result of irrational desire to harm the child permanently
Access to child	Out of home; no access to child	In home, but access to child is difficult	In home with complete access to child
Incident			
Extent of permanent harm	Abuse or neglect has no discernible effect on child	Abuse or neglect results in physical injury or discomfort; no medical attention needed	Abuse or neglect may result in death or permanent dysfunction of an organ or limb
Location of injury	Bony body parts; knees, elbows, buttocks	Torso	Head, face, genitals
Previous history of abuse or neglect	No previous reported history of neglect or abuse	Previous abuse or neglect of child	Previous abuse or neglect of child
Physical condition	Home is clean with no apparent safety or health hazards	Trash and garbage not disposed; animal droppings in home	Structurally unsound, leaky roof and windows, wall bending under weight, holes in exterior walls
Environmental			
Support System	Family, neighbors, friends available; good community	Family supportive but not in geographic area; some support from friends	Caretaker or family have no relatives or friends and are geographically isolated from community
Stress	Stable family, steady employment, nonmobile	Birth of child	Death of spouse

Adapted from Massachusetts Department of Social Services *Reference Guide for Child Abuse and Neglect Investigations* (Boston: Massachusetts Department of Social Services, 1985, p. 59).

Source: Cynthia Crosson Tower, *Understanding Child Abuse and Neglect* (Boston: Allyn and Bacon, 1989, p. 202).

Biopsychosocial Factors

Age is an extremely important variable and has several dimensions: biological, mental, and emotional. The lower the biological age, such as 2 and 3, the greater are the chances for the age to be the same on all three dimensions. However, it is possible to have a child be biologically 6 years old but emotionally and socially much younger due to the onset of the first experience that traumatized the child and hindered his or her emotional and social development.

The younger the child, the greater the risk to the child. Babies who are 2 and 3 months old can do little to run from their aggressors. It took the work of Goodwin (1982, 59–73) to specifically describe age categories and what one could expect victims to say, as described in Chapter 2.

Young children are the most difficult to interview, unless one employs the knowledge that their sense of time is limited. An interviewer must use birthdays, holidays, and schools attended as benchmarks to help identify first sexual contact. In addition, a vocabulary must be developed for talking about sexuality. What does a child call his or her anus, for example? "Stinking hole"?

Family Dynamics

Besides the trauma experienced by the victim/survivor of sexual abuse, the child sexual abuse victim-witness is often left without the supportive network of an intact family. Unlike some child witnesses in other types of court cases, these sexual-abuse child witnesses have families that are dysfunctional, even if they are intact.

It has been only recently that researchers and social service practitioners have developed theory and treatment based on family systems. Some of the research findings came from families seen in clinical settings, namely for alcohol treatment (Wegscheider 1981). In viewing families that were devastated by alcohol, for example, practitioners were better able to see families' coping styles on a continuum—with normal healthy families at one end and dysfunctional families at the other. In this manner, then, families were viewed as having "degrees" of a certain variable. For example, among 68 youth incarcerated for delinquency in Southeast Missouri, McGaha and Leoni (1995) found that 24 (63%) among the youth from alcoholic families reported that family violence was so bad that the police had to be called. Of the 68 youth, 40 (59%) indicated that they were from homes where alcoholism and/or chemical dependency was a serious problem, 30 reported at least one runaway from their family, and only 13 (45%) of the youth from nonalcoholic homes reported running away.

Family theory and therapy were important because they shifted the focus or attention from one individual—for example, the delinquent who was acting out—to the entire family, in terms of the reinforcements other family members were giving the behavior. The negative behavior was viewed only as a symptom of the bigger problem—the family. When the father and mother began counseling sessions and felt better about themselves, their relationship improved. Their behavior also improved and resulted in more appropriate parenting skills and, as a result, the negative behavior of the child often stopped.

The Family as the Focus

Family Pattern Repeats

Another key component of family therapy is the idea that family patterns tend to repeat themselves over generations. Studies done on immigrant families show how people who came to America desired to be assimilated into the emerging American way of life. Second- and third-generation Americans moved away from their families of origin when their education was completed. The erroneous belief was that each new generation would establish a new life with a new nuclear family unit free of the problems of arguing, fighting, and so forth. This geographic separation, coupled with the Protestant ethic, led people to think that their accomplishments were due mostly to their own talents. They disregarded the training in problem-solving, negotiation, and communication styles they received as members of a family. What people failed to realize was that they took their arguing skills, tendency to blame others, and so forth with them, although they were geographically separated from their families of origin (Wegscheider 1982).

In recent years greater attention has been given to the mother-child relationship and its impact on succeeding generations. Murray Bowen (1978) was the pioneer at the Menninger Clinic who investigated three to four generational views of families in treating emotional dysfunction such as schizophrenia.

In short, a dysfunctional family means that although a family is not presently alcoholic, if there is any dysfunctional coping strategy within the mother-child relationship, the child grows to become a mother or father who repeats that pattern. This is why it is crucial for us in the justice system to identify dysfunctional family elements early to provide both prevention and treatment.

Figure 5.4 represents a risk assessment developed by Rhode Island for its child welfare agencies. This instrument, like those from Oklahoma and Alaska, was based on an analysis of the relationship between family characteristics and case outcomes using large samples (that is, 1,000 to 2,000 families) of previously substantiated cases. Rhode Island's scale is particularly noteworthy because of its ability to predict the seriousness of subsequent incidents. "Just 1 percent of the low-risk cases, compared to 27 percent of the 'intense' cases, had a subsequent referral that required medical treatment or hospitalization" (Howell 1995, 206–210).

Unlike the needs scales used in juvenile justice, needs assessment in child welfare instruments focus almost exclusively on the caretaker and the family, rather than the individual child. Thus, caseworkers need to be trained in characters of healthy families as well. To evaluate the level of a family's ability to effectively operate, it is important to know how a healthy family operates.

Healthy Families

Seven concepts have been developed to describe a healthy family:

1. Healthy families **deal with tensions between individual needs and family needs.** Healthy families differentiate individual needs from the needs of the family as a whole, and family members are helped with their individual needs. An example of a family not doing very well on this variable comes from a personal experience at an amusement park in which a teenage daughter was saying to her father that some of her

Case Name	Unit	
SCR# CYCIS #	Staff Person	Date

Neglect	Score	Abuse	Score

Neglect

N1. Did the current investigation indicate neglect? _____
   a. No 0
   b. Yes . . . . +1

N2. Was the type of neglect indicated at this investigation inadequate food, clothing, medical care or failure to thrive (CANTS allegations 43,45,46,48)? _____
   a. No 0
   b. Yes . . . . +1

N3. How many early warnings were received for this household *prior* to this incident? _____
   a. None 0
   b. One . . . . +1
   c. Two or more . . . . +2

N4. How many *unfounded* investigations of this household were conducted *prior* to the current incident? _____
   a. None . . . . −1
   b. One 0
   c. Two or more . . . . +1

N5. Was neglect or sexual abuse indicated at any *prior* investigation of this household? _____
   a. Neglect . . . . +1
   b. Sexual abuse . . . . +2
   c. None of the above 0

N6. How many children were indicated for abuse or neglect in this incident? _____
   a. One or two children 0
   b. Three or more children . . . . +1

N7. Age of the *oldest* child indicated for abuse or neglect in this incident? _____
   a. Age 11 or older . . . . −1
   b. 6–10 years old 0
   c. Less than 6 years old . . . . +2

N8. Was the primary adult caretaker a perpetrator in this incident? _____
   a. No 0
   b. Yes . . . . +1

N9. Does this appear to be a stable family? _____
   a. No 0
   b. Yes . . . . −1

N10. Does any child in this family have a CYCIS contact record or a CYCIS service history? _____
   a. None 0
   b. Yes, CYCIS contact record . . . . +1
   c. Yes, CYCIS service history . . . . +2

            Total Neglect Score _____

Abuse

A1. Did the current investigation indicate abuse? _____
   a. No 0
   b. Yes . . . . +1

A2. How many early warnings were received for this household *prior* to the current incident? _____
   a. None . . . . −1
   b. One 0
   c. Two or more . . . . +1

A3. How many *unfounded* investigations of this household were conducted *prior* to the current incident? _____
   a. None 0
   b. One . . . . +1
   c. Two or more . . . . +3

A4. Has any *prior* investigation of this household indicated sexual abuse? _____
   a. No 0
   b. Yes, prior sexual abuse . . . . +2

A5. How many children were indicated for abuse or neglect in this incident? _____
   a. One child 0
   b. Two children . . . . +1
   c. Three or more children . . . . +2

A6. Age of the *youngest* child indicated for abuse or neglect in this incident? _____
   a. Age 16 or older . . . . −2
   b. Age 15 or younger 0

A7. Age of the primary adult caretaker? _____
   a. 36 years or older . . . . −1
   b. 35 years or younger 0

A8. Is there evidence that either caretaker has an alcohol or drug problem? _____
   a. No 0
   b. Yes . . . . +1

A9. Does the family appear to receive little or no external support from family, friends, or community resources? _____
   a. Some support 0
   b. Little or no support . . . . +1

A10. Does this appear to be a stable family? _____
   a. No 0
   b. Yes . . . . −1

A11. Does any child in the family have a CYCIS contact record or CYCIS service history? _____
   a. No . . . . −1
   b. Yes, CYCIS contact record 0
   c. Yes, CYCIS service history . . . . +1

            Total Abuse Score _____

Initial Abuse/Neglect Classification

Assign the family's A/N classification based on the higher of the abuse of neglect scores, using the following chart:

A/N Classification		Neglect Score		Abuse Score	
_____	Low	_____	−3 to 1	_____	−6 to −3
_____	Medium	_____	2 to 4	_____	−2 to 0
_____	High	_____	5 to 7	_____	1 to 3
_____	Intense	_____	8 to 16	_____	4 to 14

Figure 5.4
Rhode Island D.C.Y.F. Initial Family Assessment of Abuse/Neglect. (Source: Howell [1995]). U.S. Department of Justice, *Guide for Implementing the Comprehensive Strategy for Serious, Violent, and Chronic Juvenile Offenders*, p. 207).

friends were elsewhere on the grounds and she wanted to join them. The father used extremely loud language and told her in no uncertain terms that she was not going anywhere. He saw this as a family outing and the entire family was going to be together whether she liked it or not. There was public humiliation and no discussion of alternatives, such as setting a specific amount of time with her friends and the rest of the time with the family. There was obviously no preagreement. The father did not explain to the daughter that morning that her consenting to go meant she had to stay with the family for the entire time. But if the father had voiced his expectation prior to the family outing, then he could have better handled the daughter's change of mind. In a soft, private way, he would only have had to remind her of her agreement.

2. There are **clear boundaries with well-defined roles for parents and for children.** Sharing intimacy is only acceptable within clearly defined boundaries so that there is distance between parents and children. For example, parents get to set the bedtimes for the children. Children have to sleep in their own rooms. Mommy and daddy's room is off-limits unless they knock to enter and have permission to enter.

3. There are relatively equal powers between children and parents, particularly in terms of **leadership**. Children have the opportunity for feedback and power of choice. Parents, for example, can give the child a choice between milk and orange juice for breakfast, but the child is not allowed to create his own menu.

4. There is **open communication, free choice, and autonomy.** Open communication means the child feels like someone has listened to him or her. Therefore, the child is willing to share the events of the day. It also means that no topic is taboo and even the most personal parts of a person's body have a name. Contrast that with families who never discuss anything about sex and the body parts are called "down there."

5. Members find they are **understood by others.** Ideas are taken seriously. **Reflective listening** is used to help members identify their feelings and become optimistic about their situation. **Problem-solving** is used as opposed to blaming and name-calling.

6. There are **skills in negotiations.** Members share tasks and accept directions. No one family member is always stuck taking out the garbage, which is considered by some to be the "No. 1 debatable task" in the American family. When there is a problem, members reach out for input from one another and from experts in their community.

7. Healthy families **accept changes well.** They are not afraid of being close and they accept the risk of emotional injury.

Dysfunctional Families

The dysfunctional family operates on the premise that neither the father nor the mother is a whole person. Because they lack completeness and balance, the children in a family become enmeshed with the parents. They learn through life experiences to fill the gaps, so to speak, to compensate by taking on other styles of communication and coping strategies that will not upset the balance of the unhealthy family unit.

The whole person concept is predicated on the idea that each human is a composite of six characteristics or abilities: (1) emotional, (2) social, (3) physical, (4) will, (5) spiritual, and (6) mental abilities. (Think of this as a pie with six equal pieces, with each piece representing each of the above six elements.) Each ability is equally important, and behavior is the result of the interaction of several or all these abilities. In the healthy person, all of the components are equally developed and in balance. Power is balanced and self-worth is high (Wegscheider 1981).

Alcoholic Families

The alcoholic, however, is out of touch with power and substitutes a chemical for power. The areas of social, physical, emotional, will, and spiritual are poorly developed. The mental aspect dominates to the extent that the person comes across as charming and righteous. Yet the individual is preoccupied with chemicals and other addictions that stimulate denial of feelings to control pain. Such defenses as rationalization, denying, avoiding, blaming, and making excuses are used for the cover-up of both involvement with chemicals and low self-esteem. Rigidity and aggression are used to maintain control and, as a result, caring people are pushed away or kept at a distance.

The co-alcoholic, co-dependent, or enabler is the one who matches and mates with the alcoholic. Usually this person has more development in the areas of spiritual, mental, and will (excessively responsible). The co-dependent has been trained to feel responsible for everything and everyone; yet, he or she feels powerless and unworthy. There is too much reliance on the coping skills of passivity, suffering, blaming, and hoping that God will take care of everything.

Lacking both physical and emotional health and well-being, the co-dependent has no energy to deal effectively with the problems in the family. Feeling tired, weak, and fearful are both consequence and cause. The social aspect is nonexistent. The behavior of the drinker or drug abuser is certain to cause the enabler grief or embarrassment in a social situation, so the enabler withdraws from those who have offered support in the past. Thus, at home, there is a cold war of silence and avoidance or bickering and bitter quarrels. The enabler is trapped between his or her sense of "love" and the realities of exhaustion. By the time the later stages of alcoholism set in, both the dependent and the enabler are isolated, and there is a sense of loss. There is emotional and social bankruptcy (Wegscheider 1981, 89–103).

Together, the alcoholic and the co-dependent or enabler have children and pass on to these children their role models. For example, because the parents place little value on truth and honesty, their children have a tendency to lie without guilt.

In addition, each child takes on both a birth order and a specific way of responding to the dysfunctional family. There has been recent research to suggest that the four profiles developed by Wegscheider (1981) do not fit all families because of individual or unique experiences. Yet this information will help you understand how it may often happen.

The four profiles developed by the children, according to Wegscheider (1981), are called (1) hero, (2) scapegoat or rebel, (3) lost child, and (4) mascot. The hero is usually overly responsible and excels trying to be accepted by the parents. Yet nothing is ever good enough to make things right with the family; his or her efforts are inadequate to heal the pain.

Marginal notes: Co-Dependent · Hero

Usually the hero leaves the family, but not the role. In business she or he is the "type A" workaholic who is prone to heart attacks and strokes. Because intimacy—real emotional closeness—has not been encouraged in her or his family, she or he has not learned to relate to others in a way that is open and trusting. To search for the deeper meaning of life would cause the hero to face personal pain or expose the family secrets that life as a child was painful (Wegscheider 1981, 104–115).

Scapegoat or Rebel   Child No. 2 quickly realizes that child No. 1 is not getting much by being a really "good child" and thus chooses to do things differently. Trying things differently is viewed by the parents as rebellion. Whereas the first child becomes a pleaser and a leader (also called a rescuer), the second child is full of anger and gets into trouble as a way of getting attention. The anger is a mask for feelings of rejection and loneliness. Beneath the mask is hurt. So the flight from the family is to the peer group. This child also lacks honesty and genuine concern for others. It is difficult for him to build intimate, cooperative, loving relationships unless there is intervention and treatment (Wegscheider 1981, 116–126).

Lost Child   The third child, sensing that the first and second are not getting many positive strokes from their behavior, makes no demands on the family and the family ignores the child as if he or she did not exist. Through fantasy, the child becomes quiet, withdraws, and is known as the "lost child." Whereas the scapegoat (the second child) is hurt and angry, the lost child accepts exclusion as deserving. So this child experiences loneliness and worthlessness, but little anger. This child is prone to overindulgence in "goodies"; to bring "sweetness" into his or her life. The child may be overweight or an alcoholic as well.

Mascot   The fourth child tries to be the clown or mascot of the family to make everyone happy. This child tries to keep peace in the family and will sacrifice his or her own feelings and emotional growth to help hold the family together. This fourth child comes into the family at a time when Dad, for example, is preoccupied with drinking and Mom is preoccupied with Dad, and each of the other children are busy playing their own survival roles.

The research that has identified these profiles has also shown that they continue in sequence, so that child No. 5 becomes another hero, child No. 6 becomes another scapegoat, child No. 7 becomes the lost child, and child No. 8 becomes another mascot. Although there is some variation in the profiles due to sex variations and closeness of birth, the result is that these defenses compulsively cover true feelings. The children learn to live in the trap of self-delusion. More importantly, each child learns all of the maladaptive roles so that the child, upon becoming an adult, may be the alcoholic in one relationship and the co-dependent in another relationship.

McGaha and Stokes (1990) contend that children of alcoholic families are six times more likely to become dropouts or be suspended from school, and they have a higher incidence of suicide and crime participation. They tend to exhibit more aggression, hyperactivity, and depression—leading to juvenile delinquency. As a result, **youths from addictive homes are overrepresented in juvenile court as status offenders, delinquents, and abuse and neglect cases.**

Even more important to our discussion is the fact that the family may not presently be using alcohol and yet is still considered dysfunctional.

Wegscheider (1981, 21) found that out of the treated families "more than 70 percent had an alcoholic somewhere in a three-generation span and it did not seem to make any difference whether the alcoholic was recovering or still using—the families were still in stress." The family may be a second generation to the disease and still have alcoholic patterns of interaction. Or the family may not have drinking as the addiction; it may be gambling, drugs, or sex.

If you need to determine whether a family is dysfunctional, think about dysfunctionalism as if it were a continuum with degrees of dysfunction. There is no standard scale to determine a dysfunctional family per se. Plus, no matter how enmeshed (meaning that everyone is feeling for daddy instead of letting daddy suffer the consequences of his own behavior) and ineffective the family may be at handling its stresses, caseworkers are trained to notice and build upon the strengths the families do have.

Incest Families

Incest families are a special kind of dysfunctional family. For those families, the **Risk Check (RIC) List** (Figure 5.2) might be a beginning in determining the risk assessment of the child. There is a more detailed chart in Table 5.1. The family needs to be viewed in terms of the victim/survivor, the aggressor, and the silent partner.

The **victims/survivors** are not usually the initiators. They are generally too young to understand how they have been set up. Even if the child is a seductive child, a child is still not expected to have full adult comprehension and responsibility. Most of the incestuous relationships are devastating experiences, which can leave short- and long-term side effects.

Short-term effects range from irritation, infection, multiple bruises, abrasions, and bites, to vaginal lacerations, perineal tears or ruptures, severe bleeding, and hemorrhage. Other physical results are venereal disease and pregnancy. | Short-Term Effects

In *People v. Williams* (336 N. E. 2d 26, 1975), it was revealed to the court that Mr. Williams had impregnated each of his four daughters, and that one of his daughters (probably the oldest) had given birth to four of his children. Mr. Williams argued that the maximum imprisonment accorded to males versus the lower amount for females for aggravated incest was based on sex and was a violation of the Fourteenth Amendment. He lost his case. The court said it was not sex, but rather the social harm created by father-daughter incest (like unwanted pregnancy) that determined prison terms.

Beyond the mental anguish suffered by these young victims, physical reactions may include nausea, vomiting, and bed-wetting. Emotional symptoms are nightmares, fear of being alone, and panic reactions on seeing the offender.

Long-range effects to victims may last into adulthood. As grown women, victims may suffer painful complications in childbirth, or lasting discomfort or distress in the bladder and anus. Other effects include migraines, depression, self-hatred, drug addiction, alcoholism, promiscuity, impotence, prostitution, violence, and inability to trust or to be close to someone. | Long-Range Effects

The **aggressors** lack impulse control either sexually or emotionally, and they confuse their roles as protector and aggressor. For some aggressors, sexual abuse serves the needs of mastery, domination, anger, and retalia-

Figure 5.5
The effects of a
power/control-based
family. (*Source*: Domestic
Abuse Intervention
Project.)

tion, as well as sexual gratification (Groth 1977). Most will not accept responsibility for their behavior.

Forward and Buck (1978, 32) add to the profiles of incestuous fathers by showing that they are often law-abiding persons who have been physically or emotionally abused as children themselves. Although the motives may vary, one aggressor, who was Catholic, when asked by the police why he seduced his own daughter instead of using a prostitute or having an affair, replied, "What? And cheat on my wife?"

The **silent partner** is the term given to the person in the family triad who says nothing when in reality that person should protect the child. Some psychologists insist that the silent partner is a participant whether he or she knows about the incest or not.

Some authorities believe that the silent partner is consciously or unconsciously aware and is pushing the aggressor to abuse the child. Some think the silent partner has been conditioned from his or her family of origin to be part of family abuse and does not have any effective ways of coping with the misuse of power and control. In families where power and control are used, one spouse uses intimidation, emotional abuse, isolation, economic abuse, coercion, and threats to control the other. (See Figure 5.5.) Compare the family system in Figure 5.5 with the family system in Figure 5.6, which contrasts the effects of a power/control-based family and an equality-centered family. In an equality-centered family, there is respect, trust and support, honesty and accountability, responsible parenting, shared respon-

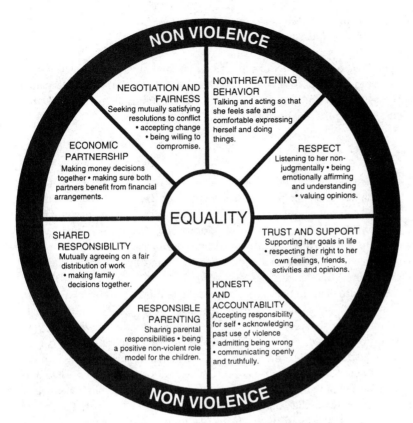

Figure 5.6
The effects of an equality-centered family. (*Source*: Domestic Abuse Intervention Project.)

sibility, economic partnership, negotiation and fairness, and nonthreatening behavior.

What effect does all this have on children? We do not know everything, but when we interview child prostitutes, we get a picture. Silbert (1989, 222), as director of Delancy Street—one of the best models for assisting female and male prostitutes—described the importance of the family by saying:

Although their lifestyles as prostitutes may be different, the backgrounds of the males tend to be quite similar to those of the females. Young male prostitutes report similarly troubled family histories. They describe a great deal of parental fighting, drinking, and emotional abuse or neglect. Their relationships with their families are poor, and they describe themselves, as did the women, as isolated among their peers. Although they come from families that appear less stable on the outside than the women did, they show similar and even greater victimization, both physical and sexual. Over three-quarters of the males involved in hustling reported that they were victims of juvenile sexual abuse. Half were involved in incest. Again, disclosure was almost nonexistent. The incest was reported by the child in only one case, and in that situation the

disclosure proved to have a negative impact on the
relationship with the person told.

Because of the impact of physical and sexual abuse on the self-worth of the child, these problems have received more attention for treatment and prevention. In addition, practitioners are becoming increasingly aware of ritualistic abuse as part of child sexual abuse.

Ritualistic Abuse

Ritualistic abuse is defined as repeated physical, emotional, mental, and spiritual assaults combined with systematized use of symbols, ceremonies, and the concept of evil, designed and orchestrated to create harmful effects. It is considered a subcategory of child abuse. It can consist of abusing a child in the form of torture, sexual assault, and/or murder. And it can be a "series of events taking place on a regular basis with multiple suspects and multiple victims" (Bass and Davis 1988, 420).

Some ritualistic abuse is based upon the family's dysfunctional patterns. It is called "intrafamilial" because it takes place within the family. For example, a husband and wife took their young daughter to the emergency room for medical treatment. The young doctor permitted them to watch while he did a pelvic examination (a special examination with medical tools in a woman's vagina) to determine the extent of her injuries. The couple then went home and incorporated that new ritual into their own sexual behavior toward the child. In *Marker v. State*, 748 P.2d 2995 (Wyo 1988), evidence of sadomasochistic materials found in the defendant's apartment were admissible on the issue of identity for aggravated assault on his 3-year-old son.

Imagine this situation. Your favorite and only brother committed suicide and several months later, at Christmas, your only gift from your parents was the same gun your brother had used. What would you think? "My parents, are they crazy?!"

Scott Peck (1983) calls it evil, and his book *People of the Lie: The Hope for Healing Human Evil* gives other case histories and definitions of evil. Forward and Buck (1989) soften the word evil by calling it "toxic." Peck is probably closer to the truth when he explains that not all evil is done in sexual ways nor does it have to be done by groups in an organized activity for evil to have devastating effects on the individual.

Like physical and sexual child abuse, ritualistic abuse can be multigenerational. This is especially true if the rituals are part of Satanism. Often these rituals are scheduled according to a set calendar and are accompanied by the wearing of robes, chanting, mock marriage ceremonies, orgies, and the mutilation of animals. Frequently they take place in cemeteries or mortuaries and center around death themes. Trickery and illusion are often involved. It's all very secretive. A lot of threats are used to ensure the victims' cooperation and silence (Bass and Davis 1988, 420).

The roots of ritual abuse can be traced back to Europe before the discovery of the New World. Reports of human sacrifice and cannibalism are found in second-century Rome and Greece. A French aristocrat born in 1404, Gilles de Rais, made confessions that sound like accounts given by today's children and adult survivors. He confessed to "sexually assaulting the children's mutilated corpses and destroying the evidence by burning the bodies" (Vargo 1992, 1).

In the 1600s another perpetrator, Catherine Deshanyes, admitted that she had participated in the ritual deaths of over 2,500 fetuses and infants. Her daughter, Maria, described some of the satanic rituals in which there was "drinking of blood and urine, animal sacrifices, orgies involving adults and children, child sacrifice, chanting and blaspheming in the name of Satan" (Vargo 1992, 1).

Satanic abuse is not well understood. Cases are not successfully prosecuted for several reasons. First, the information is so unpleasant that no one wants to even imagine that type of behavior.

Fear always springs from ignorance. Ralph Waldo Emerson

Second, lack of awareness and training on the part of practitioners (law enforcement, CPS, social workers) means that investigators do not hear the stories. The practitioners think the client is inventing the story. They don't write it down, and they don't document it or even look for physical evidence to support the victim's claim. Sometimes, the physical evidence is lacking because the cleanup job was excellent.

Third, sometimes it is many, many years later that an older woman, when having other difficulties, will reveal the memory. For example, the founder of Incest Survivors Anonymous (a national self-help organization built on the Alcoholics Anonymous model), was, at age 12, overpowered by satanic cult members and impregnated. She became a "breeder," producing babies that were later killed in her presence. Now, over age 60, she remembers abuse in rituals that included sexual abuse, torture, murder, pornography, and systematic brainwashing (Bass and Davis 1988, 417).

Fourth, there are not a lot of reported cases to study. As of 1988, only 53 cases had been reported. Of those, the two most commonly known cases are the McMartin Preschool incident (1983) and the Little Rascal case (1989).

In the McMartin case (*State v. Buckey*, 1990), one of the first of the day-care cases in the United States, Virginia McMartin Buckey and her son Raymond Buckey were acquitted on 52 out of 65 counts and the jury "hung" on the remaining 13 counts. Yet, two children who were victims stated that they had seen animals killed, had been urinated on and forced to eat feces, had been forced to simulate intercourse with other children, and they described ceremonies in which people wore robes, held candles, and forced them to drink blood. In the post-verdict press conference, many jurors claimed that they believed that some of the children had been abused. Yet they had seen the videotapes of the interviews of the children. They saw where the interviewers asked leading questions. One juror said that we never "got the children's stories in their own words" (Ceci and Bruck 1995, 251).

The American Prosecutors Research Institute and the National Center for Prosecution of Child Abuse, through grant monies of the Children's Justice Act, began to train law officers, CPS workers, and prosecutors to deal with the backlash from the McMartin case. The media focus on the trial questioned the legitimacy of the children's testimony. People just did not want to believe that adults would do such things to children!

Nathan and Snedeker (1995), a journalist and a lawyer, investigated the McMartin case along with several others and concluded that there was no evidence to support the accusations, except for parents' and professionals' panicked rumination on youngsters' behavior that sounded normal to them. In most of the cases investigated, the children never had any of the side effects associated with sexual abuse. Their question was why did so many people believe ritual abuse was true in those cases? For example:

In the spring of 1984, DA Philobosian announced that "the primary purpose of the McMartin Preschool was to solicit young children to commit lewd conduct with the proprietors of the school and also to procure young children for pornographic purposes." An assistant added that "[m]illions of child pornography photographs and films" of the victims existed. Of all the media people who trumpeted these claims, no one asked to see any photographic evidence—and, in fact, none has ever turned up, despite substantial reward offers and international searches by the FBI and Interpol. (Nathan and Snedeker 1995, 88)

In 1997, prosecutors dropped all charges against the last two defendants in the Little Rascals Day Care Center case retrial of Kelly and Wilson. Kelly, the center's owner, was convicted in 1992 after the longest, most expensive trial in North Carolina's history—nine months and more than $1 million. There is now some dispute as to what really happened. It was only after an investigation started, after intense and relentless insistence by adults, that youngsters produced criminal charges. When the children then recalled having to eat feces, being penetrated with toys, sticks, and objects, being hung from trees, and seeing infants killed, some critics thought these words were "renderings of grownups' anxieties" (Nathan and Snedeker 1995, 3).

As Nathan and Snedeker (1995, 28) so aptly point out, "the therapy model of sex-abuse intervention replaced skilled forensics personnel with social workers and others who knew nothing about how to test the validity of criminal sex-abuse charges and who unstintingly believed all of them." Perhaps what is necessary is a separation of tasks with skilled persons dealing with a particular task. For instance, law enforcement would continue to do the investigation while the therapist continues to work with the client.

Lastly, therapists find trying to deal with these children and adult survivors very difficult. For children/survivors, the norms and values of our culture are distorted and connected to torturous experiences. Terms such as love, family, hate, and killing are deprived of their usual meanings and take on new meanings. The survivors have been socialized in such a way that it is difficult for them to leave the satanic cult and function in the world outside.

In short, more needs to be done. In law enforcement, the term "ritual abuse" didn't even exist until a few years ago. There is also professional disagreement on the definition of a cult or the occult. Yet when laws are broken, crimes committed, and children are physically or sexually abused, one's religion does not matter. Illegal criminal activity, as defined by law, is clearly within the justice system's jurisdiction (*Occult Crime: A Law Enforcement Primer*, 5). Satanic abuse thus becomes both a training issue to help professionals identify incidents, and an educational issue to encourage the public

Figure 5.7
Used with permission of
Bob Gorrell, *The Richmond
Times-Dispatch.*

to report incidents. We cannot, even in the name of saving children, permit prosecutors to exploit popular anxieties about sex to perform character assassination on defendants by use of hypnosis, "guided imagery" exercises, or the jailhouse snitch as informants. In the long run, it will discredit our legal system, and when there is no law, tyranny reins.

Psychological maltreatment or emotional abuse is more prevalent and more detrimental than any other form of child maltreatment. Studies show that many victims of psychological maltreatment display antisocial behavior, and the majority of victims sustain the cycle of abuse and neglect. Current research on child development shows that foundations of personality, a way a child relates to himself and others, is established in the first two years of life through interaction with the primary caregiver, called bonding and attachment. (See "Developmental Stages of Children" in Chapter 2, "The Definition of Juvenile Delinquency, Status Offenders, Abuse, and Developmental Stages.") Emotional abuse and neglect during these early developmental stages is devastating for the developing psyche, causing damage that is very difficult to reverse.

Psychological factors are present in all types of abuse. It is the psychological consequences that define an act as abusive. An injury incurred during an athletic event might be identical to that inflicted by a parent, but the meaning to the child makes the latter abusive. Psychological damage seems to block, distort, or destroy the development of a positive sense of identity and self-esteem, knowledge, and social skills needed to ensure acceptance in a nonhostile environment and the relationships necessary to provide such learning and development (Garbarino and Vondra 1987).

> Even a dog knows when he or she is being kicked.

PSYCHOLOGICAL MALTREATMENT

Although psychological maltreatment is present in almost all cases of physical abuse, it is possible for emotional abuse to occur alone. Among child abuse and neglect categories, psychological maltreatment has been given the least attention and resources due to a lack of agreement among professionals as to the definition. Because there is a lack of definitions, states, in turn, find it extremely difficult to apply any definition in the realm of law.

Therefore, statutes usually list such harmful behavior as "rejecting, intimidating, humiliating, ridiculing, chaotic, bizarre, violent, hostile, or excessively guilt producing" (Davidson and Corson 1987, 187).

Mental neglect is defined as the failure to provide adequate nurture to meet the child's mental needs or failure to prevent the infliction of mental harm to the child, and it includes, but is not limited to, overprotection, ignoring, indifference, rigidity, apathy, and a chaotic lifestyle. Whereas emotional abuse is giving and inflicting nasty names on a child and telling him or her to go away, emotional neglect is never talking to the child.

The following eight main types of psychological abuse and neglect are the most common:

1. mental cruelty

2. sexual abuse and exploitation

3. living in dangerous and/or unstable environments where there is high violence and crime

4. substance abuse

5. negative and limiting models

6. cultural bias and prejudice in or outside of the family

7. emotional neglect and deprivation of essential love and attention

8. institutional abuse where the practices of an institution result in psychological damage to a child in their care (Brassard, Germain, and Hart 1987, 3–24)

As you look over the list, think about what those situations might look like. For example, under substance abuse, Bill, a 36-year-old schoolteacher, can still remember a sunny afternoon in third grade. He was playing in the front yard with his friends when his mother stumbled out of the house drunk and naked. She shouted at Bill for not making dinner and threw a plate at one of the other kids. Under no. 7, some judges view the frequent fighting of the parents to be emotional neglect for the child. Often, even though the child may know the parents drink and the mother is "sick" and often in bed or the father "falls asleep" at the dinner table, the child thinks it is his or her fault for all the fighting and does not blame the substance abuse!

Habit disorders such as sucking, biting, rocking, enuresis (bed wetting), and feeding disorders are common reactions to psychological abuse and neglect. Conduct disorders, including withdrawal and antisocial behavior such as destructiveness, cruelty, and stealing, are other problems. Some children may have sleep disorders or psychoneurotic reactions such as obsession, compulsion, hypochondria, and phobias. Suicide attempts are common for victims of emotional abuse.

Low self-esteem and depression are usually the most noted characteristics of these children. Experts at the NCCAN (National Center on Child Abuse and Neglect) also observed direct associations between psychological maltreatment and the potential to commit prostitution and homicide.

However, for emotional abuse to be effectively prosecuted, five main factors are required: (1) precise language in the statute, (2) guidelines for child protective agencies, (3) trained caseworkers, (4) attorneys who represent the caseworkers having a good attitude, and (5) judges with knowledge and training. It is critical for all involved to understand the devastating effects of emotional abuse and its association with other forms of child abuse and neglect and the potential for future criminal activity of children.

Widon (1992) showed that child maltreatment increases the overall likelihood of juvenile delinquency and adult criminality by 40 percent. Victims have an average first arrest age of 15.5 years, a year younger than the overall average of 16.5 years. They commit nearly twice as many offenses and are arrested more frequently than those in the control group in Widon's study (1992).

Findings of early maltreatment leading to increased rates of delinquency come from other studies as well (Smith and Thornberry 1995). In addition, research is now being focused upon adult males who were sexually abused as children to determine psychological adjustment in these men. Even though they are not confined in prison programs, they are university students with elevated scores on the Brief Symptom Inventory of somatization, obsessive-compulsive, interpersonal sensitivity, depression, anxiety, hostility, phobic anxiety, paranoid ideation, and psychoticism (Collings 1995). Because of the association of the abuse with future criminal activity of children and/or long-term psychological dysfunctions and the difficulties in prosecution, more attention is now being placed upon effective prevention programs.

One area of prevention has been dealing with dysfunctional parenting. Classes are being given to help parents understand child developmental needs, to be aware of age-appropriate childhood behavior expectations, and to develop adequate parenting skills. Some of these classes are self-help or organized programs. The most effective programs are targeted at parents expecting a child and parents considered at high-risk by the medical profession. But those programs do not meet all the needs nor identify all the parents needing assistance. Thus schools have had to develop programs for both students and the parents.

Parents need more than just knowledge. Sometimes, they have social and economic stress that places them at risk for psychological maltreatment of their children. Reducing the negative stress in the parent's life would significantly reduce the potential for child psychological maltreatment. Because research shows psychological maltreatment is the result of the unmet personal psychological needs of the parent, the most logical intervention is to meet the needs of the caretaker. Good housing and jobs for parents have an impact on children, too. Prevention programs could include encouraging social and spiritual support networks, providing home health visitors, providing tax advantages for employers who provide child care at or near the employment site, management training offered by the community or the employer, and physical and mental health fitness programs. It is less costly to the state to provide services to a family than to rear the child in foster care. And children, regardless of how much abuse occurs, would rather be reared by their own parents.

Other agencies could be supportive. Schools could have curriculum for both students and teachers. Law schools could teach child developmental stages so that the legal profession could promote a mental health model for intervention. This model would allow the state to prosecute parents that refuse to apply the available corrective and therapeutic procedures recommended by a mental health team evaluation. Ethnic and racial stereotypes and degrading references could be removed from textbooks and the public media.

Even though we know prevention before the abuse takes place is the most desired, the reality is that for some cases of abuse—physical, sexual, and psychological—treatment comes only after the abuse. Treatment is called intervention and stems from different theories.

INTERVENTION

There are costs and risks to a program of action, but they are far less than the risks and costs of comfortable inaction. John F. Kennedy

Intervention to stop the abuse of children and protect them depends upon the practice and the theories or approaches used by the helping agencies. Standardized protocols for risk assessment are now becoming more and more common in CPS agencies. CPS workers, after assessing a situation, will (1) do nothing, (2) provide services and offer future assistance, (3) leave the child at home with some safeguards such as in-home service (Home Builders), or (4) remove the child to a shelter or foster home. Rarely, but in necessary cases, the alleged offender will be removed, permitting the child to remain in the home. Unfortunately, the course of action is usually determined by the services the agency is able to provide, given the budget and the need to stretch the resources to the increasing number of reported cases.

In addition, it is important to realize that the maltreating families are heterogeneous and have different personality characteristics that contribute to the abuse and will also influence the kind of intervention. Besides needing to take into account the abusive parent, agencies need to assess the role of the child and the neglectful parent (also known as the silent partner). In some cases, a multifactor model has to be considered to address the parents' stress, social isolation, and upbringing. Today, we may use words like microsystem (the family unit itself), exosystem (the family's social system and community influence), and macrosystem (the larger culture). Regardless of the terminology, when services are provided, three of the most noted are (1) psychiatric, (2) sociological, and (3) social situational (Goldstein, Keller, and Erne 1985, 23–25).

Psychiatric

The psychiatric model looks upon the abusing parent(s) as the major cause of child abuse and the primary target of treatment. To be sure, a study of the American parents interviewed for the 1985 National Family Violence survey showed that marital violence was a statistically significant predictor of physical child abuse (Ross 1996). Thus, in this approach, the parents are viewed as having characteristics that are different from other parents. The model uses individual psychoanalytically oriented psychotherapy. The parent, like a mentally ill person, is seen as needing traditional psychodynamic verbal psychotherapy in order to change.

The goal is to get the parent to have emotional insight and understanding. Usually it is supported by home observation and direct teaching of child-rearing skills, knowledge, and attitude.

Today, the traditional view of psychotherapy has been widened to include the spiritual dimension. Formally, pain was viewed as something that broke a person down instead of breaking a person open. Part of that movement has stemmed from professionals who were reared in dysfunctional families themselves or who work with such families. They discovered that there is something inside of us so strong, wise, clear, whole, and reliable that it will rise to meet and bear the weight of whatever happens such as illness, injury, loss, or grief.

In addition, our understanding of addictions has widened. Self-help groups have modeled themselves on the AA program for alcoholics to deal with other addictions such as gambling, overeating, and sex. Sexaholics Anonymous (SA) operates to help people affected by the sexual addiction of a family member or friend. Two different groups, Daughters United and Fathers United, are self-help groups for those who have experienced family incest. The list goes on, because many people understand that their acting out behavior stems from the pains and hurts of childhood.

Sociological

The sociological model focuses on environmental stresses and cultural attitudes toward violence, as well as social class and family-community relationships in which parents feel isolated instead of being bonded to other groups in the community.

Some approaches have focused on changing our culture's acceptance of physical punishment as a child-rearing technique. In addition, this model looks at societal factors of poverty and job discrimination, poor housing, and lack of comprehensive family planning. All regard families as needing both individual and societal attention.

Social Situational

This model looks at characteristics of the child and the abuser and the interactional patterns. This approach stems from the behavioral and social learning theory that states that people learn their behavior through rewards and punishments.

Treatment concentrates on behavioral principles and techniques for changing inappropriate actions within the family and improving parenting skills. Building parenting skills includes the modification of parental disciplinary behavior so parents will stop using physical punishment. Parents receive programmed texts on child management and then are taught how to increase their children's socially desirable behavior through positive reinforcement and how to decrease their children's negative behavior through alternatives to physical punishment. Programs like Systematic Training for Effective Parenting (STEP) and Parents Anonymous (PA) use anger control and build interpersonal skills through communication to reduce isolation in the family and community.

Regardless of the theory, society today has many public agencies with knowledgeable, trained professionals available to assist parents with the challenging responsibility of raising a healthy child. Churches, public libraries, and public social service agencies can serve as resources to the community.

National organizations like Parents Anonymous (PA), Inc., is the oldest national child abuse prevention organization. PA was founded in 1970 by a single parent who wanted a safe and caring home for her children and a social worker who believed that parents are their own best agents of change. Currently, they have a national network of affiliated community-based groups with weekly meetings for parents and children. Through a system of volunteers, weekly groups are free to parents and their children who also learn healthier ways to problem-solve and, thus, grow and develop in healthier ways. Many state and local chapters operate 24-hour telephone hotlines to provide an immediate response to parents seeking help. PA also raises awareness and educates the public so that the community can work for community solutions and to encourage policymakers to promote effective services for families across America.

Both Parents Anonymous (PA) and the Nurturing Programs have been selected by the Federal Office of Juvenile Justice and Delinquency Prevention (OJJDP) as national programs for prevention of childhood problems and juvenile delinquency. In 1994, OJJDP began a collaborative effort with PA to implement the model of neighborhood-based, shared-leadership, mutual support groups in various states across the country because of the link between child abuse and juvenile delinquency.

The PA model was used to develop a parenting program inside the women's correctional center in Virginia. Known as Mothers Inside Loving Kids (MILK), the program has now grown to other prisons and jails in the same state, where fathers want to learn to be better parents, and to other states. It is an effective program (Moore and Clement 1998) that could be better promoted for there are so few programs for parents in prisons (Clement 1993).

The bottom line is that it is cheaper and better for the emotional well-being of the child to be raised in his own home than to be put into a foster home. Thus, the state would rather file a petition that the child is abused and the family is in need of services. Such an approach will work with a family willing to receive help. If, however, the act that was done to the child can be proven beyond a reasonable doubt and it is a severe crime, the state will prosecute the parent(s).

Holistic—Healthy Families

One of the most acclaimed programs on prevention of child abuse is the Hawaii Healthy Start Model. In this model, the program follows the child from birth (or before) to age 5 with a range of services, and it assists and supports other family members. Healthy Start signs up most families right after delivery of the child because they have formal agreements with all hospitals in Hawaii to enable it to perform postpartum screening. Then, paraprofessionals visit the families weekly for the first 6 to 12 months. The home visitor helps the family specify the kinds of services they want and need and the means by which to receive them. "In 1994 a confirmed child care abuse and neglect case cost the Hawaii family welfare system $25,000 for investigation, related services, and foster care. In contrast, Hawaii Healthy Start officials estimate an annual average cost of $2,800 per home visitor case" (Earle 1995, 2).

Enrolled families tend to be parents under 24 years old, low-income (50 percent receive welfare), with the father unemployed and the mother under-educated. In addition, 38 percent of the families have a history of substance abuse, 43 percent have a history of domestic violence, and 65 percent of enrolled women are single. All of these are high-risk factors, i.e., young-aged mother, single parent, undereducated, unemployed, history of substance abuse and domestic violence. Yet, after three years and 241 families served, no cases of child abuse and only four cases of child neglect were reported among the 241 families. Based on these results, the program was expanded to thirteen sites across the state. In terms of cost, at $15,000 per abuse and neglect case per year, the 42 fewer abuse and neglect cases attributable to this program between 1987 and 1991 represent a savings of over $1.26 million in child protection services (CPS) costs alone (Earle 1995, 5–9).

Hawaii Healthy Start Model is now a model for many states under the name Healthy Families. This model means:

1. increase parent/child bonding

2. higher immunization rates

3. low infant mortality rates and fewer birth complications for mothers

4. lower repeat pregnancy rates

5. 95 percent of children without developmental delays

6. children who enter school are more ready to learn

One of the reasons the U.S. Justice Department is sponsoring Healthy Families nationwide is that their research shows that children entering school healthy and ready to learn have reduced truancy rates, decreased involvement with the juvenile justice system, and lower incarceration rates. There is a two-to-one return in savings on future justice system services for every $1 invested in preventive health care, combined with child and family development services. In other words, for every $2 million in direct services, a potential future saving could be as high as $4 million.

MULTIDISCIPLINE TEAMS—JOINT INVESTIGATION

Joint investigation teams of law enforcement officers, physicians, attorneys for the state, and CPS workers have been established for cases of sexual abuse, child fatalities, and sometimes severe physical abuse and neglect. Other team members, depending upon the locality, include CASA (Court Appointed Special Advocates for the child), victim-witness coordinator, and hospital social workers. Normally, these cases are few, but because of their complexity and the potential of criminal charges, they are time-consuming and difficult. Team members usually have special training and sessions to develop bonding and positive working relationships in order to solve and treat the problems and to streamline the system. For example, a team approach can minimize the number of interviews for the victim, preserve the purity of the evidence, and expedite treatment.

The U.S. Department of Justice gives us such an understanding by the following:

*At least 33 states and the District of Columbia have
laws requiring joint investigation and cooperation
between law enforcement and child protection agencies
in child abuse cases (U.S. Dept. of Justice 1993). Most*

localities have some form of cooperation between the two agencies. Preliminary findings of a survey by the Police Foundation and National Center on Child Abuse and Neglect (NCCAN) indicate that 94 percent of the more than 800 police and sheriffs' departments contacted conduct some form of joint investigation with CPS agencies. Of the more than 400 county and state CPS agencies contacted, 89 percent have a written or unwritten agreement with their respective local law enforcement agency. (U.S. Dept. of Justice 1993)

In the state of Virginia . . . Just over half (53 percent) of the law enforcement agencies surveyed have a special unit dedicated to child abuse investigations. Such units are typical of large agencies (89 percent) rather than smaller ones (10 percent). Of the CPS agencies, approximately half (51 percent) had held inservice training in joint investigation over the prior year. (*Virginia Child Protection Newsletter* 1994, 6)

The multidisciplinary approach permits investigators to use a variety of interviewing aids, protocols, and interview approaches appropriate to the developmental stages of the child. The strengths of each team member are utilized to create a better system, as opposed to blending disciplines into a homogeneous mix in which police are not distinguishable from social workers. Even with extensive training, it takes skill and dedicated people to work as a team to deal with some of the trauma imposed upon children.

Do not ask the same questions.

Interviewing of children comes after spontaneous or accidental disclosures, or when adults have a suspicion that the child has experienced some event. Ceci and Bruck (1995), who summarize the scientific studies on children's testimony, say that children perceive adults as cooperative conversational partners who ask honest and logical questions that must have real answers. So, when they are asked the same question more than once, they think they must not have given the right answer and thus, change their answers. Children may fail to recall a number of details, yet what they do recall is highly accurate. This fact, supported by research, "has assured professionals that when children do report sexual abuse, there is no need to question their accuracy, no matter how suggestive the interviewing procedures" (Ceci and Bruck 1995, 83).

Be sensitive to power and status variables.

Some of the newest research shows that young children are sensitive to the status and power of their interviewers. The child, then, will comply with the implicit and explicit agenda of such interviewers. It is not only the actual questions but also the context of the interview. So it is extremely important that law officers or social workers make no reference to their connection to law enforcement agents. In addition, an accusatory or intimidating context leads to increased errors.

The importance of neutral, unbiased questions from the interviewer is paramount. Young children will give very accurate reports to those kinds of questions even though these reports may contain few details. The necessary training for all in the team is beyond the scope of this book.

Typically, the term *guardian ad litem* refers to an attorney representing the child in civil proceedings such as adoptions or termination of parental rights. In some states, the *guardian ad litem* may petition for the termination of the rights of the parent(s) (*Stanley v. Fairfax City Department of Social Services*, 242 Va. 60 [1991]). Various jurisdictions have differing requirements for a child advocate. In some states, the advocate must be an attorney; in others, an interested, trained adult. Whether decreed by statute or case decisions, the independent representation of the child is to see that the child's rights are being protected and the child's interests are being adequately presented to and considered at the court.

Following an investigation of all circumstances, the *guardian ad litem* is to represent the child's interest. Thus, the *guardian ad litem* interviews the child, parent(s), agency foster parents, and other material witnesses in addition to observing the child in his or her setting before making recommendations to the court.

During the court proceedings, the *guardian ad litem* examines and cross-examines witnesses at adjudicatory and dispositional hearings and may introduce and examine his or her own witnesses. (See Appendix 7B: Mock Trial in Chapter 7.) From *Matter of Jamie TT*, 59 N.Y.S.2d 892 (N.Y. Sup. App. Div. July 1993) we can get an idea of what can and should be done. In that case, the appeals court said that a child who is the subject of a child abuse petition, under Family Court Article 10, has a right to effective assistance of counsel. The *guardian ad litem* only called the witness, a 13-year-old child. She told of several incidents of sexual contact and sexual behavior on the part of her adoptive father. The adoptive father took the stand and denied everything—so it was her word against his.

Because the record showed that the lawful guardian had not prepared for the presentation of his case and did not demonstrate abuse by a preponderance of the evidence, the trial court was reversed and the matter was remanded accordingly. The county attorney failed to call numerous witnesses to the child's out-of-court statement in order to confirm the child's testimony. The attorney refused to validate the evidence from an expert witness and declined to conduct any cross-examination of the adoptive father.

In addition to *guardian ad litems*, in some courts special advocates for these abused children, called Court Appointed Special Advocates (CASA), are used. This was the brainchild of Superior Court Judge David Soukup of Seattle, Washington, in 1976. He felt that he lacked the necessary information to determine the best interests of a child being considered for out-of-home placement. He recruited and trained community volunteers. Their job was to pay attention only to the needs of the child. From national recognition and funding from foundations, the CASA program has grown to 452 programs in 48 states with 19,000 volunteers working with over 81,000 children as of 1990 (*Virginia Child Protection Newsletter* 1991).

The primary role of a CASA volunteer is to be a watchdog and make sure the court's orders are carried out by all parties and that the child does not get lost in the cracks of the justice system. In addition, a CASA volunteer can broker resources to alleviate the overloaded caseworker and provide much needed services.

To summarize, the role of the *guardian ad litem* is to be the following: (1) a fact-finder and investigator, (2) a legal representative, (3) a case monitor,

ROLE OF THE GUARDIAN AD LITEM

CASA

I am only one, but still I am one; I cannot do everything but still I can do something; I will not refuse to do the something that I can do.
Helen Keller

(4) a mediator and negotiator, and (5) a resource broker. "The appointment of a guardian is now required in every court case for a state to receive funding from the federal Child Abuse Prevention and Treatment Act" (Rubin 1985, 321).

SUMMARY

This chapter focused on child abuse and neglect—cases in which the child is in need of services but the state does not want to prosecute the case as a crime against the child. The chapter showed how a case may be investigated and processed through the court system.

Sexual child abuse was discussed first through a history of views of such abuse. The sexual fantasy hypothesis of Freud plus societal denial permitted the activity. Sexual assault centers helped to identify "father-daughter rape" or incest, which was supported by medical authorities who found venereal diseases in children under age 12.

Risk assessment was discussed in terms of sexual activity, biopsychosocial factors, and family dynamics. Types of families were discussed to show characteristics of healthy and dysfunctional families. Dysfunctional families were discussed as three typical families: (1) alcoholic, (2) incestuous, and (3) ritualistic.

Intervention and treatment were discussed in terms of three approaches: (1) psychiatric, (2) sociological, and (3) social situational. Depending upon the family and the situation, all approaches may have to be used. The Hawaii Healthy Start program was discussed to show how the effect of child abuse and neglect can be prevented so that the victims may not later perpetrate crime on others.

The chapter ended with a discussion of multidiscipline teams for investigation and the role of the *guardian ad litem*. A program for special advocates for abused children, Court Appointed Special Advocates (CASA), was discussed.

In this chapter, the child is considered by the court to be under a petition of abuse or neglect with the purpose of giving services to the family to correct the situation. The petition's purpose is not to prosecute under a criminal statute, because there may not be enough evidence or knowledge about the real offender. This type of petition serves then to protect the child and is a fallback position for the court. The attorney appointed to assist the child is called the *guardian ad litem*.

REFERENCES

Adelman, P.H. "Mary Ann and Mother: An Adolescent Turmoil to Individuate." *Adolescence* 9 (34)(1974): 199–220.

Armstrong, Louise. *Kiss Daddy Goodnight: A Speakout on Incest*. New York: Hawthorne Books, 1978.

Award, George A. "Father-Son Incest: A Case Report." *Journal of Nervous and Mental Disease* 162 (2)(1976): 135–139.

Baker, David. "Preying on Playgrounds: The Sex Exploitation of Children in Pornography and Prostitution." In Leroy G. Schutz, *The Sexual Victimology of Youth*. Springfield, IL: Charles C. Thomas, 1980, pp. 292–334.

Bass, Ellen, and Laura Davis. *The Courage to Heal: A Guide for Women Survivors of Child Sexual Abuse*. New York: Harper Collins, 1988.

Bowen, Murray. *Family Therapy in Clinical Practice*. New York: Jason Aronson, c. 1978.

Brassard, Marla R., Robert B. Germain, and Stuart N. Hart. "The Challenge to Better Understand and Combat the Psychological Maltreatment of Children and Youth." In *Psychological Maltreatment of Children and Youth*, edited by Marla R. Brassard, Robert B. Germain, and Stuart N. Hart. New York: Pergamon Press, 1987, pp. 3–24.

Browing, D.H., and B. Boatmen. "Incest Children at Risk." *American Journal of Psychiatry* 134 (1)1977: 69–72.

Brownmiller, Susan. *Against Our Wills: Men, Women, and Rape*. New York: Simon and Schuster, 1975.

Burgess, Ann W., A. Nicholas Groth, L. Holmstrong, and S. Sgroi. *Sexual Assault of Children and Adolescents*. Lexington, MA: D.C. Health and Co., 1978.

Butler, Sandra. *Conspiracy of Silence: The Trauma of Incest*. San Francisco: New Glade, 1978.

Ceci, Stephen J., and Maggie Bruck. *Jeopardy in the Courtroom. A Scientific Analysis of Children's Testimony*. Washington, D.C.: American Psychological Association, 1995.

Clement, Mary J. "Parenting in Prison: A National Survey of Programs for Incarcerated Women." *Journal of Offender Rehabilitation* 19 (1/2): 89–100, 1993.

Collings, Steven J. "The Long-Term Effects of Contact and Noncontact Forms of Child Sexual Abuse in a Sample of University Men." *Child Abuse and Neglect* 19 (1): 1–6, 1995.

Davidson, Howard, and Janet Corson. "Emotional Abuse and the Law." In *Psychological Maltreatment of Children and Youth*, edited by Marla R. Brassard, Robert B. Germain, and Stuart N. Hart. New York: Pergamon Press, 1987, pp. 185–202.

Dixon, K.N., L.E. Arnold, and K. Calestro. "Father-Son Incest: Underreported Psychiatric Problem." *American Journal of Psychiatry* 16 (1)(1978): 835–838.

Earle, Ralph B. *Helping to Prevent Child Abuse—and Future Criminal Consequences: Hawaii Healthy Start*. Washington, D.C.: National Institute of Justice, Program Focus, 1995.

Finkelhor, David. *Sexually Victimized Children*. New York: Free Press, 1980.

Forward, Susan, and Craig Buck. *Betrayal of Innocence: Incest and Its Devastation*. CA: J. P. Farger, 1978.

———. *Toxic Parents: Overcoming Their Hurtful Legacy and Reclaiming Your Life*. New York: Bantam Books, 1989.

Garbarino, James, and Joan Vondra. "Psychological Maltreatment: Issues and Perspectives." In *Psychological Maltreatment of Children and Youth*, edited by Marla R. Brassard, Robert B. Germain, and Stuart N. Hart. New York: Pergamon Press, 1987, pp. 25–44.

Geiser, Robert L. *Hidden Victims: The Sexual Abuse of Children*. Boston, MA: Beacon Press, 1979.

Gold, Steven N., Dawn M. Hughes, and Janine M. Swingle. "Characteristics of Childhood Sexual Abuse among Female Survivors in Therapy." *Child Abuse and Neglect* 20 (4): 323–335, 1996.

Goldstein, Arnold P., Harold Keller, and Diane Erne. *Changing the Abusive Parent*. Champaign, IL: Research Press, 1985.

Goodwin, Jean. *Sexual Abuse: Incest Victims and Their Families*. Littleton, MA: John Wright, PSG Inc., 1982.

Groth, Nicholas. *Men Who Rape: The Psychology of the Offender*. New York: Plenum Press, 1977.

Gutheil, T.F., and N.C. Avery. "Multiple Overt Incest as Family Defense against Loss." *Family Process* 16 (1)(1977): 105–116.

Herman, J., and L. Herschman. "Father-Daughter Incest." *Signs* 2 (4)(1977): 735–756.

Holder, Wayne M. *Sexual Abuse of Children: Implications for Treatment.* Englewood, CO: The American Humane Association, 1980.

Howell, James C. *Guide for Implementing the Comprehensive Strategy for Serious, Violent, and Chronic Juvenile Offenders.* Washington, D.C.: U.S. Dept. of Justice, 1995.

Jellinek, Michael S., Michael Murphy, Francis Poitrast, Dorothy Quinn, Sandra J. Bishop, and Marilyn Goshko. "Serious Child Mistreatment in Massachusetts: The Course of 206 Children through the Courts." *Child Abuse and Neglect* 16, (1992) pp. 179–185.

Justice, Blair, and Rita Justice. *The Broken Taboo: Sex in the Family.* New York: Human Sciences Press, 1979.

McGaha, Johnny G., and Jack L. Stokes. "Children of Alcoholism: Implications for Juvenile Justice." *Juvenile and Family Court Journal* 41 (1990): 19–24.

McGaha, Johnny, and Edward Leoni. "Family Violence, Abuse, and Related Family Issues of Incarcerated Delinquents with Alcoholic Parents Compared to Those with Nonalcoholic Parents." *Adolescence* Vol. 30, No. 118, pp. 473–481, 1995.

Moore, Alvin R., and Mary J. Clement. "Effects of Parenting Training for Incarcerated Mothers." *Journal of Offender Rehabilitation* 27 (1/2): 57–72, 1998.

Nathan, Debbie, and Michael Snedeker. *Satan's Silence: Ritual Abuse and the Making of a Modern American Witch Hunt.* New York: Basic Books, 1995.

National Center for Prosecution of Child Abuse. *Update,* June 1992, July 1992, August 1992, September 1992, December 1994.

Occult Crime: A Law Enforcement Primer, Special ed. Vol. 1, No. 6. Sacramento, CA: Office of Criminal Justice Planning Winter, 1989.

Peck, Scott. *People of the Lie: The Hope for Healing Human Evil.* New York: Simon and Schuster, 1983.

Peters, J.J. "Children Who Are Victims of Sexual Assault and the Psychology of Offenders." *American Journal of Psychotherapy* 30 (3)(1976): 398–421.

Ross, Susan M. "Risk of Physical Abuse to Children of Spouse Abusing Parents." *Child Abuse and Neglect* 20 (7): 589–598, 1996.

Rubin, H. Ted. *Juvenile Justice: Policy, Practice, and Law,* 2d ed. New York: Random House, 1985.

Silbert, Mimi Halper. "The Effects on Juveniles of Being Used for Pornography and Prostitution." In *Pornography,* edited by Dolf Zillmann and Jennings Bryant. Hillsdale, NJ: Lawrence Erlbaum Assoc., Publishers, 1989.

Smith, Carolyn, and Terrence P. Thornberry. "The Relationship between Childhood Maltreatment and Adolescent Involvement in Delinquency." *Criminology* 33: 451–467, 1995.

Snyder, Howard N., and Melissa Sickmund. *Juvenile Offenders and Victims: A National Report.* Washington, D.C.: Office of Juvenile Justice and Delinquency Prevention, 1995.

Snyder, H., and M. Sickmund. *Juvenile Offenders and Victims: 1999 National Report.* Washington, D.C.: Office of Juvenile Justice and Delinquency Prevention, 1999.

Stucker, Jan. "I Tried to Fantasize That All Fathers Had Intercourse with Their Daughters: The Story of Mary C." *MS,* 5 1977: 66–67.

Tower, Cynthia C. *Understanding Child Abuse and Neglect.* Boston: Allyn and Bacon, 1989.

Virginia Child Protection Newsletter. "Court Appointed Special Advocates."
35 (1991): 1–16.

———. "Joint Investigation: A Multidisciplinary Approach." 44 (1994): 1–16.

Vargo, Beth. "Ritual Child Abuse in Europe." *Believe The Children Newsletter,* Vol. IX, 1992.

Weeks, Ruth B. "The Sexually Exploited Child." *Southern Medical Journal* 69
(7)(1976): 848–850.

Wegescheider, Sharon. *Another Chance.* Palo Alto, CA: Science and Behavior
Books, Inc., 1981.

Widon, Cathy Spatz. *The Cycle of Violence.* Washington, D.C.: National Institute of Justice, 1992.

PRACTICE CASE

APPENDIX 5A

Charlie and Lucy Brown were married in 1989. Lucy and Charlie had two children—Peppermint Molly, now age 5, and Sam, age 3. About one year ago, Lucy got bored with Charlie and decided to raise money for her drug habit by prostitution. She left Charlie and took all the furniture from the apartment, leaving Charlie with only a baseball mitt and two children. While filing divorce proceedings, Charlie moved into his mother's small apartment until he was able to get a "low-income," three-bedroom apartment. Since Charlie has a learning disability (he cannot read or write) and a nervous condition, he has been unable to get a paying job. Thus he has been on welfare while learning to care for the children.

When Charlie goes job-hunting, he leaves the children with other male caretakers, one of whom has recently resumed psychiatric care for problems, including having been sexually abused as a child.

The Child Protective Services (CPS) has been notified of a complaint that Peppermint Molly has been coming to school with unclean, ill-fitting clothes. In addition, she has a cigarette burn on her wrist. Thus, the prosecuting attorney (PA) investigates the case.

In her investigation, the PA discovers Charlie has been beaten and abused as a child and is easily intimidated. She talks to Charlie casually and finds out that he has kissed Peppermint Molly "down there."

The PA uses dolls with the children and finds that someone has stuck "you know what" into Sam's "stinking hole." The PA finds the behavior of the daughter unusually sexy, such as lifting up her skirt and climbing all over the officer, with her panties in the face of the officer. On the testimony of these two children and their obvious knowledge of sexual activities, the PA files an emergency petition to have the children removed from Charlie Brown's custody.

At the hearing, the children are taken away from Charlie and placed in a foster home. The charges are read to Charlie and the next hearing will be in five days.

During these five days before the hearing, the PA goes to Charlie's house at about 5 o'clock in the evening with a police officer present to ask him more questions. She asks Charlie if she can search his apartment for pornographic materials. Charlie asks: "Will it get my kids back sooner?"

The PA says, "Trust me."

So Charlie signs some papers and lets her search his apartment without a warrant. She finds nothing.

Then the PA asks if he would take a lie-detector test. The PA, the police officer, and Charlie leave the apartment and go to the state police station where the test is given. Charlie tries to call his attorney but due to the hour, the attorney was never contacted.

The interview continues until 11 p.m. when Charlie comes home to make his supper. This was the same supper he was fixing when the PA and the police officer had come earlier that evening.

At the interview, Charlie was told he failed the lie-detector test and that he could be prosecuted as a criminal and get 20 years for sexually abusing his children. If he wants to get his children back, he has to cooperate. The PA feels she has a partial confession.

Using the facts as described in this case, play the roles of police, CPS worker, *guardian ad litem*, defense counselor, and prosecuting attorney, and resolve this case. If Chapter 5 does not give you enough material to answer this case, read ahead to Chapter 6, "Crimes Against Children."

CHAPTER 6

Crimes Against Children

In this chapter we will discuss how the juvenile court can make child abuse a criminal offense. This means that the juvenile court switches from a petition based on child abuse in juvenile court to a criminal proceeding based upon a criminal charge such as sodomy. In Chapter 5, "Child Abuse and Neglect," it was shown that the purpose of the juvenile court was to protect the child and preserve families with social services agencies doing the investigation, sometimes with multidisciplinary teams. In criminal court, however, the purpose is to punish the offenders, protect society, and deter other potential offenders. When a criminal case involving a child comes to juvenile court, the investigation will be done by law enforcement, and criminal rules of evidence will be used instead of civil rules. When this happens, the juvenile court holds a preliminary hearing—a hearing to determine whether there is probable cause to "hold" the accused for possible prosecution. For the offender, it is as if the process were in criminal court for adults, because the standard of proof is raised and the alleged abuser has more rights. No matter how much a child is harmed, if the court does not have enough reliable evidence to prosecute someone for the harm done to that child by the standard of "proof beyond a reasonable doubt," then the court can only find that the child is in need of services as an abused or neglected child.

First, we need to review some of the literature on violence against children and to list some of the crimes specifically. Then the chapter will discuss evidentiary problems.

Other issues will be the emotional effects of testifying, false memory, and torts. The chapter also will discuss the cycle of violence in which children are victimized and, without treatment, how they inflict pain on other children. Sometimes the child who is sexually abused acts out that behavior on other smaller children. In very rare but tragic cases, children kill the people who torture them. The policy of family reunification will precede the law case that ends the chapter. *Maryland v. Craig* shows how the United States Supreme Court tried to balance the rights of the accused with the unique problems of these kinds of crimes against children.

INTRODUCTION

Switch from a Petition of Child Abuse to a Criminal Charge Against an Adult or Youth

LITERATURE REVIEW

The National Research Council reviewed the social sciences literature and published *Understanding and Preventing Violence* (Reiss and Roth 1993, 11). Violence toward children, which includes homicides and physical and sexual assaults, is not reflected in national incidence and prevalence estimates. These statistics get hidden.

In addition, there seems to be no common agreement as to when violent behavior that occurs within a household should be regarded as family violence. Spousal assault, often referred to as marital or domestic violence, as well as physical and sexual assaults on children, or siblings assaulting children, are usually included in the definition. However, unlike street crime, family violence recurs and recurs. In contrast, victims of robbery are very unlikely to be robbed again within a six-month period of time.

What becomes problematic in legal terms are the physical and sexual assaults by relatives other than a parent or by friends who reside in the household. Legally, a cohabitant unrelated by blood or marriage, who physically or sexually abuses a child in the household, is an unrelated person. The cohabitant may abuse the trust of the child because he or she is treated as a family member, yet by law—in most states—the sexual acts are not considered to fit the legal definition of incest: the legal definition defines incest as a biological father with his daughter.

Understanding the violence done to children in families is also difficult because it is done in private places. To research it, one needs consent from family members to gather information. So it is understandable that most of the statistics come from social agencies that are called in to help a family in need. In addition, there are social and psychological processes causing family members to conceal violence, especially sexual violence.

National estimates of violence toward children come then from reports of cases known to investigatory bodies such as juvenile courts, coroners, law enforcement agencies, as well as health, education, and welfare organizations who have contacts with children. According to estimates in 1989, at least 1,200 and perhaps as many as 5,000 children died and more than 160,000 were seriously harmed as a result of violence (Reiss and Roth 1993, 228–229). In 1996, the NCCAN estimated 1,077 children were killed. (See the Introduction to Chapter 5.)

In terms of intrafamily homicide, newborns, infants, and children ages 1 to 4 are at greatest risk. The mother, rather than the father, is more prone to do the killing. Female children are more likely to be killed than males (Reiss and Roth 1993, 234).

However, a more recent national study of the extent of child deaths by parents shows that males usually assault the children by beating their heads and bodies, shaking them violently, intentionally suffocating them, immersing them in scalding water, and committing other brutal acts; mothers are held responsible for deaths caused by severe neglect. According to the U.S. Advisory Board on Child Abuse and Neglect, at least 2,000 children (a vast majority age 4 and younger) die every year and an additional 18,000 children are permanently disabled and 142,000 are seriously injured. Many of these deaths caused by child abuse and neglect are wrongly identified as accidents or erroneously attributed to natural causes because police, physicians, and coroners are largely untrained in identifying evidence of inflicted trauma and severe neglect in children. In addition, some states lack laws for felony child abuse prosecutions, and charges of homicide are routinely reduced to lesser crime offenses, according to the comprehensive national study called "A Nation's Shame: Fatal Child Abuse and Neglect in the United States" (*Richmond Times-Dispatch*, April 27, 1995, p. A6).

Physical abuse is more prevalent (more likely to be reported?) than sexual abuse for both sexes, but females currently are reported as being more sexually abused. Children from families with incomes less than $15,000 per year are reported as having a rate of physical abuse three and one-half times greater and a rate of sexual abuse six times greater than other children (Reiss and Roth 1993, 235).

Little research has been done to prove that chemical or other forms of treating depression are a means of controlling family violence, yet the following quote points to caretaker depression as being a major factor leading to abuse:

In a study of 50 mothers and fathers who had abused and neglected their children and lost custody of them by court order, 30 percent of the mothers and 25 percent of the fathers were diagnosed as suffering from major depression. An additional 17 percent of the mothers and 15 percent of the fathers showed clinical signs of a minor depression. Despite many social service contacts with almost all of the abusing families, only one parent has received any pharmacological treatment and most of the parents had no previous diagnosis of a specific affect disorder. By contrast, the comparison group appeared to have no signs of depression. (Reiss and Roth 1993, 239)

CRIMES

Children can be victims of any crime. Yet in some states, if a child is still in the womb (called a fetus), it cannot legally be killed even though an alleged offender has shot it. We will specifically discuss statutes that have been written to protect children, such as sex crimes, and then summarize the many others.

Sex Crimes

There are several specifically defined crimes that were written to protect children. They vary from state to state. Some of the early states, such as Virginia and Massachusetts, still hold to common law. Although anyone at any age can be a victim of a sex crime, in studying sexual assault offenders, we know that three-fourths of all victims are children (under 18), and almost half are under the age of 13, with almost half (47 percent) of the sexual assaults occurring in the victim's home as multiple offenses occurring over time (Poulos and Greenfield 1994). The most common sex offenses are carnal knowledge, crimes against nature, forced sodomy, indecent liberties, and child pornography.

Carnal Knowledge

Carnal knowledge is an adult having sexual intercourse, without force, with a child to whom the adult is not married. In the state of Virginia, it is with a child 13 to 14 years of age. (In other states it may be called statutory rape.)

Crimes Against Nature

Crimes against nature are also known as sodomy. This is defined as carnal knowledge of any animal, or male or female person by the anus or mouth, or voluntary submission to such carnal knowledge.

Forced Sodomy

Forced sodomy is cunnilingus, fellatio, anallingus, or anal intercourse with a person under 13 (a specific age set by statute), or against the will of the victim by force, threat, or intimidation, or through the victim's mental incapacity or physical helplessness.

Indecent Liberties

Indecent liberties are taken when an adult exposes his or her genitals to any child under a specific age (such as 14), or proposes that the child expose his or her genitals or feels and fondles, or proposes that the child perform sexual intercourse, or entices the child to enter a vehicle, room, house, or other place for any of those listed-above activities, or receives money for encouraging any person under a specific age to perform in or be a subject of sexually explicit material. To be prosecuted, the adult must do these acts with lascivious intent. Thus professionals, such as doctors, nurses, and caretakers who perform these actions with a different intent, are protected. They are not prosecuted unless lascivious intent is proven.

Child Pornography

What do your baby pictures look like?

Many of us have had our pictures taken as babies in the "buff." We may not always show these to others. Yet we know that somewhere in the treasures of our family history lies a picture of our nude body as we lay across a baby blanket. More recently, a father was taking pictures of his "baby." She was nude, lying facedown on a blanket spread across the table so that as she lifted herself up from the table with her arms, the photograph captured her dangling breasts. His "baby," as he called her, was 14 years of age. Do you think there is a difference between what your parents did and what this father did?

The challenge is how do states define child pornography in order to prosecute people who are exploiting children for sexually explicit or obscene theatrical/cinematic performances, printed materials, and other reasons. The challenge of defining child pornography will be discussed in terms of public law, types of pornography, perpetrators, victims, and the challenges of prosecuting for the criminal and juvenile justice systems.

Public Law

In 1978, President Jimmy Carter signed Public Law 95–225, an amendment to the U.S. Code concerning the use of children in obscene material. The purpose of the law was to give police agencies the power to deal with a growing threat from a multimillion-dollar industry that was connected with organized crime. Police raids of operations in several states produced evidence that "kiddie porn" was a national concern—at least 264 different child pornography magazines were available. This resulted in the founding of the

National Center on Child Abuse and Neglect, the passage of the Protection of Children Against Sexual Exploitation Act, and the passage of laws in forty-two states prohibiting the use of minors in obscene materials (Beranbaum et al. 1984).

More recently, in 1990, the U.S. Supreme Court in *Osborne v. Ohio* (495 U.S. 103) upheld the constitutionality of Ohio's statute prohibiting any person from possessing or viewing any material or performance showing a minor who is not his child or ward in a state of nudity unless the material or performance is presented for a bona fide purpose by or to a person having a proper interest therein or the possessor knows that the minor's parent(s) or guardian has consented in writing to such photographing or use of the minor. Osborne argued that the photographs in his home, each depicting a nude male adolescent posed in a sexually explicit position, were for his own personal enjoyment and were, therefore, protected under an earlier decision that permitted adults to have pornography in their own homes (*Stanley v. Georgia*, 394 U.S. 557 [1969]). The Court found that Ohio's ban was to protect the victims of child pornography and to destroy a market for the exploitative use of children. Ohio's ban encouraging the destruction of these materials was seen as desirable because research suggests that pedophiles use child pornography to seduce other children into sexual activity.

Types

Types of child pornography vary. Some pornographic materials show children in explicit sexual acts with other children, with adults, or with animals (bestiality). Others show the children in bondage with ropes and chains or appeal to sadomasochism. Because some buyers want "wet" sex, people urinate or defecate upon the children. Some of the types of pornography are simulated explicit sexual acts; some buyers want nudity. Some types are sold as being "sex education" material. For example, one book cover shows a little girl about age 6 with long blond hair. She is completely nude, has her legs spread, and is sitting on a stool. The caption of the book reads as follows:

Carol—a pretty little girl with a love of all-day suckers and bedtime stories. (Holmes 1983, 99)

Another book reads:

Perhaps the most beautiful child model ever photographed. Like a rosebud at first hint of bloom Lynne radiates delicate elegance . . . A classical grace and charm ordinarily found only in the rhythmic sophistication of the adult high fashion model. For a grand total of $21.00, the customer could obtain two 8 × 10 bordered mounting prints, four 5 × 7 glossy framing prints, and eight 4 × 5 quad book-mount prints. All of the photos were contained in an "exquisitely illustrated folio to preserve them for treasured viewing." (Holmes 1983, 99)

Child pornography is defined as "sexually explicit reproduction of a child's image, voice or handwriting." It is the record of the abuse of a child, and it can be done commercially or it can be homemade (Lanning and Burgess 1989, 238).

The distribution of child pornography comes through print and/or electronic media. Print media include magazines, still photographs, paperback books, travel guides, and listing services. Travel guides are materials developed to inform the traveler where boy and girl prostitutes might be picked up. Similar to the travel guides of legitimate groups like the American Automobile Association (AAA), which gives names and addresses of hotels and eating places, these pornographic travel guides give such information as when to go to the men's room in the basement of a particular department store in a particular city.

The electronic media can be films, slides, computers, electronic billboards, Internet, and websites. "Snuff movie" films are based upon the belief that the best way to die is by having sexual intercourse. A young person agrees to do the movie believing that this is his or her "break" into Hollywood. The victim is unaware that she or he will actually be killed as part of the film—hence, the word "snuff."

Child pornography on the Internet has also been used by adults looking for children and children looking for excitement. It seems that it is easier to protect children through proprietary environments, third-party rating systems, and phase detection systems than limit the access of the adult offender. The commercial "adult" Bulletin Board System (BBS) is big business. The owner-operator of Amateur Action BBS was reported in 1994 to have an income of $800,000. Online pornography is popular, profitable, and easily available. Thus many states are now in the process of addressing computer crimes as part of the Telecommunications Act of 1996 (PL 101–104), especially the communications decency act.

Why do adults want children as sex partners? To understand, we have some information from the perpetrators who have been caught and have undergone therapy.

Perpetrators

Immature

From interviews with convicted child molesters, three types emerge: (1) immature child offender, (2) regressed sexual preference, and (3) aggressive fixed sexual preference.

The immature child offender has never grown emotionally to accept an adult of the opposite sex as an appealing partner. For example, an inmate in Walla Walla State Penitentiary (Washington state) told the author that when he fantasized about young girls, he made no racial distinctions; he was happy with Asians, blacks, and whites. Yet he avoided sexual relationships with other adults due to feelings of inferiority, even though he seemed very bright and competent in other areas of his life.

Regressed Sexual Preference

The second type of perpetrator has enjoyed a normal childhood and good relationships with peers (including sexual). In fact, he or she may even have married. Yet the daily stress of life exacerbates feelings of inadequacy, resulting in poor coping skills. The sexual act against the child is usually preceded by some event that causes a strong sense of sexual inferiority. The offender's act against the child is an attempt to gain some sense of control (mastery) over his or her life. Usually, this offender is remorseful and ashamed of what has happened.

The third type is called "aggressive child offender" who has a fixed pref- Aggressive Fixed
erence for children. His or her need of sexual excitement may lead to a sadistic and violent act, typically involving some sort of weapon.

Although classifications are useful, a pedophile (a person who has sexual
desires directed toward children under the age of 13 of either sex) or the
hebephile (a person who is attracted to children between the ages of 13 and
15) may not conform neatly to one particular type. It is also not clear
whether sex offenders may evolve from one type to another.

Most pedophiles use their occupation as a means of finding and getting
to know their victims. Some occupations include positions of authority, such
as teachers, physicians, camp counselors, and Scout leaders. Other occupations give a pedophile the opportunity to hire youngsters. In addition, the
pedophile will use his status in the community to gain the respect of families so that parents will have no objections to their children being with the
offender. The offender is sometimes patient enough to establish this initial
groundwork in order to develop sexual relationships with lots of children
who will not be believed by the parents even if a child should tell. These
offenders are skillful in seduction and persuasion. They use bribes and
rewards to make the child feel responsible.

Pedophiles do more than just view child pornography or child erotica;
they collect it. This may mean books, magazines, articles, newspapers,
photographs, negatives, slides, movies, albums, drawings, audiotapes,
videotapes and equipment, personal letters, diaries, clothing, sexual aids,
souvenirs, toys, games, paintings, ledgers, photographic equipment, and so
on. These collections vary in size and scope depending upon socioeconomic
status, living arrangements, and age. Some keep their collection a secret and
buy only from commercial channels. The isolated collector is actively
molesting children and collecting. The so-called "cottage collector" shares
the collection and sexual activity with other individuals. He or she is not in
it for the profit as is the commercial collector. The commercial collector sells
and duplicates materials and is usually an active sexual molester (Lanning
and Burgess 1989, 236).

The Federal Bureau of Investigation (FBI) Behavioral Science unit has
been credited with providing a substantial amount of information regarding child molestation. In their terms, the situational child molester has four
subtypes: (1) regressed, (2) morally indiscriminate, (3) sexually indiscriminate, and (4) inadequate. The preferential child molester has three subtypes:
(1) seduction, (2) introverted, and (3) sadistic. However, these typologies are
limited because an actual offender may fall into a mixture of categories, and
that makes investigations more difficult. In addition, most of the research
has been collected on those presently in custody. Thus there is a preponderance of males when in fact, females do molest as well, although the
reported numbers are low. Lastly, the word molestation seems to suggest
that the children were only touched, but today the research studies report
sexual intercourse at 40.4 percent (Sapp and Kappeler 1993).

Victims

The victims include runaways and streetwise youth, the children called
status offenders in Chapter 2, "The Definition of Juvenile Delinquency,
Status Offenses, Abuse, and Developmental Stages," or the abused and

neglected in Chapter 5, "Child Abuse and Neglect." They may even include the child next door who is emotionally impoverished. Victims are found everywhere (Forward and Buck 1978). Some kids are abducted into sexual slavery by "chicken hawks," while others are seduced into posing for photographs because the persons taking the pictures are either their parents or some other trustworthy person who has befriended them, as the John Gacy case in Chicago, Illinois, taught us (Gacy was found guilty of killing 33 young boys in 1980). The children were lured to Gacy's home with the promise of jobs. Then he showed them pictures of other children to lower their inhibitions. "See, these kids do it; it must be all right." If the child liked what he saw, Mr. Gacy knew he could progress to sessions of sexual activity. If not, he would proceed with the old handcuff trick. In his home he had sexual paraphernalia such as the dildo, leg-spreader, handcuffs, chains, and the board. He told the police that he "self-pandered" his desire for erotic homosexual experimentation. Mr. Gacy tried to use the insanity defense but was not successful in his plea.

When children are prematurely introduced into adult sexuality, they may have difficulties in synchronizing the physical, emotional, and psychological dimensions of the experience. The child learns to use sex to acquire attention, goods, and services. Child molestation has some devastating effects on children, including turning them to prostitution, which may be part of a drug addiction as well. Children may suffer social withdrawal, mood swings, difficulty with peers and family, frequent urinary tract infections, and/or venereal diseases of any of the body openings. In more severe cases, the victim may suffer depression and psychosis. Today, people who are being trained in the mental health professions are learning to consider the possibility of multiple personalities stemming from early sexual abuse.

The early sexual seduction of a child can lead to overstimulation, which in turn results in guilt, confusion, and psychological disturbances. In fact, some professionals who deal with convicted offenders think that the offender, having been sexually exploited as a child, is trying to work out the problem by abusing current-generation children.

Pedophiles across the world have created a communications network that includes computer bulletin boards and organizations that fulfill their desires. Sex rings are on a continuum from solo to syndicated. In solo activities, child pornography is commonly possessed by a small group of friends.

Children abused by a sex ring usually experience more long-lasting, intense, and pervasive trauma than children abused by a single perpetrator. Because the child has been abused by so many, the child is afraid of everyone. Hunt and Baird (1990) emphasize the care practitioners must take in identifying and treating these children.

Their work is based on interviews with ten victimized children ranging in age from 18 months to 5 years. The common elements that emerged were gender confusion, inconsistency in reporting, and leakage of traumatic material. "Keith, age four, would frequently interject in sessions, 'Cut you up in little pieces.' Collen, three, said 'Blow up you house,' adding later in the session, 'Yum, yum, eat me'" (Hunt and Baird 1990, 200).

One of the difficulties in working with these children is their young age. The second is the nightmarish information that the practitioners are left to process both for themselves and the clients—the young children (Hunt and Baird 1990, 202). For example, children of sex rings have reported forced ingestion of feces, blood, and semen. Some of these materials have been smeared on their bodies. Moreover, the children may have witnessed or participated in the physical torture or destruction of living things (Hunt and Baird 1990, 205). These children need specialized practitioners to aid them.

Sometimes, the child grows older and an offender advertises through the network for another pedophile who has a sexual preference for older children, or the child is sold to a pimp for use in prostitution. Juvenile prostitution, like kiddie porn, is a very lucrative business. Some customers pay $500 a night for a child. It is the paying customers, along with the lack of alternatives for children, that make it the big business it is today.

Challenges

Child pornography involves special challenges. There are groups that lobby for the reduction of the age of consent. Organizations like the René Guyon Society, Pedophile Information Exchange (PIE), the Childhood Sexuality Circle, and the North American Man Boy Love Association (NAMBLA) are looking to change the laws to allow acceptance of sex between adults and children.

Special training is needed for professionals who work with sexually victimized children. Those who intervene, investigate, and prosecute these kinds of cases often find they need additional training from experts because of the reaction of the child. Unfortunately, the victim is the state's witness.

For some children, the seduction is so complete and the bond to his or her abuser so tight, that the child does not want to see his or her "friend" go to jail. In addition, his friend may be a pillar in the community—a devoted family man or a church or Boy Scout leader. Many people hold to an erroneous belief that only dirty old men in raincoats exhibit this kind of behavior. The child pornography victim, like the physically or sexually abused child, may suffer symptoms of the anxiety disorder called Post-Traumatic Stress Disorder (PTSD). The child may need special professional assistance for his or her own mental health, the health of the family, plus special explanations and assistance to understand the pending judicial process (Burgess, Groth, Holmstrong, and Sgroi 1978).

A complex problem like child pornography comes from the society and therefore needs to be addressed on many levels.

First, stop relying on only law to deter. As good as the legal system may be, public law does not deter a person's desire when it has reached the level of "prurient interest." In fact, the law has driven it underground and overseas.

Children of Third World countries and devastated nations of the former Eastern Block of Europe are now being used in greater numbers. Kiddie porn is a $250 million industry involving 20,000 to 30,000 children in Germany. "According to the Bangkok-based international organization ECPAT (End Child Prostitution in Asian Tourism), there are about 500,000 prostitutes 16 years old or younger in Thailand, the Philippines, and Sri Lanka. At least 50,000 are under 13," but the Southeast Women's Organization says the figure is closer to 30 million (Ehrlich 1993, 70).

Second, we must begin to work cooperatively with other advocates from the public and private sectors in local, state, federal, and international arenas. Women and children have a cash value in the "sex supply" but the industry has no rules, no scruples, and no boundaries. Children become trade goods as a hedge for a quick profit. Yet the health consequences are tremendous, because young bodies—both male and female—are not sexually developed enough to bear the effects. And then there's AIDS. In an 8- or 9-year-old, the disease runs quickly. Many countries are in danger of losing an entire generation.

Thus research and studies on the theoretical and applied will need to have a holistic approach. For that to happen, universities and law schools will need to teach trained professionals to work specifically with children and with other professionals. Pediatric law is just such a movement.

Third, we need to channel the energies and resources of the public, and especially those who have experienced some of these horrors of crimes against children, so that healing occurs and the cycle is broken. Professionals in the system need to listen to those who have experienced these crimes so as to better meet those needs. For example, Patti Limebaugh in 1980 founded SLAM (Society's League Against Molestation) because her 2-year-old granddaughter was raped and tortured by a pedophile. He had a twenty-year record and had been in prison and institutions seven times, but he was released "as a model patient six weeks before the child's death" (Huckton 1985, 92).

There are many organizations in our society aimed at helping children with specific problems. For instance, Huchton (1985) listed over fifty family-formed agencies that began as early as 1975 to specialize in the different aspects of the problems of missing children. Yet others have stopped their work due to the withdrawal of resources.

Fourth, the public needs to feel a part of the responsibility to protect children. Some states, such Washington in 1990, Louisiana in 1992, and New Jersey in 1994, have enacted legislation requiring law enforcement officials to notify the community in which a released sex offender intends to live. In July 1994, for example, 7-year-old Megan Kanka of Hamilton, New Jersey, was lured from her front yard, sexually assaulted, and murdered by a person who was a convicted sex offender and her neighbor. The Megan's Law of New Jersey requires notification when the risk is moderate to specific groups such as schools, youth organizations, and religious organizations where an encounter is likely. If the risk is high, the law calls for notifying members of the public who are "likely to encounter" the offender. Sex offender registration laws without public notification provisions have withstood most constitutional attacks (*State v. Costello*, 643 A.2d 531 [N.H. 1994]; *State v. Ward*, 869 P.2d 1062 [Wash. 1994]; and *State v. Noble*, 829 P.2d 1217 [Ariz. 1994]), but public notification undoubtedly will face constitutional challenges (National Center for Prosecution of Child Abuse, Jan. 1995, 1).

Last, public and business communities need to develop and implement prevention strategies such as communitywide parenting programs that address various causal levels of maltreatment: individual, family, community, and cultural factors. In African society, it is said that it takes a whole village to raise a child. Perhaps, we, too, ought to think more broadly.

Serial Murder

Some serial murders focus upon children. According to Hickey (1991, 166–168), in his well-researched book based upon personal interviews with 203 serial murderers, over 25 percent of all male serial killers researched had killed at least one child, whereas about 5 percent killed children only. Nearly all offenders in this subgroup that killed children were in some manner involved sexually with their child victims, either before or after death occurred. Like other offenders, these men (and one teenager) had a need to control their victims and to have power over them. In addition, the murderers follow the pattern of being intraracial (within the same race). For example, Wayne Williams of Atlanta allegedly killed black children (1980–1981). John Wayne Gacy buried 29 white victims in the crawl space and cement driveway of his home (1972–1978). Four other victims, for want of space, were discarded in the Des Planes River. (Gacy later claimed that others must have placed those bodies there because he was working 16 hours a day and was busy in community and charity affairs and helping young people!) Serial murderers of children also present themselves as nice, normal, trustworthy people, thus gaining the trust of their child victims.

For obvious reasons, the more normal the killer appears and the more caution he or she exercises, the greater the homicidal longevity. Cullen (1993, 50), in *The Killer Department*, describes the eight-year hunt by Detective Viktor Burakov for Russia's most savage serial killer. The following is a description of 14-year-old Sergei Markov's murder:

> *Near Novocherkassk, Fetisov and the other militsionery (police) left the paved road and took a dirt road to the ridge where the hunter had found the body. The decomposed remains he had seen in Donskou and other crime scenes had not prepared him for the body on the ridge. The cold weather and the snow had preserved it like a morgue refrigerator. The killer had perforated the boy's neck dozens, scores of times; the medical examiner would later count seventy wounds there, most of them light and superficial, suggesting how much the killer enjoyed seeing his knife enter his victim. Sergei Markov had suffered dismemberment analogous to that of Vera Shevkun. The killer had excised his testicles, his penis, and most of the scrotum. Turning the body over, they could see signs that his anal sphincter had been stretched and broken. Fetisov shuddered and hoped that the boy had died of his neck wounds before that had happened to him. Nearby, they found his clothes and, curiously three separate piles of human excrement.*

Whether the actual number of victims was 52, 53, or more, Andrei Chikatilo is considered the most savage serial killer to emerge from modern society. Although Pedro Alonso Lopez, who confessed to the murder of 300 girls (only 53 bodies were found), none over the age of 10, in Colombia, Ecuador, and Peru between 1973 and 1980, he did not disembowel his victims as Chikatilo did (Cullen 1993, 249).

The research on the devastating effects of children being murdered come from strong people like John Walsh, the father of 6-year-old Adam who was abducted and killed in 1981. His anger was channeled into helping create national attention and the Missing Children's Act, which brings the FBI immediately into cases dealing with missing children. Unlike the other 80 percent of parents of murdered children who go on to divorce, the Walshes fought to stay together and to cherish their memories and help the entire family, and thus all of us, to celebrate Adam's life and learn more about people who bring harm to children.

Other Crimes

Some states like Wyoming have a criminal child abuse statute making it a felony punishable by imprisonment for not more than five years if the person who is responsible for a child's welfare intentionally or recklessly inflicts physical injury, excluding reasonable corporal punishment, or mental injury upon a child under the age of 18. Bruising is considered a physical injury. In addition, killing a child under the age of 16 by abuse is first-degree murder.

There are other crimes committed against children. Some are abduction by a parent or nonparent, distribution of drugs or marijuana to a minor, and the sale of weapons, alcohol, or tobacco to minors. Children are protected under child labor laws, but some behavior in the workplace may or may not be crimes depending upon the circumstances.

Most states have a statute dealing with "causing or encouraging acts rendering children delinquent or abused." For example, in Missouri's *State v. Salata*, 859 S.W.2d 728 (Mo. App. June 1993), the defendant said he was a "toilet training expert." When arrested, he had a host of photos, magazines, and letters related to diaper training. But the defendant's photographs showed a child's excrement-smeared buttocks. Those photographs depicted "nudity" within the meaning of Missouri's child abuse law. In addition, the photos, taken together with letters describing various acts, satisfied Missouri's legal definition of conduct for the "purpose of sexual stimulation or gratification"—child pornography. Thus, the defendant's conviction was affirmed.

Another way to protect children is to make others report. All states have statutes that make it a **penalty for failure to report that a child is abused or neglected**. These statutes include physicians, nurses, teachers, social workers, mental health workers, law enforcement officers, and any others with training who have reason to suspect that a child is being abused or neglected. The statutes provide **immunity** for the person who, in good faith, makes a report. This immunity is carried to judicial proceedings as well.

However, the courts have not permitted liability to extend to the state. In *DeShaney v. Winnebago County Department of Social Services*, 489 U.S. 189, 103, L.Ed.2d 249, 109 S.Ct. 998 (1989), the U.S. Supreme Court affirmed the Court of Appeals' decision, stating that DeShaney's constitutional rights were not violated. The Court said the facts of the case were tragic (DeShaney had been beaten by his father so severely that he suffered permanent brain damage and was rendered profoundly retarded), but the social workers were not obliged to take DeShaney from his father. In other words, employees of a state's Department of Social Services have governmental immunity. See *Whitaker v. Clark*, 427 S.E.2d 142 (1993).

Last, there are crimes against children when they are killed at the hands of their caretakers. Even though there is general agreement that the actual incidence of child abuse deaths is poorly documented, we know that it does occur. The numbers of abuse-related child deaths is unknown because there is no accurate count of children who die and the cause of their deaths in the United States. In addition, it has been estimated that 85 percent of child deaths from abuse and neglect are misidentified as accidental, disease-related, or due to other causes.

To deal with children's deaths, forty-eight states have some type of death review committee, often called "child fatality review teams." Dr. Michael Durfee and a public health nurse pioneered these committees in 1978, setting up a system to retrieve cases from coroners' records in Los Angeles County. They established a protocol for review of potentially suspicious child deaths. Later, they began an Interagency Council on Child Abuse and Neglect (ICAN) that later spread to other counties in California and is now in other states.

Team members typically represent law enforcement, CPS, medical examiners/coroners, prosecutors, public health doctors, mental health specialists, educators, and pediatricians. Additional members, on a case-by-case basis, might include emergency medical technicians, fire department personnel, preschool teachers, and emergency room staff. The blend of expertise and knowledge of diverse professions can assist in understanding the cause of a child death and thereby help in the investigation and in prevention.

Although there is no uniform system throughout the United States for the investigation of infant and child deaths, many states in various jurisdictions have developed guidelines and procedures. Some have been based on the American Academy of Pediatrics guidelines. Most include determining the cause of death by an autopsy. Then there is a thorough investigation of the crime scene and interviews of children and adults in the environment. As part of the death investigation, records from other agencies are reviewed, although they remain completely confidential. Because one of the purposes is to identify factors amenable to change, strategies for prevention and education can follow. A review team can give parents peace of mind and remove any cloud of suspicion. Even if the medical examiner cannot identify a pathological condition, inflicted harm can be ruled out.

Dr. Durfee, founder of the multiagency child death review team, envisions a more elaborate system for information sharing so that cases can be managed across county, state, and national boundaries. He would like to see the efforts of the child death review team broadened to include all preventable deaths of children. He would like professional training to be more formalized and more frequent. Thus, intervention and prevention programs will follow the new understandings gained from teamwork. The work of the teams through systems intervention after a death will help with early intervention before death and thereby reduce child fatalities.

If the alleged offender of a child victim is a youth, the youth is processed through the juvenile court, as explained in Chapter 4, "Process for Delin-

PROCESS— PROSECUTION

quent (Criminal) Youth." That means that the youth would be taken into custody, go before an intake officer, be detained in the detention facility, have a hearing on the detention, and, if not waived into the adult system, have a hearing in juvenile court. *J.P. v. Carter*, 24 Va. App. 707 (1997) gives a good example of how a juvenile was criminally charged with two counts of aggravated assault (sodomy, fondling, and other sexual crimes) in juvenile court. When she was to be listed in the registry under the Child Abuse and Neglect Act, she argued that the punishment under the Act was inconsistent with the letter and intent of the Juvenile Justice Act. The appeals court affirmed the trial court by stating that listing people who have abused children, even a juvenile, in the central registry is confidential and it serves to protect all children.

If the youth is waived into the adult court, the youth's alleged crime would come before a grand jury for an indictment or filing of information by the prosecutor before having a trial, verdict, and sentence.

If the alleged offender is an adult, the adult would go through the criminal justice system. The formal criminal court procedures differ across the country. Baum (1994, 179) gives the following broad description of the stages through which felony cases usually go:

1. **Arrest**

2. **Initial appearance by the defendant in court**

3. **Preliminary hearing or examination**

4. **Grand jury indictment or filing of information by the prosecutor**

5. **Arraignment of the defendant**

6. **Procedures to prepare the case for trial: discovery, motions, conferences**

7. **Trial**

8. **Verdict**

9. **Sentencing (where defendant has been found guilty)**

Prosecuting cases with children as victims is not easy. If the alleged offender is an adult and the victim is a child, some states permit stage 3, the preliminary hearing, to be held in juvenile court where the courtroom is smaller and the child may feel more comfortable. Generally, there are more problems with prosecuting these types of cases, and these will be discussed as evidentiary problems and other issues.

Evidentiary Problems

The sexual exploitation of children in our society is still a largely unstudied and undeveloped area, worthy of independent treatment and consideration beyond what is possible in this chapter. (See Exhibit 6.1, which summarizes some of the major studies that estimate the incidence of child sexual abuse, and Table 6.1, Whitcomb 1992, 3, 57.)

Difficulties in prosecution of child exploitation cases are a major concern. In fact, the **Children's Justice Act** has provided funds for the American Prosecutors Research Institute to give training on the investigation and prosecution of child sexual abuse through its National Center for Prosecution of Child Abuse. Founded in 1985, the Center provides expert training and technical assistance and is a clearinghouse for child abuse case law, statutory initiatives, court reforms, and trial strategies. The Center also pub-

Exhibit 6.1   ESTIMATED INCIDENCE OF CHILD SEXUAL ABUSE BASED ON RETROSPECTIVE SELF-REPORTS

Author	Estimate	Victim Age Range	Study Characteristics	Caveats
Kinsey[1] (1953)	24% of women	"Pre-adolescent"	Personal interviews, 4,441 volunteer subjects	Excludes peer experiences; more than half the offenses were exhibitionism
Finkelhor[2] (1979)	19% of women 9% of men	through age 16	Self-administered questionnaire; 796 college students	Excludes peer experiences; 20% of offenses were exhibitionism
Karcher[3] (1980)	12% of women 3% of men	"Child"	Mail survey, 2,000 Texas drivers	Sexual abuse undefined
Finkelhor[4] (1984)	15% of women 5% of men	through age 16	Household survey; 521 Boston area parents	Excludes peer experiences
Russell[5] (1983)	38% of women	through age 18	Personal interviews; random sample of 933 adult women in San Francisco	Includes peer experiences; excludes exhibitionism; questions very detailed
Committee on Sexual Offenses Against Childern and Youth[6] Canada (1984)	27% of women 15% of men	before age 16	National Population Survey, 2,008 respondents	Includes peer experiences; 28% of offenses were exhibitionism; questions very detailed
Finkelhor and Hotaling et al.[7] (1989)	27% of women 16% of men	through age 18	National telephone survey by *Los Angeles Times* poll; 2,626 respondents	Includes peer experiences and exhibitionism; four comprehensive screening questions

[1]Alfred Kinsey, et al., *Sexual Behavior in the Human Female* (Philadelphia: Saunders, 1953).
[2]David Finkelhor, *Sexually Victimized Children* (New York: Free Press, 1979).
[3]Glenn Karcher, *Responding to Child Sexual Abuse: A Report to the 67th Session of the Texas Legislature* (Huntsville, TX: Sam Houston State University, 1980).
[4]David Finkelhor, "How Widespread Is Child Sexual Abuse?" *Children Today*, Vol. 13 (July–August 1984): 18–20.
[5]Diana Russell, "The Incidence and Prevalence of Intrafamilial and Extrafamilial Sexual Abuse of Female Children," *Child Abuse and Neglect*, Vol. 7 (1983).
[6]The Committee on Sexual Offenses Against Children and Youth, *Sexual Offenses Against Children* (Ottawa, Canada: Minister of Supply and Services, 1984), 179–193.
[7]David Finkelhor and Gerald Hotaling, et al., "Sexual Abuse in a National Survey of Adult Men and Women: Prevalence, Characteristics, and Risk Factors," unpublished paper prepared under Grant No. 90CA 1215 from the National Center on Child Abuse and Neglect to the University of New Hampshire, April 1989.

Source: Whitcomb 1992, 3.

lishes a monthly newsletter, *Update*, and a highly acclaimed manual, *Investigation and Prosecution of Child Abuse*. The Center does research in cooperation with academic centers, prosecutors, and specialists on legislative and procedural avenues for protecting children.

The Center is greatly needed because some child pornography magazines, for example, intentionally undermine law enforcement efforts. Articles tell readers how to park and lure or pick up children, giving instructions about games that induce cooperation from children and advice about which sexual acts leave the least incriminating evidence.

Table 6.1   SUMMARY OF PROVISIONS RELATING TO CHILDREN'S COMPETENCY

STATE / PROVISION

STATUTES WITH SPECIFIC PROVISIONS FOR CHILDREN

- Child sexual abuse victims are exempt from competency requirements
- Children must demonstrate competency before they can testify
- Other:

STATUTES THAT DO NOT DIFFERENTIATE CHILDREN

- Every person is competent, with nothing further
- Every person is competent, with minimum requirements

1 Children may testify even if they do not understand the nature of the oath.
2 Age may not be the sole reason to preclude a child from testifying.
3 Children must have the capacity to remember and relate truly the facts in question.
4 Children are presumed competent.
5 Pennsylvania case law holds that when a witness is under 14 years of age, there must be a searching judicial inquiry to make an ultimate decision as to the competency of the child. *Commonwealth v. Shorts*, 420 A.2d 694 (1980); *Roche v. McCoy*, 156 A.2d 307 (1959).

Source: Whitcomb, 1992, 57.

In addition, there are organized groups that push for the lowering of the age of consent between adults and children for sexual activity. Such groups that are more well known are the René Guyon Society, Pedophile Information Exchange (PIE), the Childhood Sexuality Circle, and the North American Man Boy Love Association (NAMBLA) (Holmes 1983, 67).

There are several problems with successful prosecution of cases involving physical and sexual abuse of children. In addition to some of the problems of normal criminal trials, children's cases have some unique points. For example, in child abuse cases in which the child has died, some courts do not hold the passive person (the person who watched while the aggressor did the act) responsible. In *People v. Wong*, 619 N.E.2d 377 (N.Y. App. July 1993), the court said that the mere fact the second defendant was in the same apartment at the time the 3-month-old child was shaken (shaken baby syndrome) was insufficient to support a criminal conviction of the second defendant. Some of the most noted points are (1) competency of children to testify, and (2) physical evidence.

Competency of Children to Testify

Court decisions regarding a child's competency to testify about certain events—and input as to whether a specific child has enough verbal skills to do so coherently—have evolved on a per-case basis. The second test is whether the child knows a truth from a falsehood and is willing to tell the truth.

Other factors that impact on a child's ability to testify are (1) age, (2) cross-examination, (3) "unavailable," (4) hearsay, and (5) identity of the perpetrator.

Age

Children as young as 3 years of age have been determined competent to testify (Goodman 1984a, 15). Older children have been found incompetent due to the inability to talk or demonstrate accuracy of recollection.

For example, in Wyoming, to be a competent witness a child must meet a five-part test: (1) understand the obligation of telling the truth; (2) have the mental capacity for accurate impression; (3) have sufficient memory for independent recollection; (4) have the capacity to express memory in words; and (5) have the capacity to understand simple questions. Thus a 3-year-old and a 5-year-old child were considered competent witnesses after the court applied the above five-part test and held that intelligence and not age is the guiding criterion (*In the Interest of CB v. State*, 749 P.2d 267, 1988).

Some who have worked with children and prepared them to be courtroom witnesses have concluded that a child's competency as a witness is dictated largely by the development of their verbal skills. The more individualized the language used with that particular child, the less likely it is that the child's story is false. Children seem to know when they are pretending. Yet practitioners need an understanding of the developmental stages of children's memory. A 4-year-old, for example, has moved from the 2-year-old stage of learning to use language as a tool for communication but will mix together important details with irrelevant details.

Goodman (1984b) provides scientific evidence debunking the myth that children are distorters of reality, misperceivers, manipulators, and fantasy-weavers simply because they do not perceive or verbalize as an adult would. This provides hope for an end to unrealistic expectations that a child victim of incest, for example, will or should recall details in the way or form that an adult would recall, disclose, or express them in language that adults use.

Research on children's understanding of time indicates that it is not until adolescence that children fully master the concept of time (Cole and Lofthus 1987). So investigators use special events to help younger children pinpoint the time. In addition, children, like adults, store only fragments of the experience due to perception and mechanisms for storing information. Perception, as a selective process, can be influenced by many other factors. But children store less of their experiences than adults and many need more guidance to stimulate memory (Lofthus and Davies 1984).

Children do not have a general memory deficit that renders their testimony untrustworthy. Even a child age 5 or below can testify when asked simple and direct questions. A pertinent example is shown by the testimony of a 5-year-old child whose father had rubbed his penis against her body while she was in the bathtub. The child did not know the word "ejaculation" or have a conceptual understanding of the physiology involved, but when asked if anything came out, replied affirmatively and said it was like "white cotton candy and was sticky" (Weiss 1983, 311).

Children do have the ability for accurate "free recall," but the amount of information they recall increases from preschool-age to adolescence. Cued recall tasks approach adult levels by the age of a normal 6- or 8-year-old child. Children distinguish real from pretend dimensions somewhere between ages 1 and 5, and they are no more vulnerable to suggestions than adults by 7 to 10 years (Lepore 1991).

Cross-Examination

Child victims also may have difficulty dealing with the direct questions prosecuting attorneys are commonly confined to on direct examination, as well as with the aggressive and argumentative leading questions asked by defense attorneys on cross-examination. Both of these question types were devised for primary use with adult witnesses.

Experience has shown, however, that victim witnesses can testify effectively without significant compromise to the search for truth if advocates for both sides are permitted to ask the child-victim witnesses leading (but not "tricky" or overly aggressive) questions. For example, asking a child if the hat worn by the offender was green or blue confuses a child if no hat was worn. (This is offering a child a choice between the truth and a "distractor.") The child, however, does not know he can say "no" to both colors; the child assumes it must be one or the other and selects one. (For greater clarification on this issue, see Exhibit 6.2, which shows the transcript of a child's testimony [Whitcomb 1992, 17].)

If the defense attacks the child's credibility by saying the child delayed his or her report of the abuse, many states permit the use of an expert witness to explain to jurors or the judge the behavior of child abuse victims in general. This means that the prosecution may not address the issue of credibility (telling the truth) of the child when it puts its case on. Later, if the child's testimony is questioned for its truthfulness by the defense

		Exhibit 6.2 EXCERPT FROM A CHILD'S TESTIMONY*
Defense Attorney:	And then you said you put your mouth on his penis?	
Five-Year-Old Child:	No.	
Defense Attorney:	You didn't say that?	
Child:	No.	
Defense Attorney:	Did you ever put your mouth on his penis?	
Child:	No.	
Defense Aitorney:	Well, why did you tell your mother that your dad put his penis in your mouth?	
Child:	My brother told me to.	

At this point, it looked as if the child had completely recanted her earlier testimony about the sexual abuse and had only fabricated the story because her brother told her to. However, the experienced prosecutor recognized the problem and clarified the situation:

Prosecuting Attorney:	Jennie, you said that you didn't put your mouth on daddy's penis. Is that right?
Child:	Yes.
Prosecuting Attorney:	Did daddy put his penis in your mouth?
Child:	Yes.
Prosecuting Attorney:	Did you tell your mom?
Child:	Yes.
Prosecuting Attorney:	What made you decide to tell?
Child:	My brother and I talked about it, and he said I better tell or dad would just keep doing it.

*L. Berliner and M.K. Barbierei, "Testimony of the Child Victim of Sexual Assault," *Journal of Social Issues*, Vol. 40 (1984): 132.

Source: Whitcomb 1992, 17.

because the child, indeed, acted like a victim, then the prosecution can use an expert witness. The expert witness, however, is limited to explaining how the characteristics exhibited by the child in the case were consistent with those to be displayed by a victim of sexual abuse. This is called a "proper bolstering of victim's testimony," because the jury can decide to give whatever weight it deems appropriate to the testimony.

To summarize to this point, courts typically view children as less likely than adults to give reliable testimony, but neither the courts nor lawmakers have ever stated a precise age at which children in general should be excluded from testifying. This means two things: (1) **competency must be determined on a per-case basis,** and (2) the **judge has considerable discretion** to determine the fitness of the young witness(es) in a particular case. Competence to be a witness is accomplished by demonstrating to the judge the **ability to distinguish truth from falsehood,** realization of what a lie is, and **an understanding of an oath to tell the truth.**

Unavailable

When a child comes to court but is unable to speak and respond to the questions, the child is considered "unavailable." In *Matter of T.P.*, 838 P.2d 1236

(Alaska Sup. Sept. 1992), the appeals court noted that the trial court made repeated attempts to have the child respond to questions and repeated attempts to prompt the child about the abuse. Despite the prodding of the trial judge, counsel, and her mother, the child refused. Therefore, the court found the child "unavailable" under Rule 804(a)(2). Then the court used the hearsay statements of the 6-year-old child in a proceeding to adjudicate the child as "in need of supervision."

Hearsay

In prosecuting crimes of a sexual nature against children, courts usually permit statements made out of court (hearsay) to ascertain the truth of the matter, so long as it is corroborated. In the above case, *Matter of T.P.*, the child made a statement to her teacher that her father had touched her in an inappropriate way. The statement was made after the child saw an animated film used to educate children about inappropriate touching and sexual abuse. The child came to the teacher crying. The teacher asked what was wrong and the child cried some more before she told the teacher.

Statements made to **teachers** or **other relatives** can be used as "spontaneous declarations." Statements made to a **pediatrician** who examines the child can be entered into court as an exception to the hearsay rule under the "medical examination" exception—statements made in the course of securing medical treatment. Both the spontaneous declaration and medical examination exceptions to the hearsay rule have been upheld by the U.S. Supreme Court (*White v. Illinois*, 502 U.S. 346 [1992]).

In *Galindo v. U.S.*, 630 A.2d 202 (D.C. App. Aug. 1993), the appeals court stated that the trial court properly considered statements made by a 3-year-old victim to her mother. The mother's testimony was admissible as proof that the child reported the sexual offense in question. But alone, it did not prove the defendant's guilt. The pediatrician's testimony was admissible under the medical-diagnosis exception to the hearsay rule; the court's holding was that it was not necessary for the mother to be the actual patient when she gave information to the doctor during the medical exam. Given the medical evidence, the statements made by the mother and pediatrician, and the child's own testimony, the court found sufficient evidence to support the defendant's conviction.

Contrast the above case with *In re Kailee B.*, 22 Ca.Rptr.2d 485 (Cal. App. Sept. 1993). The California Supreme Court said that social and home studies used by social services agencies typically contain hearsay and even multiple hearsay evidence (she said that he said that she said) but were nonetheless admissible and competent evidence on which to base a finding that a child fell within the juvenile court's jurisdiction.

In order to protect the best interests of the child, the determining factor is often not the literal interpretation of the child's statements, but rather whether those statements were in fact made, and, if they were, what could have caused the child to utter them. In this case, the $2\frac{1}{2}$-year-old was incompetent to testify, not based on the unreliability of her statements, but based on the fact that she was unable to testify in the courtroom.

Court action is considered appropriate so long as certain safeguards are maintained to protect the rights of parents. In Kailee's case, the father was not prosecuted as a criminal; Kailee was found as a dependent needing services or supervision, as discussed in Chapter 5, "Child Abuse and Neglect." The result for her father was not a criminal conviction or penalty. The court ruled that contact with her was not permitted unless it was monitored and both the father and child had undergone counseling.

The legal counsel for Kailee's father had argued that "it is better that ten guilty persons escape, than that one innocent suffer." In this situation, the court thought that "few, if any, would agree it was better that ten pedophiles be permitted to continue molesting children than that one innocent parent be required to attend therapy sessions in order to discover why his infant daughter was falsely making such appalling accusations against him." In short, the court thought that the father's argument was more accurate for a criminal setting, not juvenile court where the child was found dependent and in need of services.

Ideally, the perpetrator will confess at some point in the investigation. Then the child's out-of-court statement is sufficient corroboration to the confession and is admissible as evidence.

Identity of Perpetrator

In a criminal case, the child must identify the exact perpetrator. However, in cases of abuse where there is no criminal conviction or penalty, it is not always necessary for the court to determine who did it. For example, in *State ex rel. Juvenile Dept. v. Froats*, 844 P.2d 917 (Or. App. Dec. 1992), the court found that all of the injuries sustained by the child occurred while the mother and boyfriend were living together. Because they continued to reside at the same address, the injuries suffered by the child were attributable to one or both of them. The court has jurisdiction over the child based solely upon the allegations of abuse.

Physical Evidence

Another major problem has been physical evidence. If the case is in the criminal court, then the standard is proof beyond a reasonable doubt. As a result, some cases cannot be prosecuted under criminal charges because the proof is lacking. If the child says that she or he was sexually abused, the testimony has to be compelling and convincing, and that is very difficult for young children.

One of the investigative techniques has been the use of dolls. "Some states have statutes that give a prosecutor the right to allow child witnesses to use the dolls in court to show what happened to them" (Freeman and Estrada-Mullaney 1988, 3). Before the advent of anatomically correct dolls, police, mental health professionals, and others used dolls such as Ken and Barbie. However, even the *Teacher-a-Bodies* are not anatomically correct dolls because they are not to scale. In addition, the anatomically correct dolls have not withstood the test of researchers who find that there is very little difference between doll play of abused children and doll play of nonabused children. "Even nonabused children exhibit heightened sexual interest following a single doll experience" (Ceci and Bruck 1995, 169).

The biggest problem in physical evidence comes with situations in which the child has no extreme physical trauma. There is no venereal disease.

There are no tears in any of the child's body openings. The problem with these kinds of child abuse cases is that they often lack independent corroborative evidence. In most cases before a criminal court, the testimony of witnesses is supported, supplemented, and reinforced by physical evidence, and it is even sometimes supported by other witnesses. Even in cases where the child is the sole or primary witness to a homicide, for example, there is virtually always physical evidence that corroborates the testimony.

Unfortunately, in child abuse cases—physical and sexual—the testimony of the child victim is likely to be the only evidence of the act itself. Delays in reporting the offense further dilute the impact of the charge. For these reasons, cases where a child has venereal disease or is pregnant are more likely to be prosecuted than those cases where the victim's testimony stands alone.

For example, how does one explain to a jury that it is not normal for a medical doctor to be able to insert two or three adult fingers into the anus of a small child? Aside from the hurdle of helping the jury understand that the anal opening does not expand and retract like the vaginal area and that there has been some intrusion into that body opening, one is still left with questions of causation and proof. The defense will argue that it was caused by other things. In other words, the state has to prove forced sodomy, which means that a specific person did a specific act with *mens rea*, which is prohibited under a specific criminal law statute.

In the recent past, doctors used the test of girls' hymens measuring larger than 4 millimeters and the "wink test" (touching the anus with a cotton swab to see if it winks) to convict. But, as Nathan and Snedeker point out, there was no scientific proof:

In 1987, doctors at a children's hospital in Boston published results of their study comparing abused girls with a group seen for simple vaginal and urinary tract infections, as well as with another group who had no history of either infection or abuse. No matter what group they were in, many of these girls' hymens measured larger than four millimeters. In addition, some of the "normal" girls had bands, bumps, and tears. As for those with vaginal and urinary tract problems, their bottoms looked even more like the abused girls'. After McCann's work was published two years later, the myth of the normal four-millimeter hymen was finally laid to rest, along with synechiae, six o'clock tags, and neovascularization. Woodling's anal wink was also summarily retired, and he has not since been seen in court—though at this writing, several people convicted with his testimony, including Scott and Brenda Kniffen, are still incarcerated in California prisons. (Nathan and Snedeker 1995, 197)

Now that you understand some of the challenges of physical evidence, does that mean there will be a successful case for the state? Maybe. It depends on the child's being able to testify. For a child to actually give his or her testimony in a courtroom depends upon other issues, such as the emotional effects of testifying.

Other issues are important in criminal prosecutions. First, there are the emotional effects of testifying. Then there are the myths and reality of false memory. Last, if the case is too difficult to prove under criminal law and procedure, some victims use tort law to recover damages that at least pay for the expenses of the treatment needed to help the child deal with the abuse.

OTHER ISSUES

Emotional Effects of Testifying

Even if a child is judged competent to testify, the court must engage in a balancing test before allowing the child to testify. This balancing usually weighs the child's interests in avoiding psychological and/or emotional harm against the probative value of the child's testimony. The court has to consider whether or not the degree of possible psychological injury is substantially greater than having an average child (not abused) testify. The opinions of mental health experts will usually be used by the court to make an assessment of potential emotional and psychological damage that could occur to the child.

Stress in the Courtroom

The courtroom can be as traumatic as some of the forms of "sex-ploitation." Some of the **factors that increase stress** in the courtroom for children are as follows:

1. public setting of the courtroom
2. being unfamiliar with courtroom and court personnel
3. speaking into a court microphone
4. being sequestered with no familiar faces in court
5. different district attorney at different levels in court
6. legal and/or technical jargon
7. seeing the defendant
8. linguistic strategies of the defense
9. long delays and postponements
10. memory loss (Densen-Gerber and Hutchinson 1979, 65)

Some of the **factors decreasing stress** are as follows:

1. someone teaching the child about the court process
2. visiting and walking around an empty courtroom
3. using a private, quiet room for interviewing
4. age-related toys for children while they have to wait
5. presence of a parent or familiar person in court
6. use of clear, simple language
7. including familiar persons in the preparation process
8. keeping a written account of the testimony to refresh memory

9. instructions on how to respond to the questions (Densen-Gerber and Hutchinson 1979, 65)

Research Findings

In 1985, the Seventh National Conference on Child Abuse and Neglect opened with a point/counterpoint plenary session of the pros and cons of prosecuting child sexual abuse cases. Among the various arguments was the belief that children are harmed by the courtroom experience. The National Institute of Justice (NIJ) and the Office of Juvenile Justice and Delinquency Prevention (OJJDP) awarded three grants to empirically examine the emotional effects of the court process on sexually abused children.

Mixed Results   The research results are mixed. According to the Denver study of 218 children abused by perpetrators not living with them, testifying may impede the healing process for some children. In the North Carolina study of 100 children, victims primarily of intrafamilial abuse, results showed that testifying may speed the recovery. One of the major reasons for these mixed results is that some children testified in criminal court while others were in child protection proceedings. However, the studies did support the fact that all children scored high on measures of stress and anxiety before testifying. "Maternal support was associated with improvements in the children's mental health. Children who testified more than once tended not to improve as much as children who testified only once or not at all" (Whitcomb et al. 1994, 1).

For some children, as with adult rape survivors, it is important to testify for their own mental health. The problem is the delay in the adjudication process.

False Memory and Post-Traumatic Stress Disorder

Studies do not support the contention that the majority of delayed disclosures are fabricated. In fact, two new brain-imaging studies, conducted independently, indicate that severe, repeated sexual abuse in childhood underlies damage to a brain structure that helps to orchestrate memory. The injury to the brain may predispose people, especially children, to experience an altered state of consciousness known as dissociation and thereby develop symptoms of post-traumatic stress disorder (PTSD) (Bower 1995).

Yet the False Memory Syndrome Foundation (FMSF) argues that "decade-delayed memories" are the result of a false memory syndrome caused by a disastrous "therapeutic" program. Foundation officials are especially opposed to authors Bass and Davis (1988) for their work *The Courage to Heal: A Guide for Women Survivors of Child Sexual Abuse*, which has sold over 750,000 copies. It has a 14-step process to help victims of abuse move through the denial and pain to health and more effective strategies for dealing with life (National Center for Prosecution of Child Abuse, July 1992, 1).

FMSF argues that Bass and Davis' book promotes false memories. According to FMSF's view, *The Courage to Heal* permits unlicensed therapists to work through the book's exercises, attend incest survivor group therapy, and isolate the patient from family and friends until the fantasy is so ingrained in the mind that the abuse seems real. FMSF also denies the existence of Post-Traumatic Stress Disorder (PTSD), Multiple Personality Disorder, and even repression itself (National Center for Prosecution of Child Abuse, July 1992, 1).

PTSD, by definition, is a complex interaction of cognitive, affective, and physiological responses to an event that is outside the range of usual human experience. Victims of natural disasters and Vietnam veterans show us that some events can be distressing to almost anyone. For children, Voelm and Schwartz (1994) argue, it becomes even more masked and complicated by multiple issues of developmental stages, family dynamics, physical maturity, genetic predisposition, and cognitive skills. They think that the symptomatology and long-term sequelae exhibited in the child victim are distinct and distinguishable from the criteria established for adult diagnosis. As such, it warrants intensive study by researchers and clinicians.

The FMSF's most credible critic is the founder's own daughter, Jennifer Freyd, a psychologist at the University of Oregon (Freyd 1993). Dr. Freyd states that the FMSF is based on a personal vendetta and active denial, coasting on legitimate issues about the validity of memory. Dr. Freyd claims that her father sexually abused her as a child, but the Freyds deny their daughter's allegation and continue to take advantage of the frequent disagreement among clinical and research psychologists and the emotions of other parents who feel they have no way to prove themselves innocent. Dr. Freyd claims that there is no scientific basis for the term "false memory syndrome."

The false memory syndrome has been used as a legal defense for the alleged offender (Mitchell 1993), who perpetuates the myth while creating a business. In addition, Victims of Child Abuse Laws (VOCAL) and other similar parent groups are seen as symptoms of a "backlash" movement against the protection of children from child abuse.

One of the reasons FMSF parents have fought the charges against them with far greater success than their predecessors has been money, education, and social prestige. FMSF founder Pamela Freyd is an education researcher at the University of Pennsylvania, and her husband, Peter, is a mathematics professor there and has taught throughout the world. On the other hand, VOCAL founder Bob Bentz was employed in the paint department of a Ford automobile factory in St. Paul, and his wife worked the night shift at a print shop and are considered less influential and reliable (Nathan and Snedeker 1995, 237).

In addition, many FMSF advisory board members are prestigious academics who studiously avoid making pronouncements about issues beyond their specialties. Yet they proclaim that sexual abuse is inevitably the most devastating thing that can happen to a child so that they can argue that being falsely accused of sexual abuse is the worst thing that can happen to its members. Nathan and Snedeker (1995, 238) counter that argument by saying:

While this kind of hyperbolic rhetoric may be good organizing strategy, it puts the group in the same camp as ritual-abuse believers, who ignore research that suggests that, in general, neglect and physical abuse, which are far more common than sexual abuse, are also more destructive to children's development.

To avoid these problems of false reports, according to the National Center of Prosecution of Child Abuse, it is critical that any allegation be investigated promptly and professionally, with objectivity, by trained law enforcement and other professionals. In couples who are divorcing, however, there are estimates that the rate of invalid sexual/physical abuse claims may be as high as 33 percent (Ceci and Bruck 1995, 33). When investigations are conducted professionally and promptly, then both the needs of the children and the rights of the accused can be better protected.

Some abused children have reached adulthood but are left with the emotional scars of the trauma. Proving a criminal charge against the parent(s) is even more difficult. Thus, some adult survivors have attempted to recover the damages under a tort claim.

Torts

Torts are a part of civil law in which persons bring lawsuits for a civil wrong or injury and ask for damages. In cases difficult to prove or where alleged offenders are acquitted of the criminal charges, survivors use tort actions to regain some of the losses. Remember that most abused children do not sue anyone because the abuse is never discovered, or no one is interested or capable of bringing a legal action on behalf of the child, or the abuser has no assets.

As early as 1959, in *Gilbert v. Gilbert*, 168 C.A.2d 102, 335 P.2d 736, the California Court of Appeals upheld the judgment of $30,000 in damages for a child who lost a spleen and one kidney due to the willful and malicious misconduct of the stepfather who brutally beat the 8-year-old. The stepfather lost in his argument that he was immune (could not be sued) because a lawsuit would result in state involvement in family matters.

More recently, some children have brought lawsuits using homeowner's insurance (if the abuse occurred in the home) or car insurance policy (if the abuse occurred in the car). The legal theory is that the policy may include coverage of maltreatment judgments against the defendant who may lose the civil suit but would be indemnified for some or all of the losses by the insurance company.

Insurance companies have successfully argued in states such as California, Washington, and Wisconsin that their policies do not cover intentional acts and that such abuse is intentional. Thus, the insurance companies are not obligated to represent the insured or to indemnify any recovery against him or her as would be the case for an automobile accident.

An example of a tort is the case *Reagan v. Rider*, 521 A.2d 1246 (Md. App. 1987). Ms. Rider brought a suit against her stepfather for alleged long-term sexual abuse under the legal theory of intentional infliction of emotional distress. The jury ruled in her favor and the stepfather appealed. The appeals court found that the causation and severity of emotional distress were sufficiently supported by evidence.

In order to impose liability for the tort of intentional infliction of emotional distress, (1) the conduct must be intentional or reckless, and (2) extreme and outrageous; (3) a causal connection between the wrongful conduct and the emotional distress must be proven, and (4) the emotional distress must be severe. All four elements must be present. In 1987, thirty-seven jurisdictions recognized this particular tort as a valid cause for action.

Mr. Reagan questioned the legal sufficiency of the evidence on causation and severity of the emotional distress. His counsel argued that Ms. Rider's severe depression, which deteriorated over a three-year period and required an additional two years of therapy, was a "neurotic overreaction to trivial hurts" that "are the price of a complex society." In essence, Mr. Reagan argued that his stepdaughter had to prove that she was completely disabled before she could recover damages for intentional infliction of emotional distress.

The appeals court did not agree. In fact, they said that something less than complete emotional disablement would be sufficient to satisfy the severe emotional distress element. They noted that the testimonies of the appellee and the forensic/clinical psychiatrist were ample for the jury to make a decision based upon the behavior that occurred several hundred times from age 11 to 17, causing severe depression.

The above cited case is particularly interesting because it shows how some children turn the pain of child abuse upon themselves. Others do not. Thus, it is important to discuss how the victim can also become an offender.

Sex Offenders

VICTIM BECOMES OFFENDER CYCLE

Historically, juvenile sex offenders have been viewed as young people experimenting. Compared to violent delinquents, juvenile sex offenders have fewer alcohol and drug problems and are less often gang members. They have fewer nonviolent offenses and are therefore hidden. Because they resemble normative youth more so than do delinquent youth, the courts have been reluctant to stigmatize them. Thus, the juvenile sex offenders were ignored with the hope that the problem would go away.

It was the pioneering work of Nicholas Groth and his colleagues in the Massachusetts prison system that changed this viewpoint. Groth was director of an adult unit of sex offenders. While taking careful histories, he noticed that the adults began as youth. He also discovered that some of the adults themselves had been victimized as children. Groth and others began to push for specialized assessment and treatment strategies (Groth 1977).

Today, Groth's observations have been documented by others. Studies done on adult sex offenders show that as many as 60 to 80 percent report having offended as adolescents (Abel, Mihelman, and Becker 1985; Freeman-Longo 1983). Another professional group that has documented juvenile sex offenders involves those hospitals that have a multidisciplinary staff.

Starts Early

In addition, research has shown that there is a progression of offenses. Offenses such as obscene phone calls, voyeurism, or stealing undergarments are not necessarily harmless juvenile pranks. In some cases, the "hands-off crimes," as they are sometimes called, become more serious "hands-on crimes" like fondling or rape (Knopp 1982).

Progression of Offenses

Ryan and Lang (1991) describe the average juvenile sex offender as a male, with an average age of 14. Because juvenile perpetrators are in approximate proportion to the numbers in the general population, the offenders are likely to be white. If they have an offense history, it is more likely that their offenses are other than sexual. The victim is a 7- or 8-year-old child who is not a relative. Penetration and sufficient force are used to overcome the child's resistance.

Various Theories   There are various theories used to explain why these youth do what they do. There is some support for the victimization theory (Mones 1991; Silbert 1989; Gray 1986; Justice and Justice 1979). But not all offenders have been victims (Simons and Whitbeck 1991). Physical abuse alone or with exposure to parental and peer violence is cited as a predisposing factor. Family dysfunction as well as parental loss due to divorce, illness, death, or separation also has merit as an explanation.

The most successful treatment so far has incorporated all of those listed theories and more. Because sexual offending is very complex, sexual offenders do not respond well to the traditional one-on-one psychotherapy. In addition, there is so much denial that clinicians have begun to use physiological measurement tools like the plethysmograph. A plethysmograph is an instrument that records sexual reactions such as penile erection response. The client views a series of slides. The first slide is a picture of a dirt road. The other slides depict various degrees of force in scenes with young children, teens, and adults—both male and female. The youth is to self-report the degree of arousal, but the machine also graphs the sexual response throughout the test. Because this machine is used only for assessment in treatment and not as an investigation tool, this activity is permissible.

The Behavioral Studies Program at the Pines Treatment Center in Portsmouth, Virginia, has an innovative, multidisciplinary, and comprehensive treatment program. It is a private residential treatment approach for youth ages 10 to 19 who have sexually offended. The program accepts youth from all over the United States who are willing to show some acceptance of responsibility for their behavior. They use cognitive-behavioral techniques with an emphasis on learning appropriate ways to handle feelings such as anger through management and assertiveness training. Family theory is used if possible. Their work and data collection have been funded by research grants from the National Center on Child Abuse and Neglect (*Virginia Child Protection Newsletter* 1991, 10).

Colorado and Minnesota, as well as Virginia, also have developed treatment programs for youth sent to the state for correction. The program in Virginia has fourteen treatment objectives. A sample includes: autobiography, to examine life history; cycle of offending, to identify, analyze, and chart the offense cycle; disclosure of offense, to identify and report sexual offenses and deviant sexual behaviors; victim empathy, to examine the effects of the offense on the victim; personal victimization, to identify and study the offender's own sexual victimization, if any; fantasy and arousal, to examine the role of these issues in the sexual offense (*Virginia Child Protection Newsletter* 1991, 7).

Not all treatment objectives are met at once. Through the group process, there are developmental stages. As the youth begins to disclose more about the sexual offense, more of the defenses of denial break away. Attention can then be placed on the degree of personal victimization. Some youth are unaware that they too were violated. The involvement of the family in the therapy of the child is often a healing process for the entire family. The final stage is a precaution where the youth is led to role-playing and developing a plan to prevent reoffending.

Although most of this discussion centers on male sex offenders, there are also female sex offenders (Tracy and Shelden 1992). The incidence is smaller and the characteristics are different. For example, most of the female juvenile sex offenders that clinicians have interviewed committed their offense in concert with a male offender or a significant other, like a boyfriend or spouse (Mathew, Matthews, and Speltz 1989).

Female sex offenders

Most of this research involves small groups. Larson and Maison (1987) describe a treatment program based on sixteen women at Shakopee Correctional Facility in Minnesota. Mathews, Matthews, and Speltz (1989) had a sample of sixteen female offenders involved in Genesis II for Women, a private, nonprofit community corrections agency in Minneapolis, Minnesota.

Even though there is a scarcity of literature on female sex offenders, many people working with females see this behavior as an extension of the general violence in the family. Because some of these women are passive and feel powerless, they seemingly go along with sexual games—even if it includes the children—just to avoid having the husband get angry with them. The violence that adults do to each other is done to their children who, in turn, do it to younger children.

Widon (1995) examined criminal records on more than 1,500 individuals to determine whether the experience of abuse or neglect during childhood increased the likelihood of arrest as a juvenile or young adult. The subjects were 908 individuals who had been subjected as children to abuse (physical or sexual) or neglect, and whose cases were processed through the courts between 1967 and 1971. All subjects were 11 years of age or younger at the time of the incident(s). The results showed that of all types of childhood maltreatment, physical abuse was the most likely to be associated with arrest for a violent crime later in life. Even more important, neglect, a more passive form of maltreatment, was associated with an array of developmental problems and greater risk of later criminal violence.

From research findings and practitioners' stories, youth sometimes sexually abuse other children; some children become violent. In fact, some of these children kill other children or those who abuse them. When they do kill, their defense is similar to battered spouses. In their case, it is called the battered child syndrome defense.

Battered Spouse/Child Syndrome Defense

As the materials in this chapter have shown, battering of children and spouses is part of the bigger picture of family violence. In some states, a battered spouse who kills his or her spouse has been permitted to give testimony about the battering in order to mitigate the charge of premeditation in first-degree murder.

Testimonies of battered women, for example, have included the situation of a long-time victim of physical, sexual, and psychological abuse who loses self-confidence, feels trapped, and eventually strikes back as if in self-defense, assaulting or killing the abuser. Testimony on battered women syndrome is allowed at the discretion of judges in many courtrooms across the country, but new laws in California, Maryland, Missouri, Ohio, Louisiana, and Texas prevent judges from ruling that the testimony does not constitute legitimate evidence.

Traditional self-defense legal theories usually involve person-to-person confrontations, which are immediately violent and physically threatening. Individuals are permitted to resort to the law for their defense if a person reasonably believes there is a fear of death or great bodily harm from another who has no legal right to attack him or her. Walker (1979) was the first to describe the psychological characteristics of abused women and the battering relationships and to explain how the fear of death or great bodily harm may persist through most of their daily lives.

Without expert testimony to explain how women come to feel so defensive or fearful that they cannot leave an abusive relationship, judges, juries, and lawyers were often left wondering why the woman did not walk out long before she felt compelled to retaliate.

In the debate over battered women, Schulhofer (1995, 288–289) lists four possible variations of killing a spouse:

1. The woman who kills in the heat of a serious battering incident (that is, a "confrontational" killing).

2. The battered woman who files for divorce, moves out, and gets an order of protection, but is repeatedly pursued and beaten by her husband. Eventually, in desperation, she kills him.

3. The battered woman who kills her spouse while he sleeps.

4. The battered woman who gets a hired killer to shoot her spouse—days or weeks after a battering incident.

In the traditional self-defense doctrine, variation no. 1, she would need to show all four of these elements:

1. The threat is imminent.

2. The threat is of great bodily harm.

3. Deadly force is necessary.

4. All the above (1–3) in this list are reasonable under the circumstances.

The problem is that self-defense could be sufficient in the first variation (heat of a serious battering incident called confrontational killing) but becomes progressively weaker in the other three. The same problems the courts are having with spouse abuse become even more problematic with children who kill one or both of their parents.

The Washington State Court of Appeals, First Division, ruling February 3, 1992, in the case *State v. Andrew G. James*, No. 24252-1-I, said that the type of reasoning regarding abused women who strike out against their abusers is just as relevant in cases in which children retaliate after being abused by their parents. The court reversed the murder conviction of a youth who shot his stepfather by remanding the case to the trial court that previously erred in not allowing testimony on the "battered child syndrome."

The court said that it is unlikely the average juror would be able to understand the youth's claim that he acted in self-defense without an understanding of "hypervigilance," or "a heightened ability to discern preaggressive behavior in others, a condition that occurs with long-term abuse." Citing from the book *When a Child Kills: Abused Children Who Kill*

Their Parents (Mones 1991), the court said that other psychological effects, such as learned helplessness, depression, low self-esteem, fear of reprisal, a belief in the omnipotence of the batterer, and a belief in the futility of either resistance or flight, contribute to a child's sense of having no alternatives. Whereas women sometimes have the option of fleeing to a shelter in which their identify and location will be kept secret, such an option is "almost unknown" to children.

Because the balance of power is even more unequal in a parent-child relationship than in a marriage, the child is bound in more ways than the average person can imagine. If children run away, for example, shelters are required by law to make contact with the parents within 24 hours.

In the Andrew James case (*State v. Andrew G. James*), the stepfather, Walter Jaloveckas, had moved in with the James family when Andrew was 7 years old after the biological father had abandoned the family earlier that year. Jaloveckas became increasingly abusive with physical violence and outbursts of anger. Testimony at trial showed incidents where Jaloveckas beat or hit Andrew, his brother, their mother, smashed a stereo and bicycles with a sledgehammer, and threatened to torture, kill, or send the boys away for such transgressions as being tardy in completing chores or taking some of his marijuana. Even sadder, just as in Mones' book, the system failed the youth because Jaloveckas' actions were reported to Child Protective Services on three occasions, but CPS did not follow up on these reports. On at least two of these occasions, the mother or Andrew requested that CPS not follow up out of fear of reprisal by Jaloveckas (Sagatun and Edwards 1995, 249).

The use of experts to testify to the effects of violent abuse on the battered person does not mean that the defendant will be acquitted. The information is used only to help the jury interpret how the defendant might have perceived and responded to threats of imminent danger. The judge or jury still has to decide whether the "battered child" defense is appropriate for that particular case. Without adequate understanding of the developmental stages of children, juries and judges are left to a determination based upon stereotypes of abused children or their own childhood or children and not the actual case before them.

According to the FBI, in 1992 there were 343 cases in which a child killed a parent or someone in a guardianship position (parricides) and this number remains constant to 1997 even though the total number of murders by juveniles has doubled from 1987 to 1994. Yet these are tragic cases because the killings usually follow a history of violent abuse by that parent. In addition, as Mones (1991) has shown, some of these children have been found guilty of murder in spite of the overwhelming evidence of child torture and the lack of seriousness on the part of those receiving the complaint; the criminal justice system and society cannot accept the notion that a child could kill his or her parents under any circumstance. Even when cases of abuse are reported, the full extent of the abuse is never realized until an attorney specializing in defending children has completed an investigation.

Once the case has been successfully proven, what happens to the offender? Some groups advocate family reunification and others argue for child protection.

FAMILY REUNIFICATION

A nationally recognized authority on family violence, Richard J. Gelles, Ph.D., no longer supports family reunification as a goal for child protective service agencies. Gelles' research shows that violence, severe abuse, and homicide are distinct forms of behavior—not a linear or evolutionary pattern of violence ranging from mild and infrequent to severe and frequent. Homicide is not an extreme form of interpersonal violence. He said:

Although the compassionate approach of family reunification is attractive to those of us in the helping professions, I believe that the scientific data fail to support the models. While there are indeed many child maltreaters who can be helped to be competent parents with timely and effective social services, other parents cannot be assisted to be caring and nurturing parents.

I believe that the rigid uniform family reunification model needs to be abandoned as an official and unofficial child welfare policy. The data on child homicide clearly reveal the damage done by rigidly following the family reunification mode. Thirty to 50 percent of the children killed by parents or caretakers are killed after they have been identified by agencies and have been involved in interventions, and either left in their homes or returned home after a short-term removal.

"Child protection" and "child advocacy" needs to replace family reunification as the guiding policy of child welfare agencies. Child welfare workers need to "listen" to the actions of maltreating parents. Parents who fracture the skulls or bones of six-month-old children, who have sexual intercourse with 12-month-old daughters, and whose drug abuse patterns compromise their ability to care for their children are simply not entitled to "three strikes" before they lose their rights as parents. With severe child maltreatment, "one strike" is sufficient to warrant terminating parental rights. (National Center for Prosecution of Child Abuse, August 1992, 1)

Judge Joseph Thibodeau, Snohomish County (Washington), sentenced the defendant, Mrs. Erlandson, to an unusually long prison term. She was a nurse practitioner with no previous history of violence. The defense argued that punishment would serve no useful purpose. There were letters of support for the defendant. Yet the judge gave her 40 years. In an unusual personal statement at the sentencing hearing, he said:

Children in our society are special gifts. We must nurture our children, show them respect and must protect them to the best of our ability. Any less will result in the destruction of our society. This was a beautiful young child. One only has to view the video of . . . Easter to see what a lovely little child this person really was. She truly was a special gift to the Erlandson family. I can't bring back Kayla to life and I can't prevent future abuse of children, but I am satisfied that the Court must speak up on behalf of children. Children essentially don't have any rights. As I read the letters in support of the defendant, the theme is essentially one of total denial that this even happened. They don't mention anything about Kayla, what happened to this child. It is interesting to note in most cases the trial judges consider, we always get a letter from the victim and they always tell us what sort of trauma they went through at the hands of a defendant. In this case, obviously, the victim is not present.

It is clear that this child was an extremely vulnerable child. She came from Korea as an 18-month-old child on the 1st of October of 1990. She had a background essentially of social deprivation. She had delayed physical and emotional skills. She had a language barrier and she was new to this land. . . .

I can't imagine the pain that this child must have endured that last week before she died. There were over 30 bruises to her head, over 65 bruises to her body, all in various stages of healing. There was even a healing lacerated liver in this young child. I can't imagine the pain to the abdomen that this child endured the last week. Coupled with that, a burn, a two-inch burn on the elbow that was still weeping. One only has to touch a burner and get a superficial pain to be . . . in pain . . . the entire evening . . . Can you imagine what it would be like to have a second degree burn with three layers of skin burned away and the amount of excruciating pain that this young child endured the last several days of her life? When she . . . sustained this blunt trauma to the head, I'm satisfied that she was instantaneously unconscious.

[Kayla] would say to this court that, "When I was taken to the hospital, I essentially was brain dead . . . I can't come back, but don't let my death result in some other child enduring the same sort of abuse that I sustained." And that the Court should speak up for these children and protect them to the best of our ability. And granted, I can't stop abuse, but I surely feel that this Court should make a statement with this sentence; that there was clearly extreme cruelty . . . And I'm satisfied, when considering all of the factors in this case, an exceptional sentence of 40 years or 480 months appropriate. The Court will make such a finding. (National Center for Prosecution of Child Abuse, July 1992, 2)

Not all states under their sentencing guidelines would have permitted this. Only a minority of states have amended their first-degree or capital murder statutes to eliminate the intent-to-kill requirement when a child's death results from abuse. In those states, prosecutors must prove that the defendant physically abused the child and the abuse caused the child's death. Tennessee characterized the abusive acts inflicted by Hale in *State v. Hale*, 1992 WL 182263 (Tenn. 1992) as "misdemeanors," ruling that it was unfair to use prior uncharged misdemeanors as an element in determining first-degree murder, and it was disproportionate because the murder occurred during a misdemeanor.

The U.S. Supreme Court heard one of these cases dealing with child sexual abuse. The Supreme Court tried to balance the rights of the offenders with the special needs of children in *Maryland v. Craig.*

MARYLAND v. CRAIG

SUPREME COURT OF THE UNITED STATES

497 U.S. 836; 110 S. Ct. 3157; 111 L.Ed. 2d 666

April 18, 1990, Argued June 27, 1990, Decided

JUDGES: O'CONNOR, J., delivered the opinion of the Court, in which REHNQUIST, C. J., and WHITE, BLACKMUN, and KENNEDY, JJ., joined. SCALIA, J., filed a dissenting opinion, in which BRENNAN, MARSHALL, and STEVENS, JJ., joined, post, p. 860.

JUSTICE O'CONNOR delivered the opinion of the Court.

?

This case requires us to decide whether the Confrontation Clause of the Sixth Amendment categorically prohibits a child witness in a child abuse case from testifying against a defendant at trial, outside the defendant's physical presence, by one-way closed circuit television.

I

Facts

In October 1986, a Howard County grand jury charged respondent, Sandra Ann Craig, with child abuse, first and second degree sexual offenses, perverted sexual practice, assault, and battery. The named victim in each count was a six-year-old girl who, from August 1984 to June 1986, had attended a kindergarten and prekindergarten center owned and operated by Craig.

In March 1987, before the case went to trial, the State sought to invoke a Maryland statutory procedure that permits a judge to receive, by one-way closed circuit television, the testimony of a child witness who is alleged to be a victim of child abuse. To invoke the procedure, the trial judge must first "determin[e] that testimony by the child victim in the courtroom will result in the child suffering serious emotional distress such that the child cannot reasonably communicate." Proc. Code Ann. § 9–102(a)(1)(ii) (1989). Once the procedure is invoked, the child witness, prosecutor, and defense counsel withdraw to a separate room; the judge, jury, and defendant remain in the courtroom. The child witness is then examined and cross-examined in the separate room, while a video monitor records and displays the witness' testimony to those in the courtroom. During this time the witness cannot see the defendant. The defendant remains in electronic communication with defense counsel, and objections may be made and ruled on as if the witness were testifying in the courtroom.

In support of its motion invoking the one-way closed circuit television procedure, the State presented expert testimony that the named victim, as well as a number of other children who were alleged to have been sexually abused by Craig, would suffer "serious emotional distress such that [they could not] reasonably communicate," § 9–102(a)(1)(ii), if required to testify in the courtroom.

App. 7–59. The Maryland Court of Appeals characterized the evidence as follows:

"The expert testimony in each case suggested that each child would have some or considerable difficulty in testifying in Craig's presence. For example, as to one child, the expert said that what 'would cause him the most anxiety would be to testify in front of Mrs. Craig. . . .' The child 'wouldn't be able to communicate effectively.' As to another, an expert said she 'would probably stop talking and she would withdraw and curl up.' With respect to two others, the testimony was that one would 'become highly agitated, that he may refuse to talk or if he did talk, that he would choose his subject regardless of the questions' while the other would 'become extremely timid and unwilling to talk.' " 316 Md. 551, 568–569, 560 A. 2d 1120, 1128–1129 (1989).

Craig objected to the use of the procedure on Confrontation Clause grounds, but the trial court rejected that contention, concluding that although the statute "take[s] away the right of the defendant to be face to face with his or her accuser," the defendant retains the "essence of the right of confrontation," including the right to observe, cross-examine, and have the jury view the demeanor of the witness. App. 65–66. The trial court further found that, "based upon the evidence presented . . . the testimony of each of these children in a courtroom will result in each child suffering serious emotional distress . . . such that each of these children cannot reasonably communicate." Id., at 66. The trial court then found the named victim and three other children competent to testify and accordingly permitted them to testify against Craig via the one-way closed circuit television procedure. The jury convicted Craig on all counts, and the Maryland Court of Special Appeals affirmed the convictions, 76 Md. App. 250, 544 A. 2d 784 (1988).

The Court of Appeals of Maryland reversed and remanded for a new trial. 316 Md. 551, 560 A. 2d 1120 (1989). The Court of Appeals rejected Craig's argument that the Confrontation Clause requires in all cases a face-to-face courtroom encounter between the accused and his accusers, id., at 556–562, 560 A. 2d, at 1122–1125, but concluded: | **Procedural History**

"[U]nder § 9–102(a)(1)(ii), the operative 'serious emotional distress' which renders a child victim unable to 'reasonably communicate' must be determined to arise, at least primarily, from face-to-face confrontation with the defendant. Thus, we construe the phrase 'in the courtroom' as meaning, sixth amendment and [state constitution] confrontation purposes, 'in the courtroom in the presence of the defendant.' Unless prevention of 'eyeball-to-eyeball' confrontation is necessary to obtain the trial testimony of the child, the defendant cannot be denied that right." Id., at 566, 560 A. 2d, at 1127.

Reviewing the trial court's finding and the evidence presented in support of the § 9–102 procedure, the Court of Appeals held that, "as [it] read *Coy* [*v. Iowa*, 487 U.S. 1012 (1988)], the showing made by the State was insufficient to reach the high threshold required by that case before § 9–102 may be invoked." Id., at 554–555, 560 A. 2d, at 1121 (footnote omitted).

We **granted certiorari** to resolve the important Confrontation Clause issues raised by this case. 493 U.S. 104 (1990).

II

The Confrontation Clause of the Sixth Amendment, made applicable to the States through the Fourteenth Amendment, provides: "In all criminal prosecutions, the accused shall enjoy the right . . . to be confronted with the witnesses against him."

We observed in *Coy v. Iowa* that "the Confrontation Clause guarantees the defendant a face-to-face meeting with witnesses appearing before the trier of fact." 487 U.S., at 1016 (citing *Kentucky v. Stincer*, 482 U.S. 730, 748, 749–750 (1987) (MARSHALL, J., dissenting)); see also *Pennsylvania v. Ritchie*, 480 U.S. 39, 51 (1987) (plurality opinion); *California v. Green*, 399 U.S. 149, 157 (1970); *Snyder v. Massachusetts*, 291 U.S. 97, 106 (1934); *Dowdell v. United States*, 221 U.S. 325, 330 (1911); *Kirby v. United States*, 174 U.S. 47, 55 (1899); *Mattox v. United States*, 156 U.S. 237, 244 (1895). This interpretation derives not only from the literal text of the Clause, but also from our understanding of its historical roots. See *Coy*, supra, at 1015–1016; *Mattox*, supra, at 242 (Confrontation Clause intended to prevent conviction by affidavit); *Green*, supra, at 156 (same); cf. 3 J. Story, Commentaries on the Constitution § 1785, p. 662 (1833).

We have never held, however, that the Confrontation Clause guarantees criminal defendants the absolute right to a face-to-face meeting with witnesses against them at trial. Indeed, in *Coy v. Iowa*, we expressly "le[ft] for another day . . . the question whether any exceptions exist" to the "irreducible literal meaning of the Clause: 'a right to meet face to face all those who appear and give evidence at trial.'" 487 U.S., at 1021 (quoting Green, supra, at 175 (Harlan, J., concurring)). The procedure challenged in *Coy* involved the placement of a screen that prevented two child witnesses in a child abuse case from seeing the defendant as they testified against him at trial. See 487 U.S., at 1014–1015. In holding that the use of this procedure violated the defendant's right to confront witnesses against him, we suggested that any exception to the right "would surely be allowed only when necessary to further an important public policy"—i.e., only upon a showing of something more than the generalized, "legislatively imposed presumption of trauma" underlying the statute at issue in that case. Id., at 1021; see also id., at 1025 (O'CONNOR, J., concurring). We concluded that "[s]ince there ha[d] been no individualized findings that these particular witnesses needed special protection, the judgment [in the case before us] could not be sustained by any conceivable exception." Id., at 1021. Because the trial court in this case made individualized findings that each of the child witnesses needed special protection, this case requires us to decide the question reserved in *Coy*.

The central concern of the Confrontation Clause is to ensure the reliability of the evidence against a criminal defendant by subjecting it to rigorous testing in the context of an adversary proceeding before the trier of fact.

"The primary object of the constitutional provision in question was to prevent depositions or ex parte affidavits, such as were sometimes admitted in civil cases, being used against the prisoner in lieu of a personal examination and cross-examination of the witness in which the accused has an opportunity, not only of testing the recollection and sifting the conscience of the witness, but of compelling him to stand face to face with the jury in order that they may look at him, and judge by his demeanor upon the stand and the manner in which he gives his testimony whether he is worthy of belief." *Mattox*, supra, at 242–243. As this description indicates, the right guaranteed by the Confrontation Clause includes not only a "personal examination," id., at 242, but also "(1) insures that the witness will give his statements under oath—thus impressing him with the seriousness of the matter and guarding against the lie by the possibility of a penalty for perjury; (2) forces the witness to submit to cross-examination, the 'greatest legal engine ever invented for the discovery of truth'; [and] (3) permits the jury that is to decide the defendant's fate to observe the demeanor of the witness in making his statement, thus aiding the jury in assessing his credibility." *Green*, 399 U.S., at 158 (footnote omitted).

The combined effect of these elements of confrontation—physical presence, oath, cross-examination, and observation of demeanor by the trier of fact—serves the purposes of the Confrontation Clause by ensuring that evidence admitted against an accused is reliable and subject to the rigorous adversarial testing that is the norm of Anglo-American criminal proceedings. See *Stincer*, supra, at 739 ("[T]he right to confrontation is a functional one for the purpose of promoting reliability in a criminal trial"); *Dutton v. Evans*, 400 U.S. 74, 89 (1970) (plurality opinion) ("[T]he mission of the Confrontation Clause is to advance a practical concern for the accuracy of the truth-determining process in criminal trials by assuring that 'the trier of fact [has] a satisfactory basis for evaluating the truth of the [testimony]' "; *Lee v. Illinois*, 476 U.S. 530, 540 (1986) (confrontation guarantee serves "symbolic goals" and "promotes reliability"); see also *Faretta v. California*, 422 U.S. 806, 818 (1975) (Sixth Amendment "constitutionalizes the right in an adversary criminal trial to make a defense as we know it"); *Strickland v. Washington*, 466 U.S. 668, 684–685 (1984).

We have recognized, for example, that face-to-face confrontation enhances the accuracy of factfinding by reducing the risk that a witness will wrongfully implicate an innocent person. See *Coy*, supra, at 1019–1020 ("It is always more difficult to tell a lie about a person 'to his face' than 'behind his back.' ... That face-to-face presence may, unfortunately, upset the truthful rape victim or abused child; but by the same token it may confound and undo the false accuser, or reveal the child coached by a malevolent adult"); *Ohio v. Roberts*, 448 U.S. 56, 63, n. 6 (1980); see also 3 W. Blackstone, Commentaries *373–*374. We have also noted the strong symbolic purpose served by requiring adverse witnesses at trial to testify in the accused's presence. See *Coy*, 487 U.S., at 1017 ("[T]here is something deep in human nature that regards face-to-face confrontation between accused and accuser as 'essential to a fair trial in a criminal prosecution'") (quoting *Pointer v. Texas*, 380 U.S. 400, 404 (1965)).

Although face-to-face confrontation forms "the core of the values furthered by the Confrontation Clause," *Green*, 399 U.S., at 157, we have nevertheless recognized that it is not the sine qua non of the confrontation right. See *Delaware v. Fensterer*, 474 U.S. 15, 22 (1985) (per curiam) ("[T]he Confrontation Clause is generally satisfied when the defense is given a full and fair opportunity to probe and expose [testimonial] infirmities [such as forgetfulness, confusion, or evasion] through cross-examination, thereby calling to the attention of the factfinder the reasons for giving scant weight to the witness' testimony"); *Roberts*, supra, at 69 (oath, cross-examination, and demeanor provide "all that the Sixth Amendment demands: 'substantial compliance with the purposes behind the confrontation requirement'") (quoting *Green*, supra, at 166); see also *Stincer*, 482 U.S., at 739–744 (confrontation right not violated by exclusion of defendant from competency hearing of child witnesses, where defendant had opportunity for full and effective cross-examination at trial); *Davis v. Alaska*, 415 U.S. 308, 315–316 (1974); *Douglas v. Alabama*, 380 U.S. 415, 418 (1965); *Pointer*, supra, at 406–407; 5 J. Wigmore, Evidence § 1395, p. 150 (J. Chadbourn rev. 1974).

For this reason, we have never insisted on an actual face-to-face encounter at trial in every instance in which testimony is admitted against a defendant. Instead, we have repeatedly held that the Clause permits, where necessary, the admission of certain hearsay statements against a defendant despite the defendant's inability to confront the declarant at trial. See, e.g., *Mattox*, 156 U.S., at 243 ("[T]here could be nothing more directly contrary to the letter of the provision in question than the admission of dying declarations"); *Pointer*, supra, at 407 (noting exceptions to the confrontation right for dying declarations and "other analogous situations"). In *Mattox*, for example, we held that the testimony of a Government witness at a former trial against the defendant, where the witness was fully cross-examined but had died after the first trial, was admissible in evidence against the defendant at his second trial. See 156 U.S., at 240–244. We explained:

"There is doubtless reason for saying that . . . if notes of [the witness'] testimony are permitted to be read, [the defendant] is deprived of the advantage of that personal presence of the witness before the jury which the law has designed for his protection. But general rules of law of this kind, however beneficent in their operation and valuable to the accused, must occasionally give way to considerations of public policy and the necessities of the case. To say that a criminal, after having once been convicted by the testimony of a certain witness, should go scot free simply because death has closed the mouth of that witness, would be carrying his constitutional protection to an unwarrantable extent. The law in its wisdom declares that the rights of the public shall not be wholly sacrificed in order that an incidental benefit may be preserved to the accused." Id., at 243.

That the face-to-face confrontation requirement is not absolute does not, of course, mean that it may easily be dispensed with. As we suggested in *Coy*, our precedents confirm that a defendant's right to confront accusatory witnesses may be satisfied absent a physical, face-to-face confrontation at trial only where denial of such confrontation is necessary to further an important public policy and only where the reliability of the testimony is otherwise assured. See 487 U.S., at 1021 (citing *Roberts*, supra, at 64; *Chambers*, supra, at 295); *Coy*, supra, at 1025 (O'CONNOR, J., concurring).

III

Maryland's statutory procedure, when invoked, prevents a child witness from seeing the defendant as he or she testifies against the defendant at trial. We find it significant, however, that Maryland's procedure preserves all of the other elements of the confrontation right: The child witness must be competent to testify and must testify under oath; the defendant retains full opportunity for contemporaneous cross-examination; and the judge, jury, and defendant are able to view (albeit by video monitor) the demeanor (and body) of the witness as he or she testifies. Although we are mindful of the many subtle effects face-to-face confrontation may have on an adversary criminal proceeding, the presence of these other elements of confrontation—oath, cross-examination, and observation of the witness' demeanor—adequately ensures that the testimony is both reliable and subject to rigorous adversarial testing in a manner functionally equivalent to that accorded live, in-person testimony. These safeguards of reliability and adversariness render the use of such a procedure a far cry from the undisputed prohibition of the Confrontation Clause: trial by ex parte affidavit or inquisition, see *Mattox*, 156 U.S., at 242; see also *Green*, 399 U.S., at 179 (Harlan, J., concurring) ("[T]he Confrontation Clause was meant to constitutionalize a barrier against flagrant abuses, trials by anonymous accusers, and absentee witnesses"). Rather, we think these elements of effective confrontation not only permit a defendant to "confound and undo the false accuser, or reveal the child coached by a malevolent adult," *Coy*, supra, at 1020, but may well aid a defendant in eliciting favorable testimony from the child witness. Indeed, to the extent the child witness' testimony may be said to be technically given out of court (though we do not so hold), these assurances of reliability and adversariness are far greater than those required for admission of hearsay testimony under the Confrontation Clause. See *Roberts*, 448 U.S., at 66. We are therefore confident that use of the one-way closed circuit television procedure, where necessary to further an important state interest, does not impinge upon the truth-seeking or symbolic purposes of the Confrontation Clause.

The critical inquiry in this case, therefore, is whether use of the procedure is necessary to further an important state interest. The State contends that it has a substantial interest in protecting children who are allegedly victims of child abuse from the trauma of testifying against the alleged perpetrator and that its statutory procedure for receiving testimony from such witnesses is necessary to further that interest.

The Critical Issue

We likewise conclude today that a State's interest in the physical and psychological well-being of child abuse victims may be sufficiently important to outweigh, at least in some cases, a defendant's right to face his or her accusers in court. That a significant majority of States have enacted statutes to protect child witnesses from the trauma of giving testimony in child abuse cases attests to the widespread belief in the importance of such a public policy. See *Coy*, 487 U.S., at 1022–1023 (O'CONNOR, J., concurring) ("Many States have determined that a child victim may suffer trauma from exposure to the harsh atmosphere of the typical courtroom and have undertaken to shield the child through a variety of ameliorative measures"). Thirty-seven States, for example, permit the use of videotaped testimony of sexually abused children; 24 States have authorized the use of one-way closed circuit television testimony in child abuse cases; and 8 States authorize the use of a two-way system in which the child-witness is permitted to see the courtroom and the defendant on a video monitor and in which the jury and judge are permitted to view the child during the testimony.

Their Agreement

The Court of Appeals appears to have rested its conclusion at least in part on the trial court's failure to observe the children's behavior in the defendant's presence and its failure to explore less restrictive alternatives to the use of the one-way closed circuit television procedure. See id., at 568–571, 560 A. 2d, at 1128–1129. **Although we think such evidentiary requirements could strengthen the grounds for use of protective measures, we decline to establish, as a matter of federal constitutional law, any such categorical evidentiary pre-requisites for the use of the one-way television procedure.** The trial court in this case, for example, could well have found, on the basis of the expert testimony before it, that testimony by the child witnesses in the courtroom in the defendant's presence "will result in [each] child suffering serious emotional distress such that the child cannot reasonably communicate," § 9–102(a)(1)(ii). See id., at 568–569, 560 A. 2d, at 1128–1129; see also App. 22–25, 39, 41, 43, 44–45, 54–57. So long as a trial court makes such a case-specific finding of necessity, the Confrontation Clause does not prohibit a State from using a one-way closed circuit television procedure for the receipt of testimony by a child witness in a child abuse case. Because the Court of Appeals held that the trial court had not made the requisite finding of necessity under its interpretation of "the high threshold required by [*Coy*] before § 9–102 may be invoked," 316 Md., at 554–555, 560 A. 2d, at 1121 (footnote omitted), we cannot be certain whether the Court of Appeals would reach the same conclusion in light of the legal standard we establish today.

We therefore **vacate the judgment of the Court of Appeals of Maryland and remand the case for further proceedings not inconsistent with this opinion.**

Decision

It is so ordered.

DISSENT: JUSTICE SCALIA, with whom JUSTICE BRENNAN, JUSTICE MARSHALL, and JUSTICE STEVENS join, dissenting.

Seldom has this Court failed so conspicuously to sustain a categorical guarantee of the Constitution against the tide of prevailing current opinion. The Sixth

Amendment provides, with unmistakable clarity, that "[i]n all criminal prosecutions, the accused shall enjoy the right . . . to be confronted with the witnesses against him." The purpose of enshrining this protection in the Constitution was to assure that none of the many policy interests from time to time pursued by statutory law could overcome a defendant's right to face his or her accusers in court. The Court, however, says:

"We . . . conclude today that a State's interest in the physical and psychological well-being of child abuse victims may be sufficiently important to outweigh, at least in some cases, a defendant's right to face his or her accusers in court. That a significant majority of States have enacted statutes to protect child witnesses from the trauma of giving testimony in child abuse cases attests to the widespread belief in the importance of such a public policy." Ante, at 853.

Because of this subordination of explicit constitutional text to currently favored public policy, the following scene can be played out in an American courtroom for the first time in two centuries: A father whose young daughter has been given over to the exclusive custody of his estranged wife, or a mother whose young son has been taken into custody by the State's child welfare department, is sentenced to prison for sexual abuse on the basis of testimony by a child the parent has not seen or spoken to for many months; and the guilty verdict is rendered without giving the parent so much as the opportunity to sit in the presence of the child, and to ask, personally or through counsel, "it is really not true, is it, that I—your father (or mother) whom you see before you—did these terrible things?" Perhaps that is a procedure today's society desires; perhaps (though I doubt it) it is even a fair procedure; but it is assuredly not a procedure permitted by the Constitution. Because the text of the Sixth Amendment is clear, and because the Constitution is meant to protect against, rather than conform to, current "widespread belief," I respectfully dissent.

I

According to the Court, "we cannot say that [face-to-face] confrontation [with witnesses appearing at trial] is an indispensable element of the Sixth Amendment's guarantee of the right to confront one's accusers." Ante, at 849–850. That is rather like saying "we cannot say that being tried before a jury is an indispensable element of the Sixth Amendment's guarantee of the right to jury trial." The Court makes the impossible plausible by recharacterizing the Confrontation Clause, so that confrontation (redesignated "face-to-face confrontation") becomes only one of many "elements of confrontation." Ante, at 846. The reasoning is as follows: The Confrontation Clause guarantees not only what it explicitly provides for—"face-to-face" confrontation—but also implied and collateral rights such as cross-examination, oath, and observation of demeanor (TRUE); the purpose of this entire cluster of rights is to ensure the reliability of evidence (TRUE); the Maryland procedure preserves the implied and collateral rights (TRUE), which adequately ensure the reliability of evidence (perhaps TRUE); therefore the Confrontation Clause is not violated by denying what it explicitly provides for—"face-to-face" confrontation (unquestionably FALSE). This reasoning abstracts from the right to its purposes, and then eliminates the right. It is wrong because the Confrontation Clause does not guarantee reliable evidence; it guarantees specific trial procedures that were thought to assure reliable evidence, undeniably among which was "face-to-face" confrontation. Whatever else it may mean in addition, the defendant's constitutional right "to be confronted with the witnesses against him" means, always and everywhere, at least what it explicitly says: the " 'right to meet face to face all those who appear and give evidence at trial.' " *Coy v. Iowa*, 487 U.S. 1012, 1016 (1988), quoting *California v. Green*, 399 U.S. 149, 175 (1970) (Harlan, J. concurring).

The Court supports its antitextual conclusion by cobbling together scraps of dicta from various cases that have no bearing here. It will suffice to discuss one of them, since they are all of a kind: Quoting *Ohio v. Roberts*, 448 U.S. 56, 63 (1980), the Court says that "[i]n sum, our precedents establish that 'the Confrontation Clause reflects a preference for face-to-face confrontation at trial,'" ante, at 849 (emphasis added by the Court). But *Roberts*, and all the other "precedents" the Court enlists to prove the implausible, dealt with the implications of the Confrontation Clause, and not its literal, unavoidable text. When *Roberts* said that the Clause merely "reflects a preference for face-to-face confrontation at trial," what it had in mind as the nonpreferred alternative was not (as the Court implies) the appearance of a witness at trial without confronting the defendant. That has been, until today, not merely "nonpreferred" but utterly unheard-of. What *Roberts* had in mind was the receipt of other-than-first-hand testimony from witnesses at trial—that is, witnesses' recounting of hearsay statements by absent parties who, since they did not appear at trial, did not have to endure face-to-face confrontation. Rejecting that, I agree, was merely giving effect to an evident constitutional preference; there are, after all, many exceptions to the Confrontation Clause's hearsay rule. But that the defendant should be confronted by the witnesses who appear at trial is not a preference "reflected" by the Confrontation Clause; it is a constitutional right unqualifiedly guaranteed.

The Court claims that its interpretation of the Confrontation Clause "is consistent with our cases holding that other Sixth Amendment rights must also be interpreted in the context of the necessities of trial and the adversary process." Ante, at 850. I disagree. It is true enough that the "necessities of trial and the adversary process" limit the manner in which Sixth Amendment rights may be exercised, and limit the scope of Sixth Amendment guarantees to the extent that scope is textually indeterminate. Thus: The right to confront is not the right to confront in a manner that disrupts the trial. *Illinois v. Allen*, 397 U.S. 337 (1970). The right "to have compulsory process for obtaining witnesses" is not the right to call witnesses in a manner that violates fair and orderly procedures. *Taylor v. Illinois*, 484 U.S. 400 (1988). The scope of the right "to have the assistance of counsel" does not include consultation with counsel at all times during the trial. *Perry v. Leeke*, 488 U.S. 272 (1989). The scope of the right to cross-examine does not include access to the State's investigative files. *Pennsylvania v. Ritchie*, 480 U.S. 39 (1987). But we are not talking here about denying expansive scope to a Sixth Amendment provision whose scope for the purpose at issue is textually unclear; "to confront" plainly means to encounter face to face, whatever else it may mean in addition. And we are not talking about the manner of arranging that face-to-face encounter, but about whether it shall occur at all. The "necessities of trial and the adversary process" are irrelevant here, since they cannot alter the constitutional text.

II

Much of the Court's opinion consists of applying to this case the mode of analysis we have used in the admission of hearsay evidence. The Sixth Amendment does not literally contain a prohibition upon such evidence, since it guarantees the defendant only the right to confront "the witnesses against him." As applied in the Sixth Amendment's context of a prosecution, the noun "witness"—in 1791 as today—could mean either (a) one "who knows or sees any thing; one personally present" or (b) "one who gives testimony" or who "testifies," i.e., "[i]n judicial proceedings, [one who] make[s] a solemn declaration under oath, for the purpose of establishing or making proof of some fact to a court." 2 N. Webster, An American Dictionary of the English Language (1828). See also J. Buchanan, Linguae Britannicae Vera Pronunciatio (1757). The former meaning (one "who knows or sees") would cover hearsay evidence, but is excluded in the Sixth

Amendment by the words following the noun: "witnesses against him." The phrase obviously refers to those who give testimony against the defendant at trial. We have nonetheless found implicit in the Confrontation Clause some limitation upon hearsay evidence, since otherwise the government could subvert the confrontation right by putting on witnesses who know nothing except what an absent declarant said. And in determining the scope of that implicit limitation, we have focused upon whether the reliability of the hearsay statements (which are not expressly excluded by the Confrontation Clause) "is otherwise assured." Ante, at 850. The same test cannot be applied, however, to permit what is explicitly forbidden by the constitutional text; there is simply no room for interpretation with regard to "the irreducible literal meaning of the Clause." Coy, supra, at 1020–1021.

> **Four elements of confrontation: physical presence of the witness, testifying under oath, cross-examination, and observation of the witness's demeanor by the trier of fact. Closed-circuit TV is functionally equivalent to live testimony.**

Some of the Court's analysis seems to suggest that the children's testimony here was itself hearsay of the sort permissible under our Confrontation Clause cases. See ante, at 851. That cannot be. Our Confrontation Clause conditions for the admission of hearsay have long included a "general requirement of unavailability" of the declarant. Idaho v. Wright, ante, at 815. "In the usual case . . . , the prosecution must either produce, or demonstrate the unavailability of, the declarant whose statement it wishes to use against the defendant." Ohio v. Roberts, 448 U.S., at 65. We have permitted a few exceptions to this general rule— e.g., for co-conspirators' statements, whose effect cannot be replicated by live testimony because they "derive [their] significance from the circumstances in which [they were] made," United States v. Inadi, 475 U.S. 387, 395 (1986). "Live" closed-circuit television testimony, however—if it can be called hearsay at all— is surely an example of hearsay as "a weaker substitute for live testimony," id., at 394, which can be employed only when the genuine article is unavailable. "When two versions of the same evidence are available, longstanding principles of the law of hearsay, applicable as well to Confrontation Clause analysis, favor the better evidence." Ibid. See also Roberts, supra (requiring unavailability as precondition for admission of prior testimony); Barber v. Page, 390 U.S. 719 (1968) (same).

The Court today has applied "interest-balancing" analysis where the text of the Constitution simply does not permit it. We are not free to conduct a cost-benefit analysis of clear and explicit constitutional guarantees, and then to adjust their meaning to comport with our findings. The Court has convincingly proved that the Maryland procedure serves a valid interest, and gives the defendant virtually everything the Confrontation Clause guarantees (everything, that is, except confrontation). I am persuaded, therefore, that the Maryland procedure is virtually constitutional. Since it is not, however, actually constitutional I would affirm the judgment of the Maryland Court of Appeals reversing the judgment of conviction.

NOTES AFTER MARYLAND V. CRAIG

1. Read Coy v. Iowa (1988). The Court has in Craig (1990) taken a shift. Why? What has happened in our society in the two years between these two cases? Nathan and Snedeker (1995) credit the same activists who worked to change the rape laws with working to change laws for children. Eager child-protection advocates and prosecutors romanticize youngsters as being free of the "taint of interest" that biases adults, and they have successfully argued the need to remove children from the courtroom with high-tech assistance or hearsay from others who report what the child said.

2. Frye v. United States, 293 F. 1013, 1014 (D.C. Cir., 1923), stands for the result that an expert's claim about what is scientific is admissible in a court of

law only when other experts in the field agree. It is the rule in most federal and state courts. Thus, it has been applied to many expert witnesses and dozens of new forensic techniques, including the Rape Trauma Syndrome, the profile of a rapist, and use of anatomically correct dolls. But the long-standing requirement that scientific evidence meet minimal standards before experts may present it to the jury has often been ignored in ritual-abuse prosecutions (Nathan and Snedeker 1995, 211). Do you think *Frye* has any bearing on this case? (In the "wink test," a doctor would touch the person's anus with a cotton swab to see how large it would open or how much it would "wink." Could that just be a reflex action? What would Drs. Masters and Johnson say?)

3. Again, it is important to see the other interest groups who supported the outcome of this case. One organization that systematically targets skeptical experts has been the National District Attorneys Association (NDAA), which established its National Center for Prosecution of Child Abuse (NCPCA) in 1985. In its first year of operations, the NCPCA received some $646,000 from the Justice Department and $109,000 from the National Center for Child Abuse and Neglect. By 1988, the Justice Department had paid nearly $2 million and by 1991, almost double that (Nathan and Snedeker 1995, 235).

   So, that means the scales of justice are tipped toward the prosecutor with model statutes concerning hearsay exceptions, videotaped testimony, closed-circuit television testimony, and the competency question. To defend someone on a false charge may, indeed, be both costly and socially unacceptable.

4. The criminal law requires sacrifice of property, honor, and pride as well as acceptance of nonserious personal injury before it will tolerate the sacrifice of human life. In *State v. Schroeder*, 199 Neb. 822, 261 N. W.2d 759 (1978) the court's decision reflects the law's heavy presumption against resort to deadly force. Schroeder and a much bigger convict were locked in a cell. The bigger one told Schroeder that in the morning he was going to rape Schroeder. Schroeder, fearing for his life, during the night, stabbed the sleeping cellmate. The Court held that there was no need to instruct the jury on self-defense because the threat of harm was not imminent threat. Since people argue that women should leave home before thinking of killing their abusive husbands, courts have been reluctant to permit a self-defense argument for adults let alone children. Under what conditions and for what ages do you think that a child might have a successful self-defense argument for killing? A parent? A playmate? A stranger?

5. A woman who lost control of her car while driving drunk with five children as passengers pleaded guilty to driving under the influence of alcohol and five counts of child abuse and neglect (Associated Press, *Richmond Times Dispatch*, August 8, 1997, p. B3). Do you think the court erred in the counts of child abuse and neglect?

6. Many of the mass child-molestation cases of the 1980s have fallen apart. Prosecutors dropped all charges in 1997 against the last two defendants in the Little Rascals case. Among the others are the McMartin preschool case in California, the Margaret Kelly Michaels case in new Jersey, and the Fells Acres case in Massachusetts (Associated Press, *Richmond Times Dispatch*, May 24, 1997, p. A9). Nationwide, some experts have raised questions about the truthfulness of testimony from children who were under pressure to talk from parents, psychiatrists, and prosecutors at a

time when fears of abuse were sweeping the country and parents were hysterical. If you were able to make laws, what kinds of laws would you create to help protect the younger children and the rights of those who were accused? Would you, for example, permit children to bring tort claims, when they got older, against those who really did violate them? Who should pay for the psychological treatment for the children and the parents?

7. The Children Against Sexual Exploitation Act of 1977 requires that the defendant know that one of the performers is a minor. See *United States v. X-citement Video, Inc., et al.*, 513 U.S. 64, 115 S.Ct. 464 (1994). It would be reasonable to have a law that has the "knowing requirement to the pornographic nature of materials." Do you think it is reasonable that the prosecutor, in order to convict, must prove that the defendant knew with certainty (knowing) that one of the performers was a minor?

8. In a study done in Wisconsin with male juvenile offenders ages 12 to 19, there were no statistically significant differences between those who perpetrated sexual assaults against children and those who perpetrated them against those their own age or older. At the Ethan Allen School where the study was done by Hagan and Cho (1996), most adolescent sex offenders did not reoffend with sexual offenses but a significant number were convicted of other offenses.

✳ BRAIN EXERCISE

You have a complaint that a mother has been beating her 7-month-old child. When the child was 2 months old, he was admitted to the hospital for pneumonia, but full-body X-rays revealed previous fractures of the upper arm, shoulder blade, and shoulder socket. The child was released to the mother. Less than two months later, the next injury required a full body cast. Again the child was released to the mother. Now you want to see the child, and the mother refuses to produce the child. You go to court and ask the court to order her to show cause why she should not be held in contempt for failure to produce the child. She still refuses. What do you do and why? (See *Baltimore City Department of Social Services v. Bouknight*, 110 S. Ct. 900 [1990].)

You are the judge. In this case Jason, a 19-year-old virgin, was seduced by a 14-year-old foster child in the same home. Jason was sentenced to jail for rape. He and his family seek damages from the program placing the child with the family. What would you do? In *Feltner v. The Casey Family Program*, 902 P.2d 206 (1995), the Wyoming court dismissed the case.

SUMMARY

This chapter dealt with the difficulties in ascertaining the number of crimes against children and the prosecution of those crimes. It was shown that because statistics are often unreported or hidden in other categories of crimes, national estimates of violence toward children come from investigatory bodies such as juvenile courts, coroners, and law enforcement agencies, as well as health, education, and welfare organizations and others who have contact with children. Violence and other crimes against children are usually committed in private places by parents and others who reside in the household but are not related by marriage or blood.

The chapter discussed specific kinds of sexual crimes against children such as carnal knowledge, crimes against nature, forced sodomy, and indecent liberties. Child pornography was discussed in terms of types, perpetrators, victims, and challenges. Other crimes against children were mentioned as well as programs to deal with children's deaths—child fatality review teams.

With respect to evidentiary problems, the chapter discussed the problems associated with successful prosecution in child physical and sexual abuse cases, such as the competency of children to testify and issues of physical evidence. Competency means that a judge determines, on a case-by-case basis, whether a child is able to distinguish truth from falsehood and has an understanding of what an oath to tell the truth is. There is no specific age at which a child is considered incompetent to testify. Even though that may be the general rule, as the chapter pointed out, there are other factors that impact on a child's ability to testify, such as (1) age, (2) cross-examination, (3) unavailable, (4) hearsay, and (5) identity of the perpetrator. Physical evidence was discussed as being important, but often lacking, for corroboration.

Other issues that impact a criminal prosecution dealing with child witnesses are the emotional effects of testifying caused by the stress of being in the courtroom and the legal procedures. In terms of the argument that children are emotionally harmed by testifying, professionals will have to continue to make judgments on a per-case basis because the research results are mixed.

Regarding false memory syndrome and Post-Traumatic Stress Disorder, most studies do not support the contention that the majority of disclosures are fabricated. In fact, research shows that disclosure is complicated by multiple issues of developmental stages, family dynamics, physical maturity, cognitive skills, and so forth. False reports do happen in any crime, and special care has to be taken with these abuse cases as well.

Tort action was discussed as a way for victims/survivors to recover damages. The cited case showed how a victim turned the pain toward herself and consequently suffered severe depression.

On the other hand, some children turn the pain to others. To explain the cycle of abuse and prevention, the chapter discussed juvenile sex offenders and children who kill. Family reunification was discussed, and it was pointed out that this goal is *not* unanimously supported by leading national authorities.

The case *Maryland v. Craig* closed the chapter. It was a recent U.S. Supreme Court case in which the Court tried to balance the right of the accused to confront the child witness fact-to-face, while at the same time providing some safeguards for the vulnerability of the child.

REFERENCES

Abel, G.G., M.S. Mihelman, and J.B. Becker. "Sex Offenders: Results of Assessment and Recommendations for Treatment." In *Clinical Criminology: Current Concepts*, edited by H. Ben-Aaron, S. Hacker, and C. Webster. Toronto: M&M Graphics, 1985.

Bass, Ellen, and Laura Davis. *The Courage to Heal: A Guide for Women Survivors of Child Sexual Abuse*. New York: Harper-Collins, 1988.

Baum, Lawrence. *American Courts*, 3d ed. Boston: Houghton Mifflin Company, 1994.

Beranbaum, Tina M., et al. "Child Pornography in the 1970's." In *Child Pornography and Sex Rings*, edited by A. Burgess with M. Clark. Lexington, MA: Lexington Books, 1984.

Bower, B. "Child Sex Abuse Leaves Mark on Brain." *Science News* 147 (22)(1995): 340.

Burgess, Ann W., A.N. Groth, L. Holmstrong, and S. Sgroi. *Sexual Assault of Children and Adolescents*. Lexington, MA: D.C. Health and Company, 1978.

Ceci, Stephen J., and Maggie Bruck. *Jeopardy in the Courtroom: A Scientific Analysis of Children's Testimony*. Washington, D.C.: American Psychological Association, 1995.

Cole, C.B., and E. Loftus. "The Memory of Children." In *Children's Eyewitness Memory*, edited by S.J. Ceci, et al. New York: Springer-Verlag, 1987.

Cullen, Robert. *The Killer Department*. New York: Pantheon Books, 1993.

Densen-Gerber, Julianne, and Stephen F. Hutchinson. "Sexual and Commercial Exploitation of Children: Legislative Responses and Treatment Challenges." *Child Abuse and Neglect* 3 (1)(1979): 61–66.

Ehrlich, Paul. "Asia's Shocking Secret." *Reader's Digest* October (1993): 69–74.

Forward, Susan, and Craig Buck. *Betrayal of Innocence: Incest and Its Devastation*. CA: J.P. Farger, 1978.

Freeman, Kenneth R., and Terry Estrada-Mullaney. "Using Dolls to Interview Child Victims: Legal Concerns and Interview Procedures," *NIJ Reports* 207 (1988): 2–6.

Freeman-Longo, R.E. "Juvenile Sex Offenders in the History of Adult Rapists and Child Molesters." *International Journal of Offender Therapy and Comparative Criminology* 27 (2)(1983): 150–155.

Freyd, J. "Theoretical and Personal Perspectives on the Delayed Memory Debate." Paper presented at the Continuing Education Conference: Controversies around Recovered Memories of Incest and Ritualistic Abuse. Ann Arbor, MI, Aug. 7, 1993.

Goodman, Gail. "Children's Testimony in Historical Perspective." *Journal of Social Issues* 40 (2)(1984a): 9–31.

Goodman, Gail. "The Child Witness." *Journal of Social Issues* 40 (2)(1984b): 157–175.

Gray, Ellen. *Child Abuse: Prelude to Delinquency?* Washington, D.C.: U.S. Dept. of Justice, 1986.

Groth, N. *Men Who Rape: The Psychology of the Offender*. New York: Plenum Press, 1977.

Hagan, Michael P., and Meg E. Cho. "A Comparison of Treatment Outcomes Between Adolescent Rapists and Child Sexual Offenders." *International Journal of Offender Therapy and Comparative Criminology* 40 (2) (1996): 113–122.

Hickey, Eric W. *Serial Murderers and Their Victims*. Pacific Grove, CA: Brooks/Cole Publishing Co., 1991.

Holmes, Ronald M. *The Sex Offender and the Criminal Justice System*. Springfield, IL: Charles C. Thomas, 1983.

Huchton, Laura M. *Protect Your Child: A Parent's Safeguard Against Child Abduction and Sexual Abuse*. Englewood Cliffs, NJ: Prentice Hall, 1985.

Hunt, Patricia, and Margaret Baird. "Children of Sex Rings." *Child Welfare* 69 (1990): 195–206.

Justice, Blair, and Rita Justice. *The Broken Taboo: Sex in the Family*. New York: Human Sciences Press, 1979.

Knopp, F.H. *Remedial Intervention in Adolescent Sex Offenses: Nine Program Descriptions*. VT: Safer Society Press, 1982.

Lanning, K., and Ann Burgess. "Child Pornography and Sex Rings." In *Pornography*, edited by Dolf Zillmann and Jennings Bryant. Hillsdale, NJ: Lawrence Erlbaum Associates, Publishers, 1989.

Larson, Neal, and Sally Maison. *Psychosexual Treatment Program for Female Sex Offenders*. St. Paul, MN: META Resources, 1987.

Lepore, Stephen J. "Child Witness: Cognitive and Social Factors Related to Memory and Testimony." *Issues in Child Abuse Accusations* 3 (2) (1991): 65–69.

Lepore, Stephen J., and Barbara Sesco. "Distorting Children's Reports and Interpretations of Events through Suggestion." *Journal of Applied Psychology* 79 (1) (1994): 108–120.

Lofthus, E., and G.M. Davies. "Distortions in the Memory of Children." *Journal of Social Issues* 40 (2)(1984): 57–67.

Mathews, Ruth, Jane Kinder Matthews, and Kathleen Speltz. *Female Sexual Offenders: An Exploratory Study*. Orwell, VT: The Safer Society Press, 1989.

Mitchell, J. "Memories of a Disputed Past." *Sunday Oregonian*, 8 Aug. 1993, p. L1.

Mones, Paul. *When a Child Kills*. New York: Simon and Schuster, 1991.

Nathan, Debbie, and Michael Snedeker. *Satan's Silence: Ritual Abuse and the Making of a Modern American Witch Hunt*. New York: Basic Books, 1995.

National Center for Prosecution of Child Abuse. *Update*. June, July, August, September (1992), January (1995).

Poulos, Tammy M., and Lynette B. Greenfield. *Convicted Sex Offenders*. Richmond, VA: Criminal Justice Research Center, Department of Criminal Justice Services, 1994.

Reiss, Albert J., and Jeffrey A. Roth, editors. *Understanding and Preventing Violence*. Washington, D.C.: National Academy Press, 1993.

Ryan, G., and S. Lang, editors. *Juvenile Sexual Offending: Causes, Consequences and Correction*. Denver, CO: Kempe Center, 1991.

Sagatun, Inger J., and Leonard R. Edwards. *Child Abuse and the Legal System*. Chicago: Nelson-Hall Publishers, 1995.

Sapp, Allen D., and Stephen F. Kappeler. "A Descriptive Study of Child Molestation: Victim and Offender Characteristics." *Journal of Police and Criminal Psychology*, 9 (1) (1993): 56–62.

Schulhofer, Stephen J. "The Gender Question in Criminal Law." In Jeffrie G. Murphy, *Punishment and Rehabilitation*, 3d ed. Belmont, CA: Wadsworth Publishing Company, 1995.

Silbert, Mimi Halper. "The Effects on Juveniles of Being Used for Pornography and Prostitution." In *Pornography*, edited by Dolf Zillmann and Jennings Bryant. Hillsdale, NJ: Lawrence Erlbaum Assoc., Publishers, 1989.

Simons, Ronald L., and Les B. Whitbeck. "Sexual Abuse as a Precursor to Prostitution and Victimization Among Adolescent and Adult Homeless Women." *Journal of Family Issues* 12 (3)(1991): 361–379.

Tracy, Sharon, and Randell G. Shelden. "The Violent Female Juvenile Offender: An Ignored Minority within the Juvenile Justice System." *Juvenile & Family Court Journal* 43 (3)(1992): 33–39.

Virginia Child Protection Newsletter. "Court Appointed Special Advocates." VCPN 35 (1991): 1–16.

Voelm, Clint, and Barbara Schwartz. "Signs and Symptoms of Post-Traumatic Stress Disorder in Children." *Journal of Police and Criminal Psychology* 10 (1)(1994): 14–21.

Walker, Lenore E. *The Battered Women*. New York: Harper & Row, 1979.

Weiss, Edward H. "Incest Accusation: Assessing Credibility." *Journal of Psychiatry and Law* 2 (1983): 311.

Whitcomb, Debra. *When the Victim Is a Child*, 2d ed. Washington, D.C.: National Institute of Justice, 1992.

Whitcomb, Debra, Gail S. Goodman, Desmond K. Runyan, and Shirley Hoak. "The Emotional Effects of Testifying on Sexually Abused Children." *National Institute of Justice, Research in Brief*. Washington, D.C.: U.S. Dept. of Justice, April 1994.

Widon, Cathy S. *Victims of Childhood Sexual Abuse—Later Criminal Consequences. Research in Brief*. Washington, D.C.: National Institute of Justice, 1995.

CHAPTER 7

Other Hearings in Juvenile Court:

Child Custody, Support, and

Termination of Parental Rights

The juvenile court hears cases dealing with issues other than delinquency and abuse. There are other hearings affecting the lives of children. Those hearings are important for our consideration for several reasons. First, if you are employed by the juvenile court, you will need to have some understanding of the meaning of those hearings.

Second, domestic cases are on the increase as well as juvenile cases. In a five-year study from 1987 through 1991, a juvenile and domestic relations court in Richmond, Virginia, showed major increases in delinquency and other juvenile matters such as custody and status offenses. Domestic cases included misdemeanors, felonies, and civil and criminal support. Numerically, the history is told in Table 7.1.

Third, the other areas discussed in this chapter are intricately linked to some of the other topics discussed. For example, custody and termination of parental rights may be part of the process for parents who abuse their children. Although we often associate custody hearings with divorce, the reality is that a custody hearing can be for several reasons, including child abuse. In addition, in many divorce cases dealing with custody, accusations of sexual abuse arise that circle back into investigations by child protective services. In some states, there is a movement to put into law a rebuttable assumption that a person who maliciously makes a false allegation of child abuse with the intent to influence a judicial determination of custody is not a proper person to be awarded custody! Likewise, questions of paternity sometimes arise when parents are divorcing, when children are being placed for adoption, and when the state is attempting to get support for children in poverty.

In some states, child custody and visitation matters involve a fundamental right (*Hall v. Hall*, 708 P.2d 416, Wyo. 1985). The association with one's family is a higher state constitutional right than it is in the United States Constitution.

INTRODUCTION

Table 7.1 TOTAL DELINQUENCY HEARINGS AND DOMESTIC COURT HEARINGS

Year	Total Delinquency	Total Juvenile	Total Domestic	Total Court Hearings
1987	5,177	11,527	8,446	19,973
1988	5,818	12,244	9,146	21,390
1989	5,550	12,479	10,324	22,803
1990	6,692	14,031	11,188	26,194
1991	7,669	15,620	10,713	26,333

Last, many states are moving to family courts because they are viewed by those who use the courts (consumers) as "user friendly." Mediation is used to resolve such difficult impasses as support and custody. There is less need for lawyers so there is more money for the other expenses of living. In addition, consumers say it is quicker to get on the docket, and that is important for child support issues. Most importantly, as this book points out as one of its themes, the delinquency of a child is often related to the parents arguing over custody. So, by going to family court, all of the issues, including delinquency, custody, and divorce, can be heard by one judge at one time.

The purpose of this chapter is to discuss some of the criteria used to determine child custody and some variations on the theme called joint custody. It is in these custody hearings that many real and false charges of sexual abuse are raised. Some of the other special problems that our modern society has produced will be discussed. Attention also will be given to the **Federal Parental Kidnapping Prevention Act (PKPA)**. This was and is an attempt by the federal government to reduce the number of kidnappings of children by a parent who is in disagreement with the custody orders or the other parent. To handle some of those problems of custody and support, the **Uniform Child Custody Jurisdiction Act (UCCJA)** and the **Uniform Interstate Family Support Act** were developed. Although custody and support are separate issues, they may all be part of the hearing to end parental rights, which also is called "termination of parental rights." Termination of parental rights is the last step in the process on abused and neglected children, as discussed in Chapter 5, "Child Abuse and Neglect." Therefore, the chapter will end with a discussion of the termination of residual parental rights.

CUSTODY

Introduction and General Rules

The question of who gets the physical custody of a child is an age-old question. King Solomon of biblical times had a situation in which two women each gave birth to a child. During the night, however, one of the babies died and each woman wanted to claim the surviving child as hers. They came before the King and asked him to decide. He decided to divide the child in half so that each person could have half. The real mother, wanting the child to live, told the King not to kill the child. She would permit the other women to have the child. The King reasoned that the woman who was willing to let the child live was the real mother, and that she should have custody of the child.

Figure 7.1
Used with permission of Bob Gorrell, *The Richmond Times-Dispatch.*

"WHAT'S ALL THIS ABOUT THE BREAK-UP OF THE *AMERICAN FAMILY* ? . . . MY FOLKS ARE *ALWAYS* THERE FOR ME WHEN I FAX MOM AT WORK OR SEE DAD ON VISITATION DAYS!"

There are many judges today who wish they had the wisdom of Solomon. Two people, like a husband and wife, may both have legal rights as parents. Yet in a divorce suit, because there is only one child, the physical placement of the child can be with only one parent at a time. The judge has to decide.

In general, there are three parties to a dispute in the custody of the child: (1) the state, (2) the child, and (3) the disputing parties. Often, people think first of the disputing parties. Yet the state, under **parens patriae**, has paramount concern for the child.

The state, therefore, has developed laws and procedures for child custody. Besides issues of separation and divorce, child custody also involves temporary placements, like foster homes, for children who are being abused, or for situations in which parents need services before they can be reunited with their children. If reunification is not possible, then the children may need permanent placement called "adoption," which is done only after parental rights have been terminated.

Generally speaking, the child is the possession of the biological parent. The baby belongs to the biological mother who gave birth to the child. The parents of unwed minor children are their natural guardians, and upon the death of either parent, the survivor is the natural guardian of the child.

Centuries of child abuse have taught us that not all biological parents emotionally bond with their children so that they are protected and reared into healthy adults. Yet the general rule is that the biological parents have rights over anyone else such as a grandparent or a person called a "good friend."

Biological Parent

The general rule is that custody will go to one or the other of the two biological parents. The state looks to both of the biological parents to rear a child and financially provide for the child. If neither parent can financially provide for the child, the state will lend assistance through such government programs as Aid to Families with Dependent Children (AFDC). The parent(s) then rear(s) the child in the home with financial assistance from the state rather than putting the child into a foster home or an institution.

When the court must determine custody, it is usually between the two parents. For example, *In Interest of A.D.*, 489 N.W.2d 50 (Iowa App. June 1992), the Iowa court upheld a lower court order that placed the custody of the children with the biological father. It noted that the biological mother had made considerable progress through her substance-abuse treatment, but although she showed substantial insight into eliminating her substance-abuse problem, the court needed only to find that the father was superior.

In *Griffith v. Brooks*, 383 S.E.2d 246 (1989), the Georgia Court of Appeals held that clear and convincing evidence did not support termination of a father's right to his child. His wife, who had remarried, wanted the child adopted by her new husband. She argued that the child's father, because he was serving time for rape and aggravated sodomy, had abandoned the child. The court said that adoption laws strictly favor the rights of the natural parent.

What happens when there are no biological parents? After the Civil War and before the government developed AFDC, many children were orphaned. States then developed orphanages to rear these homeless and parentless children. From the hard lessons learned by watching children mature physically but not emotionally, we now understand the need of children to be reared by what is called a "psychological parent," and have the goal to develop the least detrimental alternatives for placement (Goldstein, Freud, and Solnit 1979).

Psychological Parent

Psychological parents are those persons who develop an emotional tie to the child because they meet its (the child's) daily needs through feeding, cleaning, and interacting with the child. (See the discussion of the psychological parent under "Placing Children Outside Home" in Chapter 2, "The Definition of Juvenile Delinquency, Status Offenses, Abuse, and Developmental Stages.")

Sometimes parent(s) have difficulties and voluntarily relinquish custody of a child, usually to his or her parent(s), the child's grandparent(s). In *In re Anthony C.*, 614 A.2d 365 (R.I. Sup. Sept. 1992), the Rhode Island Supreme Court said it was not necessary to prove a **change of circumstances**, indicating that a return of custody of the child to the mother is in the child's best interest. In that case it was only necessary that the parent show that the circumstances, which originally led to voluntary relinquishment, had changed. The mother had been 16 years of age when she placed the child in temporary custody, but she was now 21 years of age, held a job, and lived in a two-bedroom apartment. **As the biological parent, she had superior rights, and the "psychological parent" was not argued.**

List of Preferences

Oklahoma, under Section 21.1 of O.S. 10, has by statute listed the following custody preferences according to the best interest of the child: (1) a parent; (2) a grandparent; (3) a person indicated by the wishes of a deceased parent; (4) a relative of either parent; (5) the person in whose house the child had been living in a wholesome and stable environment; or (6) any other person deemed appropriate and suitable by the court. What happens when there is a contest between the mother and the grandmother? What happens when the child has become psychologically attached to the grandparent?

One of the early classical cases was *Painter v. Bannister*, 258 Iowa 1390 (1996). It showed that the grandparents had become the psychological parent. The grandparents had done all the necessary life-maintaining functions for such a long time that the child had grown to think of the grandparents as the "mother" and "father." Even though the grandparents won their case in court, in the end, they permitted the child to return to live with the father and his new wife.

Biological parents enjoy a paramount right to custody. The mere fact that someone outside the immediate family relationship might be able to provide greater or better financial care or assistance is insufficient to justify a grant of custody to that individual. (See *Uhing On Behalf of Jones v. Uhing*, 488 N.W.2d 366 [Neb. Sup. Aug. 1992].)

Courts generally agree that parents have a preferred status when compared to nonparents, but only at the initial custody hearing. Once the child has been placed with someone else, the parent has the burden of proving, by clear and convincing evidence, that any psychological harm to the child likely to result in a change in environment would be substantially outweighed by certain advantages to the child. The court has to take into consideration the age of the child and the length of the child's placement with nonparents.

Custody decisions are usually required when parents separate or divorce (*Jacobson v. Jacobson*, 314 N.W.2d 78, 1981), when a child has been entrusted to someone else with or without judicial approval (*Painter v. Bannister*), or when there has been some major change like severe sickness or accident that causes the court to intervene in light of the current circumstances. Custody decisions can also be a part of abuse and neglect cases. Please remember that a custody order as a disposition in a neglect or abuse case does not terminate parental rights. Such orders of custody are subject to periodic review hearings.

> Abuse and neglect does not mean termination of parental rights.

Test of Best Interest

Custody decisions are made at a hearing in which both sides provide testimony or expert witnesses to support a claim that one parent would be a better parent. The legal test that is used to determine child custody is called the "best interest of the child." This is a vague concept that is not clearly defined and seems to have meant different things throughout history.

At the turn of the century, the "best interest of the child" meant that the custody of a child in a separation or divorce dispute went to the father. Later, preference went to the mother under a legal theory called the "tender years doctrine."

Tender Years Doctrine

Under the "tender years doctrine," a mother of a young child was given custodial preference if other factors were equal. If both the father and mother were equal in age, physical health, and their desire to rear the child, the mother would be preferred because of the young age of the child. However, it was never determined what nurturing factors women had that men could not learn. In addition, what do tender years mean? What age is that? Are tender years 5 years? Are tender years 1 year? Are tender years 14 years?

Needless to say, some jurisdictions have abolished this doctrine as sexually discriminatory. In its place the modern statutes permit the court, in determining custody and visitation of minor children, to consider the following:

1. age and physical and mental condition of the child(ren);

2. age and physical and mental condition of each parent;

3. relationship existing between each parent and each child;

4. role that each parent has played, and will play in the future, in the upbringing and care of the child(ren); and

5. other factors as are necessary to consider the best interests of the child(ren).

Lawyers representing clients in a custody dispute look at many variables. Appendix 7A: Client Survey reveals the complexity of these cases and the evidence that has to be submitted to the court for this decision to be made. Today, many states award custody of a child with primary consideration to the welfare of the child without any presumption or inference in favor of either parent or race when deciding cases in which the parents are of different races (*Palmore v. Sidoti*, 466 U.S. 429, 104 S.Ct. 1879, 80 L.Ed. 2d 421, 1984). However, courts do not favor the parent who kills the other parent and has been convicted of first-degree murder. See *Viola v. Randolph*, 356 S.E. 2d 464 (W. Va. 1987). Today, a vast majority of states have enacted statutes that make domestic violence a relevant factor in custody decisions (Zorza 1994).

If the decision is between two fit biological parents, then the decision becomes more difficult. Sometimes there is something in one of the parent's lifestyle that causes concern, such as living in an adulterous relationship (regardless of the sexual preference). In some states, such a situation can render a parent unfit if the circumstances are seen as having an adverse impact upon the child(ren). In other words, the parent still maintains legal rights to the child(ren), but the parent is not the full-time custodial parent—bringing up the child(ren) in a home where such activity takes place. The evidence of adultery on the part of a parent is an insufficient basis to find that parent an unfit custodian. It is the child's exposure to the immoral behavior, rather than the mere existence of that behavior, that matters.

In *Roe v. Roe*, 228 Va. 722 (1985), the court applied the adverse impact theory in shifting custody of a 9-year-old daughter from her father to her mother because of the father's active and open homosexual relationship in the same residence as the child. One might interpret these cases as saying that it is not so important what goes on in the bedroom as long as it is behind the closed bedroom door.

Because the court is concerned with the "best interest of the child," the court can look to other factors for determining custody. As mentioned earlier, the combination of the child's wishes and a psychologist's testimony that transferring custody from someone who has become a psychological parent could have a long-term harmful impact on the child, are valid factors.

Thus, courts look to the relative competency of both parents, not to gender alone.

Child's Desires

Every state has a specific age at which the child is considered to have the "age of discretion." As a result, in a custody dispute or termination of parental rights, the child may give input as part of the child's pursuit of happiness and right to life—due process under our constitutional rights. The child's wishes may be made known to the court, but his or her consideration is not the controlling factor. For a case in point, read *Deahl v. Winchester Department of Social Services*, 299 S.E. 2d 863 (1983).

For example, in Wyoming, the preference of a child is considered along with the following factors:

1. the age of the child;

2. the reason for the preference;

3. the relative fitness of the preferred and nonpreferred parents;

4. the hostility, if any, of the child to the nonpreferred parent;

5. the preference of other siblings; and

6. whether the child's preference has been tainted or influenced by one parent against the other (*Yates v. Yates*, 702 P.2d 1252, 1985).

Rights of Custodial Parent

What rights does a custodial parent have? Can the parent move the children to another state?

In *Carpenter v. Carpenter*, 220 Va. 299, 1979, the Virginia Supreme Court upheld the chancellor's (the judge in the lower court) decree enjoining a custodial mother from removing the children from Virginia without the court's prior approval. The mother wanted to move to New York City to be closer to her relatives and seek better employment opportunities. She argued that she was not able to meet her household expenses in Virginia without help from her mother. Her increased earnings as a chemist in New York would enable her to provide her children with a "measurably enhanced" life. She also argued that both of the children were gifted and that New York would provide them with "a more stimulating environment" in which to develop.

The Virginia court was concerned about affording the father continuing visitation rights. In addition, the children apparently were well adjusted in the location where they had resided since their birth. The judges said that the cultural and educational advantages in New York City were not significantly greater than the cultural, educational, and recreational advantages in Tidewater, Virginia.

Later, the Virginia Supreme Court held that *Carpenter* does not preclude a judge from permitting children to be removed from Virginia by the custodial spouse, but it must be determined that removal is in the children's best interest (*Gray v. Gray*, 228 Va. 696, 1985).

In divorce cases, one parent gets custody of the child and the other parent sometimes disagrees with the judge's decision. Sometimes the action of the court makes it difficult for a noncustodial parent to sit and do nothing as was the situation in the DeShaney case. Remember, in *DeShaney v. Winnebago County Department of Social Services*, 489 U.S. 189, 103 L.Ed.2d 249, 109 S.Ct. 998 (1989), the United States Supreme Court affirmed the Court of Appeals decision stating that DeShaney's constitutional rights were not violated. DeShaney was a child who was subjected to a series of beatings by his father. The county department of social services received complaints and took various steps to protect him. Yet they left him in the custody of his father, who eventually beat him so severely that he suffered permanent brain damage and was rendered profoundly retarded.

It is not uncommon for parental abductions to involve allegations of child abuse, including sexual abuse (Forst and Blomquist 1991). Some parents take action to protect their child because taking one's own child is not considered kidnapping in common law. To handle those individuals who do not like the court's decision and take their own children to other states, the federal government stepped in to assist with this problem: hence the Federal Parental Kidnapping Prevention Act (PKPA).

Federal Parental Kidnapping Prevention Act

In December of 1980 President Carter signed the Federal Parental Kidnapping Prevention Act (PKPA). Family abductions are done by a parent or relative. The motives vary from genuine concern for the child to revenge directed against the legal guardian. The children are, unfortunately, used as psychological weapons against the parent who has the custody. As society has become more mobile, the problems of family abduction have also increased. Children who are victims of family abduction may be told that the other parent does not love them or that the parent has died. Because the child is not permitted contact with those left behind, the child suffers feelings of guilt and isolation. The children sometimes have their names changed and their identities altered. One young child was discovered when he wrote his name on his papers at school. He forgot the new name he was supposed to use, and instead he wrote another name not listed on the school records.

The PKPA states that it is the intent of Congress that the Fugitive Felon Act (18 U.S.C. § 1073) apply "to cases involving parental kidnapping and interstate or international flight to avoid prosecution under applicable state felony statutes."

The act also requires that full faith and credit be extended to custody determinations of other jurisdictions. In some states, abduction or kidnapping (the terms are considered synonymous) by a parent of his or her child is a felony and can also be punishable as contempt of court.

Obstacles to the Law

In 1988 Congress directed the Office of Juvenile Justice and Delinquency Prevention (OJJDP) to conduct a study to identify legal, policy, procedural, and practical obstacles to the location, recovery, and return of children abducted by parents. The OJJDP was also asked to recommend ways to overcome or reduce these obstacles. The American Bar Association (ABA) administered the study and reported that laws are not working properly.

Those obstacles fell into three broad categories: unfamiliarity, noncompliance, and inconsistency and ambiguity. Unfamiliarity was documented by a national survey of judges who reported that in 60 percent of the cases in which counsel should have raised PKPA, it was not raised. Inconsistency means that federal and state laws lack uniformity. In addition, statutes vary from state to state. "The lack of clarity and specificity regarding law enforcement's role in enforcing child custody orders has led to a growing concern over civil liability suits" (Girdner 1993, 21).

Other Studies

Barrett and Sagatun (1990), in studying the case histories of forty-three families from 1983 to 1987, determined that child abduction has a devastating effect on the family and, most importantly, on the child. Yet cases are complex with legal, psychological, and social issues. Their research showed that an equal number of precustodial and postcustodial incidents occurred that it is hard to tell which ones do more damage. More children were taken by mothers than fathers. The psychological and social profile of the parent was one in which power struggle with revenge constituted a stronger motive than affection for the child.

Domestic Kidnapping

Finkelhor, Hotaling, and Sedlak (1990), in their final report on missing children, looked specifically at family abduction on a national level. They concluded that most abductions were perpetrated by men: noncustodial fathers and father figures. Most victims were ages 2 to 11, with slightly more at the younger ages. They also suggest that in half of the episodes, the custodial parent knew where the children were but just did not know how to get the child returned to proper custody. The regional disparities, with the South overrepresented, suggest that "the more traditional legal system in the South makes noncustodial fathers pessimistic about getting a favorable outcome, so that they take matters into their own hands" (Finkelhor et al. 1990, 8).

International Kidnapping

Janvier, McCormick, and Donaldson (1990) studied domestic and international kidnapping and found that male parents (81 percent) were more likely to be the perpetrator in international kidnapping. Domestic kidnapping is more likely to be perpetrated by a female parent (61 percent). A child under the age of 11 is more likely to be kidnapped after the divorce in a domestic case and before the divorce in an international case. Boy children are preferred victims in international kidnappings. Inconsistencies of state laws, fear for the child's safety, and the lack of funds to continue the search for the child are common problems for left-behind parents of domestic and international cases.

The most important point of the research of Janvier, McCormick, and Donaldson is that domestic and international kidnapping are very different. Both have different variables and factors, but each could benefit from stricter enforcement of the laws in place and the creation of new custody protection laws.

In February 1992, the National Center for Prosecution of Child Abuse also became concerned about family violence and parental abduction. They believed that there was strong evidence of connections among parental abduction, child abuse, and domestic violence. The estimated number was over 345,000 children abducted every year. An estimated 2 to 33 percent of parental abduction cases involved allegations of child abuse, but an even greater percentage reportedly involved a violent relationship between the parents. "Three-quarters of abducting fathers had a history of violent behavior compared with one-quarter of abducting mothers" (*Update*, Vol. 5, No. 2, Feb. 1992).

In addition to the federal response, states and the District of Columbia have some form of criminal custodial interference statute. At least twenty-four states included protection of the child or self as a defense to criminal charges. The "protection of the child or self" defense frequently requires a reasonable person standard; that there was a reasonable belief in the imminence of danger to the child or fleeing parent. That means that it is not a violation of the statute for a person fleeing domestic violence to take a child along to housing provided by a domestic violence program. Some states require that the fleeing person register with the police "within a reasonable time" (*Update*, Vol. 5, No. 2, Feb. 1992).

In some jurisdictions, prosecutors have developed a working relationship with local shelters. This permits the exchange of information and allows professionals to make decisions on the specifics of each case. Some jurisdictions have developed more sensitive responses to take into account both the seriousness of the crime and the individual circumstances. Life on-the-run is better and safer than life at home when there is domestic violence, but not all parental abductions involve family violence, and it is the child who suffers the greatest harm.

Joint Custody

Joint custody is a popular concept and an increasingly used method for dealing with children of divorce today. In the past, custody was awarded to the person who was not at fault in the marriage. As more and more marriages end with divorce on no-fault grounds, as opposed to fault grounds like adultery, both parents want to have the same child, or the same dog, or the same Ming vase.

In some states, there are pending bills to make a law that there will be a rebuttable presumption in favor of joint physical and legal custody when determining custody of a minor child in a divorce proceeding. If that occurs, then both parents will have to take more responsibility in parenting.

Although not always clearly defined and understood by those who undertake to use it, joint custody provides for equal sharing and decision-making between separated or divorced parents. If the couple could not harmoniously make decisions in the best interest of the child while they were married, it is highly unlikely that they will when divorced. So some states require parents to take mediation and dispute resolution classes on the effect of separation and divorce on their minor children, family relationships, and finances. Clearly, this is a move to help the parents realize that although the marriage may be over, the responsibilities of rearing the child(ren) are not.

Yet some parents want to shift physical custody on a regular basis, with each parent having control while the child is with him or her. In other cases, the child moves from parent to parent. The child literally has two bedrooms, two sets of clothes, two sets of whatever. The child has to remember which day he or she goes to mommy's house and which day to daddy's house.

In other cases with joint custody, the children live in the original house and the parents take turns coming in to live in the house with the children. The mother and father each has an apartment elsewhere.

Obviously, joint custody helps the court avoid an agonizing choice. It keeps from wounding the self-esteem of either parent and it avoids the look of sexual discrimination. Parents may consent to having joint custody. But in reality, how does it affect children?

Experts in the field argue that children, especially younger children, need stability in a home environment. The decision to separate may be necessary for the parents' well-being, but the "shuffling back and forth" makes the children continue to suffer from the poor choices of the parents. Thus, older children may take to the frequent changes more easily than younger children.

In addition to cooperation, there must be agreement about child-rearing practices as basic requirements for joint custody. If and when a parent chooses to separate geographically, then there are special difficulties for interstate enforcement under the Uniform Child Custody Jurisdiction Act.

Uniform Child Custody Jurisdiction Act

The Uniform Child Custody Jurisdiction Act (UCCJA) has been adopted by all fifty states. By agreement of the states, this act restricts judicial power to alter custody decrees rendered in another state. By comity (not as a matter of right, but out of deference and goodwill), courts are obligated to enforce the custody decree of another state that had jurisdiction to render such a decree.

This act and its agreement were the result of public concern over the fact that thousands of children were and are shifted from state to state and from one family to another every year while their parents or other persons battle for custody. One parent, unhappy with the custody decision in one state, would snatch the child or keep the child during a so-called visitation. The fugitive parent and child would move to another state and the parent would ask that state's court to grant custody. The courts would get into arguments among themselves. This was called multistate jurisdictional squabbles. A parent who did not like the decision in one court would take the case elsewhere to see if he or she could get a more favorable decision. This was called "forum shopping."

Children were psychologically harmed as parents continued the emotional war and moved the child. Stability and security were lacking. This unfortunate disarray was aided by the courts until most recently when all fifty states passed the UCCJA. To better understand how the UCCJA works, let us look at (1) grounds for jurisdiction, (2) physical presence of the child, (3) declining jurisdiction and modification of decree, and (4) international application.

Grounds for Jurisdiction

The UCCJA provides a hierarchy of situations when a court is competent to decide child custody matters. The first is called **home state of the child**. The court in the home state is able to decide the child custody if that state (1) is the home state of the child at the time of commencement of the proceeding, or (2) had been the child's home state within six months before commencement of the proceedings and the child is absent from this state because of his removal or retention by a person claiming his custody or for other reasons, and a parent or person acting as parent continues to live in this state.

The second is "**best interest of the child**." For this to happen, the child and his parents, or the child and at least one contestant, have a significant connection with the state and there is available substantial evidence concerning the child's present or future care, protection, training, and personal relationships.

The third condition in which the court may make a decision is the **physical presence of the child plus necessity**. If the child is in the state and has been abandoned, or if there is an emergency, then the state can act. In our mobile society, when a child is a passenger in a car with his or her parents and the parents are killed in an automobile accident and the child is injured, then the state in which the child is present can take jurisdiction. There is necessity.

The fourth time a court can take jurisdiction is when there is **no other forum**. If it appears that no other state would have jurisdiction or another state has declined to exercise jurisdiction on the grounds that another state is the more appropriate forum, then that other state may act.

Physical Presence of the Child

Physical presence of the child in the state of the child or of the child and one of the contestants alone is not sufficient to confer jurisdiction. Physical presence of the child, although desirable, is not a prerequisite for jurisdiction to determine custody. If there is abuse, neglect, and abandonment, then there must be both physical presence and necessity. Another exception is no other forum.

Declining Jurisdiction and Modification of Decree

Jurisdiction can be denied if it is an inconvenient forum. It can also decline if there is wrongful conduct by a noncustodial parent. Most courts will not modify a custody decree made in another state unless it appears to the court that the court rendering the first decree did not have jurisdiction in accord with UCCJA or the present state has the jurisdiction.

International Application

The UCCJA is designed to have application in cases of disputes where parents take children across state boundaries into other countries. Section 23 of the Act provides:

The general policies of this Act extend to the international area. The provisions of this Act relating to the recognition and enforcement of custody decrees of other states apply to custody decrees and decrees involving legal institutions similar in nature to custody institutions rendered by appropriate authorities of other nations if reasonable notice and opportunity to be heard were given to all affected persons.

There have been other acts or treaties passed on the international level. In 1980 the Hague Conference on Private International Law, Fourteenth Session, made some agreements on International Child Abduction. There is also a European Convention drafted by the Council of Europe.

Before we discuss support, let us look at one case that uses both the PKPA and UCCJA: *In re Allan C. Johnston*, 3 Va. App. 492 (1986). The facts are that Alan and Cynthia Johnston were married in 1969. They had one child, Amanda, when they divorced in 1971. The custody of the child went to the mother. In 1980, custody was transferred to the father by consent of both parties.

Amanda, now 15, was living in Arkansas with her father. She went on a date with a boy her father had forbidden her to see. Upon finding out about the date, her father physically abused her. Six months later when Amanda used the car (previously always with her father's permission), the father threatened similar punishment. Amanda contacted her mother and went to reside with her.

A preliminary protective order was issued *ex parte* (on one side only; done for the applicant) to prevent contact between Amanda and her father. He, of course, objected to the court's jurisdiction. He was served with a petition to change custody, and he filed a writ of prohibition in Circuit Court citing the PKPA and UCCJA. (A writ of prohibition requires that no other remedies or redress are available and that the party must be aggrieved.) Upon hearing evidence, the Circuit Court denied the father's writ and he appealed.

The Appeals Court affirmed the decision of the Circuit Court. The judges said that the Arkansas Juvenile and Domestic Relations Court had the appropriate jurisdiction to decide the custody matter. There was no proof that the father would receive an unfair hearing. In fact, all the delays had been implemented by the father and, therefore, he could not consider himself aggrieved. A writ of prohibition is an extraordinary remedy and is acceptable only if the party is aggrieved and there are no other remedies or redress.

SUPPORT

Support is the amount of money one parent pays to the other to help pay for the costs of bringing up the child. In many states, there are now support enforcement bureaus along with support enforcement officers and prosecutors. It is a class six felony for nonsupport for six or more months in a twelve-month period, or for being $2,000 or more in arrears. Parolees are not excluded. If there is a court-ordered child support as a condition of parole, failure to comply may result in the arrest and return of a parolee to a state correctional facility.

Support is not the money or property given to each person as a property settlement in a divorce. Property settlement is the division of the property gained by the husband and wife while they were married. Some states have equal distribution so that the judges evaluate the net worth of the couple and divide the proceeds in half so that each partner gains an equal share from the split of the partnership.

According to the Internal Revenue Service (IRS), alimony is considered income to the former spouse receiving the money. For the ex-spouse paying it out, it is a deduction to be taken before determining adjusted gross

Figure 7.2
Used with permission of
Bob Gorrell, *The Richmond
Times-Dispatch.*

"AND AS FOR THE *PROPERTY SETTLEMENT*, LITTLE BILLY GETS THE HOUSE AND
STOCKS, BUT YOU RETAIN THE *BATMAN ACTION FIGURES....* "

income. Those payments then are taken into consideration when paying income taxes.

On the other hand, child support is not alimony. One parent pays support and the other receives it without any taxation consequences to the party receiving the money.

Greif and Demaris (1991) studied situations in which the single father with full custody received child support. They found that it occurred for the following reasons:

1. A father receives support if the mother's (no longer a wife to this man) income is known and it is less than or equal to the father's income because she is court ordered to pay.

2. Some received support if they shared in the child care prior to the breakup.

Of those fathers who have court-ordered support, 62 percent of the fathers said their ex-wives never contributed to other child-related expenses; 7 percent always; and 31 percent sometimes.

The reality is that not all parents who have been ordered to pay child support do so. In fact, states have had to develop a state agency to collect and monitor child support payments, partly because of the Revised Uniform Reciprocal Enforcement of Support Act, better known as RURESA or the Uniform Interstate Family Support Act.

Uniform Interstate Family Support Act

This is another example in which all the states have agreed to cooperate with each other, in this case for the enforcement of support monies for children because a mobile society creates ongoing need for enforcement across state lines. This act provides for an enforcement method for support duties imposed by law through the courts. Better known as the "runaway pappy act," it permits a prior support order to be registered in the state of the child and be enforced just as if it were originally granted in that new state. A support order can be modified in the future.

Remember, both the custody of the child and the amount of the child support can always be modified if there are **changes of circumstances**, because the court is always interested in the "**best interest of the child**." The court will not usually otherwise change a divorce decree or the property settlement.

Nonpaying fathers often get themselves into trouble when they do not pay their child support. Some are under a false belief that once the child is 18, the debt will be forgiven. That is not the case. In *Brown v. Brown*, 240 Va. 376 (1990), the father filed a partition suit to force the sale of the marital home after he was divorced from his wife. To his amazement, his wife filed a cross-bill for delinquent child support citing the Juvenile and Domestic Relations Court order. So when the house sold, she got her half of the profit as her property settlement, then she got back child support from his half.

Many states follow the "parental generosity rule," which provides that child support awards are not based solely on need, but also on ability to pay. Evidence of a parent's significant increase in income is sufficient to warrant an increase in child support even without proof of any additional needs of the child. The theory is that such an increase would have been shared had the family unit remained intact.

In addition, courts will not decrease child support payments if the decline in income is due to the parent's own misconduct or if he or she takes a job beneath his or her training and education (for example, if a doctor quit the practice of medicine and became a dishwasher at a fast-food chain).

Parents who remarry do so at their own peril. Case law supports the idea that the first obligation is to the children from the first marriage.

If a party wants a reduction in child support payments, he or she must prove a material change of circumstances that justifies the reduction. Parents are not required to prove the reduction is in the best interests of the child. The mother and father cannot privately and contractually alter or modify any terms of child support without court approval. The state has an interest in seeing that children are supported.

Think of it like this. Child support is for the support of the child with the custodial parent receiving the money and standing in the shoes of a trustee, administering the money to the children based upon their needs and welfare. Child support is a legal obligation parents owe to their children. If a woman makes less money than the man and the man has physical custody of the child, she still has to pay a proportion of her monies for child support just as a man must if the situation were reversed.

Even the federal government has waived its sovereign immunity to permit garnishment of federal wages to satisfy alimony or child support obligations. Waiver of sovereign immunity means that a parent can garnish 60 percent of the ex-spouse's wages from the federal government—but not all of it—for child support.

What happens if one or the other of the parents say the child is not theirs? In some divorce suits, the wife will ask for a divorce and child support. The husband, wanting the divorce as well, may agree to the divorce. Yet he will argue that he is not the father of the child with the hope of avoiding child support.

Paternity is a critical issue for both the divorcing husband and the unwed father who never did marry the mother of the child. As an introduction to the law case *Stanley v. Illinois*, 405 U.S. 645 (1972), let us review the modern tests to determine paternity.

Illegitimacy and Paternity

Stanley can be best understood in the historical context of problems in establishing paternity and the resulting problems of illegitimacy. Illegitimacy has created a huge class of persons who are socially, economically, and legally penalized not by virtue of their own misconduct, but rather by the misconduct of their procreators, judged by a double standard of morality. Pressures to change came from the past illegitimate birth rates. Other factors are common law, U.S. Supreme Court decisions, the duty to support, ways to identify the father, and more modern blood tests such as HLA (Human Leucocyte Antigens) and DNA tests.

Past Illegitimate Birth Rates and Cost to the Taxpayers

In 1940, the ratio of illegitimate to legitimate births in the United States was 38 per 1,000. In 1958, the ratio had gone up to 49 illegitimate births per 1,000 births. By 1973, the ratio had climbed to 129 per 1,000. In 1980, in the State of Virginia, for example, resident illegitimate births were 191 per 1,000 live births (Virginia 1980 Statistical Annual Report).

The national ratios had tremendous impact on state and local governments as they tried to provide financial assistance to these children. Not all illegitimate children are on public welfare. Yet for those who were, the cost was tremendous. For example, in 1982, the Virginia Department of Welfare, in unpublished available data, reported that 55 percent of 45,008 children were illegitimate at an average monthly cost to the state per child of $125.52. When that cost is multiplied by the total number of illegitimate children, the amount is $5,635,902 per month, or $67,630,821 per year.

The mothers of these children are usually very young. For every 1,000 females aged 15 to 19 in 1992, the Centers for Disease Control and Prevention reported 60.7 births, which was down from 62.1 the previous year. But 7.1 percent of these babies are born too small. Low birth weight babies are at risk for developmental problems and death during early infancy (*Richmond Times-Dispatch*, 26 Oct. 1994, p. A18). And that means additional monies for health care and treatment. With this huge bill on the taxpayers, judges and other interested people began to push for more identification of fathers and agencies to enforce child support. This was not easy for many reasons, including common law.

Common Law

Under common law, the putative father was under no obligation to support or contribute to the support of his illegitimate child. The child was considered to be *filius nullius*, which means the child of no one.

In the Jewish tradition, a child born to a woman who was not married was excluded from the congregation for ten generations. It also meant that the child could not inherit from either parent. In addition, the child had to bear the stigma of being a bastard. The words "illegitimate" were written on the birth certificate. All of these social sanctions were supposed to penalize the parents but in fact hurt the child who had nothing to do with the behavior of his or her parents. It took the action of the U.S. Supreme Court to help.

U.S. Supreme Court Decisions

Things began to change. Besides the financial pressures being placed on the taxpayers, cases came before the Supreme Court. From 1968 through 1978 there were thirteen cases in which the United States Supreme Court had to consider the constitutionality of alleged discrimination on the basis of illegitimacy. Let us look at a few of those cases to get an idea of the issues and the rationale used by the Supreme Court.

Levy v. Louisiana, 391 U.S. 68 (1968), the court held (6–3) that under the Equal Protection Clause of the Fourteenth Amendment a state may not create a right of action in favor of children for the wrongful death of a parent and totally exclude illegitimate children from the benefit of such right. In that case, Louise Levy gave birth to five illegitimate children and they lived with her. She supported them through her work as a domestic servant and treated them as any good parent would; that is, she took them to church and enrolled them, at her own expense, in a parochial school. When she died and others filed for the children in her behalf for monies from the insurance company, the district court dismissed the suit. The Court of Appeals affirmed by arguing that the word "child" in the statute meant "legitimate child." They based their denial to illegitimate children on moral and general welfare reasons because, they reasoned, it discourages bringing children into the world out of wedlock.

Glona v. American Guarantee, 391 U.S. 73 (1972), argued and decided with *Levy* that a state may not, where the claimant is plainly the mother, deny relief under the wrongful death statutes because the child, wrongfully killed, was born to her out of wedlock. The Court saw no rational basis for assuming that if the natural mother is allowed recovery for the wrongful death of her illegitimate child, the cause of illegitimacy will be served. In their minds it was farfetched to assume that women have illegitimate children so that they can be compensated in damages for their death.

Later, in 1972, the Court permitted an illegitimate child to sue to recover under Louisiana's workers' compensation laws for the death of the natural father, on an equal footing with the father's dependent legitimate children (*Weber v. Aetna*, 406 U.S. 164). In this case, the man, who was killed on the job, had two families. The first family included a woman he had legally wed and with whom he had children. In his second family, he had children by the woman but never married her. When the man died, the state wanted to give all the benefits to the legal wife and her children. The other children, although they got as hungry as their half-brothers and half-sisters, were denied monies by the state because their father had never married their mother. Thus, the court reversed the lower court and allowed illegitimate children to sue.

In 1973 in *Gomez v. Perez*, 409 U.S. 535, 35 L. Ed. 2d 56, 93 S.Ct. 872, the lower court's decision was reversed. The appellant filed a petition seeking support from the appellee on behalf of her minor children. After a hearing, the state trial judge in Texas found that the appellee was the biological father of the child and that the child needed support. But because the child was illegitimate, "there is no legal obligation to support the child and the Plaintiff takes nothing." The Supreme Court held that "once a state posits a judicially enforceable right on behalf of children to needed support from their natural fathers, there is no constitutionally sufficient justification for denying such an essential right to a child simply because its natural father has not married its mother. For a state to do so is illogical and unjust."

By 1976, the Court was not willing to say that the classification based on illegitimacy was "suspect" and justifications must survive "strict scrutiny." Instead, they argued in *Mathews v. Lucus*, 427 U.S. 495, that the classification fell in the realm of less than strictest scrutiny but that such scrutiny is not a "toothless one."

In 1981, the United States Supreme Court struck down as offending due process a Connecticut statute that required the costs of blood tests to be borne by the party requesting them. The statute denied indigent defendants the right to demand blood tests. Defendants in paternity actions in Connecticut faced an unusual evidentiary obstacle because in that state the testimony of the putative father alone was insufficient to overcome the mother's *prima facie* case. The Court saw the new blood testing system to be important in proving or disproving paternity. They said that there are seldom accurate or reliable eye witnesses to sexual activities, and the self-serving testimony of a party is of questionable reliability.

Duty to Support

Today, statutes in all states impose a duty of support upon the mother and the father even if they are unwed. As a result, the biggest challenge is determining who the unwed father is. In the past, it was easy to determine who the mother of the child was; she was the one who gave birth to the child. The father was not so easily identified. The charge of paternity was easily brought against a man even though it was hard to prove. In addition, people die and memories fade. What was there to protect a man from the personal vengeance and dislike of a woman raising a false charge of paternity against him?

Ways to Identify the Father

Ways to identify the unwed father included such things as evidence of the alleged parent consenting to or acknowledging the common use of such parent's surname, open cohabitation (living together as if married), and anthropological evidence. Anthropological evidence was claimed when the mother took the baby into the courtroom and tried to show how the baby or child had the father's head shape, size of ears, and so forth. In addition, there were blood tests.

About 1910, it was first discovered that there are four distinct types of human blood: A, B, AB, and O. By determining the blood types of both parents through simple laboratory procedures and applying the laws of heredity, it became possible to determine the blood type of the offspring. Use of parent's surname, living together, anthropological evidence, and blood tests obviously left substantial margin for error.

HLA Blood Tests

Today, through medical science's increasing success in organ transplants for humans, three groups of tests have been developed, encompassing more than sixty genetically independent blood-group systems that can also be used in paternity evaluation. These procedures include tests for red blood cell antigens and human leukocyte antigens (HLA), and electrophoresis to identify serum proteins and red blood cell enzymes.

It is now possible to exclude paternity for 99 percent of wrongly accused men. A man is excluded if both he and the mother lack a blood factor (antigen) that the child possesses. A man also can be excluded if certain substances (antigens), which must be transmitted by him, are not present in the child.

By collecting a blood sample from the mother, the baby (older than 6 months), and the alleged father, the probability of paternity can be determined. The probability of paternity is an estimate of the likelihood that the alleged father is the biological father of the child. This probability is determined by calculating the chance that the alleged father could produce a single sperm containing all the genetic information a child would have received from a true father. It might look like this:

Mother	A28,Bu51,Aw32,E14
Child	A28,Bu51,Aw36,B17
Alleged Father	A2,Bu62,Aw36,B17

The chance of paternity with such configurations is 99.98 percent. As one judge said when he saw scores like that, regardless if the couple had been married or not and this was a custody dispute, he would open up the top drawer of his desk, get out the cigars, and pass them around. The judge had found himself a "daddy."

Many states now use this more modern blood test because of its accuracy. Yet one has to make sure the alleged father had his own blood sampled and not that of a paid individual. The tests have to be offered by a duly licensed and certified practicing physician or other qualified scientist.

Some courts, like that in Prince George's County, Maryland, have a blood-taking unit in the basement of the Circuit Court. In Prince George's County, attendants from Johns Hopkins Hospital are under contract with the court to draw blood. This procedure has reduced the time lag from complaint to support for court orders from years to less than a month (*Washington Post*, 24 July 1982 at A1 Col. 3).

In one case, a couple were divorcing and the man told the judge that he was not the father. Because that seemed to be a routine ploy, the judge demanded blood tests. When the tests were analyzed and sent to the court, the report supported the claim that the man was not the father. It also said that the mother was not the mother but rather next of kin. With that information, the judge discovered that the couple had taken the woman's sister's baby to rear so that they could get welfare payments.

What this couple did not know was that blood tests called genotyping include more than routine blood testing. Therefore, these tests are useful in excluding a close relative of the accused as a potential father as well. Thus, HLA and genotyping should be performed for cases in which other procedures have proved ambiguous.

DNA Tests

In November of 1990, defendant W.R. Boyd, Sr., filed a motion seeking permission to exhume the body of J.R. Boyd, Jr., in order to perform DNA sampling and testing to determine his biological relationship with this man who had died and left a large sum of money in the estate. When people die without wills, their estates usually go to their spouses and children and if none living, then to parents and brothers and sisters before ending up in the state's coffers. In this strange situation, the child died before the parents died and left enough money for people to argue over. Since Boyd, Sr. was not considered socially the father of this wealthy child, he would have to prove it biologically through DNA tests. The North Carolina Court of Appeals affirmed the lower court that permitted it (*Batcheldor v. Boyd*, 423 S.E. 2d 810 [1992]).

Before we move on to the law case *Stanley*, unwed fathers, and termination of parental rights, let us look at *Michael H. et al. v. Gerald D.*, 495 U.S. 604, 109 S.Ct. 2333 (1989). In 1981, Victoria D. was born to Carole D. who was married to and resided with Gerald D. in California. Although Gerald was listed as the father on the birth certificate, a blood test showed a 98.7 percent probability that Michael H., with whom Carole had had an adulterous affair, was Victoria's father.

During Victoria's first three years, she and her mother resided at times with Michael, who held her out as his own (told people she was his), at times with another man, and at times with Gerald, who also held her out as his own and with whom they have lived since 1984. Michael then wanted to establish his paternity and right to visitation. The court-appointed *guardian ad litem* filed a cross-complaint asserting that Victoria was entitled to maintain filial relationships with both Michael and Gerald.

In the lower court, Gerald won and Michael's and Victoria's motions for visitation were denied. The highest court affirmed. They said that the California statute creating presumption that a child born to a married woman living with her husband is a child of the marriage did not violate the natural father's due process rights. Second, children do not have a due process right to maintain filial relationships with both a natural father and a father by marriage. The statute did not violate the child's equal protection rights.

> Common law presumes that if a child is born to a man and woman who are married, the child is a product of that man and woman—a legitimate child.

What you have is a common law presumption of legitimacy. Many states have a strong public policy against bastardizing a child. Society has historically projected that a marital family is better than a second relationship like the one with Michael.

With this as an introduction, read *Stanley*. It deals with a man who fathered three children in 18 years with Joan Stanley. He never married the woman. Then she died. If you were the State of Illinois with three children who had no mother, what would you do with them? Read to see what happened.

STANLEY V. ILLINOIS

SUPREME COURT OF THE UNITED STATES

405 U.S. 645; 92 S. Ct. 1208; 31 L. Ed. 2d 551

October 19, 1971, Argued April 3, 1972, Decided

PRIOR HISTORY:

CERTIORARI TO THE SUPREME COURT OF ILLINOIS.

DISPOSITION: 45 Ill. 2d 132, 256 N. E. 2d 814, reversed and remanded.

SYLLABUS: Petitioner, and unwed father whose children, on the mother's death, were declared state wards and placed in guardianship, attacked the Illinois statutory scheme as violative of equal protection. Under that scheme the children of unmarried fathers, upon the death of the mother, are declared dependents without any hearing on parental fitness and without proof of neglect, though such hearing and proof are required before the State assumes custody of children of married or divorced parents and unmarried mothers. The Illinois Supreme Court, holding that petitioner could properly be separated from his children upon mere proof that he and the dead mother had not been married and that petitioner's fitness as a father was irrelevant, rejected petitioner's claim. Held:

> *Summary of the Entire Case*

1. Under the Due Process Clause of the Fourteenth Amendment petitioner was entitled to a hearing on his fitness as a parent before his children were taken from him. Pp. 647–658.

(a) The fact that petitioner can apply for adoption or for custody and control of his children does not bar his attack on the dependency proceeding. Pp. 647–649.

(b) The State cannot, consistently with due process requirements, merely presume that unmarried fathers in general and petitioner in particular are unsuitable and neglectful parents. Parental unfitness must be established on the basis of individualized proof. See *Bell v. Burson*, 402 U.S. 535. Pp. 649–658.

2. The denial to unwed fathers of the hearing on fitness accorded to all other parents whose custody of their children is challenged by the State constitutes a denial of equal protection of the laws. P. 658.

JUDGES: White, J., delivered the opinion of the Court, in which Brennan, Stewart, and Marshall, JJ., joined, and in Parts I and II of which Douglas, J., joined. Burger, C.J., filed a dissenting opinion, in which Blackmun, J., joined. Powell and Rehnquist, JJ., took no part in the consideration or decision of the case.

OPINION: MR. JUSTICE WHITE delivered the opinion of the Court.

Joan Stanley lived with Peter Stanley intermittently for 18 years, during which time they had three children. When Joan Stanley died, Peter Stanley lost not only her but also his children. Under Illinois law, the children of unwed fathers become wards of the State upon the death of the mother. Accordingly, upon Joan Stanley's death, in a dependency proceeding instituted by the State of Illinois, Stanley's children were declared wards of the State and placed with court-appointed guardians. Stanley appealed, claiming that he had never been shown to be an unfit parent, and that since married fathers and unwed mothers could not be deprived of their children without such a showing, he had been deprived of the equal protection of the laws guaranteed him by the Fourteenth Amendment. The Illinois Supreme Court accepted the fact the Stanley's own unfitness had not been established but rejected the equal protection claim, holding that

> *Facts*

Stanley could properly be separated from his children upon proof of the single fact that he and the dead mother had not been married. Stanley's actual fitness as a father was irrelevant. *In re Stanley*, 45 Ill. 2d 132, 256 N. E. 2d 814 (1970).

? Stanley presses his equal protection claim here. The State continues to respond that unwed fathers are presumed unfit to raise their children and that it is unnecessary to hold individualized hearings to determine whether particular fathers are in fact unfit parents before they are separated from their children. We granted certiorari, 400 U.S. 1020 (1971), to determine whether this method of procedure by presumption could be allowed to stand in light of the fact that Illinois allows married fathers—whether divorced, widowed, or separated—and mothers—even if unwed—the benefit of the presumption that they are fit to raise their children.

I

At the outset we reject any suggestion that we need not consider the propriety of the dependency proceeding that separated the Stanleys because Stanley might be able to regain custody of his children as a guardian or through adoption proceedings. The suggestion is that if Stanley has been treated differently from other parents, the difference is immaterial and not legally cognizable for the purposes of the Fourteenth Amendment. This Court has not, however, embraced the general proposition that a wrong may be done if it can be undone. *Cf. Sniadach v. Family Finance Corp.*, 395 U.S. 337 (1969). Surely, in the case before us, if there is delay between the doing and the undoing petitioner suffers from the deprivation of his children, and the children suffer from uncertainty and dislocation.

It is clear, moreover, that Stanley does not have the means at hand promptly to erase the adverse consequences of the proceeding in the course of which his children were declared wards of the State. It is first urged that Stanley could act to adopt his children. But under Illinois law, Stanley is treated not as a parent but as a stranger to his children, and the dependency proceeding has gone forward on the presumption that he is unfit to exercise parental rights. Insofar as we are informed, Illinois law affords him no priority in adoption proceedings. It would be his burden to establish not only that he would be a suitable parent but also that he would be the most suitable of all who might want custody of the children. Neither can we ignore that in the proceedings from which this action developed, the "probation officer," see App. 17, the assistant state's attorney, see id., at 29–30, and the judge charged with the case, see id., at 16–18, 23, made it apparent that Stanley, unmarried and impecunious as he is, could not now expect to profit from adoption proceedings. The Illinois Supreme Court apparently recognized some or all of these considerations, because it did not suggest that Stanley's case was undercut by his failure to petition for adoption.

Before us, the State focuses on Stanley's failure to petition for "custody and control"—the second route by which, it is urged, he might regain authority for his children. Passing the obvious issue whether it would be futile or burdensome for an unmarried father—without funds and already once presumed unfit—to petition for custody, this suggestion overlooks the fact that legal custody is not parenthood or adoption. A person appointed guardian in an action for custody and control is subject to removal at any time without such cause as must be shown in a neglect proceeding against a parent. Ill. Rev. Stat., c. 37, § 705–8. He may not take the children out of the jurisdiction without the court's approval. He may be required to report to the court as to his disposition of the children's affairs. Ill. Rev. Stat., c. 37, § 705–8. Obviously then, even if Stanley were a mere step away from "custody and control" to give an unwed father only "custody and control" would still be to leave him seriously prejudiced by reason of his status.

We must therefore examine the question that Illinois would have us avoid: Is a presumption that distinguishes and burdens all unwed fathers constitutionally repugnant? We conclude that, as a matter of due process of law, Stanley was entitled to a hearing on his fitness as a parent before his children were taken from him and that, by denying him a hearing and extending it to all other parents whose custody of their children is challenged, the State denied Stanley the equal protection of the laws guaranteed by the Fourteenth Amendment.

?

II

Illinois has two principal methods of removing nondelinquent children from the homes of their parents. In a dependency proceeding it may demonstrate that the children are wards of the State because they have no surviving parent or guardian. Ill. Rev. Stat., c. 37, §§ 702–1, 702–5. In a neglect proceeding it may show that children should be wards of the State because the present parent(s) or guardian does not provide suitable care. Ill. Rev. Stat., c. 37, §§ 702–1, 702–4.

The State's right—indeed, duty—to protect minor children through a judicial determination of their interests in a neglect proceeding is not challenged here. Rather, we are faced with a dependency statute that empowers state officials to circumvent neglect proceedings on the theory that an unwed father is not a "parent" whose existing relationship with his children must be considered. "Parents," says the State, "means the father and mother of a legitimate child, or the survivor of them, or the natural mother of an illegitimate child, and includes any adoptive parent," Ill. Rev. Stat., c. 37, § 701–14, but the term does not include unwed fathers.

Under Illinois law, therefore, while the children of all parents can be taken from them in neglect proceedings, that is only after notice, hearing, and proof of such unfitness as a parent as amounts to neglect, an unwed father is uniquely subject to the more simplistic dependency proceeding. By use of this proceeding, the State, on showing that the father was not married to the mother, need not prove unfitness in fact, because it is presumed at law. Thus, the unwed father's claim of parental qualification is avoided as "irrelevant."

Procedure

In considering this procedure under the Due Process Clause, we recognize, as we have in other cases, that due process of law does not require a hearing "in every conceivable case of government impairment of private interest." *Cafeteria Workers v. McElroy*, 367 U.S. 886, 894 (1961). That case explained that "the very nature of due process negates any concept of inflexible procedures universally applicable to every imaginable situation" and firmly established that "what procedures due process may require under any given set of circumstances must begin with a determination of the precise nature of the government function involved as well as of the private interest that has been affected by governmental action." Id., at 895; *Goldberg v. Kelly*, 397 U.S. 254, 263 (1970).

The private interest here, that of a man in the children he has sired and raised, undeniably warrants deference and, absent a powerful countervailing interest, protection. It is plain that the interest of a parent in the companionship, care, custody, and management of his or her children "come[s] to this Court with a momentum for respect lacking when appeal is made to liberties which derive merely from shifting economic arrangements." *Kovacs v. Cooper*, 336 U.S. 77, 95 (1949) (Frankfurter, J., concurring).

Notice the use of the former law case *Meyer*.

The Court has frequently emphasized the importance of the family. The rights to conceive and to raise one's children have been deemed "essential," *Meyer v. Nebraska*, 262 U.S. 390, 399 (1923), "basic civil rights of man," *Skinner v. Oklahoma*, 316 U.S. 535, 541 (1942), and "rights far more precious . . . than property rights," *May v. Anderson*, 345 U.S. 528, 533 (1953). "It is cardinal with us that the custody, care and nurture of the child reside first in the parents, whose primary function and freedom include preparation for obligations the state can neither supply nor hinder." *Prince v. Massachusetts*, 321 U.S. 158, 166 (1944). The integrity of the family unit has found protection in the Due Process Clause of the Fourteenth Amendment, *Meyer v. Nebraska*, supra, at 399, the Equal Protection Clause of the Fourteenth Amendment, *Skinner v. Oklahoma*, supra, at 541, and the Ninth Amendment, *Griswold v. Connecticut*, 381 U.S. 479, 496 (1965) (Goldberg, J., concurring).

Nor has the law refused to recognize those family relationships unlegitimized by a marriage ceremony. The Court has declared unconstitutional a state statute denying natural, but illegitimate, children a wrongful-death action for the death of their mother, emphasizing that such children cannot be denied the right of other children because familial bonds in such cases were often as warm, enduring, and important as those arising within a more formally organized family unit. *Levy v. Louisiana*, 391 U.S. 68, 71–72 (1968). "To say that the test of equal protection should be the 'legal' rather than the biological relationship is to avoid the issue. For the Equal Protection Clause necessarily limits the authority of a State to draw such 'legal' lines as it chooses." *Glona v. American Guarantee Co.*, 391 U.S. 73, 75–76 (1968).

These authorities make it clear that, at the least, Stanley's interest in retaining custody of his children is cognizable and substantial.

For its part, the State has made its interest quite plain: Illinois has declared that the aim of the Juvenile Court Act is to protect "the moral, emotional, mental, and physical welfare of the minor and the best interests of the community" and to "strengthen the minor's family ties whenever possible, removing him from the custody of his parents only when his welfare or safety or the protection of the public cannot be adequately safeguarded without removal. . . ." Ill. Rev. Stat., c. 37, § 701–2. These are legitimate interests, well within the power of the State to implement. We do not question the assertion that neglectful parents may be separated from their children.

But we are here not asked to evaluate the legitimacy of the state ends, rather, to determine whether the means used to achieve these ends are constitutionally defensible. What is the state interest in separating children from fathers without a hearing designed to determine whether the father is unfit in a particular disputed case? We observe that the State registers no gain toward its declared goals when it separates children from the custody of fit parents. Indeed, if Stanley is a fit father, the State spites its own articulated goals when it needlessly separates him from his family.

In *Bell v. Burson*, 402 U.S. 535 (1971), we found a scheme repugnant to the Due Process Clause because it deprived a driver of his license without reference to the very factor (there fault in driving, here fitness as a parent) that the State itself deemed fundamental to its statutory scheme. Illinois would avoid the self-contradiction that rendered the Georgia license suspension system invalid by arguing that Stanley and all other unmarried fathers can reasonably be presumed to be unqualified to raise their children.

It may be, as the State insists, that most unmarried fathers are unsuitable and neglectful parents. It may also be that Stanley is such a parent and that his children should be placed in other hands. But all unmarried fathers are not in this category; some are wholly suited to have custody of their children. This much the State readily concedes, and nothing in this record indicates that Stanley is or has been a neglectful father who has not cared for his children. Given the opportunity to make his case, Stanley may have been seen to be deserving of custody of his offspring. Had this been so, the State's statutory policy would have been furthered by leaving custody in him.

Carrington v. Rash, 380 U.S. 89 (1965), dealt with a similar situation. There we recognized that Texas had a powerful interest in its electorate to bona fide residents. It was not disputed that most servicemen stationed in Texas had no intention of remaining in the State; most therefore could be deprived of a vote in state affairs. But we refused to tolerate a blanket exclusion depriving all servicemen of the vote, when some servicemen clearly were bona fide residents and when "more precise tests," id., at 95, were available to distinguish members of this latter group. "By forbidding a soldier ever to controvert the presumption of nonresidence," id., at 96, the State, we said, unjustifiably effected a substantial deprivation. It viewed people one-dimensionally (as servicemen) when a finer perception could readily have been achieved by assessing a serviceman's claim to residency on an individualized basis.

"We recognize that special problems may be involved in determining whether servicemen have actually acquired a new domicile in a State for franchise purposes. We emphasize that Texas is free to take reasonable and adequate steps, as have other States, to see that all applicants for the vote actually fulfill the requirements of bona fide residence. But [the challenged] provision goes beyond such rules. 'The presumption here created is . . . definitely conclusive—incapable of being overcome by proof of the most positive character.' " Id., at 96.

"All servicemen not residents of Texas before induction," we concluded, "come within the provision's sweep. Not one of them can ever vote in Texas, no matter" what their individual qualifications. Ibid. We found such a situation repugnant to the Equal Protection Clause.

Despite *Bell* and *Carrington*, it may be argued that unmarried fathers are so seldom fit that Illinois need not undergo the administrative inconvenience of inquiry in any case, including Stanley's. The establishment of prompt efficacious procedures to achieve legitimate state ends is a proper state interest worthy of cognizance in constitutional adjudication. But the Constitution recognizes higher values than speed and efficiency. Indeed, one might fairly say of the Bill of Rights in general, and the Due Process Clause in particular, that they were designed to protect the fragile values of a vulnerable citizenry from the overbearing concern for efficiency and efficacy that may characterize praise-worthy government officials no less, and perhaps more, than mediocre ones.

Procedure by presumption is always cheaper and easier than individualized determination. But when, as here, the procedure forecloses the determinative issues of competence and care, when it explicitly disdains present realities in deference to past formalities, it needlessly risks running roughshod over the important interests of both parent and child. It therefore cannot stand.

Bell v. Burson held that the State could not, while purporting to be concerned with fault in suspending a driver's license, deprive a citizen of his license without a hearing that would assess fault. Absent fault, the State's declared interest was so attenuated that administrative convenience was insufficient to excuse a hearing where evidence of fault could be considered. That drivers involved in accidents, as a statistical matter, might be very likely to have been wholly or partially at fault did not foreclose hearing and proof in specific cases before licenses were suspended.

We think the Due Process Clause mandates a similar result here. The State's interest in caring for Stanley's children is de minimis if Stanley is shown to be a fit father. It insists on presuming rather than proving Stanley's unfitness solely because it is more convenient to presume than to prove. Under the Due Process Clause that advantage is insufficient to justify refusing a father a hearing when the issue at stake is the dismemberment of his family.

III

The State of Illinois assumes custody of the children of married parents, divorced parents, and unmarried mothers only after a hearing and proof of neglect. The children of unmarried fathers, however, are declared dependent children without a hearing on parental fitness and without proof of neglect. Stanley's claim in the state courts and here is that failure to afford him a hearing on his parental qualifications while extending it to other parents denied him equal protection of the laws. We have concluded that all Illinois parents are constitutionally entitled to a hearing on their fitness before their children are removed from their custody. It follows that denying such a hearing to Stanley and those like him while granting it to other Illinois parents is inescapably contrary to the Equal Protection Clause.

Decision | The judgment of the Supreme Court of Illinois is **reversed** and the case is **remanded** to that court for proceedings not inconsistent with this opinion. It is so ordered.

MR. JUSTICE POWELL and MR. JUSTICE REHNQUIST took no part in the consideration or decision of this case.

MR. JUSTICE DOUGLAS joins in Parts I and II of this opinion.

DISSENT BY: BURGER

DISSENT: MR. CHIEF JUSTICE BURGER, with whom MR. JUSTICE BLACKMUN concurs, dissenting.

All of those persons in Illinois who may have followed the progress of this case will, I expect, experience no little surprise at the Court's opinion handed down today. Stanley will undoubtedly be surprised to find that he has prevailed on an issue never advanced by him. The judges who dealt with this case in the state courts will be surprised to find their decisions overturned on a ground they never considered. And the legislators and other officials of the State of Illinois, as well as those attorneys of the State who are familiar with the statutory provisions here at issue, will be surprised to learn for the first time that the Illinois Juvenile Court Act establishes a presumption that unwed fathers are unfit. I must confess my own inability to find any such presumption in the Illinois Act. Furthermore, from the record of the proceedings in the Juvenile Court of Cook County in this case, I can only conclude that the judge of that court was unaware of any such presumption, for he clearly indicated that Stanley's asserted fatherhood of the children would stand him in good stead, rather than prejudice him, in any adoption or guardianship proceeding. In short, far from any intimations of hostility toward unwed fathers, that court gave Stanley "merit points" for his acknowledgment of paternity and his past assumption of at least marginal responsibility for the children.

In regard to the only issue that I consider properly before the Court, I agree with the State's argument that the Equal Protection Clause is not violated when Illinois gives full recognition only to those father-child relationships that arise in the context of family units bound together by legal obligations arising from marriage or from adoption proceedings. Quite apart from the religious or quasireligious connotations that marriage has—and has historically enjoyed—for a large proportion of this Nation's citizens, it is in law an essentially contractual relationship, the parties to which have legally enforceable rights and duties, with respect both to each other and to any children born to them. Stanley and the mother of these children never entered such a relationship. The record is silent as to whether they ever privately exchanged such promises as would have bound them in marriage under the common law. See *Cartwright v. McGown*, 121 Ill. 388, 398, 12 N. E. 737, 739 (1887). In any event, Illinois has not recognized common-law marriages since 1905. Ill. Rev. Stat., c. 89, § 4. Stanley did not seek the burdens when he could have freely assumed them.

Where there is a valid contract of marriage, the law of Illinois presumes that the husband is the father of any child born to the wife during the marriage; as the father, he has legally enforceable rights and duties with respect to that child. When a child is born to an unmarried woman, Illinois recognizes the readily identifiable mother, but makes no presumption as to the identity of the biological father. It does, however, provide two ways, one voluntary and one involuntary, in which that father may be identified. First, he may marry the mother and acknowledge the child as his own; this has the legal effect of legitimating the child and gaining for the father full recognition as a parent. Ill. Rev. Stat., c. 3, § 12, subd. 8. Second, a man may be found to be the biological father of the child pursuant to a paternity suit initiated by the mother; in this case, the child remains illegitimate, but the adjudicated father is made liable for the support of the child until the latter attains age 18 or is legally adopted by another. Ill. Rev. Stat., c. 106 3/4, § 52.

Stanley argued before the Supreme Court of Illinois that the definition of "parents," set out in Ill. Rev. Stat., c. 37, § 701–14, as including "the father and mother of a legitimate child, or the survivor of them, or the natural mother of an illegitimate child, [or] . . . any adoptive parent," violates the Equal Protection Clause in that it treats unwed mothers and unwed fathers differently. Stanley then enlarged upon his equal protection argument when he brought the case here; he argued before this Court that Illinois is not permitted by the Equal Protection Clause to distinguish between unwed fathers and any of the other biological parents included in the statutory definition of legal "parents."

The Illinois Supreme Court correctly held that the State may constitutionally distinguish between unwed fathers and unwed mothers. Here, Illinois' different treatment of the two is part of that State's statutory scheme for protecting the welfare of illegitimate children. In almost all cases, the unwed mother is readily identifiable, generally from hospital records, and alternatively by physicians or others attending the child's birth. Unwed fathers, as a class, are not traditionally quite so easy to identify and locate. Many of them either deny all responsibility or exhibit no interest in the child or its welfare; and, of course, many unwed fathers are simply not aware of their parenthood.

Furthermore, I believe that a State is fully justified in concluding, on the basis of common human experience, that the biological role of the mother in carrying and nursing an infant creates stronger bonds between her and the child than the bonds resulting from the male's often casual encounter. This view is reinforced by the observable fact that most unwed mothers exhibit a concern for their offspring either permanently or at least until they are safely placed for adoption, while unwed fathers rarely burden either the mother or the child with their attentions or loyalties. Centuries of human experience buttress this view of the realities of human conditions and suggest that unwed mothers of illegitimate children are generally more dependable protectors of their children than are unwed fathers. While these, like most generalizations, are not without exceptions, they nevertheless provide a sufficient basis to sustain a statutory classification whose objective is not to penalize unwed parents but to further the welfare of illegitimate children in fulfillment of the State's obligations as *parens patriae*.

Stanley depicts himself as a somewhat unusual unwed father, namely, as one who has always acknowledged and never doubted his fatherhood of these children. He alleges that he loved, cared for, and supported these children from the time of their birth until the death of their mother. He contends that he consequently must be treated the same as a married father of legitimate children. Even assuming the truth of Stanley's allegations, I am unable to construe the Equal Protection Clause as requiring Illinois to tailor its statutory definition of "parents" so meticulously as to include such unusual unwed fathers, while at the same time excluding those unwed, and generally unidentified, biological fathers who in no way share Stanley's professed desires.

Indeed, the nature of Stanley's own desires is less than absolutely clear from the record in this case. Shortly after the death of the mother, Stanley turned these two children over to the care of a Mr. and Mrs. Ness; he took no action to gain recognition of himself as a father, through adoption, or as a legal custodian, through a guardianship proceeding. Eventually it came to the attention of the State that there was no living adult who had any legally enforceable obligation for the care and support of the children; it was only then that the dependency proceeding here under review took place and that Stanley made himself known to the juvenile court in connection with these two children. Even then, however, Stanley did not ask to be charged with the legal responsibility for the children. He asked only that such legal responsibility be given to no one else. He seemed, in particular, to be concerned with the loss of the welfare payments he would suffer as a result of the designation of others as guardians of the children.

Not only, then, do I see no ground for holding that Illinois' statutory definition of "parents" on its face violates the Equal Protection Clause; I see no ground for holding that any constitutional right of Stanley has been denied in the application of that statutory definition in the case at bar.

As Mr. Justice Frankfurter once observed, "Invalidating legislation is serious business. . . ." *Morey v. Doud*, 354 U.S. 457, 474 (1957) (dissenting opinion). The Court today pursues that serious business by expanding its legitimate jurisdiction beyond what I read in 28 U.S.C. § 1257 as the permissible limits contemplated by Congress. In doing so, it invalidates a provision of critical importance to Illinois' carefully drawn statutory system governing family relationships and the welfare of the minor children of the State. And in so invalidating that provision, it ascribes to that statutory system a presumption that is simply not there and embarks on a novel concept of the natural law for unwed fathers that could well have strange boundaries as yet indiscernible.

NOTES AFTER STANLEY

1. *Stanley* seems to say that men have a right to be a father and that right includes a responsibility. Some states constructed statutes requiring notice to an unwed father, regardless of his contacts with the child, if the mother was putting the child up for adoption. "Notice" has been given

by way of a certified letter (if the man's name and address were known) to other less personal publications, if there is evidence to show that the father's identity cannot be determined.

For example, an unwed mother surrendered her child to the city division of social services in the Family Court for purposes of adoption after giving the unknown father notice of the hearing in the local newspaper for a period of four weeks. The *guardian ad litem* for the unknown father objected to the termination of the unknown father's parental rights and sought an appeal on the grounds that the unknown father had not been given sufficient notice of the proceedings.

The Court of Appeals that heard the case determined that parental rights of the father may be terminated even though the parent has not entered into an entrustment agreement if the court finds, based upon clear and convincing evidence, that it is in the best interest of the child and that the (1) identity of the parent is not reasonably ascertainable, and (2) the parent is given notice of termination proceedings through an order of publication, published at least once per week in a newspaper having general circulation in the area for a period of four weeks (*Unknown Father of Baby Girl Janet v. Division of Social Services of the City of Lynchburg*, 442 S.E.2d 407 [1992]).

2. *Stanley* is an important case because it lays the legal groundwork for men to have rights to their children. This will lead to other law cases and the movement toward setting aside the "tender years" doctrine (which assumes the mother to be the best custodial parent) in custody decisions.

3. The serious student might want to ponder what Mr. Stanley was really like. If you were a Supreme Court justice, would you have decided this case differently if you knew that Mr. Stanley was, as a matter of fact, an alcoholic who wanted the children only for the welfare payments?

4. When the case went back to Illinois for a fitness hearing, the state found that Mr. Stanley was, indeed, unfit to parent the three children—an alcoholic who wanted the welfare payments.

✳ BRAIN EXERCISE

Your friend is a senior in college. It is his final semester and he is planning to graduate and get married the weekend after graduation. Then, one day, just before graduation, he comes to you. He has just received a telephone call from his old girlfriend whom he knew in Georgia where he did his basic training for the military last summer. She called to say that she had delivered a baby girl—his daughter. What advice do you give him?

Termination of parental rights is either voluntary or involuntary. Terminating parental rights is one of the most critical issues facing the juvenile and domestic relations courts. Whereas the governmental policy is to foster the preservation of the family, the reality is that the interests of the parents, the child, and the state clash.

The state employs the "best interest of the child" test. Yet it is vague, not clearly defined.

Terminating parental rights is more than finding a parent unfit. It is an issue that can have far-reaching consequences. As the court in *Weaver v. Roanoke Dept. of Human Res.*, 220 Va. 921, 926, so aptly stated:

TERMINATION OF RESIDUAL PARENTAL RIGHTS

Who has no faults? To err and yet be able to correct it is best of all.
Yuanwu

*. . . terminating parental rights renders the parent "a
legal stranger to the child" . . . and severs "all parental
rights."*

To better understand termination, it will be discussed in terms of voluntary and involuntary termination, the burden on social services, and the
standard of proof. Appendix 7B: Mock Trial shows how these factors work
together, although it does not cover voluntary termination. As the word suggests, voluntary terminations usually have no contests and are usually done
for adoption cases.

Voluntary

Voluntary is when one or both parents sign papers giving up the right to be
a parent to another person. Sometimes the voluntary termination is given
so that another couple may adopt the child. Sometimes, it is given by the
father of the children, who has not paid any child support, to the mother's
second husband who is willing to adopt and support the child(ren).

In *Unknown Father of Baby Girl Janet v. Division of Social Services of the City
of Lynchburg*, 442 S.E. 2d 407 (1992), the Court of Appeals of Virginia upheld
the lower court that terminated the parental rights of the unknown father.
In that case, an unwed mother surrendered her child to the city division
of social services for the purpose of adoption, giving the unknown father
notice of the hearing in the local newspaper for a period of four weeks. The
guardian ad litem for the unknown father objected to the termination of the
known father's parental rights and sought an appeal on the grounds that
the unknown father had not been given sufficient notice of the proceedings.
The higher court reasoned that the parental rights of the remaining parent
may be terminated, even though the parent has not entered into an entrustment agreement, if the court finds, based upon clear and convincing evidence, that it is in the best interests of the child, and that (1) the identity of
the parent is not reasonably ascertainable, and (2) the parent is given notice
of termination proceedings through an order of publication, published at
least once per week in a newspaper having general circulation in the area
for a period of four weeks.

Involuntary

Involuntary termination of residual parental rights means that children
are taken from parents (parental custodial rights) for various reasons such
as illness, mental retardation, abuse, or neglect, which is not corrected or
eliminated to the point that the child may return home safely. Yet parental
rights encompass custodial rights that cannot be severed unless the parents
(both as a couple or as individuals) have been given a substantial chance to
remedy the conditions leading to foster care placement.

Under the Virginia Code § 16.1–283, for example, parental rights may
be terminated for several reasons. One is for neglect or abuse suffered by
the child, which presents a serious and substantial threat to his or her life,
health, or development, and it is not reasonably likely that the conditions
that resulted in the neglect or abuse can be substantially corrected or eliminated to permit the child's safe return within a reasonable period of time.
For example, in *Lowe v. Richmond Department of Public Welfare*, 231 Va. 277

(1986), the termination of a mother's parental rights was upheld on the basis of clear and convincing evidence that it was not likely that her problems of alcoholism and mental illness could be corrected or eliminated in a reasonable time.

A second reason may be that the child is in a foster care home and the parent(s) fail(s) to maintain contact and is (are) unwilling or unable within a reasonable time to remedy substantially the conditions that led to the child's foster care placement.

A third reason is that the child is abandoned—usually as a baby on someone's doorstep. Legally, it also means that the identity of the parent(s) cannot be determined, diligent attempts have been made to locate them, and no guardian or relatives have come forward to identify and claim relationship with the child within six months following issuance of a court order placing the child in foster care.

Virginia's statute gives the power to the judge to terminate parental rights based on these above-mentioned conditions without a finding of "unfitness." Once a court finds that the factors in the statute are present, it is tantamount to a finding of "unfitness" (*Knox v. Lynchburg Division of Social Services*, 223 Va. 213 [1982]).

Besides social service agencies, grandparents have the right to bring an initial suit for custody when there are allegations that the child's parent is unfit. A North Carolina court argued that when the safety of a child is at issue, the doors of the courts should swing open and close the courthouse door to those who may be the most concerned members of the child's extended family. See *Sharp v. Sharp*, 477 S.E. 2d 258, 1996. Perhaps, the courts close the doors because some families continue to argue across generations.

Burden on Social Services

The burden is on the part of the Department of Social Services' representatives to show "assistance to remedy." In *Weaver*, for example, it took over three years to provide adequate housing, employment, and regular visitations with the children before the family was reunited. Thus, the parents did not have custody of the children, but they were still the legal parents of the children.

The responsibility is on the state to provide services and permit the parents a substantial chance to remedy the conditions that led to the foster care placement. In the documentation, the state, as represented by Social Services, lists and makes clear the objectives for the parents. Then the parents must agree to this plan of action.

Everyone is ignorant, only in different subjects.
Will Rogers

If your children were taken, would you agree to anything? It is probably at this step that parents need a lawyer before they sign documents agreeing to an objective that is an impossible task for them. For example, agreeing to get full employment within two years is a worthy goal on the part of the state to request of a parent. Yet if the parent has a long history of unemployment due to lack of job skills, then the state is just setting the parent up to fail by agreeing to find employment without getting assistance in training.

While the parent or parents are working toward objectives such as getting adequate housing, stable living arrangements, and paying child support, the parent or parents are to visit the child regularly. Some agencies have to provide bus tickets to financially help the parents visit the child.

Some agencies also are aware that these visits may not go very smoothly unless workers take a proactive stance, which means that the workers have to help the parents in the interaction with the child, monitor the activities, and set reasonable expectations for the next visit. Social workers have to teach the clients by showing them, doing with them, and role-playing with them. In short, parenting is a skill and practice is necessary.

An example of a case deals with Ms. Logan, a 26-year-old divorcee with a ninth-grade education. She gave birth to her third child Michael on January 26, 1986. Michael was diagnosed as suffering from cerebral palsy. The Department of Human Development became involved as a result of concerns over Michael's medical care and possible neglect. Ms. Logan was ordered to undergo a mental health evaluation and to take Michael to his medical appointments at the hospital. She was evaluated as suffering from a personality disorder that causes significant impairment in social and role functioning. On June 19, 1987, the court determined that Michael was a neglected child and ordered Ms. Logan to take Michael to all of his necessary medical and therapy appointments. She failed to abide by the order, so her residual parental rights were terminated to only that child, and Michael was placed in the Department's custody. The Court of Appeals affirmed the lower court (*Logan v. Fairfax County Department of Human Development*, 409 S.E. 2d 460 [1991]).

Standard of Proof

The standard of proof in hearings to terminate parental rights is not proof beyond a reasonable doubt. As a parent, you might want this highest standard of proof, but this is too difficult a standard for the state. With that high a standard, some children would be left in miserable situations. Therefore, the state has to prove that the parents failed to do what they were supposed to do by a lesser standard of proof called **"clear and convincing."**

In *Santosky v. Kramer*, 455 U.S. 745 (1981), the U.S. Supreme Court decided that before a state could sever completely and irrevocably the rights of parents to their natural child, due process required that the state support its allegations by at least clear and convincing evidence. It is the standard used in the mock trial in Appendix 7B. In addition, parents have a right to an attorney to represent them because this is such an important, critical decision.

What the state has to prove is that this particular parent was given chances. The state can provide homemaking services or public health nursing to help an inexperienced mother through the early part of child-rearing. The state is under a good faith effort to implement a **reunification** and **rehabilitation** plan that means an honest, purposeful effort, free of malice or design to defraud or seek an advantage. (See how this applies to the mock trial in Appendix 7B.)

If, however, the parent is unable or unwilling to make reasonable progress toward the elimination of the conditions that led to the child's foster care, then the state requests that the judge terminate the parental right due to **failure to rectify.**

If a mother is put in jail for petit larceny charges, it is reasonable that the conditions that resulted in neglect will be substantially corrected or eliminated once the woman has served her time in the county or city jail. If, however, the woman has committed murder and has a life sentence, what then?

Sometimes, the state does have to take physical custody of the child and then later terminates the parental rights so that the child can be put up for adoption. This is known as **least restrictive alternatives**. This is often done with single mothers who are addicted to alcohol or drugs, because the needs of the parent are as paramount as the child's. There is not enough time to get the parent to a level of effective parenting that could begin to meet the needs of the child without risking the child's health and development. It would also be done in cases where the mother is institutionalized for long periods of time for criminal activities or mental illness. Yet each case has to be handled on a case-by-case determination.

In *In re Valerie D.*, 613 A.2d 748 (Conn. Sup. Aug. 1992), the Supreme Court of Connecticut said that the termination of the mother's parental rights had to be reversed. The mere fact that the mother had ingested cocaine several hours before the onset of labor was simply insufficient to support the order. Although some states allow termination of parental rights based on prenatal care or the lack thereof, this state court was unpersuaded.

Termination of residual parental rights of one parent does not affect the parental rights of the other parent. Unfortunately, in some cases, the state has to find the other parent to determine willingness and ability. Then the process begins again with the previously absent parent—setting up objectives and giving the parent a chance to comply before the state can request a fitness hearing.

Sometimes the lack of the father's financial support and his failure to communicate with the child are enough evidence for the court to terminate his rights. When the social workers call the father and ask if he wants to be the father, the workers find that many want the children as if they were trophies. Their own expressed behavior is such that they really do not care for the child. At that point, the local judge and the state have to look at what is best for the child.

SUMMARY

This chapter discussed custody, support, and termination of residual parental rights in terms of three interests: (1) the state, (2) the parents, and (3) the child. As the cases show, there is, at times, disagreement among these three parties. So the courts, through law and process, try to create a balance where parents have rights and children may be reared in a safe environment to successfully grow and develop.

Custody was discussed in terms of its definition and criteria. This discussion showed that the biological parent was preferred, yet the list of preferences gives credence to others because of the psychological bonding and the "best interest of the child" test. Custody was also discussed in terms of the Federal Parental Kidnapping Prevention Act (PKPA)—a federal act addressing the problem of parents kidnapping their own children from the other spouse who may have physical custody of the child. Joint custody with its strengths and weaknesses was also discussed. Then, the Uniform Child Custody Jurisdiction Act (UCCJA) was discussed in terms of grounds for jurisdiction, physical presence of the child, declining jurisdiction, and modification of decree and international application. The UCCJA was a joint effort on the part of courts throughout the United States to stop forum shopping and multistate jurisdictional squabbles.

Support was discussed as money for the rearing of the child(ren). Again, the federal government has had to assist, passing the Revised Uniform Reciprocal Enforcement of Support Act (RURESA). Paternity and illegitimacy were discussed in terms of the high rate of illegitimate births, the common law not to support illegitimate children, the U.S. Supreme Court decisions, and more recently, the duty of the father to support if he can be identified. Thus, ways to identify unwed fathers, including the HLA and DNA tests, were discussed. The law case *Stanley v. Illinois* is an example of how a state deals with these issues of children and their parents.

The chapter closed with the rights of parents in hearings to terminate residual parental rights. Termination was discussed in terms of voluntary, for adoptions, or involuntary, when parents fail to rectify the situation and it is the least restrictive alternative for the welfare of the child. Parents were shown to have the right to an attorney and for the state to prove its case by "clear and convincing" evidence. In addition, the state has to make a good faith effort toward reunification of the child with the family and to rehabilitate the parents for the safety, health, and welfare of the child.

Deadliest of all sins is the devastation of a child's spirit. Eric Erikson

Truly, the well fare (welfare) of children is not separate from the economic factors of support or the emotional or economic needs and issues of the parents. When families have housing problems, economic problems, emotional problems, and an inability to parent children, then children have housing, economic, and behavioral problems. When children have no hope or chance to develop their potential, then children physically grow but usually give our society trouble. Then we, as a society, have a chance to make a choice. We can choose to give in to our fears, or we can choose to give children the attention and the second chance they need to become the productive persons that they can become and that we deserve.

REFERENCES

Barrett, L., and I. Sagatun. "Parental Child Abduction: The Law, Family, Dynamics, and Legal System Responses." *Journal of Criminal Justice* 18 (1990): 433–442.

Finkelhor, David, Gerald Hotaling, and Andrea Sedlak. *Missing, Abducted, Runaway, and Throwaway Children in America.* Executive Summary. Washington, D.C.: U.S. Dept. of Justice, 1990.

Forst, Martin, and Martha-Elin Blomquist. *Missing Children: Rhetoric and Reality.* New York: Lexington Books, 1991.

Girdner, Linda. "Parentally Abducted Children: Roadblocks to Recovery and Reunion." *Juvenile Justice* 1 (1993): 17–23.

Goldstein, Joseph, Anna Freud, and Albert J. Solnit. *Beyond the Best Interests of the Child.* New York: The Free Press, 1979.

Greif, Geoffrey L., and Alfred Demaris. "When a Single Custodial Father Receives Child Support." *The American Journal of Family Therapy* 19 (1991): 167–175.

Janvier, Rosemary F., Kathleen McCormick, and Rose Donaldson. "Parental Kidnapping: A Survey of Left-Behind Parents." *Juvenile and Family Court Journal* 14(2)(1990): 1–14.

Update. Alexander, VA: American Prosecutors Research Institute's National Center for Prosecution of Child Abuse, Feb. 1992.

Virginia 1980 Vital Statistical Annual Report. Richmond, VA: Center for Health Statistics, 1981.

Washington Post, July 24, 1982, A1, Col. 3.

Zorza, Joan. "Using the Law to Protect Battered Women and Their Children." *Clearinghouse Review*, April 1994, p. 1437.

Instructions to Client

The categories listed below have been compiled by lawyers across the United States and represent the most important issues to the court in the determination of custody disputes between natural parents. Please consider each of the categories and provide me with your written summary of evidence you wish to present on each subject. Please provide names, addresses, and telephone numbers of witnesses who have information in each of these categories. Include as many witnesses as possible—we will decide at a later date whether to contact the witnesses.

1. Emotional and physical health of parents.

2. Preferences of child—predicated upon age, maturity, and motivation.

3. Physical environment of parents.

4. Economic environment of custodial parent.

5. Interaction and interrelationship of child with parent, siblings, and any other person who may significantly affect the child's best interest.

6. Home giving moral and spiritual training.

7. Home that will show more love and affection.

8. Educational needs and opportunities.

9. Whether change of custody will require removal from surroundings, both physical and familial—namely, stability.

10. Necessities—meals, clothing, and health care (physical well-being).

11. Stable, consistent supervision, care, and guidance.

12. Child's adjustment at home, school, and community.

13. Mental and physical health of child.

14. Age and sex of the parents/child.

15. Parents' ability to discipline selves and children.

16. Religious needs.

17. Personal habits of the custodial parent a child may acquire by example (character).

18. Comparative empathic and emotional responsiveness of respective parents toward the child.

19. Economic environment of noncustodial parent.

20. Which parent would better promote relationship between the child and noncustodial parent.

21. Social adjustment record (employment, residency).

22. Enhancement of child's particular talents and motivation of same; background of child.

23. Wishes of the child's parent. Possible marriage.

24. Splitting of siblings—yes or no.

25. Recommendations of trained social worker, family court counselor, psychiatrists, and psychologists. Length of time child is in the custody of one parent. Presence of psychological parent.

26. Home that has built-in playmates.

27. Motivation of parent in seeking custody.

28. Reasons for divorce.

29. Tender years doctrine. Fitness of parent.

30. Intellectual and emotional history of child.

31. Parent's communication with people in general and children in particular.

32. Security. Regular visitation. Basis and need for change of custody.

33. Automatic review by the court at specified periods of time. Free from child abuse. Past history of custodian.

34. Third party's interest.

35. Economic environment of child. Custody to one; no visitation to the other parent unless a sincere interest by the noncustodial parent in the welfare of child.

36. Preschool child with mother—female child with mother, male child with father after school age (age 6). Other considerations are: Unconditional placement, drinking habits, biological parent.

APPENDIX 7B: MOCK TRIAL

Purpose: To gain an understanding of hearings to terminate parental rights by taking a part as one of the attorneys, one of the parents, or as the judge.

Documents:

1. Foster Care Service Plan: Part A, Part B, and Part C.

2. Foster Care Service Plan: Review.

3. Permanent Foster Care Placement Agreement.

4. Court Order.

5. Petition for Review and Disposition Hearing of Foster Care Service Plan.

These official documents have been included but have not been filled in to fit this particular case. As a student you might want to fill them in so you can see the work that precedes this hearing.

Instructions:

1. The case will begin with the bailiff calling court to order. "Please all rise for the Honorable __."

2. The judge will call the case.

3. The incident occurred in the City of Your State. It is being tried or heard in the Juvenile and Domestic Relations District or Family Court of that city. This permits the court to have jurisdiction. The case must proceed under the laws of your state.

4. The court needs to decide how to swear in the witnesses. In some courts, the judge swears everyone in at the beginning by asking for all persons who are going to give testimony or speak to raise their right hand. If the judge does not want a group swearing-in, then the judge will have to swear in each witness before he or she takes a seat in the witness box or seat. (You don't need a Bible. Just ask if people swear to tell the truth.)

5. Proper respect to the court means that every time an attorney talks to the judge, the attorney is to stand and address the judge as "Your Honor."

Facts:

Bobby Foster is 5 years old, born in 1996. He has been in foster care since June 1999 as a result of abuse and neglect on three (3) separate occasions, when both parents were found to have neglected the child. He was placed in DSS (Department of Social Services) custody.

DSS is currently petitioning for termination of parental rights, alleging the parents have failed to comply with the goals set in the reunification plan of the foster care plan.

The parents oppose the termination. They claim they tried to comply to the extent possible.

Before the Court are as follows:

☐ Raymond Blue, Esquire, representing DSS.

☐ Stephen Green, Esquire, representing the parents.

☐ Kathy White, Esquire, *Guardian ad litem*.

White: (Preliminary motion to admit representation of print media to observe proceeding.) Mr. Blue and Mr. Green object.

Your Honor, I would like to request my client, Bobby Foster, be allowed to exercise his right to a public hearing in this case.

Blue: We object, Your Honor. Termination proceedings should be closed to protect this child.

Green: I agree with counsel for the Department.

White: Your Honor, I believe it is my responsibility to represent the child, and I would appreciate counsel for the parents and the Department representing their own clients rather than mine.

Judge decides.

Blue: Your Honor, I would like to request a continuance. Dr. O'Neill has been unavoidably detained and his testimony is crucial to our cause.

White: I object, your Honor. Dr. O'Neill was properly subpoenaed. We have waited four (4) months for this court date. I am fully prepared and insist on going forward.

Green: We do not object to the continuance, your Honor.

Judge decides.

The parties may want to give more information on why they want a continuance. If the judge does decide to grant the continuance, everyone gets out their calendars and finds a date they can all meet again.

Assuming the judge does not continue, then move on with the script.

Green moves to withdraw on basis that he has learned that the position for the parties (husband and wife) may be in conflict.

Green: Your Honor, I would like to withdraw as representing both Mr. and Mrs. Foster. It has come to my attention that they are not united, and therefore, we may have two persons who each need to be represented.

White and Blue: I object.

Judge decides.

White: Your Honor, as the *guardian ad litem*, it is my position that the Government has the burden of moving forward at this time since they are asking for the termination.

Blue: Your Honor, our pleadings clearly establish failure of the parents to comply with the foster plan. If they deny this allegation, let them show how they have indeed complied.

Green: Your Honor, the Department clearly has the burden of going forward. They pray for relief, not us. Let them show their case by **clear and convincing evidence**.

Judge decides.

Blue: As a point of clarification, Your Honor, since we are claiming the parents have failed to comply as required by statute, we would like for the Court to initially rule on whether we may limit our case to this issue since the finding of abuse was made several months ago and is surely now a final order. We do not wish to burden the Court with a second "**best interest**" finding.

Green: I object, Your Honor. Clearly the Government must continue to show that it is in the child's best interest to suffer the severance of his parental ties before the court considers such a drastic action.

Judge decides.

Green: Your Honor, before we proceed any further, it is the parents' wish that you talk with Bobby. As you know, Bobby is 5 years old, and though not presumed to testify, we believe that his views should become known in this matter.

White: I object, Your Honor. Having Bobby testify in open Court would be very traumatic for him.

Green: But, Your Honor, we are not necessarily asking that Bobby testify in open Court, subject to cross-examination. Why, we would even be pleased if Your Honor would see Bobby in chambers, in the presence of the *guardian ad litem*.

White: Again, Your Honor, I must object. Speaking with the child serves no purpose. He is a child of **tender years**, with three (3) incidents of abuse and neglect during his short life. As *guardian ad litem*, I fear that guilt will pervade this child's emotions for the rest of his life—that somehow he will feel he caused this permanent separation, by retelling a horrifying tale that no Court could ignore.

Judge decides.

Blue: Your Honor, the Court and counsel each have had an opportunity to review the foster care plan. With that in mind, I would like to call Veronica Rowe, foster care worker for the Department of Social Services, to the stand.

The Court needs to decide who will swear in this witness.

Blue: State your full name and occupation.

Rowe: Veronica Rowe, foster care worker for the Department of Social Services.

Blue: How long have you worked with Bobby Foster and his family?

Rowe: Since his last placement in June of 1999.

Blue: And, of course, you prepared a foster care plan with the parents for the reunification of the child with them, which was filed in a proper and timely manner with the Court?

Rowe: Yes, I did.

Blue: Looking at that plan, what sorts of rehabilitative services were you looking to help in this effort?

Rowe: Well, as you can see, and I quote:

"The parents will participate in family counseling with a therapist with a forte in dynamics of intrafamilial discord so that parents will learn developmental emotional dynamics for proper growth of the child's psyche. Parents will participate in a Parenting Education Group with a goal toward developing motivational nurturance skills, including controlling the vitriolic impulses to child responses commensurate with Bobby's normal expressions to stimuli."

Of course, there were several goals, evident by a reading of this document, which was signed by the parents. Over 12 months transpired, and still no significant progress toward these goals. Accordingly, we changed our goal to adoption because of the parents' failure to comply, except for some supervised visitation over the last four months of the initial plan.

Blue: Is Bobby adoptable now?

Rowe: Yes, as a matter of fact, his foster care parents are totally bonded to Bobby, and he to them. I feel they would be suitable prospective adoptive parents for Bobby.

Blue: Thank you, Ms. Rowe. Your witness, Mr. Green.

Green: Isn't it a fact, Ms. Rowe, that you did not explain to the parents what was meant by the goals you just quoted?

Rowe: Well, yes, but this is a clearly written plan, typical of any properly presented thesis for reunification within DSS guidelines and proper licensing procedures.

Green: No further questions. Your witness, Ms. White.

White: Aren't Mrs. Foster's parents, that is, Bobby's maternal grandparents, desirous of participating actively in Bobby's upbringing?

Rowe: I understand they are, although the DSS has not made a home study as to the suitability of this placement with the grandparents.

White: How long have they expressed this interest, Ms. Rowe?

Rowe: Frankly, Ms. White, I just learned of this last week during a supervised visit with the child. Mrs. Foster has always gotten along terribly with her parents from when she was 14 years old with a constant runaway problem, not to mention delinquency. What is more, I just discovered that Mrs. Foster is now living with her parents.

White: But isn't it a fact that Mrs. Foster's parents are quite well-to-do now, and live in a lovely section of the city, and could give the best that life has to offer to their grandchild—their own flesh and blood—Bobby Foster?

Rowe: I suppose. But, I can't figure out why this sudden interest in the child after all these years. Now? How and why this mother is suddenly living at the home with the parents? I don't understand these grandparents' motive, nor those of the mother.

White: No further questions, Your Honor.

Blue: Your Honor, may I ask a few more questions on redirect?

Judge signals affirmatively.

Blue: Ms. Rowe, referencing once again the Foster Care Plan and its goals, why did you require that Mr. Foster attend Parents Anonymous?

Rowe: Well, as you know, that is a support group for parents who physically and sexually abuse their children. Mr. Blue, the first time Mr. Foster sexually abused Bobby, he also scalded him with hot bath water because Bobby didn't show signs of enjoyment of the abuse. And that was just the first time! The second time, Mr. and Mrs. Foster attempted to . . .

Green: I object, Your Honor. Counsel for the Department of Social Services is obviously wanting to use the gravity of the abuse in the past as the issue in termination here. That's improper. For the Court to decide, it must be based solely on whether the parents complied with the goals of the Foster Care Plan, which, by the way, are incomprehensible to my mind, not to mention to the minds of my clients, Mr. and Mrs. Foster.

Blue: But Your Honor, the gravity of the offense is a significant issue here. With abuse like this, can the Court ever be sure that such sadistic behavior won't occur again?

Judge decides.

Judge: If counsel has no other questions, you may step down from the witness box, Ms. Rowe, and return to your seat in the courtroom.

Blue: That is our case, Your Honor.

Judge: Mr. Green, do you wish to call any witnesses?

Green: Yes, Your Honor; I call my client, Mrs. Foster, to the stand.

The Court needs to decide who will swear in the witness.

Green: Would you please state your full name for the Court.

Mrs. F.: Mrs. Lula Foster.

Green: Mrs. Foster, do you love your son?

Mrs. F.: Yes. More than my own life. He means the world to me.

Green: Do you remember meeting with Ms. Rowe in developing the Foster Care Plan?

Mrs. F.: Yes, sort of.

Green: What do you mean by that?

Mrs. F.: Well, Your Honor. I don't read too good. I don't always understand too good what people tell me. Some people call me slow. And all those big words and all, well, I just didn't understand what I was supposed to do. And, I was afraid to ask. I mean, I didn't ever hurt Bobby none. It was all my husband's fault. He has such a temper. I quit school early because I wasn't doing too good. I got into lots of trouble and my parents practically disowned me since I was 14 even though they was loaded with money. Why, I couldn't help it about my drug addiction five years ago. I knew I should have spent the money on food for Bobby, but I just couldn't help it. Please, Your Honor, don't take my baby away from me.

Green: No further questions. Your witness, Ms. White.

White: Mrs. Foster, why haven't you visited Bobby more?

Mrs. F.: Because I didn't have no way to get to see him until I moved in with my parents a while back.

White: Do you really think you can take care of Bobby now?

Mrs. F.: Oh, yes. And what I can't do, I know my parents will help me with. Your Honor, please give me this last chance.

White: No further questions, Your Honor. Your witness, Mr. Blue.

Blue: Mrs. Foster, isn't it true that you came here to Court today saying you didn't know what you were supposed to do, when all along you understood this Foster Care Plan?

Mrs. F.: No. Really. Honest, I didn't understand.

Blue: Aren't you really just stalling for time because you figure that now that your parents and you have made up, you can use their interest in this child to reunite you with Bobby without having to do anything that the Foster Care Plan says you should do—a Foster Care Plan, which by the way, you yourself signed?

Mrs. F.: No, I promise. Everything's on the level with me and my folks now. I want Bobby with me.

Blue: You really have no intention of ever living up to your end of the bargain that you agreed to in the Foster Care Plan, isn't that true, Mrs. Foster?

Mrs. F.: No, honest, Your Honor, I didn't understand all this too good.

Blue: No further questions.

Judge: If counsel has no other questions, you may step down from the witness seat and return to your seat next to your attorney in the courtroom.

Any other evidence you wish to present, Mr. Green?

Green: Briefly, Your Honor. I would like to call Mr. Foster.

Court has to decide who will swear in the witness.

Green: Just one question, Mr. Foster. Did you participate in developing this Foster Care Plan and did you understand it?

Mr. F.: Heck, Your Honor. I don't known about all this stuff. I can't half read, and if they'd have just done and told me what to do, I'd have done it. Anyhow, me and Lula is aiming maybe to get back together, so we can be a family again.

Green: No other questions. Your witness, Ms. White.

White: Your Honor, any questions I would have would probably be argumentative and futile. Therefore, I'll defer to Mr. Blue.

Blue: Mr. Foster. You didn't do anything in almost two years to get your son back, did you?

Mr. F.: Well, I gave him a baseball glove for Christmas. All these people been on my back, heck, I didn't know what I was supposed to do.

Blue: How are you and Mrs. Foster going to get back together again if she's living with her parents? They hate you, don't they?

Mr. F.: I can't stand them either, and when Mrs. Foster gets our Bobby back, I feel sure she'll come back to me. Why, we're a team.

Blue: No further questions, Your Honor.

Judge: Any other witnesses, Mr. Green?

Green: No, Your Honor.

Judge: Since there are no other witnesses, then I will now hear closing arguments. I begin with you, Mr. Blue.

Blue: Your Honor, we have proved our case. These parents have failed to meet the goals of the Foster Care Plan, which they both signed. It has been almost two years since the abuse and neglect incident. It is time to provide permanency for this child while he is still adoptable. The parents have, without excuse, failed to substantially remedy the circumstances that caused Bobby's foster care placement within a reasonable period of time, and I urge the court to terminate the parents' rights. Consider the terrible abuse this child has been through, and let's plan now for a healthy future with people who can and want to be parents to Bobby.

Judge: Mr. Green, your closing argument, please.

Green: Your Honor. The law provides that the Foster Care Plan be clear and understandable so that it is possible to attain and to be practical for all the parties concerned. It is supposed to be specific in its goals so that one can monitor the behavior of the parents against the goals. Surely, the Court can see that this is clearly not the case with the plan at hand. The Department of Social Services has not met its burden, and, accordingly, we urge the Court to deny termination of parental rights here today. Or, in the alternative, we request at a minimum that the case be continued for six months to remand all parties to write a workable plan as required by law and to give my clients an opportunity to show the Court that they can meet those goals. This Court is in the business of reuniting families, not tearing them apart simply because they have marginal cognitive and training skills.

Judge: Does the *guardian ad litem* wish to say anything in closing?

White: Yes, Your Honor. The Court has heard today reference regarding the maternal grandparents and their interest in the child. As *guardian ad litem*, I have had a chance to investigate their home and to interview them, and I feel that it is in the best interests of Bobby to stay with this extended family, if possible. The law certainly welcomes this, Your Honor, especially when compared to the possibility of termination of all family ties. I think the maternal grandparents are suitable, and I would urge this Court to take this matter under advisement for six months and order an investigation into the suitability of these grandparents to have custody. I would propose we continue this case to a date certain, in about thirty to forty-five days, to allow the Department of Social Services time to investigate this prospective home with Bobby's family.

Blue: But, Your Honor, I must say as part of closing that the *guardian ad litem* takes me by surprise. Surely, the Court can see such placement with the grandparents will result in nothing but a sham—a manipulative effort by the parents to sidestep the requirement of law as outlined in the plan for the best interests of Bobby.

Green: Oh, come on, Joe [or Jane, or whatever is the judge's first name], you can see my colleague here is getting paranoid. He's acting just like that guy in *L.A. Law* we watched together over beer at my house.

Blue: Your Honor, I move for an immediate mistrial. You and Mr. Green are obviously socially connected and personal friends, so much so that he calls you by your first name in open Court.

Judge decides.

Judge decides the following points brought out on closing:

1. Merits of the DSS argument for termination.

2. Merits of the parents' argument that no termination can occur because of an unclear plan.

3. Merits of the *guardian ad litem's* argument for placement with maternal grand-parents, especially considering Mrs. Foster's new residence there.

4. Merits of granting DSS motion for a mistrial on grounds of Mr. Green's social familiarity with the judge.

AFTER THE JUDGE DECIDES THE CASE, THE FOLLOWING MAY ALSO OCCUR:

Losing Lawyer: Your Honor, I wish to note an appeal. What's more, I am requesting an immediate stay of the Court's order pending an appeal, as is the right of the Court, especially when a child's welfare is at stake until the final determination.

Winning Lawyer: Your Honor [if case is continued], this is not a final order of Court, therefore it cannot be appealed.

OR

Your Honor [if case is decided], I request an appeal bond, and I oppose any stay of the Court's order.

Judge decides.

With the final decisions by the judge, the judge declares the case over.

Judge: This Court is adjourned. Bailiff, please clear the courtroom for the next case.

Source: Virginia Supreme Court, *Training for New Judges*, 1993.

CHAPTER 8

Legal and Policy Issues That Affect Children

It is 10:25 at night when an undercover agent purchases $50 of crack cocaine from a young black male. The agent call(ed) us [Dr. William J. Chambliss and students riding with the Raid Deployment Unit (RDU) of Washington, D.C.] and tells (told) us that the suspect has just entered a building and gone into an apartment. We go immediately to the apartment; the police enter without warning with their guns drawn. Small children begin to scream and cry. The adults in the apartment are thrown to the floor, the police are shouting, the three women in the apartment are swearing and shouting "You can't just barge in here like this . . . where is your damn warrant?" The suspect is caught and brought outside. The identification is made and the suspect is arrested. The suspect is sixteen years old. While the suspect is being questioned one policeman says: "I should kick your little black ass right here for dealing that shit. You are a worthless little scumbag, do you realize that?" Another officer asks: "What is your mother's name, son? My mistake; she is probably a whore and you are just a ghetto bastard. Am I right?" The suspect is cooperative and soft spoken. He does not appear to be menacing or a threat. He offers no resistance. The suspect's demeanor seems to cause the police officers to become more abusive verbally. The suspect is handled very roughly. Handcuffs are cinched tightly and he is shoved against the patrol car. His head hits the doorframe of the car as he is pushed into the back seat of the patrol car. One of the officers comments that it is nice to make a "clean arrest." When asked whether it is legal to enter a home without a warrant, the arresting officer replies: "This is southeast (Washington) and the Supreme Court has little regard for little shit like bursting in on someone who just committed a crime involving drugs . . ." Who will argue for the juvenile in this case? No one can and no one will. (Chambliss 1997, pp. 147–148)

How youth are treated is a combination of philosophy, policy, and law. Sometimes the philosophy is enacted into law. The most noted example is the work of Cesare Beccaria (1738–1794). As an Italian jurist, he founded the

INTRODUCTION

Classical School of Criminology. Instead of reviewing criminals as a manifestation of demons or unknown supernatural forces, he argued that people use reason and logic with the desire of pleasure to commit crimes. By giving punishment that reduced the pleasure, a society could reduce crime. Secondly, bad laws corrupt and inconsistently administered criminal justice systems cause contempt and disrespect for the law. Even reasonable people are inclined to violate the law. The majority of these themes running through his book called *Crimes and Punishment* was "to make the punishment fit the crime." The idea of giving punishment as pain to stop the pleasure of crime because men are rational beings became the foundation of the criminal justice systems of many European and western countries, including our own. It provides the rationale for the use of punishment in the control of crime and offenders. Regardless of the fact that critics, both then and now, argue that this philosophy of mankind is faulty and class-biased, it provided support for the most fundamental assumption of the criminal justice system—prisons and jails were to be painful and not offer treatment.

Policy isn't always law, but sometimes the practice of a certain group impacts another person as if the policy were law. The end result of the RDU (Raid Deployment Unit) of the Washington Police Department with its verbal abuse and lack of an arrest warrant will matter little when the youth goes before the intake officer in the juvenile court.

Law and policy can also be influenced by research. In terms of delinquency, for example, the major research done by Cloward and Ohlin in their book *Delinquency and Opportunity: A Theory of Delinquent Gangs* (1960) argued some of the key ideas that led to President Lyndon Johnson's War on Poverty. It also led to the development of the Office of Economic Opportunity where legitimate opportunities in education and training were to be open to the economically disadvantaged as a way to empower youth and divert them from criminal activity.

Yet sometimes the research shows something that is the opposite of the prevailing policy. For example, the best available data from victim surveys conducted every year since 1973 (not the other official data collected by the F.B.I. as "crimes known to the police"), show that there has been no significant change in the crime rate in the last twenty years (Chambliss 1997, 155). Yet we have developed a policy that is best expressed by Rogers (1997) as "the greatest correctional myth of winning the war on crime through incarceration."

The recent politicization of crime has meant that the policy of the 1970s and 1980s has resulted in more punishment with no treatment programs. From the early 1970s to 2001, we have tripled the prison population nationally, but there has been a systematic withdrawal of social supports and public services for the most distressed communities and disadvantaged. We have the highest incarceration rate of any society in the free world. We "increased by 167 percent between 1980 and 1992, with the greatest percentage increase in (minor) drug law violations" (Chambliss 1997, 151). The political interests of politicians from Goldwater to Clinton in making crime (and drugs) a public issue to gain electoral advantage over their opponents has distracted us from confronting the systemic factors of crime. It has also diverted attention from other politically dangerous topics such as the budget deficit. Thus the words were "get tough on criminals" so as to produce a safer society.

So ask yourself this question: If there has been no significant change in crime rates for the last twenty years, how come we hear so much about crime and the need for money to produce a war on crime? If experts in criminal justice argue against this indiscriminate strategy of "locking up more offenders for longer periods of time regardless of their crimes or threat to public safety," how come it is still happening? Why are so many youth considered adults and sent to an adult criminal court instead of the juvenile court? Why are there no treatment programs, only more punishment?

Part of the answer is that crime became a national political issue that created a moral panic that produced a crime industry so powerful that it has become immune from the budgetary cuts experienced by the other public services. With more than $31.2 billion for 1992 (local, state, and federal budgets) being spent on prisons, the economic realities for education and other budgets are staggering (DiMascio 1997, 2). This "get tough" approach has also been applied to juveniles, even though we know that only a small number of offenders create the greatest concern for the public. The majority of the juveniles need only minimum intervention, not harsh and longer sentences.

Thus, one needs to ask this question: Who benefits from such policies? When you think you have an answer, think about why. Why would a political process permit the passage of laws that provide law enforcement agencies with greater intrusion into people's lives without safeguards?

The present-day get-tough, lock-them-up policy and the derogatory names it uses for various populations in criminal justice, make it seem as if there is a dangerous class of persons who need to be socially controlled by tactics of terror and repression in order to sanitize society. As the RDU incident that opens this chapter illustrates, the intensive surveillance of black neighborhoods has institutionalized racism by defining the problem of crime as if it were all a problem of young black males (Miller 1996). Young African-American and Latino men as well as other minorities are arrested for minor offenses over and over again so that they can be given long prison sentences. Yet we know that if the wrongdoings of middle- and upper-class people were measured or enforced like the crimes of poor people, they would amount to far more criminality and damage than the conventional crime we worry so much about (Elias 1997 [citing Frank 1985; Green and Berry 1985; Horchsteder 1984; Mokiber 1988; Feiman 1984]). Strange that drug lords become millionaires. It seems like the rich get drugs while the poor get prison.

The reason there is a disparity between research and its application is because of policy and how policy is developed. Courses in public policy abound. The purpose of this chapter, however, is to focus the definitions and some of the literature on public policy as a lens upon the criminal justice system, especially that of children and youth. Then you will be better able to understand how the states and federal government permit the juvenile court to operate today, and you will be able to redefine certain behaviors as needing official attention. To do this, it is important to understand the sources of law; what public policy is and how it operates; the theories of how laws are made; and the impact these policies have on children and their families. First, let us briefly review the sources of law before discussing policy, and theories of lawmaking and its impact.

SOURCES OF LAW

Laws cannot make men love me. But, they sure can help prevent them from lynching me. Martin Luther King, Jr.

Constitutions and Statutes

When judges and lawyers use the term "law," they mean written and un-written law. In written law, the two major sources are constitutions (state and federal) and statutes. Each state has a constitution as well as the federal government. States may always give their citizens more rights than they have under the federal, but not less. For example, the Wyoming Constitution gives its citizens a higher right when it views all confessions as coerced. A special burden is placed on the prosecutor to prove to the court by clear and convincing evidence that the confession was made with free will and voluntarily. In some states, the defendant has the burden to prove it wasn't free will and voluntary before the burden shifts to the prosecutor to defend the action of the police.

Statutes are enactments of Congress and the legislatures of the states. These acts or laws are printed and bound in an orderly fashion by chapter headings, section numbers in volumes, with an index of their contents. Of these general statutes, the laws may be compiled without revision while another type may be revised statutes. Codes of a state and the federal government are the complete system of statutory law. So, when one wants to know what definition of a crime a state may use, one consults the codes of that state.

✻ BRAIN EXERCISE

Facts: In 1985 Wisconsin passed a "grandparent-liability law." Parents are to pay child support for the offspring of their teenage children to reduce the state's high teen-pregnancy rate. Question: What do you think would be the impact of such a law?

Answer: In the first twenty-two months, only twenty-one grandparents were forced to pay an average of $80 a month (*U.S. News & World Report*, July 24, 1989 p. 26). Obviously, there must be more effective ways to reduce teen-pregnancy than just passing a law.

Acts made by state and federal governments are laws. Yet, throughout this book, you have been reading law cases with decisions of a court such as the United States Supreme Court. Their decisions made law and other lower court decisions can also be law.

Court Decisions

In some cases, the justices of the U.S. Supreme Court applied the "common law" or unwritten law through their reasoning. Their decision creates a new law through the concept of "precedence." That means that a future case will have the same decision as the past case if the question, issue, or dispute is basically the same as the earlier case heard by the court. Courts write up their decisions with the idea that attorneys will consult these cases when advising their clients. The more the attorney's present case is actually alike in facts or issues to an earlier decision of the court, the more the attorney can predict the outcome of the present case.

Since these decisions are open to the public and are considered in the public domain, any individual can research their particular problem or legal question. A person reads previous cases to get an idea of the merit of his or her own case. Yet it is wise to consult an attorney, because in some cases, the ideas that you might want to use to support your case are considered "dicta" by the previous court. Dicta are extra words to the decision of that case. Thus dicta are not normally used to support one's present case.

Although legislators are the only ones who are supposed to make law, judges can make law by their decisions. One of the most noted decisions by the United States Supreme Court that virtually changed the policy in every police department was *Miranda* (384 U.S. 436 [1966]). The Court ruled that persons arrested for serious crimes must be informed of certain rights. They have the right to remain silent (Fifth Amendment right); the right to know that anything said to an officer can be used against the person in a court of law; and the right to know that a person has a right to an attorney to discuss whether she or he should confess to a crime. (This right to an attorney is different from the right to an attorney under the Sixth Amendment.)

Judge's Law—Juvenile Waiver

In terms of juveniles, *Kent v. U.S.* (383 U.S. 541 [1966]) is a good example of how a court made a new law. That decision made a waiver hearing of a delinquent youth from a court of original jurisdiction (meaning the juvenile court in the local area of a state is required to first hear the juvenile's case) mandatory upon states that had this "original jurisdiction." The U.S. Supreme Court saw that this hearing was necessary for "due process," because the youth waived into a criminal court as an "adult" could be sentenced to the death penalty. To have such a major decision without some kind of ceremony or hearing was not permissible. Our system of justice and even-handedness required the states to provide such a hearing. In that hearing, it was important for a juvenile to have the assistance of counsel or the hearing would be meaningless in terms of protecting the youth's rights.

"Due process of law" is in the Fifth Amendment of the United States Constitution. Later, the Fourteenth Amendment made some of the federal standards apply to the state. When a state is going to take away someone's liberty, what kind of a process would you want it to provide?

Let's ask the question differently: If your liberty was going to be taken away, what kind of a process would you want to receive? Remember, the issue is not your skin color or your mother's marital status; the issue is what kinds of steps, such as notice, hearing by an impartial person, and appeal to another impartial person, would you want? What would make you think and feel that you were fairly treated and that the state was not abusing its power? Apply your answers to the present situation where statutes permit mandatory waiver or concurrent jurisdiction so that youth are waived to the adult court without any of the procedural safeguards given in *Kent*.

New State Statutes Overrule Court and Judges' Decisions

Today, many states, including those with original jurisdiction, have now passed new statutes that abolish waiver hearings known as judicial waiver for such youths of certain age that have done certain major crimes. This is called legislative waiver. In Virginia, a 14-year-old or older youth is automatically waived when charged with crimes such as murder and rape. The juvenile court doesn't have to have a waiver hearing as it did under *Kent*. Under the new state laws in many other states, the juvenile court only has to verify that the youth is a certain age and is charged with a certain crime as required by the statute of that state. Thus, the states have now created new laws that override the requirements set forth by *Kent*, that is, to have a waiver hearing to end the power of the juvenile court so the youth can be prosecuted in the adult court.

Is a legislative waiver better than a judicial waiver? It depends on the study. For example, Osbun and Rode (1984, 199) supported the judicial waiver and its traditional discretion over legislative waiver because a hearing before a juvenile judge does a better job "in identifying the more serious juvenile offenders." However, Fagan and Deschenes (1990) found an absence of uniform criteria among juvenile court judges. Variables such as age, offense, and race significantly differ among youth who are transferred and those who are not.

More recently, in a study done by tracking specific youth into the adult court to determine exactly how much punishment the youth received, Clement (1997) found that 26 percent of those youth, waived in a state that was using judicial waiver, were found not guilty or had their cases dismissed. Contrast that finding with Hamparian et al. (1982), who found that 91 percent of the waiver youth were convicted in the adult court.

In reality, new statutes effectively end *Kent* even though the U.S. Supreme Court has not overturned that decision. Unless the state or the Supreme Court finds these statutes that permit automatic waiver unconstitutional, the states have reduced the rights of juveniles that were originally granted by the Supreme Court.

One ought to wonder why a state would want to increase an adult criminal population by reducing the age of waiver to 14, 15, and in some states as low as age 12 or 10. Since the actual number of youth who commit heinous crimes is very low, one has to wonder if there isn't another agenda. For example, we now know more about the developmental stages of children and the torture that is done to some children by their own family members. When a youth who has been sexually/physically tortured kills his or her parent or guardian, why does society want to continue to punish the youth? With our understanding of children who seek to defend themselves in this way (battered child syndrome) from psychological and sociological research, why isn't the legal *mens rea* concept of guilty mind used to mitigate a youth's behavior?

Paul Mones' (1991) book, *When A Child Kills,* gives us some answers. He showed the bias and lack of understanding of the judges and prosecutors in his excellent examples of dysfunctional families and the torture many children have had to endure even after reaching out to public officials, such as police, child protection workers, schoolteachers, friends, and others. Likewise, people who work with juveniles in the court systems are often ignorant of the medical research that was done on fourteen juveniles on death row that showed that many other important variables are ignored, such as head injuries (Lewis et al. 1988).

This type of bias becomes evident in Wilkins, the youth from Missouri who was sentenced to capital punishment in *Stanford v. Kentucky* (see Chapter 4, "Process for Delinquent (Criminal) Youth"), who later appealed that decision through a writ of *habeas corpus* (*Wilkins v. Bowersox*, 933 F. Supp. 1496 [1996]). In that case, we get even a clearer idea of how juveniles are mistreated by the process of the system. To remind you, at age 10, Wilkens was committed to a mental institution for several years and then released. (Some may say he was never treated even if he wasn't mistreated in the mental institution.) Thus, it was no surprise to those who knew this young man that his behavior would get him into trouble again. When he did, however, the prosecutor who had been the public defender (defense) for the youth used the state's power to seek the death penalty for the youthful defendant after he committed a predictable murder. Wilkins won his appeal based on this conflict of interest of the prosecutor. This is how the Court said it:

The prosecutor's conflict of interest presents a very
serious issue. It seems incredulous to imagine a former
defense attorney, privy at one time to the thoughts of a
juvenile defendant so disturbed that he is committed to
a mental institution, to then turn prosecutor and
accuser seeking the death penalty for his former client
without disclosing the relationship to the court and to
counsel. This is particularly disturbing in this case
because petitioner (Wilkins) waived counsel, entered a
guilty plea to a capital charge, waived mitigation and
was sentenced to death. The presence of a former
defense attorney and confidant at the opposing table
would certainly inhibit a defendant from trusting his
present counsel or taking counsel's assertions of
confidentiality very seriously. (933 F. Supp. 1523)

The United States District Court for the Western District of Missouri, Western Division, went on to explain that this structural defect defied the analysis used to determine if there had been "harmless error." To them, the entire conduct of the criminal proceeding was, beyond a reasonable doubt, a conflict of interest caused by the prosecutor's prior representation. They granted Wilkins's petition for writ of *habeas corpus* (writ is a legal device to challenge the detention of a person taken into custody by granting a hearing to determine if the person is being legally held). The court suggested that the State of Missouri withdraw his plea of guilty and afford a new trial.

Wilkens's case may seem unusual. Yet, "according to the National Coalition for the Mentally Ill in the Criminal Justice System, there are about 33 percent more mentally ill individuals in jails than in mental hospitals. In addition, 60 percent of those in the juvenile justice system have a diagnosable mental health problem" (DiMascio 1997, 22).

The news media also plays a role in fanning the fears of youthful killer, and the confusion between what is mental illness and what is rational behavior. "Between 1990 and 1993 the number of crime stories appearing on ABC, CBS, and NBC newscasts increased from 737 to 1,698" (Chambliss 1997, 162). More recently, in many states, the news media will take crimes committed by 18- and 19-year-olds and make these headlines: "TEENAGERS COMMIT MURDER." In all states, 18- and 19-year-olds never go to the juvenile court because they are considered adults at age 18. Why then would the news continue to call these legal adults "teenagers"? Could it be that by calling legal adults teenagers, the media blurs the line between and among the ages of 15, 16, 17, 18, and 19?

Knowing that most of the general public do not note this distinction in ages, the media is using its power to enflame citizens' fears of violent youth. In this manner then, the idea is planted that children and youth no longer need protection. The society is led to believe that more severe punishment is the answer, contrary to the research and our understanding of the developmental stages of children and youth.

In addition, have you noticed the shift in the media from the term youth to "predators," as if the troubled youth or drug-addicted teenager is a tiger or a "mad" pit bull dog? Why then these shifts in terminology that promote policy shifts?

PUBLIC POLICY

To better understand how laws are used to impact children and their families in terms of policy, it is important to know how public policy is defined, what the process is, and who has the power to influence the process. First, let us discuss the definition of public policy.

Public Policy Defined

The commonsense definition is that "public policy is whatever the government chooses to do or not to do" (Dye 1981, 1). However, it is important to realize that among respected political scientists, there are multiple definitions and disagreements as to how the policy process works. It is beyond the scope of this book to resolve all the theoretical disagreements. Rather, the aim is to put public policy into a context that practitioners and ordinary citizens can understand in order to make it work for the needs of a population that has few advocates—children and youth.

Governmental Activities

In the definition of public policy stated above, there are three important governmental activities. First, public policy is a by-product of those who can legitimately act in the name of the government. Secondly, it is a deliberate course of action or inaction designed to achieve a specific purpose, usually a predetermined goal that may or may not be supported by scientific research. Thirdly, some level of authority in the government implements the public but without discretion. They "are not subject to arbitrary interpretation of individuals regardless of their official capacity" (Hojnacki 1997, 5–6).

Political System

Public policy is the result of our political system. Initially, the founding fathers, through the United States Constitution, designed a "republic" in which a separation of powers was to occur among the three main branches of government: executive, legislative, and judicial. (Notice that the word democracy is missing in the Constitution, by consulting the United States Constitution in Appendix II.) A Republic was to be a system of checks and balances among those with federal powers. In addition, the states were to be respected and honored as being better able to handle some matters for their citizens, such that the federal government did not completely overpower the individual states. In the 1790s, senators were sent by their respective states so that a state could recall a senator that didn't act according to the needs of the state. Madison's Federalist Papers Nos. 62 and 63 expressed the concern of their time that if the Senate became an elite group of tyrants due to their six-year terms, the only check on their power was a recall by their state legislatures.

However, in 1913 the Seventeenth Amendment to the U.S. Constitution was passed. Members of the Senate are no longer elected by the legislatures of the various states, but, instead, by popular vote. Over the years, senators have in fact become part of an elite group not subject to recall by their states. They have thus built power. Their power is most noted in the selection and confirmation process of Supreme Court Justices. In the book *The Bench Warmers*, a study on how Supreme Court Justices are selected, the question is posed: "What is the best way to become a United States Supreme Court Justice?" The answer is to choose as your roommate or first law partner someone who will become a future senator.

With all the bureaucracy and power of the federal government, the federal government is given even more power through income taxes. Taxes from citizens are funneled through Washington without any clear budget or accountability to the citizens. One of the original amendments to the Bill of Rights, later dropped, was for a balanced budget. In 1999, the national debt was over $5 trillion. In addition, the federal government uses these moneys as a carrot in the "carrot and stick approach" to problems. For example, states will be denied their allotted monies to repair or build roads (highway monies) unless they pass certain laws consistent with federal mandates. Why did fifty states pass some type of legislation for child protection? Answer: To get federal highway fund monies!

Historically, the United States had been a hard money country until the establishment of the Federal Reserve Bank (FRB) on December 13, 1913, when the country left "gold-backed" money for "paper money." The power to make money was given to the FRB, an independent, privately owned and locally controlled corporation. With paper money that is not backed by gold (removed by early 1970s), the monetary value fluctuates. In this century, paper money has depreciated over 87 percent. Let's calculate how that would work. For example, with 5 percent inflation, 5 percent devaluation applies to the money you earned that year and to that which is left over from the previous years. At the end of the first year of calculation, a dollar is worth 95 cents. At the end of second year, that 95 cents is reduced again by 5 percent and its real worth is 90 cents. In this manner, then, a person can work twenty years, and the government will have 64 percent of every dollar the person saved over all the years. When the FRB prints the money for the American people, they then charge the government a fee for their services that become part of the national debt. Although the Federal Reserve System reports to Congress like other governmental agencies, they are financially independent (Trescott 1998).

Give me control over a nation's currency and I care not who makes its laws. Baron M.A. Rothschild (1744–1812)

With the federal government controlling the purse, states are not always able to act in their own best interests. States, like families, find they are working harder and are still in debt—and in need of money.

Substantive and Procedural Policy

Another way to describe public policies is to view them as substantive or procedural. Substantive policy deals with the construction of interstate highways, payment of food stamps, and welfare benefits that are administered by the states. Procedural policy deals with the process of how a state legislature or a city council functions.

How Policy Impacts Society

Public policy has also been viewed or defined in terms of how it impacts a society. For example, distributive policies involve the delivery of public goods and services such as the U.S. Postal Service and public access to rivers and streams. Redistribution policies have been such "entitlement" programs as Medicare and veterans benefits.

A third category of impact is regulatory policies that are designed to control behavior. The most usual example is a criminal code. Criminal codes also involve some protections for citizens, even for federal crimes, such as the need for a search warrant with an affidavit based upon probable cause (Fourth Amendment). However, the Food and Drug Administration and the Internal Revenue Service (IRS), both regulatory in practice, are not held to higher standards and procedures for search warrants. The FDA can go into any store or doctor's office and take whatever it wants. The IRS would confiscate property (bank accounts, houses, and places of business) without a hearing and without warning. (A corporate income tax was included in the Payne-Aldrich Tariff Act of 1909 and then passage of the 16th Amendment brought about the IRS. Then personal income was included in the Underwood Act of 1913 such that personal income tax is the largest single source of internal revenue in the United States.) Citizens voluntarily give up their Fourth Amendment rights to the privacy of their papers and their effects. In 1998, Congress held hearings on the IRS because many citizens had more rights with other creditors and were more fairly treated than they did with the IRS. There were more laws and rights governing transactions between creditors and debtors that are followed by the courts than with the IRS and its agents. For example, debtors have a right to a hearing to determine if in fact a certain amount is owed before a judgment is given to someone to go after the assets of the debtor. In that hearing, debtors have a right to notice so that they can make preparations. In some cases involving the IRS, testimony before Congress was that people got notice when they saw the padlock on their business doors. When a regulatory agency has such tremendous power, it becomes overly burdensome upon the average citizen, who may not know how to respond, nor have the financial resources to hire the help of others to correct the situation.

Policy also impacts a society through self-regulatory policies such as the licensing requirements used by state governments. Professional occupational groups such as medical doctors and lawyers are regulated by the states. Being licensed to practice law in one state, for example, does not permit one to practice in another state unless one has fulfilled all the requirements of that state including taking its respective exams. Other nonprofessional occupational groups might be licensed as well, such as barbers and hairdressers, who must take specific classes and pass examinations before being allowed to offer their services to consumers.

WHAT THE POLICY PROCESS IS

The process for creating public policy is not as clearly defined as the process for passing a particular state or federal law, even though the two procedures share similarities. The policy process is ongoing so that different issues are being discussed in formal and informal meetings; through citizen groups and decision-makers; by commissions doing research and holding public hearings; and through governmental agencies to determine the impact of policy on systems and resources. The policy process may look at short-term and long-term consequences. The problem with the process is that there is not a single public policy process—there are thousands.

In addition, other groups and individuals can initiate policy by using petitions to put certain matters on the ballot. California has been one of the states most noted for having citizens who bring concerns to the general public through a referendum so that citizens can vote on the issue directly. Yet how referendums or, more broadly, the policy process works is directly related to our understanding of who has the power to influence the process.

Who Has the Power to Influence the Process

All persons in the United States have the right to influence the politics of the country for any reasons—social, religious, or environmental. People across the country try to influence the course of government in their towns, cities, states, and federal government. In fact, the public policy process is designed to discourage any group or small number of groups from dominating the process, but the reality is that considerable political skill and resources are necessary to have an impact on policy. Four interest groups giving us some understanding of who has such influence and skill to influence public policy are: (1) corporate, (2) membership-based, (3) single groups, and (4) public groups (Hojnacki 1997, 14–17).

Corporate

Large corporations sponsor the most intense professional lobbying activities for several reasons. First, they are the best organized and financed. Secondly, corporations stand to gain or lose lots of money depending upon what the government does or doesn't do. Corporations use their wealth to employ experts who are well paid to influence every phase of the political process. Corporations have political action committees (PACs) that channel large amounts of money to political candidates through campaign coffers. When elected, the officer holders are provided with opportunities to earn extra money. Sometimes they make speeches at meetings and conventions for which they are paid honorariums. The lobbyists continue to provide research and advice for the office holder and help broker deals with other office holders and those who have money to provide honorariums. In return, lobbyists become high-level administrators for the new agencies because they are politically appointed and represent the affected businesses and industries. Most of this is done below the level of public visibility.

Membership-Based

These special interest groups that lobby for their needs draw their strength from their representation of a large voting mass of persons such as labor unions, or teachers (National Educational Association), or retired persons (American Association of Retired Persons). They don't have the resources of the corporate interest groups, yet they, too, provide monies as contributions to political campaigns. However, they have to answer to their membership, so they can't do all that corporate lobbyists can do. In addition, their membership may diminish and so may their power and influence.

Single Groups

Groups like the National Rifle Association and environmental advocacy groups like the Sierra Club focus their attention on a narrow range of governmental activities. They tend to use their monies to gain "public support rather than trying to 'buy' the support of legislators who are already in office" (Hojnacki 1997, 15).

Public Groups

Public interest groups ("PIGs") like Common Cause and the U.S. Conference of Mayors have limited public support and resources to use. They usually are a small part of an overall lobbying effort. Pulling these smaller groups together can have greater impact, but it takes time for each vested-interest group to see the importance of cooperation.

Besides groups, the local media can be influential by choosing specific stories to cover and interviewing specific persons to be the "expert." Whereas local media outlets might be interested in the "truth," the reality is that they lack the resources for true investigative reports. On the other hand, the media in large cities are usually operated to make profits. The end result is that there is a lack of investigative reports.

A bank is a place that will lend you money if you can prove that you don't need it. Bob Hope

Bankers are also very influential because they provide the money for local business and industry to own property and build factories, and for individuals to buy a house through home mortgages and other financial products. The board of directors for a bank is usually comprised of persons who represent business, industrial, and institutional leaders. On the local and state level, these leaders know other important persons in the community, what they are doing, and how to work with others for the benefit of their own needs. With the takeover and buyout of many smaller banks and savings and loan institutions, financial power is becoming concentrated in the hands of a few banks who become even more powerful.

The reasons that some have more power to influence the political policy process are many. Yet most discussions about political power begin with an analysis of economic-based interest. One of the obvious reasons is that there is an unequal distribution of income.

UNEQUAL DISTRIBUTION OF INCOME

Renny Golden (1997) in the book *Disposable Children, America's Welfare System*, helps us understand that the lack of treatment for youth in the juvenile justice system is really part of a bigger problem of viewing children in general, and children from poverty classes in particular. While some of the book focuses upon the horrible welfare system of Chicago, the rest of the book grounds the reality that the city in the book could be any city in the United States because of the unequal distribution of income. Golden (1997, 68) stated: "Not since the Census Bureau began in 1947 has the gap between the rich and the poor been more exaggerated. The richest 20 percent of the nation receives over 48 percent of the national income, and the poorest

20 percent receives 3.6 percent." Part of the unequal distribution was the result of politicians who have been cutting federal programs of economic aid to families (formerly Aid to Families for Dependent Children [AFDC] now called Temporary Assistance to Needy Families [TANF]) and other individuals who have emergencies or are disabled. They use the theory that they were an "underclass" and were to blame for their own condition while they gave bailouts to corporations.

In truth, the federal program of financial assistance to families accounts for approximately 1 percent of the federal budget. Yet the richest "$1\frac{1}{2}$ percent of Americans have amassed nearly half (48 percent) of the nation's financial wealth," and the "world's richest 101 individuals and families now control wealth valued at some $454 billion" (Golden 1997, 69). This mass of wealth in an elite group "has created a global class more politically and economically powerful than any elite sector in history" (Golden 1997, 69).

Most ignorance is vincible ignorance; we don't know because we don't want to know.
Aldous Huxley

Let's get an idea of what wealth is. A one-year all-event special suite that permits sixteen persons to watch events at Madison Square Garden in New York City sells for only $325,000 (BBC radio broadcast, March 16, 1999). Who could afford it?

It is estimated that Bill Gates of Microsoft is worth perhaps $59 or 60 billion. This is considered new money. Many people in technology have reached high monetary status as well as drug lords. Yet the worth of these billionaires pales in the shadow of J.D. Rockefeller, Sr. (1839–1937). His corrected wealth is perhaps $200 billion. Even though the U.S. Supreme Court in 1910 broke up Rockefeller's Standard Oil Trust, the Rockefellers still control them all, such as Standard Oil of New Jersey, now called Exxon; Standard Oil of Indiana, now called Amoco; and Standard Oil of Ohio, now merged with interests of the British royal family and called British Petroleum (BP). Besides these oil interests located in Kuwait, the Rockefellers were wise to own pharmaceutical companies in the late-nineteenth century, and then use their influence to have medical schools teach classes in pharmacy:

The Rockefeller Institute for Medical Research was established in New York in 1902 and by 1928 had received from John D. Rockefeller $65 million in endowment funds. In contrast, as late as 1938, as little as $2.8 million in federal funding was budgeted for the entire U.S. Public Heath Service. Therefore, it is easy to see that Rockefeller family investment in health science research predated, and far surpassed, even the federal government's. (Horowitz 1996)

When the tax law changed and federal income tax came into being in 1913 (it was suppose to be temporary), the Rockefellers protected their family wealth. By rolling their money into a foundation, the money was forever exempt from income taxes. Other famous foundations have been the Mellon (Gulf Oil and Mellon National Bank) and Ford Foundations.

With the accumulated devaluation and control of the United States' money by the FRB and the shift to others who hold great wealth, the middle class is quietly disappearing into the lower class for several reasons. First, globalization of the economy has meant an economic transformation in which blue-collar jobs have been eliminated while the real wages of working Americans, between 1972 and 1994, fell 19 percent. This has pushed more women into the work force to help support the family. In 1960, women with children were 18 percent of the work force, whereas in 1995, they were 63 percent. Despite this increase in two-wage-earner families, the median family income fell 6 percent in the first six years of the 1990s as people pay income taxes. What makes this so strange is that under economic nationalism, from 1865 to 1913, tariffs, *not income tax*, produced 50 to 90 percent of the federal revenue with a U.S. growth average of 4 percent a year (Buchanan 1998).

Secondly, the U.S. government gave benefits to some U.S. corporations under the theory of simulating job creation. Six billion dollars was given as grants to such corporations as General Motors and International Business Machines (IBM). However, after receiving $58 million, IBM "cut its own research budget by a third, laid off its workers and made a $3 billion profit in 1994" (Golden 1997, 69).

Today, more Americans work in government than in manufacturing. This has led to our becoming the world's greatest debtor nation instead of its greatest creditor nation because we buy products made in other countries. The NAFTA (North American Free Trade Agreement, 1994) treaty was sold to the public as a treaty to open Mexico to U.S. exports. In 1996, we shipped 46,000 cars to Mexico. But Mexico sent 550,000 cars back to us, in part because General Motors has built fifty plants in twenty years in Mexico. Volkswagen also produced 450,000 vehicles in 1998 by paying an average wage of $1.69 an hour (one-third of the U.S. minimum wage) (Buchanan 1998).

Many of these plants in Mexico, unlike those in the U.S. that are restricted by the air and water laws, are able to develop and operate while abusing the land and its natural resources as well. Thus there is no cost to the Mexican company to clean up the air or water and that cost is not passed on to the consumer.

This shift from the true wealth of a nation residing in its factories, farms, fisheries, mines, and the genius and capacities of its people, to developing industry as the heart of economic power, has been called by some "economic development" or "public-private partnerships." Others call it corporate welfare.

Corporate Welfare

The definition of corporate welfare is any action by local, state, or federal government that gives a corporation or an entire industry a benefit not offered to others, such as an "outright subsidy, a grant, real estate, a low-interest loan, or a government service. It can also be a tax break—a credit, exemption, deferral or deduction, or a tax rate lower than the one others pay" (Barlett and Steele 1998, 2).

An eighteen-month *Time* magazine (November 1998) investigation by Barlett and Steele found that the federal government pays out $125 billion a year in corporate welfare. The companies can sell their goods to foreign buyers, engage in foreign transactions that are insured by the government, and are excused from paying a portion of their income tax if they sell products overseas. In other words, the companies get tax dollars from the government to carry out ordinary business operations, with additional perks to upper management including tax write-offs for business expenses.

The government says this is necessary to create "new jobs," but jobs have disappeared and the stockholders of the corporations gain the profits. Five billion dollars went to the Export-Import Bank of the United States to subsidize companies to sell goods abroad. Five of the bank's biggest beneficiaries (AT&T, Bechtel, Boeing, General Electric, and McDonnell Douglas, now part of Boeing) accounted for 40 percent of the loans. The result was that more than a third of a million jobs disappeared (Barlett and Steele 1998).

Remember, in corporations, the corporation sets the salaries of the employees as a business expense. From its revenues (money taken in from the sales of its products), it deducts the expense of doing the business. In addition to the salary of the employees, the building of the factory and the land that it sits on, the upkeep of the buildings, and the raw supplies to make the product are also deducted. What is left is considered the profit. The profit, known as dividends, is then dispersed to the shareholders, those buying stock in the corporation. Then the individual stockholder pays the tax on the dividend like anyone would pay tax on interest from a bank savings account.

The corporations don't really lose. If the expenses outweigh the profits, the corporation may declare bankruptcy and reorganize under certain chapters of the tax laws. But corporations are not like partnerships, so the executives are not held personally liable for the debts of the company.

This governmental policy for corporations may seem useful, but let us look at an example from Pennsylvania. In 1997, $307 million in economic incentives were given by the federal government to Kvarner ASA, a Norwegian global engineering and construction company, to open a shipyard in the former Philadelphia Naval Shipyard. If Kvarner ASA employed 950 people, the subsidy would be $323,000 for each job. If each job paid $50,000 a year and each worker paid $6,700 in local and state taxes, how long would it take to earn back the money granted to create that job? Answer: Nearly a half century of tax collections from each individual, assuming that all 950 workers are recruited from outside Philadelphia and will relocate in the city, rather than from existing jobs within the city (Barlett and Steele 1998, 4–5).

Thus, the real increase in jobs has not come from the Fortune 500 companies who have received "corporate welfare." Instead, the increase has come from market forces that created jobs, such as 10 million jobs since 1990 from small and medium-size companies, from high-tech startups to franchised business providing needed services like cleaning.

So why does this corporate welfare continue? First, it sounds good. Second, there is an army of bureaucrats estimated at 11,000 organizations and agencies with access to city hall, statehouses, the Capitol, and the White House. They work to expand their activities through seminars, conferences, training sessions, and trade associations. They legitimatize the activity by publishing their own journals, newsletters, and attractive Web sites. Using the words "economic incentives" or "empowerment zones" the ultimate get-rich scheme is accomplished by companies receiving public services at reduced rates while the rest of society pays the full cost. (Corp-Focus is a moderated list service that distributes the weekly column "Focus on the Corporation" by editor of *Corporate Crime Reporter* Russell Mokhiber. Send e-mail to listproc@essential.org.)

The financial squeeze comes because individuals and families pay the real costs of what the government does through their taxes, but their real wages have not increased in twenty years due to these hidden increased taxes. According to a recent Cato Policy Analysis paper on "The Hidden Burden of Taxation," the government takes an average of $4.10 per hour from the average manufacturing wage earner with almost half of that amount not itemized on the employee's pay stub. The concealment thus masks the true cost of government (federal and state income and medicare) and the cost of services (in taxes on phones, gasoline, airfares, etc.). As corporations expand globally and use computerized technology, they get the cheap labor they need at the expense of the American taxpayer. Thus, groups of U.S. persons are no longer needed in the global economy even as cheap labor. Jobs are gone. Low-income families in the United States and throughout the world especially suffer (Cleaver 1997).

Many countries appeal to the United States for aid, and to the International Monetary Fund (IMF), to help keep their economic systems going. South Korea received a $58 billion loan package in 1998. Yet some consider South Korea to be like a patient who has received a blood transfusion but the doctors have done little to stop the hemorrhaging. In some analysts' minds the basic problems in South Korea remain untreated, and the corporate conglomerates sprawl inefficiently across many industries. South Korea's big five corporations (Hyundai, Samsung, Daewoo, LG, and SK) have done little to create a more open and competitive economy and they are grossly overleveraged (their average debt ratio is 520 percent) and do little to cut debt (Weinberg 1999). The United States continues to lend money when it has its own $5 trillion debt. This continues because of a purposeful "wall of silence."

Wall of Silence

The concept of an individual with a conscience is one whose highest allegiance is to his fellow man. Ralph Nader

A wall of silence obscures the fact that 40 percent of America's children live below the poverty level. When Reagan and then followed by Bush were presidents in their own terms, we were told by the media that there were at least 3 million homeless in American—women with children and white-collar workers who had lost their jobs. They were people who were unable to support a family on the minimum wage. The day after Clinton's inauguration, the homeless' plight disappeared from the public's attention. Mass media withdrew its coverage. Although urban poverty is more visible, concentrated, and expanded than poverty in rural areas, people in poverty are considered by some to be "underclass" and as receiving their "just deserts," while at the same time giving government officials justification to be harsh and punitive in their responses (Golden 1997).

In addition, many of the former programs including welfare (AFDC now TANF) and food stamps have been cut or drastically reduced with no effective replacements. Homelessness is on the increase among both those who have and don't have jobs. Among those who do work and are homeless, the minimum wage with no benefits does not provide enough money to pay for the increases that have occurred in basic housing and food needs.

Today, the poor are trapped in deteriorating housing projects and neighborhoods that resemble refugee camps or concentration camps, depending upon your perspective. African-American, Latino, Native American, and other minority children live as if in another nation; they are separated from the mainstream of the culture. Families become broken not by a death of a parent or by divorce but by parents working several jobs. Single parents face even greater hardships, especially women. Women still do not earn, on average, the same money as men do (Golden 1997).

Golden (1997, 74) summarized the current situation this way:

By the 1970's, child poverty rates began to climb as deindustrialization obliterated blue-collar jobs. Job flight resulted in disintegration of neighborhoods or rural counties. When community cohesion is demolished, social fragmentation and chaos set up conditions that isolate families. The children of these families are referred to as being "at risk"—not at risk of poverty, but at risk of social failure; dropping out, being abused, becoming homeless. They become part of the disposable population no longer needed in the economy.

Judith Weitz, coordinator of "Kids Count," sponsored by the nonprofit Center for Study of Social Policy, measured the social and economic conditions for children under 18 for each state and the District of Columbia. The 1980s found an increase in the percentage of children in poverty, juveniles who are incarcerated, out-of-wedlock births, and teen violent deaths. These increases were attributed to the recession of the early 1980s, wherein a substantial number of families experienced sharp cuts in their incomes and never fully recovered, and the states declined in their Aid to Families with Dependent Children (AFDC) Program, the major welfare program for low-income families (Thorton and Voigt 1992, 39). That was followed by the 1990s—another "terrible decade for children."

The plight of children is also global. As mentioned in Chapter 6, "Crimes Against Children," children live in the streets of many third world countries. They are silent victims of corrupt police and international syndicates with organized sex tours for Western pedophiles. Poverty and lack of education make children—both boys and girls—candidates for the streets and international sex trade. While the Child Sexual Abuse Prevention Act of 1994, 18 U.S.C. 2423 (b), extends the Mann Act to provide for imprisonment for not more than ten years, a fine or both for adults who conspire to travel abroad with the intention of engaging in sex with a minor (under 18), or engage in sex with a minor within U.S. territories, it is purely symbolic. Effective enforcement at national and international levels is difficult. Foreign countries are reluctant to enforce laws barring sex with a minor. Like us in America, they have difficulties with investigations including obtaining evidence and witness testimony.

The media, who rarely target global corporations as major contributors to the nation's socioeconomic woes, has fostered this wall of silence. These corporations use their money and influence to buy up the media and then to affect elections of politicians. Like the old Mafia who bought favorable decisions from judges for their members, corporations use the financing of election campaigns to ensure that those future political candidates will be endeared to them and thus pass laws that enhance the corporation's ability to maintain their power. Thereby a "power elite" is created and permitted to work in silence.

POWER ELITE

One such power elite group is the Council on Foreign Relations (CFR). CFR has nearly 3,000 members who are individuals but represent some of the most powerful corporations. As a private group, they control over three-quarters of the nation's wealth. The CFR runs the State Department and Central Intelligence Agency (CIA) and has members in the president's administration. The end result is that they all act in the best interest of the Council and not necessarily the best interest of the American people or groups such as families and children. The Council on Foreign Relations' British Counterpart is the Royal Institute of International Affairs. Together, they continue to make high profits because they can network and strategize when and where to buy and sell goods, services, stocks, etc. at the expense of British and American citizens (Dye 1976, 1995).

Economics and politics are the governing powers of life today, and that's why everything is screwy. Joseph Campbell

Because the CFR is so well organized and focused upon its goals, most of its desires become the law and policy of the United States. Dye, a noted researcher on who's running America, documents that about 100 members of the CFR who surround the president in different kinds of capacities are called "the Secret Team." They carry out psychopolitical operations in state department and intelligence organizations. President Truman issued an executive order establishing the Psychological Strategy Board. Gordon Gray and Henry Kissinger, members of the CFR, ran this board. Then President Eisenhower issued an executive order changing its name to the Operations Coordination Board, which then became bigger and more powerful under the leadership of Gray and Kissinger. President Kennedy abolished the board, but it became an ad hoc committee called the Special Group (Dye 1976). (See also Round Table Web site at http://www.geocities.com/CapitolHill/2807/CFRClinton.html for more information.)

Since the Special Group was not formed by Executive Order, it cannot be abolished. Instead, it continues and uses something called psychological warfare.

Psychological warfare (spin doctors) uses favorable and unfavorable truths and leaves out facts completely to shape public opinion to support their goals. For example, as early as President Wilson, the Inquiry's (the forerunner of the CIA) director was Edward Mandel House. He was a political advisor and friend of President Wilson who later traded off most of Wilson's ideas (called Fourteen Points) to establish the League of Nations at the Paris Peace conference. President Wilson caught on to the betrayal. He was so upset that he suffered a stroke and refused to speak to Edward Mandel House again. At that time, the American people did not want to belong to the League of Nations that could force them to go to war and be turned into an international police force. Thus America did not join the League of Nations, and the CRF had to devise new plans and strategies. The Rockefeller Foundation funded the project of War and Peace studies (a total of 362 meetings) with nearly $350,000 to the State Department such that in 1945, the CRF attended the San Francisco conference to establish the United Nations. This time, the American people were never asked whether or not they wanted to join and pay them money. Today, as members of the United Nations, there is still debate as to the rights of our sovereign government.

The United Nations imposes policy upon all countries that affect children and their families.

The United Nations has been one of the world organizations focusing attention on the needs of women and children worldwide. They recognize and publish the fact that women make up half of humanity, two-thirds of the world's work force, yet earn about one-tenth of the world's income and own less than a hundredth of its property (United Nations Report of 1979, as cited by Eakins 1992, 73). Yet desirable changes come very slowly in many countries where the power is in the hand of "power elites" who benefit from the status quo.

Different scholars have identified this "power elite" yet they mention few names. Carroll Quigley (1966), in his book, *Tragedy and Hope: A History of the World in Our Time,* tried to help us understand the magnitude of the power elite by his twenty-year study of the power structure of the United States and Great Britain through their government papers and reports. He was sympathetic to those governments for he saw them controlling citizens' freedoms and choices within narrow alternatives. He argued that there are not two major political parties in the United States. The power elite would contribute to both and allow an alternation of the two parties in public office in order to conceal their own influence. But they would control the selection of the politicians while misleading the electorate to believe that they were exercising their own free choice. In his mind, having two parties with opposing ideas and policies was foolish. It was acceptable only by academic thinkers. In reality, he argued, the two parties should be almost identical; then the American people would be led to believe that they could "throw the rascals out" at the next election. The American people would vote and the votes might change a certain number of politicians. But there would be no profound or extensive shifts in policy. The capitalists or the industrial-military complex group would still be in charge to make their profits and gain.

Unlike Quigley, Thomas Dye (1976) gave names. His systematic work, begun in 1976 and published in six editions, gives names to those who are truly running the United States. If one were to use his work and create a sociogram (a wheel showing who talks with whom and how that one wheel of influence is connected to another), one could put together the formal and informal connections that people make and use to fulfill their purposes. A power wheel of influence might include some of the following persons: Edward Bronfman, Robert Rubin, and Alan Greenspan. Since the Jewish lobby is very influential in Washington, DC, then Edward Bronfman, who is a leader of the World Jewish Congress, head of Seagrams, and leading shareholder in Dupont, would be part of this elite group. Robert Rubin of the IMF, who gained experience and contacts while at Goldman Sachs, might be another. While he was Secretary of the U.S. Treasury, Rubin assisted a former client (government of Mexico and client of Goldman Sachs) with a bailout by the United States and the IMF—the Government of Mexico. Alan Greenspan of the Federal Reserve Bank might be another.

In summary, policy is what a government does or does not want done. The people who have the power to influence that process are many. Yet the most noted of those have been the "power elite" who use their money, influence, and contacts to continue policies that contribute to the continuation of their power and financial benefits.

The UN is but a long-range, international-banking apparatus merely set up for financial and economic profit by a small group of powerful One-World Revolutionaries, hungry for profit and power.
Curtis Dall, F.D. Roosevelt's son-in-law, as quoted in his book, *My Exploited Father-in-Law*

THEORIES OF LAWMAKING

In politics, nothing happens by accident. If it happens, it was planned that way.
Franklin D. Roosevelt

Many theorists have addressed theories of "how laws get made." There are two major groups that have application in this discussion—the consensus model and the conflict model.

Consensus Model

The first is the consensus model, which assumes that our society has a shared culture and agrees on fundamental values and the acceptance of the political organization. William Chambliss (1984) explained this model as viewing laws as created by a consensus of the society where the values and perspectives of the public are expressed. The state is value-neutral because the legal system uses the law that the people have decided is in the best interest of the public. This process of lawmaking in a pluralistic society is based upon mediation between the competing interest groups.

Political scientists have also done research into community decision-making. Robert Dahl's (1961) research in Hartford, Connecticut, showed a pluralistic-based intergroup conflict model.

In 1977, women of the United States came together in Houston, Texas, to create an agenda and proposed legislation to President Carter. The "International Women's Year Conference" had all the makings of a consensus model at work. Federal money was given to a national committee to organize and create this conference. The national committee drew up how each state was to elect or select a group of women to go and give input on all the important issues concerning women. The national committee also selected delegates at large from the United States that represented other populations, such as welfare mothers or rape survivors. At the conference, the delegates sat within their respective states while the delegates-at-large sat in special seating behind the state representatives. On the stage a person would read the proposed legislation. Delegates were to respond by going to the strategically located microphones to stand in line and wait for a turn in the given time allotment to add to the discussion. However, there were few microphones. Certain delegations that might speak against an issue such as Utah on abortion were farthest from the microphones. In addition, access to the aisles was purposefully limited by special assigned persons sitting in the seats located nearest the aisle.

This was supposed to be an open debate leading to better ideas, but in reality, it was window dressing—a show. All the proposals had been decided in form and content ahead of time because no new proposals were permitted from persons at the microphones when one could get to it. Everything had been organized and purposefully planned to make sure that there was a certain outcome and only that outcome. The voting that took place was decided by a majority vote as if a consensus had occurred when in fact it never had. (Personal experience.)

Consensus, the coming together on an issue, may have been the style of lawmaking in the early part of our history or on specific issues. However, others have noted the community elite as a dominant force in community decision-making, as the work of Floyd Hunter (1953) in Atlanta, Georgia, argued. In federal lawmaking, researchers, beginning in the 1930s and gaining more acceptances through the 1970s to the present, have noted a "power elite." These theories and research have been labeled the conflict and radical model.

Conflict and Radical Theory Model

The conflict and radical theorists argue that certain groups in a society have economic and political control. These groups make sure that their behavior is not labeled as criminal and that the behavior of others becomes legally labeled. Thus, persons who drive while intoxicated and kill others are not viewed as murderers. On the other hand, the survivor of a bar fight where persons have been drinking and a fight ensues with someone being killed is considered a murder. In both situations, there are dead bodies. Yet, because they are defined differently in law, the consequences are different.

There are many shades of difference among the various writers in conflict and radical criminology groups, and these differences are beyond the scope of this book. Yet there are some common themes, like the connection between poverty and inequality leading to crime and the law and justice system serving only the interest of the ruling class. Two of the most noted forerunners of the conflict and radical theory model were Karl Marx (1818–1883) and Friedrich Engels (1820–1895). Marx noted that in a capitalist society, the class that owns and controls the means of production (the bourgeoisie) also seeks to maximize its profits. In order to do so, they have to exploit a working population (the proletariat) to the point that they are not able to gain wealth or property. Then the ruling class has an inordinate amount of influence over a society's political institutions, especially rule making, so as to protect its economic interests.

Marx and Engels understood that a capitalist society had a special interest in creating crimes. Without crime, capitalism would not survive, because crime serves a useful purpose in the society by creating an entire criminal justice system to deal with these offenders. There are jobs for the captors and the professors who teach the courses for those who work in the system. Even torture permitted a host of honest workers to produce instruments for the states to use.

William Bonger (1876–1940), a Dutch criminologist, analyzed the crime rates of European capitalist states during the early 1900s. In addition to the crime rates, he noted a psychological-spiritual dimension brought about by capitalism—demoralization. Demoralization is the despair that a parent feels when she or he cannot feed her or his child(ren). Despair is more than sadness. It is a fear that one may die of hunger or lack of medical attention. Despair leads a parent into thinking that being a prostitute would at least put food on the table.

More recent theorists such as Thorsten Sellin (1938), George Vold (1958), and Austin Turk (1969) argued that crime and delinquency are products of conflicts between groups of unequal power. Yet they saw society divided into many groups, not just two that competed for power. Such was the case during the time of their writings, when our society in the 1960s and 1970s had many groups in political struggle—the civil rights movement, the campus student groups, the women's movement, the anti-Vietnam War movement, the deinstitutionalization of the mentally ill movement, the children's rights movement, and others as well.

Despite some of their critics, conflict theorists, especially in juvenile justice, have made significant contributions to our understanding. For example, Anthony Platt (1974) analyzed the child-saving movement of 1850s–1890s as it became the first juvenile court in Illinois (1899). As discussed in Chapter 1, "History and Treatment," the movement had visible supporters from the educated middle class, but its reform was really geared towards backing the wealthy and powerful. Platt argued that what was happening to juveniles was what industrialists were trying to do to the economy; they were achieving "order, stability, and control while preserving the existing class system and distribution of wealth" (1974, 367).

By creating a process through the juvenile court, there had to be assurance that there would be enough youth to pass through the system. Thus, new categories of youthful misconduct previously not deemed a problem became officially labeled, especially those that had a moral offense. In 1917 most states having a juvenile court also passed legislation to deal with "delinquent," "dependent," and "neglected" children. The *parens patriae* doctrine gave the court a tremendous amount of power to control, in a legal sense, the children of working class and immigrant families.

Platt (1974) depicted the early juvenile court as a device "to maintain racism, sexism, and working-class powerlessness" (384). As explained earlier in Chapter 2, "The Definition of Juvenile Delinquency, Status Offenses, Abuse, and Developmental Stages," the juvenile court in the 1960s and 1970s did deal with such issues as the vagueness of the statutes and equal protection arguments. Yet these efforts did not erase racism, sexism, and the creation of an "underclass."

Today, most juveniles are still from the ranks of the urban poor, lower classes, and minority groups. Most of the studies done on waiver show that the persons waived into the adult courts are minority males (Clement 1997). Today, as well as in the past, youth come from broken homes and homes where there is unemployment. These youth, who are not taught the proper demeanor of dress and speaking to elders, especially police officers, are more likely to be labeled as "unsalvageable" even by those working with youth, such as public defenders (Platt, Schechter, and Tiffany 1978) and probation officers in the court.

In addition, the state's programs, even the most innovative, have too few beds and too long a waiting list. For example, when I worked with a family whose oldest son had sodomized the younger brother, I argued with the probation officer to place the youth in the newer program that Virginia had created for sexual juvenile offenders. The probation officer said the youth didn't fit the criteria because he wasn't as bad as the others were. When I confronted him with the fact that the youth had not become a "pan sexual" (a man who had sex with his daughters, sons, and then the family dog before his wife called an agency where I worked), the probation officer told me the real truth. The real reason was that there wasn't enough money for this youth. Because of the youth's older age, the hope was that he would grow out of this behavior as he began to date girls. If not, they reasoned, he would grow out of the age of jurisdiction for the court and thus, would be someone else's problem, not theirs.

Having money helps people with money avoid the juvenile justice system by using an attorney in the very early stages of intake so as to take advantage of referrals to private psychiatrists and military schools. Remember that the intake stage of the juvenile court doesn't give children a constitutional right to an attorney. Yet this is the stage where the attorney can play a critical role for several reasons. First, the probation officers are often so overwhelmed with high caseloads that they welcome someone else who can do the research on the case and make recommendations. Secondly, the attorney can help explain to all parties the law and gain their cooperation in developing a plan for the youth. The attorney can identify the many good counseling and treatment programs that can be utilized when one has the money or the medical insurance, and he or she can make the arrangements for admission.

If a parent doesn't have money, what happens? Golden (1997) gave a good example from Chicago where the "get tough" campaign began in 1980 and continued into the 1990s. The 119 percent increase in the number of youth committed to the Illinois Department of Corrections was accomplished at a time when the actual felony arrests for youth crime rate had dropped 8.5 percent. "Governor Edgar's Task Force on Crime and Corrections reported that Illinois had built fifteen prisons in the last fifteen years but that the prison and jail system is still overcrowded and the streets less safe" (Golden 1997, 140). Instead of responding to what we know about children, their developmental stages, and their cries for help with early intervention programs, we permit the fears of others to rule "with legislation to lock up 11-year-olds" (Golden 1997, 140).

In addition, we know that many youth as well as adult prisoners have substance-abuse-related problems, yet we do little to provide drug treatment programs. Most juvenile courts never had the budgets or professional staff necessary to create programs or to refer youth to agency programs. Massachusetts is the only state that has really created a community-based program for juvenile offenders during the 1970s–1980s and still maintains it.

What these theorists and researchers were doing was looking to our history and to the values and beliefs that underlie the present social definitions and responses to crime. While some sociologists of crime had a fascination with the study of mentally ill persons, prostitutes, and other deviants, others looked at the unethical, illegal, and destructive actions of powerful individuals, groups, corporations, and institutions. Sutherland (1949) was the first to use the term "white-collar crime" to show that wealthy businessmen do illegal activities. However, they are not seen as criminals because of their respectable position in the community. The laws are not changed accordingly, nor does the process equalize persons before the law.

For example, if you get arrested for using a gun to steal money from someone on the street, expect to spend a lot of time making license plates for the state. You may get paid as much as 43 cents an hour. Upon release, your skill at license plate making will be useless because only the state makes that product. Your slave labor has benefited the state, and you have a record that makes it difficult to get real employment.

However, if you take millions of dollars from consumers as a top manager in a corporation, very little will happen to you. For example, from 1977 to 1983, Beech Nut, who made baby food, produced a so-called 100 percent "apple" juice for babies that was really 100 percent sugar water. It made $60 million through its misrepresentation. Then they denied any knowledge of the fraud to the Food and Drug Administration (FDA). After obstruction of justice with the FDA, the Justice Department brought criminal charges against the company and two of its executives. The corporation pled guilty and paid a fine of $2 million out of its $60 million profit. Had the two executives been friendlier with the FDA, they probably would have avoided their conviction of conspiracy, mail fraud, and violating food and drug laws. In a rare situation, each were fined $100,000 (which was probably paid by the corporation) and given a one-year jail sentence (Voigt, Thornton, Jr., Barrile, and Seaman 1995, 356, citing *Consumer Reports*, 1989b, 294–296).

To know that you do not know is the best. To pretend to know when you do not know is a disease. Lao Tzu

Only today is there a renewed interest in unethical or immoral behavior of powerful persons as violations of law. Some of that renewed interest is due to the understanding that the economic and social losses associated with individuals and organizations who are profiting by committing crimes through legitimate businesses far exceeds the human injuries and property losses incurred from street crimes. One of the most documented ones has been the now defunct Bank of Credit and Commerce International (BBCI). Spanning more than a decade, it laundered money for drug dealers and dictators. In that process, they bribed bank regulators and officials in Latin America, Asia, and Africa. The result was that they defrauded foreign depositors of billions of dollars, sold illegal military arms, and made money. Some of the money was used for dubious loans and charity donations like $8 million to President Carter's Global 2000 Fund. During the 1980s, BBCI secretly bought interest in banks in Georgia, Florida, California, and Washington, D.C., after specifically being barred by the federal banking regulators to buy banks in the United States. The Federal banking regulators viewed the ownership too murky (some was secret ownership and secret customers) and its capital structure too flimsy. In December 1991, Clark Clifford, former Secretary of Defense and advisor to several Presidents, and his law partner, Robert Altman struck a deal with the Manhattan district attorney after trying to buy the First American Bank. They plead guilty to conspiracy, bribery, a scheme to defraud, and concealing facts from federal banking regulators. They forfeited $550 million (Voigt, Thornton, Barrile, and Seaman, 1994, p. 359).

IMPACT ON CHILDREN

You must be the change you wish to see in the world. Mahatma Gandhi

Law and public policy both have impact upon children and youth. Although most of this textbook focus upon children in the justice system, it is obvious that what happens to children in their families, schools, and peers (community environmental influences) puts them at risk for juvenile delinquency, substance abuse, school drop-out, and teen pregnancy (Hawkins and Catalano 1992).

The Office of Juvenile Justice and Delinquency Prevention (OJJDP) incorporated Hawkins and Catalano's review of over 30 years of work on risk factors from various fields to use the public health model with delinquency prevention (Wilson and Howell 1997). This public health model used most successfully with combating heart disease grew out of the work of Dr. Hans Selye. He found that there were two earlier identifiable stages that a person went through before the collapse stage of the heart attack. His research into stress and distress pushed the medical profession to work on preventive measures in the earlier stages to reduce individual and social costs. Doctors and nurses began to identify risk factors and populations at greater risk for heart disease. As they saw all the violence done to and by youth (the so-called "gun and knives clubs"), they began to use this public health model for juveniles. Known today as environmental medicine, it looks for prevention programs throughout the developmental stages of children. It incorporates physical health with mental and emotional health because they are interrelated.

Yet, many others countries, including the United States, through their laws and policies have some real challenges before them to deal with some of the basic needs of children. In this section, we will discuss how specific laws or policies have impacted children in the United States and other countries.

The United States

We like to think that we are an advanced society and that we make rational laws to build up all persons within our society. Yet, that is not always the case. We have a disparity. Take, for example, when a state will provide economic and medical assistance to one group of citizens but not another group of citizens. Such was the case in California, in the spring of 1999, when over 28,500 farm workers and their families in the San Joaquin Valley were devastated by the freeze that hit the citrus industry. Already without food and work for the previous two months, the freeze meant another nine or more months of unemployment. Since the state has no disaster unemployment assistance, the families faced the loss of their homes. If the state were to request federal funds, the monies would go primarily to the growers and not the thousands of workers. (Personal email message from Dr. Don Patterson of the National Farm Worker Ministry, phone: 941/206-8247.)

Sometimes laws and policies that are passed look good "on their face" but later we learn that an intricate system of control outside the spotlight of public scrutiny and without accountability has developed. For example, vaccines for children have been historically viewed as the proper role for a society to prevent epidemics and for the federal government to "provide for the general welfare." In the past, many persons were required to have a smallpox vaccination to enter school. Today, however, there are many required vaccines. Parents and caretakers have no informed medical choice because a national enforced program that benefits pharmaceutical corporations overrules even doctors who might otherwise act in the interest of their patients.

A national campaign to enforce mandatory vaccination laws began with the Jimmy Carter Administration and escalated during the 1990s. Today, most states require children to be injected with about 33 doses of 9 or 10 different viral and bacterial vaccines, including three doses of hepatitis B in order to enter public school. Only 10,637 cases of hepatitis B were reported to the Centers for Disease Control (CDC) in 1998, including only 279 cases in children under the age of 14. Hepatitis B is neither fatal nor epidemic except among high-risk groups of adults, especially drug users (*New York Times*, July 30, 1997). Thus, parents are required to pay $120 ($40 each) even though more than 24,000 reports of hospitalizations and injuries, including about 400 deaths, following hepatitis B vaccinations has been reported since 1990 to the U.S. Government Vaccine Adverse Event Reporting System (*Science* 1998, p. 630).

There is no scientific evidence that increased use of vaccines always promotes health because no vaccine is 100% safe or effective. Some have more side effects than others, including whooping cough, which causes brain damage to children. Virginia's Lieutenant Governor John Hager is in a wheelchair because he acquired polio from the vaccine given to his infant son. The National Vaccine Injury Compensation Program has paid out $925 million in claims for vaccine-caused injuries and death but very few doctors report vaccine-associated health problems (Schlafly 1999).

A doctor must sign an exemption to the required vaccinations. All but two states permit a religious exemption and some 16 permit a philosophical exemption but this is not an exercise of free choice when one has to plead with governmental officials to tolerate an exception. Recently, a New Jersey court upheld the right of a private school to deny admission to a student who objected to taking a vaccine (Schlafly 1999).

The 1993 Comprehensive Childhood Immunization Act gave the Department of Health and Human Services (HHS) $400 million to assist states to computerize state vaccine databases, or registries, to tag and track children's vaccinations. Using the carrot approach, the CDC withholds money grants if the state health officials don't show proof of compliance. In addition, the states received amounts of $50, $75, or $100 per child who is fully vaccinated with all federal recommended vaccines, including hepatitis B. In 1995, HHS gave states the power to access newborn babies and their Social Security numbers to create a centralized database on every child's medical records (Schlafly 1999).

This vaccine policy was set by a quasi-governmental group of mandatory-vaccination promoters called the Advisory Committee on Immunization Practice (ACIP). ACIP's stated purpose is "to increase the safe usage of vaccines," not to promote the health of Americans or information to aid informed choices for patients. No wonder; the members of the ACIP have financial ties to the drug corporation. The pharmaceutical corporations spent $5.3 billion in 1998 by sending their representatives into doctors' offices and hospitals to gain their support as well as lobbying thousands of state legislators and federal and state bureaucrats (*New York Times*, Jan. 11, 1999, p. 1).

It is the mandatory feature of vaccines that makes it so profitable for the industry. *The Cincinnati Enquirer* in January 15, 1999, wrote an exposé on how the hepatitis B mandate was lobbied through the Ohio legislature, by passing the proper committee, with no notice, study, or debate. In addition, Congress in 1986 gave pharmaceutical corporations immunity from any liability related to vaccine side effects. In 1995, the American Academy of Pediatrics (AAP) agreed to endorse the vaccine schedules determined by federal authorities because HMOs require pediatricians to achieve a near-perfect vaccination rate of their patients as a condition of their HMO contract with on-site inspection of records to verify (Schlafly 1999).

Taken all together, immunity from damages in civil law suits, coercive state laws, and federal mandates make vaccines a very profitable industry for drug corporations. Meanwhile, there is little opposition.

Without scientific research and large clinical studies done by independent, non-government, non-industry-financed scientists, little will be known about side effects and long-term effects of vaccines and multiple vaccinations. Parents then become at the mercy of the state. The state is held "hostage" by the federal government because of the needed money to operate the state.

While the general public may have little knowledge about adverse reactions following vaccinations, Dr. Horowitz (1996, 1996b), has published several books based upon his research. Author of the best-selling book *Emerging Viruses: AIDS & Ebola—Nature, Accident or Intentional?*, a Harvard graduate, and independent investigator, he is an internationally recognized authority in behavioral science and public health education.

In 1990, Leonard G. Horowitz, D.M.D., M.A., M.P.H., was chief professional advisor to the largest dental and medial catalog supply company in the world when a Florida dentist infected one of his patients with AIDS. His job was to develop patient and professional educational materials to help calm the public's fear of visiting dental and medical offices. He also investigated the Centers for Disease Control and Prevention's official investigation on the case. In his expert opinion, the case was maintained as an "unsolvable mystery" because they didn't want to deal with the fact that the ex-military dentist believed he was dying of a virus that the government had created. The dentist had in his possession incriminating documents and was so enraged that he intentionally injected his patients with HIV-tainted anesthetics as if a game to trap the government. This is documented in three published scientific reports and his book *Deadly Innocence: The Kimberly Bergalis Case—Solving the Greatest Murder Mystery in the History of American Medicine* (1995).

By investigating that case, Dr. Horowitz was led to investigate a greater mystery—the origin of AIDS. In his latest book *Emerging Viruses: AIDS and Ebola* (1996b), he documented the Department of Defense's (DOD) development of synthetic biological agents—bioweapons as alternatives to nuclear weapons. He published the contracts of DOD and National Cancer Institute under Dr. Robert Gallo who along with other Litton Bionetics researchers set about to develop immune system raging AIDS-like viruses. He explained how they took monkey viruses that were humanly benign, recombined them with DNA, RNA, and enzymes from other animal viruses that cause leukemias, lymphomas, and sarcomas. Then they jumped species and cultured them in human white blood cells in some studies and human fetal tissue cells in others. Thereby, they produced immune-system-destroying, cancer-causing viruses. In his opinion, vaccines like flu, DPT, polio, and hepatitis B have been seeded with toxic genetic poisons. Through these genetically reengineered viruses for decades, a person is given AIDS, cancer, and other conditions that significantly impact the immune system. He argued:

In fact, today's live viral vaccines, including the oral polio vaccine required by law be given to our children, are still littered with simian (monkey) virus contaminants since they are developed in monkey kidney cells, and the U.S. Food and Drug Administration turns a blind eye to as many as 100 live monkey virus contaminants per vaccine dose, and is barred from telling health professionals and even health scientists this truth because of pharmaceutical industry dictated proprietary laws and non-disclosure agreements. (Horowitz 1996) (See website: www.tetrahedron.org)

In addition, when the drug industry creates a new vaccine such as chicken pox, the radio and newspaper advertising is designed to frighten parents about a disease that is mild for children. Chicken pox usually occurs with children between ages 1 and 9 who recover without complications and have lifelong immunity. Yet, the selling point used by public health officials has not been the health of the child but, rather, the saving of lost wages for a mother who has to stay home with a sick child. Thus, emotions like fear and guilt are used as hooks to grab parents and other caretakers into acceptance.

For example, the March 1999 "Vaccines" feature in *Parenting Magazine* was published by a subsidiary of Time, Inc. whose parent company is a corporate member of the Council on Foreign Relations. In that article the "science writer" told parents that infant and childhood vaccines are nearly risk free. "Unstated was the ongoing virtual holocaust of vaccine-induced injuries affecting our youth that is earning vast fortunes for Merck and other Time's supports" such as "epidemics of chronic fatigue immune dysfunction (CFIDS), fibromyalgia, lupus, Guillain-Barré, Crohn's disease, rheumatoid arthritis, type-1 diabetes, and other autoimmune related disorders besides autism, attention deficit and hyperactivity, and several vaccine-linked cancers including lymphoma, leukemia and sarcoma" (Horowitz, email, April 7, 1999).

Why are American infants being injected with hepatitis B vaccine only hours after birth (even when their mothers test negative for hepatitis B) and the French Health Ministry has suspended it in schools in France because of evidence they cause neurological disorders and multiple sclerosis (*New York Times*, Oct. 3, 1998)? If hepatitis B were primarily an adult disease transmitted through bodily fluids, wouldn't it be more useful to identify the risk populations for vaccinations? Such at-risk populations might be needle-sharing drug addicts, highly promiscuous (heterosexual and homosexual), health care and custodial workers exposed to blood, or babies born to already-infected mothers.

In short, under the present policy and law, parents and caretakers have to present proof of a child having received three hepatitis B shots before being admitted to daycare, kindergarten, fifth grade, and high school. If the French Health Minister has evidence that it impacts the children's ability to learn (hence, it will impact their ability to control their own behavior), then could this mandatory policy really create more long-term problems including a constant juvenile and adult prison population? Since there is a movement of medical doctors, researchers, nutritionists, authors, and attorneys for alternative therapies even for cancer (Cancer Control Society, Los Angeles, CA), could the law and policy be a "smokescreen" for another hidden agenda? Could not one argue that there is a conflict of interest when the pharmaceutical industrialists create the problems and then manufacture the solutions that only cause more sickness and death?

Other Countries

Law and policy affect children in other countries. In this section, we will look at Palestinian children from the West Bank and Gaza in the occupied territories of Israel. Other examples will come from countries like China, Iraq, Ethiopia, North Korea, and Russia.

Israel's Policy toward Palestinian Children (Before, During, and After the Intifada)

Before *Intifada*

Palestine was the name given to the land located south of Lebanon, northwest of Egypt, from the Mediterranean Sea inward to Jordan. One of the major cities is Jerusalem. In 1948, the name of the land was changed with the establishment of the state of Israel. When Israelis took over the government and had the first Arab-Israeli war, they forced approximately half of the Palestinians (750,000) to leave their homes, properties, and livelihoods. Most of the Jewish communities established between 1948 and 1953 were established on former Arab property. Over 380 villages and large parts of 94 other towns and cities were taken under Jewish control. The second Arab-Israeli war in 1967 forced another 325,000 Palestinians into other Arab countries into refugee camps. In addition, the systematic policy of deportation and demolitions of homes has caused an annual forced migration of 21,000 (www.pna.net).

Since the inception of the United Nations in 1948, the Palestine refugee problem has been on the agenda because it is the oldest and largest refugee problem. Today, Palestinians total approximately 4.7 million persons, of which 3.4 million are registered with the United National Relief and Works Agency for Palestine Refugees in the Near East (UNRWA). More than 40% are refugees in Jordan, 38% in the Occupied Palestinian Territory (land in Israel that is given to Palestinians to live on), 10% in Lebanon and Syria, and others in Egypt. Others migrated to Europe, the United States, Canada, and South America (www.pna.net).

In terms of law and policy impacting children, it is important to look at the 38% that live in what is now called the occupied territory—the West Bank and the Gaza Strip. It was this group of people who were systematically physically and economically abused. They are considered citizens of Israel in paying taxes but they receive none of the benefits including voting in the elections. As the young children watched how the military mistreated their parents by pulling them out of their beds at night with no arrest warrants and putting their loved ones into jail for "administrative reasons," their sense of injustice turned to anger and then rage. When that rage was put on a stone and thrown at the soldiers, an uprising started on December 9, 1987, that gained support by many others in other cities. It became known as the *Intifada*.

During the *Intifada*

The Radda Barnen Swedish Save the Children studied the status of Palestinian children early in the uprising to determine what happened when military forces' response to demonstrators turned into relentlessly punitive, at times, lethal measures against an entire population, half of whom were children (Nixon 1990). Their four-volume documentation of the first two years showed the grisly effects of state-sponsored violence.

Their research is important because many human rights organizations overlook the special vulnerability of children to army and police violence. With this documentation, it is easier to see how a government contributed to the violence, directly as well as indirectly. It also shows why some youth, not belonging to any particular terrorist group, have become Israel's worst nightmare. If children reared in terror and torture in a dysfunctional family will use that violence against others, what will happen to these children if those controlling the society use terror and torture with them?

As Nixon (1990, p. 10) explained in the introduction concerning the international conventions on human rights and the policy of the Israeli government:

The question of how this situation arose is not addressed here, however . . . It is a report about the violation of children's rights . . . Whatever the reasons for that conflict and however the parties got there, at some point, which the conventions define, certain behavior is not acceptable. The conventions state that at some point reasons do not matter, they are irrelevant. And this is especially true for children, who can in no way be seen as cause or reason for a conflict. There is a point where no reason is good enough and it becomes necessary to stop discussing why something is happening and find out what is happening. That is what this report attempts to do.

In Part I (two volumes), a case-by-case study and statistical analysis of the circumstances were done on how many children under the age of 16 had been shot to death, how many had been injured, and how many were killed or injured by the tear gas. The field work and data collection were compared with official Israeli and soldier reports. The army's claim that soldiers are not permitted to shoot at children under any circumstance or that shot and beaten children were an "exceptional" case contradicted indisputable facts such as the number and content of child medical records. The denial of tear gas killing children was at variance with soldiers' accounts. Thus, the researchers raised serious questions about the credibility of official reports but not the fact that there was systematic government-sponsored violence against people who lived on the land (Nixon 1990).

For example, the Israeli Ministry of Justice issued a four-page paper in response to persistent criticism from various human right groups on their policy on children. The paper used the argument that children were being recruited by the Palestine Liberation Organization (PLO) and they would roll tires into the road and set them aflame, make roadblocks out of boulders, and throw stones. Israel's argument was that since the child was in "harm's way," it was the inciters who should be held responsible for the injury or death of the rioting child (Nixon 1990).

Yet, the report documents 159 child gunshot deaths in the first two years from indiscriminate beating, tear gassing, and shooting of children at home just outside the house, playing in the street, sitting in the classroom, or going to the store for groceries. These children were shot for flashing V-for-Victory signs, chanting nationalist slogans, taunting and jeering at soldiers, doodling Palestinian flags in school notebooks, violating curfew, or participating in demonstrations, whether stone-throwing or not. Military personnel were responsible for 94% of the children's deaths (Nixon 1990).

Almost all of the children shot dead were hit by directed gunfire to their head or neck. Of the estimated 50,000 to 63,000 injured children (one out of

We begin from the recognition that all beings cherish happiness and do not want suffering. It then becomes both morally wrong and pragmatically unwise to pursue only one's own happiness oblivious to the feelings and aspirations of all others that surround us as members of the same human family. The wiser course is to think of others while pursuing our own happiness. The Fourteenth Dalai Lama

every 15 to 20 children) requiring medical treatment, an estimated 6,500 to 8,500 were wounded by gunfire. (In U.S. population terms, these numbers represent 9,680 American children killed and 3–3.8 million American children injured.) A sample of the 822 child gunshot injury records in the first year showed that the children, aged 3 to 15 years, had been shot in the upper body, including the head, or suffered multiple gunshot wounds (Nixon 1990).

The report described some of the case histories such as this injury of a 4-year-old boy in the Jabalia Refugee Camp in Gaza (Part 1, Vol. 1, p. 23). He had been playing with his small plastic gun with his ten-year-old cousin on the sidewalk. A combined foot-and-mobile patrol passed slowing in front of them with four soldiers riding in the jeep and nine soldiers walking behind it. As children do, the little boy raised his arm and made a clicking noise as if he were using the plastic gun. When the child did it a second time, three soldiers went after the child. One grabbed the plastic toy, threw it to the ground, and stomped on it, smashing the toy. The second soldier started screaming at the child as to where was his father. The third soldier picked the child up off the ground from behind while the second soldier beat his outstretched arm with his wooden truncheon. When the jeep backed up, a soldier appearing to be the officer demanded to know where the father was. While the neighbors came out of their two- or three-room dwellings that housed 10 to 15 people, the soldiers were still beating the child's arm and slapping him across the face. An aunt came running down the street to wrestle with the soldier holding her nephew. At that point, the soldier lifted the child in the air and dashed him to the ground, while the solder that had been slapping his face struck him on his left shoulder with the butt of his rifle. When the three soldiers were finished with the boy, they joined the patrol that was keeping the crowd back. The child's arm was fractured. In the hospital, it was set and put in a cast. The family says that the child now cries much of the time. He has developed a fear of strangers (Nixon 1990).

Situations of this kind produce more long-lasting consequences. For example, the soul or the inner child of the person is also fractured. Yet little has been done to help with those problems.

Israel also used collective punishments that served multiple purposes and evolved into a general policy of governmental violence. They included house raids, house-by-house beatings, mass arrest, tax raids, cuts in food, water, and electricity supply, prohibited access to jobs, school, and medical care, and psychological assaults. The object was to use "curfews" for extensive periods of time like weeks and months to "crush" the community into submission through a policy of impoverishment and violence. That meant that the Gaza Strip was under night curfew for 21 of the 24 months and day curfews for 41% of the months March through June 1989. Over 19,000 children in four West Bank refugee camps spent 61% of the months September through November 1989 under day curfews. Children living in these camps experienced almost 20 times more curfews than children in other communities did. In Gaza refugee camps, an average of ten to fifteen people lived in very small two- or three-room dwellings, often without toys, books, or television or electricity for television. Not allowed to go to school and confined to the house, children would either be hyperactive and uncontrollable during curfew or they would become listless, emotionally withdraw, and stare off into space for hours on end (Nixon 1990).

Dr. James Garbaino, President of the Erikson Institute for Advanced Study in Child Development, expressed concern about the violation of one's home. It is a known fact that it is critical for a child's development to have sanctity of home and parents or caretakers who protect children from the stress of living in a dangerous environment. In his words, the children of Palestine (Muslim and Christian) had more than violations of homes as safe places; there was also a "violation of the 'family' as a psychological system" (Nixon 1990, Part II, 59).

The government also used sieges, house demolitions, economic and administrative sanctions, and obstructed access to medical and health care. In two years, at least 1,098 houses had been demolished or sealed for "security" or "licensing" reasons that left at least 9,766, including 4,883 children, homeless. As the report so aptly stated:

Each one of these measures constitutes an assault on
the well being and at the times the very lives of
children, whether directly or indirectly through the
effects on the family unit. Whether considered singly or
together, the collective punishments imperiled the
ability of families to care for, nourish, and protect their
children. (Nixon 1990, Part I, Vol. 1, p. 7)

In addition, children aged 5 to 15 years were held in prison and detention centers where they were subjected to sensory deprivation, death and rape threats, violent beatings, and other brutal assaults. Other children were put through an unofficial, unsupervised, and short-term detention in temporary military posts and bivouacs. Although held for short periods of days usually by small numbers of soldiers and sometimes by settlers (Jewish immigrants) in this "non-judicial track," they were beaten and confined for purposes of extra-legal punishment, assault, and intimidation. Since they were not officially detained, their families were not notified and thus, lawyers and international bodies have no information about them or access to them (Nixon 1990).

Torture for "Security" (Phillips 1995) gives us more understanding as to what it was like to be detained or arrested by a military force. A systematic and institutionalized use of torture included physical brutality (beatings, electric shock, hanging detainee with hands tied behind the back, submerging nose and mouth under water, burns, extraction of nails and teeth, sexual assaults, and insertions of objects into the orifices of the body), sensory deprivation (long waits in the sun during the day, blindfolded and tied for prolonged periods, being prevented from sleeping up to eight days, no water or food for periods of four, seven, and eight days), and psychological abuse (mock executions, threats to throw a person out of a window, use of insulting language, rubbing the head with vomit, and being present at the torture or inhuman or degrading treatment of relatives or friends).

Shabeh combined several of these abuses. A person has his head covered with a sack that has been urinated or vomited on (very bad smelling) that reaches to the chest. In addition, the hands are tied or cuffed to a pipe fixed to a wall where the person is kept for consecutive days without benefit of food, water, or toilet.

Shabeh causes extreme pain and is considered similar to the interrogation techniques defined as torture by the European Commission on Human Rights. Yet, Israel maintained that in the absence of peace, any international treaties applied only to areas where Israeli law is applied. Local laws and international humanitarian laws were separate from laws of war that apply to situations of international armed conflict even though these citizens paid taxes to Israel and Israel was supposed to be providing services. Al-Haq took the position that protections "afforded by human rights treaties to which Israel is a party is applicable to all individuals under Israeli jurisdiction" (Phillips 1990, 31). For citizens, Israel cannot "claim an exception on domestic law, security, or any other grounds" (33).

Al-Haq documented that Israel detained on "security" grounds (not carrying their Israeli-issued identity card, possessing a book or other published material without a permit, raising the Palestinian flag, throwing stones) more than 80,000 Palestinians (about 24 percent of the male population between the ages of 15 and 54) between December 1987 and May 1992. Their study is important because it focused upon the initial period of detention before formal interrogation. In other words, the detainee is already in custody and thus illegal treatment cannot be justified as necessary to effect an arrest. In addition, they document that 85 percent were subject to torture or ill-treatment that was largely standardized in Israeli prisons, military detention facilities, police stations, and jails even though they were under the general administration of different branches of the Israeli government. This wasn't a handful of "rough cops" that were exceeding orders. It was a systematic practice that was "sanctioned at some level as deliberate policy" (Phillips 1995, 45, quoting 19 June 1977, *The Sunday Times*).

After *Intifada*

In preliminary research, Palestine has a physical disability population near 6 percent, compared to the international percentage of 2.5–3 percent (*The Jerusalem Times*, Feb. 19, 1999, p. 9). Yet, the true size of the problem, types and categories, and causes of the disabilities are unknown due to lack of studies and statistics. Those who did sustain disabilities during the *Intifada* were the working youth that have no adequate rehabilitation facilities. They become neglected on all levels. In addition, they add to the high unemployment rate as well as the high demands for services.

When we lack information on physical disabilities, it also means we lack information on more hidden disabilities and other mental health problems. Yet, from some of the information that led to the uprising, we can gain a sense of the mental instability. Amar Abu Zayyad in *Children of Israel, Children of Palestine* said that when his father was administratively arrested (taken into custody, convicted, and sentenced without a trial), he was full of anger; he was age 8. His father was taken to Nablus to a prison where the child was permitted to visit. Upon seeing the conditions, Amar vomited. His father would in six months' time be released. Yet, he said that the prison aroused such feelings of hatred toward all Israeli people that he dreamed of killing them all. The only way he could ease the sufferings of his people was to find a weapon. Since Israel had long confiscated all weapons and used them against the Palestinians, Amar was left with only the many rocks upon the ground. He took the rock to be his weapon (Holliday 1998).

Ideas must work through the brains and arms of good and brave men (and women), or they are not better than dreams. Ralph Waldo Emerson

Since Israel controls all the means for importing raw materials and exporting finished products, they would not allow the Arabs among them to develop their own industrial infrastructure that might compete with their economy or serve as the basis for an independent state. The Palestinians could work as laborers for Israel such as on their former owned farms and orchards. But, they had no independent economic base. Then Israel used its military power (rubber bullets are not rubber—only the tip) and its domestic intelligence service to disrupt any Palestinian attempt at mass organization. When the PLO, in late 1960s, engaged in some acts of bomb explosions and airplane hijacking, the press was quick to associate "terrorism" with "Palestine" even though 99 percent of the Palestinian people have never been involved in terrorist activity. The fusion of the two words "Palestinian" and "terrorist" became known worldwide (Freedman 1994).

Between 1977 and 1984, the ratio of "spontaneous incidents" as opposed to organized groups against Israelis was 1:11. In 1986, the year before the uprising, the ratio was 18:1. An example of this type of "spontaneous incident" is a sixteen-year-old Palestinian schoolboy who walked up to an Israel solder patrolling the busy Manara traffic circle of the center of Ramallah in the West Bank and put an ax into the soldier. That December 18, 1986, event was especially upsetting for Israel because they found out that no one paid him to do it. Not one faction of the many in the Palestinian Liberation Organization (PLO) had enlisted him (Freedman 1994). He was acting on his initiative of his own anger and rage.

If children were responding that way before the uprising due to the mistreatment to them and their family members, one can only guess as to the long-range consequences that will occur due to the treatment during the *Intifada*. Several theories might apply. Social learning would say that if you can do it to my loved ones, than I can do it to others once I have some power. Thus, one would expect more domestic violence and child abuse cases from these populations. They are at-risk to abuse power because they have been taught by the examples of others.

Another theory already mentioned would point to the disruption of the mental development of the child. They would argue that the child has become disconnected to the inner part of oneself (some call it the inner child or the soul) to the point that the ability to use both hemispheres of the brain is damaged. The feelings of rage or emotions of the right hemisphere are so overwhelming that the left hemisphere cannot input any logic. It is as if the child has lost his or her conscience. Or, the child never developed a sense of trust. In reality, the child has shut it off much like child sexual assault victim/survivors who dissociate or have multiple personalities in order to deal with the horrors that they have had to experience.

In this context, children reared in fear may take it out on others. Recent research into why some American police officers do or don't interdict for child abuse, neglect, and sexual exploitation is related to the way they were disciplined as children (Clement and Osborne 1998). Using a police population of 191 street officers, it was statistically significant that those who did not interdict when medical attention was denied were made to hurt others for punishment, paddled, switched, hit with rulers, mouths washed with soap, and made to wear funny clothing. In reality, as young children, these persons who later become police officers have learned to detach from their feelings. The more emotional detachment is used as a coping style, the more the belief system develops that disconnecting from one's feelings is useful. Yet, the extensive body of research on police stress reaches other conclusions. When the officer is not fully present in the moment, there may be more on-the-job accidents, citizen complaints, disciplinary problems, and/or excessive sick leave. The officers' excessive anxiety can result in an overreaction to a situation.

Using that research on the three soldiers who abused the four-year-old, it would seem that the soldier who did the verbal abuse was probably verbally abused as a child. The other soldier who used physical punishment probably had physical punishment done to him instead of more positive methods like being talked to, having time-out, or certain privileges taken away. The third soldier went after the plastic toy by smashing the gun. He was probably releasing his fear and anger as some people do when they punch holes in the wall or throw dishes against the walls instead of hitting people.

So, those who are fearful discipline others in fear and thereby, teach others to fear. Khader and Qous (1997, 16) stated it this way:

History has proven that peace remains ink on paper if
children from both sides continue to fear each other. If
we want to remove this fear, we must attack the root of
the problem that created such fears and justifies these
total closures. The root of the problem is Occupation.
Eliminating occupation alleviates fears of violence. It
remains an enigma that Israel expects Palestinians to
behave while it continues to occupy their lands,
expand settlements, mistreat, and humiliate their
people.

Applying the theory and research of dysfunctional families in Chapter 5, one might argue that the long-range consequence of rearing children in "fear" by abusive power is to create world problems. Individuals who lack a sense of security that comes from a balance of power and spiritual values of compassion manage others by a domineering style. Their "insecurities" become expressed as they try to control everything and everyone around them instead of focusing upon their own behavior and taking control over their own fears. The ultimate consequence of rearing children with "fear" tactics might mean that as fearful people, they create wars with others.

Red China

The Communist Chinese government has a "one child" policy per couple. The World Health Organization (WHO) of the United Nations released statistics that showed that in 1994, 117 boys were born for every 100 girls. The natural process is that girl babies have a higher survival rate. Usually, more boy babies are prone to spontaneous abortion and early premature births. Since boy babies are biologically weaker at birth, they have a higher infant mortality rate. From ages 1 to 5, male children have higher rates of death. To have more boy babies when the natural process is to have more girl babies means that something is being done to purposefully change the normal outcome.

According to WHO, 50 million women were estimated to be "missing" in China. Missing is a polite word for gender-cide. Some were killed while still in the womb because of ultrasound technology that revealed the baby's sex. Others were starved to death after birth, victims of violence, or not medically treated when they became ill (Associated Press in Sydney, Australia, Aug. 13, 1998).

Besides gender-cide, even under a supposedly "moderate" regime, religious persecutions and repressive labor camps produce cheap goods sold to the West, including the United States. One can bet that many children are used in those camps to make profits for others.

Countries in the Far East like Red China are also part of an underworld economy. Activities like drug trafficking, smuggling, sale of human beings and body parts, counterfeiting, prostitution, and pornography are merged with legitimate economic activity in China. The international movie *Indochine* depicted the real reason Indochina fell; it was part of the war over the drug trade. The person who controlled the land could also control the high-purity heroin.

Iraq

Dr. Haifa Ashahine, a senior gynecologist at the Saddam Hussein Children's Hospital in southern Iraq, is no longer shocked to find a child without a brain or with a giant head, stump arms like those of a thalidomide victim, two fingers instead of five, a heart with missing valves, or missing ears. Children in different villages with the highest concentration in southern Iraq born to different families are being born blind or with internal congenital defects in the heart and lungs. Mothers as young as 20 are giving birth to Mongol or Down's syndrome-type defects, which usually doesn't happen. Research showed that the number of these kinds of births has tripled since the Gulf War (North 1998).

Now, both in Britain and the United States, veterans of the Gulf War are coming forward with reports of miscarriages late in the pregnancy, sick and dying children similar to those in Iraq. The theory of this gene-twisting force is the ammunition coated in a radioactive material known as depleted uranium (DU).

So far, only one British soldier has been tested for DU—Ray Bristow, who served with his unit on the notorious Basra Road. Bristol's test was carried out by Dr. Asaf Darakovic, associate member of the American College of Physicians and professor of radiology and nuclear medicine at Georgetown University in Washington, D.C. He told Bristow last month that a test had revealed the level of radioactivity in his urine was 100 times greater than was safe. Dr. Darakovi also told Bristow that of 24 servicemen he tested for radioactivity from the 144 New Jersey Transport and Resupply Corps, 14 out of 24 tested positive for radioactivity. (North 1998, 6)

When the United States adopted uranium-tipped tank-piercing bullets, the radioactive materials may have poisoned more than just the environment of Iraq. When DU-tipped bullets hit the tanks, they explode and send millions of tiny radioactive particles into the atmosphere. For the persons who were there or came later, they breathed in the particles that affected their health. Organs most susceptible to radiation are the kidneys and the reproductive organs (the gonads and ovaries). In addition, the radioactive half-life is at least 4,000 years. So it spreads and becomes part of the food chain of the dates, oranges, and tomatoes. There seems to be no way to control the spread. Now, the birth of deformed babies is not confined to the south of Iraq or even to Iraq. Yet, it would cost billions even if it were feasible to clean up the radioactive mess in the Persian Gulf, said Leonard Dietz, an atomic scientist who wrote a report for the U.S. Energy Department (North 1998, 5).

Ethiopia

Ethiopia, once Africa's breadbasket, is now Africa's basket case with street orphans who have no future. Street children are in many cities in the world such as Moscow, South Africa, Congo, hundreds of other Third World countries like Brazil, and even parts of the United States. Yet, Kaye Corbette, a journalist, returned to Addis Abada in 1998 to see what the new government had done for the people. She found the city, meaning New Flower, to have only dominant smells of stale urine and fear. She thought that the war forced many Ethiopians into Addis since begging on the streets was more appealing than being shot by rebels or being drafted into their armies. Although homeless children wandered the streets, they were more fortunate than the multitude of young boys being kidnapped and placed in military compounds either by government forces or those of the rebels. The government elite occupied some of the most beautiful buildings. But the human refuse either have a place in corrugated tin lean-tos which housed upward of 20 people in tight quarters or the streets. Human and animal excrement filled the rut-filled streets. Pickpockets worked the streets but with little success with the tourist trade almost nonexistent. "Parents had been known to break the bones of babies at birth in order for them to join the brigade of 'monkey children,' who walked on all fours as beggars and were the main source of income for some families" (World Net Daily, Nov. 4, 1998).

Seven years ago, Corbette wrote that the "world pictured Ethiopia as starving, bloating children with swarms of flies in their eyes." In 1998, even with a new government, little has changed. The new government is just as oppressive and "ranks as one of the worst human rights offenders" (World Net Daily, Nov. 4, 1998).

North Korea

In North Korea, Doctors Without Borders, a European charity, withdrew their team of 13 professionals including nine doctors. Orphaned and homeless children have been collected into centers known as "9–27 camps" (named after the date in 1997 when Kim Jong II ordered their establishment). The medical, nutritional, and sanitation problems are "horrific" according to interviews with North Korean refugees from the centers who have escaped into China. The concern is that the North Korean government has adopted a double standard policy of feeding children from families loyal to the regime while neglecting others. The pullout is especially worrisome because a food crisis is killing 300,000 to 800,000 North Koreans a year, according to a report by an U.S. congressional delegation in August of 1998 (Pomfret 1998).

James Pringle, a reporter for the *Times* and *Sunday Times* on the border of China and North Korea, saw through his binoculars the effects of a Stalinist regime that prefers to see children die rather than open its impoverished country to the world. While the privileged ruling class and military leaders are fed from overseas aid in the capital Pyongyang, nothing is getting through to the remote border province where famine has occurred for four years. One of the few signs of life was an ox cart that was being used to pick up the bodies of the dead. He had seen the cavalcade of human skeletons tottering out of Cambodia's jungles in 1979. He had seen the children with distended bellies in African famines. Unlike those of other Third World tragedies, Pringle reported that this was a famine in an industrialized state where people starved and died quietly in their homes. If they try to escape across the border, Kim Jong II, the leader of the People's Democratic Republic of Korea, has ordered a "shoot-to-kill" policy for the border guards against the people (Feb. 2, 1999).

Russia

Expert Professor R. J. Rummel estimated that the Communist Party of the Soviet Union over six decades murdered nearly 62 million beings. This death by governments or "democide" (the systematic mass murder by government of the helpless people it controls) was more than four times the battle dead for all nations during the Second World War. The Communist party gained power by promising the peasants land, in terms the promisers knew to be a lie. Once they gained the power, they took the land from the peasants that the government already owned and exterminated those who resisted (Hoar 1998).

Russia called it "social engineering." It was forced collectivization and forced famine that resulted in at least seven million deaths in the Ukraine. Even though the people had land, the government did not permit them to grow what they wanted on the land, much like we do to American farmers under a new definition of the "commerce clause" of the Constitution that production will disturb "commerce." However, when the famine came, starving people were imprisoned for harvesting food from what had been their own land. For example, a woman who cut a hundred ears of ripening corn from her own plot after the recent death of her husband from starvation was sentenced to ten years. Another Soviet scholar quotes a sentence of ten years' forced labor without the right to amnesty. Plus, all the property was confiscated when a person gathered seventy pounds of wheat stalk to feed his family (Hoar 1998).

Presently, Russia is portraying itself as an emerging democracy, with a budding middle class and a market capitalist system. Russia's ruling elite uses the words of privatizing, democratizing, and McDonaldizing. The West has loaned Russia over U.S. $200 billion since 1991. Half is owed to the U.S. government, IMF, and other institutions. The other half is owed to European and American banks with German banks, the biggest holder of Russian debt, facing a $52 billion loss. Yet, most of that money never made it for the health and education needs of the people and their children. Instead, the money went to several groups. The first was Russia's seven super tycoons who are mostly Jewish and led by Boris Berezovsky. Another group were bankers and, of course, politicians. The Mafia that controls 60%

of all business took the rest (Margolis 1998). (Remember that the American Mafia went global in the 1950s and 1960s and, according to some experts, was part of the reason for the death of President John F. Kennedy because he was trying to get rid of them. See *Double Cross* by Gigolo.)

Conclusion

What are all these countries missing? Obviously, a real free market in a capitalist system must have clear laws. Private ownership permits each individual to be rewarded for individual effort. A free press that does investigatory journalism permits people to think and make decisions for themselves. An honest government maintains order and enforces rules for all so that prosperity can occur. If governments want people to buy commodities, the people have to have jobs that permit them to provide for the basic necessities of their families. When a government permits a group of persons to be the "slave labor" in order to keep the prices low, they also deny them the opportunity to buy the very products that would bring prosperity for the government. People in leadership in governments like parents in a family must be interested in the good of all, not just power.

Power for its own sake without limits means that governments can be as abusive as parents or caretakers who abuse their children. From the research that was done on the men who abused their wives and created the Power Wheel as shown in Chapter 5, power creates a false sense of control and pride. The intoxication process means that the desire for power constantly increases and grows subtler. The thrill of victory or the sensation of trampling someone who is helpless becomes such a drive that people who crave this power don't realize they have lost their own soul. Like any intoxicant, abuse of power leads to addiction. Just as persons who are on some type of illegal drug, power-intoxicates are spurred to do greater and greater violence. They become drunk with the pleasure it provides for them until it brings their own demise.

The end result is a legal system that we presently experience that is based on greed, bias, artificial technicality, and human blindness. Whereas justice is viewed as being blind, what we are experiencing is a distorted legal system. The system isn't just an injustice even though it is legal.

On the other hand, one can have power and control in the power wheel of equality. Support for this type of policy change comes from several authors. Harris (1997) argued for using an approach that has three simple beliefs: (1) all people have equal value as human beings, (2) harmony and felicity are more important than power and possession, and (3) that the personal is the political. French (1985) called this way of looking at the world feminism—not just a prescription for granting rights to women— a far broader vision of equality from the recognition that all humans are equally tied to the human condition of becoming.

The wedding was lovely. Invite me to the marriage. God

Following the power and equality models, one can ask this question: How can a society create a different set of structures and relations that permit the full realization of the human potential in individuals and societies?

The answer to that question will take effort. We may choose to discard some of our current thinking and tendencies. We may have to put less emphasis on "making money" and put more on how one develops one's self by the choices one makes. We may have to be more honest with ourselves, with each other, and expect the same in return from those in leadership positions.

An honest man is one who knows that he can't consume more than he had produced. Ayn Rand in *Atlas Shrugged*

We might have to give up our idea of get-rich-quick schemes. We might have to enter into business where we earn our benefits instead of trying to take them from others. Ayn Rand (1957) in *Atlas Shrugged* had one of the characters portray how an industry's distribution was supposed to be decided by voting of the voice of the people—the workers. No rules to the game, no rhyme or reason but each person could demand how much they wanted to be paid from the pot of profits. It was suppose to be all one big family of workers like pouring water into a tank but there was a pipe at the bottom draining it out faster than it could be poured in. The worker said that the owner of the company passed off this plan as if it were virtue when they all knew that they would be ashamed to admit otherwise. The worker summed it up this way:

> *There wasn't a man voting for it who didn't think that under a setup of this kind he'd muscle in on the profits of the men abler than himself. There wasn't a man rich and smart enough but that he didn't think that somebody was richer and smarter, and this plan would give him a share of his better's wealth and brain. But while he was thinking that he'd get unearned benefits from the men above, he forgot about the men below who'd rush to drain him just as he hoped to drain his superiors . . . we got what we asked for. By the time we saw what it was that we'd asked for, it was too late (616).*

We still have time to create the community, the state, the nation, and the world we want for our children and ourselves. As you have seen parents that you had wished that they could have been yours, we can create a world for our children and our children's children that we wished we could have grown up in if we would be willing to change some of our thinking. Just as we help parents change their way of thinking in rearing children, we can have healthy families that desire healthier societies.

If you always do what you've always done, you'll always get what you've always got. David Icke

The values of compassion and loving, healthy, person-oriented values that can be affirmed in the family and the home must also be in the halls where public policy-making, diplomacy, and politics are practiced. The challenge is to take the lessons learned with helping families and individuals to make free will choices to be healthy and apply them to societies where process is as important as product or outcome, where logic and compassion are integrated, and where power (left brain or male aspect) is balanced with emotions (right brain or female aspect). We can discover how to behave as befits our values and desires for harmony as we recognize our interdependence. Such a world would have universal support for the development of the uniqueness of each child as an investment in the child. That investment would be far cheaper than the present cost of all our challenges and would bring richer and greater dividends to our communities and our future.

In an interview over his recent book *The Truth Shall Make You Free*, David Icke, an English author, said:

You know, you would think, hypothetically, that some of the people within the Rockefeller or Rothschild hierarchy might consider how much more money they might make if people were freely allowed to explore their own talents and creativity in a relaxed, fun, fulfilling way. These people who own the world's money might actually make more money if people were happier expressing their uniqueness and individuality in their lives (July/August 1996, 1).

SUMMARY

This chapter attempted to focus attention on policy issues dealing with children and youth. Realizing that one can take classes in public policy, the purpose of this chapter was to specifically deal with issues of children and youth as it related to policy. The chapter had two major parts. The first part dealt with sources of law, policy, and theories of law making. Sources of law were defined as written and unwritten law with written law as being constitutions, statutes, and court decisions. Policy was defined simply as what governments do or don't do. Sometimes the policy becomes law and other times it works as a quasi-legal agency that has more power because the people have fewer protections under their constitutions, state and federal.

In terms of policy, the types of policies were discussed along with what the process is and who has the power to influence the process. In terms of who has the power, four groups were discussed: (1) corporate, (2) membership based, (3) single groups, and (4) public groups. Part of that discussion was the unequal distribution of income, the wall of silence, and the power elite. Two theories of law making were discussed as the consensus model and the conflict model from the conflict and radical theorists.

The second part of the chapter focused upon specific policies as they related to children in the United States and other foreign countries. Other countries discussed were Israel, Iraq, Ethiopia, North Korea, and Russia. The ways governments are relating to children was compared to the information on dysfunctional and healthy families as discussed in greater detail in Chapter 5.

To avoid a legal justice system that is based on greed, bias, artificial technicality, and human blindness, it was advocated that we grow healthy societies. Instead of abuse of power, equality can permit healthier communities, states, nations, and a world. The values of compassion and loving, healthy, person-oriented values that can be affirmed in the family and the home can also be in the halls where public policy-making, diplomacy, and politics are practiced. The challenge is to take the lessons learned with helping individuals and families choose healthier coping styles and apply them to societies where process is as important as product or outcome, where logic and compassion are integrated, and where power (left brain or male aspect) is balanced with emotions (right brain or female aspect). We can discover how to behave as befits our values and desires for harmony as we recognize our interdependence. Such a world would have universal support for the development of the uniqueness of each child as an investment in the child. That investment would be far cheaper than the present cost of all our present challenges and would bring richer and greater dividends to our communities and our future.

REFERENCES

Barlett, Donald L., and James B. Steele. "Corporate Welfare." Internet special report, 18 Nov. 1998, from an article in *Time*.

Buchanan, Patrick J. "Free Trade Is Not Free." Address to the Chicago Council on Foreign Relations, November 18, 1998.

Chambliss, William J. *Criminal Law in Action*, 2nd ed. New York: John Wiley and Sons, 1984.

——. "Policing the Ghetto Underclass" in *Public Policy, Crime and Criminal Justice* by Barry W. Hancock and Paul M. Sharp, eds. Upper Saddle River, NJ: Prentice Hall, 1997, 146–166.

Cleaver, Tony. *Understanding the World Economy: Global Issues Shaping the Future*. New York: Routledge, 1997.

Clement, Mary J. "Five-year Study of Juvenile Waiver and Adult Sentencing: Implications for Policy." *Criminal Justice Policy Review* 8 (2)(1997): 201–219.

Clement, Mary J., and William Osborne. Unpublished manuscript. "Street Interdiction of Child Abuse and Neglect—Statistical Analysis." Paper presented at annual meeting for the Academy of Criminal Justice Sciences, March 1998.

Cloward, Richard, and L. Ohlin. *Delinquency and Opportunity. A Theory of Delinquent Gangs*. New York: Free Press, 1960.

Dahl, Robert. *Who Governs? Democracy and Power in an American City*. New Haven, Conn.: Yale University Press, 1961.

DiMascio, William M. *Seeking Justice, Crime and Punishment in America*. New York: The Edna McConnell Clark Foundation, 1997.

Dye, Thomas R. *Who's Running America?* Englewood Cliffs, NJ: Prentice-Hall, 1976.

——. *Understanding Public Policy*, 4th ed. Englewood Cliffs, NJ: Prentice Hall, 1981.

——. *Who's Running America? The Clinton Years*, 6th ed. Englewood Cliffs, NJ: Prentice Hall, 1995.

Ekins, Paul. *A New World Order*. New York: Routledge, 1992.

Elias, Robert. "Crime Control as Human Rights Enforcement" in *Public Policy, Crime and Criminal Justice* by Barry W. Hancock and Paul M. Sharp, eds. Upper Saddle River, NJ: Prentice Hall, 1997, 386–396.

Fagan, J., and E.P. Deschenes. "Determinants of Judicial Waiver Decisions for Violent Juvenile Offenders," *Journal of Criminal Law and Criminology* 81 (2) (1990): 314–347.

The Federalist Brief, the Internet's Conservative Journal of Record, 13 October 1998, http://www.Federalist.com.

French, Marilyn. *Beyond Power: On Women, Men and Morals*. New York: Summit Books, 1985.

Friedman, Thomas. *From Beirut to Jerusalem*. New York: HarperCollins, 1995.

Golden, Renny. *Disposable Children: America's Child Welfare System*. Belmont, CA: Wadsworth Publishing Co, 1997.

Hamparian, D.M., L.K. Estep, S.M. Muntean, R.R. Priestino, R.G. Swisher, P.L. Wallace, and J.L.White. *Youth in Adult Courts: Between Two Worlds*. Columbus, Ohio: Academy for Contemporary Problems, 1982.

Haris, M. Kay. "Moving Into the New Millennium," in *Public Policy, Crime and Criminal Justice* by Barry W. Hancock and Paul M. Sharp, eds. Upper Saddle River, NJ: Prentice Hall, 1997, 397–410.

Hawkins, David, and Richard Catalano, Jr. *Communities That Care*. San Francisco: Jossey-Bass, 1992.

Hoar, William P. "The Pattern of Terror by Design." E-mail message to Mary J. Clement of Sept. 9, 1998.

Holliday, Laurel. *Children of Israel, Children of Palestine*. New York: Pocket Books, 1998.

Hojnacki, William P. "The Public Policy Process in the United States," in *Public Policy, Crime and Criminal Justice* by Barry W. Hancock and Paul M. Sharp, eds. Upper Saddle River, NJ: Prentice Hall, 1997, 5–21.

Horowitz, Leonard G. *Deadly Innocence: The Kimberly Bergalis Case—Solving the Greatest Murder Mystery in the History of American Medicine.* Sandy Point, ID: Tetrahedron, 1995.

——. Unpublished manuscript of speech "Kissinger and Rockefeller Connections to American Central Intelligence and the Origins of AIDS and Ebola" in Washington, D.C., Labor Day Weekend, 1996a.

——. *Emerging Viruses: Aids & Ebola—Nature, Accident or Intention.* Sandy Point, ID: Tetrahedron, 1996b.

Hunter, Floyd. *Community Power Structure.* Chapel Hill: University of North Carolina Press, 1953.

Khader, Khader, and Mousa Qous. "A Message of Warm Peace," *Palestine Report* 5 (36), 1999, 16.

Lewis D., J. Pinkcus, B. Bard, E. Richardson, L. Prickep, M. Feldman, and C. Yeager. "Neuropsychiatric, Psychoeducational and Family Characteristics of 14 Juveniles Condemned to Death in the U.S.," *American Journal of Psychiatry* 145 (5) (1988): 584–589.

Margolis, Eric. "Summit of the Doomed." Eric Margolis, 1998, <margolis@foreigncorrespondent.com>

Miller, Jerome. *Search and Destroy: African-American Males.* Cambridge: Cambridge University Press, 1996.

Mones, Paul. *When A Child Kills.* New York: Simon and Schuster, Inc., 1991.

Nixon, Anne Elizabeth. *The Status of Palestinian Children during the Uprising in the Occupied Territories.* New York: The American and Radda Barnen Swedish Save the Children and the Ford Foundation, 1990.

North, Gary. "Institute for Christian Economics." 1998. Website: http://www.garynorth.com

Osbun, L.A., and P. Rode. "Prosecuting Juveniles as Adults: The Quest for Objective Decision." *Criminology* 22 (1984): 187–202.

Phillips, Melissa. *Torture for Security: The Systematic Torture and Ill-treatment of Palestinians in Israel.* Ramallah, West Bank: Al-Haq, 1995.

Platt, Anthony. "The Triumph of Benevolence: The Origins of the Juvenile Justice System in the U.S." in *Criminal Justice in America* by R. Quinney, ed. Boston: Little, Brown, 1974.

Platt, A., H. Schechter, and P. Tiffany. "In Defense of Youth. A Case Study of the Pubic Defenders in Juvenile Court" in *The Children of Ishmael: Critical Perspectives on Juvenile Justice* by B. Krisbrg and J. Austin, eds. Palo Alto, CA: Mayfield, 1978.

Pomfret, John. "Aid Group Pulls Out of N. Korea: Rulers Said to Block Access to Hungriest," *Washington Post*, 9/30/98.

Quigley, Carroll. *Tragedy and Hope: A History of the World in Our Time.* Rancho Palos Verdes, CA: G.S.G. & Associates, 1966.

Rand, Ayn. *Atlas Shrugged.* New York: Signet, 1957.

Rogers, Joseph W. "The Greatest Correctional Myth: Winning the War on Crime Through Incarceration," in *Public Policy, Crime and Criminal Justice* by Barry W. Hancock and Paul M. Sharp, eds. Upper Saddle River, NJ: Prentice Hall, 1997, 300–313.

Schlafly, Phyllis. "Whatever Happened to Informed Medical Choice?" and "Vaccines a Miracle of Modern Medicine?" *The Phyllis Schlafly Report*, February 1999.

Sellin, Thorestein. *Culture, Conflict and Crime.* New York: Social Science Research Council, 1938.

Sutherland, E.H. *White Collar Crime.* New York: Holt, Rinehart and Winston, 1949.

Thornton, William E., and Lydia Voigt. *Delinquency and Justice*. New York: McGraw-Hill, Inc., 1992.

Turk, A.T. *Criminality and the Legal Order*. Chicago: Rand McNally, 1969.

Voigt, Lydia, William E. Thornton, Jr., Leo Barrile, and Jerrol M. Seaman. *Criminology and Justice*. New York: McGraw-Hill, Inc., 1994.

Vold, George B. *Theoretical Criminology*. New York: Oxford University Press, 1958.

Weinberg, Neil. "Symptom Therapy." *Forbes Global Business and Finance*, January 11, 1999, 22.

Wilson, John J., and James C. Howell. "Serious and Violent Juvenile Crime, A Comprehensive Strategy," in *Public Policy, Crime and Criminal Justice* by Barry W. Hancock and Paul M. Sharp, eds. Upper Saddle River, NJ: Prentice Hall, 1997, 314–327.

CHAPTER 9

For the Sake of Children:
Key Elements for Innovative
Prevention Programs

No one knows what triggered his rage on the chilly autumn evening two years ago when 12-year-old Billy McClellan torqued himself into an uncontrolled frenzy, beat his younger brother to the ground, punched his fist into a wooden china cabinet and cornered his foster sister against the kitchen counter, a butcher knife aimed at her chest. "Help me," she pleaded to the stunned babysitter. It took two police officers to carry Billy to the patrol car. "I'll get you for this," he screamed at them. (Vobed-jda 1998, 9)

The purpose of this chapter is to present some of the pioneering work of many experts who are working with children, youth like Billy and their families. Some of this brain and emotional development research is very new and gives us greater understanding of how to meet some of the unique needs of children. For example, Goleman (1995), in his book *Emotional Intelligence*, would call Billy's behavior an example of a neural hijacking. This is where the emotions trigger a center in the brain declaring an emergency but without giving the neocortex, the thinking brain, the chance to fully understand what is happening. The person has no chance to evaluate whether holding a knife to another's chest, like Billy did, is really a good idea. This center in the brain is called the amygdala and it acts as a storehouse of emotional memory.

To understand youth like Billy, we will need to know more about brain development, emotions, and the interplay between them. Thus, this chapter will focus on research on the brain and emotions because both impact the way we learn and deal with life situations. Some of these newer approaches are extremely effective. They are offered by far-thinking specialists and

INTRODUCTION

No matter how vast your knowledge or how modest, it is your own mind that has to acquire it . . . Your mind is your only judge of truth. John Gault in Ayn Rand's *Atlas Shrugged*

entrepreneurs, some of whom have finally moved into the mainstream of educational systems.

Remember, juveniles are not necessarily monsters. Data from the Federal Bureau of Investigation's Uniform Crime Reporting Program and the National Juvenile Court Data Archive, maintained for the office of Juvenile Justice and Delinquency Prevention by the National Center for Juvenile Justice, indicate that offenders under age 15 are not significantly younger than those of ten or fifteen years ago, and that the actual number of offenders remained relatively small as compared with the caseload of older juvenile offenders. Offenders 14 and younger still account for three of every ten juvenile arrests for violent crime index offenses (such as murder, rape, and robbery) and four of every ten arrests for property offenses. Thus, "juvenile courts and juvenile justice agencies should continue preventive services and early intervention" for youth 14 years and younger (Butts and Snyder 1997, 10).

As discussed in the preceding chapter, there is a disparity between the statistics and the public's awareness that is often used to drive public policy. Although many justice professionals remember a 12-year-old killer, the actual numbers are few. Delinquency caseloads have doubled nationwide since 1970. A professional with twenty-five years of job experience can "expect to see twice as may 12-year-old killers in 1995 as 1970, simply due to this increased workload" (Butts and Synder 1997, 11). Other factors include the mass media, which has increased the reporting of youth crime, especially violent crimes. The details are repeated when the youth is arrested, the trial takes place, and at the sentencing. "Growing publicity" may suggest to the public that juvenile crime is dramatically increasing, but that is not borne out by official statistics. In fact, Snyder (1997, 1) showed that for 1996 "all measures of juvenile violence known to law enforcement—the number of arrests, arrest rates, and the percentage of violent crimes cleared by juvenile arrests—are down."

The purpose of this chapter is to give information on what a holistic program would look like to help children like Billy. In Billy's particular case, he became more defiant and aggressive, a pattern psychologists say is common among abused children as they approach adolescence. What is especially troubling for the family is that the parents adopted Billy as part of a state's efforts to receive federal monies ($4,000 to $6,000 per child) instead of the state paying to keep the youth in foster homes. But when the family had trouble, as illustrated by the quote at the beginning of this chapter, the boy was placed in a treatment center two hours from home. The McClellans were then charged $534 a month to help pay for Billy's treatment. Because of the huge, unexpected costs for medical and psychological treatment for their child, the McClellans are filing a "wrongful adoption" lawsuit claiming that critical information was withheld from them during the adoption process. Later the family received the summaries that had been omitted from the adoption materials, including information that Billy had had a rectal exam when he was 4 indicating that he may have been raped, that he had attempted to hang a family dog, tried to fondle girls' breasts and buttocks at one of his foster homes, and ate dirt (Vobejad 1998, 9). Getting the court to set aside the adoption of the child may be the McClellans' legal solution, but children like Billy become our challenges.

In this chapter, some of the reasons for behavior such as Billy's will be discussed in terms of our present understanding of brain development, such as whole brain learning, physical exercise such as the cross-crawl that accesses right and left brain hemispheres, and neurological organization. The implication of this research will be discussed in terms of the different approaches necessary to allow all kinds of learning and the development of multiple intelligences, as well as new educational techniques like mindmapping and accelerated learning. Then emotions will be discussed in terms of emotional intelligence and a new emotional therapy.

In this approach, the goal is to give you an understanding of what would be some of the key elements needed to work with troubled youth. Since juvenile offenders are at-risk of continued criminal involvement and are more amenable (treatable) to services and sanctions, it is important to develop and maintain early and effective interventions, as well as graduated sanction programs.

Before we discuss some of the research on the brain and emotions, we need to understand what prevention is. You will learn that prevention has three levels with the third level (tertiary) supposed to be treatment because its goal is to prevent or stop future criminal activity. Since the problems of youth are often complex, they need the interaction and cooperation of several agencies—hence the term "community involvement." At times, only the term crime prevention will be used. Yet the term "crime prevention" is a generic term, so it also includes the crimes committed by those under 18 years of age, that is, delinquency as defined in many states.

CRIME AND DELINQUENCY PREVENTION

In the early 1960s, criminal justice was a "closed system." Police were considered the experts. They would solve the problem. In addition, criminal justice had little emphasis upon community building to study social problems and generate prevention or intervention programs. Crime and delinquency prevention was not part of sociology and would not come into its own until criminal justice programs were more established and legitimate. In the 1960s and 1970s crime prevention was not a household word even though most school children were aware of fire prevention.

There is no security in life, only opportunity.
Mark Twain

In 1971 crime prevention began as a national institute (National Crime Prevention Institute, School of Police Administration, Louisville, KY) that trained police officers in "target hardening" (hardening the targets of criminals by better hardware like dead-bolt locks, etc.). They had classes on crime prevention to appraise crime risks and remedial strategies. Crime was defined as occurring when the following three elements were present: (1) criminal desire, (2) criminal skill, and (3) opportunity. Breaking any one of these three elements, especially decreasing the opportunity for a criminal to commit a crime, would be crime prevention. Thus most of the preventive techniques were focused upon making the opportunity more difficult. For example, for house breaking, hardware such as better locks for doors and windows was seen as the answer.

After training, the police went back into their communities to teach better ways to make houses, garages, and businesses more secure through mechanical devices. However, crimes such as rape and sexual assault were also occurring on the streets or in people's homes regardless of good door and window locks. As crime victim and survivor advocacy groups brought the crime problem to the public's attention, the research showed that sexual assault victims did not stay around for the court trial unless there was support for his or her mental, physical, and emotional needs. If police didn't work with other agencies in the community, the police were going to lose their court cases and criminals would go free (Hageman 1978, 1981).

Thus there was a push for criminal justice to view crime prevention more broadly especially by others in allied fields such as the medical and public health authorities. The public health model began to be applied to criminal justice.

Three Levels of Crime and Delinquency Prevention

Today, crime and delinquency prevention has three levels: (1) primary, (2) secondary, and (3) tertiary. Borrowing from the medical model, crime prevention can be at the primary level, where everyone gets education on how to prevent crimes, much as fluoride is added to the public water to prevent tooth decay. For example, Officer Friendly programs teach children in the first, second, and third grades about bicycle safety, how to cross streets, and what to do and not do with strangers. Older children may get drug programs such as D.A.R.E. (Drug Abuse Resistance Education).

The secondary level focuses upon the persons who are at risk to become victims or offenders like Billy McClellan. Billy McClellan had a shattered thighbone at age 2, and burns and bruises all over his body at age 4. He had been taken by authorities twice from his mother and stepfather because of abuse, placed with his father and his stepmother, and then removed again. Billy, like the capital murderer Wilkins in Chapter 4, "Process for Delinquent (Criminal) Youth," had all the early signs for later violent behavior. Chapter 6, "Crimes Against Children," presented the argument that children who are victimized (maltreatment), if there is no intervention for that pain, may grow up and project that pain onto society or onto themselves in slower methods of self-destruction such as prostitution and drug abuse (Simons and Whitbeck 1991; Smith and Thornberry 1995; Kelly, Thornberry, and Smith 1997).

The tertiary level deals with the person caught committing a crime so as to prevent future occurrences. The following list of generalized descriptions shows the many sentencing options used with juveniles as tertiary prevention—stopping future crimes:

1. Probation—person released into the community to report to a probation officer specific times during the month depending upon the offense. This is the most widely used, less expensive option, but it is usually for first-time, nonviolent offenders. Probation is intended to reflect the best interests of the offender, the victim, and the community. Thus probation balances factors such as community protection, accountability, and individualization so that the youth will live more productively and responsibly in the community.

2. Intensive Supervision Probation—person released into the community with a probation officer who sees the client three to five times a week. Because the caseload is small, the probation officer makes unscheduled visits to the home or workplace. This option is used with property offenders, but the programs vary in structure and administration.

3. Restitution and Fines—person required to make payments to crime victims or to the court. This option may be used alone or in conjunction

with other options. Day Fines, most commonly used in European countries, have been developed by the Vera Institute of Justice for implementation. Judges in Phoenix, Arizona, for example, fine a low-risk offender according to occupation and family size. Victim-offender mediation, where offenders and victims meet face-to-face, enables offenders to take more responsibility for their behavior and pay restitution to the victim (DiMascio 1997, 36–37).

4. Community Service—person required to work a specific number of hours in a specific task in the community as part of other options or alone, depending upon the offense.

5. Substance Abuse Treatment—person agrees to be referred to a court or private outside agency for substance abuse. It can be used alone, in conjunction with other options, and/or as a diversion option so that if the client completes the program, the prosecutor may drop the initial charges.

6. Day Reporting—person required to report to a central location every day and file a daily schedule with a supervision officer showing how each hour is spent at work, in class, in outpatient substance abuse treatment, support group meetings, and other activities. The concept was first developed in Great Britain and began to be used in the mid-1980s with other populations such as senior citizens. "By 1994, more than 50 programs were operating in 20 states" (DiMascio 1997, 39).

7. House Arrest and Electronic Monitoring—person released into the community with electronic devices like a bracelet that transmits a signal to a computer that monitors the location of the offender or mandates that the offender call into a particular number and speak over the phone by a certain time or risk getting picked up and placed in jail. The typical offender in this option is a 15-year-old male who is considered a medium risk and who has done a property crime. Some programs combine electronic monitoring with probation or intensive probation.

8. Foster Homes—person who is dependent, neglected, or delinquent but not considered dangerous and is able to live with a family in a foster home. The person's own home circumstances do not permit the child or youth to live with the natural family until the problems causing the out-of-home placement are corrected. Usually probationary supervision, counseling, educational, and vocational services are available. Foster parents are selected and licensed by the states with some sort of training and minimal payment for expenses of feeding and housing the child.

9. Halfway House—person lives in a residential setting wherein one's liberty is controlled and there is mandatory participation in house activities such as group meetings, group therapy, and other classes for personal growth and control like writing résumés and applying for jobs. Halfway houses can be used after a prison or jail sentence or as a last chance to avoid revocation of probation. Many of these programs require the offender to work in the community to pay victim restitution or child support, for example, and to learn how to manage finances and life activities. Depending upon the community, residential programs vary in their emphasis upon work, education, community service, and treatment.

10. Forestry Camps, Outward Bound, or Wilderness Programs—a person lives in a camp where there is park development or farming with supplemented programs of individual and group counseling, recreational, educational, and religious programs. VisionQuest's (a for-profit organi-

zation based in Tucson, Arizona) two wilderness camps are located in the mountains of New Mexico and Pennsylvania. The Wagon Train, considered the most visible of all their programs, travels fifteen to twenty miles per day and transports youth from the East to the West just as the early pioneers on the frontier did over a hundred years ago. Each group of youth and staff have responsibility for the wagon, horses, mules, and other equipment for the camping and cooking of the food. Other wilderness programs include rock climbing and water rafting where youth learn to work with others (Robert 1988).

11. Boot Camp—person goes to a specific camp where rigorous military-style regimen is used to change attitudes and behavior and instill discipline. Originated in 1983 in Georgia and Oklahoma, camps for juveniles and adults are run by more than thirty states and the Federal Bureau of Prisons. Research shows that rearrest rates of boot camp graduates are similar to those of former inmates, mainly because the programs do little to address the job and literacy needs of the offenders (MacKenzie and Souryal 1991; MacKenzie and Shaw 1990).

12. Jail—person is locked up in a secure institution wherein one loses all liberties and others have control over one's life. The jail is maintained in the community for persons awaiting trial, for short-term (one year or less) sentences, and for those being transported to federal and state institutions called prisons.

13. State Juvenile Correctional Institutions (Prison)—person is locked up in a secure institution operated by the state or federal government. When juveniles are waived into the adult system and are found guilty, they can be sentenced to state prisons with other adult offenders or they can be sentenced to the juvenile correctional facility, depending upon the state's law. The sentences are longer at these institutions because a person's offenses are considered more serious. In *Harris v. Wright*, 93 U.S. 581 (1996), the United States Supreme Court affirmed the decision to sentence a fifteen-year-old to a mandatory life imprisonment without possibility of parole for a felony murder (murder occurring during a robbery).

14. Capital Punishment—person is tried in criminal court (adult) and sentenced to die. First, the person is sent to a state prison, and when all appeals have been exercised, the person is given the state's mandated method of ending the person's life. Since this punishment occurs only with adults, the youth has to be waived into the criminal court and tried as an adult.

Most of the emphasis in criminal justice has been at this tertiary level, resulting in the huge incarceration rate and the movement of more youth into the adult system as discussed in Chapter 8, "Legal and Policy Issues That Affect Children." The youth with drug-related problems with little or no money for good attorneys usually are the ones who get caught, with little or no treatment to get to the cause and core of their pain. The "laws impact large numbers of low-level offenders: nonviolent individuals who have no substantial role in drug trafficking operations but who may sell small quantities of drugs in order to support their own habit" (DiMascio 1997, 27).

Contrast those who get caught with those who do not. In one of Detroit's most dangerous neighborhoods, Taylor's (1990) six-year study of the Young Boys Inc. and the Pony Down gangs showed that they were being quickly and silently replaced by far more sophisticated and highly secretive business operations. The Detroit gangs transformed themselves from opportunistic street punks into sophisticated drug-dealing empires that rake in hundreds of millions of dollars a year that are less obvious to the police. They have become more covert, use violence only to protect their dealing turfs, and are more profitable enterprises.

The American public, however, still holds to the idea that the juvenile justice or adult justice systems of incarceration are going to be "rehabilitative." Public opinion studies show that the American public is less punitive than many political leaders believe. Even though they may be fearful of crime, they still hold "rehabilitation as a primary goal of criminal justice" (DiMascio 1997, 44). In a national survey of 1,003 Americans, more than a third agreed that three-quarters of anti-drug funds should be spent on prevention, education, and treatment, and 80 percent would spend at least half of the money on those areas. Fifty-three percent thought that drugs were more of a public health problem and could be better handled through prevention and treatment outside the criminal justice system. Yet only one-third of the federal anti-drug funds were spent for prevention, education, and treatment (DiMascio 1997, 44).

An even stronger cry for primary and secondary prevention tactics come from the survey sponsored by U.S. Senator Paul Simon, D-Ill., of 157 prison wardens in eight states. They responded that 50 percent of those under their supervision would not be a danger to society if released. In addition, 71 percent were for supporting the improvement of public schools and 62 percent favored increasing job opportunities as a way to fight crime (DiMascio 1997, 44).

Community Involvement

Besides these three levels of crime prevention, the criminal and juvenile justice system has sought to accomplish its prevention goals through community involvement. The community was to come together around a particular crime problem and decide collectively how to prevent and intervene most effectively. Especially today, we realize that policing agencies and other criminal justice agencies don't have all the resources to solve all the problems in the community; the community needs to be involved.

Community involvement means that the school systems and the medical and public health systems would work with criminal justice agencies such as police and juvenile court personnel like judges and probation officers. It means the involvement of other social welfare agencies and anonymous groups such as Parents Anonymous (PA), Alcoholics Anonymous (AA), Narcotics Anonymous (NA), and their subgroups. For example, Parents Anonymous of Virginia began a parenting program in 1970 called Mothers Inside Loving Kids (MILK). It is a child abuse prevention program for female inmates in a Virginia state prison, and is also a crime prevention program for the mother and the child. For the few selected felons, the program was tertiary because it helped women get in touch with some of their own unmet needs of their inner being (called the "inner child"). Through classes a woman learned the normal developmental stages of children and thus reduced her own unrealistic expectations of what children can do at specific ages. She received education and training in communications skills. For her children, the all-day visitation programs (only four a year) amounted to secondary prevention, because research shows a highly significant statistical relationship between criminal activity and having a member of one's family in prison, especially a parent (Clement 1993).

However, the use of community involvement has not been fully realized. In 1997, the Edna McConnel Clark Foundation published facts to dispel several myths about corrections systems. Realizing that prison is a necessary component of a criminal justice system, they also showed how the emerging prison-industrial complex has demanded such a growing proportion of tax revenues that states and localities are forced to make a tradeoff between prison and education or other services. The research showed that many other ways could be successfully used with less cost to the taxpayers. But, although "28 states have passed community corrections legislation and many others have created various kinds of intermediate sanctions between probation and prison, such punishments are not yet being used for a large number of offenders in the United States" (DiMascio 1997, 34).

Needless to say, the more we understand ourselves, others, and our communities, the better we can plan and implement meaningful prevention programs. We begin this chapter on innovative programs to assist you in that purpose. For example, one of the most critical factors associated with delinquency is failure in the school system. "Of all delinquency cases adjudicated in juvenile court in 1995, 28% resulted in residential placement and 53% were placed on the probation caseload" (Sickmund 1997, 1). What kinds of learning could happen for youth on probation or in residential placements?

Obviously, learning can take place in the classroom, but most of it doesn't. A youth may be declared poor in math, but he may do really well as a runner for gambling and thus have a better sense of math than is being taught in the schools.

The American Educational System has been strongly criticized but our purpose is to show what good things can happen. For example, Lou Gerstner, CEO of IBM, wrote a blunt assessment of the inadequacies of the current system in his book *Reinventing Education: Entrepreneurship in America's Public Schools* (1994). He argued that the rest of the society has seen tremendous changes in the last 25 years, but not in the educational system. It has been left behind in terms of systemic and radical change in public education that stifles initiative, teamwork, and creativity. Since he knows there is a direct link between education and income such that people who have a better education have better jobs and get better pay, he puts money where his mouth has spoken of the needed reforms. He has launched Next Century Schools, a program that channeled more than $30 million to 43 innovative schools like the School District of Philadelphia, the Charlotte-Mecklenburg School District in North Carolina, and many others across the country. In 1996, he hosted an Education Summit at IBM headquarters in New York where he had assembled 41 governors, 48 chief executives, 35 education experts, and the President of the United States. He is using his position in business as a lever for change and encouraging other business leaders—the ultimate recipients of education—to press for change (Wheelan, 1997).

What would be some of the key elements of more effective education? One of the key elements of a successful program would be to honor the uniqueness of a child's developmental stages. A part of that would be to incorporate our newer understanding of the working of the brain.

In this section we will discuss some of the pertinent research on the development of the brain and how it learns effortlessly and effectively through whole brain learning, physical exercise such as the cross-crawl, neurological organization, and other learning brain research. The work of Piaget will be discussed, then the work of Doman and Dennison. The implications of this research will be discussed in terms of the different approaches that are needed to increase learning and the enhancement of multiple intelligences. A discussion of new educational techniques like mindmapping and accelerated learning will end this section. First, let us begin with cognitive development and the historical work of Piaget before discussing whole brain learning.

BRAIN

In the world of the future, the new illiterate will be the person who has not learned how to learn. Alvin Toffler

Cognitive Development

Piaget (1971) was the one of the early researchers who noted that as children developed physically, they had accompanying regularities in thinking, or *schemata*. Just as Erikson (1963) discovered a specific task for each age of development, so did Piaget. In Piaget's scheme, the first stage of cognitive development, from birth to 2 years, involves the emphasis of the child on the development of all the modalities of sense. Yet if one hides a toy from the child's eyes, the child thinks it is gone—as in the motto, "Out of sight, out of mind." In the early part of these two years, the child begins as a passive responder and emerges as an initiator after two years of being filled with stimuli. In this first stage, called *sensorimotor*, the task is the conquest of objects as the child puts everything into his or her mouth as a method of exploring.

The *preoperational* stage is from ages 2 to 7. In this stage the emphasis is upon language development, with symbols being clearly understood and manipulated by age 7. Emotions such as anger and happiness are expressed in actions not words. The terrible twos (a name given to the age two development wherein children use temper tantrums to get their way) is a challenge for parents to correct their child without unduly hurting the child's body or spirit in the process.

In this cognitive development stage of 2 to 7 years, the child's thinking is very concrete. If a child sees a toilet seat at home in the shape of a circle, the child believes that all toilet seats are circles. When a child then is exposed to a toilet seat in a public restroom that isn't a complete circle, the child may think the toilet seat is broken when in fact it is only a partial circle. Children have the ability to learn rules but it is usually more like obeying the letter of the law and not the spirit of the law. Their thinking isn't very advanced, so they can reach conclusions that are not true, or that are hurtful for others. Remember the earlier example of the 5-year-old, when visiting a neighbor's home to play with the 4-year-old, heard the newborn baby crying and put the baby into the washing machine. The father was asleep on the davenport when the child turned on the washing machine. The prosecutor didn't charge the child with murder because of the child's lack of *mens rea*. The father was not charged with neglect because it was thought he had suffered enough from the death of his child. To understand why the 5-year-old did the act it would be necessary to understand what connections he had put together. What did he see or think he saw as to why babies stop crying?

In addition to immature reasoning ability, such as putting a baby into a washing machine to stop it from crying, children are vulnerable to being used by adults. Children respect adults and feel inferior and limited in comparison.

The third stage is called *concrete operational* and comprises the years from 7 to 11. In this stage the child has a more sophisticated level of reasoning. The child can use his or her imagination or mentally think about things before acting out. The child can reason about rules and argue. Children now expect mutual respect from adults and become highly indignant when denied that respect. Ages 7 and 8 are when children will have multiple arguments with people over what they consider to be "just." "Is that fair?" they will ask.

In the fourth stage, *formal operational*, ages 12–15, the thinking processes use advanced symbolizing and the conquest of thought. At this stage, the child is able to understand abstract ideals, theories, and principles even when they are contrary to facts. This advanced thinking permits the youth to understand probability, analogies, and hypothetical problems. Reasoning in math and sciences is more developed as the youth checks out the various theories and begins to develop new ones.

In this age of 12 to 15 years old, the cognitive development is expanded for adolescents, as is the social milieu of social and environmental factors that interact with the adolescent's physical and mental processes of thinking. Youth question authorities as they formulate their values of social justice. No longer bound by concrete reality, they begin to imagine all sorts of social and interpersonal possibilities. This new way of thinking permits them to be concerned with entrance into adulthood and the choosing of a career.

Although adolescents have greater cognitive development than younger children, they are still not like adults because they are still preoccupied with themselves. They believe that their appearance and behavior are being viewed by an imaginary audience of their peers who are as concerned with his or her thoughts and behaviors as the youth is. This egocentrism is also expressed in a personal way, because the youth thinks that his or her feelings are unique. No one has ever been in love with someone like a teenager has. These youth can think they are exceptions to the rules. Their assumption that "It would not happen to me" explains why some adolescents take such undue risk that results in their addiction to drugs or death.

Piaget (1971) suggested that for an adolescent to reach this later stage of cognitive development, the sociocultural and educational experiences have to be encouraged. If children have traumas at early ages, they may not be able to attain this level of thinking despite innate intelligence or neurological readiness. Kohlberg and Gilligan (1971) argued that nearly half of American adults never advance to the formal operational level of thinking.

Bernstein (1975) argued that the level of language expression has an impact on cognitive development. When people use a public language that is simple and composed of short sentences that are often unfinished or poorly constructed, their level of expression restricts more advanced intellectual thinking. If a person doesn't use adjectives and adverbs, this permits only a simple expression of ideas and simple reasoning. If a person rarely uses impersonal pronouns ("I think" instead of "one thinks that") and simple conjunctions like "so," "then," and "because" are overly used, the thinking will lack complicated analysis and hypothetical reasoning. The language will restrict abstract thought. People with more language development can paint pictures with their words giving shades of meaning and intonation. Language that allows for subtle and complex distinctions permits those who possess the skill to advance their intellectual capabilities.

Whole Brain Learning

Whole brain learning is the simultaneous use of the right and left sides of the brain. But we never fully understood the importance of the right side or left side of the brain until we noticed the devastating effects on those who had the membrane cut between the two halves.

Right and Left Sides of the Brain

Roger Sperry was awarded the Nobel Prize in Physiology and Medicine in 1981 for his contribution to our understanding of the importance of the right brain. His began his study in 1960 at the California Institute of Technology. In the initial stages, Dr. Sperry and his pupils were amputating or cutting the membrane of the corpus callosum, which links the left and right brain, for the treatment of epilepsy. At first, the patients with split brains showed no unfavorable side effects. That was short-lived. Within a few months, major personality disorders emerged and patients couldn't control elimination functions of the bladder and bowels. Since Sperry and his colleagues were able to medically research and study people with split brains, something that no one since has been able to do, they found that the left and right brain each had its own distinctive functions and different types of memory circuits.

The left side of the brain is considered more logical, sequential, and linear. The right brain is more intuitive, feeling oriented, and creative. Harmony and melody were seen as right-brain activities. The left brain likes details, and the right brain prefers to see the whole of something or the bottom line. Although persons have brain dominance, a preference for using one side over the other, the best use of the brain is the crossover and the use of both hemispheres together. For example, the right brain, like the mainframe of a computer, has more power for memory than the left brain. Turning on the right brain permits persons to store more memory, but the left brain is necessary to trigger it for retrieval of information. Music has its own left/right brain split such that the strengthening of the bridge between the two hemispheres also strengthens a diverse range of other mental skills. "The bridge (corpus callosum) between the two sides of the brain is 15% larger in adults who started playing the piano before the age of eight" (Freeman 2001, 51).

A controversy has been created by some who paint all learning as "old left-brain way" versus the "updated right-brain" approach. Jensen (1994, 4), citing the work of Levy, DeBono, and Iacciono, emphasizes that "each side of the brain relies on the other and each is part of a larger whole." It is really a matter of timing and the degree of involvement of both sides of the brain, not that one side is better than the other.

Cross-Crawl between Right and Left Sides

The discovery of the importance of the ability to cross over and use both sides of the brain together was also noted by Glenn Doman. He was a physical therapist working on brain-injured children in Philadelphia. He wanted to research the impact of his physical therapy on the children. He compared the children that he had worked on with the children who had no treatment upon leaving the hospital after their brain injury. To his amazement, he found that his work had little significant effect. In other words, there were some children who went home from the hospital and were in as good a shape as some of the children he had worked with. To his credit, he was willing to learn why.

By studying other children in different cultures, it soon became clear that a particular kind of movement, called cross-crawl, was critical for brain development. Doman's research, estimated to have taken seventy-five human years, delineated the very early stages that children need to be stimulated in order to maximize growth and development in motor, language, visual, auditory, and tactile development. He found that babies soon after birth would move across their cribs or floor in a cross-crawl fashion (left hand with right foot and right hand with left foot movement). He then used that pattern of movement as a technique to assist children whose brains were injured. Then, he worked with children who were mentally retarded, autistic, hyperactive, and/or had learning disabilities. Yet the research and exercises were also beneficial for all children, as evident by Doman's books: *How to Teach Your Baby to Read* (1991), *How to Multiply Your Baby's Intelligence* (1992a), *How to Teach Your Baby Math* (1992b), and *What to Do About Your Brain-Injured Child* (1990).

Today, Glenn Doman is director of the Institute for Human Potential in Philadelphia. At the Institute, the multi-professionally trained staff assesses a child's particular difficulties. Parents are shown how to do the cross-crawl with their child if the child cannot do it for him- or herself. The staff help the parents recruit volunteers to help the family give continued care around the clock to help the child develop the neurological patterns necessary for brain development (like jump starting a car) by doing this cross-crawl. The cross-crawl permits the brain to develop the neurological patterns necessary to maximize learning potential. The theory is that this contralateral movement activates speech and language centers of the brain.

Another characteristic of the Doman approach is to use a card, called a bit card, on which only one bit of information is written. A series of bit cards are read to the child, even in the womb, and shown to the child when born. Although it may seem strange, this practical approach means that when a young child has seen bit cards on the symbols for chemistry, later, when the child is in high school and is taking chemistry, the brain has already stored information about chemistry symbols. Ca for calcium doesn't seem foreign for the student. Doman's approach is theoretically supported by University of Chicago neurobiologist Peter Huttelocker's research on the brain growth in fetal brain tissue and newborn brain tissues. For example, a 28-week-old fetal brain tissue had 124 million brain connections, a newborn 253 million, and an 8-month-old in fact had 572 million. Thus, when Doman encourages parents to read to the baby in the womb, he is helping the child to be stimulated in the brain to help keep the brain cells alive. Huttenlocker's research showed that the fetal brain overproduces cells for the purpose of finding a job to do in the body. Lack of stimulation and interaction with the outside world causes the death of brain cells. Thus, depending upon the quality and quantity of the stimulation afforded by the caretakers for the child, the future number of brain cells could vary by as much as 25 percent (Jensen 1994, 235).

In the past, medical doctors have disagreed on how to deal with children who have had brain injuries, and some view Doman's work with caution. Yet the more recent research of the biopsychosocial characteristics of fourteen juveniles sentenced to death in four states, research that uses medical neurological examinations and biographic case inventories should help us move from neglect to prevention. Eight subjects had injuries to the head—the cranium—that were severe enough to result in hospitalization and/or indentation of the skull. Subject number 1, for example, was in an automobile accident at age 12 wherein he lost consciousness. In addition, he had repeated blows to his head by his father in infancy. The objective evidence was a deep indentation of the cranium behind the right ear. This work details the nature of the trauma for fourteen youth to help us understand that severe head injuries may influence subsequent violent acts (Lewis et al. 1988).

Besides physical injuries to the brain, the brain's physical and cognitive development is also based on stimulation. What happens if a parent doesn't read to a child at very early ages in their development and the child has lost some brain cells? What can a person do with the brain cells that are left? Is there any hope?

Yes. Since the brain is a muscle, it needs to be constantly and consistently stimulated. The "brain exercises" in this book that you are reading in the other chapters are part of that theory. In addition, there are some other physical exercises like the cross-crawl that can help make the brain exercises easier and learning easier.

Dr. Paul Dennison, a former associate with Doman, used the cross-crawl as a major component in his Educational Kinesiology (Edu-K) program. In 1987, the Educational Kinesiology Foundation in Ventura, California, began earnestly researching the experimental and field studies of those who had for the previous twenty years been using the cross-crawl as part of the Brain Gym exercises. Brain Gym is a series of physical exercises for the brain. They were developed as simple and enjoyable movements and activities that could be used with students to enhance the students' experience of whole brain learning. Brain Gym exercises work on the theory of stimulating both the expressive (right) and receptive (left) hemispheres of the brain to advance integrated learning. The premise is to make all types of learning easier, especially academic skills. By doing the exercises, students of any age tap into the body and brain's hidden potential (Dennison and Dennison 1989).

However, not everyone can do the cross-crawl easily. Asking some people to do the cross-crawl increases their stress and weakens them when they are tested by holding out their extended arms and asking them to resist the pressure of the therapist's hand. To correct the person's inability to do cross-crawling effortlessly, Dr. Dennison developed the Dennison Laterality Repatterning technique. The trained therapist first determines if a client is strong when doing the cross-crawl. If not, the client is told to march in place with the same arm and leg coming up (homolateral) and is then tested. Then, the client is told to march in place with the opposite arm and leg coming up (cross-crawl). Depending upon the response, the therapist leads the client in other physical exercises that help the brain "switch on," so that both the left and right sides of the brain can communicate fully with each other. The repatterning reestablishes the innate pattern of the brain to induce whole-brain movement as opposed to one-side-at-a-time processing. The object is to get a client who is stuck either in the right brain and is overly emotional or the left brain and is too logical to move into a cross pattern where she or he can access some logic and feelings and thus problem-solve stressful situations effortlessly.

Brain Gym is used in school systems throughout the United States, mostly on the West coast. In addition to research done in the states, research studies have been done in school districts in Canada, Israel, and Australia. One of the important contributions from this work has been the identification of persons who are homolateral in the at-risk populations in juvenile detention centers. For example, in Weber, Utah, Robert Eyeston found in 1988–89 that 539 of the 552 participants tested as one-sided processors. In his 1987–88 study, he found that 257 of 270 were "switched off" from the necessary brain integration mechanism necessary for complete learning. In contrast, youth of the same age that are in school have very few numbers with homolateral processing (Educational Kinesiology Foundation of North America).

For some, doing the cross-crawl while humming (another right brain activity) and moving the eyes up, down, to the left, and then to the right are simple, easy ways to stimulate both brain hemispheres. However, for others, the wiring in the brain is more complex. Perhaps there has been something as simple as a fall, a high fever, or a blow to the head, and more organization is needed for the neurological connections to take place. Thus a person needs more basic organization of the neurological wires to help make better connections to learn and have better coordination.

Neurological Organization

Is there anyone so wise as to learn by the experience of others?
Voltaire

The Neural Organization Technique (NOT) of Dr. Carl A. Ferreri of Brooklyn, New York, is based on the principle that the body is an integrated whole. Physical, environmental, emotional, and chemical (dietary) trauma can disturb these automatic functions. At first, Dr. Ferreri worked as a very skillful, licensed chiropractor. Then he had twelve young men, all about the same age, who were having troubles in school because of learning disabilities. As he worked on them he began to discover more, but even the initial treatments permitted the youth to do better, as documented by their school records. Following up on his earlier observations, Dr. Ferreri found that the body and its multitude of functions work with the precision of a computer. Just as computers have programs, he found that some programs were built in and others were developed, learned, or put together as the need arose. Yet there were primary "programs" with extensions for the others.

Further investigation recognized the specific neurological functions had priority of the program and its integration with each of the others. It wasn't just a matter of correcting the spine. There were reactive muscle systems, ligaments, bones, and joint interlinks that needed to work in harmony with each other or the client would be forever returning for an appointment. His approach called N.O.T. (Neural Organization Technique), reorganizes the nervous system so that one can function in the way the body was designed to function.

Dr. Ferreri's work, which is taught to many different types of practitioners around the world, also recognizes that sometimes there is a link to an earlier event that locks the problem into the body. A present traumatic incident in the dark or at night can be directly related to an emotional response in the body that causes an emotional reaction that has a physical manifestation such as a curvature of the spine called scoliosis, or to another physical problem tied to a past incident or trauma that occurred in the dark or at night. However, if the therapist never uses the fact that the event occurred at night when making physical adjustments on a person with the eyes open in the light, the real problem never gets addressed. The movements of the eyes, closed or open, in the light or in the dark, help the body to understand the adjustment.

Part of Dr. Ferreri's technique involves eye movements to the left, to the right, and up and down. This technique is not usually done by other licensed chiropractors, but his work in helping people to learn with less effort is supported by scientific research on multi-path learning. Jensen (1994), who compiled the work of Hart, Caine and Caine, Botella and Eriksen, as well as Nobel Prize-winning scientist and co-discoverer of DNA's double-helix formation Francis Crick, said that the functions of the brain are massively parallel. What stimuli come in through the eyes to the brain travel a million axons all working together. The tasks for therapists have been to determine what is needed for a specific client because the interconnections in the brain are not the exact same ones for all others.

The Learning Brain

The Learning Brain (Jensen 1994) is an important resource book for those "in-the-trenches." Jensen compiles all the astonishing discoveries made weekly in the fields of biology, physics, cognitive science, psychopharmacology, neurology, and genetics that give us insight about how you and I might learn. In that book, the learning brain is seen as being impacted by sixteen major factors. The first chapter, for example, focuses on physiology and biology. Each of the sixteen chapters has several topics that are explained in terms of the research, an example, the implications for learning and teaching, and action steps.

The only person who is educated is the one who has learned how to learn . . . and change. Carl Rogers

Obviously, it isn't feasible to summarize Jensen's entire book. Yet let's look more closely at his discussion on nutrition. From the early work of the 1970s done on nutrition, we know that brain size and weight vary in humans. It has been long established that babies with low birth weight will also have a smaller brain and fewer brain cells. Low-birth-weight babies, when they do grow and attend school, find that they make more errors in their school work and have less ability to problem solve. Jensen takes us a step farther.

Besides oxygen, the brain also needs amino acids to help the neurotransmitters enable the brain to perform calculations, increase attention span, and expand conscious awareness. But foods like sugar can disturb the thinking process by stressing the already weak wiring in the brain. Children with food allergies would have additional problems in learning and thus behaving. Although some chemical dynamics may be very individual, what one chooses to eat, drink, ingest through the air or any other way effects the operations of the brain. Some things remain a constant, such as the brain's need for nourishment. Jensen (1994, 158), citing Jenkins et al. in the *New England Journal of Medicine*, recommended a diet of "nibbling versus gorging" to increase metabolic functioning throughout the day. The group of students on a diet of seventeen small snacks per day had better cognitive functioning, fewer discipline problems, and an enhanced sense of well-being. Yet to do that students would need to be permitted to have access to nutritious snacks and to eat them at breaks or during long exams. It is important to know what some of the implications are from this brain research for parents, students, teachers, and those working with youth.

In short, brain development and learning are more complex than previously thought, and specialists in other alternative medicines are needed to help with all those who play a part in the learning process for children. The brain is an electrical system, but not one like the simple early telephone systems. The visual centers have over thirty interconnected brain centers, each with its own map. "The electrical and chemical dynamics of the brain resemble the sound, light and patterns of a jungle" (Jensen 1994, 8). Some children, like Billy who began our chapter, need more attention, with their parents gaining greater access to professionals who can diagnose the stressors affecting such children more quickly and easily.

Implications for Models of Education and Learning

Cognitive development is dependent on physical maturation, innate intelligence, and environmental or educational stimulation. Taken together, these variables have important implications for models of education. This is true for all children and youth and especially for treatment of delinquents in long-term juvenile institutions, for they have historically lower levels of education than comparable youths in the general population.

In more recent years, greater numbers of incarcerated youths need special educational services as do many of America's students. The National Commission on Excellence in Education confirmed that mediocrity in American education has become the norm, and that many of our children are educationally handicapped regardless of race or class (U.S. Department of Education 1983).

In terms of primary and secondary crime prevention, different approaches in education are necessary to allow students to learn in their dominant styles of learning while stimulating their weaker areas to enhance learning. Some of the implications of whole brain learning, multipath learning, and variances in brain size, weight, and wiring are that different approaches are needed to allow learning in the schools, in the home, and in detention centers and correctional centers for youth. Let's use this information with left-brain and right-brain dominant individuals.

Left- and Right-Brain Dominance

According to the Dennison approach, left-brain dominants process information either by (1) logic or (2) analysis. Logical individuals need and want systematic structure with a set outcome. Having instructions to follow gives them their greatest means of comprehension. Analytical individuals love to debate, and as children they take toys apart just to see how they work. These individuals will get into a discussion and convince you of one side. Once you are on that side, they switch to the other side of the issue. They don't require a set outcome. They seem to comprehend information by understanding the how and the why behind things. By debating or picking an argument, they are learning and gaining greater comprehension and a broader understanding.

Right-brain dominant individuals process information in other ways, predominantly operating from (1) intuition or (2) emotion. Intuitive individuals just have a sense of knowing. They aren't good at telling you how they know or how they did it. They know the end result or outcome, but they usually need help in establishing a step-by-step procedure to accomplish a project. As visionaries, their learning styles are uniquely their own and were once more highly valued in a rural society. Much of today's society is left-brain, linear, and logical in its presentation.

The emotional individuals process information most easily through their feelings. They comprehend best those things to which they can attach emotionality. They learn best in a classroom when the teacher puts more feeling into the lesson or tells stories evoking emotions. Thus they easily comprehend subjects that allow them to express emotions, such as music, art, literature, and psychology.

Primary Means of Accessing Data

In addition to being dominant in one of the above four modalities, an individual will have one or more of the following primary means of accessing, comprehending, and communicating data: (1) auditory, (2) verbal, (3) visual, and (4) kinesthetic.

The auditory person is one who can hear and mentally connect. They don't have to study; they just listen. It is the weakest modality for the majority of persons, even though it is the predominant style taught in school systems.

Verbal persons talk to hear themselves. In hearing, they comprehend what they are saying. These individuals real aloud or mouth their words in a manner that allows the connection in the brain of the circuits that then permit them to mentally comprehend. These students add to any discussion not because they may have new information to share. They do it with the hope that by expressing themselves, they will finally get it. It is the act of talking, not what they are talking about, that helps the individual to clarify his or her thoughts. For this type of individual, a teacher should wait for them to reach the bottom line. Anything between the beginning and end usually doesn't make much sense.

Visual learners learn by seeing. All of us receive information to our brains through our eyes. Our eyes can register 36,000 visual messages per hour with nearly 90 percent of the information coming through the eyes, where the retina accounts for 40 percent of all nerve fibers connected to the brain (Jensen 1995, 310). The brain can quickly respond to color, shape, and size. That is why some modern parking decks have a specific floor labeled as a number, with a flower design, and in a different color. Yet if a visual person had to assemble a child's bicycle, he or she would be get frustrated if you read the instructions to him or her. People who learn best through visual processes would rather see a picture to make something or see a map about how to get somewhere. Taking written notes in a classroom allows the visually dominant person to "see" what is being said.

People who have a kinesthetic dominance process, comprehend and communicate through movement or while moving. They are action and motion, for as they do the motion, the brain functions more effectively. If they are forced to sit and be physically inactive, they will probably create action in their minds such as daydreams. They learn through "hands-on-doing." They may appear to be impatient. However, physical activity allows them to access a part of their brain where they more easily process data and information.

Helping people understand their specific dominance, preferences, and "wiring" means that they are more accepting of their way of learning. They are better able to understand why some people do something more easily than they. As one appreciates one's own differences, it becomes easier to understand why one likes to do certain things. Critical judgments disappear, and people are more patient with themselves and others.

When people learn differently than what is the state-sanctioned way of learning, they often experience feelings of low self-esteem and anger. As they watch others their frustration in trying to copy the others' way of learning only adds to their feeling of being the "odd man out." In the author's experience at law school, very few professors used the blackboards or any other multiple teaching strategies. Thus in an occupation that demands creativity, the way the students are being taught actually works against that purpose. In the end, our entire society then suffers.

Besides adverse affects for our society, certain groups within the society have special difficulties. As explained in Chapter 4, "Process for Delinquent (Criminal) Youth," delinquents who have reading or learning challenges vary in degrees and categories. Some of these youth have a high IQ and are often very sensitive. They notice changes and feel deeply. So any criticism by their teachers, classmates, parent(s), and siblings causes deep wounds that need to be healed. Only when they work with a therapist who understands and identifies their strengths do they begin to value their own differences and the society's need for those differences. Once one can understand one's strengths in learning, one can then use one's most dominant way of learning to enhance and build up a strength in something that was weak. This is the importance of the work of Gardner and others who espouse multiple intelligences.

MULTIPLE INTELLIGENCES

The Eliot-Person Preschool on the campus of Tufts University in Massachusetts uses a curriculum that intentionally cultivates a variety of kinds of intelligences. Project Spectrum, the school's curriculum, recognized the work of Harvard Graduate Professor of Education, Howard Gardner. Gardner defined intelligence as the ability to (1) use a skill, (2) fashion an artifact, or (3) solve a problem in a way that is valued by the particular culture of that individual. In his research of over 200 "smart" ways of doing things and thinking, he grouped them into the following seven intelligences:

1. mathematical-logical: ability to solve problems, do math, proving, cause-effect, prediction, reasoning, analysis.

2. spatial: movement, sense of body and distance, drawings, dance, sports, parallel parking, use a map to find one's place, making graphs, mindmaps or memory maps.

3. bodily-kinesthetic: acting, sports, role-playing, exercise, games.

4. musical-rhythmic: rhymes, music, clapping, composing, raps, humming.

5. verbal-linguistic: stories, speech, debate, dialogs, language, reading.

6. interpersonal: social skills, empathy, building with relationships, partners, teams, win-win cooperation.

7. intrapersonal: introspection, ponders or reflects before speaking, journal writing, visualization, self-discovery. (Gardner 1985; Jensen 1994; and Lazear 1995)

Many intelligent persons have been labeled as "slow" because the teacher did not tap into all these intelligences. In fact, most people who have a dominant style of learning make it a dominant style of teaching. Assessments in the classroom may be so narrow that the student is never allowed to demonstrate what she or he has learned. A learner who is low in interpersonal or verbal-linguistic skills may be poor at explaining what he knows. If he is strong on spatial, he may be able to make a graphic of what he knows. Some students are too right-brained to answer multiple choice questions correctly. When given an essay or a paper to write, they will do very well, but with multiple choice questions they can argue how several of the answers might be right.

Lazear (1994) helped teachers, students, and parents assess their strengths and actively increase their capacity in the other intelligences through his book and workbook called *Seven Pathways of Learning*. This broader approach permits a richer picture of a child's ability and potential for success. It permits a person to assess his or her strengths and then develop ways of increasing skills in the other weaker areas.

According to Gardner, education should contribute to a child's development to help him or her towards a field where these talents are best suited. Since there are many ways to succeed and many different abilities, we should promote this multi-dimensional approach instead of an "IQ way of thinking" that people are either smart or not, are born that way, and that there is nothing you can do about it. Gardner's book refuted the IQ view that there was one monolithic kind of intelligence that was crucial for life success. The intelligences are more than seven, for there is no magic number to the multiplicity of human talents. Knowledge of a child's strengths permits parents and teachers to encourage a passion to develop beyond proficiency and on to mastery (Goleman 1995).

Jensen (1995) explained how a school's faculty can motivate good, curious people when school is more like real life and when a school provides an environment responsive to student goals. At present, some schools create a negative social comparison so that students who aren't as "smart" as others are identified, classified, grouped, labeled, evaluated, compared, and assessed as being "at-risk" learners. In those schools, the emphasis is upon avoiding failure and hassles rather than on learning. When those "at-risk" students move to a more responsive environment, their behaviors change. But the changes would need to occur with the teachers and a bottom-up administrative "approach wherein students experience that their beliefs, goals, and values are consistently integrated into school design" (Jensen 1995, 279).

Changes for students would also mean changes for teachers and administration. Yet if school reform and restructuring are not based on recent brain research, a school with punitive systems and tactics can be more like a prison than a place of learning. By having curriculum mandates, students have less choice and less chance for "buying" into the program. High stakes testing means that teachers teach for the test and students' brains become minimized instead of expanded.

On the other hand, a school with the support of the community could create an exciting and vibrant environment. Teachers would then have the support to infuse learning with emotion, energy, and enthusiasm. The peer group would be used for approval and responsibility so that there would be the maintenance of a learning environment that used the differences of learning for everyone's advantage. By getting people in the community to support positive changes and focus on learning, students and others can be hooked into being learners for a lifetime. Lifetime learning is exciting and rewarding, and research suggests that as you use your brain, you prolong your life.

Ayn Rand, in her novel *Atlas Shrugged*, had one of her characters say it this way:

I came here to bring up my sons as human beings. I would not surrender them to the educational system devised to stunt a child's brain, to convince him that reason is impotent, that existence is an irrational chaos with which he's unable to deal, and thus reduce him to a state of chronic terror. (724)

EDUCATIONAL TECHNIQUES: MINDMAPPING AND ACCELERATED LEARNING

The use of graphic organizers like mindmapping, webbing, or mindscapes has been found to help learners understand and recall information better primarily because the student is permitted to develop the map in terms of their own dominance (Jensen 1994). Mindmapping is a color-coded (right-brain activity) whole brain approach to outlining and note-taking.

Tony Buzan, the editor of the *International Mensa Journal*, was challenged in the 1960s to develop techniques that could enhance intelligence. He developed mindmapping with the following elements:

1. Central focus of an image or graphic representation of the problem or information being mapped is placed in the center of the page.

2. Ideas are allowed to flow freely without judgment.

3. One key word is printed per line.

4. Key word ideas are connected to the central focus with lines.

5. Color is used to highlight and emphasize ideas.

6. Images and symbols are used to highlight ideas and stimulate the mind to make other connections. (Wycoff 1991, 43)

Each mindmap is unique. It is a product of the person who produces it. It is not an end product, like an outline that can be sold to someone else.

Rather it is a process wherein doing it allows you to make new connections in your thinking and in your organizing in your brain. The process of drawing helps you make associations and create new pathways of thinking. The use of symbols instead of words helps you to view the mindmap as if it is in a code that has special meaning with immediate recall.

A mindmap provides four primary tools for improving memory recall and learning: (1) repetition, (2) association/connection, (3) intensity, and (4) involvement. Information that involves more than one of our senses will be remembered more quickly. It creates images in your brain while you organize the material as you receive it, so that you make associations and connections with material from other sources. Besides increasing memory and organization skills, it promotes creativity.

In addition, a mindmap can be used with many subjects including math. Victor Shatalov, considered to be one of the most successful mathematics teachers in the world, has been using mindmapping for his university-level math classes for years. In his lectures in the former Soviet Union, he would tell other teachers, a thousand at a time, how he got his students to excel, even those who had previously failed. As he explained the mindmapping technique, he pointed to how the students were able to perform complex and creative problems. The originality of the students told him that they had a true depth of knowledge of the mathematics involved (Soloveichik 1979).

Accelerated learning has many different names, commercial uses, and a journal, *The Journal of the Society for Accelerative Learning and Teaching.* Evelyn Woods' Reading Dynamics classes were probably a forerunner to the idea that one can see and read more quickly than by saying each word as one reads. More recently, Paul Scheele of Learning Strategies of Minnesota has developed what is called "Photoreading." It is based on the state of consciousness known as "flow." The flow state is a timeless, pleasure-producing experience wherein you lose yourself in the doing. Before relaxing into a flow state, the reader asks specific questions that she or he wants to learn from a particular book. By doing a simple relaxation technique to reach the flow state, the reader goes through the book turning the pages at a specific rhythm and movement so as to imprint the brain. Like taking a snapshot of each page, the reader moves through the material with ease and soon finds the answers to the desired questions. Accelerated learning makes reading easier and more fun with greater recall by using the mindmap technique.

An early pioneer in accelerated learning was Bulgarian Dr. Georgi Lozanov who taught Russians how to speak foreign languages better than anyone else. He did it by speaking theatrically with musical interplay. The music of the Classical (circa 1750–1825) and Romantic (circa 1820–1900) periods was used to introduce new information while the music of the Baroque (circa 1600–1750) period was better for a passive review at the end of a session. He developed a way of delivering information in rhythm with music that activated long-term memory and engaged the brain's most receptive states. When the music was slower or pausing, the material was delivered with enthusiasm and drama. In this manner, a teacher can deliver 60 percent of the content in 5 percent of the time (Jensen 1995, 218).

The theory is that specific frequencies of the instruments playing music from composers such as Mozart, Beethoven, Hayden, Handel, and Bach resonate with the brain frequencies or wavelengths to make learning easier. By resonating with the four-four beat, one is empowered, more aware, and alert. In addition, one's heart rate is synchronized with the beat of the music. Music tapes produced by Ostrander and Schroeder using that classical music are called "Super-Memory" and are used to enhance memory and creativity.

Jensen (1995, 212) provided the following supportive research for the use of learning with classical music:

The Soviet discovery called Kirlian photography uses an electronic imaging process instead of light to process film after exposure to humans and plants. Biophysicists discovered that all living organisms have a brilliantly colored, light-filled energy pattern that emanates from and surrounds them. What's more, this pattern can be easily photographed! Before and after pictures were taken with subjects listening to baroque music (Bach's Brandenburg Concertos). The differences are startling. The "after" photos of the biofield, done using Kirlian photography, show a more aligned, organized, fluted and harmonized pattern of energy emanating from the listener. Music can indeed affect the body.

Music is also considered a universal language. Clynes studied forty Central Australian Aborigines of the Warlbiri Tribe to document their ability to recognize musical sounds of joy, love, reverence, grief, anger, sex, and hate. "Their scores were equal to university students at the University of New South Wales, MIT, and the University of California at Berkeley" (Jensen 1995, 216).

EMOTIONS

The old model was that the mind was completely separate from the emotions and the body. Now we understand that the body, mind, and emotions are really interrelated, and that what happens in one area has impact in the others (Jensen 1994, 37). If learning is pleasurable, we want more. If it is boring or painful, we want less. Secondly, when we are feeling positive, we are better able to sort out our experiences and recall them with greater clarity. Jensen suggested that teachers and trainers pay more attention to the emotional state of the learner. Since "emotions require contexts for expression or they will disable a learner within minutes," Jensen suggested how to construct safe ways to express emotions and permit learners to praise themselves and each other about their successes. This leads to self-confidence and motivation to learn more.

Body, Mind, and Emotions Interrelated

As explained in the first part of this chapter in the discussion of physical and cognitive development, how the brain decides if something is important or not is a physiological response, with physical and emotional side effects. According to Dr. Martin L. Rossman (1980, 21) in *Healing Yourself*, studies in England and the United States have found that from 50 percent to 75 percent of all problems presented at a primary care clinic "are emotional, social, or familial in origin, though they are being expressed by pain or illness."

In addition to emotions being the cause and core of many illnesses, we also know how emotions can sometimes cause even the most rational person to act irrationally at times. Once the dust settles after an argument, we are left wondering how it could have happened. What was the reason? Why all the emotions?

To understand the emotions, we need to realize that the hippocampus, amygdala, and cerebral cortex are all involved because they acquire, store, and recall human memories. Upon seeing something, the visual signal goes from the retina in the eye to the thalamus, where it is translated into the language of the brain. The hippocampus remembers the dry facts. But if there is an emotion like fear, hate, love, or another feeling involved, the amygdala, which stores these emotional memories, sends a signal to activate the emotional centers. For survival, a smaller portion of the original signal can move through the thalamus to the amygdala to have a quicker transmission but with less precision. It is an alarm that triggers secretion of the body's fight-or-flight hormones that then send other biochemical messages to help the body move quickly and the heart beat faster. All of this drives the rest of the brain into a state of an emotional emergency without the use of the rational mind.

Short-term memory occurs when a neuron's electrical signal remains charged for days and even weeks. But long-term memory has to convert electrical traces into verifiable physical-chemical traces. Like making a tape of one's voice, the brain makes a memory tape that is preserved within the neuronal membrane by the alternation of potassium channels. Protein activates the memory by permitting sensory cells to convert stimuli from the external world into electrical signals within the brain. Without adequate protein, the synapses as well as the body's muscles are less able to perform learned behavior.

The emotional content of material to be learned influences the future memory because past emotional experiences are recorded and stored in the brain. Traumatic events from childhood usually have intense feelings that can be relived and reexperienced in the present if triggered appropriately. Called "flashbacks," these past traumatic "re-living" experiences in the present are one of the major symptoms of Post-Traumatic Stress Disorder (PTSD).

If the amygdala is cut from the brain, one loses the ability to gauge the emotional significance of events. One young man had the operation to control severe seizures, but the result was a complete disinterest in people and the loss of any feeling about feelings.

Dr. Joseph LeDoux at the Center for Neural Science at New York University was the first to map the brain at work and, as a result, shift the limbic system from being the center of the emotional brain to the rightful center—the amygdala. This is why the emotional brain, as seen in Billy's case, took control over what he did before the thinking brain, the neocortex, had a chance to make a decision. Fear, for example, can cause automatic reactions because they are etched in our nervous systems as part of the fight-or-flight and survival-versus-death responses. Goleman (1995) called it emotional intelligence.

Emotional Intelligence

Emotional intelligence is a new concept. Intelligence has been dominated by IQ tests and research on hundreds of thousands of people. This was supported by academic psychology that was dominated by behaviorists such as B. F. Skinner. For scientific accuracy, behavior was to be studied from the outside. The inner life, including emotions, could not be researched. Yet we know that grades, IQ, or SAT scores, despite their use and popular justifications, do not always predict who will succeed in life. "The link between test scores and those achievements is dwarfed by the totality of other characteristics that he brings to life" (Goleman 1995, 36).

With modern technological advancements, the psychological science turned to how the brain registers and stores information. Gardner's elaboration of intelligences, as discussed earlier, was still based on a cognitive-science model of the mind. His focus was on knowing about feelings, not on the role of feeling as intelligence. Gardner did appreciate the fact that many people with IQs of 160 may work for people with much lower IQs if they have poor intrapersonal intelligence. He saw intrapersonal intelligence as the ability to know one's feelings well enough to make good choices about who to marry and what job to take. He did support the need to train children to have higher intelligence in their emotions, even though he recognized that his work has more to do with an awareness of one's mental processes, or metacognition (Goleman 1995, 45).

According to Dr. LeDoux, the leading authority on the amygdala, the emotions that young children experience are stored as emotional memories or "wordless blueprints" that are triggered later in life. During the early period of the growth of the brain, in utero the child's amygdala matures very quickly and is closer to being fully formed at birth. Yet the hippocampus and the neocortex that are used for rational thinking have yet to be fully developed. At that point, there may not be any matching set of articulated thoughts. Instead, emotion can be an emotional outburst that takes over, based on neural bits and pieces of sensory information that have not been fully sorted out and integrated into a more rational understanding. As in the old game show called *Name That Tune*, in which a person uses a snap judgment to guess a song based on only a few notes of the song, "a whole perception is grasped on the basis of the first few tentative parts. If the amygdala senses a sensory pattern of import emerging, it jumps to a conclusion, triggering its reactions before there is full confirming evidence—or any confirmation at all" (Goleman 1995, 27).

An example of this automatic reaction that has been implanted in our nervous systems may be found in the tragedy that occurred in the Crabtree family. Matilda Crabtree was only 14 when she played a practical joke on her father that brought her death. All she did was jump out of a closet and yell "Boo" when her parents came home at 1:00 in the morning after visiting friends. But her father and mother had thought she was staying with friends. When they came home and heard noises while entering their house, her father reached for his .357 Magnum and went into her bedroom to investigate. When she jumped from the closet, her father shot her in the neck. Twelve hours later she died (Goleman 1995, 4–5).

Goleman (1995, 31) argued that children can have high IQ scores but still be at risk for academic failure, alcoholism, and criminality, because "their control over their emotional life is impaired." Emotional distress can create deficits in a child's intellectual abilities. Emotions like anxiety and anger sabotage the ability of the prefrontal lobe of the brain to maintain a working memory. Being emotionally upset cripples the capacity to learn.

Goleman (1995) cited a study done on primary school boys who had above-average IQ scores but were doing poorly in school. The neuropsychological tests showed impaired frontal cortex functioning. They were impulsive and anxious, and those emotions were expressed in their disruptive behavior.

In short, IQ tests tap the cortical areas and not the emotional brain that controls rage and compassion alike. The emotional circuits are created and reinforced, and they become knee-jerk reactions because of our experiences throughout childhood.

Goleman (1995) stated that psychologists Sternberg and Salovey have taken a wider view of intelligence. Salovey agreed with Gardner that old concepts of IQ are based on the very narrow activities of math and linguistic skills. Doing well on IQ tests or doing well on LSAT tests for law school only predict one's ability to do well in a classroom or on a bar examination to practice law, but they are less and less predictive of one's ability to perform activities that diverge from academe, such as the actual practice of law. Salovey listed the following five main domains as being important:

1. Knowing one's emotions, as in self-awareness, so that one recognizes a feeling as it happens. Conscious emotions, unlike unconscious ones, become strong enough to break into the awareness to register in the frontal cortex. Once an emotion registers, it can be evaluated, and one can decide whether one wants to continue in the same mood.

2. Managing emotions so as to shake off anxiety, gloom, or irritability and thus keep the channels of the brain open for more learning. This means holding back powerful negative emotions so as not to interfere with concentration on whatever task is at hand. Ventilating anger doesn't cool a person down because it pumps up the emotional brain's arousal and leaves a person feeling angrier. It is better to cool down and then, in a more constructive manner, talk with the person to settle a dispute. In social work terms, people "mirror" to us that which they dislike in themselves but are unwilling to acknowledge. Cognitive therapy helps people to identify their thoughts, challenge their validity, and make more positive choices. Relaxation techniques work well with anxiety but not depression. Depression, a low-arousal state, needs high arousal with such activities as aerobics.

3. Motivating one self, delaying gratification, and stifling impulsiveness by getting into the "flow" state to produce outstanding performances of all kinds.

4. Recognizing emotions in others, especially the ability to use empathy to build relationships with others and to be successful in such callings as the caring professions, teaching, sales, and management.

5. Handling relationships that undergird leadership and managing emotions in others. (Goleman 1995, 46–47)

Test your emotional intelligence. How long can you wait for something you want? Pretend you are a 4-year-old. As part of an experiment you are

Don't suppress anger. But don't act on it.
Chogyam Trungpa

given the choice to wait until the teacher comes back from running an errand and get two marshmallows for a treat, or eat one now and then get the other one when the teacher returns. What do you choose?

Psychologist Walter Mischel developed this "marshmallow test" during the 1960s at a preschool on the Stanford University campus. The youth were tracked adolescents to identify the dramatic behavioral differences between the grab-the-marshmallow preschoolers and their gratification-delaying peers. Some twelve to fourteen years later, those who had resisted the temptation at age 4 were more socially competent, less apt to regress under stress, embraced challenges and pursued them instead of giving up even in the face of difficulties. Even a decade later, they maintained their ability to delay gratification to achieve their goals. On the other hand, those who grabbed for the marshmallows were easily upset by frustrations. As adolescents, they thought of themselves as "bad" or unworthy and were prone to be jealous and to overreact to irritations by starting fights. Poor impulse control in childhood is a more powerful predictor of delinquency than IQ. IQ is a good predictor of SAT scores once a child learns to read. Some think that IQ cannot be changed. But "there is ample evidence that emotional skills such as impulse control and accurately reading a social situation can be learned" (Goleman 1995, 93).

If you did take the marshmallow like a third of the research population, is all doomed? Is there no hope? Well, it depends.

C. R. Snyder of the University of Kansas posed a hypothetical situation to test for students' ability to have hope. He gave the students the following proposition: you had your goal set on getting a B in a class when your first exam score is returned as a D. It is worth 30 percent of your final grade. What do you do after learning about the D? The responses showed that some had the ability to motivate themselves, feel resourceful enough to find other ways to reach their objectives, and break the huge task into smaller, manageable pieces (Goleman 1995, 97–98).

Hope is more than being optimistic. It is the belief that you have both the will and the way to accomplish your goals. Optimism is an attitude that helps buffer a person against falling into apathy, hopelessness, or despair in the face of tough-going circumstances or events. Hope, along with its near cousin optimism, pays dividends in life if it is realistic. Synder found that given the same range of intellectual abilities, the emotional attitude of hope made the critical difference. It was a better predictor of students' first-semester grades than were the scores on the SAT, "a test supposedly able to predict how students will fare in college (and highly correlated with IQ) (Goleman 1995, 98).

Hope and optimism, like helplessness and despair, are learned. Why are some children missing hope? Why do some children show concern when another of their playmates at the day-care center cries? Why do some of the other children react with expressions of fear, anger, or a physical attack?

Children, even very little ones in day-care centers, treat others as they are learning to be treated by their families and caretakers. Children who are callous with other children are only doing what their parents, who have been critical and harsh in their punishments to them, have been doing. It stands in sharp contrast to the empathy displayed by children of the same age whose parents nurture, encouraging their toddlers to show concern for others and to see how meanness makes other children feel. Yet if the child experiences a daily diet of physical beatings or being beaten at the whim of a parent's mood, those are the emotional lessons that will dominate. Children who are or were disciplined capriciously, even as adults today, often see that threats are everywhere and may strike at any time just like their parents did. It is sad for the child and our society, because that kind of abuse "warps a child's natural bent toward empathy" (Goleman 1995, 225).

How does one get such children who have become adults to become more empathetic? According to Goleman (1995) empathy builds on self-awareness and can be taught to most people. The exception to this general rule is what Goleman (1995, 56–57) calls Alexithmics, who have no awareness of what they are feeling, nor any awareness of what anyone else might be feeling in a situation. It as if they are emotionally tone-deaf. They do not have the ability to read body language or nonverbal cues. They lack sensitivity, whereas others can be taught empathy from early childhood experiences or other training classes as adults. For example, children can be taught through discipline with words like "Look how sad you've made her feel" instead of "You are such a bad child." When people give names to the emotions and point out the impact, the child walks away with a greater repertoire of empathic responses. Attunement is shaped between the child and the caretaker through their psychological interaction and that is why the psychological parent is so critical to a child's development and placement in or out of a home.

If children are taught to avoid expressing feelings ("Boys don't cry," or "You shouldn't feel that way"), the child loses coping skills for such relationships as adult intimacy. Examples of these types of children are those who have suffered emotional neglect in their homes, have been moved from foster home to foster home, or have been reared in orphanages. Adults who are classified as having a mental illness called "borderline personality disorder" usually have a preoccupation with the feelings of others. They learned at an early age to be vigilant (watchful) to cues that signaled a parent's upset that would lead to another beating or some other kind of threat. When the FBI developed their psychological profile technique by interviewing serial murders, one of the characteristics they discovered in the earlier lives of these killers was this lack of emotional attunement. This is why FBI Agent Douglas (1995) doesn't argue that serial murders are mentally ill even though their behavior is usually very bizarre, violent, and cruel to the victims.

This lack of emotional attunement or empathy is also part of other offenders in the juvenile and criminal justice system. In doing some research on the most vicious wife batterers, this lack of empathy was discovered somewhat by accident. Normally, when a person needs to be empathic, a person needs to become calm and be receptive to the subtle signals of feelings from another. In monitoring the physiological responses of husbands, it was found that as their anger mounted, their heart rate dropped. Instead of going higher, as in ordinary cases of increasing rage, these men became physiologically calmer. Thus their violence was calculated. Their acts of violent abuse were a method of controlling their wives by instilling fear. They also used calculated violent abuse with others, such as in their work with other friends and children. For them, any reason was good enough for them to strike out at someone. Once they started, nothing seemed to restrain their violence (Goleman 1995, 124).

Perhaps such wife abusers are doing in adulthood what may have occurred to them as children. When an adult may have beaten the child until the adult was exhausted from doing the beating or through with feeling angry, it leaves the child's soul scarred.

PSYCHOLOGICAL THERAPIES

In some cases where there has been emotional impairment, people don't develop emotional intelligence and the resulting empathy until they have had many years of personal and/or group therapy. Insight therapy is the name given to many therapies that permit a person to understand why they behave the way they are behaving. In this section, some of the traditional insight therapies such as cognitive therapy and transactional analysis and a newer approach that uses right-left brain integration to address emotions based upon belief systems will be discussed.

Traditional Therapies

The greatest gift we have is the ability to choose. Good habits are the keys to success. Bad choices lead to failure. Coach Herman Boone, Disney film *Remember the Titans*, 2000

Cognitive therapies like Ellis' (1975) Rational Emotional Therapy (RET) are based on an individual's thoughts behind the emotions. In RET, the client is shown how an assumption about oneself or others is really impacting an interaction. After an event or interaction, a person may say: "I was devastated. It was awful." The therapist knows that events are only events. It is the person who gives it meaning through his or her own thinking. The therapist then slows the process down from the triggering event to the final feeling of being angry to help the client see how thoughts of being an innocent victim or pride such as righteous indignation fueled the flames.

In this model, people are taught to monitor their own thinking. By noticing their own thinking and taking responsibility for those thoughts that run throughout the mind, they are better able to detoxify their self-talk statements. In order to accomplish this with others, it may mean that there needs to be more structure to conversations that have controversy. It may mean having "time-outs." It may mean using communication skills such as parroting and paraphrasing to make sure that one understands the other's position.

For some individuals, nondefensive listening and speaking skills don't really get to the heart of toxic emotions. Eric Berne (1961), the originator of transactional analysis (TA), used the concepts of parent-, adult-, and child-ego states. According to Berne, the ego states are present behaviors that are linked to past experiences and feelings. For example, the parent-ego state contains all the behavior, feelings, and attitudes we learned and are now modeling directly after emotionally significant persons who served as our biological and psychological parents. The adult-ego state contains behavior dealing with the facts of current reality by asking such questions as: How? Why? When?

In Berne's model, the child-ego state contains all the behavior and feelings we had as very small children. Here was the "not okay" child, the wounded child that was hurt in childhood, as well as the curious, playful child. One of the key ideas of TA was this question: When a stressful event knocks on your door, which ego state answers first?

If your adult-ego state answers the door of life with a rational brain asking questions, then one will probably have greater success than answering with an emotional child-ego state. Therapy is for those who have difficulties in their lives or are not as successful as they want to be.

Newer Therapy

A newer technique that incorporates the Doman and Dennison's right- and left-brain learning styles, repatterning of the brain for whole brain learning, and the identification of stress is called the Results System. The effectiveness of these newer techniques was conducted on a group of drug-abusing women offenders in a therapeutic unit of the Virginia Department of Corrections. Stephanie Johnston, a local therapist, volunteered her time and for six months gave sessions for a random sample of 10 inmates as individuals (Group A) and for 10 inmates as a group (Group B). Then they were compared to the women who received only the traditional approaches of psychotherapy as done by the social workers (Group C). In addition, pre/post-test questionnaires of 130 items each were administered, testing for self-esteem, life satisfaction, alcohol and drug use, passive dependency, dysfunctional attitude, and spousal abuse. To measure additional changes, monthly client progress reports, which were developed by the social workers managing the unit, were used to show changes on 10 dimensions: anxiety, avoidance, denial, in touch with feelings, anger, openness, self-initiative, setting boundaries, responsibility, and peace/contentment. The contrast "t" test showed statistical significant changes for anxiety, peace/contentment, and self-esteem (Clement 1997).

Because the sample sizes were so small, it takes real changes in order to get statistically significant numbers. Thus, one knows that there were real changes but why? One of the reasons the women changed so quickly was that the particular therapy was geared to their unique learning styles. Secondly, the Result System uses a form of biofeedback to break through the denial to identify a specific time or place wherein a person walked away from a situation telling him- or herself something like "I am not good enough." The goal is to identify a belief and replace it with more helpful and positive beliefs like "I am good enough" so as to attract situations in which the new belief can prove its truthfulness (Clement 1998b). Let's see how it worked in one case study—Inmate #108.

CASE STUDY

Inmate #108 was a 33-year-old African-American woman who tested to be left-brain dominant. She had a very difficult time holding onto a right attitude about life. She earned her label as a woman "with bad attitude." Acting like she was "big and bad," her attitude was not very helpful with the arresting officer or the sentencing judge. Her attitude was established at age 17 when she was living with her boyfriend. In her mind, it was a good year even though she was pregnant and didn't want to be. Her father died, but she didn't feel very close to him. Her grandmother also died. She was the one she really felt close to. In her grandmother's passing, she deadened her feelings as well.

In her family, she learned that people don't have feelings. If a person has a feeling, then the person is going to act on it, and it usually was violent. In her effort to get the family together after the grandmother's death, she decided to have a "welcome home" party for her brother who had just been released from prison. Her mother protested because she knew that they all had a drinking problem. When the family members drank, they acted out their anger. Bringing up a subject that someone else didn't like meant "combat" for the hearer—as if the person had said, "I'm looking for a fight." At this party, another brother got into a fight with the mother's live-in boyfriend. During the fight, the boyfriend was killed.

The mother blamed the daughter because she was the one who had the party. Both the mother and daughter were required to go to court to testify. Their relationship was strained even further. In the 17-year-old's mind, she was "people pleasing"—trying to get the family to be connected to each other because she was really lacking emotional support. She had no one to turn to in an estranged family and she was pregnant, selling drugs for her boyfriend.

From that year forward, she created a belief system and put it into an emotional "concrete" that the rest of her life would be forever like that year. Her beliefs were that separations were inherent to relationships, and that resolutions of conflicts with anger are expressed with physical violence.

At age 28, acting on those beliefs gained at 17, she killed another brother when she found him sexually abusing her daughter. This discovery triggered more than the emotions that any parent would feel, including a delayed reaction to being sexually abused as a child. The whole family dynamics were layered with unresolved guilt. In addition, Inmate #108 had a very heavy sense of responsibility. She was angry with herself, yet she projected it onto others and thus alienated herself from others. By rejecting the positive support of others, she was punishing herself.

In her first emotional therapy session using a biofeedback method of identifying stress, the counselor was able to identify her learning styles and this "so-called good year" of age 17. In a guided visualization exercise, this inmate was helped to see herself as God would see her. In doing that she could see and feel that God had forgiven her and that He wanted her to forgive herself. Some of the changes that ensued included greater trust in herself and then in others. Since trust is usually developed at a very early age (about age 2), one can only imagine that in this woman's family, no one had any trust for self or others.

This first therapy session was unusually intense and lengthy for several reasons. First, her family, for the first time since she had been incarcerated, was coming to visit. They had forgiven her, and they wanted her to know they loved her. Secondly, she had been in a mental hospital for two years when she was released into this prison special unit called a therapeutic community (TC). Yet the social workers in the unit knew that she was like a powder keg that needed immediate attention or she might explode, hurting herself or someone else. At the end of this session, she was more relaxed and began to gain a sense of peace. Later sessions would go more deeply into her beliefs such as:

☐ feeling responsible for the actions of others

☐ feeling guilty over the inability to change situations

☐ a pattern of acting out anger in a self-destructive manner

☐ a pattern of shutting down her emotions

☐ a pattern of withdrawing from others

☐ a pattern of abusive relationships

☐ heavy alcohol use

☐ a pattern of being out of control

☐ her inability to take care of herself and her children

☐ her perception that she had to fight to survive

☐ using drugs and alcohol to anesthetize her emotions

☐ denying her feelings and not allowing herself to express her feelings to others

Through an emotional replacement technique in the Results System that matched her learning style, she was able to feel strong in the belief that "others take responsibility for their own well being" and "I take responsibility for my own well being." She regained her belief that "I trust there is a power greater than myself at work in my life," and "I allow others to take responsibility for their own well being." Once she believed that "I make choices that lead me to my highest good" and "I want to be successful," she would actually attract situations to prove them true.

After many sessions over the five-month period of this newer therapy being used with women in prison, she no longer had to act out and be labeled as "crazy." Her change would mean effective change in her family and in her family of origin, for she would teach others that there were other ways. Her own children, the next generation, would have some degree of knowledge to operate in a healthier, more supportive fashion. Her instant-gratification choices of the ego, such as drugs and sex at an early age, kept her in a cycle of perpetuating her self-destructive behavior. Her ego needed attachment because inside she felt like a scared child. She was a typical co-dependent female who was using her sex to control others around her.

In the prison environment, if you had looked at her in a "wrong way," she could have easily made you "dead meat." But now that the pain, guilt, and anger had been dealt with, her real personality could come forth. Her sensitivity to pain was so great that she thought that the way to deal with life was to give pain to others. Once she had dealt with her own pain in this therapy, she opened her heart; she was a positive influence to others. She was a helping, giving person who was empathetic. She was able to connect with her own inner strengths. Obviously, there were other inmates who had positive changes as well. Yet, prison is a very difficult place to help people change. Clients are in the system involuntarily. They fear anything they say will be used against them. The system is authoritarian and coercive so that the normal response to this abnormal living arrangement is depression.

EDUCATIONAL APPROACHES FOR EMOTIONAL MATURITY

Given the movement of state, local, and federal correctional agencies away from rehabilitation and toward control, professionals in the juvenile and criminal justice systems need to advocate for change. We who know can play the role of the reformer to work outside the correctional system to promote change as well as to advocate a more humane system inside. Another way is to promote change at the primary and secondary levels of prevention such as through education.

As to be discussed in this last section, prevention can become simple and easy, given the right types of programs, while children are young—either in their family and/or in the school system. And, it will be less expensive than the cost of one child for one year in a treatment facility like Paint Creek Youth Center for serious juvenile offenders for $29,653 (1988 dollars) or the regular correctional juvenile facility in Ohio at $26,137. (Greenwood and Turner 1999, 314)

We all learn our emotional approaches through our families, schools, and others. In families, research supports the generally held idea that those couples who are more emotionally competent in marriage are also the most effective in dealing with their children. The three most ineffective parenting styles are when parents ignore feelings altogether (theirs and/or their children's), or are too laissez-faire, or show no respect for how the child feels. Contrast those three styles with saying the following to a child: "I realize you are angry. You have a right to feel angry, yet you do not have a right to beat up others while you are feeling angry. Talk to us about your anger. If not, go to your room and when you are through being angry, come out and talk to us."

Obviously, the shaping of emotional intelligence comes in our earliest years. Children with more stable experiences have more to build with.

Readiness for school is more than an ability to read. According to a report from the National Center for Clinical Infant Programs, the following key ingredients are crucial for how a child learns:

1. Confidence—a sense of control and mastery of one's body, behavior, and world.

2. Curiosity—the pleasure of discovery and the desire to do more.

3. Intentionality—the wish and capacity to have an impact.

4. Self-control—a sense of inner control.

5. Relatedness—the ability to engage with others to feel a sense of being understood.

6. Capacity to communicate—the ability to verbally exchange ideas and feelings.

7. Cooperativeness—the ability to balance one's own needs with those of others. (Goleman 1995, 220–221)

We have seen how other families have reared bullies. We know that the more brutal, shocking, and horrendous the events, the more trauma to the psyche. Vietnam veterans are only one of many groups that have experienced Post-Traumatic Stress Disorder. Some of the biological research shows that those with PTSD have brains that have undergone a lasting change. Among Holocaust survivors, nearly three-quarters still have active PTSD symptoms even a half-century later. The positive finding in that research was that one-fourth of the survivors no longer had the symptoms. Something in their lives counteracted the problem, or the emotional circuitry was reeducated (Goleman 1995, 237).

For children who have experienced shootings in schools, one way for them to heal emotionally is to permit them to play games wherein they can rewrite the script of what happened and thereby lessen their feelings of helplessness. By repeating the traumatic experience in a context of low anxiety, the child has the ability to desensitize the experience. Art is also used with such children because the emotional brain is highly attuned to symbolic meanings.

One of the ways one can tell that healing has occurred is that persons who suffered a traumatic experience find that the triggering events (remembering the past experience) become less distressing. They begin to talk about it with less emotion. They may even be able to see the humor in the situation. For that to happen, it means that the alarm signals have learned a new, healthier response. Goleman (1995, 260) stated it this way:

It stands to reason that the key skills of emotional intelligence each have critical periods extending over several years in childhood. Each period represents a window for helping that child instill beneficial emotional habits, or, if missed, to make it that much harder to offer corrective lessons later in life. The massive sculpting and pruning of neural circuits in childhood may be an underlying reason why early emotional hardships and trauma have such enduring and pervasive effects in adulthood. It may explain, too,

why psychotherapy can often take so long to affect
some of these patterns—and why, as we've seen, even
after therapy those patterns tend to remain as
underlying propensities, though with an overlay of new
insights and relearned responses.

Of course, there is no one single pathway to violence or criminal behavior. Many factors put a child at risk. Yet, like a bad storm, one can see that children who are disruptive as first-graders—unable to get along with other kids, abusive to teachers, and having a hard time learning academic material—will only continue to have difficulties unless someone or something intervenes.

Classes in anger control that have been offered in juvenile detention facilities for several decades are now being used with students in the public schools. Duke University, for example, had training sessions for forty minutes twice a week for six to twelve weeks for anger-ridden grade-school troublemakers. The youth were taught how to take a teasing scene where they might lose their temper and monitor their feelings and rehearse other possible behaviors. As one gains more control over one's temper, one also gains more self-esteem. Thus the boys are willing to learn friendly responses that preserve their dignity instead of hitting, crying, or running away in shame (Goleman 1995, 274).

In Raleigh, North Carolina, and Jacksonville, Florida, their program is called "Self-Enhancing Behavior in Students." Modeled after the Systematic Training for Parents (STEP), the program shows teachers the four goals of a child's misbehavior: (1) attention, (2) power, (3) revenge, and (4) avoidance of failure. The goal is to help teachers realize that there are a variety of causes and forces operating in a number of directions and that all actions—verbal and nonverbal—are motivated at some level of our motivational system. Then the teachers are taught intervention strategies. They are redirection, reflection, interpretation, humor, antiseptic bounce, restructuring the classroom program, direct appeal to values, appeal to group or individual goals, planned ignoring, signal interference, reality appraisal, positive notes, and phone calls home to praise students, hurdle help, counseling, and behavior contracts (Cities in Schools Fall Training Event, Oct. 7–9, 1992 in Atlanta, GA).

Other schools have developed more intense classes under names such as "social development," "life skills," "social and emotional learning," and "personal intelligences." The Office of Juvenile Justice and Delinquency Prevention (OJJDP) has information on "Preventing Violence the Problem-Solving Way" (Shure 1999). For more than two decades the research has identified specific interpersonal cognitive problem-solving skills that related to high-risk behaviors. A primary prevention program for children ages 4 to 7 and their parents is called "I Can Problem Solve" (ICPS) and was developed from that research. In 1997 it was recognized as an exemplary juvenile delinquency prevention program by OJJDP.

Treat people as if they were what they ought to be, and you help them to become what they are capable of being.
Goethe

For older children, information on emotional literacy courses can be obtained from the Collaborative for the Advancement of Social and Emotional Learning (CASEL), at the Yale Child Study Center in New Haven, CT. Self Science at the Nueva School in San Francisco is another example. Their goal is to raise the level of social and emotional competence in children as a part of their regular education by using the tensions and traumas of children's lives as the topic of the day. The core curriculum they use on impulse control, managing anger, and finding creative solutions to social problems have usually been designed by research psychologists as experiments (Goleman 1995).

The litmus test is to make these highly focused programs generalized as a preventive measure. In this manner, then, an entire school population is taught by teachers and supported by student peer groups. Instead of being tertiary prevention and dialoguing with offenders to prevent future occurrences, the program becomes primary to prevent children from becoming offenders in the first place.

Students in Self Science, for example, learn to resolve disagreements and resentment before it becomes an out-and-out fight. For that to happen, students need to be taught how to express their feelings or to express their point of view without dumping on the other person or accelerating the conflict. Being assertive is taught in the third grade. Active listening has to be practiced, as well as being a self-observer, especially when one is flooded with other thoughts or feelings of being upset. Maintaining your own self-control without screaming, blaming, or shutting down in defensiveness is indeed a worthy goal to teach the children of the future.

Although Nueva is a small private school, emotional literacy can also be part of the inner city. Augusta Lewis Troup Middle School in New Haven, Connecticut, is about 95 percent black and Hispanic. It is as far from Nueva School socially and economically as it is geographically. Yet the same excitement about learning occurs. For these students, however, some of the topics are less academic. Some of the students are struggling with having AIDS themselves from their mothers. In New Haven, the emotional literacy class is a separate topic in some grades, and in others the social development curriculum blends into the standardized traditional courses such as reading, health, or math. Some schools, like the Child Development Project based in Oakland, California, created by a team directed by psychologist Eric Schaps, integrate the lessons into the entire school curriculum instead of as separate subjects with specific class time (Goleman 1995).

Discipline problems in the schools are a good place to begin with teaching both the teachers and the students more effective ways to resolve conflicts. By using the situations of life itself as teaching moments, teachers can model more impartial and fair ways to settle disputes and to support negotiation for more complex issues.

Resolving Conflict Creatively Programs in several hundred New York City Public schools and others across the country are conflict-resolution courses to deal with violence in the school systems. These programs were developed to help reduce schoolyard arguments from escalating into hallway shootings. Although the prevention may be focused on violence, promoters of the program realize it has a wider mission. When individuals can recognize and expand their range of feelings by putting names to them, they can also become more empathic (Goleman 1995, 319). That translates into someone caring about me, and thus I become caring about others.

More importantly, emotional literacy means that schools have an expanded mission with consistent messages about emotional competence in all parts of the students' lives. Coaches use the same techniques to resolve conflicts on the playing field as the teachers do on the playgrounds and in the classrooms. In the New Haven schools, the parents are taught the methods so they can be used with the children at home. These parallel lines of reinforcement are especially important for community building. Thus emotional learning theory is being applied in other school systems (Goleman 1999) and with parenting programs (Elias, Tobias, and Friedlander 1999; Ruskon 1998).

When youth feel part of a bigger picture, it lays the foundation for their support and their willingness to be volunteers as "peer counselors" to assist others. Youth, teachers, administrators, and parent(s) begin to create a world of "justice." In a North Carolina middle school, for example, with more than 700 students, the Program for Young Negotiators is a process curriculum with several other conflict resolution programs. Within a single school year, using this whole-classroom methodology that teaches students the foundation abilities, principles, and one or more of the three problem-solving processes of conflict resolution, "inschool suspensions decreased 42 percent and out-of-school suspensions decreased 97 percent" (LeBoeuf and Delany-Shabazz, Fact Sheet #55, OJJDP, March 1997).

This shift in crime prevention programming on the federal level to a more emotional and educational component is most evident in the new Juvenile Mentoring Program (JUMP) recently authorized through Congress to the OJJDP. Federal monies are dispersed to local educational agencies to support the implementation and expansion of collaborative mentoring projects to provide one-to-one mentoring for youth at risk of delinquency, gang involvement, educational failure, or dropping out of school. Mentoring is not a new concept; programs like Big Brothers/Big Sisters were founded in 1904. What is new is the formal and informal networking with many community groups to provide significant adult role models for at-risk youth under the sponsorship of federal monies. The goal is to get the presence of a mentor in a youth's life to help reduce isolation and provide the needed supervision and support that cannot always be given in single-parent households or in households where both parents work. As stated earlier, it is the lack of parental supervision that is highly correlated with delinquency, and not that a mother works or doesn't work. Yet in low-income families, youth have fewer options for supervision (*Juvenile Mentoring Program, 1998 Report to Congress*).

One way to learn emotional intelligence is through relationships with caring adults such as those available through a mentoring program. Yet, as this chapter has shown, there are other ways to learn these skills. What is important is that we begin to teach youth so that once they learn emotional intelligence and skills, they become second nature to them. These skills become valuable for the future marketplace as well as for parenting their own children-to-be. With emotional competency skills, one can manage others with more success and less stress—by balancing the feelings of the heart and the right brain with the logic of the left brain.

When we do it unto the children, we do it unto ourselves.

In conclusion, it is important to understand where we have been and where we might be going. Our Founding Fathers knew very little about the emotional and physical developmental stages of children and their learning styles. They thought children were "small" adults. Their thinking was expressed in the United States Constitution that didn't guarantee a separate court of system of justice for juvenile offenders. Around the turn of the twentieth century, states by statute created a juvenile justice system. But by statute it can be changed or even abolished and that is what has been happening. Perhaps a better way to think about this (in)justice system for youth is in the context of the society with its multiple philosophies, values, power structures, and the manifest and latent role of youth. We still have not put the vast wealth of knowledge and research about children into practice. Thus, the Billy of the introduction of this chapter may someday be your child or relative.

We have yet to build a society wherein life is valued and uniqueness is cherished. When we do, then the justice system for youth will be part of the grander scheme of how we hold people accountable for their behavior at appropriate developmental levels with humane controls. Then prevention programs will be standard operating procedures; what we have called "prevention" will be normal practice. Young people will become whole-brain functioning persons using their heads and hearts to address the challenges of the present society by problem-solving in creative ways. Greater peace, harmony, and prosperity will flow to us all for we have treated our children as we would have wanted to be—celebrated and encouraged to be all that we can be.

SUMMARY

This chapter focused on crime and delinquency prevention in educational approaches that use the new research on the brain and emotions. Crime and delinquency prevention was discussed in terms of three levels: (1) primary, (2) secondary, and (3) tertiary. An additional component was community involvement, which may be engaged to help define the problem and allocate resources to a new approach to fit the unique needs of a group of people.

The cognitive development of children was discussed in terms of whole-brain learning, neurological organization, the learning brain, implications for models of education and learning, and newer educational techniques such as mindmapping and accelerated learning. Emotions were discussed in terms of emotional intelligence and some of the psychological therapies used to assist people with their irrational thinking. A newer therapy called the Results System was explained with a case study.

The chapter ended with examples of schools that are promoting emotional intelligence as prevention strategies for children, as well as JUMP programs sponsored by the Office of Juvenile Justice and Delinquency Prevention (OJJDP). These examples showed the active cultivation of the interrelationship of the mind, body, and brain.

REFERENCES

Berne, Eric. *Transactional Analysis in Psychotherapy*. New York: Grove Press, 1961.

Bernstein, Basil. *Class Codes and Controls: Theoretical Studies Towards Sociology of Language*. New York: Schocken, 1975.

Butts, Jeffrey A., and Howard N. Snyder. "The Youngest Delinquents: Offenders Under Age 15." *Juvenile Justice Bulletin*, September 1997.

Clement, Mary. *Counseling Resistant Clients*. Unpublished manuscript. 2001.

———. *Soul Soaring: New Techniques for Diagnosing and Overcoming What Separates You From Harmony Within*. Richmond, VA: The Oakleaf Press, 1998a.

——. "Multiple Measures in Determining Effectiveness in Correctional Treatment Programs." *Journal of Offender Rehabilitation* 27 (3) (1998b).

——. "New Treatment for Drug-Abusing Women Offenders in Virginia." *Journal of Offender Rehabilitation* 25 (1/2) (1997): 61–81.

——. "Parenting in Prison: A National Survey of Programs for Incarcerated Women." *Journal of Offender Rehabilitation* 19 (1/2) (1993): 89–100.

Dennison, Paul E., and Gail Dennison. *Brain Gym: Teacher's Edition*. Ventura, CA: Edu-Kinesthetics, Inc., 1989.

DiMascio, William M. *Seeking Justice: Crime and Punishment in America*. New York: The Edna McConnel Clark Foundation, 1997.

Doman, Glen. *What to Do about Your Brain-Injured Child*, 3rd Ed. New York: Penguin Putnam, 1990.

——. *How to Teach Your Baby to Read*. Philadelphia: The Better Baby Press, 1991.

——. *How to Multiply Your Baby's Intelligence*. New York: Doubleday, 1992a.

——. *How to Teach Your Baby Math*. Philadelphia: Inst. Achieve Human Potential, 1992b.

Douglas, John, and Mark Olshaker. *Mind Hunter: Inside the FBI's Elite Serial Crime Unit*. New York: Scribner, 1995.

Educational Kinesiology Foundation of North America. "Field Studies and Experimental Research on Educational Kinesiology." Unpublished materials.

Ellis, Albert. *Humanistic Psychotherapy: The Rational-Emotive Approach*. New York: McGraw Hill, 1974.

Elias, Maurice, Steven Tobias, and Brian Friedlander. *Emotionally Intelligent Parenting*. London: Hodder & Staughton, 1999.

Erikson, Eric. *Childhood and Society*. New York: W. W. Norton, 1963.

Ferreri, Carl. *Neural Organization Technique: Basic 2 Procedures*. Brooklyn, NY: Ferreri Institute, 1998.

Freeman, Peter. "Rock and Roll Animal," *The Bulletin*, January 9, 2001, p. 51.

Gardner, Howard. *Frames of Mind*. New York: Basic Books, 1985.

Goleman, Daniel. *Emotional Intelligence*. New York: Bantam Books, 1995.

——. *Working with Emotional Intelligence*. New York: Bantam Books, 1999.

Greenwood, Peter W., and Susan Turner, "Evaluation of the Paint Creek Youth Center: A Residential Program for Serious Delinquents." *Criminology* 31 (1993): 263–279.

Jensen, Eric. *The Learning Brain*. San Diego, CA: Turning Point Publishing, 1994.

Juvenile Mentoring Program, 1998 Report to Congress. Washington, DC: U.S. Department of Justice, Office of Juvenile Justice and Delinquency Prevention, 1998.

Kelly, Barbara T., Terence P. Thornberry, and Carolyn A. Smith. "In the Wake of Childhood Maltreatment," *Juvenile Justice Bulletin*, August 1997.

Kohlberg, Lawrence. "Moral Development and Identification." *Child Psychology: Yearbook of the National Society for the Study of Education*. Chicago: University of Chicago Press, 1963.

Kohlberg, L., and C. Gilligan. "The Adolescent as a Philosopher: The Discovery of the Self in a Post Conventional World." *Daedalus* Fall (1971): 1051–1086.

Lazear, Paul. *Seven Pathways of Learning: Teaching Students and Parents about Multiple Intelligences*. Tucson, Arizona: Zephyr Press, 1994.

Lewis, D., J. Pinkcus, B. Bard, E. Richardson, L. Prichep, M. Feldman, and C. Yeager. "Neuropsychiatric, Psychoeducational, and Family Characteristics of 14 Juveniles Condemned to Death in the United States." *American Journal of Psychiatry*, 145 (5) (1988): 584–589.

MacKenzie, D.L., and C.C. Souryal. "Boot Camp Survey: Rehabilitation, Recidivism Reduction Outrank Punishment As Main Goals," *Corrections Today* 53 (1991): 90–96.

MacKenzie, D.L., and J.W. Shaw. "The Impact of Correctional Boot Camp Programs," *Justice Quarterly* 7 (1) (1990): 125–150.

Piaget, J. "The Theory of Stages in Cognitive Development," in *Measurement and Piaget* by D. Green, editor. New York: McGraw-Hill, 1971.

Roberts, Albert. "Wilderness Experiences, Camps and Outdoor Programs," Chapter #10 in *Juvenile Justice: Policies, Programs and Services* by A.R. Roberts, ed. Chicago: The Dosey Press, 1988. Condensed version as "Wilderness Programs for Juvenile Offenders: A Challenging Alternative," *Juvenile & Family Court Journal*.

Rose, Colin. *Accelerated Learning*. New York: Dell Trade Publishing, 1987.

Rossman, Martin L. *Healing Yourself*. New York: Pocket Books, 1990.

Shure, Myrna. "Preventing Violence the Problem-Solving Way," *Juvenile Justice Bulletin* April 1999.

Sickmund, Melissa. "Offenders in Juvenile Court, 1995." *Juvenile Justice Bulletin* December 1997.

Simons, Ronald L., and Les B. Whitbeck. "Sexual Abuse as a Precursor to Prostitution and Victimization Among Adolescent and Adult Homeless Women," *Journal of Family Issues* 12 (3) (1991): 361–379.

Smith, Carolyn, and Terrence P. Thornberry. "The Relationship between Childhood Maltreatment and Adolescent Involvement in Delinquency," *Criminology* 33 (1995): 451–467.

Snyder, Howard N. "Juvenile Arrests 1996." *Juvenile Justice Bulletin*, November 1997.

Soloveichik, Simon. "Odd Way to Teach, But It Works." *Soviet Life Magazine*, 1979.

Taylor, Carl S. *Dangerous Society*. East Lansing, MI: Michigan State University Press, 1990.

United States Department of Education. *A Nation at Risk*. Washington, D.C.: National Commission on Excellence in Education, 1983.

Vobejda, Barbara. "When Foster Kids Can't Beat the Demon." *The Jerusalem Post*, December 16, 1998, p. 9.

Wheelan, Charles. "Lou Gerstner's Toughest Turnaround." *US Airways Attaché*, November 1997, 90–92.

Wycoff, Joyce. *Mindmapping: Your Personal Guide to Exploring Creativity and Problem-Solving*. New York: Berkeley Books, 1991.

APPENDIX I

Problems to Solve

Some students find learning easiest when they are given a real personal problem or someone else's dilemma to solve—like a puzzle. The following topics or problems could be used instead of a research paper because research will be necessary to resolve the problem.

1. You have been approached by a parent group of your state. They want to have a law passed that gives them a right to parental notification if their child should seek an abortion. How do you advise them?

2. School authorities are concerned about weapons and drugs in the schools. They want you to draft a policy and a form to be sent home with each student at the beginning of the school year to implement their policy to search student lockers in the high schools without warning and on a periodic basis. What advice do you give them?

3. A legislative committee is studying the problem of hardened juvenile criminals and wants to expand the transfer proceedings, including lowering the age of waiver to the adult court. What do you recommend? Are there other ways to deal with these violent juvenile offenders?

4. *McKeiver* did not give juveniles the right to a jury trial. Other states have used the jury trial quite successfully. As a staff attorney to a legislative committee concerned with juveniles, you are requested to research the problem and create a proposal. If not a jury of peers, could an advisory panel be used for the judge?

5. Compare the statutory schemes and the literature of status offenders in other states. How should the juvenile court in your state deal with status offenders?

6. Choose your best friend who has a small child, and pretend she is a battered wife who is trying to get a divorce. Discuss with her options for the custody of the child. Should she go for joint custody?

7. You are out partying one night when you notice a homeless child. Then you look again and see that his mother is also homeless. What do you do? What can the city or state do? Should the child be taken away from her because of her unwillingness to provide for the child?

8. Some of the babies being born today are victims of Fetal Alcohol Syndrome (FAS). An advocate group for the unborn wants alcoholic mothers to be locked up in jails until their babies are born. What is being done in other states for this national problem? What do you recommend for your state?

9. You have been appointed as a CASA volunteer to work with a 6-year-old who has been sexually abused by her stepfather. A decision was made to seek removal of the child from her home to protect her from further abuse while civil abuse proceedings are initiated in juvenile court. In your investigation, what factors would be most important? Are there any other alternatives? What can you do to help her? What recommendations would you make to the Department of Social Services and the court?

10. You represent the 8-year-old who went into his neighbor's house, took the goldfish, and chopped it up and smeared it on the kitchen countertop. You successfully get him off on the burglary charge. Is your real duty finished? What else could and should you do?

11. You meet a 12- or 13-year-old at the Burger King who looks very hungry. Your heart swells inside so you decide to buy him some lunch and talk to him. You find out he is being abused and has given up, so he is on the run. What would you do? Who would you call in your community to help him?

12. Your best friend has a teenage daughter or son who is interested in making extra money. They heard about this "swell company" that wants young models; they pay really good money and the travel is exciting. Why and how would you investigate?

13. Two women live together in a lesbian relationship, and one agrees to conceive a child by artificial insemination for them both to raise. The child is born, but three years later the couple end their relationship. Both want full custody of the child. You are the law clerk for the judge. What is the case law in other states on this issue? What legal reasons would you give to support your finding? (See *Curiale v. Reagan*, 222 Cal. App. 3d 1597, 272 Cal. Rptr. 520 [1990].)

14. You have a complaint that a mother has been beating her 7-month-old child. When the child was 2 months old, he was admitted to the hospital for pneumonia, but full-body X-rays revealed previous fractures of the upper arm, shoulder blade, and shoulder socket. The child was released to the mother. Less than two months later, the next injury required a full body cast. Again the child was released to the mother. Now you want to see the child, but the mother refuses to produce him. You go to court and ask the court to order her to show cause why she should not be held in contempt for failure to produce the child. She still refuses. What do you do? (See *Baltimore City Department of Social Services v. Bouknight*, 110 S. Ct. 900 [1990].)

APPENDIX II

The Constitution of the United States of America*

WE THE PEOPLE of the United States, in Order to form a more perfect Union, establish Justice, insure domestic Tranquility, provide for the common defence, promote the general Welfare, and secure the Blessings of Liberty to ourselves and our Posterity, do ordain and establish this CONSTITUTION for the United States of America.

Article I.

Section. 1. All legislative Powers herein granted shall be vested in a Congress of the United States, which shall consist of a Senate and House of Representatives.

Section. 2. The House of Representatives shall be composed of Members chosen every second Year by the People of the several States, and the Electors in each State shall have the Qualifications requisite for Electors of the most numerous Branch of the State Legislature.

No Person shall be a Representative who shall not have attained to the Age of twenty five Years, and been seven Years a Citizen of the United States, and who shall not, when elected, be an Inhabitant of that State in which he shall be chosen.

Representatives and direct Taxes shall be apportioned among the several States which may be included within this Union, according to their respective Numbers, which shall be determined by adding to the whole Number of free Persons, including those bound to Service for a Term of Years, and excluding Indians not taxed, three fifths of all other Persons. The actual Enumeration shall be made within three Years after the first Meeting of the Congress of the United States, and within every subsequent Term of ten Years, in such Manner as they shall by Law direct. The Number of Representatives

---

*Due to limited space, this is not the entire U.S. Constitution with 27 Amendments but only the first 10 and the 14th Amendment.

shall not exceed one for every thirty Thousand, but each State shall have at Least one Representative; and until such enumeration shall be made, the State of New Hampshire shall be entitled to choose three, Massachusetts eight, Rhode Island and Providence Plantations one, Connecticut five, New York six, New Jersey four, Pennsylvania eight, Delaware one, Maryland six, Virginia ten, North Carolina five, South Carolina five, and Georgia three.

When vacancies happen in the Representation from any State, the Executive Authority thereof shall issue Writs of Election to fill such Vacancies.

The House of Representatives shall chuse [choose] their Speaker and other Officers; and shall have the sole Power of Impeachment.

Section. 3. The Senate of the United States shall be composed of two Senators from each State, chosen by the Legislature thereof, for six Years; and each Senator shall have one Vote.

Immediately after they shall be assembled in Consequence of the first Election, they shall be divided as equally as may be into three Classes. The Seats of the Senators of the first Class shall be vacated at the Expiration of the second Year, of the second Class at the Expiration of the fourth Year, and of the third Class at the Expiration of the sixth Year, so that one third may be chosen every second Year; and if Vacancies happen by Resignation, or otherwise, during the Recess of the Legislature of any State, the Executive thereof may make temporary Appointments until the next Meeting of the Legislature, which shall then fill such Vacancies.

No Person shall be a Senator who shall not have attained to the Age of thirty Years, and been nine Years a Citizen of the United States, and who shall not, when elected, be an Inhabitant of that State for which he shall be chosen.

The Vice President of the United States shall be President of the Senate, but shall have no Vote, unless they be equally divided.

The Senate shall chuse [choose] their other Officers, and also a President pro tempore, in the Absence of the Vice President, or when he shall exercise the Office of President of the United States.

The Senate shall have the sole Power to try all Impeachments. When sitting for that Purpose, they shall be on Oath or Affirmation. When the President of the United States is tried, the Chief Justice shall preside: And no Person shall be convicted without the Concurrence of two thirds of the Members present.

Judgment in Cases of Impeachment shall not extend further than to removal from Office, and disqualification to hold and enjoy any Office of honor, Trust or Profit under the United States: but the Party convicted shall nevertheless be liable and subject to Indictment, Trial, Judgment and Punishment, according to Law.

Section. 4. The Times, Places and Manner of holding Elections for Senators and Representatives, shall be prescribed in each State by the Legislature thereof; but the Congress may at any time by Law make or alter such Regulations, except as to the Places of chusing [choosing] Senators.

The Congress shall assemble at least once in every Year, and such Meeting shall be on the first Monday in December, unless they shall by Law appoint a different Day.

Section. 5. Each House shall be the Judge of the Elections, Returns and Qualifications of its own Members, and a Majority of each shall constitute a Quorum to do Business; but a smaller Number may adjourn from day to day, and may be authorized to compel the Attendance of absent Members, in such Manner, and under such Penalties as each House may provide.

Each House may determine the Rules of its Proceedings, punish its Members for disorderly Behaviour, and, with the Concurrence of two thirds, expel a Member.

Each House shall keep a Journal of its Proceedings, and from time to time publish the same, excepting such Parts as may in their Judgment require Secrecy; and the Yeas and Nays of the Members of either House on any question shall, at the Desire of one fifth of those Present, be entered on the Journal.

Neither House, during the Session of Congress, shall, without the Consent of the other, adjourn for more than three days, nor to any other Place than that in which the two Houses shall be sitting.

Section. 6. The Senators and Representatives shall receive a Compensation for their Services, to be ascertained by Law, and paid out of the Treasury of the United States. They shall in all Cases, except Treason, Felony and Breach of the Peace, be privileged from Arrest during their Attendance at the Session of their respective Houses, and in going to and returning from the same; and for any Speech or Debate in either House, they shall not be questioned in any other Place.

No Senator or Representative shall, during the Time for which he was elected, be appointed to any civil Office under the Authority of the United States, which shall have been created, or the Emoluments whereof shall have been encreased [increased] during such time; and no Person holding any Office under the United States, shall be a Member of either House during his Continuance in Office.

Section. 7. All Bills for raising Revenue shall originate in the House of Representatives; but the Senate may propose or concur with Amendments as on other Bills.

Every Bill which shall have passed the House of Representatives and the Senate, shall, before it becomes a Law, be presented to the President of the United States; If he approves he shall sign it, but if not he shall return it, with his Objections to that House in which it shall have originated, who shall enter the Objections at large on their Journal, and proceed to reconsider it. If after such Reconsideration two thirds of that House shall agree to pass the Bill, it shall be sent, together with the Objections, to the other House, by which it shall likewise be reconsidered, and if approved by two thirds of that House, it shall become a Law. But in all such Cases the Votes of both Houses shall be determined by yeas and Nays, and the Names of the Persons voting for and against the Bill shall be entered on the journal of each House respectively. If any Bill shall not be returned by the President within ten Days (Sundays excepted) after it shall have been presented to him, the Same shall be a Law, in like Manner as if he had signed it, unless the Congress by their Adjournment prevent its Return, in which Case it shall not be a Law.

Every Order, Resolution, or Vote to which the Concurrence of the Senate and House of Representatives may be necessary (except on a question of adjournment) shall be presented to the President of the United States; and before the Same shall take Effect, shall be approved by him, or being disapproved by him, shall be repassed by two thirds of the Senate and House of Representatives, according to the Rules and Limitations prescribed in the Case of a Bill.

Section. 8. The Congress shall have the Power: To lay and collect Taxes, Duties, Imposts and Excises, to pay the Debts and provide for the common Defence and general Welfare of the United States; but all Duties, Imposts and Excises shall be uniform throughout the United States; To borrow Money on the credit of the United States; To regulate Commerce with foreign Nations, and among the several States, and with the Indian Tribes; To establish a uniform Rule of Naturalization, and uniform Laws on the subject of Bankruptcies throughout the United States; To coin Money, regulate the Value thereof, and of foreign Coin, and fix the Standard of Weights and Measures; To provide for the Punishment of counterfeiting the Securities and current Coin of the United States; To establish Post Offices and post Roads; To promote the Progress of Science and useful Arts, by securing for limited Times to Authors and Inventors the exclusive Right to their respective Writings and Discoveries; To constitute Tribunals inferior to the Supreme Court; To define and punish Piracies and Felonies committed on the high Seas, and Offences against the Law of Nations; To declare War, grant Letters of Marque and Reprisal, and make Rules concerning Captures on Land and Water; To raise and support Armies, but no appropriation of Money to that Use shall be for a longer Term than two Years; To provide and maintain a Navy; To make Rules for the Government and Regulation of the land and naval Forces; To provide for calling forth the Militia to execute the Laws of the Union, suppress Insurrections and repel Invasions; To provide for organizing, arming, and disciplining, the Militia, and for governing such Part of them as may be employed in the Service of the United States, reserving to the States respectively, the Appointment of the Officers, and the Authority of training the Militia according to the discipline prescribed by Congress; To exercise exclusive Legislation in all Cases whatsoever, over such District (not exceeding ten Miles square) as may, by Cession of particular States, and the Acceptance of Congress, become the Seat of the Government of the United States, and to exercise like Authority over all Places purchased by the Consent of the Legislature of the State in which the Same shall be, for the Erection of Forts, Magazines, Arsenals, dock-Yards, and other needful Buildings;—And To make all Laws which shall be necessary and proper for carrying into Execution the foregoing Powers, and all other Powers vested by this Constitution in the Government of the United States, or in any Department or Officer thereof.

Section. 9. The Migration or Importation of such Persons as any of the States now existing shall think proper to admit, shall not be prohibited by the Congress prior to the Year one thousand eight hundred and eight, but a Tax or duty may be imposed on such Importation, not exceeding ten dollars for each Person.

The Privilege of the Writ of Habeas Corpus shall not be suspended, unless when in Cases of Rebellion or Invasion the public Safety may require it.

No Bill of Attainder or ex post facto Law shall be passed.

No Capitation, or other direct, Tax shall be laid, unless in Proportion to the Census or Enumeration herein before directed to be taken.

No Tax or Duty shall be laid on Articles exported from any State.

No Preference shall be given by any Regulation of Commerce or Revenue to the Ports of one State over those of another: nor shall Vessels bound to, or from, one State, be obliged to enter, clear, or pay Duties in another.

No Money shall be drawn from the Treasury, but in Consequence of Appropriations made by Law; and a regular Statement and Account of the Receipts and Expenditures of all public Money shall be published from time to time.

No Title of Nobility shall be granted by the United States: And no Person holding any Office of Profit or Trust under them, shall, without the Consent of the Congress, accept of any present, Emolument, Office, or Title, of any kind whatever, from any King, Prince, or foreign State.

Section. 10. No State shall enter into any Treaty, Alliance, or Confederation; grant Letters of Marque and Reprisal; coin Money; emit Bills of Credit; make any Thing but gold and silver Coin a Tender in Payment of Debts; pass any Bill of Attainder, ex post facto Law, or Law impairing the Obligation of Contracts, or grant any Title of Nobility.

No State shall, without the Consent of the Congress, lay any Imposts or Duties on Imports or Exports, except what may be absolutely necessary for executing its inspection Laws: and the net Produce of all Duties and Imposts, laid by any State on Imports or Exports, shall be for the Use of the Treasury of the United States; and all such Laws shall be subject to the Revision and Controul [Control] of the Congress.

No State shall, without the Consent of Congress, lay any Duty of Tonnage, keep Troops, or Ships of War in time of Peace, enter into any Agreement or Compact with another State, or with a foreign Power, or engage in War, unless actually invaded, or in such imminent Danger as will not admit of delay.

Article II.

Section. 1. The executive Power shall be vested in a President of the United States of America. He shall hold his Office during the Term of four Years, and, together with the Vice President, chosen for the same Term, be elected, as follows:

Each State shall appoint, in such Manner as the Legislature thereof may direct, a Number of Electors, equal to the whole Number of Senators and Representatives to which the State may be entitled in the Congress: but no

Senator or Representative, or Person holding an Office of Trust or Profit under the United States, shall be appointed an Elector.

The Electors shall meet in their respective States, and vote by Ballot for two Persons, of whom one at least shall not be an Inhabitant of the same State with themselves. And they shall make a List of all the Persons voted for, and of the Number of Votes for each; which List they shall sign and certify, and transmit sealed to the Seat of the Government of the United States, directed to the President of the Senate. The President of the Senate shall, in the Presence of the Senate and House of Representatives, open all the certificates, and the Votes shall then be counted. The Person having the greatest Number of Votes shall be the President, if such Number be a Majority of the whole Number of Electors appointed; and if there be more than one who have such Majority, and have an equal Number of Votes, then the House of Representatives shall immediately chuse [choose] by Ballot one of them for President; and if no Person have a Majority, then from the five highest on the List the said House shall in like Manner chuse [choose] the President. But in chusing [choosing] the President, the Votes shall be taken by States, the Representation from each State having one Vote; A quorum for this Purpose shall consist of a Member or Members from two thirds of the States, and a Majority of all the states shall be necessary to a Choice. In every Case, after the Choice of the President, the Person having the greatest Number of Votes of the Electors shall be the Vice President. But if there should remain two or more who have equal Votes, the Senate shall chuse [choose] from them by Ballot the Vice President.

The Congress may determine the Time of chusing [choosing] the Electors, and the Day on which they shall give their Votes; which Day shall be the same throughout the United States.

No Person except a natural born Citizen, or a Citizen of the United States, at the time of the Adoption of this Constitution, shall be eligible to the Office of President; neither shall any Person be eligible to that Office who shall not have attained to the Age of thirty five Years, and been fourteen Years a Resident within the United States.

In Case of the Removal of the President from Office, or of his Death, Resignation, or Inability to discharge the Powers and Duties of the said Office, the Same shall devolve on the Vice President, and the Congress may by Law provide for the Case of Removal, Death, Resignation or Inability, both of the President and Vice President, declaring what Officer shall then act as president, and such Officer shall act accordingly, until the Disability be removed, or a President shall be elected.

The President shall, at stated Times, receive for his Services, a Compensation, which shall neither be encreased [increased] nor diminished during the Period for which he shall have been elected, and he shall not receive within that Period any other Emolument from the United States, or any of them.

Before he enter on the Execution of his Office, he shall take the following Oath or Affirmation:—"I do solemnly swear (or affirm) that I will faithfully execute the Office of President of the United States, and will to the best of my Ability, preserve, protect and defend the Constitution of the United States."

Section. 2. The President shall be Commander in Chief of the Army and Navy of the United States, and of the Militia of the several States, when called into the actual Service of the United States; he may require the Opinion, in writing, of the principal Officer in each of the executive Departments, upon any Subject relating to the Duties of their respective Offices, and he shall have Power to grant Reprieves and Pardons for Offences against the United States, except in Cases of Impeachment.

He shall have Power, by and with the Advice and Consent of the Senate, to make Treaties, provided two thirds of the Senators present concur; and he shall nominate, and by and with the Advice and Consent of the Senate, shall appoint Ambassadors, other public Ministers and Consuls, Judges of the supreme Court, and all other Officers of the United States, whose Appointments are not herein otherwise provided for, and which shall be established by Law: but the Congress may by Law vest the Appointment of such inferior Officers, as they think proper, in the President alone, in the Courts of Law, or in the Heads of Departments.

The President shall have Power to fill up all Vacancies that may happen during the Recess of the Senate, by granting Commissions which shall expire at the End of their next Session.

Section. 3. He shall from time to time give to the Congress Information of the State of the Union, and recommend to their Consideration such Measures as he shall judge necessary and expedient; he may, on extraordinary Occasions, convene both Houses, or either of them, and in Case of Disagreement between them, with Respect to the Time of Adjournment, he may adjourn them to such Time as he shall think proper; he shall receive Ambassadors and other public Ministers; he shall take Care that the Laws be faithfully executed, and shall Commission all the Officers of the United States.

Section. 4. The President, Vice President and all civil Officers of the United States, shall be removed from Office on Impeachment for, and Conviction of, Treason, Bribery, or other high Crimes and Misdemeanors.

Article III.

Section. 1. The judicial Power of the United States, shall be vested in one supreme Court, and in such inferior Courts as the Congress may from time to time ordain and establish. The Judges, both of the supreme and inferior Courts, shall hold their Offices during good Behaviour, and shall, at stated Times, receive for their Services, a Compensation, which shall not be diminished during their Continuance in Office.

Section. 2. The judicial Power shall extend to all Cases, in Law and Equity, arising under this Constitution, the Laws of the United States, and Treaties made, or which shall be made, under their Authority;—to all Cases affecting Ambassadors, other public Ministers and Consuls;—to all Cases of admiralty and maritime Jurisdiction;—to Controversies to which the United States shall be a Party;—to Controversies between two or more States;—between a State and Citizens of another State;—between Citizens of different States;—between Citizens of the same State claiming Lands under Grants of different States, and between a State, or the Citizens thereof, and foreign States, Citizens or Subjects.

In all Cases affecting Ambassadors, other public Ministers and Consuls, and those in which a State shall be Party, the supreme Court shall have original Jurisdiction. In all the other Cases before mentioned, the supreme Court shall have appellate Jurisdiction, both as to Law and Fact, with such Exceptions, and under such Regulations as the Congress shall make.

The Trial of all Crimes, except in Cases of Impeachment, shall be by Jury; and such Trial shall be held in the State where the said Crimes shall have been committed; but when not committed within any States, the Trial shall be at such Place or Places as the Congress may by Law have directed.

Section. 3. Treason against the United States, shall consist only in levying War against them, or in adhering to their Enemies, giving them Aid and Comfort. No Person shall be convicted of Treason unless on the Testimony of two Witnesses to the same overt Act, or on Confession in open Court.

The Congress shall have Power to declare the Punishment of Treason, but no Attainder of Treason shall work Corruption of Blood, or Forfeiture except during the Life of the Person attainted.

Article IV.

Section. 1. Full Faith and Credit shall be given in each State to the public Acts, Records, and judicial Proceedings of every other State. And the Congress may by general Laws prescribe the Manner in which such Acts, Records and Proceedings shall be proved, and the Effect thereof.

Section. 2. The Citizens of each State shall be entitled to all Privileges and Immunities of Citizens in the several States.

A Person charged in any State with Treason, Felony, or other Crime, who shall flee from Justice, and be found in another State, shall on Demand of the executive Authority of the State from which he fled, be delivered up, to be removed to the State having Jurisdiction of the Crime.

No Person held to Service or Labour in one State, under the Laws thereof, escaping into another, shall, in Consequence of any Law or Regulation therein, be discharged from such Service or Labour, but shall be delivered up on Claim of the Party to whom such Service or Labour may be due.

Section. 3. New States may be admitted by the Congress into this Union; but no new State shall be formed or erected within the Jurisdiction of any other State; nor any State be formed by the Junction of two or more States, or Parts of States, without the Consent of the Legislatures of the States concerned as well as of the Congress.

The Congress shall have Power to dispose of and make all needful Rules and Regulations respecting the Territory or other Property belonging to the United States; and nothing in this Constitution shall be so construed as to Prejudice any Claims of the United States, or of any particular State.

Section. 4. The United States shall guarantee to every State in this Union a Republican Form of Government, and shall protect each of them against Invasion; and on Application of the Legislature, or of the Executive (when the Legislature cannot be convened) against domestic Violence.

Article V.

The Congress, whenever two thirds of both Houses shall deem it necessary, shall propose Amendments to this Constitution, or, on the Application of the Legislatures of two thirds of the several States, shall call a Convention for proposing Amendments, which, in either Case, shall be valid to all Intents and Purposes, as Part of this Constitution, when ratified by the Legislatures of three fourths of the several States, or by Conventions in three fourths thereof, as the one or the other Mode of Ratification may be proposed by the Congress; Provided that no Amendment which may be made prior to the Year One thousand eight hundred and eight shall in any Manner affect the first and fourth Clauses in the Ninth Section of the first Article; and that no State, without its Consent, shall be deprived of its equal Suffrage in the Senate.

Article VI.

All Debts contracted and Engagements entered into, before the Adoption of this Constitution, shall be as valid against the United States under this Constitution, as under the Confederation.

This Constitution, and the Laws of the United States which shall be made in Pursuance thereof; and all Treaties made, or which shall be made, under the Authority of the United States, shall be the supreme Law of the Land; and the Judges in every State shall be bound thereby, any Thing in the Constitution or Laws of any State to the Contrary notwithstanding.

The Senators and Representatives before mentioned, and the Members of the several State Legislatures, and all executive and judicial Officers, both of the United States and of the several States, shall be bound by Oath or Affirmation, to support this Constitution; but no religious Test shall ever be required as a Qualification to any Office or public Trust under the United States.

Article VII.

The Ratification of the Conventions of nine States, shall be sufficient for the Establishment of this Constitution between the States so ratifying the Same.

Done in Convention by the Unanimous Consent of the States present the Seventeenth Day of September in the Year of our Lord one thousand seven hundred and Eighty seven and of the Independence of the United States of America the Twelfth. In witness whereof We have hereunto subscribed our Names:

Amendment 1

Congress shall make no law respecting an establishment of religion, or prohibiting the free exercise thereof; or abridging the freedom of speech, or of the press; or the right of the people peaceably to assemble, and to petition the Government for a redress of grievances.

Amendment 2

A well regulated Militia, being necessary to the security of a free State, the right of the people to keep and bear Arms, shall not be infringed.

Amendment 3

No Soldier shall, in time of peace be quartered in any house, without the consent of the Owner, nor in time of war, but in a manner to be prescribed by law.

Amendment 4

The right of the people to be secure in their persons, houses, papers, and effects, against unreasonable searches and seizures, shall not be violated, and no Warrants shall issues, but upon probable cause, supported by Oath or affirmation, and particularly describing the Place to be searched, and the persons or things to be seized.

Amendment 5

No person shall be held to answer for a capital, or otherwise infamous crime, unless on a presentment or indictment of a Grand Jury, except in cases arising in the land or naval forces, or in the Militia, when in actual service in time of War or public danger; nor shall any person be subject for the same offence to be twice put in jeopardy of life or limb; nor shall be compelled in any criminal case to be a witness against himself, nor be deprived of life, liberty, or property, without due process of law; nor shall private property be taken from public use, without just compensation.

Amendment 6

In all criminal prosecutions, the accused shall enjoy the right to a speedy and public trial, by an impartial jury of the State and district wherein the crime shall have been committed, which district shall have been previously ascertained by law, and to be informed of the nature and cause of the accusation; to be confronted with the witnesses against him; to have compulsory process of obtaining Witnesses in his favor, and to have the Assistance of Counsel for his defence.

Amendment 7

In Suits at common law, where the value in controversy shall exceed twenty dollars, the right of trial by jury shall be preserved, and no fact tried by a jury, shall be otherwise reexamined in any Court of the United States, than according to the rules of the common law.

Amendment 8

Excessive bail shall not be required, nor excessive fines imposed, nor cruel and unusual punishments inflicted.

Amendment 9

The enumeration of the Constitution, of certain rights, shall not be construed to deny or disparage others retained by the people.

Amendment 10

The powers not delegated to the United States by the Constitution, nor prohibited by it to the States, are reserved to the States respectively, or to the people.

Amendment 14

All persons born or naturalized in the United States, and subject to the jurisdiction thereof, are citizens of the United States and of the State wherein they reside. No State shall make or enforce any law which shall abridge the privileges or immunities of citizens of the United States; nor shall any State deprive any person of life, liberty, or property, without due process of law; nor deny to any person within its jurisdiction the equal protection of the laws.

*Glossary**

ACQUITTAL—Court judgment that a person is not guilty of the charges filed.

ADJUDICATION—Court judgment that a juvenile is either (1) delinquent, (2) a child in need of services, (3) innocent of any charges, or (4) abused or neglected.

ADJUDICATORY HEARING—The court hearing to determine whether a youth is guilty or not guilty.

AFTERCARE COUNSELOR—Court worker who maintains contact with a youth and provides guidance, information, and supervision after commitment to the State Department of Corrections.

AFTERCARE SUPERVISION—Supervision a child receives from a court service worker from the time of commitment until release from the juvenile justice system. In some cases, the judge can order the Department of Social Services to supervise the case. Now called parole.

AKA—Stands for Also Known As. *See* alias.

ALIAS—Any name used for an official purpose that is different from a person's legal name.

ALLEGATION—Statement that a law has been broken (made by person bringing forth a charge); assertion before proving or without proof.

ALLEGED OFFENDER—Person who has been charged with a delinquent offense but has not yet been convicted of the offense.

AMICUS CURIAE—"Friend of the Court." Usually a brief written by parents not actually litigating the case to provide information to judges to aid in the decision of the court.

APPEAL—A request that a case be sent to a higher court for review or rehearing with the purpose of having the judgment, decision, or order of a lower court set aside (reversed) or modified.

---

*For more words and greater detail, be sure to see the website, "Juvenile Law Dictionary," at www.bh.com/companions.

APPELLANT—Person who asks for an appeal from one court or jurisdiction to another court having appellate jurisdiction, or the person in whose behalf this is done.

ARRAIGNMENT—A hearing before a court having jurisdiction in a criminal (adult) court in which the identity of the defendant is established, the defendant is informed of the charge(s) and of his or her rights, and is requested to make a plea.

ARREST—The taking of a person into custody for the purpose of charging him or her with an offense or starting court proceedings.

ASSIGNED COUNSEL—A lawyer appointed by the court to defend a person who has been brought before the court. In some cities the person paid to defend is part of the Public Defender's office.

ATTACHMENT—A document ordering a person's arrest for failing to appear for a court hearing, breaking probation, or violating a court order.

ATTORNEY—A person trained in law and licensed by the state who can advise, represent, and act for persons in legal proceedings.

BAIL—Money posted as security with the court to assure the appearance in court of a person being released from custody.

BEHAVIOR MODIFICATION—Treatment program designed to change a youth's behavior by awarding and withholding privileges.

BOND—The amount of money paid as bail to secure a person's release from custody and guarantee that the person will appear for the next scheduled hearing.

CAPITAL OFFENSE—A criminal offense punishable by death or imprisonment for life.

CASEWORKER—A professional counselor who helps a youth develop an appropriate treatment program to meet his or her specific needs. Probation officers, welfare workers, social workers, and learning center counselors are often referred to as caseworkers.

CERTIFICATION—*See* transfer or waiver hearing.

CHANGE OF VENUE—The movement of a case from the jurisdiction of one court to that of another court that has the same subject-jurisdictional authority but is in a different geographic location.

CHAPLAIN—A member of the clergy who conducts religious programs and counsels youth in a learning center, detention home, or other facility.

CHARGE—A formal allegation that a person has broken a law or committed an offense.

CHILD IN NEED OF SERVICES (CHINS)—A youth who misses school regularly, often disobeys his or her parent or guardian, runs away from home, and/or commits any other "status offense." CHINS are frequently referred to as status offenders. A status offense would not be an illegal act if committed by an adult.

CIRCUIT COURT—Adult court of record.

CITATION—A written order to appear in court to answer a charge.

COMMITMENT—An order by a judge at the dispositional hearing that transfers a juvenile's legal custody to the State Department of Corrections or a child welfare agency. The juvenile is then placed in a residential treatment program, group home, or foster care.

COMMITMENT-SUSPENDED—A court decision to enter a commitment order into a youth's record but without sending the youth into state care.

COMMONWEALTH'S ATTORNEY—A lawyer who represents the Commonwealth in criminal trials in order to enforce the laws of the Commonwealth. In other states, the lawyer is called a prosecuting attorney.

COMMUNITY-BASED PROGRAM—A facility or treatment program located in or near a youth's home.

COMMUNITY YOUTH HOME—A community-based residential treatment program for youth that usually has a capacity of five to fifteen youths and is operated locally.

COMPLAINANT—The person filing a complaint with the court.

COMPLAINT—A formal written accusation filed in court charging that a certain person committed a specific offense.

CONFIDENTIALITY OF RECORDS—Refers to privacy of official juvenile records, which can be seen only by authorized persons.

CONFINEMENT—Physical restriction of a person to a clearly defined area from which he or she is lawfully forbidden to depart and from which departure is usually constrained by architectural barriers like walls and/or guards or other custodians.

CONTROL UNIT—A security cottage housing students at a learning center, which operates a program dealing with more aggressive behavior and/or running away. These cottages are more restrictive to a person's individual freedom than regular cottages. *See* cottage.

CORRECTIONAL CENTER—An institution that provides residential treatment, custody, and care programs for juveniles committed to the State Department of Corrections or Youth Corrections. In other states, this same kind of facility may be known as a "training school" or "learning center" and now "prisons."

CORRECTIONS—A generic term that includes all government agencies, facilities, programs, procedures, personnel, and techniques concerned with the intake, custody, confinement, supervision, treatment, and presentencing or predisposition investigation of alleged or adjudicated adult offenders, delinquents, or status offenders.

COTTAGE—The youth's actual place of residence while at the Reception and Diagnostic Center of the state correctional facility (prison). Each cottage has other youth residents and its own staff.

COUNSEL—*See* attorney.

COURT—A setting in which formal testimony and evidence can be heard before a judge so that a legal decision can be made on the disposition of a case.

COURT-APPOINTED COUNSEL—A lawyer appointed by the court to represent defendants unable to afford private attorneys.

COURT SERVICE UNIT—A collective term for a part of the juvenile court that includes intake, probation, aftercare, counseling, and other related services.

CRIME—An act in violation of a law; also referred to as an "offense."

CRISIS HOME—A house used for temporary supervision and counseling for a runaway youth or a youth with family problems until he or she can be returned to the family or until a more permanent placement can be found.

DEFENDANT—The person accused of committing an offense.

DEFENSE ATTORNEY—An attorney who represents the defendant in court.

DELINQUENT ACT—An act committed by a juvenile for which an adult could be prosecuted in criminal court.

DEPARTMENT OF CORRECTIONAL EDUCATION—The state agency responsible for the academic and vocational instruction of juveniles committed to the Department of Corrections.

DEPARTMENT OF CORRECTIONS—The state agency given legal custody of a youth when committed to state care by the juvenile court.

DEPENDENT—A juvenile over whom a juvenile court has assumed jurisdiction and legal control because his or her care by parent, guardian, or custodian has not met a legal standard of proper care. Being a dependent is not an offense.

DETENTION HEARING—A hearing before a judge to determine whether a juvenile should be placed in detention, continue to be held in detention, or released until the adjudicatory hearing.

DETENTION HOME—A facility that provides temporary care in a restrictive, secured environment for juveniles in custody awaiting court action. Also known as a "juvenile facility."

DETENTION, LESS SECURE—Home that provides temporary care for youths who are not in need of secure detention. Youth are housed here pending court disposition or return to another environment.

DETENTION ORDER—The official legal paper signed by a person authorized to detain youth. Detention orders contain such information as the youth's name and address, birth date, offense, and the detaining jurisdiction; sometimes referred to as an "attachment."

DETENTION, OUTREACH—One kind of detention that provides intensive supervision and places restrictions on a youth in his or her own home instead of placing the youth in a detention home.

DETENTION, SECURE—One kind of detention that provides intensive supervision and places the child in "lock and key" confinement pending disposition or transfer to another agency.

DIRECT DISCHARGE—A release from a learning center with no continuing supervision or treatment.

DISCIPLINARY HEARING—A hearing held in a learning center when a youth is accused of breaking a rule. This procedure helps protect the rights of the accused youth.

DISMISSAL—A decision by a judge to end a case without determining the juvenile innocent or not innocent. The judge may dismiss the charges even if the juvenile is found not innocent.

DISPOSITION—A court decision on what will happen to a youth who has been found not innocent. The court can release, confine, fine, or order treatment as part of a disposition.

DISPOSITIONAL HEARING—A court hearing to determine the most appropriate action in a case where a juvenile has been found not innocent.

DIVERSION—An official removal of a youth from the juvenile justice system by referring the youth to a nonjustice treatment program or simply discontinuing the case.

DUE PROCESS—Refers to protection of a person's basic rights such as notice, a hearing before an impartial judge, and appeal.

EMANCIPATION—The act by which one who was under the power of another is rendered free. Usually used in reference to the emancipation of a minor child by the parents, which involves an entire surrender of the right to care, custody, and earnings of such child as well as a renunciation of parental duties. May be done whole or in parts depending upon the age of the child and the circumstances.

FAMILY COUNSELING—Counseling directed at resolving a family's problems. Usually two or more family members participate in counseling sessions led by a trained counselor.

FELONY—A criminal offense that is more serious than a misdemeanor and that can carry harsher penalties. Usually the penalty is punishment in a penitentiary for one year or more. However, due to overcrowding in the prisons, some people are serving their time of more than one year in the county jails.

FINE—A penalty imposed upon a person convicted of a crime or traffic violation requiring payment of a specified sum of money to the court.

FOSTER CARE—A formal arrangement whereby a judge places custody of a child with the local department of social services. Foster parents then provide a home and care for children who cannot live with their families.

GROUP HOME—A relatively small residential facility or treatment program, usually serving ten or fewer youths.

GUARDIAN AD LITEM—An attorney representing a child in civil proceedings such as adoptions or petitions of child abuse.

GUILTY—A finding by the judge that a defendant did commit the offense he or she has been charged with.

HABEAS CORPUS—A writ or order issued by the court directing the release of a person being illegally held in custody.

HALFWAY HOUSE—A residential program designed to provide treatment before a youth's return to his or her community after having been in the state correctional facility (prison or jail).

HEARING—A court proceeding in which charges, evidence, and arguments are heard.

INDIGENT—Persons who do not have enough money to hire a lawyer.

INTAKE—A youth's first contact with the juvenile court in which the juvenile referral is received and reviewed and a decision is made to file a petition or divert from court.

INTAKE UNIT—The juvenile court staff who receive and review a referral and decide whether to file a petition for a court hearing.

INTERSTATE COMPACT—The agreement between all fifty states to provide for the return of runaways to their home states or to provide for the transfer, probation, or aftercare supervision when a youth moves from one state to another.

INVESTIGATION—An examination of information and evidence to determine facts.

JAIL—A locally operated secure confinement facility for adults and, under certain conditions, for juveniles.

JUDGE—The court official who conducts hearings on a case and makes the final decision on what will happen to the offender.

JURISDICTION—The territory, subject matter, or person over which lawful authority may be exercised as determined by statute or constitution. It is the power of the court to render a decision in the case before it.

JUVENILE—A person younger than the age set by statute for an adult. In some states it is under 18 and in others it may be age 16.

JUVENILE RECORD—The official written file containing a court summary and information on a juvenile.

LAW—The set of rules to govern people's actions that are enforced by police and the court.

LAWYER—*See* attorney.

LEGAL CUSTODY—A legal status assigned by the court that gives a person or agency the legal right to determine where and with whom a youth shall reside as well as the legal responsibility to provide adequate shelter, protection, medical care, food, and education for the youth.

LEGAL RIGHTS—Rights provided for and protected by law, which cannot be taken away except in circumstances prescribed by other laws.

MISDEMEANOR—An offense that is less serious than a felony and carries lesser penalties. The maximum sentence is twelve months in jail.

OFFENSE—An act committed or omitted in violation of law.

PARENS PATRIAE—"Parent of the country." Historically, a form of guardianship in English Poor Laws. Today, it is used in juvenile courts to give states the power to intervene for children's sake.

PENALTY—A punishment given by the court to a convicted offender.

PENDING STATUS—The status of a youth who is residing at the Reception and Diagnostic Center until space becomes available at an appropriate correctional facility.

PERMANENT STATUS—The status of a youth who enters a learning center to participate in a treatment program.

PETITION—A document filed at court intake alleging that a juvenile is delinquent, in need of services, or abused or neglected, and asking that the court assume jurisdiction over the juvenile. A petition is similar to a warrant filed on an adult.

PHYSICAL ABUSE—Nonaccidental injury resulting from acts of either commission or omission by the parent, guardian, or person having charge over a child.

PLEA—A defendant's formal answer in court to the charges brought against him or her such as guilty or not guilty.

PREDISPOSITIONAL—The period of time from when charges are filed until the court makes a decision in the case.

PRIMA FACIE—"At first sight or appearance" or "on its face." Sufficient or adequate on its face without further investigation or inquiry. For example, a three-month-old baby who has been diagnosed by medical professionals with gonorrhea of the mouth looks like a case of child sexual abuse. On its face, this case that strongly suggests sexual abuse will prevail until contradicted and overcome by other sufficient evidence.

PROBABLE CAUSE—Based on evidence presented, there is reason to believe that the alleged offense occurred.

PROBATION—The conditional court supervision of a juvenile found not innocent. Rules are established and must be followed for an indeterminate period.

PROBATION COUNSELOR OR OFFICER—A juvenile court employee who works with juveniles on probation. Also know as "P.O."

PROBATION VIOLATION—A juvenile's failure to follow the rules of probation such that the juvenile is returned to the court for the judge to reevaluate the case and perhaps give a stronger warning or more structure in terms of sending the youth away to a correctional facility.

PROSECUTOR—The lawyer presenting the state's evidence in criminal trials. In some states also known as the "Commonwealth's attorney."

PROTECTIVE CUSTODY HEARING—A hearing to determine who has physical custody of a child, such as the state, parents, or an interested adult.

RECIDIVISM—A return to criminal behavior after conviction and treatment.

REFERRAL TO INTAKE—An agency or individual's request that a court intake unit take appropriate action with a juvenile who is alleged to be a delinquent, a child in need of services, or abused or neglected.

RITUALISTIC ABUSE—Physical, emotional, mental, and spiritual assaults combined with systematized use of symbols, ceremonies, and the concept of evil, designed and orchestrated to attain harmful effects.

RUNAWAY—A juvenile who has left his or her parents' or guardian's home without their consent and has not returned within a reasonable period of time.

SOCIAL HISTORY—The court service unit's investigation and reporting of the mental, physical, and social background of a juvenile and the circumstances of the offense.

STATUS OFFENSE—An act that is an offense only when committed by a juvenile, such as truancy or running away.

SUBPOENA—A summons requiring attendance and testimony in a court case.

SUMMONS—A document requiring that a person appear in court at a specified time to testify.

TRANSFER OR WAIVER HEARING—A hearing to determine whether a youth's case should be handled by the juvenile court or transferred to the circuit court for trial as an adult.

TRUANT—A juvenile between the ages of 6 and 16 (ages set by the statutes of the state) who has unexcused absences from school.

UNOFFICIAL HANDLING—The processing of a case through juvenile court intake without a formal court hearing before the juvenile judge.

WARD OF THE STATE—A juvenile who is placed in the legal custody of an agency such as the State Department of Corrections or Youth Corrections or a local department of social services.

WITNESS—A person who has personal knowledge relevant to a case and is called upon to give that testimony under oath to tell the truth in a court of law.

Source: *Dictionary of Criminal Justice Data Terminology*, Second Edition, U.S. Department of Justice, 1981, and *Step by Step: A Guide through the Juvenile Justice System in Virginia*, prepared by Virginia Department of Children, 1987.

Index

Index of Cases

Author Index